"Turn of the Century Scrapbook
of Jonathan Streeter Gates"

By William Preston Gates

© Gates Publishing Company • Glens Falls and Bolton, New York

Published by
GATES Publishing Co.
William P. Gates
1 Glenwood Ave.
Queensbury, N. Y. 12804
518-798-3609 Glens Falls
518-644-9410 Bolton

Library of Congress No. 99-073215
ISBN # 0-9672397-0-2 (Softcover Edition); ISBN # 0-9672397-1-0 (Hardcover Edition)

Front Cover Design - Len Frazier of the Chronicle
Front Cover Photo of J.S.G. by Fred Thatcher, 1880s
Typist for Introduction and Index - Pat Schrade
Back Cover Photo of Author by Dawn K. Gates Macey, 1999

From the Fall of 1998 and during 1999, The Chronicle Newspaper published one article each week from this scrapbook of over 1,350 articles. All of the published articles are included in this book, along with over one thousand additional articles and photos.

Jonathan Streeter Gates, 1880s

Acknowledgements

I would like to thank the following friends and family for their support, motivation, encouragement, ideas, historical interest or helpful involvement as I compiled this book. I especially want to thank Jane Gabriels for encouraging me to produce it and Cornelia Wells (of "Trees" Gift Shop, Bolton Landing) for showing me that there was a population in this area that would appreciate it. I also wish to thank Mark Frost and the "Chronicle" for publishing my weekly articles and for his continual encouragement. To my sister, Jeanine Gates Garnsey, my sincere thanks for her record-keeping assistance during the distribution of this book.

Ted & Alice Ackary	Mark Frost	Sam & Pat Hoopes	Jim Pepper
Ron & Carol Alcan	Jane Gabriels	Doug & Trinket Houghton	Jim Perkins
John Austin	Zandy Gabriels	Pam Kenyon	Ken Potter
John Babe'	Gordon Garlick	Joe King	Mark & Mary Radloff
Pat Babe'	Jeanine & Sam Garnsey	Ed Kluck	Deanne Rehm
Elsie Baldwin	Allison Karen Gates	Bud & Ruth Kober	Royce & Julia
Jody & Steve Balsamo	Barbara M. Gates	Dick & Mary Kowell	Remington
Barbara Batt	Clifford R. Gates	Brian Kristel	Anita Richards
Janine Black	Jack W. Gates	Sandy & Ruth Lamb	Andy Roden
Donna Boggs	John A. Gates	Harvey Lambeth	Pat Schrade
Bolton Book Club	Lindsey Erin Gates	Steve Lapham	John & Pat Sheppard
Steve Boyce	Matt W. Gates	Barbara Gates Lawrence	Ed & Carol Sheridan
Dennis Brower	Michael Shane Gates	James & Mary Lawrence	Kathy Simmes
Ralph Brown	Mike T. Gates	Jeff & Sharon Lawrence	Henry Smith
Jack Bryan	Robert T. Gates	Frank Leonbruno	Ed Stanilka
Ann Buckell	Ryan Walter Gates	Gary Loke	"Staples" Queensbury
Betty Buckell	Walter Edward (Bud)	Danny Lombardo	Pat Steele
Wendy Burkowski	& Toni Gates	Dawn Gates Macey	Bill & Barb Streever
Mildred Busman	William M. Gates	Lawrence (Bus) Macey	Edna Steves
Henry Caldwell	Linda Gatewood	Jeff Maranville	Lynn Steves
Ted & Jane Caldwell	Brian Granger	John Maranville	Sally Swetland
Jerry Cashion	Cathy Hackert	Linda Marcella	Dick & Pat Swire
Leon Chase	Jean Hadden	John Mason	Lee Taber
Mark Collins	Tony & Lisa Hall	R. Paul McCarty	Drew VanDerVolgen
Pat Collins	H. Russell	Eugenia McCaw	Kate Van Dyck
Sarah Combs	& Isabelle Harris	David & Meredith	Marilyn Van Dyke
Tom & Kathy Conerty	Annie Hawkins	McComb	Cornelia & John Wells
Don Cornell	Evelyn Hersh	Willie Bea McDonald	Maragaret J. Weston
Theta & Tom Curri	Tony Hinman	John & Anita McGilvray	Bill White
Mark Curri	Historical Museum of	Dick & Mary Merrill	John & Merle
William Dow	Bolton	John & Lisa Miller	Whittaker
Darrell Finlayson	Donnie Hoffman	Bill Morgan	Hugh Wilson
Len Frazier	Kam Hoopes	Jim & Sally Pelligrini	Ike Wolgin

Deceased Family who have preserved the scrapbooks for 100 years before me.

Jonathan S. Gates	Zilpha E. Gates Francis
Zilpha E. Reynolds Gates	Walter (Smokey) Gates
Walter E. Gates	William B. Gates
Nettie G. Harris Gates	Robert A. Gates

INTRODUCTION

Jonathan Streeter Gates was born in Bolton, New York, on Lake George, August 2nd, 1847. He was one of seven children born to John and Hannah Gates, both descendants of Bolton's earliest families. Jonathan's great-grandfather, also named John, was one of the first settlers to move into the Bolton area after fighting the Revolutionary War.

According to Jonathan's diaries and journals, he spent his childhood, as most young boys of that era did, working on the Coolidge Hill family farm, tending to the animals and cutting wood for cooking and heating during the long winters. Like most Boltonians, he had a strong love for Lake George, its beauty, its bounty, and its history.

Coolidge Hill House

Jonathan's mother taught him to enjoy books, reading, and writing. He valued his one-room-school education and was appreciative of the power of books and the written word.

When he was 14 years old, the Civil War irrupted. He was too young to fight, yet old enough to learn and understand the waste of war and the soldiers' longing for peace and home. He watched relatives and friends leave to fight, some of them never to return. This experience helped to teach him to respect the fragility of life and reinforced in him the importance of "family." His brother, Isaac Streeter Gates, wrote of his feelings regarding "home," "war," and "slavery" in his own journals during the Civil War.

Slavery

Slavery is a social, political, and moral evil. It is a social evil, because It disturbs not only the peace of the domestic circle but of society at large.

Isaac S. Gates

War

There is that about it which is dazzling and splendid to view; but if we happen to get on the battle field amid the deafening roar of cannon, and the sharp crash of small arms, and the heavy tramp of men and horses, the groans and wails of the wounded and dying. Then imagine what our condition must be if with all this we to are in the last agonies of death with a victorious enemy rushing upon us eager for blood.

One of the primary settlements around Bolton at that time was in the area known as the "Huddle." It is located approximately one mile south of the present Bolton Landing. Young Jonathan would go to the Huddle General Store to meet friends, buy supplies, candy, or just to catch up on the news and gossip. The Huddle Store was located on the south corner of Gristmill Road, between Gristmill Road and Huddle Brook.

When Jonathan completed his schooling, he decided that the life of a farmer as a full-time occupation was not for him. Undecided about his future, he tried his hand at teaching in the Huddle one-room schoolhouse, which was located in the "hollow," south of the Huddle Cemetery. For a time, teaching satisfied him, and it gave him time to read and expand his skills into other interest areas such as mathematics.

In 1872, at the age of twenty-five, Jonathan became romantically interested in Zilpha Elizabeth Ferris Reynolds, a young girl who lived across from the store on the lake side of the road. Her father, Eli Reynolds, owned a large lakeshore farm that included a mile-long portion of Huddle Bay.

Jonathan Streeter Gates
1873

Zilpha Elizabeth
Ferris Reynolds
1873

Homestead on lakeside of road.

It was in this Homestead that Jonathan and Zilpha were married on "the twenty-seventh day of September, 1873." At the age of twenty-six, Jonathan began writing in his diaries and journals more frequently from 1874 onward. He wrote extensively and almost daily of his everyday life, his wife, and of his only child, a son named Walter Edward. Included in Jonathan's diaries are the names and activities of the people he knew, details of his move into the Homestead, and his growing desire to own the General Store in the Huddle.

Walter E. Gates as a young boy.

Walter as a teenager.

In 1874, he purchased the "Huddle General Store." He ran the store without partners for ten years, up to 1884 under the new name, "The Gates Store."

As business increased, he decided to take on a partner, a Mormon named Morgan Tanner who was a descendant of John Tanner, another early Bolton settler. The store's name was changed to "Gates, Tanner, and Co."

First Store, south corner of Grist Mill Road
Jonathan Streeter Gates, 2nd from left
Walter E. Gates, 4th from left

Jonathan's son Walter was now old enough to help in the store. Around 1884, increased traffic from the steamboats was causing Bolton Landing to the north to experience more growth. Bolton Landing was named for the steamboat landing, which was constructed there to accommodate the larger steamboats plying the waters of Lake George during the second half of the 19th century. These large vessels required deeper water and open space for maneuverability. Jonathan expanded his business by purchasing an old store already located there on the west side of Main Street. This store had been operating since 1845 and had been run by Steven and Truxton Pratt, then Sidney Mead, respectively. It was located in the lot directly left of today's World War I Monument. (The buildings were removed in 1974.)

First Bolton Landing Store

Another brother, George Streeter Gates, also became a partner at this time. George moved into the house attached to the Bolton Landing Store, and he operated this store for the partnership.

From left to right:
Morgan Tanner
George S. Gates
Jonathan S. Gates

Soon afterwards, the Gates brothers bought out Morgan Tanner and both stores were renamed "Gates Brothers & Co." At this time, the old store was moved back on the lot, a new larger store was built onto the front of it, and the house received a gabled roof and front porch. (One of the original "Gates Brothers & Co." signs is on display at the Bolton Historical Museum.)

Bolton Landing Store
1884

Bolton Landing Store 1888

Behind Homestead, Lakeside

Jonathan S. Gates, Zilpha E. Gates supported by chair, and Walter E. Gates

In 1899, tragedy struck. Jonathan's wife Zilpha became quite ill. She could walk only with the assistance of a chair, which she pushed along ahead of her. Zilpha died on May 5th, 1899 at the Homestead. She was 50 years old.

A copy of the original obituary for Zilpha Elizabeth Gates

*Jonathan S. Gates
at Zilpha's grave
in Huddle
Cemetery
1899*

Jonathan and his son, Walter, were now alone. Walter became a partner in the store business and did additional work now to help his father after Zilpha died.

Five years later, Walter Edward met and married Nettie Gertrude Harris of Harris Bay and Harrisina across the lake in Queensbury. They met at the "Hundred Island House" Hotel, which was located on the present Knapp Estate property below Shelving Rock Mountain. They married at the Harris Homestead in Harrisena, Queensbury, February 23rd, 1904.

At the home of the bride's parents, Mr. and Mrs. Daniel Harris, in Queensbury, Walter E. Gates of Bolton and Nettie G. Harris were married by Rev. Dwight A. Parce of Bolton, February 23, 1904. *mary 27- 1904*

Nettie Gertrude Harris   *Walter Edward Gates*

Nettie moved into the old Homestead to live with her new husband and Jonathan. There she raised their four children, Walter Ferris, Zilpha Elizabeth, Robert Alexander, and William Beckers.

With two successful stores, a growing young family around him and son Walter taking over more and more of the work, Jonathan had once again found some contentment in the evening hours. Now, he devoted even more time to his hobby of scrapbooks and journals. The articles he collected include Bolton, all surrounding towns and counties, pictures, people, postcards, letters, and news events of local, national, and international interest. His scrapbooks are packed full and cover well over 2,000 pages. (The articles in this book represent approximately 10% of his collected materials.)

In 1919 tragedy struck again. Jonathan's only child, Walter, contracted the deadly Spanish Influenza on a trip to Glens Falls. The Spanish Flu killed over 40 million middle aged healthy men around the world after World War I. The following account from his diary shows that Walter was only ill for eight days before he died on January 17, 1919.

Tue. Jan. 7, 1919 — Walter and Nettie went to Glens Falls.

Thur. Jan. 9 — Walter commensed to be sick last night. He was in terrible pain.

Friday Jan. 10 — Walter is not much better with rheumatism or whatever it is. His feet and legs are numb.

Mon. Jan. 13 — Walter is growing weaker. Dr. Rogers is telephoning Dr. Chapman to come.

Wed. Jan. 15 — Dr. Chapman came. Bled his arm.

Thur. Jan. 16 — Walter is failing fast. I had Dr. Jones and Goodman from Warrensburgh.

Fri. Jan. 17 — My poor boy Walter died at three o'clock this morning. Oh how sad I am. He was all I had to live for. How lonesome it leaves me.

Jonathan was devastated. 1919 complicated his life further because he sold his lakeshore property to Dr. William Beckers so that Dr. Beckers could build his "Millionaire's Row" mansion, Villa Marie Antoinette, named for his wife. Dr. Beckers agreed to move the Gates Homestead across the road in 1919 to where it stands today.

MORTUARY
8 tun Jan. 2, 1919.

The funeral of the late Walter E. Gates was held from his late home in Bolton Sunday, the Rev. Mr. Prudum officiating. The floral tributes were many and beautiful, showing the high esteem in which Mr. Gates was held by all who knew him.. Very few business men are held in greater esteem than was Mr. Gates. His integrity was never disputed and his efforts untiring to please all.

He will be greatly missed not only by the peoples of Bolton but by the summer colony, the greater part of whose grocery trade he held. He is survived by his father, Jonathan S. Gates; his wife, Nettie Harris Gates. and three young children.

A copy of the original obituary for Walter E. Gates.

*The Homestead during the move
in 1919 across the road to its
present location.*

After Walter Edward died, Dr. Beckers became a friend and protective figure for Nettie, her children, and Jonathan. A personal letter from Dr. Beckers was tucked into the scrapbooks, which stated how terribly he would miss Walter Edward. Nettie's fourth child was born four months after her husband's death. This child, a boy, was born in rooms over the store while the Homestead was being moved. Dr. Beckers gave him his name. "William Beckers" Gates was my father, born May 24, 1919.

After the Homestead was moved, Nettie did not like the feeling of having her home crowded onto a small plot of land. She felt closed in. She explained her feelings to Jonathan and he arranged to have the store moved back from the road to its' present location. He also had the front porches removed from the store to help open up the view from the Homestead.

VIEW OF STATE ROAD, BOLTON, N.Y.

The Huddle Store

Another view of The Huddle Store

With his only son dead and gone, Jonathan sold the Huddle Store soon afterwards, but kept the Bolton Landing property and buildings. Jonathan continued his scrapbooks right up to his sudden death on December 11th, 1921. From 1921 to 1954, Nettie continued to tuck interesting local articles between the pages of Jonathan's scrapbooks and later, her daughter, my Aunt Zilpha Gates Francis, also added occasional articles from 1955 into the 1960's. My uncle, Robert Alexander Gates, added additional material to the collection and preserved everything in the Homestead until his death in 1996. He preserved his brother Walter's (Smokey's) photos, programs, and articles on the "El Lagarto." Smokey was a mechanic on this Bolton based Gold Cup Speedboat throughout its racing years. (The El Lagarto is now on display at the Adirondack Museum in Blue Mountain Lake, New York.) Robert also preserved unusual antique artifacts from all around the Lake George area and collected articles and photographs of "Bill Gates Diner" operated by his brother William and sister-in-law Dawn Gates. This diner is the last Hudson Valley Trolley. Bill and Dawn (my parents), ran it from 1949 to 1981 on Bolton's Main Street with considerable help from my brother, Walter Edward II, sister Jeanine Marie, and me. It also rests now at the Adirondack Museum.

As I write this in the Spring of 1999, the year of Bolton's Bicentennial, I continue to discover more old photos and articles tucked into remote corners of the 1830 Gates Homestead in the Huddle. There is far too much material to fit into this one book, so I have selected a representative sample of Jonathan's articles from 1899 to 1917 to recreate the flavor and nature of Jonathan's original scrapbooks for you and to help you turn back time to the years around 1900.

The articles are in their original, imperfect condition so you can experience them as they first appeared long ago. This book gives you far more than a recounting of the history of the greater Lake George, Glens Falls area. It gives you a glimpse into the heart and soul of the man who collected this history for us all, my Great Grandfather, Bolton's Jonathan Streeter Gates.

William Preston Gates
Great Grandson

THE MOHICAN'S REVENGE.

An Ancient Legend of Bolton on Lake George Retold.

One more tale of legendary Lake George is printed below. It was written by the late Robert C. Alexander, editor of the Mail and Express, and first appeared in that paper. Mr. Alexander was a friend of many Glens Falls people and an ardent lover of Lake George. The "fateful rock" mentioned in the legend is on the shore of the lake directly in front of "Buena Vista," the Alexander cottage in Bolton bay.

High on a wooded point of rock jutting out into Bolton bay is perched a modest summer cottage. Behind it stretches the "forest primeval of murmuring pines and hemlocks." In front is spread out a varied picture of island, lake and mountain, which Charles Dudley Warner declares to be unsurpassed on Lake George. In the immediate foreground is the gem-like Leontine islet, with its single hermit tent gleaming white amid the overhanging pines. Directly over it, but two miles distant, is Green island, and on it the spacious Sagamore hotel, thronged with gaily dressed visitors. Beyond is the mighty dividing wall of the Tongue mountain range, separating the lake from the great Northwest bay, while across the lake, still further on, looms Black mountain, in all of his stern and lonely majesty. Between these two mountain ranges are the clustering islands in the Narrows, while around them all are poured the silvery waters of the "Holy Lake," which lies among its guardian hills "like a sparkling eye in the smiling face of happy childhood."

The lawn before the cottage slopes gradually toward the lake until it meets the edge of a miniature palisades, fifteen feet in height, over the vertical face of which a plummet would sink in thirty feet of water. At one point a natural ledge two feet in width inclines gradually to the water along the face of the cliff, and there alone is the steep wall of rock accessible. Farther along, the cliff runs out into a natural breakwater, behind which is a quiet cove where the boats are moored.

Moonlight on Lake George! Who can resist its alluring fascination? We push off from the dock and slowly paddle out "into the view." A long line of Japanese lanterns light the piazza, from which comes the sound of merry voices and laughter. From the Lake View hotel, across Concordia bay, come to us bright music and a piano accompaniment. Now the stillness is broken by the rollicking cries of a band of college students camping on Sweetbriar island, now by the blast of a horn from the cottage which reverberates around the sides of Bolton bay until five distinct echoes are returned. Only a gentle ripple disturbs the mirror-like surface of the water, but still enough to break into a thousand silver dimples the reflected moonbeams. We rest on our oars; we watch the diamonds drop from the blades, and listen to the gentle lapping of the waves against the boat.

At length the various sounds from the shore we have left grow gradually distant and confused, until they seem to be but one low and dreamy accompaniment of something more distant, more weird, yet more real. Though but a stone's throw from the rocky point, it seems to have receded into the past until it is dim and indistinct. We feel as if today touched yesterday—that far-off yesterday before the white man came to summer at Lake George and mocked the grandeur of nature's domes anl arches with his flimsy architecture. More beautiful then than now, the queen of lakes rested calmly amid the virgin forests and almost untrodden mountains. Not yet had the deadly crack of the rifle or the boom of cannon echoed from crag to forest the stern notes of war. Not until fifty years later did the first white man look on this historic lake, when Father Jogues was brought a captive to its shores, and called it St. Sacrament. As we pause in reverie, and dream, and listen, we seem to hear sad music around us, and we know that the quiet bay and the shelving rock we have just left have a tale to tell of that distant yesterday. With every breeze the gloomy pipes whisper it to the waves, and the waves repeat it with tremulous horror.

It is the hunting ground of the Mohicans. All is solitude and loneliness. The sun is just beginning to penetrate the gloomy forest, and the birds are singing their matins. Early as it is we discern a dusky figure gliding stealthily among the tree trunks. His moccasins make no sound as he softly treads upon the leaf-strewn ground, avoiding the dead sticks and twigs which might crackle under his foot. He stoops to put aside the clinging boughs which obstruct his path, and thus reveals his stalwart figure and muscular limbs. He is armed with bow, tomahawk and scalping-knife and is in all the hideousness of war paint. It is plain to see that it is one of the young braves of the tribe of the Mohicans.

A stag bounds across the path of the savage, but almost unnoticed. It is evidently no mere hunting expedition, but some secret errand which brings him thus early from the Mohican camp-fire to the shores of the Horicon. Cautiously he moves among the trees until his eyes catch the gleam of the crystal water. Near the shore he reaches a point with which he seems to be familiar. He crouches down behind a great mossy boulder, and waits hour after hour, attentive to every sound, and with all the tireless patience of the Indian warrior. He hears naught but the sighing of the breeze through the boughs, the ripple of the water on the rocks, the chirrup of a squirrel overhead.

But hark! A rustic in the shrubbery, the crackling of a twig, and suddenly an Indian girl, bright and beautiful of face and form, whose single deerskin garment scarcely concealed her lithe and graceful figure, sprang into view like a Naiad of the wilderness.

"But ne'er did Grecian chisel trace
  A Nymph, a Naiad, or a Grace
  Of fairer form or lovelier face."

Her rich black hair decked with ornaments indicative of rank, fell like a mantle over her bare shoulders, while her bright eyes shone like stars in the night. She has now reached the point of rock, and, shading her eyes with her hand, looks expectantly down the lake. The crouching Indian, as she passed near his hiding place, caught his breath and clasped his breast as if in pain, but made no other movement. He has recognized Katonah, the fair daughter of the Sagamore of his tribe.

As the maiden stands and watches a dark object is seen moving out of Ganouskie bay, and, turning the end of Green island, rapidly approaches her. It is a canoe, containing a single dusky figure. Hidden for a moment by Leontine island, it appears, and a few more vigorous strokes bring the frail craft close to the shore. The newcomer is a manly young brave, whose face lights up with joy as he sees the fair watcher on the rock. He reaches the foot of the sloping ledge, leaps ashore, dashes eagerly up the face of the cliff and clasps the willing maiden in his arms. His accents, as the lovers converse in subdued tones, are softer and less guttural than those of the Mohicans. A year before in one of the northward forays of the latter, this young chief, Chourongay, had been taken back a captive, and closely guarded in the camp of his enemies. Escaping soon afterward, he rejoined his tribe, and gained not only his liberty but the heart of the lovely Katonah. Nor was this the first time the lovers had met at their favorite trysting place.

Meanwhile malignant hate and ungovernable passion distort the visage of the ambushed Mohican, and murderous gleams flash from his eyes as he watches every movement of the unconscious lovers. With fiendish deliberation he fits an arrow to his bow, take careful aim, and with a sharp twang the arrow speeds on its murderous mission. Startled by the sound, the Huron quickly turned, and the shaft mean for his own heart penetrated the breast of Katonah, who, with a faint cry, sank bleeding at his feet. With a cry and rage of horror, Chourongay faced his assailant, who was already leaping towards his rival. The tomahawk of the Huron whirled about his head and flew like an arrow at the head of the Mohican, but a panther-like movement of the latter avoided the weapon, which however, severed the war-plume from his scalping tuft and buried itself in a tree trunk behind him. Each now drew knife and dashed to the encounter. The Huron, more powerful than his antagonist, seized the Mohican's upraised arm, caught h.m around the neck, and by a tremendous muscular effort bore him to the earth, and his gleaming blade flashed above his enemy's face. It fell, not upon the throat but on the shoulder of the Mohican, who by an agile movement, dodged the descending blow. Then, throwing his sinewy arms around the Huron he drew him close to his breast and repeatedly plunged his knife into the back of his adversary until the grip relaxed, the body rolled away and the prostrate Mohican arose, bleeding, but victorious. His whoop of triumph rang out over the lake, as he took the scalp of his victim and hurled his body far out into the water.

As it disappeared in the lake the victor turned to the lifeless form of the Indian girl, and cried, "O Katonah, Laughing Eyes, treacherous and beautiful as yonder waters. Even here, beside the silvery Horicon, but a few short moons ago, you promised to wed the Soaring Eagle, and light his wigwam with your flashing eyes, and for you he would hunt, and fight and get honor. By yonder sinking sun, by the moon and the stars, and by these holy waters, you swore to be mine, and called down the curse of Manitou if your words would be false. But you forswore your oath, and fled the wigwam of the Sagamore, your father, to dally with his enemy and mine. Like a snake he stole into the tent of the great chief and stole the heart of Katonah, Laughing Eyes. The Mohican never forgives nor forgets. The Soaring Eagle is avenged. Yonder below the dark water lies his body, and already his spirit has fled toward the setting sun. Now must we follow him. My spirit, and not his, must pass with yours through the land of shadows to the happy hunting grounds, for Manitou has made you mine."

Even as he spoke he clasped to his breast the lifeless form of Katonah, and leaped with her from the rock. Over their heads rolled the waters of the Horicon, and through the shadowy pines floated a solemn requiem for the dead.

* * * * *

A cloud has overspread the face of the moon, and now leaves us in its shadow. Again music and shouts of laughter meet our ears, and we row rapidly back to the cottage, whose genial lights cast a faint glow over the water. Past the fateful rock, around the breakwater and into the dock, and quickly we rejoin the merry company on the piazza. Yesterday and today

have met, but the tale of yesterday is told, while that of today is to be continued. We have to do with the unfinished, not with the finished.

Blood-stained lake of yesterday, thou art but a direful dream! Ours is the beautiful, dimpled lake of today, which ripples so merrily and carelessly under yon fatal rock. We will gather up the pleasures of the present, which are all around us, and forget the bloody scenes that are of yesterday, dim and fanciful.

Zilpha Elizabeth Ferris was born in Chester April 23, 1849, the daughter of Allen and Laura Loveland Ferris. Her parents dying when she was quite young, she was adopted by relatives in Bolton, where in 1873 she married Jonathan S. Gates. Mrs. Gates was a woman specially endowed to make home happy. Her kindness was unceasing, her charities always ready, her hospitality made sunshine for all who entered her beautiful home on whatever errand intent. To the community in which she dwelt her loss is irreparable. Her fatal illness was protracted through many weeks of great suffering, borne with heroic patience while it exhausted every resource of medical skill and tender, assiduous care. The worn body gave up the struggle on May 5, and she is gone. She leaves a husband to inconsolable grief and one only child, a son, Walter, who knows what the best of mothers is like. She is also survived by one brother, John Ferris, of Igerna. The funeral was held from the house on Sunday and was attended by a great assemblage from this and nearby towns. The interment was in the Huddle cemetery.

Warrens OBITUARY. *News*
Nov. 9th 1899

Robert C. Alexander, editor-in-chief of the New York Mail and Express, died Saturday evening at his home in New York after an illness dating back two years. He went abroad last July and was under medical treatment in Germany until the middle of September, when he came home and went to his summer home at Bolton, on Lake George. He remained there until October 26, when he returned to New York greatly improved in health and confident of his ability to resume his work. During the next few days he spent several hours at his desk, but he contracted a cold during the wet and chilly weather that then prevailed, and by the following Friday was confined to his bed. From that time life gradually ebbed away.

Mr. Alexander was born July 7, 1857, at West Charlton, Saratoga county, N. Y. He entered Union college in 1876, and was graduated from there at the head of his class in 1880, and later from the Albany Law school, with the degree of LL. B. After practicing in Elmira for a short time he went to New York. In March, 1895, he assumed the duties of editor of The Mail and Express. Two years later he, with Robert E. A. Dorr, purchased the paper, and since that time he had been a leading force in its development and progress.

The Late Isaac Streeter.

The news of the sudden death of Isaac Streeter, of Bolton, Wednesday morning, brought a shock of surprise to many of his friends in this village, where he was known, as well as to his relatives and friends in Bolton, where he had been a life-long resident. Deceased was an upright citizen, a member of the society of Friends by belief, and respected by all who knew him. Over two years ago he was seriously injured while blasting a rock, and never fully recovered from the effects of the accident. He married, in 1861, Alice Goodman, daughter of the late Oton Goodman, of Bolton, who, with a sister, still survive him. Funeral this morning. *he died Feb. 28*
1894

MOHICAN PROPERTY SOLD.

9/9
25/

The Mohican House property, at Bolton, has been purchased from the Glens Falls Insurance company by W. K. Bixby, of St. Louis, Mo., and by him presented to his wife. Mr. Bixby is president of the American Car company, of St. Louis, a combination of companies manufacturing cars, and his wife is a sister of Miss Roxie G. Tuttle and W. S. Tuttle, of this village. It is probable that the hotel will be torn down and a handsome summer cottage built, although this will not be done at once. Mr. and Mrs. Bixby will spend the summer at Bolton, and arrangements for building the house may be made at that time. The property is very desirable for a cottage site.

---

he died JOHN STREETER. *Feb 27*

John Streeter, an old and highly respected citizen of Horicon, died at his home in that place Monday morning, aged seventy-four years. He leaves a widow and six children. The funeral was held yesterday morning at 11 o'clock. *1901*

G. F. Times *1901*
Thursday June 13th OBITUARY.
Putney.

Joseph Putney, aged 85 years, died at his home in Bolton, Tuesday. Mr. Putney was born in Warrensburg, but had resided in the town of Bolton for more than sixty years, and he was highly respected. He is survived by his wife, one son, David T., and a daughter, Rebecca A. Putney. The funeral was held today at 10 o'clock at the Trout Lake Methodist church.

OBITUARY.

JOHN DAVID GATES.

John David Gates, aged sixty-six years, died at 5:40 o'clock yesterday morning, at his home on Hudson street. He had been in poor health for several years, but the immediate cause of death was the grip, with which he had been ill since Monday night. Mr. Gates was born in Bolton and always lived there until he removed to this place four years ago. He was twice married, his first wife being Mrs. Sarah Beadenell, of Warrensburgh, to whom he was united January 27, 1861. His second wife, who survives him, was Mrs. Amelia E. Pendell, also of this place. They were married in 1883. Besides his widow he leaves one daughter, Mrs. R. T. Taylor, of Bolton. Four brothers also survive him—Johnathan S., George S., Dodge S., and Joseph Gates, all of Bolton. The deceased was at one time prominent in the political affairs of his native town and served two terms as supervisor. He was a modest, unassuming citizen, upright in all his dealings and thoroughly respected by all who knew him. The funeral will be held from the house to-morrow afternoon at 2 o'clock. The Rev. T. S. Rush, D. D., pastor of the Presbyterian church, will officiate. Interment in the Warrensburgh cemetery.

—William E. Spier, a prominent citizen of Glens Falls, whose death in New York was announced yesterday, had been ill a little more than a week, an abscess forming in his left ear. An operation was performed Saturday and he rallied. It was believed that he would recover, but Tuesday afternoon his condition became worse and he failed rapidly until the end. He became a member of The Morgan Lumber Company at Glens Falls in 1873 and later engaged in the manufacture of shirts and collars. He also manufactured paper. He was prominent in the organization of The Glens Falls Paper Mills Company in 1882, and became its President in 1885. In 1898 he was chosen Treasurer and a Director of The International Paper Company. He was also a Director in The Trust Company of America and the First National Bank of Glens Falls, besides holding interests in many other corporations. Recently he became interested with ex-Senator Miller and John W. Mackay in mining matters in the Southwest. He was the owner of Suburban Farm, near Glens Falls, and had bred light harness horses there. He had owned Attograph, 2:16½; Robert McGregor, 2:17½; Delmar, 2:16¾, and Directum, 2:05¼, the present head of the stud, with Abdell, 2:23. In 1898 Mr. Spier made a sensation by buying by telegraph the then champion trotting stallion Directum. The horse was in California; and the dispatch was sent from the trotting meeting at Lexington, Ky. Mr. Spier was born May 16, 1849, at Northville, Fulton County, his parents being Elias and Harriett Spier. He married Ida Morgan, daughter of James W. Morgan. She and one son, Lester Morgan Spier, survive. The funeral will take place Saturday morning at 10 o'clock from the Glens Falls residence, the remains arriving to-morrow by special car. Spier Falls was named in honor of the deceased by Eugene L. Ashley.—Daily Times, May 9.

MAN WHO WROTE "SUWANEE."

Though He Has Been Dead Since 1864, His Ballads Are Still Popular All Over the Land.

Milwaukee Sentinel.

In one of our largest music houses the other day I chanced to overhear a young lady giving an order for several songs, says a well-known Milwaukee musician. As she read off the list I paid no special attention until my ear caught the titles, "Old Kentucky Home," "Gentle Annie" and one or two others.

"What!" I said to myself, "are Foster's songs still sold?" I had had a general idea that they were sung from memory when sung at all, or that a few copies, yellow with age and reposing at the bottom of the piles of music in some old-fashioned parlors, were all that remained of the once popular ballads. But a few words with the clerk proved to me that I was wrong. He told me that it was no rare thing for people to ask for them; that, if not in stock, they could still be obtained of Foster's publishers.

This set me to thinking of the young composer and the melodies which won for him a world-wide fame.

Stephen Collins Foster was born in what is now part of Pittsburg, July 4, 1826, and died in New York, January 13, 1864. He was educated at Athens Academy and Jefferson College. He was not distinguished for unusual scholarship, but was a quiet, serious boy, with a fondness for scribbling on scraps of paper in odd corners. His first published song was "Open Thy Lattice, Love," written in 1842, when he was little more than sixteen years old, and his last work, "Beautiful Dreamer," appeared in 1862.

It is the ballad writers of a time that most directly address the people. Foster had a word to say, and though more than fifty years have passed since he wrote his best songs, they still have power to speak to us. The opening notes of "Nelly Gray" or "Hazel Dell," or "Suwanee River" will cause a hush to fall upon the gayest company, and in almost every breast will be conjured up some memory, sweet or sad, of days gone by.

Stephen Foster was not a musical prodigy; he had not even a good technical knowledge of music. His talent lay rather in the possesion of an exquisite taste and in a natural use of the simple rules of harmony—also in his ability to fit words and notes together. By the very mesmerism of his own heart-power he gave to his songs a life and feeling that was wonderful and that has made them live. They had a spirit and inspiration which made them genuine works of art; for what can art do better than to reach the heart?

The popularity attained by Foster's compositions may best be judged by noting the following figures: Of "Suwanee River" there have been sold considerably over 400,000 copies; of "My Old Kentucky Home," more than 300,000 copies; "Massa's in the Cold, Cold Ground," 250,000 copies. Nearly 100,000 copies of "Old Dog Tray" were sold in six months.

The inspiration for "Massa's in the Cold, Cold Ground" came to Foster at Covington, Ky. He heard an old slave bewailing the death of a kind master, and that he and several other slaves, aged and worn out in faithful service, would pass into the hands of less kind owners. "Old Kentucky Home" is said to have been suggested to Foster on hearing an old negro speak with love and longing of his former home in Kentucky. Foster took frequent journeys for the purpose of acquainting himself with slave life in all its phases, therefore his work bore the impress of truth.

His body was taken from New York to Pittsburg for burial, and reposes in the old Allegheny cemetery, near the arsenal.

Mr. Brown was familiarly known as "Uncle George." He was of a genial disposition and made many friends. From the day he entered the hotel business he gained for his house a reputation for comfort and hospitality which was recognized by all who ever had occasion to enter its doors. Before the building of the railroad to Caldwell the Halfway House enjoyed a patronage second to none other in this locality, and its proprietor was known far and near.

The deceased is survived by his wife, who is now critically ill; one son, Stewart Brown of Whitehall, and three daughters, Mrs. James T. Crandale of Caldwell, Mrs. A. P. Scoville of Glens Falls and Mrs. Duane Buckbee of French Mountain.

JOSEPH HASTINGS, HERO.

Tribute of Colonel Cunningham to a Brave Color Bearer.

Joseph Hastings, aged 74 years, died at his home in North Bolton, Monday. Deceased was a veteran of the war of the rebellion, having served as color bearer in the 118th regiment. He was a member of Post Randall, G. A. R., of Bolton and a member of Bolton Lodge, I. O. O. F. The funeral was held Wednesday at 1 o'clock at the North Bolton Methodist Episcopal church, Rev. Charles Kennedy officiating.—Bolton Correspondent.

Asked about the above which appeared in The Times of a recent date, Colonel J. L. Cunningham said:

Yes, the first I knew of the death of Joseph A. Hastings of Bolton was from the brief notice in The Times.

"Old Joe Hastings," as his veteran comrades fondly called him, was a gentle, modest, unassuming man, without brag or bluster, counting the doing of duty, however trying, or dangerous, only what was to be expected of a soldier. I considered him a hero, for he rendered splendid and conspicuous service as the color bearer of our old 118th regiment, New York Volunteers, all through its term of service.

He enlisted in Company D of that regiment at Horicon, and when the regiment was organized at Plattsburg, Hastings, who lacked but a half inch of being six and a half feet in height, was elected and appointed sergeant of its color guard, which was made up of the tallest men of the regiment. He received from the state the bright and new silken regimental colors, bore them in every one of the moving engagements in which the regiment participated, cared for them in camp and on the march through the three years of service and returned them, torn and worn and tattered, to the state authorities. This is an unusual record. He had been in all the battles which were finally inscribed on the regimental colors, which are now, with others, in the capitol building at Albany. I do not know as any other of our original color guard came back with Hastings. Large men did not, as a rule, stand the hardships of soldier service as well as the smaller and more compactly built, but Sergeant Hastings was seldom off duty from sickness and, I think, was never in hospital. It would be a severe illness that would make him resign the colors to other hands.

At the second battle of Fair Oaks, Va., October 29, 1864, the regiment lost in killed, wounded and prisoners, 111 officers and men, and every regiment of our brigade lost its colors except the 118th. When nearly surrounded and successful resistance was no longer possible, orders were given for every man to act for himself, Sergeant Hastings and his color guard made such a daring and rapid retreat under a concentrated fire upon its escaping colors as to win the admiration of all who saw it, whether friend or foe. The colors were saved, as they were at Drury's Bluff, by Hastings' brave purpose to keep them out of the enemy's hands.

Conspicuous in height, and as color bearer always in the center of the regimental line, he was, of course, more of a target than any other man of the regiment, yet he escaped wounds, except a slight hurt from a sharpshooter's rifle in the trenches before Petersburg. It was said of the 118th that its colors were carried higher than those of any other regiment of our corps, because of the unusual heighth of their bearer. Hastings was a cheerful, uncomplaining soldier, known and respected by every comrade. His only "kick" was because the quartermaster's department never provided trousers of sufficient length for his use. He was obliged to draw two pairs, using one to splice the legs of the other, although his officers usually provided him, at their own cost, with a tailor made suit of good material to measure.

He received after muster-out a commission from the governor of the state with a rank of brevet lieutenant, because of his meritorious service. No better soldier, or gentler spirit served his country in the civil war than Color Sergeant, Brevet Lieutenant, Joseph A. Hastings.

She died BOLTON. *July 2 '01*

—Mrs. Maria Putney, widow of Joseph Putney, died at her home on the shores of Trout Lake, July 2, aged 88 years. She survived her husband just three weeks. The funeral was held at the Trout Lake Methodist Episcopal church July 4. She was buried in the Bolton cemetery. Rev. Charles Kennedy conducted the service, assisted by Rev. C. Lewis. *July 4*

—Mrs. Eliza Bennett, wife of John Bennett, died July 4 at her home on the shore of Trout Lake, aged about 40 years. She leaves besides her husband one daughter, Mrs. Milo Cardle. She was buried in the Bolton cemetery. The funeral services were conducted by Rev. D. A. Parce.

Troy Times Obituary. *Friday July 19 1901*

—Amasa Howland, a pioneer paper manufacturer of the upper Hudson, died at noon Tuesday after an illness of three months at his residence in Sandy Hill, aged seventy-four years. At the time of his retirement from the presidency of The Howland Paper Company he was the most prominent representative of the paper industry in northern New York. Mr. Howland leaves two sons, J. Edward and Fred D. Howland. The funeral was held yesterday afternoon.

Glens Falls Times July 23rd 1901

GEORGE H. CRAMER.

Life of the Well Known Trojan Who Died at Lake George.

The Troy Record of last evening says:

George H. Cramer, one of Troy's oldest and wealthiest citizens, died at a late hour last night at his summer villa, Trinity Rock, on Lake George, a short distance from Caldwell. The news of his death was received by his friends in Troy this morning and is heard with general expressions of regret.

Mr. Cramer was in his eighty-sixth year. He was born in the village of Waterford, Saratoga county. He spent most of his early life in that village, and later on took up his home with his father, John Cramer, in this city. His father was prominently identified with the wealthy citizens of Troy when the municipality was young. His financial interests included stock in the Saratoga County bank, of which he was president. John Cramer was also one of the directors of the old Rensselaer and Saratoga railroad at its incorporation. He was active among those who purchased the old construction bridge between Troy and Green Island when the city of Albany was attempting to turn trade from the northern part of the state from Troy, its natural channel, to Albany by building rival railways, one of which reached from Albany to Schenectady. John Cramer was also a member of the original board of trustees of the Rensselaer Polytechnic insitute. The Rensselaer and Saratoga railroad, which was incorporated in 1832, was a short railroad line of twenty-six miles, and when George H. Cramer became old enough to engage in business he became interested in this road, and at the time of his death was

---

president of the board of directors. He was also president of the Albany and Vermont railroad and the Saratoga and Schenectady railroad, all of which are portions of the Delaware and Hudson system today.

The deceased acquired his fortune from his railroad interests and the iron industries. In the year 1838 Mr. Cramer became junior partner in the firm of Green & Cramer, dealers in and importers of iron and steel, with an etablishment on River street near its junction with First street. This firm subsequently dissolved, Mr. Cramer leaving in 1852. It is now known as Hannibal Green's Sons. The deceased was a trustee of the Troy Savings bank and had been president of the United National bank since 1889, when he succeeded E. Townsend Gale. Prior to this he was a director, having been elected to that office at the bank's organization in 1865, when it was formed by the consolidation of the two banks then known as the Farmers' bank and the Bank of Troy. He served as a director in the bank until May, 15, 1889, when he was chosen president.

The deceased was a charter member of the Troy club, where Mr. Cramer was fond of visiting with his friends in this city. He was also connected with the Young Men's association and was a contributor to the library which that association has sustained.

Mr. Cramer married Miss Henrietta Knox Cannon, daughter of LeGrand Cannon and sister of LeGrand B. Cannon of New York city. LeGrand Cannon was one of the early settlers in this vicinity and possessed immense property interests in Troy. He was the owner of the Cannon place block and at his demise left a large estate to his daughter, Mrs. Cramer. The deceased was executor of this estate. Mrs. Cramer died on September 9, 1900, at Caldwell, and her remains were interred in the family plot in Oakwood. He was a member of St. Paul's Episcopal church in this city and his family also attended St. James' Episcopal church at Caldwell during the summer months.

The deceased had owned the estate on Lake George for thirty-five years past and had his winter residence at 19 Third street in this city.

Mr. Cramer suffered a stroke of paralysis about five years ago and has gradually failed in health since. For the past year he has been practically blind. At his death bed last night were his three children, LeGrand C. Cramer of this city, Miss Henrietta Cramer and Mrs. D. V. R. Johnston of Albany and three grand children, all the children of his son, LeGrand C. Cramer.

The deceased during his life was of a retiring disposition and though energetic in business he cared more for his home life. Acts of charity and philantrophy characterized his whole career and though never making an ostentatious display of his generosity, many persons have cause to remember him for his acts of kindness. When engaged in his business pursuits and social life he was modest and unassuming.

The directors of the United National bank will meet tomorrow to take action on his demise. The funeral will be held at 10 o'clock Wednesday morning at the home at Trinity Rock and interment will be in Oakwood cemetery.

July 18th 1901

Capsized on Lake George

The steam yacht Cyric, owned by B. Burgess Warren of Philadelphia, who is also the owner of the famous fast yacht Ellide, was capsized Thursday afternoon in Lake George, a half-mile east of Dome Island and opposite Camp Andrews, where the water is more than 100 feet deep. Mr. Warren was on a fishing trip, when a heavy thunderstorm, accompanied by a strong wind, suddenly passed over the lake. The canvas curtains had been pulled down and fastened to keep out the rain.

A terrific gust of wind struck the yacht, and not finding a vent through the upper works forced the boat over, and it rapidly filled. The boat was kept afloat by a large air-tight compartment in the bow. Besides Mr. Warren there were on board Capt. Alexander Taylor of Bolton, engineer John Mead of Caldwell and the steward, Robert Thompson. Thompson tore open the curtains and seized Mr. Warren, who had a narrow escape. The men clung to the bow and were rescued by John Harris of the Sagamore after they had been in the water more than forty minutes. After the storm had passed the yacht was towed ashore. *Troy Times*

Glens Falls Times
Aug. 17th 1901
NS FALLS DAILY TIMES. SA

DEATH OF A. NELSON CHENEY

THE STATE FISH CULTURIST EXPIRED SUDDENLY THIS MORNING AT HIS HOME.

Death Due to Heart Failure—Mr. Cheney Had Been Indisposed for Several Days — Deceased Widely Known, Personally and Officially.

A. Nelson Cheney, state fish culturist, died this morning at 1:15 o'clock at the residence of his daughter, Mrs. Walter P. Leavens, Park avenue, with whom he made his home. Death was sudden and was due to heart failure.

Mr. Cheney was born fifty-three ago in this village and Glens Falls had always been his home, although much time had been spent in travel in the performance of his official duties. His parents were Albert Nelson and Annah Hunt Cheney. His father was one of the pioneer lumber merchants of this locality.

The deceased was widely known and throughout the country his name was probably more familiar than that of any other resident of this locality. He had made a life study of fish and their habits and he was everywhere recognized as an authority on matters piscatorial.

In 1895, when the reorganization of the state fisheries, forest and game commission was accomplished and the office of state fish culturist created, Mr. Cheney's appointment to this official position was made and universally declared to be eminently fitting. The public records show that Mr. Cheney performed well the duties of his office and all know that since 1895 the fishing interests of the state have been cared for as never before.

Mr. Cheney had often served with distinction on committees and commissions at various expositions in this state and throughout the United States and had only recently returned from such a mission at the Pan-American exposition.

Mr. Cheney has been a large contributor to literature pertaining to fish. His articles were to be seen in nearly all numbers of Forest and Stream, Outing, The Angler and The Fishing Gazette, London, as well as in other periodicals. Several years ago, with Charles F. Orvis, a well known writer on piscatorial subjects, Mr. Cheney completed a volume on fishing and various phases of angling. The volume, which was designated as "Fly Rods and Fly Fishing," was a collection of short articles several of which were from the pen of the deceased.

A BOLTON MAN INJURED.

Glens Falls Times

RUFUS RANDALL MEETS WITH AN ACCIDENT WHICH MAY RESULT FATALLY.

Aug 12 1901

Was Visiting Relatives in Glens Falls And Met With a Mishap on the Trolley—Jumped From a Car in Motion—Details of the Affair.

Rufus Randall, a prominent farmer of Bolton, lies in a critical condition today at the home of his son and daughter, Mr. and Mrs. Isaac Tripp, 130 Bay street.

On Thursday Mr. Randall, accompanied by another son and daughter, Mr. and Mrs. E. M. Pratt, came to Glens Falls to visit his brother, A. G. Randall, and Mr. and Mrs. Tripp. Yesterday afternoon he visited his son, Clarence Randall of Sandy Hill and returning home from that village by trolley he met with an accident which caused injuries of a serious and probable fatal nature.

Mr. Randall, who was on a car in charge of Motorman Leach and Conductor McLead, rode up Glen street and through Sanford to Bay street and when near the corner of the two latter thoroughfares motioned to the conductor that he wanted to get off. He immediately arose to his feet and stepped down onto the running board. Then before the car could stop it is said he stepped or jumped to the road. Several pedestrians say that he jumped with his back to the front of the car.

Mr. Randall fell violently backward, striking on his head, the blow rendering him unconscious. The motorman and conductor picked up the injured man and helped him to the home of Mr. Tripp, where he still lies in an unconscious condition.

Dr. Bullis was summoned and in the evening Dr. Fitzgerald and Dr. McLaughlin were called in consultation. The injured man is suffering with concussion of the brain and little hope is given of his recovery. He has been delirious and at times has been very violent.

Mr. Randall is 59 years old. He is well known in Glens Falls and throughout the county.

G. M'KINLEY, THE STUDENT

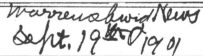

The Dead President Was a Classmate of Colonel Howard.

In a pleasant conversation with a Times reporter today, Colonel H. A. Howard related many striking incidents of the life of President McKinley as a law student.

The dead president and Colonel Howard were members of the class of '67 in the Albany Law school.

Colonel Howard recalls McKinley as as the one man of the two hundred students who most impressed him during their school work in pursuit of legal knowledge.

He was somewhat short in stature, but had a most pleasing appearance. In this latter respect he was exceptional. He always acted as though he thought the time too short in which to accomplish what he had undertaken. He would always be the last man to enter the class room, apparently holding back for more time and thorough preparation. When the class was dismissed he was the first one out, eager to be at the next thing which he had to do.

So, in going to and fro between school and his boarding house he was always in haste. From this habit he gained the nickname of "The Trotter." His classmates would follow him at times and when he reached his lodging place he would turn and laugh good-naturedly and disappear. As a student he was careful, had a clear grasp of his subject, leaving the impression that he had devoted a great deal of time on his lessons. He understood his work perfectly. He was a hard worker and had an energetic way of accomplishing his tasks.

Colonel Howard spoke of the way in which they missed him after school was over and the men were gone.

No one seemed to think much of his making such a great career although each one appreciated his excellent spirit and method of work.

Warrensburg News
Sept. 19th 1901

FATAL ACCIDENT AT CORINTH.

Former Warrensburgh Young Man Killed by Fall While Painting.

Albert D. Noble, of Corinth, while painting the outside of one of the International Paper company's buildings at that place, about 10 o'clock Saturday morning, fell from a ladder and sustained injuries which caused his death at 4 o'clock in the afternoon.

In order to reach a high place in a gable Mr. Noble had constructed a staging made by lashing the ends of two ladders together and swinging them in a horizontal position across the end of the building. He then placed a shorter ladder on the staging and leaned it against the structure. Upon this he was standing while a fellow workman stood at the bottom to steady the ladder. Without warning the horizonal ladders broke in the center and the two men were precipitated into a flume. Mr. Noble struck on his back across the edge of the flume while his more fortunate companion fell in the water and escaped with comparatively slight injuries. Mr. Noble was carried to his home, where he was attended by several physicians, but nothing could be done for him. He was partially paralyzed because of the injury to his spine, and though conscious part of the time was unable to move or talk after he was injured.

MAY BE ANOTHER MURDER.

W. News Sept. 19

S. H. Nichols Shot by Dr. Lincoln at West Stony Creek.

1901

From Harrisburgh lake, in the town of Stony Creek, comes the news of a crime, probably a murder, committed at that place late Tuesday evening, when Dr. Henry M. Lincoln, of Wilton, shot Seth H. Nichols, proprietor of the Lake house, on Harrisburgh lake. The shooting occurred, it is said, either while the two men were engaged in what started as a friendly scuffle, or as a result of the efforts made by Nichols to separate Lincoln and another man when they were quarreling. Mr. Nichols is said to have been wounded in the left side and hand, and his injuries were of a serious and perhaps fatal character. The injured man is about forty-five years of age and a son of Riley Nichols, of Adirondack. For about fifteen years he has been employed at West Stony Creek, where he ran the hotel at that place for Oscar W. Ordway. A year ago he purchased the property. His wife was Miss Ida Davis, of Bolton, and they have seven children. Dr. Lincoln, who is about forty years old, came from one of the best families in Saratoga county and was well educated and a man with bright prospects until, a few years ago, he became the victim of bad habits which shattered his health. Last winter he was taken to a sanitarium for treatment and an affair in which he became involved, in Norfolk, Va., gave him an unenviable reputation. Through the treatment he improved in health and resumed his practice, but his old habits again overcame him and for some weeks past his condition has been precarious.

WALKER-STEWART.

Miss Bessie Stewart, daughter of Horace Stewart, proprietor of the Stewart house, at Bolton Landing, and Howard Cyrus Walker, of that village, were married yesterday morning at 11:45 o'clock at the Presbyterian manse, Glens Falls, by the Rev. John R. Mackay. *1901*

1901

"THE WARREN RECORDER,"

G. F. Times Oct. 7th

Warren County's First Newspaper, Printed at Caldwell in 1825.

Says the Warrensburg News:
Perhaps few people in this vicinity are aware that Warren county had a newspaper seventy-six years ago. We have upon our desk, however, an interesting relic in the form of "The Warren Recorder," published at Caldwell and dated Friday, October 21, 1825, being No. 1 of the second volume of the first newspaper published in Warren county. The paper is loaned to us by Martin Granger, of Pottersville, and was preserved by Mrs. Granger's father, John P. Prosser, of Bolton, who was supervisors' clerk for twenty-eight years. While yellowed by age and in a somewhat dilapidated condition, the paper is still readable throughout its four pages and proves to be a well-edited and nicely gotten up sheet for the time. The terms of subscription are named as two dollars per annum, accompanied by the interesting announcement that "Most kinds of country produce will be taken in payment for papers." The pages are devoid of news items, most of the space being taken up by legal notices and an account of a Republican convention for Saratoga county, held at Ballston, Spa., September 21, 1825, when John Cramer was nominated as a candidate for senator in the fourth senatorial district. Then follows an address prepared by a committee appointed for the purpose. Among the most interesting of the other contents is "A Dream," which was experienced by Mr. Prosser. The dream seems to have been in the form of an allegory, in which the dreamer was "seated on the rock Horeb" and given a sling and seven smooth stones with which a Being of wondrous beauty directed him to slay a large he goat having his feet placed on the carcass of a huge bear,

---

W News The Marion House Sold. *Oct. 31*
William A. and Henry L. Sherman, of Glens Falls, have sold the Marion house, on Lake George, to H. Wronkrow, a New York banker and real estate man. The hotel was managed last season by A. H. Russell, formerly of the Lake house, Caldwell. *1901*

Enrolled HIRAM GRAY. *Nov. 3rd*
Hiram Gray, of Pottersville, who died from the effects of injuries received from a fall from his wagon, was buried Sunday of last week in a Warrensburgh cemetery, up the river. Deceased was seventy-three years old and leaves a wife and one son, Leroy. *1901*

Died MRS. DELILAH NOBLE. *1901 Nov. 3*
Mrs. Delilah Noble, wife of William Noble, deceased, died at her home in Warrensburgh, near the West river, Sunday morning, aged eighty-one years. The funeral was held Tuesday afternoon at 1 o'clock from the house, the Rev. C. A. Johnson officiating. Mrs. Noble is survived by one brother, Horace Stewart, of Bolton; two sons, Sidney and Edward Noble; two step-daughters, Mrs. William Swan, of Warrensburgh, and Mrs. Charles Harris, of Thurman. *1901*

Glens Falls Times
Oct. 21st 1901

GLENS FALLS DAILY TIMES, MO

NEW LAKE GEORGE STEAMER

CONTRACTS HAVE BEEN AWARDED AND THE WORK OF CONSTRUCTION HAS BEGUN.

Boat to be Called Sagamore and Will be Built on Pine Point, Caldwell—Craft to be Similar to the Lake Champlain Steamer Chateaguay.

The Lake George and Lake Champlain Transportation company has awarded contracts for the construction of the new Lake George steamboat to take the place of the ill-fated Ticonderoga, which was destroyed last August by fire.

The new boat will be christened the Sagamore, this being the name of one of the Indian tribes which in years gone by roamed the shores of the lake.

The hull and frame of the new boat, which will be of steel, are being built by Harlan Hollingsworth & Co. of Wilmington, Del. The engines will be built by Fletcher & Son, New York city. This company has built engines for several of the fastest steamboats afloat. The work of building the new boat will be done on Pine Point at Caldwell, and the craft is to be completed and ready for commission on July 1, 1902.

The Sagamore will be a model craft and will be built after the pattern of the Lake Champlain steamer Chateaguay, with improvements over that boat.

There will be three decks, the hurricane deck being open to the public. The dining room on the main deck will seat ninety people.

The boat will be licensed to carry about twelve hundred passengers.

Captain E. S. Harris will command the new craft and Captain White of the ill-fated Ticonderoga will succeed to the commandership of the Horicon.

The Sagamore will cost $150,000. The executive board of the Lake George and Champlain Transportation company decided upon the name "Sagamore" for the new steamer. The board consists of Horace G. Young, president of the company; Dr. W. S. Webb, vice-president, and General Manager George Rushlow. Sagamore was selected after deliberation and the consideration of various names. The name is euphonious, easily pronounced and especially appropriate.

LAKE PROPERTY BOUGHT. *1901*
Oct. 19
Albert Comstock of New York city has purchased of Mrs. White of Providence, R. I., the Bell point property on the Bolton shore of Northwest Bay, Lake George. Mr. Comstock is well known in Glens Falls and vicinity. Mrs. Comstock was formerly Miss Caroline Ranger of this village.

ACCIDENT ON BRANT LAKE.

Orville Duell of Horicon Shoots Himself While Hunting.

While duck hunting on Brant Lake, Monday morning, Orville Duell, the 16-year-old son of Oscar Duell, accidently shot himself, the bullet entering the abdomen and coming out through his back. Young Duell was with his brother Robert and they had rowed out some distance on the lake in quest of game. Coming to where some ducks could be seen Robert asked his brother to hand him the gun, which lay in the bottom of the boat. As the younger boy picked up the firearm, with the muzzle pointed toward him, the trigger was in some way pulled, discharging the weapon. The bullet, a 44-calibre, struck him in the stomach. Duell was taken to his home, where Dr. Stafford attended him. Later Dr. Perkins of Pottersville and Dr. Thomson of Glens Falls were called and an operation was performed. The lad, though somewhat improved, is still in a very critical condition.

The Fastest Craft Afloat. *1901*

The diminutive steam yacht Ellide, owned by E. Burgess Warren, of Philadelphia, who summers at the Sagamore on Lake George, was for a time the fastest American craft afloat. On her official trial the Ellide steamed at a rate of over forty miles an hour. When Captain George B. Harris used to let her out at only a thirty mile clip last summer the staid old steamer Horicon would seem to be just lazily ambling along when doing her best. But the Ellide must give the laurel to a new mistress of the waves, the Arrow, owned by Charles R. Flint, a New York capitalist. Both boats were designed by the same naval architect. The Arrow can cut through the water at the rate of fifty miles an hour and is easily the speediest vessel in the world.

THANKSGIVING DAY FIRE.

Residence of Mr. Tippetts of Caldwell Burned to the Ground.

A serious fire visited Caldwell early last evening when the handsome residence at the corner of Helen and Church streets, owned by the Daniel Ferguson estate and occupied by William H. Tippetts and family, was burned to the ground. A part of the contents was saved.

Mr. and Mrs. Tippetts and children were in Glens Falls for Thanksgiving, and during their absence the fire occurred, it being supposed that the flames started from a defective chimney.

GATES-ROGERS. *1901*

The marriage of Miss Edith Frances Rogers and John Gates, both of Hill View, was solemnized at the home of the bride's mother, Mrs. F. E. Truesdale, December 1. Rev. Milton Tator officiated.

RATHER UNIQUE COTTAGE.

To Stand on an Imposing Site at Shelving Rock, Lake George.

George O. Knapp, of Chicago, owner of the Hundred Island house, Lake George, and also owner of a cottage on the hotel grounds, will build another summer dwelling, the new building to stand on an imposing site on the side of Shelving Rock mountain. The site decided upon for the structure is the first lookout which is on the path leading from the Hundred Island house up Shelving Rock mountain and about a quarter of a mile from the hotel grounds. A private cable road will be constructed and Mr. Knapp, with the members of his family or guests, can reach the lofty heights of his cottage without an effort. The basement of the cottage will be made large enough to admit the cable car, so that the car can be taken without leaving the inner walls of the house.

The Ellide (Record, 40.2 miles an hour), Lake George, N. Y.

HIS SKULL FRACTURED.

HOWARD DUDLEY, OF BOLTON, THROWN FROM A WAGON.

Struck Heavily on His Head and Right Shoulder—Serious and Painful Accident—Injured Man's Condition is More Favorable This Morning.

Howard Dudley, of Bolton, was thrown from a wagon yesterday and had his skull fractured by the fall. He is now confined at the Warren house, in this village, suffering greatly, but with chances in favor of his recovery.

The accident happened yesterday afternoon about 3 o'clock. Earl Dudley, a younger brother, who is in the employ of the Hudson Valley railway; Judd S. Fish, who had come from Corinth; Ransom Wells and Howard Dudley, who had been in the woods working for Stillman Lanfear, on his lumber job near Indian Lake, decided to drive from this place to Bolton Landing. They hired a team and two-seater at Potter's livery stable and started soon after dinner intending to go by Hill View, over the mountain road.

Earl Dudley and Wells were in the front seat, the former driving, Fish and Howard Dudley were seated behind. After they had gone a short distance on the cross road, the young men, who are all residents of Bolton, decided to take another route home, turned around, and just over the break of the sharp pitch by Jay Crandall's, in North Caldwell, the pole strap broke letting the wagon onto the horses. The team made a lunge and the end of the pole striking an obstruction in the road caused the conveyance to take a "header."

The two men in front and Fish behind jumped in time to save themselves from serious injury, Wells being somewhat hurt about his legs.

Howard Dudley was thrown out, striking heavily on his head and right shoulder. He was picked up in an unconscious condition, bleeding profusely from his wounds.

After breaking away from the wagon the horses ran to the foot of the hill and jumped the road fence into a field, where they were caught, as soon as they had recovered from their fright, by Charles Hall, who came to the assistance of the victims of the accident.

The wagon was a complete wreck, but the harness was patched up and another vehicle borrowed in which the injured man was conveyed back to this village. Dudley was still unconscious when taken into the Warren house.

Dr. Logans was called and found the patient suffering from compression of the skull over the right eye. The injury is a very serious one; the upper lip was badly cut; other bruises about the face will only cause temporary disfigurement.

Dudley is twenty-one years old and a son of Mr. and Mrs. Peter Dudley, of Bolton. He has a rugged constitution which will favor his recovery. He is receiving every attention at the Warren house and this morning a slight improvement was noticeable.

TROLLEY RUNS TO RIVER.

THE FIRST CAR CAME THROUGH FROM GLENS FALLS TUESDAY.

Dec. 24th/1901

Distinguished Passengers Aboard--Prominent Warrensburghers Enjoy Return Trip--Ticket Offices Established Here--Rates of Fare by Ticket and Coupons.

Tuesday was a red letter day in Warrensburgh's march of enterprise. It was about 3:00 o'clock in the afternoon when the first car of the Hudson Valley Railway system, No. 33, reached the Schroon river and was stopped—not by obstructive local policy or dormant public spirit, the bridge is not completed, that was all, or "33" would have come whizzing on through Main street to the Adirondack hotel.

The car was in charge of Crosby Taylor, motorman, and Charles Hartman, conductor. The passengers were Hon. A. B. Colvin, president of the road, and daughter, Miss Frances Colvin, accompanied by Miss Kate Lee; J. A. Powers, chairman of the executive committee; Treasurer Cowles; Superintendent Kinmouth; H. E. Smith, secretary to the president; Rev. John R. Mackay; W. H. Parker and William A. Wood, of the Times Publishing company.

The party was driven from the present terminus of the road to the Adirondack hotel, where the officers of the road had a consultation with Hon. L. W. and James A. Emerson in regard to some detail matters of special moment.

A ticket office was established at the Grand Army house in addition to the one at the Adirondack hotel.

Negotiations were opened with Lockwood's stage for the transfer of passengers from Thurman station to Warrensburgh, and it is announced that special rate tickets will soon be issued for the benefit of persons living at Thurman and points north who may prefer to take the trolley at Warrensburgh for Glens Falls and points south instead of going by the Adirondack railway to Saratoga and then up.

Car No. 33 left on the down trip at 4:15 having on board Congressman Emerson, James A. Emerson, Supervisor Weinman and Superintendent of the Poor A. L. Soper, in addition to the passengers up. With a significant snap the brakes were loosed; of a sudden the clamor of a gong and then the car became the god-child of Miss Colvin, who manipulated the lever for a distance in honor of the event. Congratulations among the group of passengers were in order; the car not being specially decorated for the occasion they exchanged figurative boquets of speech.

The advent of the trolley, which will give Warrensburgh the benefit of railway facilities for freight as well as passenger traffic, says the Glens Falls Star, is one of the most important epochs in the history of this village, and the advantages which it will afford in the matter of shipments and in providing an easy means of communication with the outside world, will doubtless result in a notable development of the industrial interests of the place.

Warrensburg news

THE deer season closed several days ago, but we learn from "Squint Eyed Bob," the poet of the Adirondacks, that there is one man who is still hunting contrary to law. Says Bob:

There is a man in our town,
Who thinks he is awful cute.
He has tramped the woods many a mile,
A deer for to shoot.

Thinking that it is up to the game protector to do something, the poet prods that official with these lines:

Now if we had a game protector
That was worth a single pin,
He would rally out and hustle about,
And take such fellows in.

The game protector, we dare say, thinks someone ought to hustle about and take "Squint Eyed Bob" in.

Dec. 5th/1901

G, DECEMBER 27, 1901.

MANY DEER KILLED.

The Hunting Season of 1901 Witnessed the Destruction of 6,150.

Reports received by the state forest, fish and game commission from the express companies operating in and out of the Adirondack region show that during the past hunting season 1,286 deer were handled, including 1,062 carcasses, 103 saddles and 121 heads. This was 84 more than was handled by the express companies during the season last year.

This means that about 6,150 deer were killed during the past season, as for every deer killed about four are eaten in the camps or reach places on the outskirts of the woods by means other than the express companies. Fifty-three deer were shipped from Childwood, 45 from Big Moose, 91 from Beaver River, 76 from Northville, 63 from Newton Falls, 99 from North Creek, 27 from Racquette Lake, 20 from Paul Smith's, and 32 from Piercefield. The commissioner has been informed that one buck shot weighed 333 pounds. Hunters who get a deer weighing 275 pounds think they have bagged unusually big game.

Warrensburg News
Jan. 23th/1902

WIZARD OF LAKE GEORGE.

A QUEER CHARACTER INVOKES THE AID OF A WITCH.

Indulges in a Special Incantation Once a Week--Then He Burns Panther Hairs in Honor of This Marvelous Woman--His Life Regulated By an Old Panther Skin.

In the mountains back of Shelving rock, on the east shore of Lake George, lives a curious character known to residents thereabout as Josh Richards. He is a hunter, mystic, trapper, philosopher, and necromancer.

As a general thing, he indulges in a special incantation once a week, on which occasion he plucks three hairs from the hide of an Adirondack panther and burns them, with appropriate ceremonies. The invocation or incantation is intended to propitiate a mythical witch supposed to inhabit undiscovered caverns on Black mountain. Josh believes that as long as he continues the sacrifice the woman will aid him in all of his pursuits.

"Josh, how do you know that the witch isn't a humbug?" he was asked recently.

"Umph!" he replied. "I've tried her. When I forget to burn panther hairs, she forgets me, and I come home empty handed."

Then he proceeded to give a few instances of how his faith in the witch had been rewarded and how she had helped him out of several difficult scrapes. Once he had an interview with a large bear in the woods on Mount Erebus. He was getting the worst of the argument when he thought of the witch. He called to her for help, and all at once the hug of the animal grew weaker, and he was enabled to introduce his hunting knife between the bear's ribs without any great amount of trouble.

Said Josh in an earnest kind of way:

Don't talk to me of the witch not being the cause of my good or bad luck. She knows the woods by heart and manages things to suit herself. When I got away from that bear, I was black, blue and green all over. But I got his hide, just the same, and that's what's left of him over there by the bunk. When I got home that night, I burned six hairs in her honor—she just loves the smell of panther hairs—and when I got out of bed the next morning I was trim as a whistle.

One night she came to me in a dream. I saw her just as plain as I see the nose on your face, and she says, says she: "There; next time you goes fishing take a lot of 'lasses and smear it on the boat just above the water line." I did it and come near drowning. The lake was alive with shad flies. The critters settled on the sides of the boat, and there they stuck fast until the craft was covered. The trout was hungry and jumped for the flies so fast that they came tumbling into the boat one after the other. When the first three or four come in, I up with a club and knocked daylights out of them, but I had to drop that and take to the oars. When I reached shore, the boat was loaded to the water's edge with hundreds of the big jumping fish. If I had had another rod to row, I would have sunk sure.

Then he proceeded to give a few more instances of where, how and when he had received aid from this most marvelous of women; how through her assistance, he once made his escape from the den of a bear back on Shelving rock, and, on returning home one dark night and finding his shanty in flames, how he called on the witch and out of the clear sky came down a thundering big rain and put out the fire in a jiffy. At another time when provisions were low and he was in danger of starvation, as the deepness of the snow prevented a visit to Fort Ann, where he usually obtained his food, he burned several hairs from the mangy old hide, went to bed, and when he got up the next morning there before his door, not thirty feet away, stood a big buck ready to be shot. He blazed away and had venison enough and to spare for several weeks.

All of his actions and indeed his whole life are regulated by that old panther skin. When it first came into his possession, it was covered with hair and was considered rather a good looking skin as panther skins go. Today it is nearly bald, and if Josh lives a few years more he will be obliged to sacrifice bear hairs or invest in a new panther skin.

OFFICERS OF THE SAGAMORE.

The Champlain Transportation company has named the following officers for the new Lake George steamer, Sagamore: Captain, E. S. Harris; clerk, John W. Gillett; first pilot, Warren Rockwell; second pilot, Walter Harris; steward, Herbert I. Vail. Captain F. G. White of the ill-fated Ticonderoga will succeed to the captaincy of the Horicon. John Washburn will be the pilot.

THE RAILROAD BRIDGE COMPLETED
1902

First Electric Car Ran Into Warrensburg Saturday Afternoon—Other Notes.

The Hudson Valley railway bridge over the Schroon river at Warrensburg was completed Saturday afternoon, and the first car, in charge of Motorman Lester Brownell and Conductor John Mead, passed over the structure at about one o'clock. The cars for Warrensburg leave Glens Falls fifteen minutes after the even hour, and run into Warrensburg as far as the residence of L. W. and J. A. Emerson.

The waiting station at French Mountain is nearing completion, and it is expected that it will be ready for use the latter part of the week.

Master Mechanic Singleton, of the Hudson Valley has been in town for a day or two getting the two new smoking compartment cars, Nos. 34 and 35, ready for use. He says that they will be put on the road this week.

A restaurant has been opened at the waiting station on the electric road at Thomson.

The through theater cars will be put on the electric road again tonight. One car will leave Fort Edward at 7:20, and another Sandy Hill at 7:37. A special car will also leave Caldwell at 7:30.

GLENS FALLS' POPULATION.
Jan 25, 1902

The population of Glens Falls has been officially declared to be 13,355. The village board met last evening and the report of the enumeration recently made was submitted by Clerk Dillon. The figures were approved.

W. news **GEORGE W. SEAMAN.** *mar 6*
Our Bolton correspondent writes as follows:

George W. Seaman died at his home in Bolton Sunday in the seventy-sixth year of his age. He moved from Glens Falls to this place nearly forty years ago. He conducted a tannery for several years of which he was one of the firm of Ferguson & Seaman, his partner being Hiram Ferguson, of Albany. Mr. Seaman was supervisor of the town of Bolton for several terms and was postmaster for about ten years. He was a very companionable man and enjoyed the esteem of his neighbors and friends. He is survived by his widow and the following children: Mrs. Leroy N. Smith, of Schaghticoke; Mrs. Addison Comstock, of Ballston; Mrs. S. B. Bradley, of Wheaton, Ill.; William A. Seaman, of Michigan; Allen T. Seaman, of Kniman, Ill.; Mrs. Millington, of Pittsburg, Pa. Jennie A. and Hiram F. Seaman, of Bolton. Funeral services were held Tuesday afternoon. *1902*

Star mar, 5th 1902
A ONE-TIME ACTIVE FIGURE.

In Town Affairs—Death of William Benedict Gurney.

William Benedict Gurney died at his home, 10 Charlotte street, yesterday forenoon at 11:45 o'clock. The deceased was born at Claverack, Columbia county, on January 7, 1822, and was therefore eighty years of age. He came to Queensbury with his parents when six years of age, and had lived in this town continuously since. For many years Mr. Gurney was an active political worker, and held the offices of highway commissioner and justice of the peace for several terms. He was first married in 1849 to Ann Robison, of Washington county, who died in 1853, leaving three children, Edgar B., Mary J. and Belle. His second wife, Miss Mary Alston, with whom he was united in 1855, is also dead. Five children—Ella, Abbie H., Elizabeth R., Helen A. and George E.—were the fruit of this union, all of whom except Ella are living.

Mr. Gurney was an active figure in the affairs of the town until restrained by the infirmities of age. He moved from what was known as Gurney lane to Glens Falls a few years ago. The funeral will occur from the house Thursday afternoon at two o'clock.

"I love you more than words can tell,"
At last he summoned pluck to say.
She hung her head and murmured. "Well,
Perhaps there is some other way."
—Brooklyn Eagle.

ENING, MARCH 6, 1902.

AN ACCIDENT AT CALDWELL

CLARENCE HASTINGS FALLS FROM A STAGING, RECEIVING SERIOUS INJURIES.

Accident May Result Fatally—The Man Falls Fifteen Feet, Striking on His Head and Shoulders—Picked Up in Unconscious Condition.

Clarence Hastings, who has made his home in Warrensburg and Bolton, received serious if not fatal injuries today at Caldwell.

Hastings has been employed on the construction of the new summer home of Royal C. Peabody of New York, which is building on the Bolton road, and this morning while at his duties received injuries which may result in his death.

MURDER IN WARRENSBURG
G. F. Star — Apr, 24th

JOHN L. CREEDON KILLS POWELL H. BRACE.
1902

Sequence to a Row With a Traveling Minstrel at the Riverside Hotel—Murderer Gives Himself Up to an Officer.

The usual quiet of the village of Warrensburg was disturbed last evening by a drunken melee which culminated in a murder, and added another homicide to the annals of crime in Warren county. The victim is Powell H. Brace, who for three years had been proprietor of the Riverside hotel, in that place. The murderer is John L. Creedon, a man of twenty-eight years, who was reared in Smiths Basin, but has lived at different times in Glens Falls.

Creedon was employed as a laborer in the construction of the Caldwell and Warrensburg branch of the electric road. Subsequently he secured employment in the graphite mines owned by Glens Falls parties and located near Pottersville. He left the mines last Saturday and took a train to Thurman, whence he went by stage to Warrensburg. He arrived at the Riverside hotel late in the afternoon and passed the night there. Sunday morning he took the nine o'clock car to Glens Falls. He spent Sunday in this village, and was seen on the streets in an intoxicated condition. It is supposed that he also spent Monday and yesterday here. He is known to have been in town a portion of the time at least. At five o'clock last evening he reached Warrensburg on an electric car, and went directly to the Riverside hotel, where his trunk had been left by Expressman James Potter on Saturday.

Among the hangers-on at the hotel when Creedon put in an appearance was Joseph Morrissey, a colored minstrel, who claims Binghamton as his home, but who travels about from place to place singing and playing on a banjo. At Creedon's request Morrissey sang and played for a time. Creedon then invited the minstrel to the bar, and both had drinks. The negro afterwards resumed his singing. Creedon remarked that he did not know how to sing, and ordered him to stop. Morrissey refused to obey, and Creedon became abusive. Finally the negro struck Creedon in the face. The two grappled, and fell to the floor, Creedon on top. At this juncture Landlord Brace came into the office, adjoining the bar-room, where the men were scuffling, and, pulling Creedon off of Morrissey, ordered Creedon to leave the house. This was about 7:45 o'clock.

Mrs. Sarah Hastings, or Fish, the cook, hearing the disturbance, called Creedon out on the piazza and asked him to keep quiet. He remained on the piazza only a moment, when he returned and demanded a drink. Lewis Putnam, the bartender, refused to serve him, and ordered him out. At his request, Creedon's trunk was taken from the office and placed outside on the stoop.

Creedon went out, opened the trunk, and took out a revolver. With the weapon in his hand he went to the office door, and was about to enter, when Landlord Brace stepped up, and, with a warning gesture, ordered him not to come inside. Creedon shouted, "I'll put you out of business." Before the spectators could realize what he was doing, Creedon had raised the revolver and fired. The ball entered Brace's left side, several inches above the heart. Brace reeled into the parlor, where he fell on the floor. Dr. C. B. Cunningham was called, but the man died in about fifteen minutes.

Meanwhile Creedon had run as far as the river bridge and then retraced his steps and went to the Patnode barber shop, where he asked for an officer. From there he went to J. H. Pasco's livery stable. To Mr. Pasco and James Davison he explained that he had shot Brace, and wanted to give himself up to an officer. He was taken to Constable William H. Straight, at the Adirondack hotel. Officer Straight later turned Creedon over to Deputy Sheriff Stone, who took his prisoner to the county jail. Creedon said a man handed him the revolver to shoot Brace, and he committed the crime in the excitement. Creedon seemed much concerned about the effect his act would have on his aged mother. He claimed to have dropped the revolver where the shooting was done, but this is not probable, as the weapon could not be found last night.

The Dam at Spier's Falls

Times

The foundation of the dam at Spier's Falls, on the Hudson River above Glens Falls, has been completed, and now a solid wall of masonry is stretched entirely across the river. The "big hole" at the site of the dam presented an engineering difficulty of magnitude. From the bottom of the hole to the crest of the dam the masonry will rise 157 feet. The dam at the base will be 115 feet through, while at the crest it will be only eight feet. The dam will be finished within a few weeks, a force of 300 men being employed at present.

THE HORICON REMODELED

G. F. Times May 26

LAKE GEORGE STEAMER BEGINS HER SEASON OF 1902 AS A NEW BOAT. *1902*

Her Hull With the Exception of the Keel is Entirely New—The Boat Has Been Thoroughly Overhauled and Much Improved.

The Lake George steamer Horicon today began her season of 1902, practically a new craft.

The boat has been on the dry dock all winter and yesterday afternoon when she tied up at Caldwell after sailing up the lake from Baldwin she presented a greatly improved appearance.

With the first voyage of the Horicon, always the last week of May, one realizes that summer is near at hand and yesterday afternoon as the boat steamed up from Baldwin preparatory to making her initial trip she was saluted from many points and her reception at Caldwell was cordial. The trip from Baldwin to Caldwell was made in little over two hours.

This morning at 9:30 o'clock the Horicon left the railroad dock at Caldwell for her first trip. She was due to arrive at Baldwin at 12:30 when the return trip was immediately begun.

Captain E. S. Harris was in command and will run the Horicon until July 1 when, with his crew, he will go aboard the new Sagamore. Captain White of the ill-fated Ticonderoga will then assume command of the Horicon.

The Horicon was much changed by the ship builders during the winter months. Her hull, with the exception of the keel, was built entirely new. All of her upper work was overhauled and new suspension frames were erected. The wheel bearings were also replaced new. The decks below were overhauled and replanked where needed. The engine and boilers were likewise overhauled. The boat was newly painted throughout and a new carpet of deep red was laid in the state room.   z

With all her improvements and new parts the Horicon is as good as the day she was launched in 1877.

The Horicon tied yesterday afternoon on the west side of the railroad dock, while the Sagamore is building on the east side. Both craft were visited by many Glens Falls people during the afternoon. The new boat is 205 feet long. Her beam measures 30 feet while her width over all is 54 feet. The Horicon is 204 feet long. Her beam measures the same as the Sagamore, but her width over all is 50 feet.

Jonathan S. Gates of Bolton Landing, Warren county, New York, has in his possession a powder horn, which this John Gates, who was his great-grandfather, carried through the revolutionary war. In accordance with the custom of the soldiers of this war, this horn has an inscription, which is as follows:

"John Gates, his horn.
July year 26th 1777.
In Boston state, I wrote this date.
Upon a hill so high.
So take it not for fear your lot
Will be in misery.
To all men to whom these"——

XIV. STEPHEN GATES (Nathaniel (18), Samuel (12). Simon, (11). Stephen (10), etc.) Born July 20, 1737, married ——, died 1779. His son:

XV. CAPTAIN AARON GATES, born near Chatham (a few miles from Amenia), N. Y., April 3, 1776; married Martha Kellum (who was born Sept. 22, 1783) March 3, 1798. (The writer is informed by his cousin, Charles Gates, of Warrensburg, Warren county, N. Y., that Capt. Aaron's father and mother died about the time he was 3 years old. Whether Stephen Gates died in the military service I have been unable to ascertain.)

STEAMER HORICON", LAKE GEORGE. N.Y.

1903

DEATH OF MR MEYER.

about Feb. 6 1903

A Well Known Summer Resident of Lake George Passes Away.

Theodore F. Meyer of Yonkers, whose death was briefly announced in these columns on Monday was one of the well known summer visitors at Lake George. He had spent the summer months at that resort for several years at Alma farm, which was owned by him. This has been one of the largest and best known stock farms in this section of the state. In recent years Mr. Meyer has been unable to take an active interest and the stock has been sold.

In speaking of the death of Mr. Meyer the New York Tribune in the issue of Monday says:

Theodore F. Meyer, who died at his home in Yonkers on Saturday, was well known to members of the legal profession here, having been an active member of the local bar for many years. Born in Bremen fifty-eight years ago, the son of the late L. H. Meyer, then United States consul there, Mr. Meyer was educated in Germany. He subsequently entered Columbia and was graduated from there. He read law in the offices of Burrill, Davidson & Burill, and subsequently formed a partnership with the late Judge Sinnott, the firm being Sinnott & Meyer. Mr. Meyer has a large corporation practice, among his clients being the Pittsburg, Fort Wayne and Chicago railroad, the Chicago, Denver and Rio Grande railroad, and the Rio Grande and Western, the latter being organized under his supervision. Mr. Meyer continued active practice until a few years ago, when a stroke of apoplexy put an end to his activity. The stroke left him paralyzed on his right side, but his brain was unimpaired. He leaves a widow, two sons and four daughters.

Sher— **OBITUARY.** *Deed 1903*

Feb 18

Penfield.

Mary S. Penfield, aged eighty-two years, died at the Algonquin hotel, Bolton Landing on Wednesday evening. She is survived by her son, E. G. Penfield, proprietor of the Algonquin, and by two other sons and two daughters, none of whom, except the first named, are residents of this county. A short funeral service will be held at Bolton Landing on Sunday, and on Monday the remains will be taken to Waterville, he rformer home for interment.

REV. JAMES W. GRANT.

The Rev. James W. Grant, a venerable and respected clergyman of the Baptist denomination, died at his home in Whitehall Wednesday of last week. He was born at Bolton in 1822 and was a son of the Rev. William Grant, who was a famous exhorter of his day. Both father and son were preachers of the old school type.

BLACK BEAUTY A WONDER.

Glens Falls Star Mar. 12

Her Performances in Races as a Green Mare. *1903*

Black Beauty is a black mare, 15½ hands high; weighs 1,050 pounds; is six years old; is owned by George Streeter, of Hague. Speaking of this mare as a race horse, she never started in a race until the races at Hague on February 24, 1903, when she went against F. Walker's Cuyler Brown, G. Stewart's Alexander Wilkes, R. Bolton's Dan Theron, and won the race in three straight heats, going the last mile in 2:33½. This mare had no training for this race, and was worked out only once before the race.

In regard to the race that she started in at Bolton on Thursday, March 5, 1903: Between the time she started at Hague and Bolton she was not trained, nor had she had a work-out.

In going to Bolton to race her it was understood that she would not have to start against horses that could go better than 2:35. But after getting up there it was found out that the horses she was to start against from Glens Falls that they call Muggins and Victor had been a race at Caldwell on Tuesday, March 3, better than 2:30. After all of this Mr. Streeter decided to start in the race. So at 2:30 o'clock the judge called them up for the word, and you would think to see Black Beauty score that she was an old race mare. They only scored a few times, when they got the word, and it was a horse race until they finished. A blanket would cover all three of them, going the mile in 2:29. The second heat was a good race up to the three quarter, when she got a little tired, but the heat was made in 2:31½. The third heat was the horse race. The second time they scored they got the word, and a better race never was seen over ice or turf. The three horses were all in a bunch up to the three quarter, going the first half in 1:11½, and to the three quarters in a 2:22 clip, finishing the mile in 2:29. A good many thought that if Black Beauty had the pole that heat she would have won the heat. If anyone would like to know how this mare is bred they can find out by inquiring of George Streeter, of the Phoenix hotel, Hague, N. Y.

W Nems July 2nd 1903

Lake George Children Wed.

A pair of Lake George children, Cleon West and Frances Weaver, aged respectively eighteen and sixteen years, went for a drive on Monday evening of last week and worried their parents by not returning until the next day, when they sought the parental blessing as a newly married couple. They were wedded by the Rev. Milton Tator, of Hill View, to whom they gave their ages as eighteen each.

Completing a Private Park.

George O. Knapp of Chicago, owner of Shelving Rock, the large landed estate at the Narrows on Lake George, has decided to close the Hundred Island House and to make the property a part of his private estate. The Hundred Island House has been a hotel at Lake George for more than twenty-five years, but will not receive guests this year and will probably be torn down to make room for buildings connected with Mr. Knapp's estate. The Shelving Rock property, which includes Shelving Rock Mountain, is 3,000 acres in extent, and its development was begun nine years ago when Mr. Knapp purchased the hotel and neighboring land. Extensions and improvements, including such features as twenty miles of drives, have made this one of the handsomest private parks in the country. Henry E. Nichols, who has been manager of the Hundred Island House since Mr. Knapp took possession nine years ago, will remain as manager of the Shelving Rock estate. He has been Mr. Knapp's representative in conducting the extensive improvements to that property. *Mar. 10, '03*

F. A. Star 1903 **OBITUARY.** *July 3* Eli Reynolds

Eli Reynolds, an old and highly respected citizen of Hill View, died Tuesday after an illness of some weeks. He was eighty-nine years old. He is survived by his widow and one son, Amos Reynolds, of Glens Falls. Interment in Warrensburg cemetery.

MARCUS E. GRANGER is no more. He was one of the best-known and most jovial characters in Warren county and his rotund form and hearty laugh will be greatly missed. As a fiddler for country dances Marcus was in his happiest mood and he enjoyed the merrymaking of the young people as much as they. Then it was that his laugh became infectious, his smile beatific. His famous fiddle told the story of his life, it breathed his sunny disposition. The violin is the aristocrat of the mansion, but give us the fiddle, the democrat of the unpretentious home. As violin, it weaves its garlands of roses; as fiddle, it scatters its modest violets. As violin, it is held in awe by those cultured in music for its wondrous powers; as fiddle, it is loved by the millions for its simple melodies. "Marcus and his fiddle furnished the music." To how many comes back those happy days agone! A shifting of the bow—the music eddies into a mournful tone—a fiddle-string snaps—Marcus is dead. *1903*

THE PRESIDENT'S GUEST.

MIKE CRONIN TELLS OF HIS VISIT TO THE WHITE HOUSE.

Enjoyed A Two Hours' Talk With Mr. Roosevelt While "Big Guns" Waited--Exchanged Opinions With Chief Executive on Various Important Subjects.

There was no prouder man in Warrensburgh Monday than M. F. Cronin, of Aiden Lair Lodge, Minerva, who was on his way home from attending the Sportsmen's show, in Madison Square Garden, New York city. He was the center of an admiring crowd at the Adirondack hotel, who listened breathlessly to his vivid recital of his recent noted visit to President Roosevelt.

While in New York "Nervy Mike" took a run over to Washington to see the Chief Executive.

Bubbling over with gratification he related how the President had conferred with him on such subjects as the protection of forests and the preservation of fish and game. With a gesture of pride he repeated the President's congratulations on his having raised five children and his evident belief in Mr. Roosevelt's own doctrine as to the duty of an American citizen in that respect.

"Don't think for a minute I am stuck on myself," apologized Mike, "or that I think I'm any better man than I was before I was entertained by the President. But I'm so tickled over the way he treated me, just as if I was his own brother, that I can't help letting the gladness stick out. Mr. Roosevelt is certainly a man of nerve, as I discovered on the last twenty miles of that ride of ours over the rocks to North Creek, but he is also a man of heart and the way he made me feel at home was a caution.

"You see the other night when he spoke to the Methodists in the metropolis—you published it, how he noticed me struggling with the cops, who wouldn't let me get look at him —he invited me again to go down and see him. I'm glad I went.

"When I arrived in Washington I put up at one of those swell apartment houses—not a hotel, you know—where a lot of those high guys like Senator Gorman and that push stop. You ought to have seen the door attendant nearly turn pale when I wrote on the back of one of my cards, 'Just arrived,' and told him to take it to the President, but when he got back with one of the President's cards with 'Come at once,' written on it, I thought that he would turn inside out trying to be polite.

"I got to the White House all right, and I tell you the President made me feel right at home. We spent two solid hours talking and some of the biggest in the land had to sit outside and twirl their hats. After our little chat he sent me to the house of representatives with his private secretary, and I noticed that our congressman, the Hon. L. W. Emerson, seemed to be just about as important as any of 'em. Of course, Essex county is in another district now, but we wouldn't be surprised to see 'Lou' try again, especially after that crooked postmaster over at Fort Plain, who turned him down last summer at Saratoga, has been found out at last.

"It may conceited in me to say it, but the President and I are interested in many of the same subjects. We talked about good roads—our ride when President McKinley lay dying led up to it—the protection of the Adirondack forests, and the necessity of the state purchasing the lands that are for sale and dedicating them to the public comfort as a play ground and health resort.

"In the Adirondack region there are sixty preserves," said Mr. Cronin as he brought out a newspaper clipping for reference, "with an aggregate acreage of 789,993 acres held as private property by Sportsmen's clubs or individuals.

"The private preserves in the Adirondacks, with a slight exception, have been established within the last sixteen years—most of them within eleven years—and the comparatively sudden exclusion of the public from its own camping grounds has provoked a bitter hostility on the part of the hunters, fishermen and guides who ranged formerly over this territory. The sportsman who returns to some favorite haunt only to find himself confronted with the words, 'No Thoroughfare,' turns back with a resentful feeling, while the guides, who were wont to conduct their patrons wherever game was plentiful, view with threatening looks the hired gamekeepers that guard the forbidden lands.

On the other hand, the owners of the preserves point to the protection of the forests, fish and game afforded by them and to the large number of guides and woodsmen to whom they furnish constant and lucrative employment. In 1899, the dry season in which forest fires were raging in the Adirondacks to an unusual extent, it was noticed that there were no fires on the private preserves, aside from incipient ones that were extinguished before any serious danger was incurred. This was due to the large number of forest patrols employed by the owners of these tracts.

"It is not necessary that the state should purchase these private holdings in order that the tree growth may be protected, for the owners can be relied upon to preserve the forest conditions that are so essential to the enjoyment of their property. The acquisition of these high priced lands may be deferred until the rest of the Adirondack park has been bought. But the tenure of title to these private preserves is not permanent like that of the state preserve; these properties change hands frequently; public sentiment is always gratified when any of this territory is opened to the public; so it would be well if the state kept a fund on hand, available at all times, for the purchase of such tracts whenever any portion is thrown upon the market.

'The President said the people should be careful about fires and that every citizen should extend his utmost power to prevent them, each man constituting himself a fire warden, an especial protector of this great means of earning a livelihood.

"Well, to change the subject, the President asked, 'How's Mrs. Cronin? And Rosey? And Katharine? And Arthur? And little Add?' He remembered them all.

"'Well Mr. Roosevelt,' I said, 'you see I believe in your idea of an American's duty in welcoming all the little ones that come along.'

"'That's all right,' he said, 'I admire you for it.'

"'You have got me beaten by one, though, sir.'

"'Don't worry about that,' said he, 'you'll be catching up to me the first thing you know.'

"'And between you and me,' said the noted Adirondack guide to THE NEWS man, "I'm on my way home now thinking there may be something doing. I see the stork has been walking in Warrensburgh lately. Never mind, I've been married seventeen years. Mrs. Roosevelt and her children met my wife and her children at the time President McKinley was shot. They were guests of Dean Sage, of Albany, at Hewitt pond.

"But I wouldn't change places with the President. I have less responsibility and a pleasanter place to live. His life is a hard one."

Who shall judge man from his manners?
    Who shall know him by his dress?
Paupers may be fit for princes,
    Princes fit for something less.
Crumpled shirt and dirty jacket
    May beclothe the golden ore
Or the deepest thought and feelings—
    Satin vest can do no more.

Truth and justice are eternal,
    Born with loveliness and light;
Secret wrongs shall never prosper,
    While there is a sunny right.
God, whose world-wide voice is singing
    Boundless love to you and me,
Links oppression with his titles
    But as pebbles in the sea.

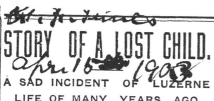

STORY OF A LOST CHILD.

Apr 15 1903

A SAD INCIDENT OF LUZERNE LIFE OF MANY YEARS AGO RECALLED.

Account of Story as Written in 1826 by Josiah Fasset—The Mysterious Disappearance of the Little Daughter of Alexander Dean, Jr.

Away back in 1826 there disappeared mysteriously as if swallowed up by the earth the little daughter of Alexander Dean, Jr., of Luzerne. The child was never found and to this day interest in the sad mysterious affair occasionally revives.

The solemn news I now relate,
'Twas in Luzerne, in New York state,
A girl was lost, has ne'er been seen,
The child of Alexander Dean.

One-half mile this child did steer,
She was sent by her parents dear;
On her return to find her home,
She miss'd her way and never come.

'Twas in April, on the fifth day,
Then this poor child did stray away;
She was six years and nine days old,
This from her mother I was told.

Her parents now in keen distress,
Go searching through the wilderness;
Determin'd for their loss to find,
But still they leave the child behind.

Hundreds of men were rais'd around,
Slowly a marching o'er the ground;
And here they strove but all in vain,
They ne'er could find their child again.

Now they go searching different ways,
Till there was spent full nineteen days;
Now they had trac'd the green woods through,
They had to bid this child adieu.

Although she's gone, yet seems to speak,
Parents no longer for me seek;
For I am lost, shall ne'er return,
I must leave you now all to mourn.

Oh! my parents you did engage,
Fanny to find upon the stage;
But as for me, you'll ne'er obtain,
Your loss is my eternal gain.

Farewell to all beneath the sun,
My time is past, my work is done;
Now I am gone you plainly see,
To dwell in long eternity.

And now my friends have all been kind,
Searching with us our child to find;
Although we've rov'd the mountains o'er,
We must leave her forevermore.

Oh! now our child is took away,
And turning to its mother clay;
While we feel the chastizing rod,
We'll say like Job, "blessed be God."

Now we are in a lonesome state,
Our troubles now they are so great;
Fanny is gone, who was our child,
Oh! may we now be reconcil'd.

Lord, help us now to spend our days,
That we may live thine holy ways;
Oh! may we now prepared be
To meet her in eternity.

ADRIFT ON A RAFT

Apr 23d 1903

Two Bolton Boys Have a Trying Time on Lake George Saturday.

One of the heaviest winds known for several years came up suddenly Saturday afternoon at Bolton, on Lake George. The lake was quickly transformed into a seething mass of foam. Two boys, Don, son of H. F. Seaman, and Lee, son of James Brown, got on a raft in Finkle's bay and paddled about. Finally, they concluded to go it alone and untied the rope by which the raft was moored to the dock and started to cross the bay. At once the wind caught them and swept them out into the broad waters of the lake. How they kept themselves on the raft; why it, a boy-made thing, was not wrenched asunder, are mysteries beyond mortal calculation. But a speck on the lake was discovered and it was followed and the boys transferred to the boat and brought home. Great praise is due Walter Pratt, himself hardly beyond boyhood, who went out to the rescue with only a small boy, into a seething turmoil of water which few men would have cared to enter.

BOLTON.

Wednesday Mar, 11 1903

—Mrs. Gilbert Carpenter who has been visiting her many friends in this place returned to her home in Queensbury Wednesday.

—Reuben and Horace Smith of Igerna visited their cousins, Jonathan S. and Walter E. Gates, Thursday.

—Herbert Beswick, aged nineteen, son of Byron and Eliza Beswick, died Friday night. The funeral was held Sunday at 1 o'clock p. m., at the home. Interment in the Beswick cemetery.

—Mr. and Mrs. Ralph Stone and children of Warrensburg visited Mr. and Mrs. Joseph H. Gates, Saturday.

—In the town race of the horse trot Saturday Walter E. Gates' horse Bob, who was driven by W. H. Clothier, won in three straight heats with Fred Stewart's mare So So second and Eldee Pratt's Belle Harkaway third. Time, 2:50, 2:48 and 2:46.

—George B. Fuller, who has been visiting friends in this place for a few days, returned to the Alma Farm yesterday.

OBITUARY.

1903 June 25th

CHARLES GATES.

Charles Gates died at his home in Lewisville Friday night after a brief illness of blood poisoning, aged sixty-six years. He leaves a widow, two daughters, Mrs. Fred Wells and Miss Minnie Gates, and one son, Myron J. Gates, all of this place. He is also survived by one brother, Henry Gates, and a sister, Mrs. Jane Hall, both of Caldwell. The funeral was held at his late home Sunday afternoon at 2 o'clock, and was conducted by the Rev. N. M. Learned. The Odd Fellows lodge, of which the deceased was a member, attended in a body, and followed the remains to their last resting place in the village cemetery.

LLOYD-PRATT.

July 16 1903

Miss Pearl Pratt, youngest daughter of Mr. and Mrs. John Pratt, of Bolton, was united in marriage Sunday to Leslie Lloyd, also of that place. The ceremony was performed by the Rev. Richard Palmer, at the home of the bride. The house was prettily decorated with flowers. Miss Lola Lloyd, sister of the groom, was bridesmaid, and Selah Pratt, brother of the bride, was best man. The happy couple went immediately to their future home, a good farm and house, equipped with everything to begin with. They received many useful and beautiful presents from relatives and friends, together with good wishes for a long and happy life together.

GRAND ARMY HOUSE SOLD.

Aug 20 1903

"Uncle Pat" Heffron to Retire September 1—Mac R. Smith to be His Successor.

"Uncle Pat" Heffron, who fifteen years ago established the Grand Army house, and who has since conducted it and with the assistance of his estimable helpmate, "Aunt Mary," has made it one of the most popular hotels in this section, has sold the property to Mac R. Smith and will retire from business. Mr. Smith will take possession September 1. Mr. Heffron's retirement will be regretted by his hosts of friends and patrons. His genial disposition has endeared him to all with whom he has come in contact and the home-like accommodations and excellent cuisine of his hotel have become widely known through the "drummers" and other satisfied patrons who have at various times enjoyed his generous hospitality.

Mr. Heffron, who is a veteran of the Civil war, has not enjoyed good health of late and Mrs. Heffron, who has been housekeeper since the establishment of the hotel, is also in poor health. Their condition, they hope, will improve when they are relieved of the work and cares of their present positions.

Mac R. Smith, who will succeed Mr. Heffron, has had some experience in the hotel business, having successfully managed the Palisades, a summer resort at Brant Lake, Horicon, for two seasons. He is a companionable young man and will undoubtedly make a popular and successful landlord.

LAKE GEORGE BOY KILLED

HORRIBLY BURNED BY EXPLOSION OF FIREWORKS.

Entire Stock In Small Store Set Off by Shot From a Toy Pistol—Young Fred Alston Was Overcome by Powder Fumes and Unable to Escape.

An explosion of fireworks in the store of Henry W. Sisson, at Lake George, Monday afternoon, caused the death of Freddie Alston, the seven-year-old son of Mr. and Mrs. William Alston, of that place, and completely wrecked the interior of Mr. Sisson's establishment, involving a loss of about $300.

Mr. Sisson is a photographer. A few weeks ago he moved his studio into the small stone building just north of the county clerk's office. This building is one of the village landmarks. It was built in 1830 and was formerly used as the office of the Caldwell estate by the late William Caldwell.

A few days ago Mr. Sisson put in a stock of fireworks as an adjunct to his regular business. Tuesday afternoon about 4 o'clock he started down the lake to take some pictures, leaving the store in charge of Fred Barber, a fifteen-year-old boy. He had been gone but a short time when several boys, among whom was Freddie Alston, entered the store. One of them bought a toy pistol and loaded it with blank cartridges. He pulled the trigger several times but the cartridge failed to explode. Going into the store he laid the weapon on the counter with the intention of selecting another. One of the other boys picked it up and pulled the trigger while the pistol was aimed at a bunch of torpedoes. This time it went off. Sparks from the cartridge ignited the fireworks and in a moment rockets and cannon crackers were exploding on all sides. The store was instantly filled with smoke and the fumes of burning powder.

All the boys rushed for the door and escaped except young Alston, who was overcome by the smoke and fumes. It was not known that the boy was in the burning building until after E. J. Worden, proprietor of the Worden house across the street, had brought the flames under control by means of a fire extinguisher. About that time the boy recovered consciousness and gave several shrieks. William Varnum rushed into the building and rescued the lad, who had again lapsed into unconsciousness.

Washington's Leap.

In 1775 there lived in a Virginia town a rich and eccentric old farmer whose daughter was the loveliest maiden in all the locality. The beautiful Annette was 18 years of age and had many suitors for her hand and heart. On her nineteenth birthday the old man invited all the youth of the village to a grand haymaking frolic.

"Now, my lads," said the old man, after the banquet was some time over, "I've got something to say to you. It seems that a good many of you have been casting sheep's eyes on my Annette. Now, boys, I don't care anything about money or talents, book learning or soldier learning. I can do as well by my girl as any man in the country, but I want her to marry a man of my own grit. I got my old woman by beating the smartest man on the Eastern Shore. Now, listen. I've taken an oath that no man shall marry my daughter without jumping for it. There you are, boys; yonder's the green, and here's Annette. The one who jumps farthest on a dead level shall marry her this very evening."

"Twenty-one feet and a half. A magnificent leap!" cried the judge. "Hoorray for Harry Carroll!"

Hands, hats and handkerchiefs were waved wildly by the delighted villagers, and the eyes of the happy Annette sparkled with joy.

Now, just before Harry had leaped a stranger had entered the throng unperceived. He was a tall, gentlemanly young man in a military undress frock coat, who had at that moment arrived on horseback before the inn. He was just in time to witness Carroll's great leap.

The man's handsome face and easy address at once attracted the eyes of the maidens, while his manly and sinewy frame, in which were happily united symmetry and strength, called forth the admiration of the young men.

"Mayhap, sir stranger, you think you can beat that," said Charlie Simms, remarking the manner in which the new comer scanned the arena. "If you can outleap Harry Carroll, you beat the best man in the colonies."

"Is it for amusement you are pursuing this pastime?" inquired the youthful stranger, "or is there a prize for the winner?"

"The sweetest prize man ever strove for," answered the judges. "Yonder she stands."

The stranger cast a respectful glance at the blushing maiden, and his eyes looked admiration.

"Are the lists open to all?" he asked.

"All, young sir," replied Annette's father with interest. "If you will try, you are free to do so. Here is my daughter, sir; look at her and decide."

With a smile the newcomer threw off his coat, drew his sash tighter around his waist and stepped forward. All hearts stood still as the young man bounded forward.

"Twenty-two feet and an inch!" The judge's words were received with murmurs of surprise and wonder. Not without a feeling of pity for poor Harry, all crowded around the new victor, offering him their congratulations. Resuming his coat, the stranger sought with his eye the fair prize he had, although nameless and unknown, so fairly won. She leaned upon her father's arm, pale and distressed

Poor Harry Carroll stood aloof, gloomy and mortified, admiring the stranger for his ability, but hating him for his success.

"Annette, my pretty prize," said the victor, taking her passive hand, "I have won you fairly, but I think there is a favored youth among the competitors who has a higher claim than mine. Young sir," he continued, turning to the surprised Harry, "methinks you were the victor in the list before me, and as such, with the permission of this worthy assembly, you receive from my hand the prize you have so well and honorably won."

The youth sprang forward and grasped the stranger's hand with gratitude, and the next moment Annette was weeping from pure joy upon his breast. The place rang with the acclamations of the delighted people, and amid the excitement the newcomer withdrew, remounting his horse, and rode briskly out of the village.

That night Harry and Annette were married. Several years later Harry Carroll became Col. Harry Carroll. One evening the colonel was sitting on the piazza of his handsome country house, when a courier rode up and announced the approach of General Washington and suite who would crave the colonel's hospitality for the night.

That evening at the table Annette now the dignified, matronly and still handsome Mrs. Carroll, could not keep her eyes from the face of her illustrious visitor. "I suspect, colonel," said the general, "that Mrs. Carroll thinks she recognizes in me an old acquaintance, but I have become, by dint of camp fare and hard usage, too unwieldy to leap again 22 feet one inch, even for so fair a bride as one I wot of."

George Washington was indeed the handsome young athlete whose mysterious disappearance in the native village of the lovers is still traditionary.

COLDEST SUMMER ON RECORD.

Figures Supplied by the Weather Bureau in New York.

With yesterday the last day of the month, August and the summer of 1902 pass into history as the coldest recorded by the weather bureau.

June reached the record of 1881. July was just a little bit off normal, but not enough to keep its fellow months of the summer from taking the average temperature a fraction below the figure reached in 1897.

The average temperature during June, July and August, figuring the last day of the present month at the normal, as recorded by the weather bureau in New York, was sixty-nine degrees. In 1897 the average temperature was recorded at three-quarters of a degree higher. The average temperature during August has been 69.5 degrees, nearly two degrees lower than the lowest mark the month ever reached. In 1897 and eight times previous to that year the average temperature for August was recorded as seventy-one degrees.

POWER IS USED.

1903

TROLLEY CARS OPERATED BY ELECTRICITY FROM SPIER FALLS DAM.

LIGHTS LAST EVENING.

Red Letter Day in History of Hudson River Water Power Company—First Power Delivered Yesterday Afternoon—Trolley Cars Run Today.

The Hudson Valley Railway company is today operating its cars under power from Spier Falls.

Last evening lights were furnished from Spier Falls for Saratoga, Ballston and Glens Falls.

Yesterday afternoon at 3:03 o'clock the first power was delivered from the big dam up the river. At that hour Katherine R. Ashley, daughter of President Eugene L. Ashley, closed the switch which connected the monster generators with Glens Falls. This important step was taken in the presence of Miss Ashley's parents, her grandmothers, Mrs. Demmis Ashley and Mrs. P. A. Hitchcock, Dr. and Mrs. Lemon Thomson, Mr. and Mrs. Clarence M. Wilmarth and a number of employes of the Hudson River Water Power company.

After midnight the connections between Spier Falls and the Queensbury power house of the Hudson Valley Railway were perfected and this morning at 3:30 o'clock the first car under the new electrical power was run out of the sheds and to the village.

President Ashley is a motorman as well as a dam builder and he ran the car to Glens Falls. His passengers were employes of the railway and power company and it is said today that several have promised themselves never to ride on another trolley car of which Mr. Ashley is the motorman.

The car developed wonderful speed and there was no slowing up for curves much to the discomfort of the passengers who were compelled to hold fast for their lives. However, Mr. Ashley only smiled and well he might. He had accomplished a great work.

Throughout the day 1,500 horse power was furnished the trolley line.

Three of the big 5,000 horse power generators are now operating at Spier Falls.

On Friday 10,000 horse power will be delivered to the General Electrical works at Schenectady.

HAD A KILLING TIME.

R. *Sope Wird*

Colonel (who detests motors)—Well, and how did you enjoy your ride?
Flossie—We've simply had a killing time of it.
Colonel—Animals or old women?—Judy.

A FRACTURED SKULL *1903* *Spt 4* AND BROKEN ARMS

TERRIBLE FALL OF WILLIAM SCHERMERHORN AT BOLTON.

PICKED UP UNCONSCIOUS

Trephining Performed and Patient Recovers Consciousness—His Condition Remains Very Critical.

William Schermerhorn, a well known contractor, of Caldwell, was seriously if not fatally injured at Bolton yesterday. He is a foreman on the building of Villa Solitude, owned by Herman Broesel, and at half-past five o'clock he was on a third story scaffolding. He started to leave the scaffold and crawl up on the plate, when some one spoke to him from below. He turned and stepped back upon an insecure board, which gave away, precipitating him thirty-three feet to the ground below.

Mr. Schermerhorn struck head first upon a pile of brick. Dr. D. L. Rogers was summoned, and the unconscious man was at once taken to the Seeman cottage, where all that could be was done to relieve him. Dr. Thomson, of Glens Falls, was at once called, and upon his arrival at eight o'clock a careful examination was made. The skull is terribly fractured over the right eye and in the temporal region. It was indented fully three-quarters of an inch. Both forearms were also fractured. The surgeons trephined the skull, removing ten or more pieces of the bone There was also a considerable hemorrhage. After the operation the patient recovered consciousness. From so great a fall it may develop later that there are internal injuries. His condition is very critical.

Mr. Schermerhorn is forty-two years of age, and has a wife and eight children.

MIDDLEWORTH'S, WEST SIDE, LAKE GEORGE, N. Y.

PARK FOR BURG.

MISS WOODWARD MAKES A FINE GIFT TO THE UP-COUNTY TOWNSHIP.

TWO ACRES IN TRACT.

The Prospective Park is Located Opposite J. P. Baumann's Residence—A Refuge for the Weary—Commissioner Smith Now Opening Streets.

Miss Elizabeth B. Woodward has given to the town of Warrensburg about two acres of land, corner of Hudson street and the Big Turn, for a public park, which will doubtless be known to the present and future generations as "Woodward park," in honor of the generous donor.

The idea is a good one, says the Warrensburg News, and in keeping with town's improvements of late. A public park will add beauty to the village and be a joy for the summer season when it will be a refuge for the weary. It will also afford a haven of rest for the older set, tired mothers, and a place of recreation for restless children.

As a public benefactor, therefore, Miss Woodward is justly entitled to the gratitude of an appreciative people.

The park will be located across the street from the residence of J. P. Baumann and will be about the shape of a right angle triangle, formed by the junction of Hudson street, the Big Turn, and a new street now being opened, which will be known as Park street.

Commissioner S. F. Smith has been doing good work this week in laying out a street through Miss Woodward's property from Hudson street just opposite Mr. Baumann's residence, extending in the same direction toward Main street as the Big Turn.

At right angles to this street, an appropriate name for which is needed, Mr. Smith has run one street south past Lewis Thomson's tenant houses toward Second street.

Park street opens on the Big Turn, opposite Henry Smith's residence and intersects the new street a few rods from Hudson street.

These streets are fifty feet wide, with six feet on either side for walks.

Miss Woodward will cut up her property into building lots.

Big Hotel Closed. 1903

After a most successful season the Fort William Henry hotel has closed and the gaiety at Lake George is over. Manager W. W. Brown closed the doors Saturday.

ROBINSON'S LOST POND

Article in "The News" Brings Out Another Interesting Story.

GLENS FALLS, N. Y., Aug. 31, 1903.

EDITOR NEWS:—My attention was called to an article in your valuable paper in regard to what is now called Robinson's lost pond, stating that the eyes of only four mortal men have ever looked upon its waters, as far as is known. I have heard my father say that my uncle, Calvin Baldwin, went with an Indian called Sabael, not far from the year 1808, from the place then known as Penilton, to Cold River and thence to this pond. After they had found the pond the Indian told Baldwin that there was a salt spring near them, but he could not take him to it unless he would go blindfolded, for it would not be allowed by his tribe. So my uncle allowed himself to be blindfolded, and for about half an hour the Indian led him through the forest. He then halted and removed the bandage from his eyes and there was the spring as Sabael had described it to him. After a short stay they returned to the pond, as they had come, and went home.

Mrs. E. H. Johnson, one of Calvin Baldwin's daughters, and the only surviving member of a large family, who is living with her daughter, Mrs. Frank Murray, in Glens Falls, told me that her father some years after succeeded in again finding the pond, but could not find the spring, and this was the same pond the Indian called "Lost Pond." Sabael said, "Me lose him many moons." P. BALDWIN.

THE LOVE OF LATER YEARS.

What of the strong man's stubborn passion,
  When Love comes singing sweet and low?
What of the long-established fashion
  When Love comes pleading: "Let it go?"
From habits that enslaved before
He turns as one new-born, to sigh,
He dreams of wildwood haunts no more,
  His gun and rod uncherished lie.

The thunders of applause that shook
  The halls of state for him are all
Forgotten when she turns to look
  And when he hears her softly call;
The wisdom that he had he lays
  Aside, forgetting to be wise,
He craves no honor but her praise,
  His universe is in her eyes.

Frisky Old Horsemen. Oct 15

There are many who probably thought that W. S. Stewart, of this place, and Mr. Crandall, of Warrensburgh, both of whom drove in the races at Huber's park, for men of their years, were rather frisky. And so they are. We dare say there are not many occasions on which two such men compete in the same race. However, there are older drivers than they, for the Vergennes Vermonter of last week says: "The oldest horseman in the country is said to be Charles Taylor, of White River Junction, who drove a trotter last week at the Springfield fair, although ninety-seven years of age."—Ticonderoga Sentinel.

1903

Coal Discovered in Bolton.

Thomas Ramsey, Edward Sexton, Marvin Scribner and Moses Finkle, of Bolton, are making arrangements to develop a mineral deposit recently discovered at Padan Aram, between Bolton and Horicon, which they believe to be coal. The mineral burns readily and makes a hot and lasting fire. Dec 13/25 1903

A Subject for Antiquarians.

GLOVERSVILLE, N. Y., February 16.—THE STAR: In regard to article which I saw in your paper about the Lake house: The Gazeteer of the State of New York says: "Warren county was formed from Washington on March 12, 1813; named in honor of General Joseph Warren, of the Revolution." It also says that the court house was built in 1816 and 1817. The first courts were held at Lake George Coffee house, and the first judge was Henry Spencer. My grandfather told my father that the first courts were held in what is now known as the Lake house.

Yours truly,
MAY W. HUBBELL.

PLANK ROAD NOW OPEN. Jan 6 1904

Money Paid Over Yesterday and the Keepers Opened the Street at Four O'clock.

The amount of the award of the commission appointed to assess the damages in the condemnation proceedings, $15,000, was yesterday paid to President Colvin, of the Plank Road company, and at four o'clock he issued orders to the gate keepers to collect no more tolls. A survey is to be made to determine the exact length of the road in the two towns, so that the costs may be assessed on the town in proportion to the distance in each town. It is about seven to three.

SPORTS AT LAKE GEORGE. Star Aug. 19 1904

Good Races Yesterday—Vinco to Try for the World's Record.

A large crowd witnessed the sports of yesterday at Lake George, there being two good races. The match between E J. Worden's Free delivery and J. B. Wilson's chestnut colt for $200 a side was won by the former in straight heats. Time, 2:34½, 2:32½, 2:32. There were six starters in the town race, George Stanton's Gipsey Girl won in straight heats, J. N. Hubbell's Buckskin Joe taking second place and William Hamlin's Claribel third. The other starters were Earl Mattison's Grey Eagle, Samuel Weller's Skip and John Smith's Claude.

A match has been made for Saturday between J. J. Cunningham's Vinco and Wyreka, in which it is said the former will make a try for the world's ice record.

FOURTEEN DEGREES BELOW THE RECORD

Jan th 1904

WEATHER BUREAU THERMOMETER INDICATED THIRTY-SIX BELOW.

OTHERS ARE LOWER STILL

Warrensburg Has One Which Registered Forty-six Below—The Lowest Point Reached Here Was Forty.

Professor C. L. Williams' thermometers, furnished to him by the weather bureau, had not yet found their level when THE STAR went to press yesterday. The new record made yesterday was thirty-six degrees below zero. The lowest previous record was twenty-two degrees below zero on February 25, 1894.

Other thermometers were not as modest. At Warrensburg the highest reported was at the pulp mill, where forty-six degrees was registered. Here in Queensbury forty-two is reported from the Haviland place, and in the village at William Doty's residence it was forty degrees below, and thermometers in all parts of the village marked from thirty-four to that figure. Gansevoort reports forty-five and Fort Edward and Sandy Hill follow closely in its wake. At Hadley and North Creek the forty-five degree point was reached. At six o'clock last evening it was as cold as it was at the same hour Monday evening, but it did not increase during the night as it did the night before, and it is not at all likely that this morning will be as cold.

The intense cold greatly delayed the steam roads yesterday, it being impossible to make steam rapidly enough to maintain speed.

M. B. Little and other old citizens recall that forty-one years ago this winter there was a cold wave, which was then called a cold spell, in which the thermometers here reached the forty degree below zero point.

Star Feb 18th 1904

Some Changes in Queensbury.

There will be a good many changes in Queensbury this spring. Myron Langworthy will move on the Howard farm, Bay road; Gilbert Carpenter will move on the Numan farm, Ridge road; George Chase will move on the Baker farm, Bay road; Bradford Thornton, now on the Baker place, will move to his home here; Clarence Ross will move in the Langworthy house.—Queensbury correspondent.

RECORD BREAKING WEATHER.

W. News Jan. 7th 1904

Tuesday Morning the Coldest Ever Known in Warrensburgh.

Forty-seven degrees below zero, recorded Tuesday morning at 6 o'clock by a reliable spirit thermometer at the Schroon River Pulp and Paper company's mill in Burnhamville, stands as the record for cold weather in this town. Never before was such weather known in this locality by any man now living and it is safe to say that the temperature has not been so low here since the glacial age. Neighboring towns report from 35° to 43° but Warrensburgh alone claims the distinction of 47°. At various points in the village the mercury registered 40° and all the way from that to 46°. In Glens Falls 43 was the lowest claimed and the northern towns were apparently contented with anything from 26° to 35°.

At 11 o'clock in the forenoon the mercury had managed to crawl up to 35° and at 12:30 to 30°, and it was only a few degrees warmer at any time during the day.

Yesterday morning at 5 o'clock 32° was recorded and then the mercury began to raise slowly but surely until last night when it came up with a rush At 1 o'clock this morning it was 10° above zero and at 7 o'clock it remained the same.

The cold wave arrived with the snow storm Saturday and it will long be remembered as the worst ever known here.

There was no suffering in Warrensburgh as everybody had plenty of fuel and by feeding fires almost continually managed to keep fairly warm.

G. F. Star Nov 17th 1903

ARGUMENT OF A HORSE CASE.

Celebrated Action of Riddell Against Jenkins in County Court.

At a special term of county court held yesterday, the case of Dr. Riddell, of Luzerne, against Rev. C. L. Jenkins, of Indian Lake, was argued. This has become a well known case in the county, and attracted much attention when tried before Justice F. B. Potter and a jury in Chestertown. The plaintiff alleged defendant sold him a horse afflicted with the heaves, guaranteeing the animal to be sound. In the justice's court plaintiff recovered a verdict of eighty dollars, including costs, from which an appeal was taken, both on the law and the facts. The arguments were made yesterday by Counselor J. H. Cunningham, for the plaintiff, and Counselor M. S. Bevins, for defendant. The former was given ten days in which to file a brief.

ROYAL POTTER.

Dec. 3

Royal Potter, who lived in Wardboro, Hague, near the Bolton line, died on Tuesday, the 24th ult., at his home there, aged about sixty-five years. The deceased had been ill several months, due to hardening of the lungs. The funeral was held last Thursday at the house. A widow, who was formerly Miss Mary Dalrymple, of Bolton, survives; also, one son, Clinton; two daughters, Mrs. Myrtle Ross, of Hague, and Mrs. William Wallace, of Ticonderoga, and brothers and sisters in the West. *1903*

W. News Oct. 29 1903

BOY BURIED IN SAND.

Bolton Youngster Meets With Serious Accident While at Play.

THE NEWS correspondent at Bolton Landing writes that Tuesday morning before school some little boys went to play in the sand hill near Asa Dickinson's place. Many sand swallows have nests there and the boys were trying to get at them. Quite a heavy shelf of grass and sand projected over the nests, as a great deal of sand has been dug out and carted away, leaving a big hole where the boys were. All at once the heavy shelf broke and fell down completely burying little Arthur Lamb. His brother and a little companion tried to dig him out, but couldn't, and so one ran for help while the other dug, but it was fully ten minutes before he was taken out, apparently dead, and carried home, where he lay unconscious all day. Towards evening he could understand what was said to him and speak a little. Dr. Rogers was in attendance all day and towards night Dr. Hunt, of Glens Falls, was summoned. The boy is about six years old. He is a son of Town Clerk Edward N. Lamb.

ANOTHER HOTEL SOLD.

The Warren House Purchased by Ashley T. Kellogg.

The Warren house property was sold Monday by George C. Waters & Company to Ashley T. Kellogg. The price is not stated but it is believed to be about $10,000. This is the third hotel that has changed hands in Warrensburgh within two months, the Grand Army house having been purchased by Mac R. Smith and the Adirondack hotel by O'Connor Brothers.

Waters & Company bought the Warren house of Mr. Kellogg about three years ago. They have been successful in their management of the property and the house has been well patronized. Mr. Kellogg will take possession November 10 and will on that date assume his former position as landlord.

Last week Waters & Company sold to James W. Potter a building lot between the hotel and the Kellogg building. The price paid was $1,500. Mr. Potter expects to build a handsome residence on the lot in the spring.

THE SAGAMORE,

(GREEN ISLAND, LAKE GEORGE.)

MYRON O. BROWN,
Proprietor.

Bolton Landing, N. Y.,

THE U. S. GRANT CABIN TO BE EXHIBITED.

The old cabin built in St. Louis county, Missouri, by Ulysses S. Grant before he had won fame as a commander is shown in the illustration. It will be one of the exhibits at the world's fair, and after the close of the exposition will probably remain permanently in St. Louis. The man on horseback in the illustration is General Frederick D. Grant.

Star Dec 19

Held for the Grand Jury.

Fred A. Bentley, of Lake George, charge with blackmail by Peter Riley, proprietor of the Cold Brook house, yesterday waived examination before Justice Stearns and was held in $1,000 bail to await the action of the grand jury. In default of bail, Bentley was placed in the Lake George jail.

1903

L. Times Jan'y 6th 1904

HILL VIEW.

Miss Cora Earle and Wallace Gates were united in marriage Sunday evening by Rev. Milton Tator.

A BOY'S HORRIBLE DEATH.

HEAD IS BLOWN OFF BY DYNAMITE CARTRIDGE.

Young Paul Millington, of Riparius, Believed to Have Taken His Own Life—He Preferred a Dreadful Death to Possible Blindness.

Paul Royston Millington, the thirteen-year-old son of Mr. and Mrs. Chauncy Millington, of Riparius, was instantly killed at that place Saturday morning by the explosion of a dynamite cartridge.

It is believed that the boy took his own life. This theory is supported by the fact that he had been despondent for some time, and by remarks that he had made.

Two years ago while playing in the woods a branch struck young Millington in the eye, destroying the sight. Several months ago the other eye began to trouble him and it was feared that he would become totally blind unless relief could be obtained. Last summer he was taken to the Albany hospital, where he underwent an operation. Lately it became apparent that another operation would be necessary. The boy was aware that the result would be doubtful and brooded over his trouble. Often he told his playmates that he expected to be blind. "Then I will die," he would add.

Saturday his father told him that a second operation had become necessary and preparations were at once begun to again visit Albany.

"I'd rather die than go to the hospital again," cried the boy. "I won't go. I'll kill myself," he added.

The boy had said this before and the father paid little if any attention to his son's remarks.

A little later the Millington household was startled by a heavy explosion. Mr. Millington hurried to the barn yard and then to the field in the rear. There he found his son. The boy was dead.

Young Millington had procured a dynamite cartridge with cap and fuse and going to the rear of the barn had placed the explosive on a rock. Then he lighted the fuse and taking his stand beside the rock with his head close to the cartridge, awaited death.

The back of the boy's head was literally blown off. Particles of brain matter and pieces of his skull were scattered in every direction. Death was, of course, instantaneous.

The funeral was held Monday from the Methodist Episcopal church at Wevertown, the Rev. R. G. Adams officiating. The pall bearers were schoolmates of the deceased—Claude Beach, Frank and Edward Harvey and Harry Raymond. Interment was made in the Bates cemetery.

FROZEN TO DEATH ON A RIVER BOOM

Star Nov. 28

SAD FATE OF FORMER JUSTICE JOHN N. HALL.

1903

PROBABLY BEWILDERED

When he Found he Had Taken a Wrong Car to South Glens Falls, and Wandered Out on the Ice.

John N. Hall, a well known resident of French Mountain, met a terrible death Thursday night in the icy waters of the river. He was found frozen stiff at 10:30 yesterday morning a few rods above the paper company's barn on the Saratoga county side. How he came there is a mystery. Various rumors were heard, among them one that he was robbed and thrown down the bank. This story obtained little credence, however, as the man's watch was not taken.

Mrs. Charles Cornell, who lives on the lower end of First street, near the river, was awakened about 2 A. M., by sounds which she thought were groans, coming from the direction of the river. She awakened her husband, but as the noise ceased for a time, no investigation was made. Mrs. Cornell heard the sounds again about four o'clock.

Michael Holleran, while driving close to the river, discovered a man lying motionless thirty feet from shore, with his head, shoulders and chest resting on a big boom and his hands clinging to it. Mr. Holleran called Dr. White and a crowd soon collected. The physician found that the man had died probably from exposure and exhaustion and not from drowning and that he had been dead for several hours. He had the two inches of ice, which had formed around the body, chopped away. Then he ordered the remains taken to the paper company's barn. From letters in his pocket, Dr. White ascertained the man's name, and he notified Mrs. Hall and summoned Coroner McCarty, of Saratoga.

News Feb 10 1903

SAD RUNAWAY ACCIDENT.

A FORMER WARRENSBURGH BOY KILLED AT NEWCOMB.

Gilbert Carpenter Thrown from Wagon Saturday Night While Bravely Trying to Hold His Frightened Horses—Died from His Injuries at Noon Sunday.

Gilbert Carpenter, aged nineteen years, a son of Mr. and Mrs. Benjamin Carpenter, of Bolton, was killed in a runaway accident Saturday night, at Newcomb Lake, where he was employed by H. K. Perrine, of Albany.

Young Carpenter was driving a team of horses on a lumber wagon. Saturday night, about 5 o'clock, he had finished his work for the day and was driving into the barnyard to unhitch his team. The horses, being very spirited, were prancing and playing, when the wagon struck against a pair of bob-sleighs setting in the yard. This frightened them and they ran across the yard and around the corner of the barn, the boy pluckily clinging to the reins and striving to gain control of them.

As the horses turned the corner the wagon struck the barn with great force and rebounding was hurled over a stone wall. The young driver was thrown from his seat onto the whiffletrees, between the horses and the wagon, and was in that position when the wagon struck the stone wall. Truman Brown, grandfather of the deceased, had just entered the yard and was near when the accident occurred. He went to the boy's assistance and extricated him from the wreck of the wagon. He was carried into the house, where it was discovered that one leg was broken and his spine was seriously injured. His father, who is employed by Superintendent of the Poor A. L. Soper, was notified of the accident by telephone and started for Newcomb in the night, arriving there in time to see his son before he died.

ANOTHER COLD WAVE NO RECORDS BROKEN

BUT HORICON CLAIMS FORTY-SEVEN DEGREES BELOW.

HOW READINGS DIFFER

Contrast It With the Temperature Enjoyed by Warren County Sojourners in the South.

While no local cold weather records were broken yesterday morning, it was cold enough to satisfy anyone. But at Horicon the spirit, not mercury, because that was out of business at six o'clock yesterday morning, was read at forty-seven degrees below by L. D. Waters. Four hours later it was at thirty-two degrees. At eleven o'clock Monday evening it was thirty-three degrees below.

The reading of Professor C. L. Williams' thermometer yesterday morning was twenty-seven degrees below, nine degrees higher than during the cold wave of two weeks ago. At 7:15 it was twelve degrees below and at nine o'clock it was eleven degrees below. At D. P. DeLong's it was thirty-two degrees below and at the tollgate thirty-four degrees below. At the Rockwell house barber shop it was eighteen degrees below at eight o'clock and twenty-one degrees below at J. P. Bickley's market. It was thirty-eight degrees below zero at the St. James hotel, Fort Edward, forty-one degrees at Moses Kill and fifty-two degrees at Fort Miller bridge.

Those who hugged coal stoves or shivered while moving about out of doors, last night, will envy the people of Florida their delightful weather conditions. Lewis Burgess writes:

St. Augustine, Fla., January 16 — The Star—Gentlemen: My communication to you in regard to weather related to New York and not to this place. There, at the city hall, it was reported eight degrees, as I wrote you, not eight degrees above. That was quite too cold for this place. Now, at 2 P. M., it is seventy degrees. That was Tuesday morning, January 5. Trains coming to the south are well filled.

Yours truly,
L. BURGESS.

—Wallace Gates, of Hill View, has bought the boarding house kept by Mrs. Warner, 26 South street, and will conduct the place in future. *Feb 2 1904*

—19—

G. F. Star Dec 20 1903

Length of New Brooklyn Bridge, 7200 feet

Length of Old Brooklyn Bridge, 5925 feet

Width of Old Brooklyn Bridge, 85 feet

Width of New Brooklyn Bridge, 118 feet

THE NEW BROOKLYN BRIDGE.

The new bridge over the East river, connecting the boroughs of Manhattan and Brooklyn of the city of New York, is said to be the finest example of suspension bridges in the world. It was seven years in building and cost about $11,000,000.

FORTY-SEVEN YEARS AGO

News Jan 28th 1904

Great Similarity Between Winter of 1856-57 and 1903-04--What to Expect.

It is not only the severity of the cold but the unbroken succession of weeks without a thawing day that makes the present winter remarkable. The January thaw appears to have been indefinitely postponed.

Last week THE NEWS called attention to the fact that the winter of 1856-57 had all the familiar twinges in the zero brand of cold snaps that have been experienced so far this winter. It is, therefore, reasonable to infer that the similitude may keep up during the coming spring and summer.

The spring of 1857 was a very early one. In consequence of the great amount of snow and ice there was a big freshet. The old covered bridge across the West river between Warrensburgh and Thurman was carried away February 19. The prospects for a big freshet this spring are also good.

The summer of '57 was cold and the hot season was marked by periodical frosts which almost ruined the crops. The corn crop was a complete failure. Reasoning from analogy, the gospel of the weather prophet, next summer is liable to be discouraging to the farmers in this vicinity.

THE LAKE HOUSE MUST GO

Dec. 10 — 1903

OLD LAKE GEORGE HOTEL TO BE TORN DOWN OR REMOVED.

Building and Its Furnishings to be Sold at Public Auction--Hotel Built Over a Century Ago--To be Replaced by Private Mansion or Club House.

The Lake house, at Lake George, one of the oldest summer hotels in the state, will be torn down or removed this winter. The hotel property is owned by the Cooper Realty company, of Brooklyn, of which Charles C. Cooper is president. Yesterday the company held an auction sale on the property which is continued today. The hotel and its contents will be sold to the highest bidder with the proviso that the purchaser of the building must remove it before March 1, 1904. C. W. Cool is the Glens Falls agent of the Cooper company.

Just when it was built no one seems to know. Capt. E. S. Harris, whose knowledge of matters along the lake is as thorough as anyone's, says he has known the house for seventy years, and that it was an old structure when he was a boy. There are no records of any description in the county clerk's office which will give an inkling as to when it was built, probably about 1792, but the books show that in 1805 all pieces of property which were surveyed in the village had the southwest corner of "The Coffee House" as a starting point.

Later, in some of the descriptions the words, "The Coffee House, better known as the Lake House," appear, which establishes the fact that both were the same structure.

For many years the Lake house dock was the only place where a steamboat could land at the head of the lake and it was the starting place for the old Mountaineer, built about 1824, the original steamboat on the lake of any size. The first steamboat on Lake George was the James Caldwell, built about 1816.

The property during all these years has been in many hands and has had its days of prosperity and its days of adversity.

The first conveyance of the property on the county records is 1819, when Samuel Payne disposed of the building together with some thirty acres of land surrounding it to James Caldwell, the consideration being $7 600.

At this time the building was a two story affair and consisted of that part of the present building known as the office. Subsequently it was raised another story, and at different times additions have been built, until it reached its present size.

In 1823 John Baird bought the hotel and in 1826 he leased the building to George R. Baker, together with the furniture, and one half interest in the steamboat, "Mountaineer." The rent was $1 500 a year and the term of the lease was five years.

In 1830 the property evidently went into the hands of the owner, and at that time he conveyed the property to his daughter, Margaret Putnam, of Saratoga Springs, reserving to himself and wife a life estate.

Another interesting matter which the deeds show is the tenacity with which a mortgage hung over the property. In 1823 a mortgage of $2,000 is recorded. During all the changes of ownership up to 1879, this incumbrance still existed, but in that year it was satisfied.

Mr. Sherill was in possession of the property until his death in the early sixties. After his death the house was leased to various parties, and in 1893 Daniel and Henry F. Peck secured the property on a mortgage foreclosure sale, and soon after that the house passed into the hands of the Horicon Improvement company.

Herbert Irish, of Lake George, was Sunday the victim of a fatal railway accident in Whitehall. Mr. Irish was employed as brakeman on train No. 42, which runs between Whitehall and Mohawk. At the time of the accident the train was being made up, and Brakeman Irish, standing on the side of the engine, was caught between the boiler and a freight car standing near the point of a switch and crushed to death.

Silas Burch's Courtship.

When I was courtin' 'Mandy Glenn
(I was a shy young feller then.
"Retirin' " as a settin' hen).

I used to squirm, an' sweat, an' mop
My face till I would almost drop,
But still the question wouldn't pop!

Seemed to be somethin' on my chest,
An achin' underneath my vest,
That bothered me like all possessed!

But 'Mandy used to set an' smile,
An' watch me freeze, an sweat, an' bile,
An' know what ailed me all the while!

One night as we was goin' to church,
She slipped an' gave a sudden lurch,
Plumb to the arms of Silas Burch!

Well, sir, I—kissed her quicker'n scat!
Before I knew what I was at.
The question? Wa'n't no need o' that!
—F. L. Rose, in Chicago Record-Herald.

Miss Ada Enches, who has been housekeeper for J. S. & W. E. Gates for over two years, has returned to her home in Glens Falls.

A SOCIAL FUNCTION 4,7 Star
Feb. 6 1904
FIFTY YEARS AGO

SOME OF THE BOYS OF THOSE DAYS
WHO PARTICIPATED.

NEARLY ALL AT REST NOW

The Managers From Glens Falls, Sandy
Hill, Fort Edward, Lake George,
Warrensburg and Vicinity.

Glens Falls had some pretentious social functions half a century ago, even though a comparatively small place. Sternberg's hall, which stood at the corner of Glen and Park streets, on the site of the N. H. Murray block, was the scene of many of the brilliant gatherings attended by the early settlers. Charles Taft is the owner of an elaborately printed invitation for one of these events which makes interesting reading for the older residents. It was found in the Joseph Mead house, at the corner of Bay and Maple streets, when the structure was torn down a few years ago. The heading, in gold-bronzed fancy type, reads as follows:

THE OLD FOLKS' BALL.

The pleasure of your company is respectfully solicited, at an "Old Folks' Ball," to be held

AT STERNBERG'S NEW HALL,
WEDNESDAY EVEN'G, NOV. 29, 1854.

Star A Large Load of Logs. *Feb 22nd 1904*

The largest load of logs ever drawn in the town of Newcomb was hauled by a team in charge of William Noonan, who was employed on the Thomas Dillon job by Finch, Pruyn & Company. The load consisted of 187 pieces and measured forty-three markets. The loading was done by John Moynihan, who is considered an expert.

Star OBITUARY. *Apr. 14th 1904*

Henry Gates.

Henry Gates, a resident of Warrensburg, died on Friday at the residence of Wilber Cole, at Igerna, of pneumonia, after an illness of five days, aged sixty-three years. The remains were brought to the home of Mrs. Alice Gates, widow of a brother of the deceased, in Warrensburg, and the funeral occurred on Sunday under the auspices of the Post Charette, G. A. R., the Rev. Mr. Warren officiating. The deceased is survived by a sister, Mrs. James A. Hall, of Lake George.

G. F. Times

ENING, APRIL 16, 1904.

CHAMPLAIN CLEAR OF ICE.

The Lake Has Been Closed for Nearly Three Months.

The ice in Lake Champlain has disappeared, the strong northwest wind having sufficed to clear the water of the ice that had been gradually disintegrating for the past few days. The lake closed over on January 19, which was just a month earlier than last year. It opened a month and one day later than last year. The following table shows the dates on which the lake has closed and opened since 1816:

1816—Broad lake closed February 9, opened April 5.
1817—Closed Jan. 29, opened Apr. 16.
1818—Closed Feb. 29, opened April 15.
1819—Closed Mar. 4, opened Apr 17.
1820—Closed Feb. 3, opened Mar. 12.
1821—Closed Jan. 15, opened Apr. 21.
1822—Closed Jan. 24, opened Mar. 30.
1823—Closed Feb. 7, opened Apr. 5.
1824—Closed Jan. 22, opened Feb. 11.
1825—Closed Feb. 9, opened Apr. 1.
1826—Closed Feb. 1, opened Mar. 24.
1827—Closed Jan. 21, opened Mar. 31.
1828—Not closed.
1829—Closed Jan. 31, opened Apr. 4.
1830—Closed Jan. 15, opened Apr. 12.
1831—Closed Jan. 16, opened Apr. 10.
1832—Closed Feb. 6, opened Apr. 17.
1833—Closed Feb. 2, opened Apr. 6.
1834—Closed Feb. 13, opened Feb. 20.
1835—Closed Jan. 10, Feb. 7; opened Jan. 23, Apr. 12.
1836—Closed Feb. 27, opened Apr. 21.
1837—Closed Jan. 15, opened Apr. 26.
1838—Closed Feb. 2, opened Apr. 13.
1839—Closed Jan. 25, opened Apr. 6.
1840—Closed Jan. 25, opened Feb. 20.
1841—Closed Feb. 18, opened Apr. 19.
1842—Not closed.
1843—Closed Feb. 16, opened Apr. 22.
1844—Closed Jan. 25, opened Apr. 11.
1845—Closed Feb. 3, opened Mar. 26.
1846—Closed Feb. 10, opened Mar 26.
1847—Closed Feb. 15, opened Apr. 23.
1848—Closed Feb. 13, opened Feb. 29.
1849—Closed Feb. 7, opened Mar. 23.
1850—Not closed.
1851—Closed Feb. 1, opened Mar. 12.
1852—Closed Jan. 17, opened Apr. 19.
1853—Closed Feb. 19, opened Apr. 9.
1854—Closed Jan. 27, opened Apr. 11.

1855—Closed Jan. 25, Feb. 5; opened Jan. 26, April 20.
1856—Closed Jan. 22, opened Apr. 18.
1857—Closed Jan. 18, opened Apr. 4.
1858—Closed Feb. 12, opened Apr. 4.
1859—Closed Jan. 11, opened Mar. 31.
1860—Closed Feb. 2, opened Apr. 1.
1861—Closed Jan. 25, opened Apr. 13.
1862—Closed Feb. 5, opened Apr. 22.
1863—Closed Feb. 4, opened Apr. 25.
1864—Closed Feb. 17, opened Mar. 7.
1865—Closed Jan. 18, opened Apr. 5.
1866—Closed Jan. 30, opened Apr. 10
1867—Closed Feb. 20, opened Apr. 8.
1868—Closed Jan. 7, opened Apr. 15.
1869—Closed Jan. 19, Feb. 1; opened Jan. 26, Apr. 20.
1870—Closed Feb. 25, opened Apr. 10.
1871—Closed Jan. 24, opened Mar. 12.
1872—Closed Jan. 8, opened Apr. 22.
1873—Closed Jan. 29, opened Apr. 25.
1874—Closed Feb. 1, opened Mar 27.
1875—Closed Jan. 16, opened Apr. 30.
1876—Closed Feb. 5, opened Apr. 24.
1877—Closed Feb. 15, opened Apr. 5.

1878—Closed Jan. 31, Feb. 15; opened Feb. 1, March 1.
1879—Closed Jan. 30, opened Apr. 22.
1880—Closed Feb. 2, opened Mar. 7.
1881—Closed Jan. 16, opened Apr. 21.
1882—Closed Feb. 4, Feb. 25; opened Feb. 8, March 4.
1883—Closed Jan. 26, opened Apr. 22.
1884—Closed Jan. 8, opened Apr. 19.
1885—Closed Jan. 29, opened Apr. 25.
1886—Closed Jan. 24, opened Apr. 15.
1887—Closed Jan. 9, Feb. 13; opened Jan. 12, April 27.
1888—Closed Jan. 22, opened Apr. 24.
1889—Closed Feb. 7, opened Apr. 11.
1890—Closed Feb. 10, Feb. 21, Mar. 7; opened Feb. 11, Feb. 28, Mar. 12.
1891—Closed Jan. 27, Feb. 14, Mar. 8; opened Jan. 31, Feb. 27, Apr. 2.
1892—Closed Feb. 14, opened Apr. 3.
1893—Closed Jan. 16, opened Apr. 12.
1894—Closed Feb. 6, Feb. 12; opened Feb. 10, March 15.
1895—Closed Feb. 7, opened Apr. 19.
1896—Closed Feb. 17, opened Apr. 17.
1897—Closed Jan. 31, opened Apr. 10.
1898—Closed Jan. 30, opened Mar. 16.
1899—Closed Feb. 1, opened Apr. 20.
1900—Closed Feb. 28, opened Apr. 19.
1901—Closed Feb. 1, opened Apr. 11.
1902—Closed Jan. 30, opened Mar. 28.
1903—Closed Jan. 24, Feb. 19; opened Jan. 30, Mar. 12.
1904—Closed Jan. 19, opened Apr. 13.

LAMB-WARD.

Lyman Ward, of North Bolton, has issued invitations to the marriage of his daughter, Thirsa, and Bert W. Lamb. The ceremony will take place on October 12 at 8 p. m.

A Hotel Man's Big Laker.

J. Ben Hart, of The Wawbeek, while fishing Friday in upper Saranack lake in front of his hotel, caught the biggest lake trout that has been taken from that water in several seasons. It measured forty two inches in length and weighed thirty one and three quarter pounds. Mr. Hart said that his friends styled him a liar when he talked of Adirondack fish, and that he was pleased to have an opportunity to illustrate his integrity. *Mar. 31, 04*

AN ADIRONDACK INCIDENT.

The Late Senator Quay's Experience With a North Creek Stage Driver.

The late Senator M. S. Quay and a shrewd Adirondack stage driver once figured in the following incident, says a Philadelphia paper. When the senator went to the Adirondacks some years ago to prepare for the return home of his family, he rode up to Blue Mountain Lake from North Creek in a coach that was distressingly tardy and which was following after another that, if possible, was even slower. He chafed for a time at the pace and then hit upon a plan he thought would serve to speed both teams. He leaned over to the driver and offered a dollar if the latter would get in ahead of the team in front. The driver smilingly agreed and then raised his voice to say: "Hey, I say, Bill! Bill! Turn yer rig to the side of the road, will yer? There's a guy here says he'll give me a dollar if I pass ye."

Aug 11-1904

A Noted Divine to Preach at Riverbank.

The Rev. C. F. Wilcox, Ph. D., will preach at the Middleton schoolhouse, Riverbank, next Sunday morning, at 10:30 o'clock. Dr. Wilcox is at present pastor of the Third Avenue Methodist Episcopal church, Watervliet, and is classed as one of the ablest preachers in the Saratoga conference. He began his professional career in Warrensburgh in the seventies in an humble way and has worked himself up until he is now classed among the eminent divines of his church denomination. Riverbank is Mrs. Wilcox's native home and the residents of that place will enjoy a rare intellectual treat listening to Dr. Wilcox's sermon.

Star
Mr. Bixby Buys St. Louis Mansion. '04

W. K. Bixby, president of the American Car and Foundry company, who owns a beautiful summer residence at Bolton, has purchased a palatial residence in St. Louis. The price paid is said to have been $600,000.

The poor man has one happy thought
As he eats bread and water—
As long as he is poor no duke
Will ever wed his daughter.
—Detroit Tribune.

OLD LOG MARK IN DISUSE

news Sept 29. 1904

Every Lumberman and Log Driver Interested in the New "F."

Every lumberman in the Adirondacks will be interested in the fact that thousands of the logs which will be sent down the Hudson river to the Big Boom next spring will bear a new lumber mark.

The marks which have for years been stamped into all the logs cut in the north woods by Finch, Pruyn & Company, of Glens Falls, and with which every riverman and log driver is as familiar as he is with any of the things of his daily life, will disappear.

The new mark which the company adopts is simply the letter "F."

The old marks were "25" and the bar "L". The last mentioned was a letter "L" with a heavy dot or bar in the center and has been in use for years.

The new mark is necessary in order to settle up the affairs of the partnership and start the log accounts of the new corporation correctly. It will be two or three years yet before the logs with the old marks stop coming through the Big Boom, as it takes about that length of time for a log to get through to the mills after it is put in the river.

News Aug 25, 1904
Burned By Gasoline Explosion.

George Granger, engineer on J. B. Simpson's steam yacht Fanita, on Lake George, was severely burned about the face and hands Tuesday. He was starting a fire and used gasolene, and an explosion followed.

Star
OBITUARY.

Daniel Harris.

Daniel Harris, of Bolton, aged sixty-nine years, died about midnight Tuesday night. The funeral will be held to day at one o'clock at his late home. In his death Bolton loses a good citizen, a kind neighbor and a firm friend. He is survived by his wife, four sons and four daughters, Mrs. James Snow, of West Day; Mrs. Leonard Dingman, of Stony Creek; Miss Julia Harris and Mrs. Walter Gates, of Bolton; George Harris, of Queensbury; Benjamin Harris, of Sandy Hill; Martin Harris, of Staten Island, and Daniel, Jr., of Bolton.

Mail
James Brown.

James Brown died at his home at Bolton Landing last Thursday. Deceased is survived by his wife and six children, Mrs. George Mills, of Glens Falls; Percy and Harry Brown, of Schenectady; Claude Brown, of Glens Falls; Ralph and Lee Brown, of Bolton; two brothers and four sisters, Fred Brown and Mrs. Dennis Moore, of Long island, Lake George; Mrs. William Hall, of Luzerne; Mrs. George Gates and Mrs. Truxton Braley, of Bolton. His mother, Mrs. Margarette Brown, of Long island, Lake George, also survives. *1904*

---

news WALTER M. PECK. Oct 6

Walter M. Peck, formerly a well-known business man of Glens Falls, died Saturday, in San Francisco, from the effects of a surgical operation performed two days previously. The deceased was forty-three years old, a native of Glens Falls, and had lived there a greater part of his life. Several years ago he was a prominent member of the Horicon Improvement company, which conducted the Lake house and the Prospect mountain cable railway at Lake George. He leaves a widow and one son, his mother, Mrs. Addie M. Peck, and brother, Harry M. Peck, all of Glens Falls. *1904*

Star OBITUARY. Sept 12th 1904
Mrs. Julia Tuttle.

Julia Tuttle, aged fifty-eight years, wife of Sidney Tuttle, of San Antonio, Texas, formerly of Glens Falls, died Friday night at the summer home of her sister-in-law, Miss Roxie Tuttle, in Bolton. The remains were taken on Saturday to Rome, N. Y., where the funeral occurred yesterday.

CONDUCT WASHINGTON HOTEL.

M. O. and W. W. Brown Lease The Dewey—Assume Management Soon.

M. O. Brown and son, W. W. Brown, two well-known hotel proprietors, have leased from George R. Jones, in Washington, D C, the Dewey house, one of the largest and best hotels in that city. It has 150 guest rooms and 52 private baths. The hotel is situated at the corner of Fourteenth and L streets. W. W. Brown is in Washington now arranging to assume the management about December 1. He will be joined by Mr. and Mrs. M. O. Brown and Mrs W. W. Brown and son, Willard, this week.

M. O. Brown was a former landlord at the Rockwell house, and for many years conducted the Sagamore on Lake George. *Star Nov 22 1904*

LUZERNE'S NEW HOTEL

Star Dec. 8 1904

Will Be a More Pretentious Establishment Than First Supposed.

The new Rockwell house at Luzerne is to be of larger dimensions than at first reported. The dining room is intended to seat 100 persons and the hotel will be designed to accommodate 150 guests. H. W Linindoll, who has so successfully conducted The Elms at Luzerne for several seasons, will manage the new hotel, and will no doubt regain the prestige enjoyed by the old Rockwell hotel in years agone, when guests from all parts of the United States, and also from foreign countries, thronged its corridors and piazzas. It is the intention of the management to make the Rockwell one of the best hotels in the Adirondack foothills, and with the experience and ability that will be brought to the task there is little doubt that the effort will be successful.

Death of Chief Joseph, Tribal Head of the Nez Perces Indians.

With the death of Chief Joseph, the famous leader of the Nez Perces, the United States has lost its most celebrated Indian. Joseph, since the death of Red Cloud and Sitting Bull, has been the most discussed American Indian. He was the last of the great warrior chiefs. Descendant of a long line of fighters, chieftain since early manhood of the Nez Perce tribe, and followed with constant devotion by his dwindling people, Chief Joseph was the last Indian leader who dared to put up a real fight against civilization; and in his desperate Waterloo he put up a fight that gave Gen. Nelson A. Miles and Gen. O. O. Howard all they could do to crush him. Chief Joseph it was who, when the United States took away the reservation given him and his people by grant, dug up the hatchet after years of peace and made the last fierce struggle between red and white. Now that Chief Joseph is dead, the mantle of his diluted power falls to his son, Flo-Cut, of a generation which knows little of the old-time warfare.

Red Cloud, perhaps, was the most famous of latter-day Indians. From the time of Red Cloud's death Joseph typified the Indian nation, for he was the last of the really great chiefs. No one knows how old he was, but he is believed to have approached fourscore. He died near Spokane, Washington, in the little reservation set by for his tribe after his Waterloo in the Bear's Paw Mountains, in the Yellowstone, in 1877.

It is thirty-one years since President Grant awarded the Wallowa Valley, near Snake River, in Oregon, to the Nez Perces. The tribe settled down in the valley and began to prosper. In 1875, scarcely two years after the award, the Government told them to move on. Chief Joseph refused to surrender the valley to the whites who began to take up land in the now public domain, and in 1877 the Government got a reminiscent little taste of Indian fighting.

General O. O. Howard was ordered out against the militant old chief. To the astonishment of the country at large Chief Joseph, instead of exterminating himself in a fruitless exhibit of savagery, put up a wily game, and completely outwitted Gen. Howard and skipped unscratched into Big Hole Basin. There Gen. Gibbons and his militia met Chief Joseph of the Nez Perces, and one of the bloodiest battles of Indian history took place. Gen. Gibbons was wounded and the troops repelled.

Joseph, who now retreated toward the Yellowstone, was followed by Gen. Howard.

It was here that Gen. Miles took a hand. He was near the Missouri River, and when he learned the situation he undertook the campaign which made him famous. It ended with a five-days' siege near Bear's Paw in the Yellowstone and the subjugation of the fierce old warrior. Chief Joseph handed over his rifle to Gen. Miles at 10 o'clock in the morning of Jan. 4, 1878.

For twenty-five years Chief Joseph stayed among his people quietly, living peacefully on the reservation mapped out for them near Spokane, and making only one long journey away, when he visited New York at the time of the Grant celebration, in 1897. To Gen. Miles, who afterward became his close friend, and who always calls him "The Napoleon of Indians," Joseph had said: "From where the sun now stands I fight no more against the whites." And his word was kept.

Chief Joseph was famous for his face and figure. He was tall, straight as an arrow and wonderfully handsome, his features being as clear cut as chiseled marble. He never spoke a word of English, but some of his sayings, translated, have become famous. He used to say: "Look twice at a two-faced man;" "Cursed be the hand that scalps the reputation of the dead;" "The eye tells what the tongue would hide;" "Firewater courage ends in trembling fear;" "Big name often stands on small legs;" "Finest fur may cover toughest meat;" "When you get the last word with an echo you may do so with a squaw."

Star Nov 2 1904

THE DEER WAS WOUNDED

AND THEN ANOTHER HUNTER CAME AND CARRIED IT AWAY.

Exasperating Experience of Galloway C. Morris, of Lake George—He Ran Short of Cartridges and Lost Big Game.

On Sunday afternoon a deer strayed upon the premises of Galloway C. Morris, who resides on the Bolton road, Lake George. Mr. Morris procured a rifle and a few cartridges, and the deer was driven into the lake. He succeeded in wounding the animal, and, his cartridges being exhausted, he went back to procure a fresh supply. As he returned to the water front George Granger, of Bolton, came along in a steam launch, killed the deer, loaded it into his boat and steamed away. Mr. Morris was in Glens Falls yesterday, and in speaking of the incident he expressed strong disapproval of the action of Mr. Granger, characterizing it as unsportsmanlike. Just the same, several residents of Bolton are enjoying choice venison steaks and cutlets.

Rugge Thomson, son of Dr. Lemon Thomson, has returned from the Boreas river with a handsome buck which weighed more than 200 pounds. Mr. Thomson was away from home only a few days on his hunting trip, and killed the deer when he had been but a few hours in the woods.

Star Dec 22 1904

THE FINAL SUMMONS.

Miss Thankful Smith.

Miss Thankful Smith died of paralysis yesterday morning at her home on East street, Fort Edward. She was born on December 24, 1848, at Bolton. She was for about 15 years a teacher in public schools and for the past 23 years had spent the summer with Mr. and Mrs. M O. Brown at the Sagamore and other hotels conducted by Mr. Brown on Lake George.

Hotel Change at Hague.

Mr. and Mrs. Truman Waters, who have been in partnership with George Streeter as proprietors of the Phœnix hotel at Hague for the past two years, have moved to Horicon. Mr. and Mrs. Frank Owens, of Graphite, will move into the hotel and take the place of Mr. and Mrs. Waters.—Hague correspondent.

Star Dec 23 1904

J. B. Wilson, of Bolton, has sold his trotting horse Ned Wilson to Leonard Bibbey, of Fort Edward. Consideration, $400.

Glens Falls Star Nov 24 1904.

PARADISE BAY SOLD.

George O. Knapp, of Chicago, Buys Surrounding Property

TO CONVERT IT INTO BIG PARK.

The 400 Acres Just Added to His Property Gives Him About 3,500 Acres With a Six-mile Frontage on the Lake—Thanksgiving in Camp.

H. E Nichols, acting for George O Knapp, president of the People's Gas company of Chicago and owner of the Hundred Island house at Shelving Rock, Lake George, has just purchased the prettiest bit of American scenery and by many tourists said to be the most beautiful in the world—Paradise bay. He plans to make a big park of all his property, consisting of 3,500 acres with a frontage on the lake of six miles

Hall & Anderson a few months ago purchased of the H. G. Burleigh estate a large tract of land fronting on the lake. Soon afterward Mr. Nichols obtained an option on it and now part of the tract has passed to Mr. Knapp. Mr. Nichols was in town yesterday. In conversation with a STAR man he spoke enthusiastically of the plans for constructing drives and adding to the beauty of the property by removing dead trees, clearing out considerable brush and in every possible way adding to the natural attractions of the place.

This plan has been carried out extensively on Mr. Knapp's other property, with pleasing results.

The new tract begins at the northerly boundary of the Knapp property, extends along the shore three miles to Black Mountain and back on the mountain for a quarter of a mile. It contains about 400 acres, and the land is heavily wooded.

A force of men has already been set to work building roads and making preparations for extensive work next spring.

Mr. Knapp and party of eight guests arrived in Glens Falls last evening They were joined by Mr. Nichols and arriving at the lake hurried down to Shelving Rock.

At Mr. Knapp's beautiful camp high up on the mountainside they will spend Thanksgiving and probably remain until next week.

TWO ACCIDENTS, BROKEN BONES.

James L. Maranville and Sheriff Bowyer Meet Similar Misfortunes.

James T. Maranville, proprietor of the Lake George and Bolton stage line, had his left leg broken just above the ankle yesterday afternoon. The accident occurred at Lake George. Mr. Maranville had a hay rigging on his wagon which he had loaded with shingles at the D. & H. freight depot. He was going down the Fort William Henry hill in the southern part of the village when a bundle of the shingles slid from the front part of the load and struck the horses. They started to run and swerved across the road on to the railroad track. The wheel caught the rails and threw Mr. Maranville off in front of the wagon. A wheel passed over his left leg with the result stated. He was taken to the residence of Dr. Bean, where the broken bone was set, and afterwards was conveyed to his home in Bolton.

Sheriff W. W. Bowyer while driving in the town of Horicon Sunday afternoon, was thrown from his wagon and had his left shoulder broken. He was going from the west side of Brant lake to Adirondack over a very rough road when a jolt of the wagon broke the kingbolt and the sheriff was thrown out and struck on a rock. He clung to the reins and succeeded in holding the horse and regaining his seat in the carriage. He returned to Horicon and from there telephoned to Dr. C. J. Logans, of this place, to meet him in Chestertown. Dr. Logans responded promptly and with Dr. E. L. Stafford, set the broken bones. Sheriff Bowyer returned to Lake George Monday.

A Three Million Dollar Estate.

An adjournment was taken until January 30 in the matter of probating the will of the late J. W. Finch at Glens Falls Monday. Judge S. Brown appeared for the executors, of whom he is one, the others being the sons, George R. Finch and J. T. Finch, and Mrs. T. H. Foulds. It is estimated that Mr. Finch left an estate of more than $3,000,000.

A Practical Farmer.

John Grant Haviland, of Ridge road, is known as one of the most progressive farmers in northern New York. The appearance of his farm house and outbuildings shows that he merits his reputation. Mr. Haviland has recently been making improvements on his place. He has erected a silo of 110 tons capacity and has built a basement under his principal barn. This basement is 30 by 126 feet in dimensions and provides warm and comfortable quarters for 42 cattle and four horses. It is supplied with running water and has all the latest improvements in the way of feed racks and other fixtures.

FELL UNDER THE WHEEL

SAD DEATH OF A WELL-KNOWN CITIZEN OF WARRENSBURG.

While Hauling a Heavy Load of Coal His Horses Started Suddenly, Throwing Him from Wagon—His Skull Crushed.

Albert H. Alden, a well-known resident of Warrensburg, met a sudden death in that village at half-past 2 o'clock yesterday afternoon.

Mr. Alden was driving home from Lake George with a load of two tons of coal. He had reached what is known as Osborne hill, in Warrensburg village, when his horses started suddenly and he was thrown from his seat. As he reached the ground a wheel passed over his head, crushing his skull and killing him almost instantly. Dr. Goodman was summoned, but his services were not required. Alfred Hammond and Charles Wells placed the body in C. E. Lavery's delivery wagon and conveyed it to the late home of the deceased in Lewisville. Coroner Burt, of Lake George, was notified.

The deceased was about 65 years old. He is survived by his wife, three sons, John S., of Waterford, and Seth and William Alden, of Warrensburg; a daughter, Mrs. G. W. Farrar, of Warrensburg; three sisters, Mrs. Alzina Fuller, of Warrensburg; Mrs. Martha Williams, of Troy, and Mrs. Harriet Bonelle, of Fort Dodge, Iowa.

THE MO...

SILVER BAY HOTEL

It Is Now the Property of a Religious Association.

A LAKE GEORGE CHAUTAUQUA

The Association for Christian Conference Purchases the Property, Having Secured the Necessary Funds—An Ideal Spot to Hold Conferences.

The Silver Bay Association for Christian Conference and Training having secured the last installment of the necessary $100,000, the Silver Bay hotel, on Lake George, has passed into possession of the association. The purchase price, it is understood, was $70,000. The remaining $30,000 will be used to improve the property.

Silver Bay is one of the most beautiful spots on a lake famed for beauty. The property purchased includes a hotel and seven cottages, with accommodations for several hundred guests, and the appurtenant lands comprise over 1,000 acres in part covered with timber. It is an ideal place for a Christian summer school. On the property is a lake 1,000 feet above the level of Lake George, the mountain lake containing a number of islands suitable for campers. They will be utilized for camping purposes during the coming summer. It is the intention of the managers to offer to working girls special privileges during a portion of the summer. The hotel will be open to young men as a vacation resort during August. In June and July those attending the various conferences will find hotel accommodations there.

The conference program for the coming summer will be as follows: Preparatory school girls, June 23 to July 3; eastern college women, June 23 to July 3; secretaries and workers of city Young Women's Christian associations, July 4 to 17; missionary conference of young people, July 21 to 30; general secretaries, physical directors and workers of the Young Men's Christian associations, August 1 to September 15.

MR. MILLER ACCEPTS

Says He Is Willing to Meet Lake George Wrestler.

WILL PUT UP $1,000 TO $500

The Schuylerville Athlete Stipulates That the Match Must Take Place in Glens Falls or Schuylerville—Best Two of Three Falls to Decide.

Adam Miller, a Schuylerville hotel keeper and well-known athlete, indicates his willingness to meet Mr. Bull, a Lake George wrestler, in a catch-as-catch-can match, best two falls in three. Mr. Miller explains the terms upon which he will make the match in the following note:

To the Editor of THE STAR:

A few lines to let you know that a man by the name of Bull has challenged me to wrestle catch-as-catch-can. I accept the challenge and am ready to wrestle him best two falls out of three. I will bet $1,000 against $500 that I can beat Bull. The match to take place in Glens Falls or Schuylerville. Money to be posted in the office of your paper. This challenge is open to all woodchoppers such as Bull is at Lake George.

Respectfully yours,
ADAM MILLER,
Hotel Windsor, Schuylerville, N. Y.

P. S.: A Mr. Brown, of Lake George, is willing to back Mr. Bull. He wants me to wrestle at Lake George, but I insist that the match must take place at Glens Falls or Schuylerville.

A YOUNG MAN'S TRAGIC DEATH

Drawing Gun Toward Him When It Suddenly Discharged.

TORE HOLE THROUGH BREAST.

Was Returning to Town With a Load of Wood — His Father With Him When Fatality Occurred—Parents of the Young Man Stricken With Grief.

A sad accident occurred at 2 o'clock Saturday afternoon on Hall hill, Luzerne mountain, which resulted in the death of George Smith, a young man 18 years old, residing on Bay road, Glens Falls.

Young Smith and his father, John Smith, went to the mountain on Saturday for a load of wood. Before starting the young man loaded his shotgun and placed it in the sleigh, so as to be in readiness for a shot at any game that might appear. They loaded the sleigh and started on the return trip in the afternoon.

At a point on Hall hill, where the decline is quite steep, they stopped the team to adjust a brake chain on the sleigh. After the chain was in place the young man said to his father, "All right; go ahead." As he spoke he reached out and attempted to draw his gun from on top of the load of wood. The muzzle was toward him, and it is supposed that the hammer caught on a knot, for the gun was suddenly discharged, the contents entering the young man's body and tearing a great hole through his right lung.

The father ran to a nearby house for assistance, and Elijah Gayger hooked a horse to a cutter and brought the young man to his home on Bay road. On the way they met Dr. Chapman, of this village, who accompanied them. The doctor saw that the case was hopeless, as young Smith had nearly bled to death on the way. The injured man was made as comfortable as possible, but death ended his sufferings at 5 o'clock yesterday morning. Dr. Chapman stated last evening that he never saw a patient with greater vitality or grit.

ANOTHER BIG DAM ON THE SACANDAGA

Plans Making by River Improvement Company for Utilizing 240,000 Horse Power.

POWER WORTH $10,000,000 IS NOW RUNNING TO WASTE.

The Plan is to Harness the Sacandaga, Racquette and Black Rivers for the Benefit of Manufacturers and Others Using Water Power — To Provide Storage for Ten Billion Gallons.

Harnessing the Sacandaga, Racquette and Black rivers in the Adirondacks and utilizing the 240,000 horse-power, worth $10,000,000 a year, now going to waste, is the task which the new state river improvement commission will begin to consider Thursday in Albany, says the Journal. The commission consists of the attorney-general, state engineer and surveyor, superintendent of public works, forest, fish and game commissioner and Wallace C. Johnson, of Niagara Falls, engineer.

The commission will take up in earnest the great work of conserving the enormous water energy now going to waste and allowing it to be used so that there shall be the minimum of flood damage in the spring of the year. Incidentally the development of plans now in sight means profit for power producers all along the upper Hudson but it will not cost the state anything and the direct benefit resulting from preventing the Hudson from overflowing its banks means a great deal to Troy, Albany and other cities and towns.

One of the first things to be taken up is a storage scheme on the Sacandaga It is proposed to build a dam costing from $300,000 to $500,000 on the west branch of the Sacandaga above Hadley, and one on the east branch of the same stream at Griffin. These dams will raise the water in Piseco lake from five to ten feet and provide storage for 10,-000,000,000 gallons of water. All this impounded water can be used in making a larger even flow over the big power dams along the upper Hudson.

CAVE WITH A HISTORY

1905

Located in the Flat Rock Below the River Bridge.

SITE WILL SOON BE BUILT ON.

A Deed Conveying the Property to the International Paper Company Has Been Filed in the Saratoga County Clerk's Office—Of Historic Interest.

A covenant against the grantor deed for $1, etc,, executed on December 28, 1904, by Frederick H. and Arabella S Parks to the International Paper com pany conveying all of the interest Mr. Parks had by virtue of the deed from William McEchron, dated July 1, 1904, in the premises lying in the Hudson river in the towns of Moreau and Queensbury, commonly known as "Cooper's Cave" or island from its having been mentioned and described by the great American legendary novelist in "The Last of the Mohicans" was filed for record in the Saratoga county clerk's office on January 24. It is made "subject to any and all rights of the public" therein, says the Saratogian.

This little lime rock islet lying at the base of Glens Falls and to the south side of the bridge connecting the sister villages has long been the Mecca of tourists from Saratoga to Lake George, both in the stage days and since steam and electricity have laid aside the jehus with their steeds and made obsolete the time-honored Concord coaches from the interest invested in it by Cooper's narrative. An old Scotch baronet, who visited the scene in 1878 and passed through the cave on his way from Montreal to New York en route home from a tour eastward around the world, said "I shall purchase a copy of 'The Last of the Mohicans' and reread the tale with renewed boyish interest, now that I have seen that wonderful cave."

The "cave," which was a fissure or orifice cut through the limestone by the swirl of the water from the falls, has been practically obliterated since the stone arch bridge, so familiar to the eye on the annual calendars of the Glens Falls Insurance company, was demolished in pursuance of the supreme court order made by the late Justice Joseph Potter in 1888, and the blasting of the rock for the pier of the new iron bridge broke down its thin and shaly rock roof. It now is swallowed in the iconoclastic maw of the "paper trust," and another American antiquity is made to be a thing of the past to exist only in legends of "Leather Stocking" and the Iroquois braves, for its side lies within the space that is to be occupied by the mammoth new paper mill that the International Paper company is preparing to erect at South Glens Falls.

SATURDAY EVENING.

KEEP GIRLS AT HOME; ADVICE GIVEN MOTHERS

REV. MR. JUDKINS SAYS THEY SHOULD BE TAUGHT THE DO-MESTIC SCIENCES.

IN LIEU OF BUSINESS.

Home Rather Than the Factory and Shops Is the Place for Our Girls—Splendid Address Made Before the Local Mothers' Club.

The Mothers' club met last evening in the assembly hall of the Ridge street school house, the lecturer of the evening being the Rev. Charles O. Judkins. The speaker dwelt on "Domestic Work for Girls in Preference to the Factory and the Shops."

Mr. Judkins took up a thorough discussion of the subject, treating it from many points of view. Many of his arguments were based on G. Stanley Hall's latest work on "Adolescence." He asked the mothers to keep their girls at home, to teach them the domestic sciences and keep them out of the factory. Girls are competing today with men in all trades, when it would be more fitting for them to learn the duties of the home. The girl's place is in the home, while the man who is the natural breadwinner, must go out into the world and fight the battle of life. How many of our girls today, trained to factory life, have made the home life a failure because their domestic training had been neglected? The girl goes into the factory or shop and all her mental faculties are thrown on the machine, and at night she is glad to seek a little rest. She has had no time for a home training. It would be far better to keep your girls on the farm, where there is no other work but that of home duties, than to live in the city and neglect her home education. A business life is work for the men, and care of the home should be in the hands of the girls.

He warned the mothers of allowing them to roam the streets, where they had no business at all. The home is the place for our girls, and not the street. Mr. Judkins also spoke on the other side of the question, that of education. Many of our girls are stunted in mental growth, while others have had their minds developed in the highest possible degree and the physical power with which to do their household duties lies dormant. Both should be developed. They go hand in hand together.

Bluffer Failed to Make Good.

James L. Maranville, of Bolton Landing, requests THE NEWS to state that he is the backer of L. D. Bull, of Lake George, in the proposed wrestling match with Adam Miller, of Schuylerville, instead of putting up for Miller, as stated in our last issue. Mr. Maranville posted a forfeit at the office of the Glens Falls Star, as demanded by Miller but the Saratoga county bluffer failed to cover it, evidently being afraid to try conclusions with the muscular Lake George woodchopper.

News HAGUE. *March 30*

Martin Dickinson, brief notice of whose death was made in THE NEWS last week, was born in Bolton, March 20, 1843, and was consequently just sixty-two years old on the day of his death, the direct cause of which was Bright's disease, although he had been ill for a long time with valvular heart disease. Deceased spent his youth in his native town until the Civil War broke out, when he enlisted to do service for his country. In February, 1866, he was married to Miss Ellen Stockton, of Johnsburgh. They resided in Bolton until 1868, when they went to Lyndonville, Orleans county, where they remained until 1880, when they returned to Bolton and for three years lived on the Alma farm. In the spring of 1883 they moved to Hague, where Mr. Dickinson was an honored citizen and respected by all. He held the office of justice of the peace for fourteen years.

A BIG HOTEL PLANNED *May 5* *Star* ROOMS FOR 1,500 GUESTS.

New Owners of the Marion House, Lake George, to Enlarge the Hotel Next Year. *1905*

Joseph H. Marville and William Morris, of Atlantic City, have purchased the Marion house, Lake George, of H. Roukow, and will open the house on June 25, after making temporary repairs. Next year the new owners plan to make the Marion house the largest hotel on the lake, and preparations are said to be already under way for the proposed changes. It is stated that the new hotel will accommodate 1,500 or more guests.

Rueben S. Ripley

Reuben S. Ripley, aged 76 years, died yesterday afternoon at his home in Harrisena after an illness of some time. Mr. Ripley was well known in this vicinity and about Lake George, where at one time he owned the famous resort known as "Ripley's Point." He was born there and spent the greater part of his life on the farm near the point.

About 20 years ago he sold the farm to Professor Gunn, but reserved the point, which shortly afterwords was sold to George Ferris.

RECALLS THE BOYHOOD OF GEORGE FERGUSON.

Times May 3rd 1905

GEORGE W. SISSON OF POTSDAM WRITES OF THE DAYS OF OLD IN GLENS FALLS.

WERE BOYS TOGETHER.

And They Attended Dr. Holden's School—A Word as to the Harrison Campaign of 1840—Some Political Meetings in Glens Falls.

Potsdam, N. Y., May 1.
Editor Glens Falls Times:

The Glens Falls Messenger brings to me the obituary notice of the death of George Ferguson. We were boys in the same school. He was one of the very few remaining native-born citizens of Glens Falls connecting the present with the preceding generation. I sometimes lapse into a reminiscent mood. It is thirty-eight years since I removed from Glens Falls, yet being a native there and a subscriber to the Messenger for over fifty years, with many ties to link me to the place, I retain my interest in and with those I have known there and in the growth and progress of the town.

My ancestors were among the earliest settlers in the town of Queensbury. I was born on Ridge street Glens Falls, in 1828, the same year that Henry Ferguson moved to Glens Falls. In 1832 my father purchased and moved to the present location of the Glens Falls Insurance company's building, which property had been owned and occupied by my grandfather, Joseph Wing, and his father, Edward Wing, previous to 1800. I came early to know the families of Henry Ferguson and Henry Philo, the store of Philo & Ferguson and the Ferguson residence being diagonally opposite my father's residence.

At that time there was a hotel or tavern where Henry Crandall's residence stands, and another opposite where Hotel Ruliff stands. It was customary each year for a company of the state militia to assemble and go through the manual exercises in the open space of Monument square.

JACOB VANDENBURGH.

Jacob Vandenburgh, a life long resident of Bolton Landing, died on the 3rd inst. of catarrh of the stomach, aged eighty-three years. Besides a widow he is survived by the following children: Mrs. L. F. Kent, of Glens Falls; Mrs. Fred Wilcox, Mrs. H. E. Chamberlain, Mrs. Jay Ross, Miss Carrie Vandenburgh, George and Edward, all of Bolton Landing. The funeral was held Saturday afternoon, the Rev. Charles Kennedy officiating. Interment was made in the Huddle cemetery.

OLD STORE, BUILT IN 1854.

NEW STORE, COMPLETED IN 1872.

News of the death of George Ferguson Friday afternoon, though not unexpected, was received with deep regret by many who had known him for years, and reminiscences were related Saturday by those who had been connected with him in the early business and social life of the village upwards of half a century ago. As related in Saturday's STAR, Mr Ferguson's father began business at the corner of South and Glen streets with Henry Philo in 1829. The old store building was constructed in 1854, after George had been taken into the firm by his father. The reconstruction of this building was begun in the fall of 1871 and finished in July, 1872. Through the kindness of James A. Holden, who owns the cuts used in the History of the Town of Queensbury, published by his father, Dr. A. W. Holden, THE STAR is permitted to reproduce the pictures of the old and new stores contained in that history. The grocery of Orville Smith now occupies the ground floor of this block.

LAKE GEORGE IS CLEAR *1905*
AFTER 135 DAYS.
Times Apr 26th

The Ice Disappeared Yesterday—Mohican Begins Trips Monday.

Lake George is now clear, the ice having entirely disappeared yesterday.

The lake closed on December 10 and was thus closed 135 days, which is a record for many years.

The Lake George steamer Mohican begins her daily trips Monday, leaving Baldwin each day at 7:20 and stopping at all landings on signal, reaching Caldwell in time to connect with the 11:25 southbound train. Going north, the Mohican will leave Lake George at 2:45, touching at all landings on signal and arrive at Baldwin at 6:30. The through line traffic will begin on May 29, on which date the Sagamore will go into commission.

Captain Wesley Finkle will command the Mohican.

CIVIL WAR VETERAN *June 1*
Star PASSES SUDDENLY AWAY.
1905

Robert Boyd Taken Suddenly Ill Yesterday Morning of Heart Trouble Lives But a Short Time.

Robert Boyd, a veteran of the Civil war, died yesterday morning at his home, 5 Gage avenue, at 6 o'clock. Mr. Boyd attended the Memorial exercises at the Empire theater Tuesday evening and appeared to be in usual good health, save from slight rheumatism, which had been troubling him for some time. He retired feeling as well as usual, but was taken suddenly ill at 2 o'clock with heart difficulty. Dr. D. M. Hall was called, but medical attendance was of no avail and death occurred about 6 o'clock.

Robert Boyd was born December 26, 1839, at Bolton. Lake George, and was therefore a few months over 66 years of age. His parents were Pliney C. and Martha (Booth) Boyd. He was one of six children,

STANDARD OIL MAN BUYS *1905*
FOURTEEN MILE ISLAND.
Star Jany 18th

Delaware and Hudson Sells Property to W. H. Beardsley for Summer Home.

The Delaware and Hudson Railroad company has sold Fourteen Mile island to W. H. Beardsley, of New York, who intends erecting a beautiful summer home and private park.

The purchaser is a director of the Standard Oil company and secretary of the Florida East Coast railroad. The sale was made at the recent trip of the railroad officials to the lake. The island is on the east shore of the lake, near the narrows, and 11 miles from Lake George village. It has an area of 12 acres, and between it and the main land there is a deep narrow channel through which the largest boats on the lake can pass.

The property was for many years owned by Erastus C. Smith, of Albany. The Hotel Kenesaw was for some time conducted there, and several years ago the railroad company acquired the property and used it as a picnic ground. The company paid $14,000 for it.

Locating Bolton-Horicon Line.

A party from Bolton, headed by Richard Brown, surveyor, were engaged Friday locating the town line between Horicon and Bolton, where it reaches the river, to ascertain in which town L. D. Tripp resides, which, according to their figures, is in Bolton. *Nov. 10—1905*

BENTLEY-SMITH. *July 6*

John Bentley and Miss Lura Smith, both of Riverbank, were married at Bolton Tuesday morning by the Rev. William W. Kennedy. *1905*

HEMAN GOODMAN *Glens Falls 1905*

Heman Goodman died in Glens Falls Thursday in the eighty-seventh year of his age. The funeral was held Sunday afternoon from his late home. Mr. Goodman was born in Bolton, this county, December 31, 1818, the son of Eleazar Goodman and Elizabeth Catlin Goodman, who came from South Hadley, Mass., and settled in Bolton in 1785. He was the last to survive of their family of ten children. He was twice married, his first wife being his cousin, Sarah Redfield Goodman, a daughter of the Rev. Eldad W. Goodman, of Bolton, who died in 1872 and was survived by two children, Elroy W. Goodman, who died in 1875, and Ellen M. Goodman, who died in 1885. His second wife, Lucy A. Hatfield, of Springfield, Mass., died in 1879. Mr. Goodman removed to Glens Falls from Bolton in 1845, and was engaged in the marble business. Of late years he has been retired. The only near relative surviving is a granddaughter, Mrs. Howard M. West, of Albany.

Horace Greeley and an Autograph.

In his "Recollections of a Busy Life", Horace Greeley tells the story of how he once dealt very effectively with a persistent autograph hunter. A gushing youth wrote to Greeley as follows:

Dear Sir—Among your literary treasures you have doubtless preserved several autographs of our country's late lamented poet, Edgar Allan Poe. If so, and you can spare one, please inclose it to me and receive the thanks of yours truly, ----.

To which Greeley replied:

Dear Sir - Among my literary treasures there happens to be just one autograph of our country's late lamented poet, Edgar Allan Poe. It is a note of hand for $50, with my indorsement across the back. It cost me exactly $50.75, including protest, and you may have it for half that amount. Yours respectfully,
HORACE GREELEY

The autograph was found among Greeley's possessions after his death.

BORN FOR A LAWYER.

1905

Why His Mother Recommended Him to Colonel Ingersoll.

Among the stories which Colonel Bob Ingersoll delighted to tell was the following, says the writer of "America's Most Popular Men:"

While studying law with a firm out west the colonel found himself alone in the office one day. He was interrupted by the entrance of a raw boned, sharp featured countrywoman, who ambled into the room leading a freckle faced, watery eyed ten-year-old boy by the hand.

"Air you the lawyer?" she began.

On being answered in the affirmative she went on to say that she had brought her boy Jim to town for the purpose of binding him out at the "lawyerin' trade." She was morally certain, she averred, that Jim was a born lawyer and that all he needed was a chance.

"But, madam," objected the colonel, "he is entirely too young to begin the study of law."

"Too young, indeed!" sniffed the fond mother contemptuously. "You don't know Jim. He was born for a lawyer."

Much amused, the colonel asked her on what grounds she based her hopes of a future at the bar for her darling child.

"Why," said she, "when he was only seven years old he struck work, and he wouldn't do another lick if he got killed for it. When he was eight he got sassy and put on more airs than a prize horse at a country fair, and now, Lor' bless me, he jest freezes on to everything he can lay his hands on."

GLENS FALLS TIMES,

Sept 18

PRETTY AUTUMN WEDDING *1905*
AT BOLTON, LAKE GEORGE.

Miss Fanny Praddow Simpson Weds Edward Perry Townsend.

A pretty autumn wedding occurred Saturday afternoon at Bolton when Miss Fanny Praddow Simpson, daughter of Mr. and Mrs. John Boulton Simpson and Edward Perry Townsend, Yale 1903, son of Mr. and Mrs. Edward Townsend of New York, were united in marriage at the Church of St. Sacrament. A reception followed at the Sagamore hotel, of which the bride's father is part owner.

Mryon T. Townsend, brother of the bridegroom, was best man. The ushers were Messrs. Harold Townsend, Robert A. Grannis, Jr., Arthur R. Van DeWater, Morton C. Fitch, Carroll J. Weddell and William P. Howe.

The bride wore a gown of point applique lace and carried a bouquet of lilies of the valley. The maid of honor, Miss Helen Simpson, sister of the bride, and the only bridesmaid, Miss Louise Townsend, sister of the groom, wore white chiffon cloth gowns and carried bouquets of white roses.

Jeptha Ross and Miss Geneva Palmer, of this place, were married July 3. *1905*

1905

1905. News Aug. 31st

YEAR WITHOUT A SUMMER.

Ice Formed In July and Corn Was Frozen In August, 1816.

Eighty-nine years ago was the year without a summer. Frost occurred every month in the year 1816. Ice formed a half inch thick in May. Snow fell to the depth of three inches in New York and also in Massachusetts in June. Ice was formed of a thickness of common window glass throughout New York on the 5th of July. Indian corn was so frozen that the greater part was cut in August and dried for fodder, and the farmers supplied themselves from the corn produced in 1815 for the seed in the spring of 1817. The old timers of Warren county will tell you that the rising generation is "not in it" with all the big snow storms when comparison is made away back in the days when they were boys.

OBITUARY.

news *aug 3 1905*

JAMES WRIGHT.

James Wright, of Chestertown, died at his home Monday morning at 2:30 o'clock from the effects of an accident which occurred Thursday. Mr. Wright was leading a cow to pasture when the animal became unruly and while struggling with her he was thrown to the ground and struck his abdomen against a large rock injuring himself internally. He was able to reach his home and Dr. E. L. Stafford was called to attend him. An examination showed that his injuries were of a very serious nature and there was little hope of his recovery. The deceased was sixty-five years old

MATRIMONIAL

Star *Nov 10 1905*

Harris-Irish.

Miss Effie G. Irish and Emmett Harris were married at the parsonage Thursday, Nov. 2. After a brief wedding trip they have taken up their residence at the home of the groom's father, Ezra Harris.—Kattskill Bay cor.

Elderly Man Struck by Car

Sept 14 05

While waiting on a platform at Batesville, above Lake George village, Sunday evening, the running board of the Warrensburgh-Saratoga trolley car leaving this village at 7:30 struck Ralph Shaw, of Lake George, seventy-three years old, who had come down to the trolley station to see his sister off. The left knee joint was fractured. *1905*

The man who has money might rest
   if he would;
And the man who has none, he might
   rest if he could;
But never till manhood has gone out
   of style,
Will the man who's a man want to
   rest all the while.
     —The Technical World Magazine.

A LIFE WELL SPENT

Star July 15 1905

Samuel Pruyn Celebrates His Eighty-fifth Birthday.

LONG ACTIVE IN THIS COMMUNITY

Born in Cambridge, He First Moved to Stillwater, Then Came to Glens Falls and Helped Organize Finch, Pruyn & Co.—Still In Good Health.

An active man of his years is Samuel Pruyn whose 85th birthday was observed a few days ago. For many years Mr. Pruyn has been among the foremost business men of the town, both in industrial and financial circles. He was born in Cambridge, Washington county, in 1820, and this and his early years were passed on the paternal acres in the town of Cambridge.

In 1850 Mr. Pruyn engaged in the lumber business at Stillwater and there he remained five years. He made little financial headway during those five years, owing to the breaking of booms and the escape of logs.

He came to Glens Falls in 1855 and engaged in the lumber business. Ten years later he formed a partnership with the late Jeremiah W. and Daniel J. Finch, under the name Finch, Pruyn & Co.

They purchased the saw mills on the north side of the river at the foot of Glen street and made extensive additions to them. There the firm contin-

ued business until a year ago, when the mills were torn down to make room for the new paper mill which will be in operation by September.

COWS GROUND TO MINCE MEAT.

Star Sept 25 1905

Passenger Train Kills Two Outright at Glen Lake While Third One Has to be Killed.

The passenger train, due from here for Lake George at 6:58 p. m., struck three cows belonging to Hollis R. Brown, at Taft's crossing, near Glen Lake, Saturday evening. Two were killed outright and Dr. Bruce Mackay, who was called, ordered the third one killed. The train was running behind time. The cows had wandered over a broken fence onto the track.

FORMER WARREN CO. MAN DEAD.

G. F. Star Sept 22 1905

Hiram Wilson Passed Away Tuesday at the Utica Hospital.

Hiram Wilson, a well known resident of this vicinity up to a few years ago, died Tuesday at Utica, where he had been confined in the hospital. The funeral was held yesterday at the home of Peter Barton, of Laurens, a brother-in-law.

Mr. Wilson was identified with local newspaper work and wrote considerable at Lake George. His mind became clouded in 1874 and much of the time since had been spent in hospitals.

He was born in Sandy Hill in 1840. He inherited from his father, the Mohican house at Bolton Landing and conducted it for seven years. In 1864 he married Miss Josephine Barton, of Laurens. Later he was customs inspector at the port of New York. Besides his wife, who resides at Oneonta, two daughters Miss May Wilson, and Mrs. F. F. Carmen, of Montclair, N. J., survive. Three sisters and two brothers also survive.

BILLINGS' ESTATE GOES TO A 12-YEAR-OLD LAD.

He is Billings Sherman, of Greenwich, and Will Get About $2,000,000 Is a Grandson.

A twelve-year old lad is the sole heir to the large estate left by the late Jesse Billings, the Northumberland farmer and merchant, who was credited with the possession of at least a million dollars worth of property, says the Saratogian. He is Billings Sherman, the deceased's grandson, and the Billings legacies will make him one of the richest persons.

He figured out the distance
Of the stars up in the sky;
He figured out our planet's age,
And when this earth will die;

He figured out the railways
And such things with patient skill—
But he never saw the errors
In his monthly butcher's bill.

FIRST OCCURRENCES.

Envelopes were first used in 1839.

The first steel pen was made in 1830.

Postoffices were first established in 1464.

The first lucifer match was made in 1829.

Kerosene was first used for lighting in 1826.

The first steamboat plied the Hudson in 1807.

The first balloon ascension was made in 1783.

Omnibuses first appeared in New York in 1830.

The first locomotive was run in this country in 1820.

The first watches were made at Nuremberg in 1477.

The first English newspaper was published in 1588.

Pins were first manufactured in this country soon after the war of 1812.

The first complete sewing machine was patented by Elias Howe, Jr., in 1846.

The first Union flag was unfurled on Jan. 1, 1776, over the camp at Cambridge.

The first newspaper printed in the United States was published in Boston on Sept. 25, 1790.

RUSSELL'S SAW MILL BURNS ENTAILING LOSS OF $3,500

Oct 9th 1905

Mill Was All Ablaze When Fire Was Discovered — Some Lumber Saved—Will Rebuild.

The steam saw and planing mill of George Russell at Ferguson Hollow, Lake George, was destroyed by fire early yesterday morning. The building caught fire about 4 o'clock and it was not discovered until fifteen or twenty minutes later. By that time it was all ablaze and though efforts were made to extinguish the fire about the only property saved was $500 worth of lumber. There was no insurance on the building and the loss will be about $3,500.

Mr. Russell expects to rebuild the mill in the same locality as soon as possible.

DEATH OF STEPHEN THOMAS.

Star Nov 29 1905

The Well Known Milk Dealer Passed Away Last Night.

Stephen Thomas, a well known milk dealer in Glens Falls for thirty years or more, died last night at 10:20 at his home on Bay road, after an illness of about a year. Mr. Thomas embarked in the milk business when a young man and continued his route up to the time he became ill.

The deceased was born on the old Col. Morgan farm on March 16, 1848.

SEPTEMBER 19, 1905

G. F. Times

LAKE GEORGE YACHT, THE FASTEST BOAT.

The Ellide Is a Hummer—A View From Albany.

That the fastest boat in the world washes regularly up and down Lake George every summer and fall is known to few people outside of those who have their summer homes on the lake or make the place the scene for a few days' outing. The yacht, a long, racy looking craft, called the Ellide, is owned by Commodore E. Burgess Warren of Philadelphia, a Lake George camper of many summers, and an enthusiastic fisherman and yachtsman. Mr. Warren recently entertained on board the Ellide Frank W. Johnston, sergeant-at-arms of the assembly and a party of Albany statesmen whom he had in tow.

"Do you know," said Mr. Warren, replying to exclamations of surprise that greeted his statement of the boat's record-breaking time, "that outside of those who come to Lake George and a few naval engineers and experts, people do not know of the Ellide's existence. Back in the nineties, when she made her test trials on the Hudson, her fame was world-wide. Every paper of prominence in the world—daily and scientific—printed something about this yacht. The clippings I received at the time would fill a bushel basket. But boats are something like human beings. They're soon forgotten when out of the public eye."

The Ellide's record time is forty miles an hour, which is yet to be beaten by any sailing craft. She is trim, eighty feet long, eight feet four inches maximum beam, with a normal displacement of about thirteen tons. Five steel bulkheads divide the yacht into six water-tight compartments. She is half machinery. Her engine is a Mosher patent quadruple expansion, having cylinders nine inches, thirteen inches, eighteen inches and twenty-four inches in diameter, and of about sixty inches mean pitch.

In addition to the main propelling engine, there is an inboard surface condenser, and six specially designed auxiliaries, including feed pumps, air-pumps, circulating-pump, bilge-pump and blower. The boiler is of the Mosher water tube type, encased in polished brass. It consists of two steam drums placed over two water drums and connected together by a number of solid drawn steel tubes so arranged that the gases pass twice the length of the boiler at right angles to the tubes before entering the stack, thus absorbing a high proportion of the heat liberated, and giving to the boiler a high efficiency. The boiler has 1,203 square feet of heating surface and 30 square feet of grate surface, and is similar to those now in use in United States navy torpedo boats.

Mr. Warren is a millionaire, who retired from business during the panic of '73 to become "a fisherman." He passed his summers on Lake George and his winters on the Florida coast. He was a close friend of the late Joe Jefferson.—Albany Journal.

MODERN CAMP TO REPLACE HUNDRED ISLAND HOUSE.

Hotel to be Torn Down Soon by Geo. O. Knapp—Structure Built Over 30 Years Ago.

George O. Knapp, owner of nearly a dozen miles of property on Lake George, near Black mountain, will soon tear down the Hundred Island house and erect on the site a large camp. The work of dismantling the hotel will begin tomorrow or Wednesday. Many of the hotel fixtures will be sold.

The hotel was built over thirty years ago by the late R. G. Bradley, of Sandy Hill, and was sold under foreclosure nearly a dozen years ago to Mr. Knapp, who happened to be visiting at the lake at the time. The house was soon afterward closed to the public and used by its owner as a summer residence together with the lodge far up on the mountain side.

JESSE BILLINGS' LIFE IS ENDED

Millionaire, Survivor of Two Murder Trials, Dead in Northumberland.

Jesse Billings, of Northumberland, famous throughout the state for his connection with the famous Billings murder case, a millionaire farmer, lumber and ice dealer, died at his home in Northumberland Sunday morning. He had been ill for some weeks with stomach trouble and this, with his age, hurried his death.

Billings was tried twenty years ago for the murder of his wife. On the first trial, the jury failed to agree and on the second, he was acquitted. Mr. Billings came from an old Colonial family. He was born in Northumberland in 1828, the son of Dr. Jesse Billings, was educated, spent his entire life and made a fortune there. Leaving school when he was 18 years old.

On the evening of Tuesday, June 4, 1878, Mr. Billings' wife, while sitting in a window, was shot dead by someone from outside. Because of the well known unhappy relations during the twenty years of maried life, Mr. Billings was arrested after the coroner's inquest charged with murder.

Judge—What's the charge? Officer—Attempting suicide. Judge—How was that? Officer—He wanted to fight me.

* * *

Lake George; Shelving Rock and Hundred Island House.

HINTS FOR FARMERS

Treatment For Splint.

It is not common for a splint to produce lameness, and therefore it would be well for you to satisfy yourself whether the lameness is caused by the splints before undertaking to treat for their removal, says the Atlanta Constitution. A peculiarity of the lameness caused by a splint is the fact that the lameness is not always continuous and is apt to be more manifest after the animal has become warmed up in his work. There will also be an increase of temperature of the affected part and a degree of tenderness to pressure. If satisfied that the splint is the cause of the lameness and the part seems hot and tender, first bathe three times a day, ten to fifteen minutes at a time, with a solution of one-half ounce of sugar of lead in one quart of water. Continue this for three or four days. Then rub on and around the splint a little of an ointment made by mixing two drams of cantharides with one ounce of lard. Keep the head tied up for twenty-four hours; then wash off the ointment and grease with lard. Repeat the blister in two weeks and continue for two or three months if necessary.

GLENS FALLS LARGER BY 2,037 POPULATION.

SPLENDID GAIN DURING FIVE YEARS IS SHOWN BY STATE CENSUS ENUMERATION.

FIGURES FOR ALL TOWNS.

Queensbury's Growth Is 1,791—But

Several Towns of County Go Backward—Secretary O'Brien's Census Report for Warren and Washington.

Population of village of Glens Falls in 1900—12,613.

Population of village of Glens Falls, June 1, 1905—14,650.

Gain in five years—2,037.

Population of Warren County.

According to figures given out yesterday afternoon by Secretary of State O'Brien, the population of Warren county on June 1, 1905, was 31,935, with a net gain of 130 persons over the figures shown by the actual enumeration, under the plan of crediting the inmates of state and county institutions, according to the city or town, and county, of actual residence at the time of admission to the institution. The distribution of the population in 1905 by towns, in comparison with similar figures for 1900, is as follows:

Towns.	State Census. 1905.	U. S. Census. 1900.
Bolton	1,561	1,363
Caldwell	1,489	1,465
Chester	1,965	2,052
Hague	1,054	1,042
Horicon	1,114	1,136
Johnsburg	2,364	2,374
Luzerne	1,371	1,341
Queensbury	16,781	14,990
Stony Creek	910	1,019
Thurman	833	809
Warrensburg	2,483	2,352
Inmates of institutions (a)	10	
Totals,	31,935	29,943

Increase—1,992.

(a) Not credited to any town in the county.

Population of Incorporated Villages.

Villages.	State Census. 1905.	U. S. Census. 1900.
Glens Falls	14,650	12,613
Lake George (a)	644	

(a) Village of Lake George incorporated March 11, 1903.

Increase for Glens Falls—2,037.

A FRACTURED SKULL

Kills William H. Morehouse, a Warrensburgh Farmer.

THROWN FROM WAGON SATURDAY

Injured Man Died Early Monday Morning—His Daughter Badly Hurt, But Chances Favor Recovery—Strap Breaking Cause of Casualty.

By the breaking of a neck yoke strap, William H. Morehouse, of Warrensburgh, was thrown from his wagon early Saturday morning and received injuries from which he died. His daughter, Lavina, was seriously injured, but her recovery is probable.

The home of Mr. Morehouse is about five miles from this village, three-quarters of a mile from the main road leading along the Schroon river and about three miles above the county home.

Saturday morning a little before 6 o'clock Mr. Morehouse and his sixteen-year-old daughter started to drive to the home of Lindsey Murdock, on Harrington hill, intending to spend the day there. But they had not gone more than half a mile from home when the accident occurred. By the breaking of the neck-yoke strap, while going down a steep pitch in the road, the wagon was thrown upon the horses which dashed wildly forward. The daughter was thrown out first. When she recovered consciousness and finally reached home in a dazed condition it was after 9 o'clock, indicating that she must have lain by the roadside for nearly three hours. She was not able to give her mother any particulars of what had happened, but her oldest brother, about fourteen years of age, started out to investigate. He found his father lying unconscious on a pile of rocks and then hurried to the nearest neighbors for help.

Assistance came quickly and Mr. Morehouse was carried to his home. The horses were found detached from the wagon and quietly browsing near the scene of the accident. Dr. Griffin was summoned and found that the man's skull was fractured and his right shoulder and arm broken. From these injuries he died early Monday morning. He regained consciousness before his death and at intervals recognized members of his family, but he was not able to talk and could give no details of the sudden and terrible casualty.

The doctor found that the daughter's right arm and shoulder were also broken. She lay in a stupor until yesterday, at times bleeding from the nose and ears. But present indications are favorable for her recovery.

Buffalo Bill's Trail Open.

New Road now Through 100 Miles of Wildest West.

Buffalo Bill has lived to see one of his cherished plans carried out. After forty years the trail which he himself mapped out through the wildest part of Wyoming has been opened as a public road.

In laying out the trail the old fighter employed no engineer. He struck out for the wildest and most beautiful scenery to be found and this road from the town of Cody to the Yellowstone passes through such ravines and along such precipices that several short tunnels have had to be cut. Part of the time the way is over mountains and part of the time along winding rivers and canons.

Upon this trail in one of the very loneliest spots, Col. Cody has built for himself an imposing mausoleum in which he will some day be buried. The tomb is located on the apex of Rattlesnake Mountain, which before this road was opened was inaccessible save to a few experienced mountaineers.

Col. Cody's trail will help the homeseekers who will go to the Wind River and Shoshone Reservaton next summer. The Government has already set June 15, 1906, as the date when the land shall be thrown open. In the meantime the United States is spending $2,225,000 on an irrigation project in this selfsame Big Horn Basin for the reclamation of near to 150,000 acres of fertile land.

The country is located in northwestern Wyoming, immediately east of Yellowstone Park. The basin contains more than 8,000,000 acres, and it is believed that at least a fourth of this can be influenced by irrigation.

That part of the Big Horn district which the United States Government is seeking to irrigate lies along the Shoshone River in Big Horn County. The main canal will be sixty feet wide at the bottom, and will extend from Rattlesnake Mountain, three miles above Cody, along the north side of the river to a terminus above Garland.

At one point the canal passes through a ravine with perpendicular walls several hundred feet high, and this at the narrowest point will be walled up by a dam 120 high as a reservoir.

New Proprietor of Warren House.

Maurice O'Connor, who recently purchased the Warren house property from Ashley T. Kellogg, took possession yesterday and assumed the management of the hotel. James Minihan, formerly clerk of the Adirondack hotel, is employed in the same capacity at the Warren. *Dec. 28th 1905*

FIRST TRAIN INTO WARRENSBURG

Came Over From Thurman on the Extension Saturday.

The first train to run over the new branch of the Delaware and Hudson from Thurman to Warrensburg was run Saturday morning, arriving in Warrensburg about noon, writes a correspondent. This was the first steam train that ever entered Warrensburg. The Thurman Warrensburg extension is about three miles long, and was begun last summer. It crosses the Hudson south of Thurman on an iron bridge that was formerly used between Troy and Green Island. The new extension connects with the Adirondack branch of the Delaware and Hudson at Thurman, and gives an outlet for a large quantity of paper, pulp, manufactured linen and other manufactured products of Warrensburg, which hitherto have been carried to Lake George by team or on trolley cars.

WEATHER LIKE SPRING.

Sudden Rise in Temperature Takes Away the Sleighing.

Yesterday was a typical spring day with the thermometer registering at noon 60 degrees above zero. The sun thawed the snow so fast that by night the streets were almost bare and many who had been using sleighs had to resort to wagons. The river raised considerable during the day.

Sleighs replaced the wheeled trucks in the fire houses Saturday afternoon. Yesterday afternoon within 24 hours the wagon took the place of the sleigh in the Ridge street house.

Another evidence of spring reached this office Saturday in the form of branches of pussy willows in full blossom. They were cut at Lake George and were sent to Glens Falls by Miss Helen Tripp, of that village.

JOHN BOTHAM TWADDLE.

Superintendent of the Warrensburgh Woolen Company's Pants Factory.

As superintendent of the Warrensburgh Woolen company's pants factory, one of the most flourishing industries of Warrensburgh, John Botham Twaddle occupies a position of considerable prominence and responsibility in this community. Mr. Twaddle came here in 1900, when the factory was first established, from Malone, where he had had an extended experience in the business as superintendent in the large factory of J. O. Ballard & Co. He came recommended as a first-class man, possessed of the technical and executive ability necessary to fit him for the position.

HOW AN ARM WAS LOST.

news Jan. 4 the

Particulars of Accident of Which H. M. Lewis Was Victim.

1906

Further particulars have been received here regarding the accident of which H. M. Lewis was the victim in Saratoga last week.

Mr. Lewis, it is stated, was feeding a planing machine when a stick got caught in the knives. He attempted to remove it without stopping the power, when the rollers caught a mitten on his left hand and drew the hand and arm into the machine. He was then unable to reach the power lever and the other workmen were in another part of the mill, so bracing his shoulder against the frame of the machine and exerting his entire strength he kept his body from being drawn between the rollers while the cruel knives stripped the flesh from his arm.

When his fellow workmen reached him the arm was so badly lacerated that there was no hope of saving it. He was taken to the hospital and almost immediately placed on the operating table. He begged of the surgeons to save the arm but they were unable to do so and it was taken off about half way between the elbow and shoulder.

Mr. Lewis is about sixty years old and is not in rugged health. It was feared that he would be unable to stand the shock, but he rallied from the operation much better than was expected and has improved so rapidly that he is now considered out of danger and will probably be able to be removed to his home within a few days.

Mr. Lewis was a resident of Warrensburgh for many years and was one of our best citizens. The news of his great misfortune was a shock to his many friends here and they sympathize with him deeply. He has been employed in planing mills since he was a boy and has never before had a serious accident.

Star April 4th 1906

Snow and Rainfall for March.

The rain and snowfall for month of March just passed compared with previous years as shown by statistics kept by Observer Cronkhite, of Gansevoort, is appended: 1906 snow 20 1-2 inches, rain 2.92 inches; 1905 snow 17 1-2 inches, rain 1.57 inches; 1904 snow 14 inches, rain 2.15 inches; 1903 snow 3 inches, rain 6.79 inches; 1902 snow 15 inches, rain 5.08 inches; 1901 snow 14 inches, rain 2.57 inches.

"Bayruth" Sold to Ohio Man. *News*

County Treasurer Frank S. Packard has sold his summer home, "Bayruth," on Lake George, near Hill View, to a wealthy man of Toledo, Ohio. The sale includes Mr. Packard's motor boats, the house furnishings and everything about the place. Possession has been given. *May 8. 1906.*

ROBERTS, TRAPPER, HUNTER HAS READ BIBLE 33 TIMES

Star Jan 9. 1906

In 35 Years Has Taken 53 Bears, 1,500 Foxes, 2,000 Raccoons and Mink. Wants Strict Game Law.

Edwin Roberts, a trapper and hunter who lives near Brant Lake, was in town the other day to dispose of about $200 worth of fox, mink and raccoon skins. Mr. Roberts is the father of Jesse Roberts, who attended the Glens Falls academy and who is now preaching in Bolton, and, is well known in the north. Mr. Roberts has lived in the woods for 35 years and has raised a large family on the small farm, with the aid of his traps and gun. He came to Warren county from Vermont and during his thirty five seasons in the woods has trapped 53 bears, over 1,500 foxes, 1,000 raccoons, 1,000 mink and many other animals.

Mr. Roberts in conversation with a Star man told many interesting stories of adventure in the woods, and one describing how he was nearly killed by a bear as large as a cow, was particularly exciting.

Besides being a clever hunter, Mr. Roberts is exceptionally well read in the Bible, and can repeat long passages. He has read every chapter of every book in the Bible thirty-three times, and he says he will keep on reading it as long as he can see the printed page.

Mr. Roberts says he is very glad that most of the hounding of deer has been stopped by law. He favors a shorter hunting season. say during the month of November, when the deer are in their best condition. He also favors a shorter season for brook trout and would limit a fisherman to a reasonable number of fish. He thinks the game laws would be more rigidly enforced if in each town a disinterested person were given authority to arrest violators of the law.

SAMUEL PRUYN, PRESIDENT OF FINCH, PRUYN & CO.

Times — Feb 5

Is Elected Today to Succeed George R. Finch, Deceased.

The directors of Finch, Pruyn & company, incorporated, met this morning in special session when Samuel Pruyn was elected president to succeed George R. Finch, deceased.

The other officers of the company are: Vice president and secretary, Maurice Hoopes; treasurer, Howard H. Pruyn. *1908*

-32-

WOMAN WHO THREW ACID HELD FOR GRAND JURY

ATTACK MADE BY JENNIE COSGROVE, ON HER HUSBAND, JAMES COSGROVE.

IN SARATOGA HOTEL

Times Feb 5-1906

Man and Wife Had Not Lived Together for Five Years—The Latter Sought Interview and at Conclusion Threw Deadly Acid.

Mrs. Jennie Cosgrove, of Warrensburg, was arraigned at Saratoga this morning, charged with assault in the first degree in throwing nitric acid in the face of her husband, James Cosgrove, of Saratoga. She waived examination before Police Justice William J. Delaney and was held to await the action of the grand jury. J. Edward Singleton, of Glens Falls, appeared as counsel for the accused.

According to the charge made by Cosgrove his wife came to Saratoga Saturday night and engaged a room in the Commercial hotel. Yesterday, it is claimed, she sent word to her husband to call on her at the hotel. He did so, bringing with him their young daughter whom he has had in charge.

In response to Mrs. Cosgrove's summons, the husband went to her room, leaving the little girl behind. He remained alone with his wife for several moments and just as he was about to depart, he says she stepped in front of him and threw the acid in his face. He received severe burns but his eyes were not injured.

Whether there was any trouble directly previous to the assault is uncertain, but it is generally known that the couple have been separated for about five years. Mrs. Cosgrove sought separation some time ago and her husband retaliated by seeking a decree of absolute divorce charging infidelity. Cosgrove is twenty-six years of age and is employed by Swift & company at Saratoga. His wife, until a day or two ago, was employed by the Empire Shirt company at Warrensburg. She is three years his junior.

Lake George Cottager Dead in Italy.

News has been received in this village relative to the death of Miss Elizabeth Warren which occurred a few days ago at San Remo, Itay. Miss Warren was a daughter of the late Dr. George W. Warren. The family was well known in town and vicinity having spent many summers at Lake George in the old Terriault cottage at Bolton. Miss Warren was 30 years old and came from an old Revolutionary family. *Star March 9 1906*

1906

HIRAM J. ROCKWELL.

—The funeral of Hiram J. Rockwell, the well known hotelman, was held this afternoon. At 1:30 o'clock there were private services at The Ten Eyck and at 2 o'clock were held the public services at St. Peter's Episcopal Church, Albany. The services, which were very impressive, were conducted by Rev. Thaddeus A. Snively, D. D., of Chicago, Ill.,

He found no greater pleasure than driving behind a pair of fast horses. Mr. Rockwell was born in Luzerne, Warren County, July 13, 1832. He early became identified with hotels and was proprietor of The Wayside at Luzerne. He later became proprietor of the Lake House and the Fort William Henry Hotel at Lake George. These hotels he conducted for some time, when he built the Rockwell House at Glens Falls. About twenty years ago he conducted the American House in this city, and during the few years he was here he made a host of friends. His next venture was at The Kenmore in Albany, which he managed with his son, Frederick W. Rockwell. When The Ten Eyck was built H. J. Rockwell & Son took charge of its management in connection with The Kenmore, which they later relinquished in order to devote all their energies to making The Ten Eyck a success.

NEW BOAT LINE FOR LAKE.

To Operate Between Kattskill Bay and Lake George Station.

Stephen Harris of Kattskill Bay has purchased a steam cabin passenger boat of John Vandenburg, of Kattskill Bay to operate this summer between Kattskill Bay and Lake George station. The boat which has been out of water for two years has been fitted up and will be ready in a week or two. Mr. Harris has obtained a license to operate it. The boat is licensed to carry 25 people and will begin operations June 15 or July 1. June 1, 1906

SUSAN B. ANTHONY DEAD; END CAME PEACEFULLY

1906

ROCHESTER, N. Y., March 13.—The long and eventful life of Susan B. Anthony closed at 12:40 o'clock this morning. The end came peacefully. Miss Anthony had been unconscious practically all of the time for more than twenty-four hours, and her death had been almost momentarily expected since last night. Only her wonderful constitution kept her alive.

Dr. M. S. Ricker, her attending physician, said Miss Anthony died of heart

SUSAN B. ANTHONY.

failure, induced by pneumonia of both lungs. She had had serious valvular heart trouble for the last six or seven years. Her lungs were practically clear, and the pneumonia had yielded to treatment, but the weakness of her heart prevented her recovery.

BIDS FOR 175 STATE ROADS, 1906 WARREN COUNTY AMONG THEM

State Engineer Van Alystyne has announced he would receive bids June 28, 29 and 30 for construction this summer of 175 roads within the state under the state aid act. Among them are six in Saratoga county and two in Warren, between Glens Falls and Lake George, 7.560 miles and Lake George and Bolton 9.740 miles.

A FEMALE PREACHER

1906

Departs for West to Engage in Missionary Work.

LEAVES HER HUSBAND BEHIND

But Takes Her Two Children and Another Man—Graphophone to Aid in the Work of Evangelizing the Wild and Wicked Westerners.

If the carefully laid plans of Mrs. William Bennett, of this village, and Fred Cooper, of South Horicon, are successfully carried out there will arrive in far off Idaho within a week or so the most peculiar combination of humanity that ever struck the wild and wooly West.

Mrs. Bennett and Cooper left here together Tuesday night on the 9:30 trolley car accompanied by the woman's two children, Eva, aged fourteen, and Richard, aged ten. Though their destination was not publicly stated Mrs. Bennett Tuesday afternoon told a friend in strictest confidence that she was going to Idaho to engage in missionary work. Regarding Cooper's destination she was somewhat reticent. She admitted that he was to accompany her, but claimed that he was going only to Fort Miller. However, it was known that some of the man's clothing was packed in one of her trunks so arranged as to protect some dishes from breakage. There is no doubt that it will remain there until the journey is ended and Cooper will be with it. The trunks, four in number, were sent away in the early evening by team to Lake George.

Cooper was dressed for his journey just as he came from the north, with flannel shirt, slouch hat and a cheap fur coat such as some lumbermen wear. His baggage consisted principally of a graphophone and forty records. It is presumed that he intends to charm the Idaho sinners with rag time selections and coon songs while his companion labors to convince them of the error of their ways.

William Bennett, the deserted husband, is said to be an honest, hardworking man, and, domestically speaking, a good provider. The couple moved here last fall, from South Horicon, and took up their residence in the rooms over Robert Swan's store on lower Main street. Bennett was employed on Dr. Nostron's place on Wall street, in the town of Bolton, and was at home only Saturday nights and Sundays. His wife worked in the shirt factory. Cooper, it is said, came here frequently and called on the woman.

THE ELK ARRIVE FOR LAKE GEORGE

Star March 22rd 1906

FIVE OF THEM TAKEN UP PROSPECT MT. FOR LIBERATION.

One Wild Buck Became Cast Wednesday Night and Died Late Last Night—The Other Five Elk Will Be Taken to Tongue Mountain Today. They Are In Fine Condition.

The arrival of ten elk at Lake George yesterday afternoon caused a great deal of excitement in the village and a large crowd soon gathered to see the animals. W. W. Burton brought them from the Blue Mountain Forest park in New Hampshire, where they were caught a few days ago. Though some of them were wild, they were crated and put in three cars for transmission. There are six does and four bucks. One of the bucks became cast Wednesday night and he was found in the morning with his head under his body. He was a wild creature and was rescued from his dangerous position with considerable difficulty.

The elk are fine, large animals. Three does and two of the bucks were taken up Prospect mountain to the big hollow late in the afternoon. When the party reached Big Bow, near the big hollow, the elk were liberated. Four of them started off up the mountain as unconcerned as if they were back in their old haunts in the big New Hampshire park. The buck which became cast the night before, was very weak and could hardly walk. He was taken back to Truman Hammond's barn, where he died at 11 o'clock.

The other five elk will be carted to Bolton and then taken across the lake to the George O. Knapp property. From there they will be taken up Tongue mountain and liberated.

The elk were sent by Austin Corbin, of New York, who is largely interested in the New Hampshire park. If the elk survive and remain in the mountains, as there is reason to believe will be the case, it is quite probable that more elk will be sent to the Adirondacks next year.

THE MADE-TO-ORDER HUSBAND.

He must be tender and true,
Never right cranky or blue;
Of looks, a fair share, I trust,
A moderate amount of "dust."
A masterful man, I ween;
Not finiky nice, but clean.
Some passion, to make life bright;
Of love a bountiful sight,
A lover of home and wife,
Of babes—if they bless our life,
One man like this would leaven
The whole of this mortal sphere.
You may find him in heaven—
I'm sure you never will here.
—Mrs. Minnie N. Ri—

CARL SCHURZ HAS SINKING SPELL

Son of Former Cabinet Officer Telephones to Doctor to Hurry to Bedside.

NO HOPE THAT PATIENT CAN RECOVER.

Carl Schurz, former Secretary of the Interior, had a turn for the worse this afternoon and it was feared that he was dying.

His son, Carl L. Schurz, left Mr. Schurz's house at 24 East Ninety-first street, and telephoned for Dr. A. Jacobi, asking him to hurry to the patient, as his pulse had become very weak.

A little earlier Andrew Carnegie had called at the Schurz residence and was allowed to see the patient.

At Mr. Schurz's bedside almost constantly are his son and his daughters, Misses Agathe and Marianne.

Dr. Jacobi this morning said that Mr. Schurz had passed a quiet night and was better. The morning bulletin read:

Mr. Schurz has been quite sick for the last few days, but he is in no immediate danger, and is, indeed, very much improved and fairly comfortable.

Dr. Jacobi said that the pulmonary oedema, which had affected Mr. Schurz's lungs, had been relieved.

The physician has given it out that there is no hope of Mr. Schurz's recovery. He is seventy-seven years old and is suffering from a stomach disorder, complicated with other diseases.

Mr. Schurz was active up to a week ago, despite his advanced years.

Star April 4th 1906

DEATH OF AN OLD RESIDENT; ELDAD GOODMAN PASSES AWAY

He Was Born in Bolton and Moved to Goodman Farm From Harrisena. Funeral on Friday.

Eldad W. Goodman, an old respected resident, died at his home on Elm street at 8:45 o'clock last evening, after a short illness from a complication of diseases. He was born in Bolton 75 years ago and when a young man moved to Harrisena. Later he moved to the Goodman farm north of the village and then seven years ago he came into the village to live.

He is survived by his wife, a daughter, Miss Ethelyn Goodman, a sister, Mrs. Alice Streeter, of this village, and a brother, Oton Goodman, of Cross Forks, Pa.

The funeral will be held from the residence, 53 Elm street, Friday afternoon at 2:30 o'clock.

HENRY GOSSLING.

Henry Gossling, aged sixty-five years, an old time resident of Lake George, died Tuesday morning at 5 o'clock at his home on the Bolton road. He was a German by birth, coming to this country when a young man and settled first in St. Louis. He afterwards came to Lake George, entered the employ of the late Colonel Price and after his death became caretaker of the Lake George property of George Foster Peabody. He lived at Lake George for about forty years. Besides his widow he is survived by one son, Walter Gossling, of Lake George. The funeral was held yesterday afternoon at 2 o'clock from the home of Mr. Peabody, Lake George. The interment was made in the Lake George cemetery.

Star April 19 1906

Ice Out of Lake George.

The ice went out of Lake George late yesterday afternoon and within a day or two many craft will be launched. The first boat on the lake, it is said, was the Knapp launch, in which Mr. Nichols rode up as far as Hill View Tuesday. Walter Harris put his boat in the water on the east side of the bay Tuesday and went across the bay to the village yesterday morning in the floating ice.

News **HENRY A. MUTHSAN.** *May 4.*

Harry A. Muthsan died Tuesday at the home of D. S. Gates, Bolton, where he had been staying for his health. At the request of Darcy lodge, No. 187, of New York, the funeral tomorrow aforenoon at the house will be in charge of Warrensburgh lodge of Masons and members of the craft are requested to meet at the lodge rooms at 8 a. m., sharp, tomorrow morning. Interment in the Huddle cemetery at Bolton. *1906*

Bolton Landing.

Mr and Mrs Fred Thatcher are home from Schenectady for the summer.

A son was born to Mr and Mrs Frank Phelps, May 7.

Mrs F R Norton went to her home in Albany Tuesday for a visit.

Mr and Mrs C E Webb and Mr and Mrs Alexander Taylor moved into their new house last week.

Mrs E M Lamb and son, Arthur, visited the former's sister, Mrs Smith Hastings of South Glens Falls, last week.

Mr and Mrs L E Taylor have moved into rooms over Gates Brothers' store.

May 16. *Star May 23. 1906*

Star **Millionaire as Pathmaster.** *May 23*

A. Thieriot of New York city is again at Chestertown, where he spends about eight months every year. Mr. Thieriot, who is a millionaire, is pathmaster for the village of Chestertown and he takes great pride in assisting in keeping the roads in excellent condition, employing men at his own expense for this purpose. He is executor of the Delmonico estate in New York.—Troy Times. *1906*

PILOT HARRIS NOW A BENEDICT; A PRETTY CHURCH WEDDING.

Miss Alice Bertha Chism of Albany, and Walter Price Harris of Lake George, Married.

The wedding of Miss Alice Bertha Chism, daughter of Mr. and Mrs. George M. Chism and Walter Price Harris, of Lake George, took place Saturday night at the Memorial Baptist church, Rev. H. C. Colebrook officiating.

Mr. Harris is head pilot of the steamer Sagamore.

RICHARD BRADLEY DEAD.

Passed Away Yesterday After Lingering Illness.

Reuben G. Bradley died yesterday at 4 a. m. after a lingering illness. Mr. Bradley was born in the town of Moreau in 1832. He was engaged in the lumber business for a number of years and in 1871 he opened the Fourteen Mile Island House at Lake George, afterwards known as Kenisaw. In 1874 he built the Hundred Island House and opened it in 1876. It was sold later to George O. Knapp. The deceased is survived by one sister, Mrs. Sarah Bradley, of Caldwell, two daughters, Miss Jennie Bradley, of Washington, D. C., and Mrs. James M. Whitman, jr., of Sandy Hill. The funeral will be held Sunday at 2:30 p. m. from the home of Mrs. James Whitman, Main street. Rev. Dr. E. R. Sawyer will officiate. *Star June 23 1906*

FRED H. PARKS LEFT $10,000 TO HOSPITAL

Star June 2.

Estate Estimated to be Between $1,000,000 and $2,000,000--- Bulk to Widow and Daughter

The will of Frederick H. Parks was admitted to probate in surrogate Jenkins court yesterday. Mrs. F. H. Parks and Frank R. Kimbley were named as executors. The estate is variously estimated to be valued between $1,000,000 to $2,000,000 but nothing definite as to its value could be ascertained. The bulk of the estate is left to the widow, Mrs. Parks and a daughter, Mrs. Florence Parks Kimbley.

To the Parks hospital is left $10,000, the income to be used for the maintenance of two beds, one in memory of the decedent's mother, Harriet Hewitt Parks and the other in memory of his father, Solomon A. Parks.

JUNE ORANGE BLOSSOMS; A DAY OF WEDDINGS.

Star June 20 1906

Four Ceremonies Performed Yesterday by Local Clergy—Tuttle-Braman Nuptials.

Miss Edith Tuttle, daughter of Mr and Mrs. W. S. Tuttle, and Robert A. Braman, of Grand Mere, Canada, were married yesterday noon at the summer residence of the bride's aunt, Miss Roxie G. Tuttle, at Bolton. The house was prettily decorated with oak leaves and daisies. There were no attendants and the ceremony, performed by Rev. Dr. Henry George, was simple. The bride was gowned in white silk mull trimmed with Duchess lace. There were many beautiful presents. After the reception the newly married couple left for a trip to the sea shore. They will reside at Grand Mere. Quite a number of guests from out of town were present. They were met at Lake George and conveyed to Bolton in W. K. Bixby's new launch. "Forward," and taken back to Lake George later in the day. The guests were Mrs. M. J. Braman, W. W. Braman, Three Rivers, Canada; Mr. and Mrs. I. G. Braman, of Watervliet; Mrs. J. W. Cameron, Miss Zaida Herrick, of Saratoga; Miss Sarah Cronkhite, of East Lake George; Mrs. W. S. Tuttle, Mrs. H. Emerson West, Mrs. Archie McEachron, Miss E. C. Boyd, Mrs. P. P. Braley, Mr. and Mrs. Andrew Thomas, Mrs. R. J. Whitby, Mrs. A. G. Sellingham, Mrs. Robert Kirkpatrick, S. B. Goodman, Misses Gertrude Whipple, Florence Batcheller, Mildred Griffith, Kate Whitby, Jessie Allen, Helen Tuttle, Kathleen Sellingham, Bertha Sellingham, Luther Tuttle, of Glens Falls; Mr. and Mrs Jay Tuttle, Sidney and Bessie Tuttle, Mrs. Sarah Tuttle, of Bolton Landing.

OBITUARY.

Star July 31 1906

Mrs. Zilpha Streeter.

Zilpha, widow of John Streeter, of South Horicon, died very sudden at the home of her daughter, Mrs. Philetus Haskins on Thursday with neuralgia of the heart. She is survived by these children: Eugene Streeter, Robert and Scott, of Horicon; George, of Hague; Mrs. Fish, of Hague; and the daughter already mentioned. The funeral was held at Horicon.

Tearing Down Hotel.

news Oct 18 1906

Workmen are tearing down the Hundred Island house, Lake George, and on the site George O. Knapp, the owner, will build a cottage. No plans have as yet been made for the new structure. For many years the Hundred Island house was a popular Lake George resort, but for several seasons past has been closed to the public.

CONTRACT FINALLY LET TO BUILD BOLTON TOWN HALL

1906 Star Aug. 13

After spending two years in an attempt to build a town hall at Bolton and contending with injunction upon injunction, the contract to build Bolton town hall was let at Bolton Saturday by the town board. Two bidders were in the field, Gifford, Williams and company, of this place, and the Schermerhorn Construction company, of Bolton. The Schermerhorn company bid was the lowest, $3,872.83 while that of the Glens Falls firm was $6.17 higher, $3,879. The contract went to the Schermerhorn company.

The structure will be one story with a finished basement for jail. It will be built of cement blocks. The hall will be used as a meeting place for the town board, for the town clerk, justices of the peace and supervisor. The board which will supervise its construction is composed of Fred R. Smith, supervisor; John Taber, S. P. Braley, Henry Roberts, H. F. Seaman, justices of the peace, and Edward N. Lamb, town clerk.

OBITUARY

news Sept 13

JOHN COOLIDGE.

John Coolidge, for many years proprietor of the Diamond Point house at Hill View, died at 1:45 o'clock Monday morning. He sustained a shock Friday evening about 9 o'clock. His right side was paralyzed. Subsequently pneumonia developed. He was unconscious when found in the pantry of the hotel and remained so up to his death. Dr. J. M. Griffin, of Warrensburgh, was in attendance day and night. Dr. T. I. Henning, of Glens Falls, was summoned Sunday in consultation, but medical skill was not able to rally the patient. Mr. Coolidge was born on Coolidge hill, Bolton, where he passed his younger days on his father's farm. He married Miss Phebe Middleton, of Warrensburgh. In the early seventies he leased the Diamond Point house and later purchased the property, which is one of the most attractive of the smaller summer resorts on Lake George. Deceased was a plain, practical man, punctual to the discharge of every obligation. He was devoted to his home and family, of whom a widow and two daughters, Misses Mary and Anna Coolidge, survive, and one sister, Mrs. M. N. Dickinson, of Warrensburgh. Jonathan M., Thomas S., and Flavel B. Coolidge, of Glens Falls, who were also born on Coolidge hill, are cousins. The funeral was held yesterday afternoon at 2 o'clock from the late home, Rev. C. W. Dunham, of this village, officiating. Interment in Warrensburgh cemetery. *1906*

-35-

A BANKER 50 YEARS; WM. A. WAIT IS DEAD

Star Oct 29, 1906

DEVOTED TO CHURCH, HOME AND BANK, A VALUABLE CITIZEN GONE

He Was a Poet by Gift, a Man of High Literary Attainments—Interested in Philanthropic Movements — Was Director in Many Institutions—The Funeral Wednesday

William A. Wait, almost a lifelong resident of Glens Falls and a banker for 51 years, died at his residence on Warren street at 4:15 Saturday afternoon. Death followed a stroke of apoplexy sustained at his place of business Thursday afternoon.

Mr. Wait's Life.

Mr. Wait was born in Saratoga November 24, 1835. His schooling was of the commonest, only lasting until he was fourteen years old. At that age he came to Glens Falls, taking a

WILLIAM A. WAIT.

job as clerk in the dry goods store of William Fonda, located where now stands the Russell and Wait store. He afterwards was clerk in the postoffice under Postmaster William Peck.

Star OBITUARY. *Oct 9 1906*

Mrs. Alice Streeter.

The funeral of Mrs. Alice Streeter was held yesterday morning at her home 108 Bay street. Rev. Dr. John R. Mackay officiated. The remains were taken to Bolton for burial. The bearers were Thomas S. Coolidge, P. P. Braley, S. B. Goodman and John Gates.

---

news BROWN-BURHANS. *Oct 4*

Willard W. Brown, formerly manager of the Rockwell house, Glens Falls, and Mrs. Viola H. P. Burhans, formerly of Warrensburgh, were married Tuesday in New York. They will be at home after November 1st at the Dewey hotel, Washington, D. C., of which the groom's father, M. O. Brown, late of the Sagamore hotel, Bolton-on-Lake George, is proprietor. *1906*

Powell Hill, While Intoxicated Started Out to Find Trouble and in a Fight With Wm. and George Banker Received Fatal Injuries.

Star Sept 5 1906

AUTOPSY SHOWED DEATH DUE TO BROKEN BACK

District Attorney, Coroner and Sheriff Making An Investigation.

Powell Hill, a mine laborer of Hague, Lake George, died last evening about nine o'clock as the result of injuries inflicted by two men who have been arrested and held to answer a charge of murder.

The cause of the trouble was a drunken brawl, according to all the reports. Word came to the district attorney yesterday morning and he left at noon accompanied by Coroner Edgar S. Bullis and Dr. Charles S. McLaughlin. At Lake George they were joined by Sheriff Bowyer. On their arrival at Hague they found that the two men who had attacked Hill, William and George Banker, had been arrested in the morning.

ER 5, 1906. *Star nov 5/190*

GRANDDAUGHTER OF COL. PRICE DIES IN GLENS FALLS

Mrs J M Fogarty Suffered Apoplectic Stroke and Fell Few Days Ago. Died at Hospital Saturday.

Mrs. J. M. Fogarty, of New York and Lake George, granddaughter of the late Col. Price, died Saturday afternoon at three o'clock at the Parks hospital after an illness of three days, following a stroke of apoplexy and a fall at Lake George a few days since.

Mrs. Fogarty spent her summers at the old Lake house and later in the Lake George Inn cottages. She was thirty-five years old and a daughter of the late Walter M. Price. Her husband, who was well known in Glens Falls, died two years ago. The remains were taken to Bullard's undertaking rooms and the funeral will be held Tuesday forenoon at 11 o'clock at the Lake George Episcopal church, Rev. E. M. Parrott officiating. The remains will be interred in the Price lot at Lake George.

"DIVORCE IS UNSPEAKABLE" SAYS REV. C. O. JUDKINS

The divorce problem was again considered last night in a sermon delivered by the Rev. Charles O. Judkins, who preached on the subject of "Good Breeding and Marriage." Mr. Judkins said that divorces were a great American fault and were fast becoming a mania which spoiled the purity of homes. "Without the pure home," said Mr. Judkins, "the kingdom of heaven cannot come to the earth."

The questions considered relative to this great problem of the day were "Are Separations Ever Right?" and "Is Divorce Ever Right?" Mr. Judkins said that there was a vast difference between separation and divorce. In separating, a couple could be true to the marriage pledge, but divorce meant an absolute breaking of something promised never to be broken.

"Separation," continued Mr. Judkins, "is bad enough for husband and wife, but an absolute breakage of that tie is unspeakable."

Mr. Judkins gave several illustrations when separation was right, and one of them was where a man and a woman were driven to it by one or the other reaching a state through drink that life with each other could not be tolerated, "but divorce," said the speaker, "is never ideally or in theory ever right, no matter what the cause to bring it about."

Mr. Judkins spoke from the fact that it ruins childhood and curses children. "There is a time coming," continued Mr. Judkins, "when we will keep our promises for better or for worse." In concluding Mr. Judkins said: "Keep divorce at a distance, for it is the greatest sin against the kingdom of heaven. Give us homes of purity so that the child can be born to breathe righteousness, then the kingdom of heaven can come to such a home."

---

oct 29 1906 **Mrs. Helen A. Stoddard.** *Star*

Mrs. Helen A. Stoddard, wife of S. R. Stoddard, the well known lecturer, writer, historian and traveler, died yesterday morning at 1:17 o'clock at her home, 36 Elm street. Mrs. Stoddard was born January 21, 1850, in South Glens Falls. Her parents were the late Thomas Potter and Judith S. Mosher Potter. During March, 1868, she married Mr. Stoddard, who with two sons, Charles H. and LeRoy R. Stoddard, of New York, survive. Two brothers also survive, George A. Potter, of Spokane, Washington, and John E. Potter, of Glens Falls.

Mrs. Stoddard was a member of the First Church of Christ, Scientist. The funeral will be held Tuesday morning at 11 o'clock at the home on Elm street. The remains will be interred in the family plot in Bay street cemetery.

Star Nov. 24th 1906

SANTOS-DUMONT MAKING A FLIGHT IN HIS NEW AEROPLANE, THE BIRD OF PREY.

M. Santos-Dumont has abandoned the dirigible balloon for the aeroplane, which rises in the air and remains without the support of a great envelope inflated by gas. In his first public flight he covered twenty-seven feet and won the archdeacon cup, which was offered to the first aeroplane heavier than air which should fly a distance of twenty-five meters. In a later flight he covered 685 feet and declared he could have gone much farther but for fear of injuring the crowd below.

NEW BANK AT 'BURG SEEMS A MYSTERY

Star Nov. 16th 1906

CHARTER APPROVED FOR A NATIONAL WITH $50,000 CAPITAL.

Five Glens Falls Men Named as Applicants But They, Interrogated, Have Nothing to Say—Reoux May be Cashier—An Institution for Lake George Rumored.

The application of Jeremiah T. Finch, Byron B. Fowler, T. S. DeLong, S. B. Goodman and J. M. Coolidge to organize the Warrensburg National Bank of Warrensburg, with $50,000 capital, has been approved by the comptroller of the currency.

This short dispatch sent out from Washington, D.C., yesterday afternoon confirmed rumors which have been afloat for the past few days of a new bank at Warrensburg and also at Lake George and incidentally added a new phase to the local political situation.

OLD STAGE DRIVER DEAD
Star Dec. 6th 1906

William Mead, Last of Ben Starbuck Line, Passes Away.

William Mead, the last surviving stage driver of the old Ben Starbuck line, which was operated from Moreau to Lake George nearly 50 years ago, died Tuesday night at 8:55 o'clock at his home in Caldwell. He was 74 years of age. He is survived by two daughters and one son, Mrs. Charles Dennis, of Lake George; Mrs. James Long, of Saratoga, and Beaker F. Mead, of Glens Falls. Two sisters and a brother also survive, David Mead, of Bay road, and Mrs. Lucy Stebbins and Mrs. Alphonsus Brown, of Lake George. The funeral will be held Friday afternoon at 1 o'clock at the home in Caldwell. Rev. Mr. Parrott will officiate. The burial will be in Gurney Lane cemetery.

TRASK BUYS AN ISLAND;
TO CAMP AT LAKE GEORGE.
Star Dec 22nd 1906

Spencer Trask, of New York and Saratoga, has purchased of Mrs. F. F. H. Myers, of Bolton and Yonkers, Three Brothers island in Lake George, near Bolton. Mr. Trask will have a summer camp on the islands the coming summer.

Against Regents' Examinations.

Rev. J. A. Hamilton, pastor of the First Methodist church, Saratoga, took occasion in a recent sermon to criticise regents' examinations. The condemnation came in the course of his sermon on "The Health Element." Mr. Hamilton opposed the examinations on the ground of health, declaring that the nervous strain that precedes such examinations is entirely too severe for pupils to undergo.

Star nov. 22 1906

Ice On Lake George Yet.
Star Dec 20 1906

Captain Stephen Harris, of the Cleo, Schermerhorn Brothers' boat, ran the craft up to the head of Lake George yesterday from Fourteen Mile island. Mr. Harris was much amused to read last evening that the lake was covered with ice, for the only ice he saw was a small strip at the Fort William Henry dock. The Cleo is hauling material for Mr. Beardsley's new cottage at Fourteen Mile island, and is probably the only power boat on the lake.

CAPTAIN HARRIS DIED YESTERDAY

Star
Dec 20 1906

WELL KNOWN VETERAN LAKE GEORGE NAVIGATOR FOUND DEAD.

Had Been Ill Recently—Commanded Big Steamers for Many Years and Piloted Craft on the Lake Since a Boy—Did Valient Work When John Jay Burned—Funeral Friday.

Captain E. S. Harris, pioneer captain on Lake George and historian of that region for many years, was found dead in bed at his home at Lake George yesterday morning. He had been suffering from Bright's disease for the past three years. He was 79 years old. Captain Harris was commander of the steamers Minnehaha and Horicon for several years, of the John Jay when it burned and the Sagamore until he retired three years ago. Capt. Harris was the author of an extensive history of Lake George giving the history of the place graphically back to its discovery in 1607.

Capt. Harris was born June 8, 1828, at Kingsbury. When four years old he moved to Lake George. As early as 10 years old he began to navigate the waters of this well known lake with his father, who had a scow built to carry wood and lumber. At 15 he began his career as fireman of the steamer William Caldwell. Aside from the duties of fireman he was called upon to make the landings with a yaul at the two wharfs, Bolton and Hague. William Potter, the pilot of the Caldwell, was his first instructor in handling a boat. After a year at firing the Caldwell Mr. Harris spent four years on excursion cruises. His life on the lake is best told in his own language:

"The first steamboat built on the lake was in the year 1815. It was the James Caldwell. It had two boilers that were set in brick work, and her smoke stack was also brick. She was used part of two seasons and then was burned. The next steamer was the Mountaineer. She was built in 1824, and continued in service until 1836. My first trip on a steamboat was made on this boat.

"In the year 1838 the steamer William Caldwell began making regular trips. In the year 1850, she made her last one.

"In the year 1848 the steamer John Jay began running through the lake. This boat was built and owned by my brother, John Jay Harris, and I was employed as her pilot, and held that position until the 29th day of July, 1856, when she was burned. This accident occurred on her trip south, the boat taking fire when passing Friends Point. The hull now lies off Calamity Point at Hague.

"The steamer Minnehaha was built in the winter of 1856-57 and began making her regular trips that season. Here began my career as captain.

"This boat was one of the fastest and finest steamers of her day, and admired by steamboat men as well as all others.

"The business on the lake having greatly increased, the large and elegant steamer Horicon was built to succeed her in the year 1876, and is still in service.

"The business on the lake still continuing to increase, it was found that in order to meet the exigencies of this business there must be added greater facilities, and in the year 1884 the steamer Ticonderoga commenced running. I was in command of her and put her in readiness for buisness. She was burned on the 29th day of August, 1901.

"At this time I was in command of the Horicon, and then done the work that the Ticonderoga did by making two trips through the lake daily.

"In the year following, 1902, there was built at Caldwell one of the finest steamboats ever placed upon an inland lake. She was named the Sagamore in honor of that noted Indian chief. This elegant and commodious steamer has a steel hull, steam steering gear, and is also provided with a very powerful searchlight. The hurricane deck can be used for sight seeing. She has the latest and most improved modern devices for trimming ship. The dining hall is on the main deck, and can seat nearly 100 guests. In all of her other appointments she is thoroughly modern and up to date. During the first trips that she made I was her captain but by overwork and severe sickness it was decided by the president of the company that in duty to myself I should retire from active service, and I was given lighter employment.

"The steamer Mohican, a propeller, early and in the latter part of the season, makes regular trips through the lake and return. During the height of the season she makes regular trips to Paradise Bay."

S. R. Stoddard in his history of Lake George says of Mr. Harris:

"Captain E. S. Harris, the commander, whose lifelong service has made him a recognized authority on matters relating to Lake George, makes the excursion through the lake specifically interesting by calling attention to remarkable features along the way and by giving with places of note, their history or the traditions connected with them."

Of the burning of the John Jay, Stoddard's history says: "Fire broke out in the engine room and could not be controlled. Captain Harris, then pilot, headed for the beach and stood at the wheel until the tiller ropes burned off, then going aft shipped the tiller and steered by guess. Blinded by the smoke he missed the beach, the boat struck on a rock and rebounding, slid back into deep water, where it burned to the water's edge and sank. Six lives were lost."

Mr. Harris often conducted excursions in the winter season for the Delaware and Hudson from vicinity points to Washington. He served as supervisor of his town, was postmaster of Caldwell under President Hayes. Three years ago he retired on account of ill health. Besides a wife, he is survived by two sons, George, of Bolton Landing, and Walter P., of New Bedford, Mass., pilot of the Sagamore during the season. The funeral will be held Friday afternoon at 2 o'clock from the Presbyterian church, Lake George, Rev. C. W. Blake officiating.

Star Oct 1 1906

CHARLES EVANS HUGHES.

JULIA SMITH.

Miss Julia Smith, of Albany and Turtle Island, Lake George, died Saturday morning after a short illness at the home of William H. Griffin, of Bolton, where she and her brother were spending the winter. Miss Smith had not been well for several years still her death was rather unexpected. She is survived by her brother, Erastus C. Smith, and also by relatives in Albany, where she was taken Monday for burial.

ADDISON ALLEN.

The funeral of Addison Allen was held Friday afternoon from his home at Bolton Landing. Mr. Allen died Christmas afternoon, after five years' illness of asthma. He was fifty-eight years of age and is survived by a widow, one brother, Fred W. Allen, and a sister, Mrs. Fred Stewart, of Bolton Landing. Interment in the Huddle cemetery.

CAPT. E. S. HARRIS.

The funeral of Capt. E. S. Harris was held Friday afternoon at 2 o'clock from the Lake George Presbyterian church, the Rev. C. W. Blake officiating. The service was largely attended by friends of the deceased. The pall-bearers were Henry Sisson, Arthur West, Fred F. Hawley, Cutler Bradley, Edwin J. Worden and R. Emmet Archibald, all of Lake George. *1/6*

BROWN'S HOTEL CHANGES HANDS

E. E. Fosmer Pays $23,000 for the Property and Will Take Possession January 1. *1/7 1907*

E. E Fosmer, a well known hotel man, last night purchased Brown's hotel on Glen street, including the block, fixtures, furnishings and good will, possession to be given January 1. The consideration is $23,000. Mr. Brown expects to leave soon after that time for the west.

Brown's hotel has been a well known hostelry for the past 15 years since it was opened as a hotel by M. J. Collins. He continued it for several years when he sold out to a nephew, M. J. Collins, jr., now deceased. Three and a half years ago he sold the hotel to Alfred Brown, who has continued it since.

PEABODY BUYS BROWN'S HOTEL.
Star — Jan 8 1907
Will Make Several Improvements and Conduct Hostelry Himself.

Newman Peabody has purchased from E. E. Fosmer, of Saratoga, the Brown hotel property, recently purchased by him for $23,000. Mr. Peabody assumed the ownership of the hotel Saturday and will hereafter manage it under his personal direction. The business will be conducted in the most modern way.

The hotel will be thoroughly renovated, repaired and several new features will be added which will make it one of the most up-to-date hostelries in this vicinity. The hotel will be known as "Peabody's Hotel."

RICHARDSON ON PEABODY.
Star — Jan 11
Tells Briefly of Work of Great Philanthropist Who Speaks Here Soon.

The annual address by George Foster Peabody at the anniversary service of the Y. M. C. A. in the Baptist church Sunday evening will be an event to hear a philanthropist of note of which many will avail themselves. Of Mr. Peabody, Rev. George Lynde Richardson says:

"George Foster Peabody, who is to make the address at the anniversary service of the Y. M. C. A., in the Baptist church next Sunday evening, is one of the most notable men of our country and time. He is a native of Georgia, but came as a young man to New York city, where he had a business career marked by conspicuous success, but a success which never involved the lowering of those high ideals by which his whole life has been consistently governed. For years he has been actively interested in many beneficent and uplifting movements, and latterly he has retired from business and given himself entirely to the service of his fellow men. Philanthropist is a much misused word; it is often applied to one who is a mere giver of money, but it means by derivation a friend of humanity and in this higher and truer significance, it describes Mr. Peabody. He has been active in the cause of education in the south, both for white children and for negroes, is a trustee of Booker Washington's great school at Tuskegee, and was recently offered the chancellorship of the University of Georgia. Mr. Peabody is a member and an active worker of the Episcopal church, and serves on the vestries of two parishes, Holy Trinity, Brooklyn, and St. James', Lake George.

"Although nominally retired from business, Mr. Peabody is one of the busiest men to be found anywhere. His beautiful home on Lake George is the center of a network of charitable and philanthropic enterprises, and he is constantly in consultation, by correspondence and in person, with the men who share his unselfish purposes and efforts for the betterment of the world, from every part of the country. He is much sought as a speaker at conventions and conferences, but does not often find time to accept such invitations. The officers of the local association, and the citizens of Glens Falls, generally, may well feel honored by the coming of such a man to address them on the possibilities of service to God and man."

Lake George Summer Resident Dead

James Hayden died at his home in New York city Wednesday. Mr. Hayden had been a summer resident of Lake George for many seasons. He was stricken with his last illness last summer at his home at the Hayden mansion on the Bolton road.

ALL NIGHT HOTEL FOR GLENS FALLS

Extensive Improvements to Peabody's Hostelry, Including Putting in Ladies' and Gents' Dining Rooms.

OPERATE ON BOTH EUROPEAN AND AMERICAN PLANS.
Star June 19.1907
Alterations to be Finished March 1, When Place Will be Ready.

Glens Falls is to have an innovation in the hotel business in the way of an all night hotel, operated on both the American and European plans. Newman Peabody who recently acquired the hotel property on Glen street formerly owned by Alfred Brown, has made arrangement for the change and work will be commenced at once on the undertaking. It is expected the remodelled hotel will be opened under the new plan about March 1.

Mr. Peabody will make many changes in the hotel. Two dining rooms will be provided, one on the ground floor for gentlemen and one on the second floor for ladies. Entrance will be had to the gent's by way of the office and to the ladies through a stairway leading from the street. Private dining rooms will also be provided on the second floor. The hotel will be open 24 hours in the day with a chef in attendance at all times. Lunches or meals will be served at all times as well as shell foods.

The cafe will be enlarged. A skylight will be constructed in the rear of the hotel. Sound proof floors will be placed.

CHARLES CURTIS, PART KAW INDIAN, WHO HAS WON A SEAT IN THE UNITED STATES SENATE.

Charles Curtis, who will succeed Joseph Ralph Burton as senator from Kansas, has been a congressman for thirteen years. He is a lawyer, is forty-seven years of age and has been a hustler all his life. His father was a white man and his mother a Kaw Indian squaw.

PICTORIAL PHASES OF THE THAW MURDER TRIAL IN NEW YORK.

Harry K. Thaw, who is being tried for the murder of Stanford White on the evening of June 25, 1906, has an imposing array of legal talent in his service, but he relies principally upon Delphin M. Delmas, a California lawyer who has been very successful in defending men who rely upon the "unwritten law" as their defense. Thaw shot White because he believed White had ruined Evelyn Nesbit, who later became Mrs. Thaw. James Fitzgerald is the judge who is trying Thaw.

Star Jan 25

'Don't worry, eat three square meals a day, say your prayers, be courteous to your creditors, exercise, go slow and go easy. Maybe there are other things that your special case requires to make you happy, but, my friend, these, I reckon, will give you a good lift.—Abraham Lincoln.

1907.

Jan, 24

Bolton Landing Hotel Changes Hands

C. E. Ingraham has purchased the Wilson hotel at Bolton Landing to take possession May 1. The hotel is the only all-year-round one in the place. *Star Jan 31 1907*

A girl fresh from college taught English,
She was pretty and just twenty-two.
If she smiled at our Professor,
He'd do what she asked him to.
We all fell slave to her charms,
Her complexion was just like a peach,
The only trouble with her was
She didn't have time to teach.
She went to all the parties
And attended many a ball,
And her mind was so filled with dresses
She couldn't teach classes at all

Bolton Horse Race Declared Off.

The race between S. M. Prouty's Max O'Rel, T. P. Braley's Lady High-flyer and Wilbur Bentley's Tomb Stone, which was scheduled for to-morrow on the ice at Bolton has been declared off, the first named horse being sick.

Feb 14—Montgomery Fish, a much respected citizen of the Huddle, Bolton, died at his home last Thursday at the age of 77 years. Deceased is survived by his wife, a son, Judson Fish, of this place; two daughters, Mrs Walter Vedder, of Philadelphia, and Miss Maude Fish, of Augusta, Ga. The funeral was held Saturday from his late home. Interment was made in the Huddle cemetery.— *1907*

Star
Fort Edward.

HOTELS CHANGE HANDS.

April 1, 1907.

Brown Takes Possession of Hudson, Holbrook to Conduct Kingsbury Inn.

Alfred Brown, formerly proprietor of the St. James Hotel in this village and for the past four years proprietor of Brown's Hotel, Glens Falls, will this morning take possession of Hotel Hudson, which he recently purchased from Harry G. Underwood. Mr. Brown is well known in this village, having by his genial disposition made a host of friends in this vicinity during his former proprietorship in this village. A number of improvements are contemplated.

Peter G. Holbrook, the retiring landlord has leased the Clark house, Sandy Hill, and will on May 1st, take possession, changing the name to Kingsbury Inn. Mr. Holbrook has for the past five years successfully conducted Hotel Hudson and made many friends who will regret his departure.

Star Feb 13 1907

CHRIST CHURCH, METHODIST EPISCOPAL, TO BE DEDICATED IN SPRING

The beautiful new Christ church, Methodist Episcopal, will be dedicated in early spring. This has been definitely decided upon, though no date has been fixed. The dedicatory exercises will continue a week.

The church has the distinction of being the most beautiful in the Troy conference, and cost over $100,000.

CHEER UP, MY GOOD WOMAN, YOUR HUSBAND HAS THE BASE-BALL FEVER, ITS NOT SERIOUS.

DOCTOR, I'M SO WORRIED ABOUT MY HUSBAND, HE'S LOSING HIS SLEEP AND WHEN HE DOES SLEEP HE HOWLS AND GROANS SO.

BANK AT LAKE GEORGE.

news Feb 28th *1907*

New Institution Organized at Meeting of Citizens Saturday Afternoon.

A large and enthusiastic meeting of citizens was held at the county clerk's office, at Lake George, Saturday afternoon, when it was voted to apply for a charter for the "Warren County National Bank," with a capitol stock of $25,000, to which amount a surplus of fifty per cent. was also voted to be subscribed.

The signers to the petition to the comptroller of the currency were Col. Galloway C. Morris, LeGrand C. Cramer, Charles J. Peabody, E. R. Ziebach, of Lake George; Hon. Edward M. Shepard, of Brooklyn, and Hon. A. B. Colvin, of Glens Falls.

The meeting organized by electing Colonel Morris chairman and Jerome N. Hubbell secretary. Messrs. Morris, Hubbell and Colvin were made a committee on subscriptions and apportionment of the stock.

TEA TABLE GOSSIP.

At a dinner recently Senator Depew told this story: A young farmer contemplating matrimony approached his father with the question: "When Sue and me are married, who ought to be the boss? I contend I ought to boss, being the man, while Sue says the women always boss the men." The old man smoked awhile reflectively and then answered: "Son, that is a question you will have to answer for yourself. In the barn are the two horses, the bay and the gray. Hitch them to the spring wagon and put in a hundred chickens. Then travel through the country and when you find a place where the woman is boss give her a chicken. When you find a man running the place give him a horse." Wondering at his father's command, but accustomed to obedience, the youth set out, stopping at each farmhouse and making his inquiries as to who was the head of the family. Toward the end of the third day he hitched his team in front of a weather-beaten shack where on a little side porch sat a hairy man in his shirt sleeves, with his feet cocked up on the railing. "Howdy," said the man, expelling a stream of tobacco juice all over the porch. "Maria, come here and git the stranger a chair." At his words appeared a meek little woman, in a sunbonnet, evidently fresh from her labors at the washtub, dragging a chair behind her in a spiritless manner. "Sit down and make yourself at home," he said, while to his wife, "Git back to the tub." "Here is where I lose a horse," said the young farmer to himself, but he boldly explained his mission. "Ho, ho," laughed the man of the house. "Maria, who's boss here?" "Why you be, Silas," replied the woman, looking up for a moment from her task. "Well, I guess there's no doubt of that," responded the young man, surveying the frail, working woman and the hulking, loafing man. "Come, select your horse." Silas went out and examined the team carefully. "Better unhitch the bay and lead him to the barn," he finally decided. Her curiosity getting the better of her, the wife had meanwhile approached and was surveying the team. "Looks to me, Silas," she said, "like that bay wasn't as sound as the gray." "O, pshaw, what do you know about hosses?" replied the lord and master. "Stranger, unhitch the bay hoss." "Come here a minute, Silas," continued his wife, and a whispered conversation took place, at the conclusion of which Silas approached the young man seeking information and, thrusting his hands deep in his trouser pockets, announced: "Wall, stranger, I've changed my mind. I guess after all I'll take the gray." "What you get," replied the young man, gathering up the reins, "is a chicken!"

The Coal Black Steeds.
Two glossy steeds for winter's needs
  Are mine to use at will.
Though hills are steep and drifts are deep,
  They bear me forward still.
"On, Left!" I cry. "The goal is nigh.
  Brave Right, a few steps more!"
Until at last, all troubles past,
  We reach the schoolhouse door.

TWINS FOLLOW TRIPLETS.
News Mar 28 1907
Nature Is Again Generous to This Family Dwelling on Oak Street.

If the walk on your side of the street should raise up a couple of feet do not get frightened. It's only Otto Fish, of this village, walking on the other side. Two baby girls—twins—were born to him Saturday and he naturally feels exceedingly weighty over the event. The father, mother and children, who have been named Fannie and Hattie, are all doing well.

By one, twos and threes, singly, in duets and triples has nature been generous with this Fish family. Clifford, the first born, is a chubby youth in his fifth year; Viola, Vernice and Vernon, the triplets, who changed the semblance of things most completely in Warrensburgh, were born June 30, 1905, while Fannie and Hattie, having initiative and impulse in common, first saw the light last Saturday.

There has never been anything like it before in Warrensburgh.

As did the triplets, so do the twins beam smilingly on all comers and, moreover, they also look like winners.

Dr. James E. Goodman was the attending physician.

AMATEURS' BIG HIT IN OPERA "MIKADO"
Star — April 17
Presentation of the Piece by Local Talent for Y. M. C. A. Benefit Delighted Large Audience at Empire.

1897

MANY LOCALISMS WERE SPRUNG, BRINGING DOWN THE HOUSE

Opera Will be Given Again Tonight—The Cast of Characters.

The pleasing and tuneful opera "Mikado" was presented by local talent to a large house at the Empire theater last evening for the benefit of the Woman's Auxiliary of the Y. M. C. A. The play was given here some sixteen years ago, but it is safe to say that the professional company at that time scored nowhere near the success of last evening.

THE FINAL SUMMONS.
New 9611
Sudden Death of Aged Methodist Minister at Bolton Landing Friday. *1907*

The Rev. Charles Kennedy, of Bolton Landing, died very suddenly Friday at midnight at his home. He had been in his usual health and retired at 10 o'clock. At midnight he was awakened by violent coughing and died before medical assistance, which was immediately summoned, could reach him. Mr. Kennedy was for many years a minister in the Methodist Episcopal church and would have been eighty years old next Sunday. He is survived by one son, George W. Kennedy, principal of the public schools of Saratoga, and by one sister, Mrs. Robert Jarvis, of Warrensburgh. His wife, who was a teacher in her younger days and for a few months thirty-odd years ago was principal of the Warrensburgh academy, died last fall. Since her death, Mr. Kennedy has been staying with his son in Saratoga. It was but a few days ago he left for Bolton Landing. The funeral was held Monday afternoon at 2 o'clock from the First Methodist Episcopal church, Bolton Landing, the Rev. Mr. Ingersoll officiating. Interment in Huddle cemetery.

Bolton Landing.
Star — May 13 1907

The services held at the Methodist Episcopal church, Bolton Landing, on Sunday, May 5, were especially interesting and impressive.——The new pastor, Rev C A Ericson, has occupied the pulpit only three Sundays, but through his earnest activity the church is gaining in life and vigor. In the morning a new pulpit, given by Dr. Sanford, of Long Island, in the name of his two daughters, was dedicated. A good sized audience listened to the appropriate words of the pastor. In the evening the house was filled, and many, not being able to find seats, went away or remained outside. Especial music was furnished, Miss Ella Lennox rendering a very pleasing solo.

Igerna.
Star — Mar. 1st 1907
John Ferris is very ill. Dr Perkins, of Pottersville, is attending him.——

New Bank Cashier Appointed.
New Apl 23 1907
R. Emmett Archibald has been appointed cashier of the new First National bank of Lake George. Mr. Archibald is a young man of splendid business ability and has a hand-shaking acquaintance with everybody he knows. He is, therefore, deservedly popular and well fitted for the position of bank cashier. The bank building will probably be located on the Hayden plot near the library building. A street is to be opened up down to the lake.

Elmwood Seminary, Destroyed By Fire Nineteen Years Ago

Star April 25. — 1907.

FRANKLIN PHOTO ELECT CO

The old Elmwood seminary building which was destroyed by fire in October, 1888, was one of Glens Falls' first educatonal institutions. The accompanying electro is reproduced through the kindness of Charles Sansouci, a member of the Glens Falls fire department, who obtained the cut at the time of the fire by wrenching it from a door of the building.

The old seminary building was located at the corner of Park and Elm streets and was erected by Miss Ann Swartout over 40 years ago. She conducted a boarding school for years and was succeeded in managing it by Miss Amy Taylor. The seminary after awhile was abandoned and Prof. Whipple for a time conducted a business school in the building. At the time of the fire the building was occupied as Wait's hotel.

The seminary in 1873 was in its most flourishing condition. Among the graduates of the institution now in Glens Falls, are Mrs. James H. Bain, Mrs. W. W. Buckingham, Mrs. L. P. Juvet, Miss Helen Chitty, Mrs. Merritt Codner, Mrs. Delbert Wilkey.

Until a few years ago the graduates occasionally held reunions here.

Star may 29

BRYAN OR ROOSEVELT.

One of Them Will Be Next President, Says Senator Bourne.

Washington, May 28.—"Unless Roosevelt makes the run next year Bryan will be elected president," declared Senator Bourne of Oregon, after a long conference with the president. "Bryan can beat any of the rest of them. The people don't know to whom to turn with assurance that Roosevelts' policies will be carried out."

"But," it was suggested, "the president has insisted that he wouldn't accept another nomination."

"Of course," replied the senator, "but the president can't stand out against the demands of the whole people. Why, it would be giving the lie to his whole life. To serve the people when they demand it, and so long as they demand it; that is the ideal citizenship, the citizenship of Theodore Roosevelt. It would be a cowardly and a weak thing for the president to refuse such a call." *1907.*

The Bargain Hunter.

From store to store she hastens
  And will think the day well spent
If on all the things she purchases
  She saves but half a cent.
                              —Judge.

A Satisfied Son

My pa ain't any millyunaire,
  But Gee! He's offul smart;
He ain't no carpenter, but he
  Can fix a feller's cart.
He ain't no doctor, but you bet
  My pa, he allus knows
Just what to do to fix a boy
  Who's got a bloody nose.

My pa ain't presidunt, becoz
  He says he never run;
But he could do as well as
  Any presidunt has done.
A presidunt may beat my pa
  At pilin' up a vote;
But he can't beat him, I will bet,
  A-whittlin' out a boat.

My pa ain't rich, but that's becoz
  He never tried to be;
He's no 'lectrician, but he fixed
  A telephone for me.
My pa ain't never wrote a book,
  But I know that he could,
Becoz the stories that he tells
  To me are allus good.

My pa knows everything, I guess
  An' you bet I don't care
Coz he' ain't presidunt or rich
  As any millyunaire;
Whenever things go wrong my pa
  Can make 'em right, you see;
An' though he ain't a presidunt,
  Pa's good enough for me.

Opening Dance at Brant Lake Hotel.

George C. Waters, formerly one of the proprietors of the Warren house, in this village, and more recently of the Clark house, Sandy Hill, has leased the Brant Lake house, at Horicon, and will open it with a public dance on Tuesday evening, June 11. Good music will be provided. *News June 6 1907.*

ORSON P. MORSE
May

Minerva's Grand Old Man Died Sunday Funeral Yesterday Afternoon.

Orson P. Morse, the only living son of Abraham P. Morse, the veteran surveyor of the Adirondacks, died Sunday evening at 5:30 o'clock, at his home in Minerva, aged eighty-six years.

His father, who named the town of Minerva, was land agent and surveyor of all the Adirondack lands in that section, drawing deeds to purchasers and going to New York twice a year to settle with the landlords, going as far as Albany on horseback. His land office is still standing at Moore's Corners, to which place he got the first mail route established via Ticonderoga and was postmaster there for forty years. He was also builder of the Westside Baptist church, which was organized in 1807, the centennial celebration of which will be held next October.

In 1844 the first party of sportsmen made a trip through to Long Lake, stopping at the Morse Inn for dinner. The only road through to Long Lake at that time was where the trees had been cut out, and the party rode on a lumber wagon, sitting on a plank with their feet resting on a chain.

Orson P. Morse died on the old hotel site. It was while working with his father that the deceased picked up his knowledge of surveying and woodcraft, of which State Engineer Verplank Colvin once remarked: "There is none qualified to examine."

Among the familiar scenes of his youth Orson P. Morse laid down life's burden with

Life's work well done
Life's race well run
Life's crown well won
  Now comes rest. *news 1907.*

The funeral was held yesterday afternoon from the Westside Baptist church, and the remains were taken to Deep River, Conn., for interment.

Troy Times May 9 1907.

There are many interesting things in Carl Schurz' autobiography, now running through McClure's magazine, and among them the following Lincoln story that is vouched for as not having been retailed before: "An Englishman who had traveled far and wide over the United States called upon Mr. Lincoln and told him of the impressions he had received of various parts of the country. Speaking of social conditions and habits, he said, among other things, that to his astonishment he had heard that many gentlemen in America were in the habit of blacking their own boots. 'That is true,' said Mr. Lincoln. 'But would gentlemen in your country not do that?' 'No, certainly not,' the Englishman replied with emphasis. 'Well!' said Mr. Lincoln quietly, 'whose boots do they black?'"

Reality.

Castles in the air you may
  Construct mid scenes of mirth,
But all the same you'll have to pay
  Your rent while here on earth.
            —Chicago News.

-42-

DRAWING IT FINE.

Burnett Arrests Boy for Leaving Fish Line in Water a Few Minutes.

Game Constable W. H. Burnett, of Lake George, on Sunday arrested a young boy by the name of Pierce Cotter, who lives near Barbers Bay on the east shore of Lake George, for having a set line, fined him $10 and told him to appear at Lake George yesterday morning. The boy had been fishing off the dock and was called to the house, and placing his pole down on the platform put a stone on it and left to do the errand. The vigilant officer spied the fishing tackle and boldly placed the young man under arrest. "Bill" would be the only man we know of who could find the proverbial "needle in the haystack." *1907*

GOSSIPY GLEANINGS.

There is a man in Brooklyn who is willing to testify to the effectiveness of advertising. In fact, his little notice rather overdid the business. But that only goes to show how many persons read the advertising columns. Frank Hinderer of Brooklyn regrets he advertised for a wife. He is forty-five and good looking. His "ad" brought 800 answers, and it was reported he had selected his bride and would marry. When a reporter saw him, however, he said: "Stop. Do not speak of the subject to me. I am trying to forget." "And you are not marrying to-day?" "I have changed my mind. This whole thing has been terrible, terrible," he muttered, clapping his hands to his head. "I never dreamed there were so many women in Brooklyn," he continued. "The postman asked me if I had opened an employment bureau. I received eight hundred offers in three weeks. Some of them called at my boarding house. I encountered them everywhere I went. Finally I had to give up my job. I dared not go home for a week. They were of all ages, from sixteen to sixty. It was one terrible time." Mr. Hinderer explained that his intentions in advertising for a wife were most innocent and well meaning. "I was engaged to marry twenty-five years ago, but the young woman died," he said, "and I vowed I'd never marry. But bachelor life is lonesome. I was earning $4 a day as harness maker and had plenty of money to support a wife. But I've changed my mind now. I shan't marry. No, indeed, nothing could induce me to."

Horses Backed Into the River

A team owned by Highway Commissioner Robert Swan and driven by R. G. Jarvis, drawing dirt from the bank just below the big rock, backed over the bank into the river Monday morning. The water is about fourteen feet deep at that point and the whole outfit was submerged when they plunged in. Mr. Jarvis swam ashore and the horses were rescued with some difficulty uninjured except for a few scratches.

RUMORS OF CONCRETE BRIDGE TO REPLACE PRESENT IRON ONE

Prominent Moreau Man Says That a Conference to Talk Over New Structure is Not Improbable.

According to rumor Saturday the towns of Queensbury and Moreau together with the Hudson Valley railway company may build a concrete bridge across the river instead of having the present iron structure repaired. As yet the town of Queensbury has taken no action toward compelling the railway company to repair the bridge.

The papers recently served by the town of Moreau notifying the company to stop running cars across the Moreau end of the bridge have had not effect yet, as the company continues to use the bridge regardless of its unsafe condition.

In conversation with a prominent Moreau man Saturday a Star reporter was informed that the papers already served would lead up eventually to an injunction, or perhaps before such proceedings were taken the parties concerned would get together in conference and plan to build a new bridge.

NEW YORK-GLENS FALLS AUTO RECORD BY J. T. FINCH'S CAR

A new record has been established by automobile from New York to Glens Falls by A. J. Tracy, chauffeur for Jeremiah T. Finch. He arrived in Glens Falls Saturday with the 40 h. p. Martin, after a ten days' trip, during which over 1,200 miles had been covered. The actual running time between New York and Glens Falls was 8 hours and 25 minutes. Mr. Tracy states that during the ten days' trip he did not have to change any adjustments on the machine

The best previous time between New York and Glens Falls was nine hours, made last week by a Ford high power runabout.

Mrs. Gates Better Today.

Mrs. Amelia Gates, who is ill with typhoid fever, at the home of her brother, George T. Lockwood, was in such a serious condition Monday that Dr. Cunningham was called to consult with Dr. Goodman, the attending physician. They pronounced the patient's symptoms unfavorable and rather against recovery, but did not discourage hope of a favorable termination of the disease. Today the trained nurse in attendance pronounced her condition considerably improved. Mrs. Gates' sister, Mrs. Caroline Jarvis, of Esterville, Iowa, arrived here Monday to assist in caring for her. *1907*

WELL KNOWN GLENS FALLS MAN RUN OVER BY AUTOMOBILE

Star July 6th 1907

D. McCarthy Was Crossing State Road When Auto, Said to Belong to Trask, Knocked Him Down

Dennis McCarthy, a well known shirt manufacturer, was severely injured by being struck by a touring car belonging, it is said, to Spencer Trask, at the crossing of the state road and the Hudson Valley tracks at Chambers', near Bloody Pond. Mr. McCarthy, left here on the 9:30 car yesterday and got off at Chambers', and as he was crossing the road the auto struck him. He was knocked down and run over, the car passing over his right leg above the knee, across his arm and chest. The scalp wound inflicted was several inches long. The bruises, while very painful, are not expected to prove serious, unless internal injuries appear or complications develop. The touring car slowed up after it hit Mr. McCarthy, but did not stop. The crew of the Hudson Valley car ran the car back and, taking Mr. McCarthy aboard, carried him along until a south bound car was met. He was transferred and brought home. Dr. Floyd Palmer attended him here.

Burton Denies Abandoning Baby.

William West Burton, of The Antlers, Lake George, whom the police of Schenectady charge with abandoning the baby found in a basket under the Union street canal bridge on the night of June 29, and which the mother claimed last week, appeared Monday at Schenectady police headquarters, and submitted to arrest. He admitted that he was the father of the child, but pleaded not guilty to the charge of abandonment. He was held in default of $3,000 bail. The mother is held as a witness. *Star July 24 1907*

A Colorado man who is visiting in Wellington told H. L. Woods this story, according to The Kansas City Star. The Game Warden of Colorado was walking out in the mountains the other day when he met a hunter with his gun. The official suggested that that ought to be a good country for hunting. "It certainly is," said the hunter, proudly. "I killed one of the finest bucks yesterday I ever saw, and he weighed over 200." It was the season when deer may not be shot without subjecting the hunter to a heavy fine. "Well, that is a fine one," said the Warden, "and do you know who you are talking to?" Being assured that he did not the official said: "Why, I am the Chief Game Warden of Colorado." The hunter was only taken back a moment when he said: "And do you know who you are talking to?" The Warden did not know. "Well, sir," said the hunter, apparently much relieved, "you are talking to the biggest liar in the whole state of Colorado."

NO AUTOMOBILES ALLOWED.

news. Sept 26

State Highway Between Lake George and Bolton Closed Temporarily by Builders.

Owing to the excessive speed at which automobiles are run over the partially completed state road between Glens Falls and Bolton, with the result that the surface is badly torn by the heavy tires, the northern portion of the highway, between Lake George and Bolton, was temporarily closed Sunday to these machines. The contractors placed a man at either end of the road, one at the junction of the new road with the Warrensburgh turnpike, just north of the village of Lake George, and another at the northern terminus, and all cars attempting to enter the forbidden territory were held up and their owners ordered to take another route.

The contractors have made complaint against the tearing up of the road by speeding on several occasions but until Sunday no action was taken to prevent the practice. Under the contract the builders are responsible for the condition of the road until it is turned over to the county, but they are not allowed to close the highway except for brief periods and this was done Sunday for the first time to prevent further damage to the macadam from the usual heavy Sunday traffic.

An amusing incident of the affair was the hold-up of the car of Le Grand C. Cramer, of Troy, whose summer cottage is located near Hill View. Mr. Cramer had started out to make the run to the Halfway house for supper, put on the refusal of the guard to let him pass along the highway was compelled to come to Warrensburgh by way of Bolton and then back down the turnpike and lower state road. He was allowed to make the return trip later in the evening over the Bolton road. Rigs drawn by horses were allowed to travel without interruption.

news July 4 1907

Lincoln's Rebuke.

The saying that there are few honest lawyers did not hold true in the case of Lincoln. A man once called to retain him on a suit.

"State your case," said honest Abe.

The man did, and then Lincoln said:

"I cannot represent you, for you are wrong, and the other party is right."

"That is none of your business if I employ you," said the client.

"Pardon me," said the man who afterward became president; "my business is never to defend wrong. I never take a case that is manifestly wrong."

"Well, but you can make trouble for the other fellow."

"Yes," said Lincoln, "I can set a whole community at loggerheads, I can make trouble for this widow and her fatherless children and by so doing get you $600 that rightfully belongs to her, but I won't do it."

"Not if I pay you well?"

"Not for all the money you are worth," was the reply.

THE CLEO RAN ONTO A LEDGE, BUT NO ONE WAS INJURED

Star July 8th 1907

While returning from a cruise down the lake the pleasure craft Cleo, owned by the Schermerhorn Brothers company, ran onto a hidden ledge off Gull rock, a half mile south of Hulett's Landing, yesterday afternoon. The impact broke some of the steam pipes connected with the engine, disabling the craft, but no one of the 30 young men aboard was injured.

Several who were at the Hulett house donned bathing suits and preservers, and acting as a volunteer crew went to the assistance of the steamer. The boat was pushed off the ledge and last night a boat from Bolton arrived and towed it back to the head of the lake.

NEW LAKE GEORGE STEAMER WILL BE SHIPPED NEXT WEEK

Star July 24 1907

The new passenger steamer for Lake George to replace the Mohican in the spring of 1908 has been completed in the building yards of the T. S. Marvel Shipbuilding company at Newburg, and the frame work has been inspected by the directors of the Lake George Steamboat company and found to be satisfactory. The parts will reach Baldwin some time next week, it is expected, and the final setting up and bolting will be commenced at once.

The boat will be ready to go into commission the early part of next season. She will be 115 feet long over all, 108 feet on the water line, 25 feet beam, moulded depth 8 feet 9 inches; draft, loaded, 6 feet; speed 15 miles an hour, and will cost $65,000.

The name of the new boat has not been definitely decided upon, but it is expected that she will be named after one of James Fenimore Cooper's famous characters of local interest in the vicinity of Lake George. It is possible that she may be called "Uncas" after Cooper's hero in "The Last of the Mohicans."

news **Barn Burned at Riverbank.** *Sept*

During the thunder storm last Thursday evening the barn of Lemuel Sherman, at Riverbank, was struck by lightning and burned, together with about eight tons of hay, a quantity of pine lumber, a lumber wagon, sleigh, etc. A cow that was in the barn was killed. The loss is estimated at $1,000. There was no insurance. *1907*

Mrs. Amelia Gates is convalescing from her recent serious illness of typhoid fever. She is able to sit up some. *news oct 17th* *1907*

Star 1907

A Shell for Union.

A shell fired from the United States ship Saratoga is in the possession of Union College and will be placed in the museum. The shell was presented to Union by Gilbert K. Harroun, "as a reminder of American loyalty, skill and intrepidity." The shell was fired in the battle of Plattsburg, on Lake Champlain, in 1814, during the war with England.

Troy 1907 Sept 19.

A Real Cardiff Giant.

Capt. George Auger, the giant actor, who is appearing in a vaudeville sketch at Proctor's this week, has attracted a great deal of attention on the street as well as on the stage because of his remarkable height. He is seven feet seven inches tall, and his claim of being the tallest man in the world seems to be well substantiated. He is about the same height as was Chang, the Chinese giant whom Barnum exploited a number of years ago. Captain Auger is a Welshman and is twenty-four years of age. He was born in Cardiff and is therefore a real "Cardiff Giant" and the only one. He weighs 325 pounds, but on account of his great height appears to be rather thin. Captain Auger was at one time a member of the London police force, but was compelled to resign because of the attention he attracted in the streets. It was then that he decided to go on the stage. His partner in the sketch that he is producing is Ernest Rommell, who is but thirty-four inches tall. The contrast between the two is extremely ludicrous.

news Sept 16

DEAD BODY FOUND.

1907

William Norton, Log Rafter at Bolton Landing, Drowned in Northwest Bay.

The body of William Norton was found near the mouth of Northwest bay creek Friday night by John Taber. He was last seen in the village on the morning of the 15th inst., when he left there in a light row boat. He had been employed during the summer rafting logs on the lake for Warren J. Smith, of Ticonderoga. The remains were taken in charge by Undertaker R. T. Taylor, of Bolton Landing and, by permission of Coroner C. K. Burt, were removed to the former's undertaking rooms, where a private funeral was held Saturday afternoon, the Rev. P. Contois officiating. Interment in Huddle cemetery. Deceased was fifty-six years of age and is survived by a daughter, Mrs. Herbert Miller, of Hague; one brother, Alva E. Norton, of Lake George, and two sisters, Mrs. Benjamin, of Springfield, Mass., and Mrs. Egglestone, of Henderson Harbor, N. Y. His father and four half sisters reside in the West.

Nuts to Crack

Why is it more dangerous to go out in the spring than any other time of the year? Because in the spring the grass has blades, the flowers have pistils, the leaves shoot, and the bullrushes out.

When does a ship tell a falsehood? When it lies at the wharf.

When is a fowl's neck like a bell? When it is wrung for dinner.

What is the only organ without stops? A woman's organ of speech.

-44-

ST PICTURE OF PRESIDENT M'KINLEY, FROM WHICH NIEHAUS' STATUE WAS MODELED.

THE very lifelike statue of President McKinley designed by Sculptor Niehaus for the national McKinley memorial, Canton, O., was modeled after a photograph of the president made while he was delivering his Pan-erican address at Buffalo the day before he was shot.

HENRY WORDEN.

A Long and Useful Life Suddenly Terminated at Lake George.

Henry Worden, a devoted churchman, a well-known citizen and contractor, a man of many friendships, whose sturdy manhood and long life has left an indelible impress, not only on the life of the little village he loved so well, but on the lives of many with whom he had come in contact in his long and zealous service of the Master, passed into rest Thursday evening at his home in Lake George.

His religious and industrial activities were singularly blended and it was his life's aim not only to build churches in a material sense, but in the higher and spiritual sense. Following this inclination, he became known as a church builder throughout his home section. He built the Methodist Episcopal churches of Fortsville, Reynolds Corners and Lake George. He finished the Presbyterian church at Warrensburgh and built the Episcopal church at this place. He also constructed the new Methodist Episcopal church in this village. He completed the Catholic church at Bolton.

Why is a pair of skates like an apple? Because they have both occasioned the fall of man.

Why can you never expect a fisherman to be generous? Because his business makes him sell fish (selfish).

Which is the most wonderful animal in the farmyard? A pig, because he is killed and then cured.

Why can a blind man always see his father? Because the father is always apparent (a parent).

Why does a horse eat in a very odd way? Because he eats best when he has not a bit in his mouth.

ROOSEVELT'S WILD RIDE.

Recalled by Sad Fate of Driver, "Mike" Cronin, Now Mentally Unbalanced.

Michael F. Cronin, proprietor of Aiden Lair lodge, Essex county, was taken to the St. Lawrence state hospital, at Ogdensburgh, suffering from insanity, as stated in The News last week. The trip from Glens Falls to the hospital was made without incident. An Ogdensburgh news dispatch says:

"Mike" Cronin, the Adirondack guide, drove Roosevelt on his famous ride through the mountains to the nearest railroad station in 1901 upon receipt of the telegram announcing McKinley's assassination.

The vice president was camping at Cronin's resort, Aiden Lair, sixteen miles from North Creek, a station on the Delaware and Hudson railroad, when late at night a courier arrived, bearing dispatches announcing the Buffalo tragedy. Colonel Roosevelt at once ordered Cronin to hitch his fastest horses and take him to North Creek, where a special train was in waiting. Within five minutes they were on their way in a light wagon drawn by a pair of roadsters. Cronin urged the horses to their utmost speed, and it was the wildest and fastest trip ever made over the mountain region by team. With the future president clinging desperately to the seat and urging Cronin on, the guide swung his horses along the road and past dangerous places without slowing down.

Once the light wagon smashed against a stone which sent it spinning along on two wheels, but the vice president only cried out encouragement to his daring companion. "If she breaks down Mike," he said, "we'll ride into North Creek on horseback." At another time during the long ride, when the horses were being given a breathing spell, the vice president told Cronin stories of his life as a cowboy on the plains, and again, as the horses dashed along, he sang "Auld Lang Syne."

North Creek was finally reached in an hour and forty-three minutes. One of Cronin's horses died soon after and later its mate succumbed from over-exertion. In due time the guide was well repaid. The president never forgot the details of the historic ride, nor his companion on that trip.

A few years later the president visited New York to give an address at Carnegie hall. Cronin was in the crowd that surged around the entrance when the president came along. Working his way well up to the front, the guide managed to get within speaking distance of the president when he appeared. He called out to Mr. Roosevelt and the president immediately recognized his voice and turned around. Cronin pushed forward and the president gave him a hearty handshake. "Hello, Mike! How are you?" he cried. "That was a bully ride we had that night, wasn't it?" The president chatted a moment or two with the guide and then passed on.

Cronin's mind has been giving away for four years, and at present he is in a state of melancholia. His delusion is that he is engaged in buying up large parcels of real estate. He is forty-five years old and has a wife and seven children. Since his mind began to fail, his wife has attended to his business matters.

YOUNG MAN DROWNED AT BOLTON LANDING

Nov. 1 — 1907

Boat in Which Herman Berthold Was Rowing Overturned and He Sank Before Help Arrived.

HAD BEEN OUT SHORT TIME; TRIED TO TURN BOAT AROUND

Body Was Recovered by Mrs William Landis Two Hours Afterward

Herman Berthold, a butler in the employ of H. Broesel, of New York and Bolton, was drowned at 3 o'clock yesterday afternoon in Lake George near Bolton Landing. The young man went out for a row and well out from shore started to turn his boat around. The boat tipped over and the rower was precipitated into the water. No one was able to get to him in time to save the lad and not being able to swim, he sank.

The body was recovered at 5 o'clock by Mrs. William Landis. Dr. D. L. Rogers, of Bolton Landing, was called. The body will be taken to New York, where the dead boy has an uncle. The boy's home is in Germany, which he left three months ago. There he has a mother. He was 18 years old.

He wooed her when her hair was brown
 And when her waist was slim,
When every other boy in town
 Was envious of him.
He walked with her in country lanes
 When she was young and glad
And youth and strength and hope and health
 Composed the sum of all the wealth
 That she had ever had.

He won her when her heart was light
 And when her laugh was gay,
When every day was fair and bright
 And care was far away.
He claimed her as his own when she
 Regarded him as one
For whom the fates had much in store,
Whom men would honor more and more
 For great things nobly done.

He has not won the world's applause,
 She knows he never can;
His step is slower than it was,
 But he's an honest man.
She wears the bloom of youth no more,
 Yet side by side they fare,
Poor, bent old husband and gray wife,
Along the humble walks of life,
 And still are lovers there.

Why did the Highlanders do most execution at Waterloo? Because every man had one kilt before the battle.

Why is a coachman like the clouds? Because he holds the reins.

Why is a committee of inquiry like a cannon? It makes a report.

TO OPEN STATE ROAD IN FEW DAYS

Star Oct 31st 1907

Work Will Probably be Finished in Less Than a Week.

It is expected that the state road between Glens Falls and Lake George will be formally opened to the public this week, probably Saturday. A strip of the road between the Halfway house and Bloody Pond has been unfinished because of the inability to get the necessary trap rock to complete the road, which was specified in the contract for the Glens Falls-Lake George but not the Lake George-Bolton road. Ten carloads of this trap rock arrived some time ago at French Mountain and the most of it is now unloaded and placed on the road. This section of the road between French Mountain and Bloody Pond has been shut off from public use for a few days while workmen are engaged on it.

The blasting on the Lake George-Bolton road will be finished this week, it is expected, and this too will be thrown open to the public, it is understood within a short time.

Oct 7th 1907

1907

PRESIDENT ROOSEVELT

CAME TO STAY.

Return of the Prodigal With Money and a Large Check.

Old home week had come, and the returned sons and grandsons were gathered together. One after another they rose and told with pardonable pride their achievements in the great world, impressing their importance on the stay at homes. At length Mr. Jameson spoke:

"I went away from here twenty years ago a poor young man, with only one solitary dollar in my pocket. I walked the four miles from my father's farm to the station, and there I begged a ride to Boston on a freight car. Last night I drove into town behind a spirited pair of horses, and my purse—guess how much my purse holds in money today, besides a large check," and Mr. Jameson looked about him with a smile.

"Fifty dollars!"

"Seventy-five!"

"A hundred!" shouted the boys, filled with admiration.

"No," said Mr. Jameson, drawing a large, flat purse from his pocket when the clamor had subsided, "none of you has guessed right. When I had paid the 25 cents to Ozzy Boggs for my refreshing drive in the coach I had, besides my trunk check (which I retained for financial reasons), exactly 4 cents. I have come back, my friends, to stay. Any little jobs of sawing and splitting will be gratefully received."—Woman's Home Companion.

New Rural Delivery at Lake George.

Star Oct 30 1907

Postmaster Hawley, of Lake George, has received official notification of the establishment of rural free delivery route No. 2, to begin service December 2. This route will cover about all the territory between Lake George and Warrensburg, going up the turnpike as far as John Andrews' corners, thence to Flat Rock and Andrew Shaw's corners to the school house From the school house the route goes to Vernon Shaw's and back; thence over Truesdale hill and return by way of Warrensburg turnpike. This route will cover a distance of 15½ miles, serve a population of 500 people and include over a hundred families.

---

news Dec 5th 1907

Lake George Hotel Man's Purchase.

An important real estate deal has been consummated by the purchase by E. J. Worden, proprietor of the Hotel Worden, of Lake George, from former Senator Cooper, of Brooklyn, of a strip on Main street, Lake George, 100 feet in width, extending from the highway to the lake front. The consideration was $8,000. The property adjoins the Warren county court house and contains on the front the Tucker cottage, lately known as the Lake George Inn, and in the rear the Orr cottage, on the old Lake house site. These cottages will be used by Mr. Worden for the accommodation of his guests.

TO LAUNCH STEAMER MOHICAN AT BALDWIN ON SATURDAY

Star Dec 12 1907

Miss Loree, Daughter of D & H R R President, to Christen it—The Name Uncas Discarded.

The launching of the new steamer of the Lake George Steamboat company will take place at Baldwin Saturday at 11 a. m. Miss Loree, daughter of President L. F. Loree, of the Delaware and Hudson company, will christen the steamer, says the Troy Times. The new steamer is to be called the Mohican, succeeding the old boat, which will probably go out of commission this year. The new boat is a twin screw propeller, with a length over all of 115 feet, breadth over all of 26 feet and 6 inches and a speed of 15 miles an hour. The hull is constructed of steel. The main deck will have a freight space forward. On the quarterdeck will be located the purser's office, the lunch counters and the officers' quarters. Aft on the main deck opening from the quarterdeck will be the ladies' cabin. The quarterdeck will be covered with rubber tiling and the ladies' cabin will be carpeted. Both of these rooms will be finished in butternut and cherry to show the natural wood. The main stairway will reach from the main deck to the promenade deck. On the promenade deck forward will be located the pilot house and quarters for officers. The promenade will be open in order to afford excursionists an unobstructed view of the scenery.

The propelling machinery will consist of two inverted, direct-acting, compound engines, high pressure cylinder, ten inches in diameter; low pressure cylinder 21½ inches in diameter; 16-inch stroke. Two water tube boilers will provide steam for the motive power.

It was at first proposed to call the new steamer the Uncas. Because, however, the name Mohican seems to be more appropriate that named has finally been selected.

A preacher came at a newspaper man in this way: "You editors do not tell the truth. If you did you could not live; your newspapers would be a failure." The editor replied: "You are right, and the minister who will at all times and under all circumstances tell the whole truth about his members, dead or alive, will not occupy his pulpit for more than one Sunday, and then he will find it necessary to leave the town in a hurry. The press and the pulpit go hand in hand with whitewash brushes and pleasant words, magnifying little virtues into big ones. The pulpit, the pen, and the gravestone are the great saint-making triumvirate." And the great minister went away looking very thoughtful while the editor turned to his work, and told of the unsurpassed beauty of the bride, while in fact she was as homely as a mud fence.

A NEW PICTURE OF THE STANDARD OIL MAGNATES WILLIAM ROCKEFELLER AND JOHN D. ROCKEFELLER.

TWO men who are vitally interested in the outcome of the ouster proceedings now pending against the Standard Oil company are John D. Rockefeller and his brother William. They were photographed recently at the home of Mrs. McCormick on Lakeside drive, Chicago. Mrs. McCormick is John D. Rockefeller's daughter. In the picture John D. is shown at the right and William at the left.

NING STAR, DECEMBER

BRIDE OF 4 DAYS 14 1907 TAKES HER LIFE

MARRIED AN OLD MAN FOR REVENGE ON DELINQUENT LOVER.

Pretty 16-Year-Old Josephine Rivers Married Old Man of 60 Because Her Lover, John Gay, Put Off Their Marriage; She Repented and It Is Thought Took Poison.

"I've done it at last," said a bride of four days, Josephine Daniels, the sixteen year old wife of J. H. Daniels, a veteran of 60 years, as she lay dying Thursday afternoon at their home, a little cabin in the town of Luzerne, about a mile and a half from the village of Corinth.

Much mystery surrounds the death of the young woman, and the people of the little community are divided as to the cause. Some say she was killed by someone, and others claim she died by her own hand.

She was Josephine Rivers, daughter of Charles Rivers, and was considered one of the belles of the country. For several years John Gay, a machine tender, in the International Paper company's mills at Corinth, had been the recognized favorite in the girl's affections, and they were together whenever he could get away to see her. They were betrothed, and were to have been married last fall, but no public announcement of the fact had been made. Recently she asked him when he intended to marry her, and he told her in the spring, and gave as his reason for the delay the fact that the mills were now running on half time and he could not support her. This brought on a lover's quarrel, and he did not call to see her again until Tuesday of this week, when great was his surprise to learn that on Monday she had married Daniels, who was visiting his nephew for the winter. A justice of the peace had tied the knot in Corinth.

He went to call on the girl and her husband at their home, and after exchanging greetings with him, the girl asked to see him alone. The husband consented and they stepped into an adjoining room.

He said, "Josie, what made you do this?" and she answered, "I don't know why I done it, but I won't live with him a week." The girl evidently regretted her hasty marriage, and longed to be free to marry her lover, or intended to make way with herself.

Thursday afternoon about 2 o'clock, a Branch girl called at the house and found the young bride acting queerly around the house. Suddenly she complained of being stiff in the limbs, and requested the girl to lay her upon the bed and summon a physician. No medical aid could be procured and after suffering several convulsions she died about 6 o'clock.

Coroner Edgar Birdsall was notified by telephone yesterday and, accompanied by Drs. Henning and Cunningham, he drove to the scene of the death. The coroner immediately held an inquest while the other physicians performed an autopsy. Gay, the jilted young man, was subjected to a severe examination, but nothing could be found to show that he had been connected with the death. About all that was learned from him, aside from the words quoted above, was that he and the girl intended to spend Christmas with the young man's aunt in Glens Falls.

The husband was found to be in a half drunken condition, and with a drunken man's grief sobbed the following, "Single on Sunday, married on Monday, a widower Thursday." Nothing of import could be learned from him, but he suspected his wife's change of heart and declared he would not bury her if she had been untrue to him.

The examination by the physicians disclosed no symptoms of foul play and they could ascribe no reason for her sudden demise. The convulsions suffered by the girl were such as follow a dose of strychnine, and, suspecting this poison had been used, the physicians brought the stomach back with them and Dr. DeRoode will make a chemical analysis of its contents today.

The young girl, although but 16, appeared to be at least 20. She was of an exceedingly dark complexion with dark hair and eye.

news STICKNEY-WRIGHT. Jan.

Prof. John R. Stickney, of Plattsboro, principal of the union school at Bolton Landing, and Miss Mary Wright, only daughter of Mr. and Mrs. C. A. Wright, of this village, were married Thursday afternoon at 5 o'clock, at the Church of the Holy Cross, the Rev. Guy Harte Purdy officiating. They are spending their honeymoon in town and Sunday will return to Bolton to resume their work in the school, Mrs. Stickney being also a member of the faculty. 1907.

FOUND DEAD IN BED

Stephen Griffing Died Alone in the Night at the Warren House.

ONE OF NATURE'S NOBLEMEN

Retired in Apparent Good Health Saturday Night, Dead Body Found at 1:30 P. M. Sunday—Was a Man of Many Virtues and Great Ability.

Stephen Boyd Griffing, aged seventy-seven years, who for the past thirty years had been station agent in the employ of the Delaware and Hudson company at Thurman and Warrensburgh, was found dead in bed Sunday afternoon in his room at the Warren house in this village. Death was due to heart disease.

A Horse's Memory.

My father had a fine driving horse that was intelligent and had learned a number of tricks. One night he was stolen, and no trace was found of him for nearly two years when, one day, father met a stranger driving the horse and of course claimed him. In the dispute which followed father remarked that if it was the horse stolen from him he would on being unharnessed go to the gate, lift the latch, open the gate, go around the barn, slide the bolt, open the door and go into the third stall. The man agreed to give the horse up on those terms. They drove home and up the lane to the barn and unharnessed the horse, when, without a moment's hesitation, he performed the feats father said he would.
—Chicago Tribune.

JUSTICE VAN KIRK DECIDES
IN FAVOR OF ANDREW THOMAS

Star Dec 19. 1907

Supreme Court Justice VanKirk yesterday handed down a decision in favor of the defendant in the case of Thomas D. Trumbull vs. Sarah S. Tuttle et al, impleaded with Andrew Thomas.

The court held that the main issue was that of priority of liens between Trumbull and Thomas. This case has been in court since 1903. Thomas got a verdict once, but a new trial was ordered. The property in which the liens are held is situated on the corner of Bay street and Hope avenue.

The court decided that Thomas' lien was prior to that of the mortgage which was held by Trumbull, and which he sought to foreclose. and that out of any sale of the property by the plaintiff in foreclosure proceedings, Thomas, lien is to be paid before that of the plaintiff.

James H. Bain appeared for T. D. Trumbull; Edward M. Angell, for H. Prior King, as executor of the estate of William Moore, and Chambers and Finn for Andrew Thomas.

A. H. RUSSELL BUYS LAKE HOUSE PLOT

1908

MOST IMPORTANT LAKE GEORGE TRANSFER IN SOME TIME

He Purchased the Entire Property From Senator Cooper Yesterday and Will Use the Low Cottage, Occupied by the Club Last Year, for His Dining Service.

The most important real estate transaction that has taken place at Lake George for some time was consummated yesterday by A. H. Russell, the proprietor of the Lake George Inn and cottage colony, when the old Lake House property was transferred to him by Senator Cooper, of Brooklyn. This property is located in the heart of the village of Lake George and consists of about 350 feet of lake shore and the same frontage on Canada street (Main street). On the site is located the McCoon cottage and Low cottage, occupied last summer by the Glens Falls club, and there is also one of the finest hotel sites on the lake.

On the west side of the street are located the five Crescent cottages with a 300 foot frontage. This lot is bounded by two cross streets. Mr. Russell has conducted the cottage colony for five years and he had the Lake House the previous six years. Mr. Russell told a Star reporter yesterday that the season of 1908 is a very promising one. Many applications for the cottages have already been received.

Mr. Russell said he expected to use the cottage occupied by the Glens Falls club last year for his dining service. He has other plans for the improvement of the property and eventually probably more buildings will be erected.

The Creation

ALL things bright and beautiful,
　All creatures, great and small,
All things wise and wonderful—
　The Lord God made them all.

Each little flower that opens,
　Each little bird that sings—
He made their glowing colors,
　He made their tiny wings.

The cold wind in the winter,
　The pleasant summer sun,
The ripe fruits in the garden—
　He made them every one.

The purple-headed mountain,
　The river running by,
The sunset, and the morning
　That brightens up the sky—

He gave us eyes to see them.
　And lips that we might tell
How great is God Almighty,
　Who has made all things well.
　　　—By C. F. Alexan

Fastest Carriage Team in County.

Thomas O'Connor, of the Adirondack hotel, is naturally a pleasant fellow to meet, but these days he is more so than ever now that he owns the fastest driving team in the county. They are a fine span of browns, as bright as a berry and perfectly mated in every particular. "Look out for 'em when they get to going," Jack Hoag, who takes care of them, said this morning.

GOODMAN FAMILY HOLD BIG REUNION

Aug 26 1908 Sun 11

A reunion of fifty descendants of Eleazer Goodman who came to this part of the country from South Hadley, Mass., and settled at Lake George, was held yesterday on the property of Walter Lawton, Basin Bay, Lake George. There were four generations represented at the gathering.

The party went from here to Basin Bay by automobile for a basket picnic. After dinner a part of the family went by auto to what is known as Goodman Corners, which is three miles north of Bolton and put up there a new sign bearing the name "Goodman's Corners." From there they went to Indian Brook and to Federal Hill, where the Goodman burying ground is located.

Eleazer Goodman came to this vicinity in 1790 and settled near Bolton on the Lake George shore. He had seven sons and one daughter, and they all lived in this vicinity.

Those present at yesterday's party were: Mr. and Mrs. Samuel Goodwin Boyd, Mr. and Mrs. P. P. Braley, Miss Frances C. Braley of Glens Falls; Mr. and Mrs. Truxton P. Braley of Bolton, Mr. and Mrs. Thomas Gilchrist, Thomas Gilchrist, Jr., Mary Louise Gilchrist of New York city; Clara Goodman Ward, of Hudson Falls; Bessie B. Goodman, William J. Goodman, Mr. and Mrs. Orgin W. Goodman, Neva E. Goodman, R. Marie Goodman, Helen M. Goodman, J. D. Goodman, Louis C. Goodman, of Fort Ann; Dr. J. E. Goodman of Warrensburg; Mrs. Julia H. Goodman, Mrs. H. T. Goodman, Miss Kathleen Goodman, of Warrensburg; Amy S. Carlton, of Granville.

Clara Goodman Maxim. Nellie Goodman Maxim and Jessie Braley, of Bolton Landing; Mrs. Emily P. DeLong, Daniel P. DeLong, of Glens Falls; Mr. and Mrs. Russell M. L. Carson. Shirley Elizabeth Carson, Samuel Goodman Carson of this city; Miss Florence E. Gale of New York; Mr. and Mrs. Samuel B. Goodman. Ethelyn B. Goodman of Glens Falls; Mr. and Mrs. Charles H. Wilson.

There were also the following guests present : The Rev. John R. Crosser, D. D., of Millport, O.; Thomas S. Coolidge and wife. Georgiana P. Coolidge. Miss Estelle C. Palmer. Mrs. Ella B. Grandey and Chester Grandey.

A Wood Chopper's Mishap.

Ralph Gates, of Hill View, while chopping in the woods Saturday, slipped on an icy limb and cut a gash in his knee about five inches long. Dr. Stiles sewed up the wound.

TEA TABLE GOSSIP.

Abstinence is becoming a marked characteristic of the commercial traveler. According to The Youth's Companion a salesman declares that twenty years ago the men on the road in his line were drinkers. To-day four-fifths of them are not. He was led to tell this story, which conveys its own moral: "I remember that the day I was taken on by our corporation I met the highest salaried salesman in the trade, a man who could have taken his choice of employers. I was bubbling over with pride and satisfaction, and, youngster fashion, I blurted out the story of my luck. He congratulated me and asked me to drink with him, by way of celebrating, and when I thanked him and told him I didn't drink he seemed half amused and half sympathetic. 'Don't drink, eh?' he retorted. 'You'll never be able to sell goods if you don't drink.' I didn't believe that then any more than I believe it now, and, as it turned out, the poor fellow himself was on the way to convince me that I was right. All at once he began to go to pieces, and within a couple of years none of his old employers would have paid him $10 a week. Fact is he wouldn't have been worth $2 to anybody. Then, again, there was a merchant up here in Westwood, a drinking man himself, who bought pretty heavy bills and whom we salesmen were all after. Some of the boys used to take him out to the saloons and fish for his trade in all such ways. I didn't. But after a year or two I noticed that he was buying more than nine-tenths of his goods from me, and one day I brought it up in a joking way. 'How about it, Mr. Larkin?' said I. 'Well, Jack, I'll tell you,' the old fellow said. 'I'm willing to go out and drink with a drummer. I'd probably drink anyhow. But when I do business I want to deal with a sober man.'"

Kenesaw Hotel Torn Down

Mii____ Jan 17 1908

Messrs J. A. and F. C. Thatcher of Bolton Landing, have just completed the demolition of the old Kenesaw hotel on Fourteen Mile island. They purchased the structure lately of W. H. Beardsley of New York, the owner, under a contract to raze and remove the material before spring. As soon as the ice is formed heavily enough the material, consisting of over fifty thousand feet of good lumber, will be moved, a portion to Ticonderoga and the remainder to this village.

F. C. Thatcher who operated the photograph studio on the Fort William Henry grounds has made arrangements for its occupancy next season and is now looking for a suitable location to erect a residence.

Valuable Bolton Property Sold.

newspaper 1.12 mii

George R. Fish, of Bolton Landing, has sold his Lake George property known as Fish's point to W. H. Moffit, of New York, for $12,500. The property, which comprises about 100 acres, is located on the lake shore not far from Bolton Landing. Mr. Moffit, it is said, will partition the property into lots suitable for summer residences. The sale was effected through Dr. D. L. Rogers, of Bolton Landing. *1908*

BOY SHOT THROUGH THE HAND WHILE AT LAKE GEORGE COTTAGE

Warren Dunn, Fifteen-Year-Old Lad, Found a Revolver and It Accidentally Exploded

Warren Dunn, the 15 year old son of Mr. and Mrs. Fred Dunn, Fulton street, accidentally shot himself yesterday afternoon in the left hand with a 32 calibre revolver, which he found at the Dunn cottage, two miles north of Lake George village, where in company with Charles Farlin and Edgar Mason, young Dunn had gone t spen the day. The ball entered the center of the hand but did not pass through, becoming imbedded in the back of the hand.

The injured boy hurried to Glens Falls for medical aid. On reaching the village he went to the Finch, Pruyn and Company grist mill on Glen street, where he told his grandfather of the accidnt. The two proceeded immediately to Dr. W. J. Hunt's office. The doctor ordered the boy taken to Parks hospital where the ball could be removed. The operation was performed by Drs. Hunt and Clarke.

ANNUAL MEETING
Of the First National Bank of Lake George

Mirror Jan 17 1908.

The stockholders of the First National bank of Lake George elected Tuesday the following board of directors: W. K. Bixbee, Hon. Addison B. Colvin, Frank L. Cowles, LeGrand C. Cramer, Jerome N. Hubbell, Clayton C. Lanfair, Galloway C. Morris, Harry C. Noyes, Charles J. Peabody, George F. Selleck, Edward M. Shepard, Elmer J. West Smith H. Wood, Edwin R. Ziebach, Lawrence Jacob.

POTATOES AND POETRY.
Local Farmer Who Is an Adept With Either Hoe or Pen.

News Jan 30th 1908

Frank L. Bennett, of South Warrensburgh, was last week awarded the first prize of eight dollars offered by a farm journal in Philadelphia for the best article on raising potatoes. Mr. Bennett is a young farmer who used brains in his business and is therefore successful. He wields the pen as well as the hoe and his literary work is quite promising. He is the author of a novel with the scenes laid around Lake George, which has not been published and also several poems. Following is his latest production in that line:

LAKE GEORGE.
Written for The News by Frank L Bennett

Horicon! I love thy fair waters.
 So beautiful with headland and bay
Thy mountains, so wooded and solemn,
 That near to the sky seem to lay.

Methinks as I look on the hill,
 On islet and water so fair;
That surely the colors of heaven
 Are resting in splendor there.

FAMOUS STOCK FARM NOW IN NEW HANDS

March 0th 1908

WHERE MAJOR DELMAR WAS FOALED AND TRAINED FOR TRACK

Warren J. Potter Purchases Suburban Stock Farm, Once the Property of William E. Spier—Will Continue it As a Breeding Place for Trotters and Pacers.—Will Regain Prestige

The Suburban stock farm, formerly the property of William E. Spier, was yesterday purchased from Dr. H. S. Paine by Warren J. Potter. The farm, which is located on the Bay road about two miles from Glens Falls, embraces some 400 acres, of which about 200 acres are tillable land, 100 acres of pasture and the remainder in timber lots. Mr. Potter will take possession April 1.

The Suburban farm has an interesting history. It came into prominence about 15 years ago, when William E. Spier, one of the organizers and the mainstay of the Northern New York Trotting Horse Breeders' association, established it as a stock farm. Here he maintained a large string of trotters and pacers of the Hambletonian and Morgan strains. It was the home of Robert McGregor, May King, Autograph, Jefferson Wilkes and other noted horses, and here Major Delmar, the world's most famous trotter, first saw the light of day and disported in the broad pastures. At present Armont and Major Allen are among the horses on the farm, and it is Mr. Potter's intention to continue breeding trotters. He has a few likely youngsters which he hopes will prove as speedy as Paul Kelly, a son of Armont.

The Suburban farm is peculiarly adapted to stock raising. It has the necessary buildings and is one of the best watered farms in northern New York, having an independent system of waterworks which receives its supply from Hunter's brook. The new proprietor is a thoroughly practical farmer, and the Suburban will soon regain its old-time prestige.

Navigation on Lake George.

The new steamer Mohican, Capt. Weley Finkle commanding, will be placed in commission May 9. As yet the successor to the late Capt. James H. Manville, of the Sagamore, has not been named, but it is understood that either Captain White or Captain Rockwell will command the steamer this summer. *News Apl 31 1908*

-49-

A RECORD BREAKER

Tuesday Night Coldest Ever Known in Town.

nurs 1908

OLDEST INHABITANT SILENCED

Forty-Nine and Fifty-Odd Degrees Below Zero Recorded and Then the Registering Fluid Sank Out of Sight Down In the Depths.

Such weather conditions as prevailed in Warrensburgh Tuesday night are left to the imagination. In the evening the mercury began to take a drop down from the cold snap which was prevailing and in the morning people simply threw up their hands in amazement.

It was a second edition of the atmosphere conditions of four years ago last month, when all thermometers in town recorded over forty degrees below zero, while at points down along the Schroon river as far as the paper mill fifty-odd degrees below are reported. Again Tuesday night Warrensburgh played another memorable game of freeze out with the north pole.

The variations in temperature recorded in the same localities in town Wednesday morning were probably due in part to the variations of inaccurate mercurial thermometers. As mercury freezes at thirty-nine and four-tenths degrees below zero it is safe to conclude that when a mercury thermometer goes more than forty degrees below, the scale is not properly marked. Scientists say that a mercury instrument does not record accurately more than thirty-five degrees below. Forty-four degrees were the fashionable figures about town Wednesday morning.

If Old Boreas reigns supreme from now until spring the winter of 1907-8 will be remembered as an unusual one. Although brief cold snaps have occurred at intervals the weather as a rule up to the past week has been unseasonably mild. Coal bins and wood sheds that at this time last year had been replenished long since, have still much to offer of their original supply, and the old saying about "half the wood and half the hay" remaining on Candlemas day (Sunday) ought to prove true with something to spare this year, that is, up to the first of the month.

From the records of years ago it is seen that mild winters and severe winters were both well known long before the memory of the oldest inhabitant of the present day, and that a winter like the one we are now having, though unusual in some respects, is just as old-fashioned as the kind grandfather liked to tell about.

The heaviest snowstorm of the season struck this locality Saturday and eighteen inches fell in most places. Sunday a high wind was experienced and the roads were blockaed.

Road Commissioner Milon U. Brown and Pathmaster James Harrison had the big Newcomb snow plow in commission Sunday and Monday making roads in the village and breaking out the highways leading to the village.

About ten inches of snow fell last night and this morning, which has delayed traffic on the railways today more than the heavier fall of Saturday.

Ever since Saturday older residents of the town have been scratching their heads and trying to remember just when there was anything like *it*.

Star may 1

MATRIMONIAL. *1908*

Stoddard-Doty.

Miss Emily Doty and Seneca Ray Stoddard, the well known artist and Adirondack illustrator, both of this city, were united in matrimony at 1 o'clock yesterday afternoon. The ceremony, which was performed by the Rev. Dr. George B. Gow at the home of the bride on Harlem street, was a quiet affair, only immediate friends of the contracting parties being present. Mr. and Mrs. Stoddard took the 2:30 train for New York, where they will tarry a week and then return to this city

---

news MARTIN GRANGER *Oct 2*

Martin Granger, of the Huddle, died Thursday at his home. The deceased was born at Indian brook, Bolton, eighty-six years and eight months ago. He is survived by his widow and two daughters, Mrs. Orson Ables, of Bolton, and Mrs. Walter P. Smith, of Pottersville. Mr. Granger was the father of the late Marcus Granger, of Glens Falls. *1908*

Now that President Roosevelt goes on record as preferring the horse to an automobile, let some one figure out how many new votes he will lose by not running again. *Star May 2 1908*

THE PEOPLE'S FORUM.

George Brayton Sows Buckwheat—Merchant Asks Question.

To the Editor of The Star:

I am 75 years old and on Saturday last I sowed 11 acres of buckwheat by hand in just four hours. When some boy or machine of any kind beats that I will sow some more.

GEORGE W. BRAYTON.

Glens Falls, June 15. *Star June 16 1908*

---

news July 9 1908

Rejected Suitor Shoots Girl at Middle Granville, Then Takes Own Life.

A shocking tragedy occurred at Middle Granville Saturday evening, when Joseph P. Morrison, of New York, shot and killed Miss Mamie Quigley, a beautiful young woman twenty-four years of age, and then committed suicide. Her refusal to marry him was the cause of the double tragedy.

Morrison arrived in Middle Granville on the evening train and went directly to the home of the girl's father, John Quigley. On Morrison's arrival, after paying his respects to the family, the different members left the porch, the mother to prepare supper, a younger sister going for the mail and another one out on the street, leaving Morrison and the girl alone. Morrison apparently was in an irritable mood, and before the last sister left he displayed a jealous temper.

Soon after the couple were alone Morrison took a Smith & Wesson revolver from his pocket and fired three shots at the girl. She ran around the house and down the lawn, crying for the Rev. Father Lynch, of the Church of Our Lady of Mount Carmel, whose rectory is across the road from the Quigley house. The mother heard the screams and thought her daughter's waist had caught fire from firecrackers. The mother reached the dying girl, who apparently had but one desire, to reach Father Lynch, and not until strong arms held her back did she stop in her efforts. Soon Father Lynch arrived and gave her the last rites of the church. The girl was conscious to the last and lived about twenty minutes.

Search was then made for the murderer and the officers were notified. Morrison ran but a short distance, when he turned the weapon upon himself. His dead body was found in a clump of bushes. Three shots had taken effect in his head. A card in his pocket showed that he resided at 509 East Sixteenth street, New York. He had been working in Saratoga.

Mr. Brayton Grows Oats, Too.

Editor Morning Star *Star aug 1908*

W. S. Newton, of Kingsbury, wishes to hear from some one having a larger crop of oats than his on 15 acres, which threshed out 607 bushels.

I had 16 acres of oats grown on my farm at Dunhams Basin, from which were threshed 962 bushels. They weighed 36 pounds to the bushel and were threshed by Fred Griffin of Adamsville, who will vouch for the same. Mr. Griffin threshed in three hours and 20 minutes 470 bushels, which speaks well for his ability as a thresher.

A. V. BRAYTON.

CHARGE OF ABDUCTION AGAINST MARRIED MAN

Frank Woodard, charged with abducting pretty Minnie Crannell, a Queensbury girl, was taken in custody yesterday in Buffalo by Constable Cornelius Buckley. The girl is not eighteen years old and had been missing from home some time, and it was not until a few days ago that her whereabouts became known, and then it was learned that she had been taken away by Woodard, who, it is alleged, has a wife and child whom he deserted.

It is alleged that Woodard and the Crannell girl were married in Canada, but this marriage can be annulled. It is possible that a charge of bigamy will also be made against Woodard. He will be arraigned before Justice of the Peace Breen today.

WOODARD TO BE ARRAIGNED ON ABDUCTION CHARGE TODAY

Post Aug 3 1908

Brought Here From Buffalo Saturday By Constable Buckley

Woodward greeted the officer, whom he knows well and made no attempt to escape. The girl, however, became apprehensive and ventured the opinion "that he wasn't very nice." Woodward was arrested at once and the girl was allowed to accompany the party.

OLD DOCUMENTS.

Star Aug 7

One 58 Years Old—The Other Dates Back to Civil War.

An interesting relic of old times came to light a few days ago in the attic of the building on Ridge street occupied by Lapham & Parks. It is a receipted bill for goods sold, and from the fact that it bears an internal revenue stamp and its ancient appearance, it probably dates back to the days of the civil war. It reads:

Peck & Byrne
  To A Vermillia, Dr.

July 3.	To 77 lbs. ham at 18c			$13 76
"	201 "	"	"	3 60
"	22¾ "	"	"	4 10
				$21 46

Received payment,
   A. Vermillia.

Another old document left at the Star office is a post coach way bill of the Starbuck stage line for June 20, 1850. It read:

Mr. Sanders, 1½ seats, Lake George to Glens Falls,	$1.13
Mr. Townsend, 4 seats, Lake George to Glens Falls,	3.00
	$4.13
	D. Gale.

MORNING STAR, AUGUST

1908

MR. SMITH'S CLAIM DISPUTED BY MANY

DUTCHESS COUNTY MAN SAYS HE IS OLDEST POSTMASTER.

Was Appointed 60 Years Ago and Has Ever Since Filled the Office—Was an Admirer of Zachary Taylor—Smiths Basin Postmaster Must Look Closely to His Laurels.

Many newspapers have declared George W. L. Smith, of Smiths Basin, to be the oldest postmaster in point of service in New York state and perhaps the oldest in point of continuous service in the United States.

Postmaster Smith was appointed April 19, 1861, by Montgomery Blair, postmaster general during Lincoln's first term, and has survived all the Democratic administrations since that time.

Before his appointment as postmaster Mr. Smith had served as clerk in the postoffice for ten years, giving him 57 years of continuous service. Smith has really served the postoffice department one year less than James G. Kerr, an octogenarian, who is now employed in the office of the superintendent of mails in Chicago, but Kerr has never risen to the dignity of being boss of a postoffice.

A Poughkeepsie Press dispatch, however, is apt to make both Smith and Kerr sit up and take notice. It says:

"The oldest postmaster in point of service in New York state and in the United States is Milo F. Winchester, of South Amenia. 'Way back in 1848 Mr. Winchester was one of the partisans of 'Old Rough and Ready', as Zachary Taylor was nicknamed. He used to sound the slogan:
'Clear the track if your toes are tender, For honest Zach can never surrender.'

"Mr. Winchester received his appointment, signed by Jacob Collamer, postmaster under President Taylor, on July 1, 1849, and he has filled the office during the intervening sixty years without a break.

"Although he has white hair, Mr. Winchester is an exceedingly well preserved man. In addition to being postmaster he was justice of the peace at South Amenia for 41 years."

"Count that day lost
 Whose low, descending sun
Views from thy hands
 No worthy action done."

Can't Beat Uncle George.

In reply to a Jenkinsville correspondent George W. Brayton writes:

"Your Jenkinsville correspondent writes that a Harrisena farmer has hens that produce what they call big eggs, 6 1-2 by 8 1-2 inches. I stepped into my henhouse yesterday, and the first egg I picked up was 7 by 8 3-4 inches in dimensions. This is about an average of my daily egg crop. I keep hens, not bantams."

Benjamin Batty, of 10 Maple street, brought into The Star office last night an egg measuring 8 1-4 by 7 inches, but not large enough to beat Uncle George's record.

BUY BLOODY POND.

1905.

State Historical Association Acquires Deed to Property.

News. July 31

Bloody Pond has been purchased by the New York State Historical association. The deed was made out and recorded a day or two ago in the county clerk's office and in the near future plans will be perfected for improvements to the property, these improvements to consist of the building of a road and fence about the pond and the making of minor changes.

Funds for the purchase of the property were obtained by Dr. Sherman Williams, Glens Falls, one of the officers of the historical association. Dr. Williams has always been active in work along this line and early this summer he started a subscription to raise $500 for the purchase and improvement of the property, the deed to lie in the name of the association. People responded readily to the call for funds and recently the total amount sought was made up. Of this amount $300 was paid to H. D. Chambers, owner of the pond and surrounding lands, while $200 will be expended on improvements. It is planned to build an iron fence about the pond and to encircle it with a macadam driveway, built from the state road to the nearest edge of the pond and around it.

The improvements will be gotten under way at once and the pond will be put in proper shape for visits from historical pilgrims before the summer is over.

Bloody Pond is one of the most famous of the points of historical interest in this section of the country. Near it, in the ravine near French Mountain, one of the battles of the French and Indian wars was fought. When the carnage was over the bodies of the dead and even the badly wounded were thrown into the pond, dyeing its waters a deep red and giving the pond the name which has clung to it ever since.

The state's purchase is directly on the line of the state road and the Hudson Valley railway, and is thus easy of access.

HEAR JACKSON CASE IN COURT AT SALEM

GRAND JURY TAKES UP CHARGE AGAINST MURDERER.

9+ times Sep+ 25

WHO CUT WIFE'S THROAT

1908

Supreme Court Term, Justice Kellogg, Presiding, Convenes at Salem, With Forty-seven Cases on Calendar—Local Attorneys in Attendance.

The Washington county grand jury, which sat today at Salem in connection with the session of supreme court, Justice Kellogg presiding, will have as its principal business the consideration of the murder case of the People against Frank Jackson, colored, who is accused of killing his wife in Sandy Hill last month. As the killing was witnessed by a number of persons, all of whom saw the accused wield the razor with which he cut his wife's throat, there is little doubt of the outcome of the case. If a true bill is found against the man, which is entirely probable, Justice Kellogg will appoint a term of court, probably within a month or two, to try the negro for his life.

Jackson's crime, it will be remembered, was committed on the lawn at the residence of Hon. Grenville M. Ingalsbe, about 7 o'clock on the morning of August 24, when Jackson, enraged at his wife for her alleged actions with other men, dragged her out of the kitchen and cut her throat. He escaped into the outskirts of the village, but was caught within two or three hours by Deputy Sheriff Mott and a posse of officers, to whom he confessed the killing, giving as his reason for the act that his wife was a bad woman.

The grand jury also has the usual number of minor crimes to investigate and an average total of excise violations. As the sitting today did not commence until afternoon, it is not expected that a report on the Jackson case or other cases will be given before the end of the week.

The court term has a total of forty-seven cases to consider, including a number of big damage actions. A number of local attorneys are at Salem in attendance at court, having cases on the calendar.

MUST MARRY IN TOWN WHERE LICENSE IS ISSUED

Star aug 27 1908

An Albany press dispatch states that residents and non-residents who desire to be married in New York state must have the ceremony performed in the town or city in which the marriage license has been procured, according to an opinion of Attorney General Jackson, which was made public by the state department of health yesterday.

KATTSKILL HOUSE BURNED.

News Aug 20 1908

One of the Oldest Hotels on Lake George, and Three Cottages, Destroyed.

The Kattskill house, one of the oldest hotels on Lake George, and three cottages, situated at Kattskill Bay, Lake George, were destroyed by fire shortly before noon Monday. The cottages burned were the Mayflower, a boarding house; the summer residence of A. R. Wing, of Fort Edward, and the cottage of John J. Allen, of Brooklyn. The guests and families escaped. The loss is estimated at $60,000.

The fire started at 10 o'clock in a clothespress on the second floor of the Mayflower. A dress hanging near a stovepipe is supposed to have become ignited from the pipe. When discovered, the entire clothespress was afire and the blaze spread rapidly. The Mayflower had forty guests and they escaped, though none of the contents was saved.

A high wind was blowing at the time and the flames quickly caught the Wing cottage, a few feet north. This was soon enveloped in flames. The Wing family, who were in the cottage at the time, escaped but saved practically nothing from the cottage.

The fire swept on and the south wing of the Kattskill house was soon ablaze. The Wing cottage is separated from the Kattskill house by only a few feet. Sufficient warning had been given the 100 guests in the latter house, so that most of them saved their personal effects and much of the effects of the hotel were also saved. With the Kattskill house burned the cottage of Mr. Allen, located in rear of the Kattskill house. The contents of the Allen cottage were saved.

The Kattskill house was an old hotel and had been conducted in recent years by the owner, A. P. Scoville, of Glens Falls. The Mayflower was conducted by Mrs. Taylor, of Fort Edward, and owned by J. B. Abbott, of Binghamton.

Mrs. William Knox, of Brooklyn, lost $15,000 in jewels and personal effects. She offered $500 for someone to save them, but the person to reach nearest to them, William Blake, of Sandy Hill, could not get within three feet of the drawer containing the valuables. John D. Whish, secretary of the State Forest, Fish and Game commission, lost $1,000 in personal effects. Mr. Scoville states that he will not rebuild the hotel.

Kattskill House

FRED G. JENKINS THE CHOICE FOR CHIEF OF POLICE

GIVEN APPOINTMENT BY BOARD OF PUBLIC SAFETY.

NAMED FOR 3 MONTHS

Probationary Period Provided By City Charter—Jenkins Who Is An Efficient Officer Was Chief Under Old Village Government—Appointment Made as Unanimous Choice of Board of Public Safety.

Fred G. Jenkins, chief of the village police force during the administration of President Horton and acting chief since the organization of the city force, was last evening appointed chief of police of the city of Glens Falls for a probationary period of three months.

THE BROESEL BOAT WINS 10 MILE RACE

aug 21 1908

BIG EVENT OF YESTERDAY AT HAGUE REGATTA.

WALTER HARRIS SECOND

Events of Sporting World—Bill Hurley To Meet Lewis in Six Round Exhibition—The Ridgewoods Have Practice Game in Greenwich.

Herman Broesel's new motorboat, the Simplex XV, won the fast ten mile race yesterday at the Hague regatta, doing the distance in 24 minutes 31 seconds. The second in the race was the Adelaid, a new Fay & Bowen craft owned by Walter P. Harris.

This race was the big race of the day and the prize was the Broesel cup, which must be won twice in succession before being given as a final trophy.

In the six mile race for the Town Topics trophy, given by Colonel W. D. Mann, the Dearie, owned by Herbert J. King, finished first.

In the three mile race the Mohican, owned by L. R. Scott, finished first, and the LaPetite, owned by Miss Sophie Mann, second.

The four-oared barge race was won by a barge captained by Bruce Carney of Sabbath Day Point.

The winners of the canoeing and rowing races were given in yesterday's paper.

---

neit nov 5 1908
Recalling Incidents of Long Ago.

M. H. Tanner, of Bolton Landing, was in town last week calling upon the friends of his boyhood. He found two persons in town, J. S. Carter and W. S. Bascom, who were schoolmates of his in Fort Edward forty-three years ago and they had a most enjoyable time in recalling the incidents and those who took part in them, in those days that are now but a memory. Mr. Tanner is a gentleman of good address and his geniality never fails to warm one's heart.—Benson correspondent, Fair Haven (Vt.) Era.

Getting Horses Ready.

Jerome Jenkins, the man who invented the quaint saying, "Let's take su'thin'," is in his old home town, Glens Falls. He is in charge of a stable of trotters and pacers for Asa Roberts, of Bolton, and will soon have a bunch in readiness for racing on the ice. *Star nov 12 1908*

Mexico nov 5 1908
A MARINER'S DREAM.
Pleasant Visions of a Naval Soldier on the Isthmus of Panama.

Cassius Wood, a Warrensburgh boy who is a private in the marine battalion stationed at Camp Elliott, Isthmus of Panama, last week sent to his sister, Miss Deffie Wood, of this village, the following poem, which was composed by his chum, private August Risch, who evidently has pleasant memories of a Thanksgiving dinner in the North:

A MARINER'S DREAM.

I was sitting down to dinner
  In a farm house o'er the sea,
To a turkey brown and tender,
  And a steaming cup of tea.
There were fritters sweetening richness
  And a row of pumpkin pies,
With the lightest, whitest biscuits,
  That were ever made to rise.

There my dear old-fashioned mother,
  In her purple painted gown,
Meekly bent her silvery tresses
  As she called the blessing down.
She was just about to help me
  To the sugar and the cream,
When the reveille awoke me
  And I found it all a dream.

Tho' today I'm in the tropics,
  Many, many miles away
From the farm-house and the turkey
  And my mother old and gray,
Clad in torn and faded Khaki
  And the raggedest of hats,
In a country where the menu,
  Runs to slush that's full of gnats

It is not the least of hardships
  Marines all have to bear,
Dreams and pleasant recollections
  Of the days of better fare
While the peaceful homefolks gather
  Round a board with plenty spread,
They are waiting in the trenches,
  Waiting for a dose of lead.

But all friends and near relations
  Far among the smiling fields,
Who are grateful for the bounty
  That the plenteous harvest yields,
Don't forget who guards "Old Glory"
  For a golden land and you
To spare a tho't at dinner
  For your absent friend in blue.

GOSSIP WORSE THAN WAR AND HELL.

Times nov 12 1908

Gossip is a humming bird with eagle wings and a voice like a foghorn. It can be heard from Dan to Beersheba and has caused more trouble than all the ticks, fleas, mosquitoes, coyotes, grasshoppers, clinch bugs, rattlesnakes, sharks, sore toes, cyclones, earthquakes, blizzards, smallpox, yellow fever, gout and indigestion that this great United States has known or will know when the universe shuts up shop and begins the final invoice. In other words, it has got war and hell both backed up in the corner yelling for ice water.—Ex.

DR. GILLETTE DEAD; OPERATION IS FATAL

nov. 12th 1908

WELL KNOWN LAKE GEORGE VISITOR PASSES AWAY.

HAD MANY LOCAL FRIENDS

Dr. Gillette, Prominent in His Profession and Insurance Circles—He Was Lover of Lake George and Did Much for its Advancement.

Glens Falls and Lake George friends have been advised of the death of Dr. Walter R. Gillette of New York, former vice president of the Mutual Life Insurance company, who passed away at Roosevelt hospital in New York ten days after an operation for the removal of an intestinal cancer.

Dr. Gillette was born in Philadelphia in February, 1840, and was the son of Rev. A. D. Gillette, D. D., for many years the pastor of Calvary Baptist church, New York.

Graduating from Madison (now Colgate) university in 1861, Dr. Walter Gillette entered the New York college of physicians and surgeons and received his diploma in 1863. He entered the army and held the position of assistant surgeon to the close of the civil war, after which he became surgeon to the postoffice department and held that office for thirteen years.

Thirty years ago Dr. Gillette was family physician to Richard A. McCurdy, president of the Mutual Life Insurance company of New York and through the friendship thus begun he became first a medical examiner, then a director and finally vice president and general manager of the Mutual Life Insurance company of New York.

From his boyhood Dr. Gillette was a lover of nature and took great delight in the beauties of his summer home on Bluff Head, opposite Sabbath Day Point, Lake George. He was a generous contributor to the fund for building Grace memorial chapel at Sabbath Day Point, in 1885, and one of its trustees from the first.

His enthusiasm for the beauties of this part of Lake George led him to purchase the large tract of land fronting on Van Buren bay and this he later sold to its present owner Silas H. Paine. He also at one time owned the Slim Point property which now belongs to the Silver Bay association.

Dr. Gillette's wife died a little more than a year ago and their surviving children are Dr. Curtanius Gillette, a successful physician of New York, Abram D., a lawyer and Mrs. Harrison K. Bird (nee Grace Gillette) also of New York.

— 53 —

CAPTAIN WESLEY FINKLE A JOLLY LAKE SAILOR

Star Nov 17 1908.

One of the youngest looking men of his acknowledged age is Captain Wesley Finkle, of the steamer Mohican on Lake George. The captain and his accomplished wife called at The Star office a day or two ago, and a reporter pumped a reluctant story out of one of the most trustworthy and efficient navigators on the state's inland waters.

Captain Finkle told the pencil pusher that he is 66 years old, but he doesn't look a minute over 50. He has been on Lake George from boyhood, and knows every rock and shoal on that beautiful sheet of water. For the past 34 years he has been in the employ of the Champlain Transportation company, 20 years as pilot and 14 years as captain. Judging by the freshness of his face, he is good for another 20 years of command.

Captain Finkle is a man whom everybody loves, and the patrons of the lake steamers hope he may live forever.

SAMUEL PRUYN'S WILL ADMITTED TO PROBATE

Star Jan 4 1908

The will of the late Samuel Pruyn was admitted to probate Saturday by Surrogate Kiley. The instrument leaves the estate to the widow, Mrs. Eliza Jane Pruyn, to be held in trust, and upon her death to be held in trust for the daughters, Mrs. Charlotte Pruyn Hyde, Mrs. Mary Pruyn Hoopes and Miss Nell K. Pruyn. The beneficiaries of the trust will receive the income from the estate, unless the trustees decide that the income is insufficient for their proper maintenance, in which event some of the principal may be used. Two grandchildren, Mary Van Ness Hyde and Samuel Pruyn Hoopes, are also made beneficiaries.

The will leaves the Pruyn home at the corner of Elm and Cross streets to the widow during her life, and at her death it reverts to the original estate. The sum of $3,000, to be paid within three months, is also left to Mrs. Pruyn.

Maurice Hoopes, a son-in-law of the testator, and Louis M. Brown are named as executors of the will.

OBITUARY.

Star Dec 2 1908.

Ezra Harris.

The funeral of Ezra Harris, who died yesterday morning at his home at East Lake George, will be held Thursday morning at 9:30 o'clock. The burial will be in the Bolton cemetery. Mr. Harris was 69 years old. He is survived by three sons and a daughter, Halsey E. Harris, of Binghamton; Emmet Harris, Winfield Harris and Mrs. Bessie Merrill, of East Lake George. Two brothers, Warren Harris, of East Lake George, and Peter Harris, of California, also survive.

COMPENSATION.

You have to pay for what you get.
  A gift comes to you free,
But if you've nothing to return
  You do not get it. See?
A stolen kiss seems cheap enough
  Snatched from a lady friend,
But often you will find it more
  Expensive in the end.

It seems an easy way to get
  The little bunch of bliss.
It's so much trouble to inquire
  If you may have a kiss.
And so by stealth you pick the prize
  Like cherries from a tree,
And, not content with one, you try
  To make it two or three.

And then you go upon your way
  As happy as a lark
And plan another theft next day
  As soon as it is dark.
A basket of the choicest fruits,
  Of peaches red and plums,
For nothing—isn't it a dream?
  But wait till pay day comes.

The tickets for the matinee
  You have to bring around,
The choicest candy in the store
  At eighty cents per pound,
And if she up and marries you
  Then, chastened, mild and meek,
You pony up without a word
  Your pay check once a week.

OBITUARY.

News Dec 10 1908

FLAVEL B. COOLIDGE.

Flavel B. Coolidge, one of the most respected business men of Glens Falls, died Monday afternoon in the Montreal General hospital, where he had been a patient for the past three weeks. The cause of death was Bright's disease. Deceased was born on Coolidge hill, in Bolton, in June, 1848, and was a son of Jonathan and Mary Coolidge. He had been a resident of Glens Falls for forty years, and had a wide circle of friends throughout Warren county. Deceased is survived by a widow, who was Cynthia Seeyle; two brothers and a sister, Jonathan M. Coolidge, Thomas S. Coolidge and Mrs. Martha Goodman, of Glens Falls; also a cousin, Mrs. M. N. Dickinson, of Warrensburgh. The funeral was held this morning from the home in Glens Falls.

WILLIAM BOYCE SUSTAINS INJURIES IN PAPER MILL

Post Dec. 22 1908

William Boyce, 35 Staple street, met with a serious accident yesterday morning while employed in mill No. 5 of the Union Bag and Paper Company, Sandy Hill. Mr. Boyce was standing on a ladder, from which he fell a distance of about six feet, striking on his head and being rendered unconscious and sustaining a deep cut in which three stitches were taken by Dr. W. Cuthbert of Sandy Hill. The injured man was brought to his home in this village.

During the past seventy-seven years great industrial changes have taken place in Sandy Hill, especially at Baker's Falls, where in 1844 the Howland Brothers manufactured the first sheet of manila rope paper. At that time the population of the entire village did not exceed 1,000. Today there are more than 6,000 progressive citizens, and three of the principal industries are located at Bakers Falls, affording employment to about 1,500 hands.

The scene at Bakers Falls indicates substantial progress, as where once the Howland Brothers' mill stood, the machinery in the plants of the Union Bag and Paper company, the Standard Wall Paper company and the Iron and Brass Works, hum with industrial activity.

The cut accompanying this sketch shows Bakers Falls in 1831. It was reproduced from an old English plate and loaned the Star by F. D. Howland. In 1831 the population of Sandy Hill did not exceed 600, and not more than 50 families resided in the vicinity of Bakers Falls. A great contrast is now seen.

Baker's Falls have brought industrial life to Sandy Hill. Without the falls Sandy Hill would not be the progressive village it is today.

The Howland Brothers in harnessing the falls for the manufacture of paper, began an industry which has made Sandy Hill. The Howlands were identified with the industrial life of the village until about 1899, when the Howland Paper company was absorbed by the Union Bag and Paper company. The Howlands figured conspicuously in the paper manufacturing business before and after the war. The firm was composed of Amasa and Enos Howland.

SANDY HILL'S GREAT PROGRESS SINCE HUDSON WAS HARNESSED

Reproduction of Old Steel Plate Made Many Years Ago---Where a Solitary Mill Then Stood There Are Several Large and Flourishing Industries.

Baker's Falls, Sandy Hill, 1831.

THE MAN WHO KNOWS.

The man who knows more.
　Than professor or sage,
Who's really a marvel
　For one of his age,
Is the chap who has never
　Been ten miles away
From where he was born
　In the fresh scented hay.

To him all the secrets
　Of earth are laid bare.
He solves every problem,
　Makes round holes look square.
Delves into the meaning
　Of passing events,
Makes doubters look doubly
　Like thirty-one cents.

Such things like the tariff,
　The trusts and their tricks
And matters financial
　To pieces he picks.
His learned opponents
　Must take to the woods
And leave him the master
　Right there with the goods.

He knows more about it,
　Not trying to boast,
Than one who has traveled
　From mountain to coast.
And why should he not,
　Let me ask, take the prize
With nothing to do
　But think and grow wise?

Times Dec. 23d 1908

J. E. GOODMAN DEAD BORN IN WARREN CO.

James E. Goodman, a native resident of Warren county, and a cousin of the late S. L. Goodman of Glens Falls, died yesterday at his home in Granville, word to that effect having been received last evening by Samuel B. Goodman.

The funeral will be held tomorrow afternoon at two o'clock at the Goodwin homestead in Granville.

The deceased, long a prominent figure in this section of the state, was born June 3, 1832, in Bolton, this county.

He was of English extraction, his ancestors being among the first to settle in this country. After receiving a common school education, at the age of seventeen he entered the State Normal school at Albany, from which he graduated in 1852. After teaching several terms he engaged in the drug business in the city of Troy, and later moved to Fort Ann, where he engaged in farming. This he continued at different places until 1884. In that year he was one of the promoters and organizers of the Farmers' National bank of Granville, and was elected its first president, a position he held for nineteen years. During his terms of office the bank grew to such proportions that it occupied a prominent place in the financies of this section. He resigned in 1903 and was instrumental in the organization of Washington County National bank of Granville, and was elected its first president, a position he held until his death. Mr. Goodman was a staunch Republican and has filled several elective offices, having been supervisor of the town of Hartford four successive terms and member of assembly in 1882. Besides that he had held many responsible positions of trust in the local life of Granville.

Star BOLTON. Feb 12

Mrs. John Vandenburgh died Friday after a long illness. She was buried Sunday in the Huddle cemetery.—— The Rev. Mr. Crossman, of the Free Methodist church returned home Wednesday from Glens Falls, where he has been holding revival services for two weeks.——James Fawden died Sunday. The funeral will be held Tuesday at his late home.——The ice houses are nearly all filled around here.——Jay Taylor spent Monday in Glens Falls.——February 9. 1909

TABLET TO COMMEMORATE PRESIDENT ROOSEVELT'S MIDNIGHT RIDE IN ADIRONDACKS.

Fac-simile of the bronze tablet erected by **Harry V. Radford** on a large bowlder on the mountain road entering North Creek from Tahawus Club.

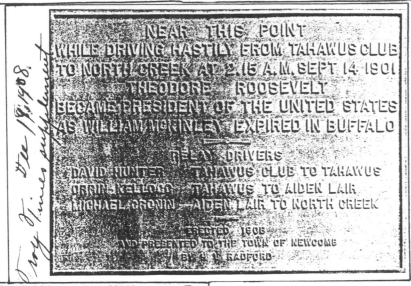

NEAR THIS POINT
WHILE DRIVING HASTILY FROM TAHAWUS CLUB
TO NORTH CREEK AT 2.15 A.M. SEPT 14 1901
THEODORE ROOSEVELT
BECAME PRESIDENT OF THE UNITED STATES
AS WILLIAM MCKINLEY EXPIRED IN BUFFALO

RELAY DRIVERS
DAVID HUNTER — TAHAWUS CLUB TO TAHAWUS
ORRIN KELLOGG — TAHAWUS TO AIDEN LAIR
MICHAEL CRONIN — AIDEN LAIR TO NORTH CREEK

ERECTED 1908
AND PRESENTED TO THE TOWN OF NEWCOMB
BY H. V. RADFORD

Troy Times supplement Dec 15, 1908.

SAMUEL PRUYN DEAD AFTER LONG ILLNESS

PROMINENT CITIZEN EXPIRES IN EIGHTY-EIGHTH YEAR.

PIONEER IN INDUSTRIES

Times Dec 24 1908

Deceased, with J. W. Finch, Founded Big Lumber and Papermaking Business—Active in Other Lines of Advancement—Was a Philanthropist.

Samuel Pruyn, one of the oldest and most prominent citizens of the community, died this morning at his home on Elm street after an illness of over a year. He was eighty-eight years of age. Death was due to general debility, caused by the extreme age of the deceased.

Mr. Pruyn was one of the pioneers of the industrial upbuilding of Glens Falls. With Jeremiah W. Finch, he was the founder of the lumber and papermaking business of Finch, Pruyn & company; with several others he bought and rebuilt as an electric line, the Glens Falls, Sandy Hill and Fort Edward street railway and in many ways he was a contributor to the material growth of his native community. He was a consistent church worker and as a philanthropist accomplished much for the needy of Glens Falls, though his good deeds in this line were never generally known. He was an ideal type of the progressive citizen, having been an active worker up to the time of his compulsory re-

tirement.

The deceased was born at Oak Hill in the town of Cambridge, N. Y., on June 19, 1820. He came to Glens Falls in his youth and in 1865, formed a partnership with Jeremiah W. Finch. This partnership, formed to conduct a lumber, lime and grist business, continued prosperously for about forty years, finally being merged into the corporation of Finch, Pruyn & company, now existent. The present business of the company, of which Mr. Pruyn was president, includes lumbering, papermaking and kindred industries and keeps five or six hundred men busy at certain times of the year. During the partnership and the incorporation, Mr. Pruyn devoted his time to the manufacturing department of the business. He was elected president of the company in 1906 and in 1907 purchased a controlling interest. In November of last year he was compelled to give up his active duties by the illness which caused his death today.

The Glens Falls, Sandy Hill and Fort Edward street railway, sold to the Hudson Valley in 1901, was rebuilt and put in condition as a modern transportation system by Mr. Pruyn and others. Mr. Pruyn was at one time a director of the First National bank and at the time of his death was a director of the Merchants' National bank. He has always retained an interest in farming.

In politics, Mr. Pruyn was for years an independent Democrat. As a trustee of the village he took an active part in introducing a water system and as a member of the board of education built the Union school on South street.

Mr. Pruyn attended and was a member of the Presbyterian church, to which he contributed liberally throughout his residence here. His parents were connected with the Dutch Reformed denomination.

Though few people know of his activities in this line, Mr. Pruyn was a philanthropist on an extensive scale. He assisted more than fifty needy families in this city and vicinity to build homes, advancing the money for construction and getting his return as best he could, and sometimes not at all. In many local contests for the public good he put his shoulder firmly to the wheel.

OLDEST STATE RESIDENT DEAD

Times Dec 29 1908

Patrick Flood Dies at His Home In Cohoes at the Age of 110 Years

Patrick Flood, in all probability the oldest resident of New York State, is dead at the home of his daughter, Mrs. Michael Mullen, in North Reservoir street, Cohoes, at the remarkable age of 110 years. Mr. Flood was born St. Patrick's day, March 17, 1798, in Kings County, Ireland, and was the son of sturdy Irish peasants.

He was eight years old when Fulton steamed up the Hudson. About 1850 Mr. Flood removed to this country, taking up his residence in Albany, and a little later removed to "The Bush," which is now a part of Cohoes. For a number of years he ran a sand boat on the Erie canal.

Getting Along.

How painlessly a fellow glides
  From poverty to riches,
To holding down a leather chair
  From toil and digging ditches!
And he can hardly realize
  That once when he was shorter
He didn't buy what he desired
  Because it cost a quarter.

Communing with a fat cigar,
  His pedals on the table,
To think that he was once in need
  Seems almost like a fable.
He wonders, if he wanted coin
  When he was poor and thrifty,
Just why he didn't write a check
  For twenty-five or fifty.

He looks about him and he sees
  Men short of food and raiment,
Without a diamond stud because
  They cannot make first payment.
He thinks that they could beat the game
  If they were only gritty,
Forgetting how he struggled on
  E'er luck on him took pity.

'Tis easy to forget the past
  And down the road go spinning
All in a handsome touring car
  When riches has an inning.
Although not many months away
  From poverty's embraces,
He feels superior to those
  Who sit in lowly places.

Mr. Pruyn was married in January, 1860, to Eliza Jane Baldwin of Cambridge. A son, John Knickerbocker Pruyn, who died when but a year old, and three daughters, Charlotte, now

Mrs. Louis Hyde Fiske; Mary Eliza, now Mrs. Maurice Hoopes, and Miss Nell Knickerbocker Pruyn, were born to Samuel Pruyn and wife. The widow and daughters all survive.

Arrangements for the funeral have not been made.

PROF. GEORGE W. KENNEDY.

The body of Prof. George W. Kennedy, whose funeral was held Friday at Saratoga, was at once taken to Troy and incinerated at the Earl crematorium. The ashes were deposited at Bolton Landing, where his parents resided for several years. Deceased was a son of the Rev. John Kennedy, a Methodist Episcopal minister, and was born at Hadley, May 6, 1862. He received his early education at the Warrensburgh academy and the Troy Conference academy. Later he attended Syracuse University, where he prepared himself for a teacher and became prominent in the educational work of the state. At the time of his death, caused by acute yellow atrophy of the liver, he was principal of the high and grammar schools of Saratoga. On July 10, 1882, Mr. Kennedy married Miss J. Luella Fonda, of Rupert, Vt., who died on June 22, 1896. On December 21, 1898, Miss Lillian Freeman, of Fair Haven, became his wife. She with two daughters, the Misses Laura and Mary F., survive. His only other immediate survivor is an aunt, Mrs. Robert Jarvis, of Warrensburgh.

OBITUARY.

THOMAS WILLIAM SUTTON

Many of Warrensburgh's older residents will be sadly interested to learn of the death of one who passed the years of his boyhood and youth in our pleasant little town. Thomas William Sutton was born in New York city in 1842, the son of Moses Sutton and his wife, Elizabeth (Taylor). When he was about three years old his parents moved to Warrensburgh. Here he grew up a light hearted, mischievous boy, full of fun, and with a few boon companions, ready for almost any prank which promised amusement. Soon after the outbreak of the Civil War he went to the front as first sargeant of "Warrensburgh's Own" Company I, Ninety-sixth N. Y. S. V. Infantry. In 1864, at Cincinnati, Ohio, he was married to his cousin, Miss Adeline E. Peckover, who died March 7, 1879. The three daughters of this union are still living: Mrs. Cora E. White, of Plymouth, N. H.; Mrs. John J. Archer, of Warrensburgh, and Mrs. Marion P. Hill, of Madisonville, Ohio. In 1879 Mr. Sutton enlisted at Columbus, Ohio, in the Twelfth regiment U. S. Regular Infantry. He was afterward transferred to the Eleventh and later to the famous "fighting Ninth," to which he belonged at the time this regiment was ordered to Cuba with the Rough Riders in 1898. In this same year he was retired by reason of sickness after serving in the regular army twenty-one years and seven months. He was proud of the fact that in all that time he was never reprimanded and was several times specially commented for honest and faithful service. Durnig his later years he suffered greatly from rheumatism and spent much of his time at the Soldier's home at Bath, where he died December 27, 1908.

A Notable Career.

Dr. Henry R. Stiles, who died at his home, Hill View, Lake George, last week, was not only a physician of some note, but a historian and a man of long and varied labors in many fields of endeavor. His principal claim to an enduring memory, however, rests on the comprehensive history of Brooklyn, which he compiled many years ago.

Dr. Stiles, who was seventy-six years of age, was born in New York city. He received his education at the New York University and at Williams College. After being graduated at the New York Ophthalmic Hospital, he practiced for a year and then went to Galena, Ill., where he remained for some years, finally moving to Toledo, O., where he edited The Toledo Blade in 1856. He returned to Brooklyn that same year, and forming a partnership with Mr. Calkins he published The American Journal of Education. In 1859 he resumed the practice of medicine. He was appointed Health Commissioner of the old city of Brooklyn and published the first history of Brooklyn. In 1873 Dr. Stiles was made medical superintendent of the Middletown Homeopathic State Hospital.

Four years later he went to Dundee, Scotland, where he was placed in charge of the Homeopathic Dispensary of that city. He returned to Brooklyn in 1881 and from that time until 1888 he practiced there and in New York city. In 1888 he removed to Lake George, where he opened an institution for the treatment of mental and nervous diseases.

Dr. Stiles was one of the organizers of the Society for the Promotion of the Welfare of the Insane in New York city, the American Anthropological Society, and the New York Genealogical and Biographical Society—of which he served as president for four years.

LINCOLN'S LAST STORY.

Told to a Congressman Night Before the President Was Assassinated.

What was doubtless the last story told by President Lincoln and which has heretofore escaped publication was recently related to the house of representatives by General Keifer of Ohio, says a Washington dispatch. A bill to reorganize the militia of the District of Columbia was under discussion. It met the criticism of General Keifer, who said it reminded him of a story told by President Lincoln the night before he was assassinated to the late Hon. Samuel Shellabarger, for many years a member of congress from Ohio.

Mr. Shellabarger, said General Keifer, called at the White House to request the appointment of a constituent to a staff position. "That reminds me of a story," responded President Lincoln. "There was a woman living on the banks of the Sangamon in the early days who had the reputation of being able to make a good white shirt. An Irishman about to get married ordered a shirt from her for the ceremony. She made the shirt and starched it, but when the Irishman put it on he found that the starch went all the way around, and he returned it for reconstruction, with the comment that he didn't want a shirt that was all collar.

"The trouble with you, Shellabarger," Mr. Lincoln remarked, "is that you want the army all staff and no army."

A PLUCKY BLACKSMITH SUBDUES KICKING HORSE

A man from out of town yesterday afternoon drove up to the door of Julien Beaudett's blacksmith shop on Park street to have his horse shod. While unhooking the horse, a fractious beast, it took fright at a passing go-cart and began running in circles, meanwhile rearing and kicking alternately, with its driver holding fast to one rein. Ernest J. Rivers, an employee of Mr. Beaudett, rushed out, seized the horse by the head and controlled it until it could be unhooked and led into the shop. The animal escaped with slight scratches, but the front of the cutter was wrecked 1909

Mrs. Alice D. Harris, aged forty-eight years, died Tuesday morning at her home in Queensbury. She had been a resident of Queensbury forty years, and was born in Bolton. She was a daughter of Almond Dickinson. She is survived by her husband, Walter Harris, two daughters and a son, Mrs. Benjamin Odell, Miss Mabel Harris and Eliphalet Harris, of South Dakota. Four brothers and a sister also survive, Sumner, Truman, Marvin and Benjamin Dickinson, and a sister, Mrs. Marena Moore, of Hill View. 1909

OLIVER'S BAR-ROOM STOVE.

A Near-Poem, Written by One of the Faithful, and Affectionately Dedicated to Oliver, "By Jove."

One of the "Committee of 47" has "writ a pome" which he asks us to publish, "by Jove"; so here goes.

A Circle gathers both day and night,
 'Bout twenty or more, by Jove,
At Oliver's, the boys sit tight
 Forninst the bar-room stove.
The boxes, chairs and desks
 Take the place of fine settees;
And here the circle spends its time
 In most luxurious ease.
There's Paul Cote, and Wilson wise,
 Talk race both night and day;
But seldom meet upon the ice,
 "Because they're not built that way."

Here's where the farming is all laid
 out;
 Here's where the hay is raised;
Here's where the cords of wood are
 cut,
 And where the stock is grazed.
Sam Carr hasn't much to say,
 But he loves the merry war;
And when he gets a mighty thirst
 The boys'll call him to the bar.
There's Johnny Smith and Jimmie
 Green,
 Who have not hired a seat,
So they have to spend their time
 A plugging on the street.
Jim ne'er has much to say
 But just drops in to while dull time
 away.
Here's where the races are all pulled
 off,
 'Stead of on the ice, by Jove;
The horses step at a fearful gait
 'Round Oliver's bar-room stove.

The women folk about the town
 Say if these great affairs
Would only happen close to home
 They'd all be millionaires.
But while they're lugging up the coal
 And cutting wood 'til they could cry
Their warriors brave are fighting still
 To see who can tell the biggest lie.
There's Tink who drops in now and
 then
 For a few hours' social chat,
And he thinks he gets the boys
 "a goin"
 'Til they don't know where they're
 at.

The nights they come, the nights
 they go,
 Spring, summer, winter, fall;
And still they meet there, thus and
 so
 These setters one and all.
Frank Caldwell drops in, face a-grin,
 To have a pleasant smoke;
And all of you who know him,
 Wait for his little joke.
I'd tell you more of what they do
 And rake them o'er, by Jove;
But I must go and take my seat,
 Near Oliver's bar-room stove.

COL. GALWAY C. MORRIS OF LAKE GEORGE MEETS DEATH

President of Lake George National Bank Dies In Philadelphia

DECEASED A VETERAN OF WAR OF THE REBELLION

Edwin R. Ziebach Will Leave Today to Attend the Funeral

Colonel Galway C. Morris, president of the Lake George First National Bank, and for the past twenty-five years a prominent resident on the store of Lake George, near tea island, died yesterday afternoon at the home of his son, Herbert Morris, in Philadelphia, where he was taken last November on account of failing health.

Colonel Morris has been president of the bank since its organization in 1907. For the past fifty years he has been exceedingly prominent among the cottagers coming to Lake George and in public affairs he always took an active part. He was a member of one of the oldest Masonic lodges in the country and several years ago he was one of the organizers and president of the Consumers' Coal Company of Philadelphia. Mr. Morris was 74 years of age and a veteran of the Civil war. He is survived by two sons, Dr. Ellison and Herbert Morris, both of Philadelphia. Mrs. Morris died at Lake George about nine years ago.

Edwin R. Ziebach, vice president of the Lake George National Bank, will leave today to attend the funeral.

A LEPROUS TRAMP STARTS A BAD FIRE

Star   Feb 15

BURNS BEAUTIFUL HAYDEN COTTAGE AT LAKE GEORGE.

1909.

Had Just Been Released from Parks Hospital and Previously Had Served a Term in Albany Penitentiary—Culprit Found in a Tree and Lodged in the County Jail.

The beautiful Hayden cottage, lo-

---

cated between the cottages owned by George Foster Peabody and Charles J. Peabody on the Bolton road, Lake George, was burned to the ground early yesterday morning by an incendiary. The fire broke out about 6 o'clock, and as the cottage was unoccupied, the Lake George authorities at once suspected that incendiarism was the cause of the fire, and started in search of the culprit.

A young man known as Jesse Bentley, and well-known in Glens Falls police circles, was found hidden in a hemlock tree a short distance from the cottage. He was taken in custody on suspicion and this morning will be arraigned before Justice of the Peace Weaver on a charge of arson.

Bentley was discharged from the Parks hospital Saturday, after several weeks' treatment for a bad skin disease which resembled leprosy. He walked to Lake George, and it is supposed proceeded down the Bolton road to the Hayden cottage in search of shelter. He broke into the cottage, and, it is believed, started a fire to warm himself.

The cottage burned belonged to the H. H. Hayden estate. It was furnished. The loss will probably amount to about $8,000.

Bentley came into Glens Falls about two months ago, fresh from the penitentiary. He applied at police headquarters for lodging. The police detected that he was afflicted with a peculiar disease, and for more than a week he was cared for, until he was removed to the hospital for treatment.

FENCE RAIL PHILOSOPHY.

A cheerful countenance always shows better on a gloomy day.

Many a man is governed by his wife's good judgment, but is too mean to acknowledge it and takes all the credit to himself.

Few people know how to enjoy riches, but everybody would be willing to take a chance.

"It is no disgrace to be poor," says the adage; but it is mighty inconvenient.

The pleasures of life, like wine, should be sipped slowly, not gulped.

It is not difficult to recover money lost in a venture, but when a good name is lost it is gone for good.

Beware of the girl who leaves the dishes for mother to wash.

A man is known by the love he bears his mother.

We may not admire a pig's manners, but there is no taint to the money his carcass brings.

Some farmers get rich by selling what they cannot eat and eating what they cannot sell.

The farmer who can find no reason for being thankful this year is certainly playing in hard luck.

The pessimist is one who is mad because other people are glad.

It is safer to trust a man with wrinkles about his eyes than one with wrinkles about his mouth.

If nobody confessed his sins we would never know how wicked this world really is.

BOY'S FATAL COAST ON CRUST

Mirror — Feb 26 1909.

MARK DALRYMPLE DIED EARLY THIS MORNING

Stick Was Run Through Boy's Body Last Sunday When Sliding Down Hill. Funeral Sunday Afternoon at 2:00 O'clock From Home, and 3:00 O'clock From St. James.

Mark Dalrymple, son of Mr. and Mrs. Elmer Dalrymple, is dead at the home of his parents as the result of a coasting accident last Sunday when he was impaled on a stick as he was thrown from a coaster.

The affair has cast a gloom over the whole community, for the lad was much loved both in his home and in the village where he was well known and admired for his manly qualities and upright life.

Mark, who was nineteen years of age, was out on the snow crust near the Cramer place on Sunday afternoon sliding on a coaster which consists of a barrel stave on which is nailed an upright block for a seat. His coaster became unmanageable and threw him over a slight declivity at the foot of which was a bush that had been partly chopped down, leaving an upright stick about an inch in diameter and a foot or so in length. The boy was impaled on this stick which entered his body at the lowest point of the abdomen, and passing entirely through, came out just below the shoulder blade. Being possessed of great pluck and invincible courage, he freed himself from the stick and ran for his home a half mile away which he reached alone and told of his injury.

Dr. C. B. Stiles of Hill View was summoned and also Drs. Cunningham and Henning of Glens Falls. As the nature of the injury required surgical treatment he was taken at once to Parks hospital. The operation revealed the fact that a large intestine had been ruptured a a great deal of lasceration of the parts was apparent.

About four inches of the intestine had to be removed, and after the operation the doctors gave but little hope of the lad's recovery. He rallied bravely and made a strong fight for life, but all in vain.

Tuesday the prospects of recovery seemed bright, but the doctors gave the family very little encouragement. The key to the situation lay chiefly in securing a resumption of the action of the bowels, and on account of the patient's robust health this was more difficult than it would have been otherwise. All Thursday the lad gradually failed and after intense suffering death came to his relief in the early hours of this morning.

DEATH IN ACCIDENT

Stephen Pasco Thrown From a Cutter and Killed.

News — Feb 11 1909.

VICTIM'S SKULL WAS FRACTURED

In Attempt to Avold Meeting a Trolley Car One of Warrensburgh's Honored Citizens Receives Fatal Injuries— Wife Escapes Hurts.

As the result of injuries received Monday afternoon by being thrown from a sleigh, Stephen Pasco, one of Warrensburgh's oldest and most esteemed citizens, died at 8:40 p. m. His head struck a tree, fracturing the skull, and he was injured internally. Mrs. Pasco, although she was severely shaken up, escaped serious injury.

The accident through which Mr. Pasco met his death occurred shortly after 3 o'clock. Mr. and Mrs. Pasco left their home at twenty minutes of that hour, driving the family horse, Maud, a spirited but perfectly gentle animal. After attending to several errands downtown, they had started homeward from Joseph Lavine's store when Mrs. Pasco called her husband's notice to the express trolley car rapidly coming down the Main street grade. Knowing his horse was accustomed to shy at the cars and the roadway being narrow, Mr. Pasco thought to avoid any possible trouble by turning into the driveway of E. S. Crandall's residence. In doing so the right runner of the cutter caught on a stone or lump of ice and overturned, throwing both occupants out. Mr. Pasco's head struck a tree and he was dragged for some distance, behind the sleigh, before his tight grip on the reins loosened. One shoe was even torn from his foot. Mrs. Pasco, who wore a heavy fur coat, struck on her side in the snow and received no serious injuries except a severe shaking up and slight injury to her left arm which was broken about five years ago.

The horse continued on up the driveway, turned around and was coming back when stopped by Mrs. Pasco.

Dr. C. B. Cunningham happened to be near the scene of the accident and he directed that Mr. Pasco be conveyed on a cot in R. D. Baker's delivery sleigh to his home on upper Main street. Later Dr. J. E. Goodman was summoned and the two physicians worked over the injured man for two hours, but without avail. His skull was fractured causing concussion of the brain. Several of his front teeth were knocked out and a number of internal injuries were found in the region of the chest.

Stephen Pasco was a vigorous man for his age. For a number of years he had not been active in business, simply passing his declining years in the comradeship of his estimable wife in ease and comfort, enjoying the fruits of their labors. He was born in Johnsburgh December 3, 1832, and was therefore past seventy-six years old. He was educated at the Warrensburgh academy and Fort Edward institute and afterwards learned the carpenter's trade. In 1857-8 he was a contractor and builder in Saratoga. In 1864 he returned to Johnsburgh, where he conducted a general store about two years and then removed to Warrensburgh to engage in the same business. With his brother, Walter Pasco, in 1873, he bought of G. T. Lewis the planing mill and sash and blind factory in Lewisville which they conducted successfully and with much profit until 1898. Mr. Pasco was married in Johnsburgh, October 19, 1859, to Miss Mary E. Ferris, of that place. They had two daughters, one of whom died in infancy and the other, Carrie Pasco, at the age of sixteen.

George K. Hawley.

The death of George K. Hawley, one of this city's most respected citizens, occurred yesterday morning at 7 o'clock at his home on Park Place, as the result of an attack of apoplexy on Tuesday night. He was born in Glens Falls March 26, 1836, and would have been 73 years of age the 26th of this month.

The deceased was a son of George G. Hawley, one of the most prominent of the early settlers of Glens Falls. Mr. Hawley, though he was the head of one of the best known families of the city and former village, always lived a quiet life, mingling very little in public affairs. However, aside from performing the duties of the average citizen, he served as an inspector of election for a number of years and before the village was incorporated in 1874 acted as fire warden. After the incorporation he was overseer of the poor for several years

Mr. Hawley was an active member of Christ church and a consistent church worker. During his more active years he was connected with a number of business interests, but of late had been in practical retirement, devoting his energies to the care of his residence property and to matters of minor importance. He was active up to the time of his death. The survivors are two sons, William G. Hawley, of this city, and Frank B. Hawley, of Boston. The arrangements for the funeral have not yet been made.

Lake George Country Club. "Perspective Sketch." Chas. S. Peabody Archt.

NEW HOME OF L. G. CLUB

A SUBSTANTIAL ADDITION TO THE LAKE.

Will Hold Opening Festivites First Week in July. One of the Finest Golf Courses in the Country. To Remain Open the Year 'Round.

The above illustration is from the architect's drawing giving a general view of the proposed club house for the Lake George Club which was organized last summer by the leading cottagers on the lake.

The formation of the club was the crystallization of a sentiment which had its first definite expression in the old Lake George Yacht club located at Basin bay, the buildings of which were burned some years ago. Pessimistic ones have been inclined to point to the rise and fall of this organization as an example of what might reasonably be expected of any similiar institution. But times have changed in the years just passed; and there is everywhere on the lake a growing sentiment for increased social life that finds its highest expression in this new movement under the conservative democratic plans of the founders of the Lake George Club.

The new club grounds will be easy of access, being directly on the state boulevard to Bolton Landing and but a three-minute walk from the Marion dock where all steamers land, and where are post, telegraph and telephone offices.

The leasing of the Marion golf links to complete those planned by the club on its own grounds will give a superb nine-hole course, which will be laid out under the direction of Mr. T. G. Pickering, America's foremost expert in these matters. At a recent visit to the grounds Mr. Pickering pronounced the situation "ideal" and promised that the Lake George Club golf course should be second to none in this section of the country.

Tennis courts will be also be laid out and this sport, which has been so admirably fostered by Manager Krumbholz of the Sagamore, will surely become one of great importance on the lake this season.

The government of the club will be thoroughly representative of the best social element up and down the shores of the lake. To preclude the possibility of the club becoming a close corporation or passing into the control of a clique, the originators devised a plan of maintenance that assures as wide a hospitality as is possible and still maintain the privileges and safeguards of a refined home.

The ownership of the club is represented by "Founders' shares" at $500 each, no person being permitted to own more than three shares. As the shares are not all sold, a number of the founders have pledged themselves to the support of the club for a period of time, at the end of which they feel certain the undertaking will have become self-supporting.

The membership of the club will be drawn not only from the cottagers on the lake, but from visitors who come for short periods. It is expected that arrangements will be made to admit to membership for as short a term as one week. The founders have not completed their plans for the government of the club, but the general thought is to keep dues down to as a low a figure as is possible and assure a sufficient income to keep up the property.

The summer home of the club will be in the Club House now in process of construction as shown on this page. The winter home will be in the Dormitory just north of the Club House which in the summer-time will be used for servants quarters and sleeping rooms for guests.

In the center of the Club House will be the assembly hall, 28x38 ft. The ceiling will be the roof timbering, finished natural, with an height of about 20 feet to the ridgepole. All interior finish will be in natural wood stained to harmonize with the general scheme.

The main Dining Room, 24x34 feet, with a roof timber ceiling, will be situate at the north of the Assembly Hall and at its far end will be an immense fireplace. The two rooms will be connected by a large archway reaching almost to the apex of the ceiling.

A gallery will surround all sides of the two rooms except where the archway connects them. On the lake side, as may be noticed in the illustration, will be numerous loggias affording delightful lounging places and extensive view of the water.

Still farther to the north will be found a Private Dining Room on the lake side, back of which will be the culinary department. The Billiard Room will be situated in the northwest wing of the structure, to the left of the illustration as shown.

Over the Billiard Room will be the men's toilet and locker rooms which will open on to a deck over the piazza. At the other end of the building over the Private Dining Room and kitchen will be found the ladies' toilet and locker rooms having two loggias, one to the east and one to the north.

The exterior of the building will present a bungalow effect in certain schemes of finish. The entire finish will be very rough, boulders supporting the piazza rails, the approach being constructed of rough-hewn stone steps, and the walls in a rough cement, the whole being in complete harmony with the natural surroundings.

The building is so situated that the genius of the architect was able to contrive out of the natural surroundings a Venetian entrance on the water where boats may run in under the east piazza and find anchorage. Here will be found a Cafe with an inside entrance to the Assembly Room. Rough-hewn rock and rustic construction will dominate here where the effect is almost that of a grotto.

The building is L shaped, the angle being formed at the main land entrance on the northwest. Its construction has been let to the firm of Smith & Worden of this village, and such favorable terms have been made by the Founders that they feel that in the completed grounds and structures the club will have a greater value than such an outlay usually represents.

The architect, Mr. Charles S. Peabody, has disposed of the box-like angles of the old Lindon Hall, now the Dormitory, in a very happy fashion. The building has been moved to a site near the lake shore north of the Club House and is pleasantly surrounded by evergreen trees. Its square roof will be replaced by a mansard which will come well down the sides, and broad piazzas will tend to give the structure a bungalow effect. This building will contain twelve sleeping rooms for guests, the top floor being given over to servants' quarters. Under the efficient management of Emil Strand, the caretaker, this building will be open the year 'round, and it is expected that many of the club members will avail themselves of this opportunity to spend portions of the winter months on the lake.

It is planned to locate the garage building on the upper side of the highway so that the guests will be free from the noise and odor of the machines.

To the south and west of the club dock is a perfectly sheltered natural harbor which will afford anchorage for a considerable number of boats. Enough docks will be constructed in this harbor to give the club members ample accommodations for their.

The founders hope for an opening of the building the first week in July and are planning an extensive program for the week.

The Lincolns and Burhans. 2

All that is left of the family of Abraham Lincoln are three persons. None of his children are living, but Robert T., his son. Robert married a daughter of Senator Harlan, of Iowa. He has a daughter Mary, who married Charles Isham. They have one child, a son named Lincoln Isham, born June 8, 1902. Charles Isham was the son of William B. Isham, of New York, and Julia Burhans, daughter of the late Colonel B. P. Burhans, of Warrensburg. The Ishams are well known in this village.—Warrensburg News.

1908
DR. C. I. FARLEY. Feb. 25

Dr. Charles I. Farley died Monday evening at his home in Glens Falls. He was seventy-seven years old Monday, his birthday. He was formerly a resident of Bolton, and he resided in Glens Falls about fourteen months. Dr. Farley had practiced medicine in Sandy Hill, Fort Edward, Bolton and in the West. He was an assistant surgeon in the army. He was a member of the Odd Fellows' lodge, in Bolton, and of the Ancient Order of United Workmen, Fort Edward.

SUNDAY AFTERNOON.

(Original verses by a Japanese who recently located in Glens Falls.)

There's not a Sunday afternoon
But finds him stepping down
Just at the corner, when the car
Comes jingling out from town;
And nudging, nodding, whispering,
The gossips watch him go
To knock once more at her dear door—
It is Belinda's Beau.

"He's on the way, he's on the way;"
Her heart begins to beat
At eager footsteps hurrying
Along the frozen street;
"He's here, he's here!" it sings for joy
At sight of him and lo,
For all it's winter roses bloom
To greet Belinda's Beau.

If it should chance the weather's fine
Beneath her dimpled chin
Her bonnet hides a monstrous muff
She slips her fingers in;
To tread with him her well-worn path
Across the sparkling snow,
That lake into a fairyland
Belinda and her Beau.

Then home they turn when early dusk
Creeps on, a starlit haze,
To stir the embers on the hearth
Into a fitful blaze;
While very near, although apart,
Before the ruddy glow
They sit, in secret silence—
Belinda and her Beau.

O, trembling, timid, happy time,
When love that dyes the cheek
And shines in sorry stolen glance,
Still hesitates to speak; ;
They part without a word, and yet
Without a word they know,
Next Sunday when it comes around
Will bring Belinda's Beau!
TOSUO TAKAHASHI.

WHAT ONE HOTEL DID.

The Sagamore Gives $41.28 to Troy Times Fresh Air Fund.

Times Oct 1/1909.

T. Edmund Krumbholz, manager of the Sagamore at Sagamore-on-Lake George, sends to the Troy Times fresh air fund $31.28, being the amount of collections from the box at the hotel for the benefit of the fund. When it is remembered that $10 had been previously received as the proceeds of an entertainment given by the little folks at the hotel and that Mr. Krumbholz donated a very large part of the dishes used at the fresh air home at Grafton, it will be seen that the Sagamore and its management have at heart the interests of the children and of the fund which helps them so usefully.—Troy Times.

J. D. CASEY HAS BACK BROKEN BY DERRICK

Post *Star* Sept 16 1909.

CONTRACTOR, WELL KNOWN IN THIS CITY, MEETS WITH FATAL ACCIDENT.

Little Falls, Sept. 15.—James D. Casey of the firm of Casey and Murray, barge canal contractors was struck down and his back broken by a derrick loaded with stone. He was standing beside a driller, Fred Laundry, whose right hand was smashed off and leg crushed and broken. A load of stone was being hoisted by the derrick from the stone pit at the mile lock. It swung up over the drill and the derrick brake slipped, letting the half ton of stone in the scoop descend on the two men. Laundry's hand was caught on top the drill and the scoop landed on Casey's head. Casey was thrown against a rock and the scoop swung against his breast and held there, resting partly on Casey and partly on the drill. The Italians swarmed up out of the pit screaming. Somebody gave the signal to "hoist." and the car was lifted, but dumped the stone, some hitting Laundry's leg. Mr. Casey is sixty-three years old. His case is hopeless.

Mr. Casey was a member of the contracting firm which built the Glens Falls-Lake George State road, and was well known in this city.

LAKE GEORGE CLUB BUILDING IN ASHES

Times Oct 30 1909.

Fire which caused a loss of about $14,000 destroyed one of the buildings of the Lake George Country club at Hill View late yesterday afternoon. The building was an immense four story structure, was formerly a part of the Marion Hotel property and was commonly referred to as the Linden or Marion farm house.

The origin of the fire is a mystery. There was a fire in the furnace, another in a fire place. A brush fire was burning near the building and it is thought that a spark probably set fire to the building. Neighbors for miles around came to the rescue, but the flames had gotten under such headway that it was impossible to save the structure.

Insurance of $10,000 was carried through the agency of Little & Loomis

FALLS DAILY TI

10 THOUSAND READY TO VOTE IN WARREN CO.

Oct 29 1909.

Nearly ten thousand voters are registered for the coming election in Warren county. County Clerk Sisson today compiled the registration totals from the city of Glens Falls and all the towns of the county and the total for the county, as officially anounced, is 9,735. This figure shows a falling off of about 400 from last year, but as 1908 was a presidential year this would be expected. The vote this year will be heavy for an election on local issues only.

The figures for the several towns and election districts are given below:

Bolton—553.
Caldwell—650.
Chester—First district, 284; second district, 354.
City of Glens Falls—First ward, 690; second ward, 745; third ward, first district, 565; second district, 411; fourth ward, 512; fifth ward, 617.
Hague—336.
Horicon—396.
Johnsburg—First district, 293; second district, 347; third district, 241.
Luzerne—448.
Queensbury—First district, 156; second, 186; third, 303; fourth, 201.
Stony Creek—313.
Thurman—289.
Warrensburg—First district, 449; second district, 396.

Basing his figures on the registration, the county clerk has ordered 14,725 ballots and 3,669 sample ballots.

The Chestnut Horse

There is an ancient tale of a band of Arabs being pursued by their enemies which sums up their theory about a horse's color. Among the fleeing band was a man with unusually keen eyesight, and from time to time he would describe to his leader the horses ridden by the enemy.

"What manner of horses do they ride?"
"Black horses."
"Then there is no need of haste."
At the noon halt the leader again asked, "What manner of horses do they ride now?"
"Bay horses."
"Then we must ride harder."
A few hours later the leader asked, "Are they horsed again?"
"They ride chestnuts."
Then, we ride for our lives.

CAR LEAVES ROAD 1 OCCUPANT HURT

Post *Star* Sept 18 1909

SERIOUS ACCIDENT JUST AVERTED AT HALFWAY BROOK LAST EVENING.

That four persons did not meet serious injury last evening in an auto accident which occurred at Halfway Brook is due to mere luck. About 10 o'clock a car driven by Ralph Gates of Hill View and containing three other passengers—two young ladies and a youth, ran over the embankment on the west side of the northern approach to the bridge which spans the Halfway Brook. The lights on the machine were burning low and in attempting to allow an automobile which was approaching from the rear to pass, Mr. Gates turned out a little too far, the dirt embankment at the end of the cement wall gave way, and the car crashed into the guard rail tearing it away and landing on its side in the ditch.

All four occupants of the car were carried over the embankment and with the exception of one young lady, who was slightly injured, all escaped without a bruise. Mr. Gates did his best to prevent the accident and stuck to the wheel being pinioned between that and a post against which the machine struck preventing it from turning entirely over. At the time of the accident the machine was running at a low rate of speed and would undoubtedly not have gone over the embankment had not the dirt given away.

The machine which is a Stoddard-Dayton, owned by D. Brereton of Bolton, is apparently but little injured and will be taken from the brook this morning.

THE ROAD TO SUCCESS.

The struggle is hard and work hours long,
But the goal I would reach is high.
I must count my crosses as stepping-stones,
On the road to success they lie.
And success isn't reached in a day or a year,
The journey is far and long;
The road is rough, and few understand,
I must go the way others have gone.

Columbus' own sailors near threw him o'er
Ere they caught the sight of his land:
John Morley wrote every day for a year
Ere was printed a thing from his hand;
And many a man has almost despaired
Before he has reached his goal:
As men, indeed, we count the few
Who have climbed to success' fold.
ELSIE D. CORNELL.

Trenton, N. J., Sept. 13, 1909.

Bolton Landing, Nov. 10.—Mrs. Jay Taylor and son, Alexander, have returned home from a visit with relatives in Albany.

Mr. and Mrs. E. N. Lamb entertained Mr. and Mrs. Ralph Brown of Warrensburg Sunday.

Mrs. Minerva Burgess has purchased Henry Menill's place on School street, consideration $2,000.

Little Miss Helen Ross is the proud possessor of a new piano.

Jay Taylor is convalescing from an attack of the grip.

Miss Charlotte Norton visited Mr. and Mrs. Will Dayo of Glens Falls from Saturday until Tuesday.

Mrs. Philetus Corporon visited Mr. and Mrs. Robert Cardle of Warrensburg last week.

A daughter was born to Mr. and Mrs. Victor Dickinson Sunday, November 7.

Among those who left for New York yesterday on the excursion trip are Mr. and Mrs. J. L. Maranville, Mr. and Mrs. David Fosmer, George Fish and Johnathan Gates.

Henry Knoblauch's new store on Main street is nearly ready for occupancy. The Bolton Supply company of which Mr. Knoblauch is a member, expects to move their goods from their store on the Sagamore road into their new quarters this week. _1909._

Woodman, Spare That Tree.

(By George P. Morris.)

Woodman, spare that tree!
  Touch not a single bough!
In youth it sheltered me,
  And I'll protect it now.
'T was my forefather's hand
  That placed it near his cot;
There, woodman, let it stand—
  Thy ax shall harm it not!

That old familiar tree,
  Whose glory and renown
Are spread o'er land and sea—
  And wouldst thou hew it down?
Woodman, forbear thy stroke!
  Cut not its earth-bound ties;
Oh, spare that aged oak,
  Now towering to the skies!

When but an idle boy,
  I sought its grateful shade;
In all their gushing joy
  Here, too, my sisters played.
My mother kissed me here;
  My father pressed my hand—
Forgive this foolish tear,
  But let that old oak stand!

My heart-strings round thee cling
  Close as thy bark, old friend!
Here shall the wild-bird sing,
  And still thy branches bend.
Old tree! the storm still brave!
  And, woodman, leave the spot;
While I've a hand to save,
  Thy ax shall harm it not!

Oct 28 1909

A Friend of Labor

Times,

In the list of nominees on the Republican county ticket there is no candidate more worthy of support than Truxton P. Braley, the candidate for sheriff. Mr. Braley is one of Bolton's solid citizens. He has lived in the lake shore town all his life through his boyhood, his school days, his young manhood and his maturity, up to his present age of 52 years. He has always had the confidence and trust of his fellow townsmen, in all matters public and private.

The only public office Mr. Braley has ever held was that of highway commissioner of the town of Bolton, to which he was elected three successive times, serving six years. His last term expired three years ago. In this office he made a record for honesty and efficiency which showed his standard of public life, namely that a public officer should serve the people of the county, working for their interests and for the proper conduct of his office.

For several years Mr. Braley has been a road contractor and landscape gardener. He also owns several cottages on Lake George. In various capacities he has had something to do with improvements to nearly all the properties on the Bolton road.

Mr. Braley has been an employer of labor extensively since he has been in the contracting business. He was the first employer in Bolton to grant a nine-hour day and the first to raise the wages of common laborers from $1.50 to $1.75 a day. He has always been popular with the men in his employ and with workmen generally in his home town.

Mr. Braley asks for election upon his record as a private citizen and a public official. He conceals nothing. He promises to administer the office of sheriff faithfully and well and for the best interests of the county. He will command a heavy vote.

FISH-PALMER.

Charles E. Fish, of Bolton, and Miss Cornelia Palmer, of Glens Falls, were married in that city December 23, at Christ church parsonage, by the Rev. C. O. Judkins.

HON. LYMAN JENKINS

new _Nov 25 1909_

Appointed County Judge and Surrogate by Governor Hughes.

Lyman Jenkins, senior member of the law firm of Jenkins, Kellogg & Barker, Glens Falls, was Saturday appointed county judge and surrogate by Governor Hughes to succeed the late William L. Kiley. Judge Jenkins was ill in bed when he received the announcement of his appointment to the office for which about every Republican lawyer in Glens Falls was an avowed candidate.

Judge Jenkins will serve until December 31, 1910. Judge Kiley's term would not have expired until two years from that date. A nomination will be made next fall for the regular term of six years. Judge Jenkins was born in Queensbury and has always been a resident of that town. He was district attorney for three terms and in 1901 was elected county judge, succeeding Judge Cheritree. Three years ago he was a candidate for renomination when William L. Kiley was nominated at the Republican county convention. He ran on an independent ticket, but was defeated by the late William L. Kiley in a three-cornered contest, Louis M. Brown being the Democratic nominee.

Judge Jenkins assumed office Monday, presiding over a term of surrogate's court. Only one matter was transacted—the issuance of a letter of administration to Samuel Turner in the estate of Clarence E. Turner, late of Johnsburgh.

In taking possession of the surrogate's chambers, one of the first official acts by the judge was to reappoint Daniel S. Cheritree clerk.

Judge Jenkins states that he will not sever his connection with the firm of Jenkins, Kellogg & Barker.

The Vanadis, one of the most valuable steam yachts on Lake George, and owned by George O. Knapp of Chicago, was destroyed by fire Friday night. The boat burned to the water's edge, while tied to the dock at Shelving Rock. The cause of the fire is a mystery, but the flames doubtless started from the boiler. The boat had made a trip Thursday evening and when left at the dock was carefully inspected by the captain and engineer. During the night the fireman and another employe of Mr. Knapp, who occupy a cottage near the lake shore, were aroused by the sound of escaping steam. They quickly dressed and found the Vanadis enveloped in flames. The men were powerless to stay the fire and the craft was completely destroyed. The boat was insured for $3,200 through the agency of Little & Loomis, Glens Falls. The Vanadis was built in 1897 by C. _Ig Bates_, of this village, at an original cost of $6,000. She had since been improved and kept in perfect repair. The yacht was of sixty foot beam. _new M/S_

FIX TAX RATE FOR THE ELEVEN TOWNS

The Board of Supervisors, in session yesterday at the armory, prepared the following tax rate for the eleven town of the county:

Bolton .027.

Caldwell, .022 in Lake George village; .024 in the rest of the town.

Chester .040.

Hague, .028.

Horicon, .030.

Johnsburg, .030.

Luzerne, .029.

Queensbury, .033.

Stony Creek, .050.

Thurman, .028.

Warrensburg, .023 in lighting district; .019 outside of lighting district.

Post Star Dec 15 1909

Supervisor Bain offered a resolution to the effect that the chairman appoint a committee of two relative to furnishing an office for the county treasurer.

The towns of Hague and Luzerne, through a clerical error, were taxed $71.87 and $53.70, respectively, more than was their proportionate share, and resolutions were offered by Supervisors Bolton and Hartman directing the county treasurer to pay the supervisors of the above towns the said amount in each case.

These resolutions are expected to be adopted at today's session. The members of the board expect to finish their work Thursday.

Her Thanksgiving.

Oh, have you got the turkey picked,
And is the oven hot
And ready for the pumpkin pies?
I'll have to bake a lot,
And currant cakes and ginger snaps,
Of each a heaping tray.
Our boys and girls are coming home
To spend Thanksgiving day.

I'll make some sugar cookies too.
They used to like them so
When they were little toddling things.
It seems so long ago!
And apple tarts for daughter Jane
With eyes of tender gray.
She's bringing both her babies home
To spend Thanksgiving day.

I rose before the peep of dawn,
I had so much to do,
But never have I felt so spry,
Though I am sixty-two.
To cook and bake and boil and brew
Seems only just like play
With all the dear ones coming home
To spend Thanksgiving day.

I thank the Lord who gives to us
The sunshine and the rain
That here in one unbroken band
I see them once again—
Our children and their children, too,
All hastening to obey
The voice of love that calls them home
To spend Thanksgiving day.

—Minna Irving.

Joseph H. Gates

Post Star   Jan 12. 1910

Joseph H. Gates, an old and highly respected resident of Bolton died yesterday afternoon at 4 o'clock in the sixty-fifth year of his age. Besides his widow, the deceased is survived by one daughter, Mrs. Ralph Stone, of Warrensburg; three brothers, Jonathan S. Gates, Dodge S. Gates and George S. Gates, of Bolton; two nieces Mrs. C.B. Taylor of Bolton and Miss Mary O. Beswick of Utica. The funeral will be held tomorrow morning at 10 o'clock.

BOLTON.

Times   Dec 23

Bolton. Dec. 22—Anson Sylvester Palmer was born May 2, 1853, at Warrensburg, and died at Bolton, December 15, 1909, aged fifty-six years. Mr. Palmer had always been a resident of Bolton and was well known here. His last sickness was for only a few days and death resulted from pneumonia and other complications. He was living with his nephew, Mr. James Palmer, when taken sick. The funeral services were held at the Free Methodist church at Bolton on December 17, at 2 p. m., by the pastor, C. E. Hudson. Burial at Bolton cemetery. *1909*

BRALEY COTTAGE DAMAGED BY FIRE AT BOLTON FRIDAY

Star Jan 1910

A cottage owned and occupied by T. P. Braley and family, at Bolton caught fire Friday morning, and but for its early discovery and the hard work of the occupants would have resulted in not only the loss of the building but of two adjoining cottages as well. The loss is estimated at about $150.

OBITUARY.

News   Jan 6

HORACE STEWART. *1910*

Horace Stewart, aged about seventy-seven years, died at his home at Bolton Landing about 8 o'clock on Wednesday evening of last week of a paralytic stroke. Mr. Stewart had been an invalid for the past two years, but was able to be around the house as usual until a short time before his death. He was born in Bolton and had spent his entire life there, having for over forty years been proprietor of the Stewart house. Mr. Stewart's wife died last spring. He is survived by one son Fred, and by three daughters, Mrs. Amy Barber, Mrs. Howard Walker and Mrs. Nelson Ormsby, all of Bolton, also by one sister, Mrs. Sarah Tuttle, and one brother, who resides in the West. The funeral was held Saturday. Interment in the Huddle cemetery.

HYMENEAL.

News   Jan 6 1910.

BROWN-TABER.

Truman C. Brown and Mrs. Matilda M. Taber, both of this village, were married at the Methodist Episcopal church Sunday afternoon at 4 o'clock. Although no invitations were issued about thirty relatives and friends were present. In the absence of the pastor, Rev. E. J. Guernsey, the ceremony was performed by the Rev. Joel Hall, of Sandy Hill. A singular fact in this connection is that Mr. Hall more than fifty years ago, in Bolton, his first charge, performed his first marriage ceremony and Mr. Brown was the bridegroom. After all these years he happened to be in Warrensburgh Sunday just in time to start Mr. Brown upon a second matrimonial voyage.

LAKE GEORGE.

Times   Jan 24 1910

Lake George. Jan. 17.—The funeral of Bolton Landing's venerable townsman, Horace Stewart, took place at 2 o'clock Saturday afternoon, Jan. 1, from his late residence. The Rev. William H. Lakin, of the Baptist church, officiated. And during the course of his remarks alluded to the noble qualities of Mr. Stewart's character, mentioning particularly his sterling integrity, his untarnishable reputation through a long career. Mr. Lakin also mentioned the beautiful home life of Mr. Stewart, who was a kind and loving husband and father. The floral contributions which were received at the Stewart homestead were many and beautiful. Among the many was a large pillow of flowers from the family, a beautiful bunch of calla lillies, carnations and many others, showing the esteem in which the deceased was held by his townsmen. Mr. Stewart had been a life long resident of Bolton Landing, was married and lived over fifty years in the house in which he died. He was about seventy-six years of age and had been in failing health for some time, nevertheless his death came as a shock to the entire village. He was loved and respected by a large circle of friends and acquaintances. He leaves 4 children to mourn his loss, one son, Fred Stewart, and three daughters, Mrs. Haward Walker, Mrs. Nelson Ormsby, Mrs. Annie Barbour, all of Bolton Landing. His loss will be keenly felt by his young grandson, Stewart Barbour. Stewart's father died four days before his birth. He was born in the home of his grandfather and had always lived with him. Their affection for each other was very deep. He with the rest of the bereaved ones has the deepest sympathy of a host of friends.

WEST BOLTON.

Fred Pratt has moved on to the Stephen Cilley farm.

Stewart Fuller has sold his farm in Johnsburgh to Henry Washburn.

Clarence Putney lost a horse Sunday morning. The animal bled to death.

Lewis Washburn, of Johnsburgh was a guest at Stewart Fuller's night last week.

Orlin Pratt, who moved to Warrensburgh a few years ago, has moved back on his farm on Lamb hill.

OBITUARY.

JAMES A. LAMB.

James A. Lamb, of Bolton, died of pneumonia Thursday at the home of his daughter, Mrs. Thomas Duell. He was seventy-three years of age and is survived by one brother, Charles Lamb, who lives at the soldiers' home, in Bath, and by three sons and four daughters—Alonzo, of Los Angeles, Cal.; Myron and Perry, of Bolton; Mrs. William Taylor, Mrs. Thomas Duell and Mrs. Joseph Morehouse, of Bolton, and Mrs. Nathan J. Kenyon, of Warrensburgh. The funeral was held Saturday, at 11 a. m., from the Methodist Episcopal church of Bolton. Interment in Warrensburgh cemetery.

JOSEPH H. GATES.

Joseph H. Gates, aged sixty-five years, died at his home in Bolton yesterday afternoon at 4 o'clock. He leaves a widow and one daughter, Mrs. Ralph Stone, of this village. He is also survived by three brothers, Jonathan S. Gates, Dodge S. Gates and George S. Gates, of Bolton, and two nieces, Mrs. C. B. Taylor, of Bolton, and Miss Mary O. Beswick, of Utica. The deceased was a life-long resident of Bolton and one of the most prominent and highly respected citizens of the town. The funeral will be held from his late home tomorrow morning at 10 o'clock. 1913

MRS. ABIGAIL HERRICK.

Mrs. Abigail Herrick, widow of Hines Herrick, died Friday night after a brief illness of pneumonia and Bright's disease, at the home of her daughter, Mrs. Edwin Osborne, with whom she resided. She was born at Lake George, June 22, 1823, and was therefore eighty-six years old. She had lived in Warrensburgh more than sixty years. Mrs. Osborne is the only surviving child. One brother also survives, John Ainsworth, of South Warrensburgh. The funeral was held at the Church of the Holy Cross Sunday afternoon at 3 o'clock, the Rev. G. H. Purdy officiating. 1910

New Boy at South Bolton.

A son was born to Mr. and Mrs. Clifton Dudley, of South Bolton, Friday. Mrs. Dudley was formerly Miss Anna Gates and is a daughter of Mr. and Mrs. Dodge S. Gates. 1910

To Make Invisible Ink.

To the Editor of "The Press."

Sir:—In reply to "Curious" for invisible ink, a solution of chloride of cobalt will answer the purpose. About one dram of the salt to one ounce of distilled water.

GEORGE W. SISSON LEADER IN LUMBER

NATIVE OF GLENS FALLS, BIG MAN IN THE TRADE.

AN INTERESTING WRITE UP

The American Lumberman, a Journal Devoted to the Trade, Gives Sketch of Glens Falls Man and Tells of Successful Business Career.

The American Lumberman, a periodical which its names signifies, is devoted to the lumbering interests, recently "wrote up" George W. Sisson of Potsdam, a former Glens Falls man, who is now one of the most prominent figures in the lumber world.

Mr. Sisson was born in Glens Falls, December 19, 1828, a son of James Sisson, one of the earliest merchants of the town, his ancestors on his father's side being descendants of Richard Warren and Frances Cook, who came to America on the Mayflower. Ancestors on his mother's side were members and strong supporters of the First Society of Friends or Quakers organized in America, that at Sandwich, Mass., in 1656.

GLENS FALLS HORSE MAKES ICE RECORD

Glens Falls, famous in former years for its fast horses, is coming to the front again and City Assessor G. Frank Bryant's Bell Ringer is turning the trick. At the races on Lake George yesterday afternoon this horse which has gained quite a reputation locally in the past few years, covered a mile in the fast time of 2:09 1-4, which breaks the world's record for ice races.

This new record was established in the named race for a purse of $100. The local horse easily won all three heats, while the second place was won by M. B. Leland's Dorothy Dix, with George R. Russell's Woodhaul, third.

The races were witnessed by a large and enthusiastic crowd of horsemen.

In the named race for a $25 purse three heats were trotted and the race was postponed until this afternoon.

A. M. FARRINGTON

Well Known Commercial Traveler Who Died Suddenly Sunday.

A. M. Farrington, of Whitehall, died very suddenly Sunday morning about 3 o'clock, having been ill but a few hours. Mr. Farrington was in his usual good health up to Saturday evening, when he was taken with an attack of acute indigestion. A physician was called and relieved him of this attack, but about 3 o'clock Sunday morning he had a sinking spell and passed away after a very few minutes. Mr. Farrington was a resident of Whitehall nearly all his life and for a number of years was engaged in the grocery and crockery business in that town and was very successful, but for a number of years has been on the road in the employ of W. E. Malloy & Company, a grocery and provision house, and was well known in Washington and Warren counties and for miles around. Mr. Farrington was a large man, weighing fully 250 pounds and appeared to be a very robust and hardy man, and one that would be able to stand a hard sickness, and his sudden taking away has caused his family and many friends a severe shock. He leaves a widow, one son and two daughters.

"The Indian's Grave."

To the Editor of "The Press."

Sir:—Inclosed find the poem "The Indian's Grave," by John Russell Hayes.

READER.

Philadelphia, September 14, 1909.

Last of her race, she sleeps in this lone grave—
Lowly and lone, and dim and half-forgot
In these last hundred Summers since she died;
Last of her race—laid here so long ago
And gently mourned by folk of alien stock.
But not of alien hearts, kind Quaker folk
Who cherished the lone Indian, cared for her,
And made her loneliness less sorrowful
Till life went out.

    And so went out a race
That through uncounted cycles had their home
Beside Wawassan's wild and wandering stream,
Tracking the bear and moose among these hills
And taking fish in those rude stone-built dams
That still remain in old Wawassan's stream,
And celebrating round their flickering fires
Strange pagan rite and solemn dance of war—
So long and long ago!—ere yet our sires
Forced Magna Charta on reluctant John
Or yielded unto Alfred's kindly law,
Yea, even ere they stormed the eastern shores
Of Britain, rovers on the wild North Sea—
So long ago this old Algonquin folk
Hunted and warred and worshiped 'mid the woods
That hid these hills in endless greenery.

What tribal memories survived in her,
That last lone Indian woman—what remote
And pale tradition from the ancient years,
Of sylvan loves and wars, heroic deeds
Of deathless chieftains, wisdom of the gods?

I think some primal feeling surely stirred
At times that lonely heart brooding the past,
When, in gray Autumn twilights by her fire
She mused and mourned, recalling how in youth
She heard the old men grieve, old women weep
O'er territory wrested from their tribe
By the intruding English. Hopelessly.
They grieved and wept—she could not understand
The great All-Father's will, she only knew
How numbers lessened, how the forest fell
And spoiled the hunting, how the fishing failed,
And how as farmland after farmland spread
Along Wawassan's shores her people waned
In ancient power and comfort.

    'Tis but little
We do, in honoring her name to-day,
Toward offering penance for he pitiless force
Exerted by our sires against her race.
To-day, among these grand old Indian hills
And by this wild and wandering Indian stream,
In reverence and sorrow let us rear
This strong, rude boulder o'er the Indian's grave—
We of the alien English paying thus
Some tribute small of honor and remorse.
Unto the noble natives of these hills
By Indian Wawassan's mourning stream.

BANKING DEVICE INVENTED BY JNO. E. PARRY AND SON

Post Star Feb, 9

APPARATUS IS SIMPLE IN CONSTRUCTION BUT GREAT TIME SAVER

1910

John E. Parry, cashier of the Glens Falls National Bank, and his son, Elliott J. Parry, through their combined efforts have invented a time computer, which is very simple in construction but will not doubt revolutionize banking methods, as to the manner of computing the number of days between stated dates, the time on notes and interest days on all money transactions. The apparatus is operated by turning a dial which mechanically and accurately gives the number of days sought in one-tenth the time that the result may be secured by the old fashioned way of figuring it out.

The apparatus consists of two circular pieces of cardboard. One is a little smaller and is suspended on a pivot above the other. The months of the year are printed in order around the edge of the smaller cardboard and 365 equally distant bisecting lines cross both pieces of cardboard toward the center.

Although the apparatus is inexpensive, the cost of the material of which it is constructed costing less than a dollar, it is very practical and a great time saver.

Mr. Parry has not yet applied for a patent, nor has he mentioned his intention of so doing, but if he does, his friends say he will realze a large sum for his trouble.

"The Poor Old Slave."

To the Editor of "The Press."

Sir:—A request has been made for this old song, one that was issued in the later 50s and even at this day the music for it can be purchased.

A. H. WAY.

Wilmington, Del., Dec. 16, 1909.

'Tis just one year ago to-day,
    That I remember well.
I sat down by poor Nelly's side,
    A story she did tell;
'Twas about a poor, unhappy slave,
    That lived for many a year,
But now he's dead and in his grave,
    No master does he fear.

CHORUS.

The poor old slave has gone to rest,
    We know that he is free;
Disturb him not, but let him rest,
    Way down in Tennessee.

She took my arm, we walked along
    Into an open field,
And then she paused to breathe awhile,
    Then to his grave did steal.
She sat down by that little mound
    And softly whispered there,
"Come to me, father, 'tis thy child!"
    Then gently dropped a tear.

But since that time how things have changed,
    Poor Nelly, that was my bride,
Is laid beneath the cold grave's sod,
    With her father by her side.
I planted there upon her grave
    The weeping-willow tree,
I bathed its roots with many a tear,
    That it might shelter me.

BOY FOUND IN SNOW AND MAY NOT RALLY

G. F. Times Feb 7

HAROLD ELDRIDGE OF WARRENSBURG THE VICTIM. *1910*

LAD OVERCOME BY FEVER

Found Lying in Snow Near Woods Back of Russell Place at the Burg, Unconscious and Suffering From Fever and Spinal Meningitis.

Harold Eldridge, a sixteen-year-old boy, lies at his home in Warrensburg in a critical condition, and it is feared that he will not recover. On Saturday afternoon he was found by John Burt lying in the snow near the woods back of the Russell place in Warrensburg. A gun was at his side and as he was unable to speak it was believed that he had accidentally shot himself. However, an examination revealed that the boy had been overcome by brain fever and spinal meningitis.

Mr. Burt carried the boy out to the highway where he secured help in taking him home. Dr. Cunningham was then summoned.

The condition of the boy this morning had not improved and owing to exposure to the weather which might have been several hours before he was found, it is believed that he will not recover.

LEVI PRATT.

Levi Pratt died Thursday night at his home on Lamb hill, Bolton, in the eightieth year of his age. He is survived by a widow, five sons and three daughters—Orlen, Bert, Judd and Fred Pratt, of Bolton, and Dennis, of Knowelhurst; Mrs. Clarence Putney, of Bolton; Mrs. William Ainsworth, of Warrensburgh, and Mrs. Ruth Hill, of Caldwell. The funeral was held Tuesday at the Lamb schoolhouse, at 2 p.m., the pastor of the Bolton Landing Baptist church officiating. Interment in Green cemetery.

COURTNEY S. COLLINS.

Courtney S. Collins, a native of the town of Chester, died Friday afternoon at his home in Glens Falls, aged seventy years. He was a former sheriff of Warren county and during his term of office for three years resided at Lake George. After his term of office expired he removed to Glens Falls, where he conducted the Collins boarding house.

O-24-3 1910

Here in Glens Falls where General Daniel E. Sickles is remembered as a former townsman there will be general approval of the plan to retire the war hero with the rank and pay of lieutenant general.

General Sickles, who is now 85 years of age and who spent his youth in Glens Falls, was admitted to the bar in 1846. He was a member of assembly, his first elective office, in 1847, sixty-three years ago.

He continued in public service as corporation attorney of New York, secretary of legation in London; state senator and four years as representative in congress before the beginning of the war between the states.

Upon the outbreak of hostilities General Sickles went to the front as a colonel and following gallant conduct at Fredericksburg he was brevetted brigadier general. He lost a leg at Gettysburg.

After the war General Sickles served as minister to Spain, sheriff of New York county and an additional term as member of congress. Since April 14, 1869, he has been on the retired list of the regular army with the rank of major general.

MRS. JOHN H. ORMSBY

Mrs. John H. Ormsby, of Bolton Landing, died Tuesday morning, aged sixty-two years. She had been in poor health for about a year. Deceased is survived by her husband and seven children—Lindsey, of Warrensburgh; Bernard, of Minnesota; Theodore, Edward, Nelson, Mrs. Benjamin Baker and Miss Nina Ormsby, of Bolton. The funeral will be held this afternoon, at 2 o'clock, from the late home, Rev. W. S. Warren, pastor of the Warrensburgh Baptist church, officiating. Interment in Huddle cemetery.

MISS LOUISE CROSBY.

Miss Louise Crosby, a former well-known resident of Lake George, died Tuesday at Winona, Minn., where she had resided for a number of years with her sister, Mrs. William H. Wyman, who is the only surviving relative. The remains will be brought to Lake George for interment in the family plot in the village cemetery. The deceased was a daughter of the late Francis G. Crosby, who founded and for many years successfully conducted the Crosbyside hotel, at the head of Lake George. *1910*

PROMINENT RESIDENT OF SANDY HILL CALLED TO THE WORLD BEYOND

Post Star ———————— *Feb 24/1918*

Eber Richards of Sandy Hill Answers Final Summons---Was One of the Pioneer Lumber Dealers of This Section of the State and a Man Respected by all Who Knew Him---

At 4 o'clock yesterday morning, at his home in Sandy Hill, occurred the death of Eber Richards, aged 73 years, one of the pioneer lumbermen of this section of the State, and a man respected and looked up to by all who enjoyed the pleasure of his acquaintance.

Born May 6, '36.

Summer Resident

For many years he was one of the best known summer residents of Lake George. He was the pioneer cottage

Eber Richards

owner at the now flourishing colony of Pilot Knob and "Commodore" Richards has given pleasure to more people in his yacht "Theta' than any other private yacht owner on the lake.

In Surrogate's Court. *1910*

Hon. Lyman Jenkins, county surrogate, at his chambers in Glens Falls Monday, admitted to probate the will of Joseph H. Gates, late of Bolton, and issued letters testamentary to Mary J. Gates.

TO QUIT GLEN STREET AFTER THIRTY YEARS

Times — Feb 19 1910.

After being located on Glen street for thirty years, the Kendrick & Brown Company is today moving to its new building on Lawrence street, near the Delaware & Hudson station. The present store will be vacated in about two weeks and will be leased to some other concern. The company is one of the oldest established in Glens Falls and has probably occupied one location longer than any other firm in the city.

The business was organized in 1880 by Samuel D. Kendrick, at present president of the company. A three story building, which it now occupies, was built at the corner of Glen and Berry streets and a mill was constructed in the rear of this store on Berry street. The plant was destroyed by fire sixteen years ago and later the company built a plant on Lawrence street.

The company's new building adjoins its plant and with the removal of the store and office the entire business of the company is practically under one roof. It is a modern brick structure or mill construction and is one of the best buildings of its kind in the city.

Lake George Printing Company.

The Lake George Printing company, of Lake George, was incorporated Friday to publish the Lake George Mirror. The capital is $5,000 and the directors are George Foster Peabody, Edwin J. Worden and D. S. Sanford, of Lake George. The other members of the company are George Knapp, of New York; Edward M. Shepherd, of Brooklyn; W. K. Bixby, of St. Louis; John Boulton Simpson, of New York; H. E. H. Brereton, of Hill View; LeGrand C. Cramer, of Troy, and Joseph Marvel, of Atlantic City. The management of the paper, with Edward A. Knight as editor, will remain the same, but there will be increased efforts to promote Lake George as a summer resort. *News Mar 3 1918*

Star Mar 10

Cooper Union Custodian Dead.

NEW YORK, March 9.—James Maginn, for forty-five years the custodian of Cooper Union, is dead. In the discharge of his duties he met many prominent persons, notably Abraham Lincoln, Dean Stanley, Ferdinand de Lesseps, Professor John Tyndall, Emperor Dom Pedro and Governor Leland Stanford. *1918-*

Benjamin Frank Lapham

By the death of Mr. Lapham Glens Falls loses one of her oldest and most respected citizens. *1910*

He was the oldest son of Jonathan and Elizabeth S. Lapham and was born on September 11, 1822, on the Lapham farm, now known as the Grant Haviland farm in the town of Queensbury.

When he was ten years old his parents removed to Glens Falls and he had since continuously resided here and for about sixty years in the dwelling on Ridge street.

His love for Lake George was proverbial, and for many years he had been president of the Glen Club and was the only survivor of the charter membership, which included the names of Orange Ferris, F. A. Johnson, William McEchron, Jerome Lapham, J. C. Clark and others prominently identified with the business growth of Glens Falls.

Memorial to Spencer Trask from the Saratogian Feb 5, 1910

HON. SPENCER TRASK

"Of his earnest efforts toward the increase of all influences for good which exist in this community, Saratoga Springs is gratefully aware."

Spencer Trask

*Killed in a Railway Accident
December 31, 1909
While on the Business of the
Saratoga Reservation Commission.*

SPENCER TRASK.

Stunned into silence is the clanging mart,
A hush falls on the templed place of art;
While church and state and many a lowly
    heart
Mourn for this hero of our later days—
Too simple for the laureled crown of praise.
Earth weeps for manhood's ripened flower,
The swift extinguishment of crescent power;
For him, loved of the gods, forever young,
From old titanic Norsemen fitly sprung—
From Vikings in the mighty sagas sung.

Large were his aims. Quickly the golden
    thought
Into a jeweled deed was wisely wrought.
Young workers in their summer homes of
    rest,
And stricken children rose and called him
    blest.
The loving servitor, the happy guest—
And from his presence drew the tonic cheer
Of a deep spring with waters ever clear.

Sad his wide domain among the hills,
His Yaddo pine to lonelier music thrills;
But sadder yet his islands on the Lake,
Where Art and Nature wedded for Love's
    sake.
When the long chains of light at twilight's
    gloom
Shall flush as rosy garlands into bloom,
And from his belfry chime the soft-toned
    bell—
Poignant the lingering echoes of farewell.
    —Ada Foster Murray, in the New
York Times.

BIGGEST TROUT EVER COUGHT IN L. GEORGE

Richard O'Brien of this city, while fishing near Victoria Lodge, Lake George, yesterday morning, caught a trout which weighs nineteen pounds, and is said to be the largest fish of the kind ever taken from the waters of Lake George.

The trout will be placed on exhibition today at the market of J. O'Leary and Brother.

FROM GLENS FALLS TO BOLTON BY AUTO

G. F. Times Apr 27 1910

The auto stage line of Miller Brothers between Glens Falls and Bolton will be put in operation next week. The firm will conduct a passenger and freight business and the cars to be used are those of the Rapid Motor Vehicle company of Pontiac, Mich. Competent men will be in charge of the automobiles and several trips will be made each day. The distance between Glens Falls and Bolton is about eighteen miles and it is doubtful if any place else in this section can more beautiful scenery be found than between those two points. *1910*

HUDSON FALLS NOW ADOPTED BY THE D. & H.

May 25 1910

The following official notice has been issued from the office of A. A. Heard, general passenger agent of the Delaware & Hudson company:

"To ticket agents, baggage agents and conductors—

"The station now known as Sandy Hill, Washington county, on the Saratoga division, has been changed to Hudson Falls. Hereafter the new name is to be used by ticket agents when issuing tickets with blank destinations and by baggage agents when checking baggage.

"The present stock of tickets, reading to Sandy Hill will be used until supply is exhausted, the new name will appear on all future issues."

$2,000,000 VALUE OF PRUYN ESTATE

SETTLEMENT OF THE ACCOUNTS OF HOOPES AND BROWN EXECUTORS.

Post Star apl 12

The value of the estate of the late Samuel Pruyn totals over $2,000,000. The transfer tax amounts to $21,-315.62 as shown by a receipt from County Treasurer Bazinet filed in the judicial settlement of the accounts of Maurice Hoopes and L. M. Brown, executors of the estate, with Surrogate Jenkins. The receipts, countersigned by the State Comptroller, reads like this:

Received of Maurice Hoopes and Louis M. Brown, executors of the last will an dtestament of Samuel Pruyn, one thousand, three hundred and fifteen dollars and sixty-two cents, transfer tax upon the estate of the said deceased.

Lewis Burgess

Lewis Burgess of Hague-on-Lake George, widely known throughout Warren County and Northern New York, died at his residence on Monday evening, May 23, after a brief illness.

Mr. Burges was born in Dresden, Washington County, in August, 1834. In company at first with Samuel Weston, who was for many years the proprietor of Sabbath Day Point on Lake George, he began the business over fifty years ago which he continued up to the time of his death. He had a winter residence in St. Augustine, Florida, from which he had recently returned.

Mr. Burgess was elected supervisor for the Town of Hague, Warren County, in 1862, 1866, 1867 and 1889 and held the office of justice of the peace for many years previous to the beginning of the present year.

He was postmaster of Hague for about thirty-two years continuously up to 1893, when his brother-in-law, John McClanathan, was appointed to succeed him, during the second term of president Cleveland's administration.

Mr. Burgess gave to the Town of Hague the lot on which the Town Hall was built in 1893 and the lot on which the fine new district school No. 1, was built in 1909. His fine residence was opposite the store where he had done business for so many years. Mr. Burgess is survived by his widow. He had no children. His funeral will be held at Hague on Wednesday, May 25 at 2 p. m. *Post Star May 25/10*

A SECTION OF GLEN STREET AS PHOTOGRAPHED IN 1864

The above reproduction from a photograph, taken in 1864, shows the West side of Glen street, just above the Rockwell House, as it appeared at that time. It will be noted that the block on which the B. B. Fowler Company's store and other large business houses now stands was then used for residential purposes. Trolley cars had not then made their appearance nor had telephone and electric light plants become established.

ALONZO LANE.

Alonzo Lane, an aged resident of North Bolton, died at his home in that place Friday. Mr. Lane had not been well for many years. He is survived by his widow and two sons. Leonard, of North Bolton, and Prof. Richard Lane, of Glens Falls. The funeral was held Sunday, the Rev. E. J. Prescott, of the Bolton Methodist church officiating. Interment in the Huddle cemetery. *news apl 1 1910*

"THE CAPTAIN'S DAUGHTER."

We were crowded in a cabin.
  Not a soul would dare to speak;
It was midnight on the water,
  And a storm was on the deep.

'Tis a fearful thing in Winter,
  To be sheltered by the blast;
And to hear the rattling trumpet.
  Thunder "Cut away the mast."

So we sheltered there in silence,
  While the captain held his breath;
And the hungry seas were roaring,
  And the breakers talked with death.

As thus we sat in darkness,
  Each one busy in his prayers.
"We are lost," the captain shouted.
  As he struggled down the stairs.

But his little daughter whispered.
  As she took his ivory hand.
"Isn't God upon the ocean
  Just the same as on the land?"

Then we kissed the little maiden.
  And we spoke in better cheer;
And we anchored safe in harbor,
  When the morn was shining clear.

Cause of Unreserved Comment.

apr 28 1910

Mrs. L. W. Emerson has sent her brother-in-law, A. H. Thomas, some seed potatoes from California, which for some utter inexplicability the bugs are not supposed to disturb. Mr. Thomas has turned the seed over to Joel F. Bennett, who is well known as an A 1 potato raiser, but Mr. Bennett is somewhat incredulous when it comes to Warrensburgh potato bugs and shakes his head in a doubtful manner. Should these potatoes, however, turn out bug-proof, they will cause wild excitement, unreserved comment and uproarious hilarity among potato growers in this locality.

Electric Light Plant at Bolton.

An electric light plant established by Henry Knoblauch, will begin operations at Bolton Landing May 1. It will be in charge of Orrin Tubbs, who moved his family there from this place yesterday. Mr. Tubbs has been employed in Bolton for a year and his family spent most of the winter there.

-69-

A SCENE FAMILIAR TO GLENS FALLS RESIDENTS

Past Star
May 6 1910

M. B. LITTLE
J. R. LOOMIS
A. Z. DeLONG
INSURAN
LOANS
REAL ES

Meredith B. Little.

We present herewith a reproduction from a drawing of Meredith B. Little, by James A. Kennedy, who is connected with the local office of the Western Union Telegraph Company.

It is, indeed, probable that no resident of Glens Falls enjoys a wider acquaintance or his more highly respected by the public than is Mr. Little. For years he has made Glens Falls his home and has always been prominently identified with movements having for their purpose the betterment of the general public.

Possessed of a benevolent spirit, he has, in a quiet yet effective manner, brought happiness to many a family, with which fate had seemingly dealt harshly. His whole life has been but an exemplification of the golden rule, as a result of which he enjoys the friendship and good wishes of all who know him.

Mr. Little was born at Williamstown, Mass, May 4, 1834. He moved to Cambridge in 1837, and resided with his grandparents on a farm at that place until fourteen years of age when he accepted a position as clerk in a store. In 1852 he moved to Glens Falls, where he has since been in the insurance business. He has represented the Glens Falls and the Home Insurance Company of New York for more than half a century. For the past twenty-five years he has believed, taught and practiced the truths of the higher Spiritualistic philosophy, being the founder of and president of the First Psychical Society of Glens Falls.

Mr. Little is a great lover of nature and spends much of his time directing the care of a beautiful flower garden which adorns the lawn at his residence on Warren street.

Terms in Measuring Electricity.
To the Editor of "The Press."

Sir:—In speaking of an electric lighting plant one of the terms used is as follows: "Twenty KVA steam driven unit." If possible, will you kindly state what the letters "KVA" stand for or mean?

ALFRED C. PRIME.
Jamesburg, N. J., Nov. 9, 1910.

It is not generally expressed in the way you name in connection with the unit. KVA is the abbreviation for kilo volt amperes, the measurement of electric energy.

News   HYMENEAL.   *Nov 10*

LAMB-SHERMAN.

Perry Lamb and Miss Lila Sherman, both of Bolton, were married on Wednesday evening of last week, at the Methodist Episcopal parsonage in South Glens Falls, by the Rev. W. J. Chapman.

1910

WILL LIGHT BOLTON BY ELECTRICITY

Times — June 29 1918

The Bolton Landing Electric Light Company, in which Seymour Taylor of this city is interested, received its big dynamo last week and will be prepared to furnish current before the end of this week. The outfit is a Fairbanks-Morse producer gas plant which will deliver a current to the main feed wires of 2,300 volts. This current will be distributed to transformers located in convenient districts whence it will be delivered at 110 voltage to the consumers. Already about 500 lamps have been ordered in the residences and cottages of Bolton Landing.

The lighting service will extend from the Algonquin hotel on the south to the summer residence of Dr. Jacobi on the north and from the lake shore to the back streets of the village itself. A regular district is to be established for the purpose of lighting the streets, the expense of same to be borne by tax levy, in the district. It will be necessary to secure a petition signed by a majority of the taxpayers in the district and this will have to be acted upon by the town board. Such a petition is now under way and will be pushed through as rapidly as possible.

The lighting company has been rapidly pushing construction work and its poles and wires are all in place and as soon as the generator is ready the power will be turned on.

Henry C. Knoblauch is president of the new company.

GIRL FALLS DOWN OLD WELL HOLE

Times — Oct 8 1918

Janet, the eight year old daughter of Mr. and Mrs. W. H. Straight, Warrensburg, had a harrowing experience a few days ago. The child stepped on some planking covering an old well in an effort to gather apples from an overhanging tree, when the boards broke, precipitating her to the bottom of the shaft, a distance of twenty feet. The boards that went down with her gave her a scant footing and enabled her to keep her head above the surface of the ice cold water. Michael O'Connor, of the Adirondack Hotel, heard the child's cries for help and going to her assistance with the aid of other men succeeding in rescuing her from her perilous position.

The child is none the worse for her experience, except for the ice bath and severe fright.

BIG LAKE HOME FOR BRERETON

Times July 18.

H. E. H. Brereton of New York and Hill View has razed the Brereton homestead on the Bolton road near Hill View and in its stead is to erect a summer home which when completed will be one of the finest residences of the Bolton road colony.

The house which will be of stone and stucco will be about one hundred feet in length and the width will vary from forty to sixty feet. One of the features of the interior of the house will be a large pipe organ. It is expected that the structure will be ready for occupancy by next summer. *1910.*

---

new **Assembly Point Hotel Planned.** *Aug*

It is said that plans are being made by Dr. D. S. Sanford, of Brooklyn and Lake George, to rebuild the hotel on Assembly Point, which was burned down about twenty years ago. Dr. Sanford owns the greater part of Assembly Point and Long Island, nearby. Thus a vast area would be improved if the hotel is built and the scheme for developing the grounds is carried out. It is stated that Dr. Sanford has been offered $100,000 for Long Island. This is the largest island in Lake George and is situated about three miles from the head of the lake. *11. 1910*

COMMITTEES OF COUNTY BOARD

Times nov, 17th 1910

APPOINTMENTS ARE ANNOUNCED
AT TODAY'S SESSION.

CHAIRMAN THURSTON

Patterson, Hall, Bolton, Van Dusen and Pitcher on Equalization Committee—Finance Composed of Bickley, Baker and Noxon.

Jesse F. Thurston, chairman of the board of supervisors announced today the standing committees for the year. The supervisors are meeting daily at Lake George and a long term is expected with plenty of hard work for the members of the board as there are many important matters to be considered.

HENRY E. H. BRERETON
Bolton Man Elected to the Assembly as Representative From Warren County.

Times ✗ Nov, 9th 1910

DEATH OF MRS. BROWN.

nurroo Jan 24 1910

Eunice Mead, wife of Alphonse Brown, died at 6:30 o'clock Saturday evening at her home in this village. Mrs. Brown was born in the Town of Caldwell in 1832 and has resided here all her life. She was the daughter of David and Maria Mead, also life-long residents of the Town of Caldwell. Besides her husband, she is survived by three daughters, Mrs. Henry E. Nichols, Shelving Rock; Mrs. Elmer J. West and Mrs. W. J. Hunt of Glens Falls; one son, Dolphus J. Brown, Lake George; one brother, David Mead, Queensbury; and one sister, Mrs. Stebbins of Lake George. The funeral was held from the late home Tuesday afternoon at 2 o'clock, the Rev. M. F. Fales of the Lake George Presbyterian church officiating. Interment was made in the Lake George cemetery.

Star July 14 1901

Henry Crandall

The above photograph of Henry Crandall, one of Glens Falls' most philanthropic residents, was snapped by a Post-Star representative while the noted benefactor was standing in Monument Square, near the library which bears his name.

Mr. Crandall is possessed of a most reserved nature. Of his many philanthropic deeds he will say nothing, yet every resident of Glens Falls knows of countless movements for the public good which have been either wholly or partially enacted through the generosity of "Uncle Henry."

The Crandall Park on Upper Glen street, the City Park on Maple street and the Crandall Free Library are only a few of the institutions which Glens Falls' residents and visitors are privileged to enjoy through the benevolence of one who stands out prominently as a self-made man.

Going the Pace.

Man toils away week in, week out
And saves and plans and frets,
And tells the world his salary
Is three times what he gets.

His wife, to prove her love for him
Before all here below,
Puts on the style she might afford
If what he says were so.
—Houston Post.

LAST TRIP MADE TODAY BY HORICON

LAKE GEORGE BOAT WILL BE DIS-
MANTLED.

Times Sept

AFTER 34 SEASONS

Old Craft Will Give Way to Modern Boat Which Will Take Her Name and be Ready for Service Next Summer—New Steamer in Course of Construction at Baldwin Will Be of Steel and Will Measure 230 Feet with 59 Foot Beam—Changes in Lake George Passenger Service.

(Special to Glens Falls Daily Times.)
LAKE GEORGE, Sept. 10—Upon her arrival at Baldwin this evening the Steamer Horicon of the Champlain Transportation Company will have completed her last regular trip of the season, and this marks the ending of her career as a passenger boat, as it is expected to have the new steel boat ready by June 1, 1911.

The Horicon will take the trip of the steamer Mohican for three days next week, while the smaller boat undergoes some repairs to her boilers, and after that will be taken to the harbor, her machinery removed and dismantled.

The Horicon was built thirty-four years ago, and has seen continuous service on Lake George every season, making the morning trip until the "Sagamore" was completed and after that taking the place of the "Ticonderoga" which was burned in 1901. She is still in very good condition, but has to make way for the more modern boats of steel construction.

The new "Horicon" which is being put together at Baldwin will be of steel construction and about four feet longer than the Sagamore measuring 230 feet in length and 59 foot beam.

The Mohican made her last Paradise Bay trip for the season this afternoon and the yacht Pampero which has been making the short trips from the Lake George dock went out of commission this afternoon.

SHE FAILED TO DECLARE HER GOWNS

LAKE GEORGE WOMAN TRIES TO OUTWIT HUSBAND.

CAUGHT BY OFFICIALS

Mrs. Herman Broesel Didn't Want Husband to Know of Paris Purchases—Denied at First Buying Costly Dress Abroad.

(Special to Glens Falls Daily Times.)
NEW YORK, Sept. 3.—Mrs. Herman Broesel of Lake George, whose husband is president of the Jefferson Bank and one of the principal members of the importing house of Boessneck, Broesel & Co., of 466 Broome street, was compelled to appear at the Custom House yesterday afternoon to explain to Deputy Surveyor Smyth why she had failed to declare for duty several fine dresses, a cloak, and some laces when she arrived from Europe on the Cunarder Lusitania Thursday night. Mr. Broesel, who was also a passenger on the Lusitania, accompanied his wife, and was present at her cross-examination by the customs officials.

As a result of the investigation all of Mrs. Broesel's trunks, as well as the one belonging to her maid, were sent to the Public Stores, where they were opened and re-examined by Customs Inspector George W. Harnisch and Deputy Surveyor O'Connor this morning.

Mr. and Mrs. Broesel and Mrs. Broesel's maid were among the first of the Lusitania's passengers to come ashore yesterday morning, and as soon as they had assembled their baggage Inspector Harnisch was assigned to make the examination. One of the trunks was a new upright one, fitted with hangers on which were suspended a dozen or more costly gowns. Inspector Harnisch found Mrs. Broesel had declared $200 worth of goods.

Harnisch looked at several of the garments that were not mentioned in the declaration, and turning to Mrs. Broesel asked her if she was certain that she had declared everything she had purchased while in Europe. Mrs. Broesel said she had, and that the garments in question were bought in this country.

Harnisch then sent for Deputy Surveyor O'Connor, and he took up the questioning of Mrs. Broesel, and again Mrs. Broesel is said to have stated that she had declared everything that she had bought while abroad. While Harnisch and O'Connor were question-

ing Mrs. Broesel, another inspector was sent to the stateroom that she had occupied on the Lusitania, and when he returned he brought with him garment labels bearing the names of three well-known dressmaking establishments in Paris. The names were those of the house of Redfern, Du May, and of Linkel.

The Custom Inspectors said that the labels were found in the Broesel stateroom and that the threads were still in them, indicating that they had been recently torn from the garments. Mrs. Broesel would not admit buying anything from these houses when confronted with the labels.

The customs men finally appealed to Mr. Broesel and advised him that the safest course was for his wife to declare any additional goods purchased in Europe which she might have failed to mention in her declaration. They told him that it might be necessary to have Mrs. Broesel searched, and he finally said that he would see if she was carrying anything in the way of dutiable goods. The customs authorities say that when he returned he had a lace table centerpiece and a shirt waist, both of which Mrs. Broesel had had concealed in her clothing.

But Mrs. Broesel would not admit that she had bought anything from Redfern, Du May or Linkel.

MORIAH VISITED BY FIRE ENTAILING $30,000 LOSS

Star

Hotel Sherman, One of the Most Up-to-Date of Adirondack Resorts is Totally Destroyed

Aug 13 1910

Hotel Sherman at Moriah, Essex County, was totally destroyed by fire last Wednesday evening, entailing a loss conservatively estimated at about $30,000. The hotel was owned by J. R. Carson who, previous to taking possession of Hotel Sherman, conducted a hotel at North Hudson which was one of the favorite abodes of hunters.

Hotel Sherman, which was some years ago known as the Magnolia Hotel, was purchased by George R. Sherman, a prominent horseman. Under his direction it was remodeled and newly furnished throughout and was one of the most up-to-date resorts in the lower Adirondacks. About a year ago Mr. Sherman sold the property to Mr. Carson. No plans for rebuilding the structure have as yet been made.

On the same night the barn of the Stickney House property at Port Henry was destroyed by fire. The Stickney House is conducted by a Mrs. King who two years ago managed Hotel Sherman for its owner.

JOHN B. SIMPSON GIVES BURNETT A GOLD WATCH

1910

Post Star Sept 22

Game Protector Burnett of Lake George is the proud possessor of a beautiful gold watch, suitably inscribed, which was recently given to him by John Bolton Simpson in appreciation of his efficient service.

HORICON BUILT 34 YEARS AGO

Times
nov(9 1910

The Lake George steamer Horicon, which will be replaced by a new boat next season, was built in 1876, and placed in service in 1877. The new steamer will be 230 feet six inches in length over all, 59 feet extreme breadth, will have three decks similar to the steamer Sagamore now plying on the lake, a main deck, saloon deck, and hurricane deck, dining room will have seating capacity of one hundred people, and will be located on main deck aft. The interior finish of the steamer will be natural wood, butternut with cherry trimmings, the decorations will be on canvas of attractive design. Will be equipped with two boilers, lobster return tublar type, 10 feet six inches width of front, 25 feet long. The engine will be a jet condensing vertical beam type, 52 inches cylinder, 10 inch stroke, patent feathering wheels, sewage tanks, trimming tanks electric lighted throughout including a powerful search light, steered and heated by steam. The vessel will be up to date in every particular, and will have all the latest features known to modern shipbuildng.

State Flowers.

THE BEST FISH STORY EVER TOLD

GRANVILLE SENTINEL HAS ONE
THAT'S ORIGINAL.

Times—Nov 19
1910

A REMARKABLE TALE

Bullhead Caught in Lake St. Catherine Lives on Air and Refuses to Die—Granville Man Taming it for Household Pet.

The Granville Sentinel has a fish story to relate this week which no unholy person can successfully question. It is a literally true story, as all fish stories published by The Sentinel are. There is a widespread and deep seated conviction among common laymen that the authors of all fish stories are eligible to membership in the Ananias club. Just why this theory or impression occupies a place in the hearts of men is difficult of explanation. It may be a remnant of original sin and therefore hereditary. Possibly it is a later day invention of satan or imported with hands across the sea.

The story as told by The Sentinel follows:

One week ago today, which according to the almanac, was last Thursday, a party of semi-professional christians was engaged in piscatorial work, or pleasure, just as one may view it, at Lake St. Catherine. An inventory of the united catch that night revealed the fact that it consisted of one two-pound bullhead that didn't know enough to die when afforded an opportunity. And therefore hangs the tale. By mistake, when the party went home, the fish was left on the kitchen floor of the cottage where the men were stopping.

Two days later members of the same party were again at the cottage and expected to find a decayed fish, but, on the contrary, it was alive and kicking. With a newspaper to prevent soiling his fingers by the handling of putrid matter, L. Carr attempted to pick up the fish and when it gave a strenuous flop the surprised Carr nearly went through the roof of the building. When placed in water the fish swam about apparently as healthy as when taken from the lake by M. S. Strong forty-eight hours previous.

The fish was brought to Granville by Mr. Carr, who is taming it for a household pet. It is yet alive and its absence from water does not seemingly affect its health. The truthfulness of this story will be vouched for by Mr. Carr and several other men of unquestioned veracity.

BRAYTON PURCHASES PARK STREET SHEDS

WILL DEAL EXTENSIVELY IN FARMING MACHINERY, SEEDS, PLANTS, SHRUBBERY, ETC.

Star two 25 1918

The Farmers' Sheds on Park street, which have been owned and conducted during the past six or seven years by William A. McCoduck, have been purchased by Albert Brayton the Lower Warren street wholesale meat dealer. Mr. Brayton will take possession of the business on January 1, 1911, but will come into possession of the property on December 1, of this year. The business will be continued as during the past, with the exception that Mr. Brayton will deal more extensively in farming machinery and other commodities such as seeds, plants, shrubbery, etc.

The buildings on the property are old, but extensive repairs will be made by Mr. Brayton, and the sheds and stables put in as good condition as possible.

Mr. Brayton is well known in Glens Falls where he resides on Sherman avenue. For many years past he has conducted a wholesale meat business on lower Warren street and is the owner of considerable farm land in this vicinity which he works. He has not decided whether or not he will devote his time exclusively to the new business.

C. E. BENEDICT DEAD AT LAKE

Times — Sept 13

The death of Charles Edward Benedict of New York city occurred September 7 at his summer home at Bolton-on-Lake George.

The deceased was born in Glens Falls in 1846 and will be remembered by many residents of this city. For thirty-five years past he has had a summer home at Bolton and each season while at the lake frequently visited Glens Falls friends.

He is survived by three sisters, Mrs. E. J. Dickinson and Mrs. W. C. Edgett of New York City and Mrs. Robert Reid of Park Ridge, N. J. *1910*

B. F. Hammond Owner of Fast Horse.

Horsemen of Warrensburgh are anxiously and patiently awaiting a public exhibtion of speed by the well-known circuit pacer, "William M," 2:10¼, recently purchased in New York by B. F. Hammond, and which arrived in town Thursday. This noted bay gelding is said to have worked a public trial at Columbus in 2:03½, making the final eighth in fourteen seconds. He has every appearance of being able to show as methodical work on the track as does his energetic namesake, William M. Condon, in the realm of retail drugdom. *News Dec 8th 1910*

A REMINDER OF OLD TIMES.

News Dec 8th 1910

Picture of Old County Clerk's Office Displayed at Lake George.

In the county clerk's office at Lake George there was hung recently a photograph of the little stone building which formerly stood for many years on the site of the present handsome structure. The picture was taken by the late Dr. W. R. Adamson, in the spring of 1885, on the morning of the day that workmen began to tear down the building to make room for the clerk's present quarters.

In front of the building is seen the late D. V. Brown, then county clerk, and his deputy, E. W. Hunt, also deceased. Sanford Brown, the clerk's son, is standing in the doorway. The new building was ready for occupancy on March 8, 1886, and the clerk moved into it on that date from the court house, where the business of the office was conducted until it was completed. The picture was presented by Dr. Adamson's son, Harold Adamson, of Glens Falls, who found the negative among his father's effects and had some copies printed from it. It is valued highly by County Clerk Sisson, who was deputy clerk for a number of years and worked in the old building under George P. Wait.

HILL VIEW DOCTOR KILLED.

News Nov 2th 1910

Plunges Over Embankment in Dark and Fractures Skull.

Dr. C. B. Stiles, of Hill View, while driving to the home of a patient near that place Friday night, guided his horse over a steep embankment in the dark and was thrown from his carriage on to the macadamized state road, striking on his head and fracturing his skull. The injury caused his death the following day.

Dr. Stiles was on his way home from a professional visit to Hill View, or Flat Rock, and stopped at the home of Edward Norton to see a patient. To reach this place he was obliged to leave the state road. While returning from the Norton home the darkness made it impossible for the physician to see the outlines of the road, and as a result he guided his horse over a steep embankment near the state highway and was thrown from his road cart and injured as stated.

The accident occurred near the Henry George place and assistance reached him soon after he fell. He was taken to his home and physicians were summoned, but nothing could be done for him and he remained in a comatose state until he died at 4:30 o'clock Saturday morning.

Dr. Stiles was highly esteemed by all who knew him and his genial presence will be greatly missed in the community in which he had long been a familiar and prominent figure.

ONLY ONE ROAD TO BE PURCHASED

Post Star Dec 17th 1910

Because of an opinion by County Attorney Davis that the Board of Supervisors can not legally purchase the Lake George-Warrensburg toll road, a resolution, introduced a few days ago to purchase same at a cost of $6,000 and the Warrensburg-Chester road at a price of $9,000, was yesterday amended in a resolution introduced by Supervisor Haselton. Mr. Haselton's amended resolution provides that Warren County acquire the rights and franchises of a toll road between Warrensburg and Chester, known as the road of the Warrensburg and Chester Road and Turnpike Company, and that a committee be appointed to consult with owners of the road with a view to purchasing same. In the event of failure to come to a satisfactory agreement, the committee is authorized to start condemnation proceedings. The Lake George-Warrensburg road is eliminated.

Winter Getting a Good Start.

Yesterday was the coldest day of the season. The thermometer registered eight degrees below zero at T. J. Smith & Son's grist mill, fourteen below at Thurman station, and twenty below was reported at North Creek. It has since moderated considerably and this morning the mercury stood at three above zero at the grist mill.

News Dec 8th 1910

LAST AND ONLY FLAG FOR PACER

Times Dec 16th 1910

LEXINGTON, Ky., Dec. 16—Star Pointer, 1.59 1-4, against time, is dead. The famous pacer dropped dead yesterday of apoplexy in the paddock at the farm of his owner, W. M. Williams, at Columbus, Tenn., where he was a pensioner, having been purchased by Mr. Williams a few months ago in order to give the great old horse the honor of dying in the state that gave him birth. He was twenty-one years old, sired by Brown Hal, dam Sweepstakes, by Snow Heels, and had during his career in the stud sired nineteen record pacers, two of his sons siring thirteen pacers and two of his dams three pacers, including Morning Star, 2.04, and Sirius Pointer, 2:08.

He was bread by H. T. Pointer of Springhill, Tenn., and had been owned by J. W. Titley, Chicora, Pa., Smith and Mills, of Boston, and Joseph A. Murphy, Chicago. Star Pointer's race record was 2:00 1-2, made October 1, 1897, at Springfield, Ill.

Star Pointer made his only appearance in Glens Falls about a dozen years ago when he went against John R. Gentry in a special purse race. Gentry had the advantage of the pole and took the two deciding heats but he was driven for all there was in him. It was in this race that Gentry made his record of 2:01 1-2. This mark which now stands as the local track record was not bested for some time after the Glens Falls race.

Telephone Penetrating Mountains.

The New York Telephone company has completed two copper circuits from Glens Falls through Warrensburgh to North Creek, thus establishing connection between the Bell lines and the southern Adirondacks. The company is constructing a line to Newcomb, thus giving Long Lake and Blue Mountain Lake connection with the Bell system. The construction is of the highest type and more than $20,000 will have been spent in the construction of these lines when they are complete. *1910*

-74-

THE NEW STEAMER HORICON LAUNCHED TODAY AT BALDWIN

Times Dec 1 1910

LAKE GEORGE BOAT CHRISTENED BY MRS. SIMS.

READY JULY 1, 1911

New Horicon Slides Down Ways and Gracefully Floats Waters of Lake— Interior and Over Deck Work to be Rushed and Steamer Will be Placed in Commission Early Next Season— Splendid Craft is a Credit to Lake George—History of Navigation in the Up-State Region.

Breaking a bottle of wine over the bows and with these words "I Christen Thee Horicon" Mrs. Clarence S. Sims, wife of the vice president and general manager of the Delaware & Hudson Railroad stood sponsor for the new Lake George Steamer 'Horicon' which was launched today at Baldwin. The ceremony went through without any interruption, the boat slid down the ways and floated gracefully out on the waters.

A large crowd gathered to witness the launching despite the inclement weather. Everything had been placed in readiness long before 11 o'clock, the hour set for the launching, and as the boat slid down into the water a cheer went up from the spectators.

The new boat will be placed in service about July 1, 1911, succeeding the old Horicon which will be dismantled. The work on the interior and over-deck will be rushed during the winter and when the craft is placed in commission next summer, the Lake George Steamboat Company will have a fleet that will compare favorably with any body of water the size of Lake George.

The new boat will replace the old Horicon which was built in 1876.

The length of the new boat over all is 230 feet six inches and the extreme breadth of hull thirty-three feet. The breadth of the steamer over guards is fifty-nine feet. It is equipped with two boilers of the lobster return tubular type, ten feet six inches wide of front, twenty-six feet long, and the diameter of the cylinder is fifty-two inches. The stroke of the piston is ten feet. The patent feathering wheels are twenty-two and one-half inches wide and have curved steel buckets.

The new boat will have three decks, main, saloon and hurricane, all of which will be conveniently arranged for the transportation of passengers, freight, express, baggage and mail. The Horicon will not be unlike the Sagamore, now in service, although some important changes will be made in the new boat. The dining room will seat about 100, and there will be better conveniences in the kitchen. The boat will be capable of developing a speed of twenty-one miles an hour. There will be a limited number of observation staterooms for private parties.

The boat will be finished in white, and the dining cabin, quarter deck and main saloon in butternut, with cherry trimming, finished in the natural wood. The boat will have a carrying capacity of 1,500 passengers.

The contract for the hull and engine was let to The W. & A. Fletcher Company of Hoboken, N. J., the hull contract being sublet to The T. S. Marvel Shipbuilding Company of Newburgh. The ship carpenter and joiner work was done by carpenters and joiners of The Lake George Steamboat Company. The boat was designed by J. W. Millard & Brother of New York under the direction of Andrew Fletcher of W. & A. Fletcher and the officers of the steamboat company. It is expected that the new boat will be ready for service about July 1, 1911.

The James Caldwell, built in 1813, was the first steamboat on Lake George, and the second was the Mountaineer, built about 1824. The next was the William Caldwell in 1833, and then came the John Jay in 1836. The Minnehaha made her appearance in 1857, and then came the Ganouski, the Horicon and the Ticonderoga, with the latter-day up-to-date steamers Sagamore and Mohican.

The Lake George Steamboat Company was formed in 1855 in accordance with an act of the Legislature passed January 14, 1854. The old company was succeeded by the present company, which was incorporated February 23, 1872. The first directors of the original company were James J. Gregory, David Banks, Jr. John F. Sherrill, J. W. Holcomb, Almond C. Farr, Hosea, F. Carr and Morris Ketchum. The Champlain Transportation Company became interested in The Lake George Steamboat Company in 1866, and its interests were assigned to the present company in 1872.

"Twixt Two Lovers."

To the Editor of "The Press."

Sir:—Kindly print inclosed jingle?
MISS JEAN McNEIL.
Eddystone, Pa., Nov. 21, 1910.

She was awfully gone on them both,
And didn't know which to take;
The minute she selected one,
For the other her heart would ache.

It was very hard to decide,
They were both such "perfect dreams,"
So stylish and up-to-date; just the kind
That all girls like, it seems.

One minute she chose the dark one,
So rich, tho' plain—but then
Her glance fell on the light one,
And she changed her mind again.

She sought her friend's opinion,
But she sadly shook her head;
"They're both so rich and handsome,
Just suit yourself," she said.

She gazed again with yearning,
That only a girl e'er knew,
And sighed for hope's returning;
Oh, why couldn't she have the two!

They both remained quite near her,
Small wonder, indeed, about that;
But it really is a very hard task,
Selecting a new Winter hat.

In a Village by the Sea.

To a little seaside village
Came a youth one Summer day,
Just to spend a short vacation, that was all.
There he met a fisher maiden;
And, to while the hours away,
At her cottage every day he used to call.
The lassie thought he meant the words
He spoke in idle jest,
And hand in hand together they would roam.
But one day there came a letter,
And, with breaking heart she read:
Just these simple words: "Good-by; I'm going home."

CHORUS.
In a village by the sea
She was happy as could be;
Like a bird, her heart was ever light and free.
Now the moon shines not so bright,
For she's all alone to-night,
Where he left her in the village by the sea.

Just a year ago this Summer
To the village by the sea,
To the cottage, came this youth so bright and free.
He had come to beg forgiveness,
For he'd learned to love her, too;
Just how dear he did not know till far away.
Her father came to greet him
As he knocked upon the door,
And together through the churchyard they did roam;
And he pointed to a grave-mound,
Said, "She bade me say to you,
Just these simple words—'Good-by; I'm going home.'"

-75-

GENERAL H. E. TREMAIN LAWYER AND SOLDIER DEAD IN NEW YORK

WELL KNOWN SUMMER RESIDENT OF LAKE GEORGE.

Times Dec 10th /8/

OWNED BIG ESTATE

His Hill View Property is Largest on the Bolton Road—Death Follows Illness of Several Months—General Tremain Was Well Known New York City Lawyer and Veteran of the Civil War—Deceased Had Received Congressional Medal for Bravery in the Battle of Resaca.

NEW YORK, Dec. 10—General Henry Edwin Tremain, a veteran of the civil war and a well known lawyer, died yesterday at his home, No. 37 Madison avenue.

General Tremain had been in poor health for some time, but he attended the fiftieth anniversary banquet of his class in the College of the City of New York two weeks ago at the Hotel Astor. He was ill from that date and died from heart disease.

Born in this city in 1840, he enlisted for the civil war as a private in the Seventh New York Volunteers, but later recruited a company and went to the front as lieutenant in the Second regiment of Fire Zouaves, known as the Seventy-third New York Volunteers.

He was on the staff of General Nelson Taylor at the siege of Yorktown. Later he was on the staff of General Pope and was taken prisoner at the second battle of Bull Run.

He was in Libby Prison, was exchanged and later was with General Sickles as assistant inspector general. He was made a major in 1863 and recommended for bravery at Chancellorsville. For heroism at the battle of Resaca he was awarded the Congressional medal of honor.

At the close of the war he was admitted to the bar and became a member of the law firm of Tremain & Tyler. He was one of the founders of the New York Law Journal, was president of the Republican Club and a member of the Society of the Army of the Republic. He left a widow.

In fact Warren county was his voting residence. His summer home and farm on the Bolton road form one of the largest properties of that colony and his estate near Hill View is known as one of the largest on the lake shore. For several seasons General and Mrs. Tremain made Glens Falls their home occupying the dwelling at 32 Sherman avenue. For a long period General Tremain was a frequent visitor to this city and was largely interested in the commercial development and the professional and social life of the community.

BIG BUILDING BOOM IS NOW IN PROGRESS AT BOLTON LANDING

Times Dec 14th 1910

Several Factories and Business Structures are Going up—Summer Residents Adding To Their Properties.

(Special to Glens Falls Daily Times.)

BOLTON LANDING, Dec. 14—The advent of electricity seems to have inspired everyone here with a desire to build, regardless of the season of the year. Zero weather is no longer a sign of cessation of any kind of outdoor work.

Truxton Braley and Dr. D. L. Rogers are breaking ground for the foundations of a large and well equipped building, steam-heated and lighted by electricity, to be used when completed for two stores, offices and apartments.

Sheridan Finkle has a large dwelling well under way and has shown very good architectural taste in the design of the building.

Orlie Vandenberg has just completed the slating of the big roof on his new barn and horse stable and will commence the foundations of his house very soon.

James Maranville has raised his stable nearly eight feet up and is adding twenty-five horse stalls in the basement for the better accommodation of his large livery business.

Antonio Knauth, of New York, is building a garage in which he expects to house one of the latest and most powerful Pierce-Arrow cars next season. Mrs. Percival Knauth, of the same place, is also building an extensive greenhouse, from which she expects to have early vegetables sent to her home in New York.

Count Mankowski has made the contract for a boat house one hundred feet long to take care of his fast motor boats.

Miss Crandall, of Albany, is building a charming residence under the able supervision of Captain Fred R. Smith, which she expects to occupy at such times when she is not traveling in Europe.

There is no lack of employment for all kinds of competent workmen and mechanics as is usually the case at this time of year and the work bids fair to continue all winter at the present rate.

A WELL KNOWN RESIDENT AT HIS JOURNEY'S END

W. Scott Whitney, Veteran of Civil War, Passes Away at His Home on Hunter Street

Star Dec 2 1918

After an illness covering a period of several years, during the last nine months of which he had been confined to his bed, W. Scott Whitney, a well known resident and Civil War veteran with an enviable record, passed away at his home on Hunter street at 4:15 o'clock yesterday morning.

Mr. Whitney, who was a former official of Warren County, was born at South Schroon, Essex County, in 1841. In 1860, he enlisted in Company I of the Twenty-second Regiment, the original Iron Brigade, and served with that regiment for two years. He was mustered out of service at the expiration of that period, but later re-enlisted in the Second Veteran Cavalry, known as the famous Morgan H. Chrysler's Cavalry, and had been promoted to the rank of second lieutenant at the close of the war. Mr. Whitney took part in the battles of Antietam and Bull Run (second engagement).

Upon his return home, he entered the Albany Business College and after graduation, taught school in the West for a number of years. He returned East to accept a position in a general store at Pottersville, but after a short time resigned his position to accept a similar one in the store of Hollis Russell in the Robertson building on Glen street. Later he entered the employ of the Morgan Lumber Company as a bookkeeper and was a short time afterward elected to the office of county clerk.

Upon the expiration of his term of office he again went West to conduct a sheep ranch in which several Glens Falls men were interested. He returned in a short time, however, to become engaged in the insurance business with D. B. Ketchum of this city.

All this time Mr. Whitney had enjoyed good health, but a few years later when he entered the employ of the Northwestern railroad, he was informed by an occulist that his eyesight was gradually leaving him as the result of injuries received in the war. He resigned his position and returned to this city where he soon became totally blind, which affliction he has suffered for about twenty-three years.

Mr. Whitney is survived by his widow and two sons, Harry and Lester Whitney, of this city. The funeral will be held from his late residence tomorrow afternoon at 2:30 o'clock. Friends are requested not to send flowers. The Rev. T. E. Williams will officiate, and interment will be in the Bay Street cemetery.

TODAY IN HISTORY

Phil. Press Dec 14 1910

The Death of George Washington
December 14

Napoleon Bonaparte said: "Posterity will talk of Washington with reverence, as the founder of a great empire, when my name shall be lost in the vortex of revolution."

Like so many other of the prophecies of the great Napoleon, it is becoming more apparent every day of its truth, and on this date, December 14, one hundred and eleven years ago Washington died at Mount Vernon at the age of 68, after an illness of only twenty-four hours.

The month of December, 1799, found Washington in the enjoyment of excellent health. His nephew, Major Lewis, writing of him as he appeared to himself and a friend at that time says: "The clear and healthy flush on his cheek and his sprightly manner brought the remark from both of us, that we had never seen the general look so well."

On Thursday, December 12, the General rode out to his farms about 10 o'clock, and did not return home until half-past three. Soon after he went out the weather became very bad, rain, hail, snow falling alternately, with a cold wind. In the evening he showed evidences of having taken cold and complained of a sore throat. He went out the following day, however, to mark some trees. Upon his retiring it was noticed that he had grown quite hoarse. Between two and three o'clock on Saturday morning of the fatal day, he awoke Mrs. Washington, and told her that he was very unwell, and had had a chill. She observed that he could scarcely speak, and breathed with difficulty. He refused to have the household aroused until morning, when Dr. Craik was sent for, who was very much alarmed at the General's condition, and advised a consultation with several other neighboring physicians.

They administered to him but the medicine seemed to take no effect. To the respectful and affectionate inquiries of an old family servant, as she smoothed down his pillow, how he felt, he answered, "I am very ill." To Mrs. Washington he said: "Go to my desk, and in a private drawer you will find two papers—bring them to me." They were brought. Upon looking at them he observed: "These are my wills—preserve this one and burn the other;" which was accordingly done.

He grew gradually worse. About five o'clock in the afternoon he said to Dr. Craik, who was at his bedside: "Doctor, I die hard, but I am not afraid to go. I believed, from my first attack, that I should not survive it. My breath cannot last long."

The doctor pressed his hand, but could not utter a word. He retired from the bedside and sat by the fire absorbed in grief. About six o'clock the consulting physicians were about his bedside, and he held out his hand to be raised up in bed. He said to the physicians: "I feel myself going; I thank you for your attentions; but I pray you to take no more trouble about me. Let me go off quietly. I cannot last long."

About ten o'clock at night he tried to speak, but he was hardly audible, and after giving a few directions, he asked the physicians: "Do you understand me?" When they replied yes, he said: "'Tis well," which were the last words the Father of our Country ever uttered.

While those about the bedside were fixed in silent grief, Mrs. Washington who was sitting at the foot of the bed, asked, with a firm and collected voice: "Is he gone?" No one was able to reply but simply nod their answer. "'Tis well," said she in the same voice, "all is now over; I will soon follow him; I have no more trials to pass through."

About twelve o'clock the body was carried down stairs and laid out in the large drawing room. The burial took place the following Wednesday, December 18, his remains being deposited in the family vault at Mt. Vernon.

The sudden tiding of his death fell like a domestic sorrow upon the hearts of the people; lamentations and solemn obsequies filled the land and, throughout the whole world the event was heard with the deepest emotion. Nearly forty years after his death and burial his remains, together with those of his wife, were reentombed, in order to their being placed in the marble coffins which had been generously offered for that purpose by a patriotic citizen of Philadelphia, to the legal representatives of the departed chieftain. This was in 1837.

"Don't Judge a Man by the Coat That he Wears."

To the Editor of "The Press."

Sir:—It pleases me to be able to furnish to "R. P." the words of the above song. This song—the words of which were written by W. H. Ashton and set to music by Charles Schultz, may now be classed among the old songs. The readers of "The Forum" will not fail to note the moral of the song.

W.

Wilmington, Del., October 20, 1909.

Don't judge a man by the cost of his clothing.
Unheeding the life path that he may pursue;
For we often admire a man who needs loathing
And we fail to give honor, where honor is due.
Though the hand may be hard, and fingers stiff-jointed,
And the coat he has on may be tatters and tears;
Yet greater than kings or princes anointed
You can't judge a man by the coat that he wears.

Give me the man as a friend and a neighbor,
One who toils at the spade or the loom or the plow;
One who earns his diploma of manhood by labor,
And who purchases wealth by the sweat of his brow.
That man will be found in the front ranks of labor,
Be known by the work which his industry rears,
And the chiefdom when won will be dear to his neighbor,
Then we'll honor the man—not the coat that he wears.

Why should the broadcloth alone be respected,
And we laugh at the man who in flannel appears;
While the angels in heaven have their limbs unprotected,
No you can't judge a man by the coat that he wears.
Then hail to the man who from honor and duty
Would wive all the laws which cold fashion impairs;
For the man is not made of gold, silver nor beauty,
Then we'll honor the man—not the coat that he wears.

RICHARD CANFIELD QUITS THE GAME OF CHANCE

Post Star Dec 29th 1910

"KING OF GAMBLERS" FORSAKES THE GREEN CLOTH AND LIVES IN RETIREMENT

YIELDS TO ENTREATIES OF 12-YEAR-OLD DAUGHTER

Turns Aside Offer of $30,000 a Year to Manage Fashionable Gambling Resort in Europe. Is Rich Enough to Live Without Worry. Has Made Money in Many Cities.

The New York Telegraph said yesterday morning:

Many friends of Richard Canfield, known all over the world by the title of "King of the Gamblers," were discussing along Broadway last night reports that he had absolutely quit games of chance forever. It was stated that the former "King" had been offered a salary of $30,000 a year to manage a gambling casino in one of the most famous and exclusive resorts in Europe, but had turned the offer down because his 12-year-old daughter had asked him to reform.

It was further said that, despite reports to the contrary, Canfield would not accept any gambling concessions from Cuba, Mexico or any other country, and that hereafter old maid or cassino would be his limit.

"What's that?" asked a man who had joined a crowd of the "King's" friends in a Broadway cafe, "Canfield has quit gambling? Is he dead?"

Canfield is now rich enough to live without worrying about wolves whetting their teeth on his door. He has everything ne wants and is content, it is said, to spend his time with his family in Providence, or with his friends here in New York.

In his earlier days Canfield had a narrow escape from being a college graduate. Had a friendly gambler not come along while the young man was in school and persuaded him that there was more money in just getting it than in enticing it selfward with the aid of a college degree.

Then Canfield went to other cities and in each he made money. He opened the Saratoga Club in Saratoga and a "clubhouse" in this city near Fifth avenue and Twenty-eighth street. Eight years ago he had a place in East Twenty-fourth street, which was Driscollized by Mr. Jerome. That was the beginning of the end of the Canfield reign.

Canfield is not and old man yet. He wants to be let alone, it is said, in order that he may enjoy himself with his family and pictures. For he is a connoisseur when it comes to art and he owns paintings and tapestry enough to make the average woman art lover go crazy with delight.

So Canfield, once "King" of them all, is to quit, rumor has it. He has no further use for the title "King of the Gamblers" and he doesn't care who assumes it. In fact, so set is he in his determination to "let it alone" that it is said he will even refuse to take a chance at a church fair.

HE'S THOROUGHLY AROUSED.

News Dec 29th 1910

"Bill Simpkins" Makes Onslaught Upon The News in Lively Manner.

Editor News: In a recent issue of The News was an item concerning the firm of Sears, Roebuck & Co., a Chicago mail order house. The News says that this house does not benefit Warrensburgh, yet this concern buys several thousand pairs of trousers from the Warrensburgh Woolen company every year, also the well known firm of Montgomery, Ward & Co., is equally large buyers of the Warrensburgh Woolen company's products. Does this injure the town of Warrensburgh? Where does The News get its support if not from the out-of-town trade? Frear's Bazaar, of Troy, and all of the big Glens Falls concerns advertise in The News, and they are all mail order houses, receiving in this way a large amount of trade from this locality. There are also many other out-of-town concerns advertising in The News. Why not give 'em all a dig when roasting the Chicago firm? If The News had to depend on Warrensburgh merchants for support I think it very doubtful if the paper would ever reach Easy street, in the vicinity of Comfortable avenue. We all notice that when a business man of Warrensburgh wants a new suit of clothes he generally goes to Glens Falls; also when one of our local merchants, who is a big kicker about the Chicago mail order house, wanted a delivery wagon he sent to Sears. Roebuck & Co. to buy it. Mr. Editor, you don't know it all.

BILL SIMPKINS

NEW TRAIN SERVICE.

News Dec 29 1910

Becomes Operative January 2 on Saratoga and Champlain Division of D. & H.

Formal announcement has been made by the Delaware and Hudson company of a new train known as No. 6 on the Saratoga and Champlain divisions, which provides an improved week day service to Albany, Troy, Boston, New York and the West. The train carries a cafe car from Plattsburgh to Albany, serving meals a la carte. The service becomes effective January 2. The train leaves Glens Falls at 9:05 p. m. and is the sleeper which the Commercial association requested the company to put into service.

Following is the schedule:

Leave Lake Placid 2:30 p. m., Saranac Lake 2:50 p. m., Lyon Mountain 4:08 p. m., Dannemora 4:44 p. m., Plattsburgh 5:35 p. m., Essex 6:31 p. m., Westport 6:50 p. m., Port Henry 7:12 p. m., Crown Point 7:26 p. m., Ticonderoga 7:53 p.m., Rutland 7:30 p. m., Whitehall 8:40 p. m. Glens Falls 9:05 p.m., Saratoga Springs 9:35 p. m., Leave Troy 10:55 p. m. Albany 11:26 p. m., Boston (via B. & M.) 7:00 a. m., Boston (via B. & A.) 6:40 a. m. New York 5:05 a. m., Binghamton 4:30 a. m., Chicago (via D. & H. and Erie) 7:57 (second morning.)

RUN DOWN BY AUTO.

news

Mrs. John G. Taylor Seriously Injured While Seeking Safety in Flight. *News*

Mrs. John G. Taylor, who was Miss Emma Reoux, of Warrensburgh, before her marriage, was considered in a critical condition for a while last week brought about by internal injuries as the result of a peculiar accident following a sleigh-ride. *1911*

Mrs. Taylor, formerly of Bolton Landing, is at present staying at Lake George. With a party of friends visiting at Ingle lodge, from New York and Long Island, she had been to Glens Falls Thursday afternoon and was returning home late at night.

The sleigh had just crossed the Hudson Valley tracks at Gage hill when the whiffletree broke and the team was stopped while the driver repaired the damage. Suddenly an automobile approached them at terrific speed and Mrs Taylor and Mrs. C. H. Taylor, of Long Island, fearing the machine would hit the sleigh, jumped to the ground and ran. The latter, who was in the lead, scrambled out of harm's way, but Mrs. John G. Taylor was run down by the auto, which then passed over her body.

Mrs. C. H. Taylor assisted the chauffeur in releasing the unfortunate woman. The latter's clothing, with the exception of her coat, was torn into shreds. She was helped to a neighboring house and later was removed to Ingle lodge. At first it was not thought that she was seriously hurt, but later it was learned that she was hurt internally.

-78-

WARREN COUNTY HOSPITAL

The above reproduction from a photograph represents "The Gables" at North Creek, now owned by Dr. Lee Somerville. The building was erected by the late Dr. T. C. Durant, at one time president of the Adirondack Railroad. The Warren County Board of Supervisors recently adopted a resolution appropriating the sum of $10,000 for its purchase, the property to be used a County Hospital for tubercular patients.

GRANVILLE SWEPT BY FIRE.

news Jan 6 1911

One of the Worst Conflagrations in the History of Washington County.

Granville was visited Monday night by the worst conflagration in its history. Summarized, the fire loss follows: Twelve buildings burned; twenty families homeless; loss, $10,000; insurance, $65,000; burned area, Main street, 200 feet east and 200 feet west of the Mettowee river, on both sides of the street; fire broke out at midnight; under control at 3:00 a. m.

The property destroyed includes: The Weinberg block, in which was located the store where the fire started, the Troy Clothing store and Dr. Williamson's dental office, the Thorne block containing Smith's bakery, and two flat houses; the Sullivan block including Sullivan's hardware store, the Howland drug store and flats; the residence of John Lloyd, the Nelson hardware store, the Granville furniture store, the Vanderwarker block, the barber shop of Mr. La Barns, the residence of William Dooley, the residence of Victor Mancini, the Valley hotel, a lagre structure, the McGraw hall, another big building, the Munson house, Barrigan's cafe, Whiting's livery stable, John Williams' blacksmith shop, and several other places.

Fire in a small village like Granville or Warrensburgh, with limited facilities to fight it is a very dangerous circumstance as has been demonstrated in both places. The trouble in

Granville Monday night is that there was no water pressure and in consequence the flames devoured property greedily. The main residential section was saved only by a sudden shift of the wind.

THE LUMBER INDUSTRY.

Was a Great Business Fifty Years Ago, as It Is Today. *news Jan 12*

Orson R. Wilsey, who is lumbering the mountain sides of Hackensack this winter, has cut about 600 markets of pine, which he sold and is now delivering to the local lumber firm of A. C. Emerson & Co.

While the price of a pine market is about $3.10 these days, and although lumber was relatively cheap something over half a century ago, the value of this primitive growth then is shown by the fact that the courts gave $1,000 an acre damages against a defendant who had cut without right the original pine timber growing on a farm in this vicinity. *1911*

Lumbering was the great industry in that day in this region, as it is to-day. Fifty odd years ago the lumber teams furnished the bulk of travel on the highways and there were inns at frequent intervals for the entertainment of the teamsters, who would stop over night wherever night overtook them.

The regular price for a man's supper, lodging and the housing of his team was fifty cents.

DEAD AT SON'S HOME

Lohn T. Rice, of Corinth, Passed Away in This Village Yesterday Morning.

John T. Rice, one of the foremost citizens of Corinth, died of pleuro-pneumonia yesterday morning, at the home of his son, Philip E. Rice, of this village. *news Feb 2 1911*

Mr. Rice arrived in Warrensburgh Saturday evening, coming here from North Creek, where he was taken ill. Upon reaching his son's residence a physician was summoned, who found his patient was suffering from pleurisy as the result of a severe cold contracted while on a business trip to the northern towns. Pneumonia developed. A counsel of doctors was held and a trained nurse engaged. Mr. Rice's condition Tuesday showed improvement, but that night the symptoms became alarming. The oxygen treatment was used and his life prolonged by this means.

Deceased was born in Port Henry, February 9, 1849. In the early fifties his parents moved to Conklingville and later to Corinth, where his father, who was killed in the Civil War, conducted a tannery. He was practically a life-long resident of Corinth and took an active interest in the town's affairs holding several offices of responsibility. He also served as school commissioner of Saratoga county. He was an elder in the Presbyterian church and a prominent Mason and Odd Fellow. A widow and a sister, Mrs. E. A. Walker, of Corinth, and a son, Philip E. Rice, of Warrensburgh, survive.

Times OBITUARY *1911*

Jan 30 Mrs. Sarah Tuttle.

The funeral of Mrs. Sarah Tuttle, who died Thursday at the home of her son, Jay Tuttle, at Bolton Landing, was held this afternoon and was well attended by friends and relatives. Mrs. Tuttle was the mother of William S. Tuttle of this city and was ninety-one years and six months old. She was the last membebr of the Stewart family and was well known in Bolton Landing and in this city. Despite her age, Mrs. Tuttle enjoyed the best of health until a short time before her death. Besides the above mentioned sons, she is survived by three daughters, Mrs. W. K. Bixby of St. Louis, Mrs. George Cronkhite of Kattskill Bay and Miss Roxie G. Tuttle of Bolton.

RANDOM THOUGHTS.

Who marries for money often doesn't get even that.

The man who hints that he could tell much if he would, probably couldn't.

Who carries evil report about others to you will carry evil report about you to others.

When a person tells you that "they say", ask him whom he means by "they."

He that farely complains will receive attention when he does.

Some men waste much time in trying to do things for which they are not fitted.—Albany Journal.

UTICA SATURDAY GLOBE, DEC 31 1910

EDWARD M. SHEPARD, of New York.
NOTED LAWYER AND AUTHOR WHO IS IN THE RACE FOR UNITED STATES SENATORSHIP.

A HUNDRED GLENS FALLS BOYS ARE GIVEN START ON ROAD TO SUCCESS

Star Jan 9 1911.

Twenty-Five Dollars Placed to the Credit of Each Boy by Henry Crandall, Originator of the "Boys' Savings Club," Great Enthusiasm shown.

When Joseph R. Duell, manager of Henry Crandall's Boys' Saving Club which was organized last Saturday called the second meeting to order this afternoon, Crandall Hall was crowded to its capacity and boys were lined out through the hall and halfway down the stairs trying to gain admission to become members. As the membership is limited to one hundred those who remained after that number were enrolled had to be turned away and there were thirty sadly disappointed youngsters who were told that the constitution limited the membership to one hundred and as that number had already joined, they could not be enrolled.

The final organization was perfected this afternoon by Mr. Duell assisted by N. S. McOmber, another prominent G. A. R. man. The boys were lined up and their names were taken down in the big book after the ob-

ject of the club had been explained to them.

The enthusiasm with which the boys entered into the spirit of the organization indicates that it will be far more successful than Mr. Crandall, whose generous philanthropy makes it possible, or Mr. Duell ever dreamed. Mr. Crandall gives each member $62.50 and the boy has to save $37.50. This money remains in the bank until the boy is twenty-one years old and there are certain rules and regulations that he must observe, such as refraining from the use of liquor, tobacco, etc. Each member receives a bank book with $25 to his credit and when he has saved $37.50 the other $37.50 will be deposited for him by Mr. Crandall.

Mr. Duell said this afternoon that meetings will be held from time to time so that the members may become acquainted and entertainments will also be held.

HORSES DROWN IN LAKE GEO. WATERS

GEO. POTTER OF BOLTON TAKES PLUNGE WITH TEAM—BARELY ESCAPES DEATH 1911

Star — Jan 19

On Monday afternoon, George Potter, a teamster of Bolton, had a very narrow escape from drowing, when the sleigh which he was driving broke through the ice and sank to the bottom, carrying the team with it.

Potter was drawing cement from Bolton to Three Brothers' Island, the summer home of Mrs. Spencer Trask, and had about a 5,000-pound load on his sleigh. At the point where the accident occurred the ice was only six inches thick and this was not enough to support the sleigh.

The heavy load caused the sleigh to sink like lead and this pulled the horses down. They made frantic efforts to save themselves, but to no avail, for they soon sank out of sight.

Mr. Potter was also precipitated into the water, but quickly recovered himself and was on the ice. He turned to help the horses, but they had gone down in the meantime and being hitched to the heavily laden sleigh, never rose to the surface.

Outside of his icy dip, Mr. Potter is none the worse for his experience. The team was valued at about $300.

"Your Kiss."

To the Editor of "The Press."

Sir:—Please give inclosed original poem, "Your Kiss," space in "The Forum."

E. ELLSWORTH CLASPBY.
Lewistown, Pa., Sept. 6, 1910.

The world hath a wealth of pleasures,
  That pleases the human eye;
There are wondrous sights daily to see,
  Beneath the blue-domed sky.
But the attractions of city or country,
  Are lacking the lasting bliss,
Of a look into your innocent eyes,
  Or taste of your loving kiss.

God gave us the hills and valleys,
  And made the meadows green;
He built the mountains, towering so high,
  And modeled the landscape scene;
But of all the works of creation,
  Excelled are they, dear miss,
By the sunny smile upon your face,
  And the sweetness of your kiss.

God molded the frame of mortal,
  A wonderful job well done;
Then took a rib and woman made,
  Poor man, an improvement upon;
And he that speaks slight of woman,
  Surely never felt the bliss
Of a look into her innocent eyes,
  Or taste of a loving kiss.

GREAT INTEREST SHOWN IN HAGUE RACE CARNIVAL

Star Feb 1, 1911

Yesterday's race meeting at Hague was a most enthusiastic one, and large numbers were present. The ice was in excellent condition,

GOOD PROGRAM ON ICE COURSE

Times

The ice race meeting at Hague came to a close yesterday. The summary:

2:29 Class.

Colonel Hank, (Brown)..	4	4	1	1	1
Putnam Jack, (Sears)....	2	1	2	3	3
Miss Bolton, (Bolton)....	1	3	3	2	2
Babbitt Sprague, (Bailey)	3	2	4	4	4

Time—2:28 1-2; 2:25; 2:24; 2:23 1-2; 2:27.

Free-For-All.

Feb 4 1911

Lambert J., (Brown).......	1	1	2	1
Con, (Towers)........	2	3	1	4
Fabiola, (Dudley)	3	2	4	2
George M., (Towers).......	4	4	3	3

Time—2:21 1-2; 2:21; 2:20; 2:27.

Green Race.

Orwell Belle, (Treadway)....	1	1	1
Betty B., (Baker)...........	2	2	3
Lady Elle, (Wallace)........	3	3	2

Time—2:40; 2:38 1-2; 2:38.

"UNCLE HENRY" CRANDALL CELEBRATES 90TH BIRTHDAY

Grand Army Men Pay Tribute to "Grand Old Man of the North"

Star Feb 14 1911.

Uncle Henry Crandall, the "Grand Old Man of the North," celebrated his ninetieth birthday anniversary yesterday. During the day Mr. Crandall was the recipient of many congratulatory messages, and about 7:30 o'clock in the evening a delegation of twenty-five members of Post E. M. Wing, G. A. R., called at his residence and presented him with a box of beautiful flowers. The presentation speech was made by Colonel Frank Bryant and Mr. Crandall, in his usual hearty manner, thanked his callers for their thoughtfulness.

WORDEN'S JOHN HENRY IS WINNER

Times

Feb 16 — 1911

The ice races at Lake George yesterday afternoon attracted a large crowd of horsemen. Following are the officials: Starter, Leonard Bibbey; judges, W. G. Leland and U. G. Smith, of Glens Falls, and John Woodward of Warrensburg.

The summary:

Named Race, Purse $50.

John Henry, (Worden)....	1	1	1
Ada McGregor, (Hall)......	3	2	2
John L., (Lucia)...........	2	3	3
Bessie F., (Finkle).........	4	4	4
Honest Dan, (Rourke).....	5	5	5

Time—2:33, 2:33 1-4, 2:33 1-2.

2:20 Class.

Colonel Hanks, (Brown)	4	1	1	1
John O., (Wilson).....	1	2	2	5
Steve, (Bailey)	2	3	3	2
Mary Fraiser, (Hall)...	3	4	4	4
Belle Ringer, (Bryant)..	5	5	5	3

Time—2:23 1-4, 2:24, 2:21 3-4, 2:27.

Uncle Henry, although ninety years of age, stands today as one of the busiest men in the State. Although not actively engaged in business pursuits, he manages to busy himself in a manner such that through his efforts untold good is almost constantly dealt out to both the old and the young. He is, in every sense of the word, a self-made man. Starting with practically nothing he has climbed step by step up the ladder of success until today he may be very appropriately referred to as a striking example of what can be accomplished through strict adherence to duty.

DEATH OF OLD TIME ENGINEER

Times. Feb 4 1911

HIRAM PHILO PASSES AWAY AT GLEN STREET HOME.

BUSY LIFE ENDED

Mr. Philo Made Original Map and Boundaries When Glens Falls Was Incorporated as Village in 1839— Was Coroner When Lake George Boat "John Jay" Burned.

Hiram Philo, one of the oldest and best known residents of the county died yesterday afternoon at 3:45 o'clock at his home, 329 Glen street. Mr. Philo was born in Halfmoon, Saratoga county on March 10, 1824.

Mr. Philo was a civil engineer, and with his father, who also followed this profession, he established the boundaries of Glens Falls village when it was incorporated in 1839. He had charge of the running out of subsequent extensions in 1874. He also surveyed nearly all of the islands at Lake George which were sold by the state.

Mr. Philo was a merchant in Glens Falls, Warrensburg and Bolton for about twenty-one years and in 1843-44 conducted a store at Glen and Warren streets. At that time he lived on the present site of No. 27 Elm street.

He was a justice of the peace in the town of Bolton for eight years, notary public for over forty and was coroner at the time of the burning of the steamer "John Jay" on Lake George, about 1856 when several lives were lost. He was trustee of schools at Bolton for seventeen years, was town clerk of Bolton several terms and was nominated twice for member of assembly and once as supervisor, declining the nominations.

He learned the civil engineering profession from his father and it is said of him that about ninety per cent. of the older deeds and title papers of property in Glens Falls were prepared by him or under his direction.

On April 17, 1844, he was married at Sandy Hill to Miss Amy Coffin. Mrs. Philo died November 17, 1900, at the age of seventy-six years.

THE BACHELOR'S VALENTINE.

All alone he sits in his room tonight,
  A bachelor by choice, is he;
Surrounded by furnishings so bright,
  A picture of luxury.
His library is certainly most complete,
  For good is his taste in books:
Many and rare, the volumes there
  As one may find who looks.
His smoking set enjoys a place
  Conspicuous to the eye;
"Dudeen" and cigars are things of
    grace
  On the stand they occupy.
His den, as 'tis called, (and rightly,
    sir:)
  Is filled with each needful thing
To fit the wants of his solitude,
  And bachelor comfort bring.
O, yes, there are photos too, galore—
  Tho' of maidens—just a few
Of his favored girl acquaintances,
  Whom he condescended to
Accept cards from, and even more
  He has them still;—yet why
He cannot tell, unless it be
  They're pleasing to the eye.
Perhaps he meets the originals
  In the city's throng each day,
Or maybe they're but memories
  Who dwell—"far, far away."
But nearby or distant, all are fair,
  From the maid of pensive face,
To the roguish lass who smiles at him
  With happy girlish grace.
  But, thoughtful eyes and laughing
    eyes
  Peep from the mantle in vain,
At "he of my tale, who chose his
    fate—
  A bachelor to remain.
          (February 14th.)
Alone he sits in his room tonight,
  But he reads no volume grand—
His glance now rests on perfumed
    squares,
  Written in feminine hand.
The inspection over, with a smile
  He gathers them up, with care,
And binding them all in one precious
    (?) lot,
  They're dispatched to the escri-
    toire's care.
And the bachelor returns to his Mor-
    ris chair
  Close by the fireside bright;
While Cupid, pausing at the door,
  Smilingly whispers, "good-night!
We'll meet again my lonely man,
  On another holiday—
When satin and lace and sentiment
  You will not store away."
          (Five years later.)
All alone (oh, no!) he sits tonight,
  But not in a den dwells he;
He's reading the evening press, just
    now,
While DOROTHY'S MAKING THE
    TEA.
  Lost in Time's sea, his once firm
    vow
—A "bachelor" to remain—
  He's a husband now, and for no
    wealth
Would he be single again.

THE CENSUS FIGURES FOR VILLAGES AND TOWNS OF COUNTY

Times Jan 24 1911

Reports Compiled and Given Out Today in Washington—Population of Glens Falls by Wards.

(Special to Glens Falls Daily Times)

WASHINGTON, Jan. 24—The popu-
lation of Warren county towns and
villages and Glens Falls city by
wards as reported today follows:
  Bolton, town—1518.
  Caldwell, town, including Lake
George village—1482.
  Lake George, village—632.
  Chestertown—1731.
  Glens Falls City by wards:
  Ward One—3,177.
  Ward Two—3,443.
  Ward Three—4,051.
  Ward Four—1,836.

Ward Five—2,728.
Hague, town—1,043.
Horicon, town—1,001.
Johnsburg, town—2,315.
Luzerne, town—1,185.
Queensbury, town—2,667.
Stony Creek, town—858.
Thurman, town—805.
Warrensburg, town—2,385.
  Hudson Falls and Fort Edward.
Kingsbury, town, including Hudson
Falls village, population 7,080.
  Hudson Falls, village, 5,189.
  Fort Edward, town, including vil-
lage, 5,740.
  Fort Edward village, 3,762.

"THE CHARMING WOMAN.

Miss Myrtle is going to marry,
  And a number of hearts she will break;
There's Lord George, Tom Brown and
    Sir Harry,
  All dying of love for her sake!
'Tis a match in all must opinion,
  Let the gossips say all that they can!
For indeed, she's a charming woman,
  And he's a most fortunate man!

Yes, indeed, she's a charming woman,
  She reads both Latin and Greek;
And I'm told that she solved a problem
  In Euclid before she could speak.
Had she been but a daughter of mine,
  I'd have taught her to knit and to
    sew,
But her mother (a charming woman!)
  Couldn't think of such trifles, you
    know.

Oh, she's really a charming woman!
  But I think she's a little too thin,
And no wonder such very late hours
  Should ruin her beautiful skin.
It may be a fancy of mine,
  But her voice has a rather sharp tone,
And I'm told that these charming
    women
  Are apt to have wills of their own.

She sings like a bullfinch or linnet,
  And talks like an archbishop, too;
She can play you a rubber and win it,
  If she has nothing better to do!
She can chatter of poor laws and tithes,
  And the value of labor and land;
'Tis a pity when charming women
  Talk of things they don't understand.

I am told that she hasn't a penny,
  Yet her gowns would make Maradas
    stare,
And I fear that her bills must be many,
  But you know that's her husband's
    affair!
Such husbands are very uncommon,
  So regardless of prudence and pelf;
But they say such a charming women
  Is a fortune, you know, in herself!

She has brothers and sisters by dozens,
  And all charming people, they say,
And several tall Irish cousins,
  Whom she loves—in a sisterly way.
Young men, if you take my advice,
  You would find it an excellent plan—
Don't marry a charming women,
  If you are a sensible man.

WHAT "TEDDY" SAID

Rooseveltian Philosophy Poe[t]ized by M. J. Fitzpatrick.

MANY SUBJECTS TOUCHED UPON

new Feb 23 1911

And Treated with Characteristic Strenuosity

—Read by Veteran Vaudeville Artist at
Club Dinner and Received with
Very Great Enthusiasm.

M. J. Fitzpatrick, the veteran actor
and vaudeville artist, who makes Warrensburgh his home, returned to this
place Tuesday from an extended tour
through the West and South, playing in
the leading vaudeville theatres of the
principal cities. Having been on the
stage and touring the country, from
Maine to California, for several decades, Mr. Fitzpatrick has circles of
friends in most places where men congregate, and one of these he struck a
few weeks ago while playing a week
stand in a Western city. A club dinner
was on during the week and the genial
"Fitz" being well known as a clever
entertainer, was invited to participate
in the pleasures of the occasion and say
a few words to his friends while the
post prandial program was in progress.

You can Molly Coddle to a frazzle
  A politician that is daft,
You can count me out a present
  For my true friend Billy Taft,
But don't you think for a moment
  That I'm politically dead,
Or I'll come back again to fool you—
  And that's what Teddy said.

-82-

Abraham Lincoln.

To the Editor of "The Press."

Sir:—It was my good fortune to have heard both the first and last inaugurals of Abraham Lincoln. He was fond of story-telling, but he knew when to use them. There were no stories in any of his messages. His stories were arguments or illustrated the subject discussed.

The first time I saw Lincoln was at his first inaugural in front of th Capitol. There were, not counting those on the platform, less than 50 spectators. When he appeared, h looked for somewhere to place hi silk hat. A stout muscular man, not many inches over five feet in height, with long black curling hair, relieved him of it. That man was "the little giant," Stephen A. Douglass, Lincoln's friend and political opponent. Both then were united against secession. Lincoln's inaugural and the many

discussions, whether it meant war or peace, are on the records of those days. A friend who then stood beside me in less than six weeks wore the gray and I wore the blue.

After the 19th of April—the date when the first blood of the Civil War, also the date when the first blood of the Revolution, was shed—a Maryland delegation visited Lincoln protesting against any more troops passing through Maryland. The President replied that they were not fish to swim under it, nor fowls of the air to fly over it, therefore, they must pass through it. Rev. Dr. Fuller, one of that delegation on returning home said, "Cursed is the people who have an ape for their President." This is an age of forgiveness yet I cannot quite forgive the doctor for those bitter words, though he has passed away, and after the death of Father Abraham, apologized for having used

them. A gentleman having requested his autograph, Lincoln wrote Mr. J. Walter S——. You ask me for my autograph here it is, A. Lincoln. In 1863 I attended a White House reception. As the visitors approached in line, each one received a vigorous grasp of their hand at the same time drawing them past the President. I was by no means small or weak but that hand-shake made my arm tingle. A Philadelphia friend attended a reception. John G—— was 6 feet 4½ inches in height, straight as a plumb line, a quarter of

an inch taller than the President. A little in line before him was a Jerseyman who was over 6 feet 3 inches and approached on his toes. "Down on your heels, Jersey, You can't pass," said Father Abraham. After looking G—— over, he said, "Mr. G——, Jersey could not pass but I reckon I will have to knuckle under to you. I first heard the Blonden story while waiting to hear election returns. I illustrates Mr. Lincoln's ready wit and apt response. Many committees waited upon him, some urging him to lean more to the North, other to the South. To one of these, he said, "If you had all you possess converted into gold and had given it to Blonden to carry over Niagara Falls on that trip, when he was half over would you shout, 'Blonden, lean a little more to the north or a little more to the south?' Would you not rather hush up until he was over?" A thrill passed through those present when the narrator added, "No man after that durst ask him any question."

In Baltimore, at the close of the war, some divinity students paid me a visit. The day before the assassination we went to Washington. After showing them the public grounds and buildings, towards the evening we reached the White House, where a crowd was assembled, calling for the President to address them. But he sent an apology. I have since thought that had he appeared he would have been then assassinated. All Washington was illuminated, rejoicing at Lee's surrender and the fall of the Confederacy. The next evening in Baltimore one of my student friends said that he was sorry that he did not remain in Washington another day to see Lincoln. I said to shock him if you had waited and gone to Ford's Theater you might have seen him there. Most pious people were then against theater-going. I had previously seen Lincoln at that theater. I little thought then of the great national tragedy that was about that time being enacted at that theater. Next morning brought the sad news. Baltimore homes, both Union and secession, were draped in mourning. I had not wept since boyhood but that day tears dimmed my eyes. I loved Lincoln.

WELL KNOWN BOLTON MAN DIES TWO DAYS AFTER WIFE

Esli Alonzo Griffin Succumbs But a Short Time After Death of Spouse

Mar 16 1911

Following his wife, who died on Wednesday last at the Utica hospital, Esli Alonzo Griffin, aged 53 years, died Friday at midnight at the home of his father, Benjamin Griffin, of Bolton Landing, interment having been made Monday in the Huddle cemetery. His wife was formerly Miss Clementine Truesdale, the couple having been married in 1880. After their marriage they lived in Glens Falls, where Mr. Griffin conducted a livery stable on Park street. Mr. Griffin was well-known throughout Warren and Washington Counties. He is survived by his father, two sisters, Mrs. Leonard Lane, of Bolton, and Mrs. Chauncey Murch, of Glens Falls, and also one niece, Mrs. Lane, of this city.

"Al." Brown for Village President.

Alfred Brown, proprietor of Hotel Hudson, at Fort Edward, has been nominated by the Republicans for president of that village. Mr. Brown was formerly proprietor of the Warren house, Warrensburgh, and is thoroughly adapted for the hotel business. Everybody likes him and calls him "Al." He is a good judge of men and knows quite a bit about the muddy science of politics. And this is one reason why he will make a good village president. *news Mar 1916*

Steamboat Service on the Lakes

news Mar 30 1916

A. A. Heard, general passenger agent of the Delaware and Hudson company, announces that the steamer Ticonderoga will begin service between Grand Isle, Plattsburgh, Burlington and Westport on Lake Champlain about April 15. The steamer Vermont on the same line will resume through service between Plattsburgh and Fort Ticonderoga on May 29. On Lake George the steamer Mohican will begin service May 1 and the steamer Sagamore May 29. The full summer schedule will be in force June 26.

CAMPAIGN COST OF SHEPARD'S RUN FOR U. S. SENATOR

Star 1911 apl 11

Albany, April 10.—The Brooklyn committee of Democrats, which advocated the election of Edward M. Shepard for United States Senator, today filed with Secretary of State Lazansky a statement showing expenditures amounting to the fund were: George Foster Peabody, William N. Dykman and A. Augustus Healy, each $500; James Shevlin, $250. Other contributors were: Alexander E. Orr and Herman A. Metz $50 each and George L. Rives, $25. The principal items of expenses were for newspaper advertising, bureau service and clerk hire.

Saturday another Shepard committee certified to the Secretary of State that it spent $4,233.79 in aid of Mr. Shepard's candidacy.

THEY HELPED THEMSELVES.

Times apl 11

Too Much of a Neighborly Spirit Lands Two Indians in Jail. *1911*

Peter Lawrence and his son, Will, two Indian residents of East Lake George were arrested last evening at their home by Deputy Sheriff William Hackett on a charge of burglary. On Saturday evening the men broke into the summer home of Mr. Knox of Troy,

JOHNSBURG FARMER MURDERED AND CHARRED BODY FOUND BY NEIGHBOR IN RUINS OF BURNED FARM HOUSE

William Hopkins, a Johnsburg Farmer, Believed to Have Been Killed by Charles Anders, an Employe, Who Sets Fire to Building in Which Men Were Staying

COUNTY OFFICIALS SEARCHING FOR ALLEGED ASSASSIN

Discovery Is Made by James Piper Whose Suspicions Are Aroused by Finding of Sleigh Belonging to Hopkins Some Two Miles Distant from Farm House. Foot-Prints in Snow Lead to Belief that Culprit, after Driving Away from Scene of Crime, Abandoned Rig and Made His Escape in the Woods Toward Northville, Details of Trouble not yet Known

Murdered by a drunken companion, who afterward set fire to and burned the house in which both men were staying, is believed to have been the fate of William Hopkins, a Johnsburg farmer, whose charred remains were found in the ruins of a house on what is known as the Jenks farm about three miles from Bakers Mills yesterday morning.

Murderer at Large

Charles Anders, of Mill Creek, a twenty-year-old youth for whom a warrant has been issued, is believed to be Hopkins' murderer, and although every effort was being made by the authorities to find him, he was still at large at a late hour last evening.

No Details of Crime

No details of the double crime have as yet come to light, and nothing definite can be learned until the apprehension of Anders is effected. The Jenk's farm, the scene of the crime, was owned by Hopkins, but was untenanted. Hopkins and Anders left North Creek Sunday evening for the farm, where Hopkins was engaged in making maple sugar for a few days. It is said that either or both men had been drinking, and a traveller at a late hour is said to have reported that he heard the voices of the men in argument when he drove by. No other evidence has as yet been secured that indicates that the men bore any ill feelings toward each other.

Piper Makes Discovery

The remains of Hopkins with his skull fratured and the burned farm house was first discovered by James Piper, who lives on the Oregon Road, a few miles from the Jenk's farm, at about seven o'clock. When Piper arose at daylight, and started toward his barn, he discovered Hopkins' team of horses in his yard. Recognizing the horses, and fearing some accident had occured to their owner, Piper started back over the road which the horses had come. At a point about two miles from his home, he discovered a sleigh to which the horses had been hitched at the side of the roadway. A man's tracks in the snow, proved that some person had driven the horses as far as this point, and had then unhitched them from the sleigh. After unhitching the animals, the driver started out across the fields and woods in the direction of Northville.

Body Is Found

Piper continued on his way to the Jenks farm, and upon his arrival found the home in ashes. A search among the embers revealed a human body, which was afterwards indentified as that of Hopkins. Although the face and body were burned beyond recognition, an indentification badge, which the man wore on his suspenders, told who he was. The crime was reported to Justice of the Peace Braley of Johnsburg, and a warrant issued for the arrest of Anders. Constable Baker was sent after Anders who is believed to be still hiding in the vicinity.

Mentally Affected

Anders, who lived with his parents on what is known as the Dallaba Place near Mill Creek is said to be eccentric, and persons who know him cite numerous instances which seem to indicate that the youth is mentally affected.

Hopkins, the victim, was about forty years of age and leaves a wife and four children.

Officials On Trail

Coroner Burt, Sheriff T. J. Smith and District Attorney John H. Cunningham left for North Creek yesterday, and every effort will be made to capture Anders.

THE DAVY CROCKETT HOUSE, SAN ANTONIO, TEXAS.

[Former home of one of the immortal heroes of the battle of the Alamo, in the Texas war fo independence, which is now preserved as a memorial to one of the most picturesque frontiersmen of the nation.]

THE center of interest in America to-day is historic old San Antonio, which is the point of concentration for the bulk of troops that have gathered in Texas to be utilized in the present emergency. Just beyond Fort Sam Houston, which may be termed the citadel of San Antonio, is a grass covered plain, 800 acres in extent, where the great camp is situated. The troops are massed by regiments, which are encamped in squads, all facing in the direction of Gen. Carter's headquarters, which are located on top of a little hill that is the only elevation to break the monotony of the landscape.

The interesting city of San Antonio consists of three parts: the old town, or San Antonio proper, between the San Pedro and the San Antonio rivers; Chihuahua, west of the San Pedro; and Alamo, east of the San Antonio. The old town is the business quarter and has in great part lost its Mexican character, having been almost entirely rebuilt since 1860. Chihuahua is almost exclusively Mexican in character and population. The houses are one story high, built partly of stone and partly of upright logs with cane roofs.

Alamo is the largest quarter of the city, is considerably larger than the other two and is mostly inhabited by Germans.

In the north part is the Alamo plaza, with the fort of that name which, 6, years ago, was the scene of a savage and sanguinary encounter between a small company of Texans and Americans, and a greatly superior force of Mexicans, which resulted in the capture of the fort and the massacre of the entire garrison. Among the valiant defenders was the famous Davy Crockett, who had gone to help the Texans in their fight for independence, and who fell surrounded by the bodies of those he had slain ere he was cut down.

The heroic valor of the garrison and the barbarity of the Mexicans thrilled the American people. The cry of "Remember the Alamo!" was heard throughout the country; and the feeling which it excited did much to bring on the war with Mexico, in which an American army swept triumphantly into the capital of the Montezumas.

Hard by this historic place is the old cabin of Davy Crockett, which has been preserved by the patriotic Texans as a lasting memorial to the hero, who lost his life in the sublime cause of liberty.

"SPRINGTIME WILL COME AGAIN."

We miss you dear little robin,
  Since you have gone away;
To the land of balmy breezes,
  To sing the live long day.
We miss your dear sweet voice,
  Coming from bush and tree;
No more we hear sweet echoes,
  Sounding across the lea.

We miss sweet roses and pansies,
  And asters of many a hue;
We miss the dahlias and peonies,
  And violets of deepest blue.
We miss the sweet scented clover,
  Casting fragrance on the air;
Since the beautiful flowers have faded,
  All seems desolate everywhere.

But the chill hand of Winter,
  Will soon be lifted again;
The snow and ice will disappear,
  From hillside, field and lane.
The robin will come from Southland,
  And herald the gladsome news;
That Springtime is near at hand,
  With flowers of many hues.

GOV. AND MRS. JOHN A. DIX.

[First lady of the State photographed with her husband just before the inauguration.—Photo copyright, 1911, by George Grantham Bain.]

AMID pomp and splendor, with cannons booming and the blare of music and enthusiastic acclaim, John A. Dix was inaugurated Governor at Albany on Monday. The occasion was unusual in that he is the first Democrat to fill the place in 18 years—since Roswell P. Flower was New York's chief executive.

The parade was the longest and most brilliant in years and a great number of strangers swelled the local crowds on the streets. The Governor's address contained several timely suggestions and emphasized the need of reducing expenses. The press of the State warmly endorses the Governor's pledges and predict for him a successful administration.

FEW HISTORICAL FACTS ABOUT WARREN COUNTY

Some Interesting Data Gathered From the Gazetteer of New York—County Will be One Hundred Years Old on *March 15 ~1911~* March 12, 1913. *True*

Town.	Males	Females
Bolton	625	512
Caldwell	452	428
Chester	993	943
Hague	309	306
Horicon	678	568
Johnsburg	1,059	924
Luzerne	666	620
Queensbury	3,237	3,201
Stony Creek	491	422
Thurman	687	572
Warrensburg	987	959
Total *In 1860*	10.184	9,485

William E. Burdett, formerly editor of The Glens Falls Daily Times, has in his possession a copy of the Gazetteer of New York, a book published in 1860, which was a gift to him from his grandfather, the late Elliott Burdett of Whitehall.

Because of the present agitation for a centennial celebration in this county in 1913, many of the facts this book contains concerning Warren county and its name, will prove interesting.

Warren county was formed from Washington county on March 12, 1813, just ninety-eight years ago last Sunday, and was named in honor of General Joseph Warren, a hero of the Revolutionary War. The first court was held at what was known as the "Lake George Coffee House" and in 1817, a court house was built at Caldwell. The first newspaper in the county was started by John Cunningham in 1813 and was known as the Warren County Patriot. Fourteen papers had been started between that time and 1860 of which number, one was the Glens Falls Messenger, which is still being issued.

The town of Bolton was formed from Thurman on March 25, 1799. Hague was taken from this town in 1810 and a part of Horicon in 1838. In 1860, there were two places of worship in Bolton, a Methodist Episcopal and a Baptist church. The first church in the town was a Presbyterian edifice with the Rev. Mr. Armstrong as pastor. This was in the year 1804 but at the writing of the Gazetteer in 1860, the Presbyterians had no meeting place in Bolton.

Caldwell was formed from Queensbury, Bolton and Thurman on March 2, 1810. The town was named in honor of General James Caldwell, a merchant of Albany, who became a patentee of 1,595 acres, of its ground, by grants issued September 18 and 29, 1787. In 1860, there were but two churches in that town, the Presbyterian and the Union.

Chester was formed from Thurman on March 25, 1799. The settlement of that town, commenced in the latter part of the eighteenth century and in 1796, the first church, a Baptist, was built, the Rev. Jehil Fox being pastor.

Hague was formed from Bolton, February 28, 1807, and was at first known as Rochester. Its name was changed April 6, 1808, and a part of Horicon was taken from it in 1838. The first settlement of this town was made in 1796 and in 1860, the Union church was the only one in the town. Horicon was taken from it in 1838, and Hague, March 29, 1838. This town was settled in the year 1790 and in 1820, the Rev. Nathaniel Streeter, a Wesleyan Methodist clergyman, organized the first church. In 1860, the four churches of the town were two Baptist, the Wesleyan Methodist and the Methodist Episcopal.

Johnsburg was formed from Thurman on April 6, 1805, and took its name from the first name of John Thurman an early settler, who settled there at the close of the Revolutionary war. The Baptist church was organized in 1793 and in 1860 there were four more churches in the town.

Luzerne was formed from Queensbury on April 10, 1792 and was known as Fairfield, but on April 6, 1808, the name was changed to Luzerne. The first settlements were made in 1770 along the Hudson River.

Queensbury was incorporated as a township by patent, May 20, 1762 and recognized as a town, March 13, 1786. Glens Falls was incorporated on April 12, 1839. The village of Glens Falls after twenty-one years of growth had a population of 3,420 in 1860.

Stony Creek was formed from Athol on November 3, 1852. The first settlement was in 1795. The first preacher in this town was Johnathan Paull, a Christian Indian. The first church, a Presbyterian was organized in 1800.

Thurman was formed April 10, 1792. Settlement was begun in the latter part of the eighteenth century. A Baptist church was the first formed there, the Rev. Jehil Fox being the first minister. This town was also named in honor of John Thurman.

Warrensburg was formed from Thurman, February 12, 1813. The village of Warrensburg constituted the greater part of the town and in 1860, the village had a population of 700. The first settlement was made a few years after the close of the Revolution. A Methodist Episcopal church, the first in the town was organized in 1796, and the Rev. Henry F. Ryan was the first minister.

The population of the county in 1860 was as follows:

MEETS DEATH BUT SAVES LIFE OF HIS SWEETHEART

Star apl 13 1911

Arthur Kingsley a seventeen-year-old youth, or Adirondack, gave up his life Sunday afternoon in a successful attempt to save, that of his sweetheart, Miss Edna Avery of Ossining young Kingsley had been visiting for several months past with his grand mother, Mrs. Freeman Webb, of Ossining and had been a constant companion of Miss Avery during that time.

The two young people started for a walk Sunday afternoon, and after walking a short distance came to the tracks of the New York Central railroad, where they decided to turn and walk along the track. The particular portion of the railroad chosen by the young people runs along the top of a high embankment. The track was a double one and when the couple saw the southbound train approaching they leisurly crossed to the other track. The noise of the approaching train deafened them and on looking up Young Kingsley saw that a north bound express was but a few feet away from them on the other track.

He seized his companion and hurled her down the embankment but could not save himself, being crushed beneath the wheels and mortally injured. So quick was his action in rescuing Miss Avery, that the young man hurled her with great force she rolling over and over the bank for nearly fifty feet, stopping within a few feet of the Hudson river.

Although badly scratched and bruised the young woman scrambled up the bank. The injured boy was removed to the home of his grandmother where he died.

Arthur Kingsley was the son of Mr. and Mrs. Charles Kingsley of Adirondack to which place the remains have been taken for interment.

—86—

THE REV. CICERO BARBER REACHES 101ST. MILESTONE

Owing to His Feeble Health, Fort Edward Clergyman Will Not Preach His Anniversary Sermon Next Sunday.

Mar 9, 1911

The Rev. Cicero Barber, of Fort Edward, will celebrate his 101st birthday tomorrow, but considering that he has earned a respite from preaching, he will not occupy the Fort Edward Methodist church pulpit on Sunday as has been his custom for many years. Mr. Barber is in feeble health and it is with regret that the people of Fort Edward reconcile themselves to the omission of the anniversary sermon.

The aged minister has led a remarkable life, one of great usefulness and help to his fellow men.

Rev. Cicero Barber is the oldest member of the Troy Conference, having been admitted to the conference in 1887, seventy-three years ago.

The Barber family has been one of considerable note in the history of this section. The grandfather of the subject of this sketch, Moses Barber, was a Connecticut citizen, and a soldier of the Revolutionary War. He was in the battle of Saratoga, where Burgoyne was met and defeated and his army and himself were made prisoners.

Dr. Isaac Barber, father of Cicero, was born in 1781, in the town of Berne, Albany county. He studied medicine and practiced his profession in Schoharie, and also represented his county in the state legislature. He was associated with Governor DeWitt Clinton and was that great statesman's frequent adviser. He was an ensign in the War of 1812, at Sackett's Harbor. He was also a great reader and a fine scholar.

The original Barbers came from Connecticut and Rhode Island, and it is found that their ancestry can be traced back to the time of William the Conqueror.

JIM EMERSON'S STORIES.

Another Good One Told by the 'Burg Statesman Appears in N. Y. Herald.

This morning's edition of the New York Herald contains another one of Jim Emerson's stories. His latest follows: *Times apl 7*

"Speaking of being pursued," said Senator Emerson, "there is a fellow named Dan Moody up in my county, who use to be a great hunter. One time he was out in the woods when a big black bear took after him. He had no gun, he had nothing, in fact, but a small pocket knife, and he knew he was in for a devil of a time. He had met black bears before.

"After he had been running for half an hour and the bear was slowly but certainly gaining on him, he decided to pray, and this is in substance what he said:—

"'Good Lord, I ain't much on praying; in fact, I don't know that I ever prayed before, but I'm in a hell of a pickle here now and I need help. I shan't ask you for anything again, I promise that, and as I was saying, I don't believe I ever asked you for anything before, but I'm going to ask you now to save me from that bear. He's bigger'n I be and it won't be a fair fight. Now, if it happens that you don't feel like helping me please don't help the bear, and jes' lay low, and you'll see the damndest fight you ever saw in your life.'"

"THE MOST BEAUTIFUL WOMAN IN AMERICA,"
WHO HAS BEGUN SUIT FOR DIVORCE AGAINST HER HUSBAND, SIDNEY C. LOVE.

"THE most beautiful woman in America"—according to Sir Philip Burne-Jones, the aesthetic English artist—has begun suit against her husband for divorce. The lady in question is Mrs. Marjorie C. Love, wife of Sidney C. Love, spectacular financier, clubman and polo player. Love began his career as a financier with nothing, quickly made a fortune of more than $1,000,000 and failed completely in 1909. He is now in the far west and there are stories in business circles to the effect that he is paralleling his wonderful rise which started 15 years ago when from a $15 clerk in Keokuk, Iowa, he came to be a manipulator in the higher realms of finance. Reports of his prosperity have reached New York and it is said that having redeemed his fortunes he declared his intention of winning back his wife's love and that he expects to come east on that mission within a few weeks.

According to friends of Mrs. Love, her husband might just as well stay where he is, as she is determined on the divorce. They have been separated for some time—in fact, have not seen each other since August, 1909. No very definite reason is given as to why Mrs. Love wishes to be freed. Two years ago society was astonished to learn that while the couple were residing in England Mrs. C. C. Burnes, of Chicago, Mrs. Love's mother, had appealed to Ambassador Whitelaw Reid to protect her daughter from Mr. Love, who, she said, "was making life unbearable for her."

"He is trying to steal their baby," said Mrs. Burnes, "and my daughter is almost distracted."

The ambassador could not interfere directly, but he found a small and exclusive hotel for Mrs. Love, her baby and her mother. Then a guard was set around the baby.

Love, of course, says all this was nonsense—that he has nothing but affection for his wife and wouldn't cause her trouble for the world.

This is the young man's second experience in the divorce court. His first wife, who was Miss Minerva Cool, of Cornish, Ohio, obtained a divorce from him in 1903 after three years of married life. In her petition for divorce she declared that he had made life miserable for her; that he had refused to support her and that she had to pawn her jewels and sell part of her wardrobe. She afterward married William H. Kemble, of Philadelphia.

TO WED MAN MANY YEARS HER SENIOR

Times Apr. 17, 1911

Miss Kathleen Douglas Figures in Romance.

WELL KNOWN HERE

Sister of Curtis N. Douglas of Albany to Marry a Wealthy Retired Business Man of New York-She is Thirty-Two Years Old and He is Seventy-nine.

Tottering slowly with the aid of a crutch and cane, George Henry Hughes, a wealthy retired business man of New York, aged seventy-nine years, caused much comment Saturday afternoon, when he entered the City Hall of the metropolis and applied for a marriage license. Mr. Hughes has chosen for his partner in joys and suffering, Miss Kathleen Douglas, a young woman of thirty-two years of age who is well known to many residents of this city.

Miss Douglas is an orphan, the daughter of the late J. P. Douglas and a sister of Curtis N. Douglas of Albany, formerly state senator. Her brother's wife is a sister of the wife of Governor Dix. Miss Douglas has earned her livelihood for several years past by writing magazine and newspaper articles, and has been greatly aided in this work by Mr. Hughes, whose ideas on many subjects are along the same lines as are Miss Douglas'

When taking out the marriage license, Mr. Hughes gave his age as "over sixty-five" and Miss Douglas gave her age as thirty-six. Their real ages were afterward disclosed to newspaper men by Mrs. Daniel Rue Chamberlain, an intimate friend of Miss Douglas, who accompanied the couple when they applied for the license. Mrs. Chamberlain stated that the wedding might be held next Wednesday and that the groom had a married daughter, nearly as old as his bride to be.

WOMAN SUES FOR BREACH OF PROMISE

May 17 1911. *Times*

A dispatch from New York today states that Miss Kathleen Douglas of Albany, who is well known in this city, has brought an action for breach of promise against George H. Hughes of New York, the millionaire head of the Oilcloth trust. Miss Douglas is thirty-six and Hughes is over eighty.

Miss Douglas and Hughes appeared at the New York City Hall for a marriage license several weeks ago, and because of the great difference in their ages this caused no little comment. For some reason unknown to her friends, the engagement was suddenly broken off a few days later.

Now Miss Douglas is suing the aged millionaire to recover $100,000.

HORSE THIEF IS CAPTURED AND IS LODGED IN JAIL

Star Sepl 18. 1911

Danny Jackson, the Spruce Mountain youth who stole a horse belonging to Paul Smith, a farmer who lives on the Chester road near Warrensburg, last Saturday night has been captured and is now in the Lake George jail awaiting trial.

"MEET ME BY MOONLIGHT.

Meet me by moonlight alone,
And then I will tell you a tale;
Must be told by the moonlight alone,
In the grove at the end of the vale;
You must promise to come, for I said,
I would show the night flowers their queen;
Nay, turn not away that sweet head,
'Tis the loveliest ev'er was seen.

Daylight may do for the gay,
The thoughtless, the heartless, the free;
But there's something about the moon's way
That is sweeter to you and to me;
Oh; remember, be sure to be there,
For though dearly a moonlight I prize;
I care not for all in the air,
If I want the sweet light of your eyes.

Both the words and music of this song, the first line of which has become one of the most familiar of all "familiar quotations," were produced by J. Augustus Wade, an English composer, who died in London in 1875, aged 75. He was extremely poor and in his last days literally went begging among the music publishers.

LOCAL MEN BUY HOTEL PROPERTY

May 8 1911

M. J. DOLAN AND STERLING F. HIGLEY TO CONDUCT GLEN LAKE RESORT

The Glen Lake Hotel property, part of which was destroyed by fire last winter, has been purchased by M. J. Dolan, Jr., and Sterling F. Higley of this city. Messrs. Dolan and Higley will cause necessary improvements to be made after which the hotel will be opened for the summer season on or about June 1.

Considerable work will be done toward improving the appearance of the property, and an effort will be made to make it the most popular resort in the vicinity. Game and fish dinners, clam chowders, bakes, etc., will be held, and picnickers will be especially catered to. Seats and benches will be placed beneath the trees and the place will otherwise be beautified.

CHARLIE BAKER HERE 1911
May 19

Charles Baker, the "Mayor of Bakers Mills," is enjoying a few days vacation in this vicinity. Monday night Charlie attended the Hurley-Henry bout at the Casino A. C., and yesterday he went to Lake George where he enjoyed himself visiting many friends. Charlie is one of the most popular men in Northern New York and is well known to hundreds of residents of Warren County as one of the squarest and cleanest trotting horse race promoters in the Adirondacks.

Mr. Baker is recovering from injuries, received in an accident at his home in Bakers Mills about a week or ten days ago, and he feels that a few days outing will do him all the good in the world.

To readers who do not know him, personally, Charlie will be remembered as the constable who pursued and caught William Andrews the accused murderer of William Hopkins of Johnsburg, after two days chase through country roads filled with drifted snow.

May Walter A. Ferris 20 '11

Walter A. Ferris, one of Hudson Falls' oldest and most highly respected citizens, died at his home, 21 Maple street, Saturday evening at 11 o'clock, after a four weeks' illness. The deceased was born at Fort Ann. He moved with his parents from that village when three years of age and has since resided here continuously. Mr. Ferris was a veteran of the Civil War. He was 83 years old.

WHEN THE "BOYS IN BLUE" WENT FORTH TO BATTLE

Stirring Incidents of Fifty Years Ago Recalled by Extract from the Glens Falls Republican of May 14, 1861, Preserved by Henry Griffing.

Henry Griffing of Warrensburg has in his possession a copy of the Glens Falls Republican published on Tuesday afternoon, May 14, 1861. The paper is prized very highly by Mr. Griffing because of the fact that it contains an account of the departure from Glens Falls, fifty years ago, of the "boy in blue" who went forth to sacrifice their lives, if necessary, that the union might be preserved and an enslaved people be set free.

Under the caption, "Under Orders—Departure of Recruits," the Republican publishes the following:

The impatience of our soldiers was relieved on Thursday last by the reception of orders from Albany to report themselves at once in that city. The order was received with great satisfaction, and preparations immediately made to leave without delay. The report having been well circulated, long before the time fixed for the departure on Friday, our streets were filled with interested and anxious spectators—men, women and children—some moved by idle curiosity, others desirous of bidding adieu to brothers, husbands, relatives and friends, and still others anxious to shake the soldier by the hand and bid him God speed on his patriotic mission.

About two o'clock p. m., Fire Companies Defiance No. 1 and Cataract No. 2 marched to the centre of the village each Fireman bearing the Stars and Stripes, and preceded by the Glens Falls Brass Band. The Military, consisting of Captain Holden and Clendon's Companies and a Company from Schroon Lake, which had marched up from Fort Edward to accompany our troops to Albany, then formed a hollow square and were addressed by Rev. H. H. Bates, in substance as follows:

Mr. Chairman:—What do we here on this occasion? What means this martial array? For what are these weapons of warfare? Do you reply that our constitutional governors calls to arms in defense of our Capitol, our Halls of Legislation, our words of declaration against Tyranny—of our perils in danger, trials, and deep adversity?—Do you say that the person of your Chief Magistrate is in danger, and that even his life is threatened? And do you tell me that your public altars and your private altars, now so richly protected by our Constitution and laws, are now about to

be thrown down—swept away by rebellious hands, aye, by a traitorous foe? You assure me our happy land —happier than all other lands—by the freedom which is guaranteed to us by thought, or word and act, in our civil position, and in our religious position, is in danger of being the prey to misrule, anarchy and political death? And is all this true? Yea, this, and more than this is true. In common with all portions of our Northern States, in the Counties of Warren, Washington, Saratoga and Essex, noble minded men, whose love of country is something more than words, have come forth from their public or secluded positions, at the call of our constitutional chief magistrate, to defend the rich gifts which Heaven has given us. These are some of the noble men before us.

Officers and soldiers—my countrymen in arms—who are about to leave us for a noble purpose, to accomplish a glorious object: In behalf of this community, and at their request, I rise to express to you the deep interest which is here taken in the common cause which now calls you from your firesides to the field of battle. Believing that through God's help our constitutional government was formed—that His succor and defence have all along been given as seals and pledges of His approbation and protection; and now that rebels and traitors threaten to destroy it, founded in God's wisdom, we say that any mode to change it, other than a constitutional mode, is an insult to Heaven's wisdom—is contrary to our native sense of true and real government. Such act is traitorous—rebellious against the constitutional authority of our country—against the God of battles, whose hand helped us in repelling Tyrants, and to cement our Union with the blood of patriots. Some tell us "the South has a right to revolutionize, as this right is inherent in all States!" If there were no constitutional government, and no right of individual suffrage under it, then I grant that revolution might be allowable as against tyranny and despotism. Southern traitors rebel against a constitution and laws of their own choice and aid in making! They seek not in a Constitutional way to correct any imaginary wrong—They point to no violation of the agreement made between us which we are not quite ready, in a

Constitutional way, to redress. But instead of Constitutionally settling our difficulties, they are irritated that in a Constitutional way a President was chosen, and our government continued! While there has been no censure for unconstitutional acts, they dare rebel, and seek to lead others to become traitors to government! Their position is one fearfully black, corrupt and traitorous in the eye of nations, and in the eye of God! O, my countrymen—soldiers in arms— the cause you have in hand is the cause of right—of Constitutional law against rebels. No page of impartial history shall record other than that their act is rebellious without a shadow of an apology. As Judas had no apology for a traitorous act, so have Southern traitrs no excuse to make, and impartial history will only record them as in truth deserving, as I trust you will give them such chastisement as shall lead them back to allegiance and loyalty to God and man, or else death. If I could see that this rebellion, this revolution, was formed on any justifiable cause —if I could see that the North had in any wise oppressed or tyranized over the South—then instead of urging you on to arms, I would here urge you homeward—to your shops and to your farms.

But as no tyranny, no oppression has ever been attempted over them, no valid excuse can be shown to God or man for rebellion against a government, in its design better than all other governments on earth.

No, my countrymen, we have, as a people, deeply pondered these things. We have consulted the statutes of men, yea, of God, and we find no ground of apology for rebellion and misrule; for revolution against constituted authority, except where Tyranny prevails. Our Fathers have an apology, for laws were imposed upon them to which they never had consented; they were crushed and oppressed by Tyrants, and nature and revelation bade them rise to arms as men, 'free born, and of an age lawful to assert their right to liberty." God nerved their arm for battle. Not for a moment then compare the position of the South, in her unholy and cowardly revolution with our fathers of old.

—89—

CHANCE FOR GRAFT.

Any Speaker Could Have Money.

That All of Champ Clark's Predecessors Were Not Millionaires Was Not Because They Could Not Have Commanded the Coin—Place Where Big Money Might Follow an Appointment or the Nod of a Head—But Most of Our Speakers Have Retired Poor, With Their Honesty Unquestioned.

CHAMP CLARK has come forward as a defender of the civic virtue of his brothers in office. During a recent visit to Philadelphia Mr. Clark took occasion to repudiate the popular idea that all public men are corrupt. To prove his contentions he cited the small worldly estates of former speakers of the House.

To be sure he did not mention his immediate predecessor in office, Uncle "Joe" Cannon, for he is a millionaire several times over. But Uncle Joe aside, a careful investigation of the personal history of all the speakers from the anti-bellum period down to the present seems to prove fairly conclusively that Speaker Clark is by no means without good material on which to base his claims that they did not grow rich in office.

SOME PROMINENT SPEAKERS OF THE HOUSE.

CHAMP CLARK.   THOMAS B. REED.

JOSEPH G. CANNON.

GEN. J. WARREN KEIFER.   CHARLES F. CRISP.

THE WORDEN, Lake George, N. Y.

Times   Apr. 28, 1911

ICE GOES OUT OF THE LAKE TODAY

The ice has been gradually disappearing from Lake George and the last went out today. The bays of the lake have been clear for some time but it was not until the past few days of warm weather that the ice in the center of the lake was affected.

This "break-up" causes much relief of the citizens of Lake George, who were fearful of a late season. It will now be possible to open the season of navigation on scheduled time and it is expected that the Mohican will make her first trip on Monday. This will be the only boat used for the first few weeks after which the Sagamore and Horicon will be pressed into service.

REBEKAH LODGE AT BOLTON.

March 25 1911   News

Calumet, No. 330. Instituted Tuesday with Thirty-five Members.

Calumet Rebekah Degree lodge, No. 330, was instituted at Bolton Landing Tuesday by District Deputy President Clara Hawley, of Lake George, and staff. This is the fifth lodge of the order established in Warren county as an auxiliary of the Odd Fellows lodges. Flourishing organizations have been in existence for some time in Glens Falls, Lake George, Warrensburgh and Chestertown. Johnsburgh is now the only town having an Odd Fellows lodge which has not also the Rebekah, which is especially for the wives, daughters and sisters of members of the three-link fraternity.

Calumet lodge starts with a membership of thirty-five and the following officers: Noble Grand, Kathleen Nelson; vice grand, Maud Vandenburgh; recording secretary, R. T. Taylor; financial secretary, Sarah Taylor; treasurer, Mrs. Tobin; inside guard, Bessie Finkle; outside guard, Benny Sherman. These were installed Tuesday evening by the district deputy. The degree was conferred on the candidates by the team of Montcalm lodge, of Lake George.

The ceremonies were witnessed by about 125 members of the order from the various lodges of the county. Mt. Hackensack lodge, of Warrensburgh, was represented by Sheriff and Mrs. T. J. Smith, Mr. and Mrs. John Beswick and Mr. and Mrs. William L. Smith.

At the conclusion of the evening's work the new lodge entertained the visiting sisters and brothers at a banquet in the town hall.

CANNON BALL FOUND UNDER THE BRIDGE

May 31 1911.

Otto Quist of this city and Royal Smith of South Glens Falls while hunting for stones Saturday on the rocks under the Glen street bridge found a cannon ball that is doubtless a relic of the early wars.

The men were looking for round stones for some minor part of the new Finch and Pruyn office and had a long pole with nails at such an angle that they would fasten over the stone and hold it. The cannon ball, which is three inches in diameter and weighs between eight and nine pounds was found in the bowl like hole commonly called the "Devil's Punch Bowl."

The relic was not badly rusted but groves had been worn by its constant rubbing against the rocks in the bottom of the hole.

RALPH SHAW.

Ralph Shaw, an old resident of Lake George, died at that place Saturday, at the home of his son, Ralph Shaw, Jr. The funeral was held from the home Monday afternoon at 2 o'clock, the Rev. Merton S. Fales officiating. Interment in the Lake George cemetery. *June 1 1911.*

JOHN BULL.

John Bull, of Bolton Landing, died Friday after a long illness of heart disease. He was about sixty years old and leaves a widow; also two sons by a former wife, Theodore Bull, of Baltimore, Md., and Charles Bull, of Lake George.

MAN'S FOOT CRUSHED BY FALLING TROLLEY WHEEL

Star May 27

While returning to this city on a Hudson Valley car which left Glen Lake at 11 o'clock last evening, Paul Enches, who resides at 112 South street, received a bad cut on his right foot when a trolley wheel fell from the pole and crashed through the roof of the car. The wheel, a heavy copper one, fell with full force on the toes and instep of his foot, crushing and lacerating them. He was removed to the Glens Falls hospital, where his injuries were treated. *1911.*

There wance was two cats in Kilkenny,
And aich thought there was wan cat
too many;
So they fought and they fit,
And they gouged and they bit,
Till, ixciptin' their nails,
And the tips of their tails,
Instid of two cats they warn't any.

NEW YORKER TO MANAGE NEW HOTEL

Times

G. J. VALLIQUETTE IN CHARGE OF FORT WILLIAM HENRY.

May — 24 1911

HOTEL ABOUT READY

Will be Opened on June 17—Two Banquets Planned for the Early Season —Delaware and Hudson Officials Well Pleased With Progress Made on Building.

The New Fort William Henry Hotel at Lake George is rapidly nearing completion. Practically all of the work on the interior is finished, and nearly all of the sleeping rooms are furnished and ready for occupancy. M. M. Kelly manager of the Fort William Henry Hotel and Hotel Champlain entertained the board of directors of the Delaware & Hudson Company on Friday and the officials expressed themselves as being much pleased with the progress made.

Although having only about eighty rooms the hotel is equipped with over fifty baths and all rooms are arranged en-suite, many of them having open fire places in addition to the steam heating system that has been installed.

The concourse and dining room from an artistic standpoint leave nothing to be desired, being finished in colonial style, and expensive oil paintings of scenic and historic interest will be hung in panels arranged for them.

George J. Valliquette of New York city, a hotel man of wide experience has been secured as manager and has engaged a competent staff to assist him. The Philamonic orchestra of the Metropolitan Opera House of New York city with Signor Ruggerio as leader, has been engaged to furnish music, and it is the intention of the management to open on the date scheduled, June 17.

Two elaborate banquets have been arranged for the early season one on June 23 when the directors and officials of the D. & H. Co., will meet for a detailed inspection of the property, and the other on June 25th, which is given by the Commercial Association of Glens Falls for the purpose of promoting better acquaintance with the officials of the Delaware & Hudson Railroad Company.

—91—

BURGLAR IS CAUGHT IN LAKE STORE

CHARLES BULL "CAUGHT WITH THE GOODS."

HEARING LATE TODAY

Discovered by Clerk at the Carpenter House—Had $32 and Bag of Groceries in His Possession—Remanded to the County Jail to Await a Hearing.

A bold attempt at burglary was made last night when the general store of H. J. Selleck at Lake George was broken into by Charles Bull, a young man, who for several years has resided in that town.

About midnight last night when Gregory Ferrio, a clerk in the employ of O. C. Lucia of the Carpenter House, was retiring he heard the sound of breaking glass and saw a light flash in the rear of the store, which is next to the hotel. Calling assistance, he stationed a guard at the front and rear of the building and went in search of Officer Hubbell, who was on duty further up the street.

When they attempted to enter they found both doors locked. The proprietor was summoned to unlock the front door, when they entered the store. Bull was found with all the money in the register, amounting to $32, in his possession, and also a bag of groceries that he had packed ready to carry away. He was at once taken to the county jail to await a hearing late this afternoon.

REV. D. W. GATES

The Rev. David W. Gates, D. D., a prominent Methodist Episcopal clergyman of the Troy conference, died suddenly Saturday at his home in Saratoga Springs. He was seventy-eight years old and retired from active work some four or five years ago. Dr. Gates was formerly presiding elder of the Plattsburgh district, and was at one time pastor of the church in Glens Falls. He was the last of his family. The funeral was held Monday and the body was interred in Oakwood cemetery, at Round Lake. *25 1911*

May

WILLIAM G. CONKLING DIES TODAY AFTER LONG ILLNESS

May 27, 1907

William G. Conkling of New York died this morning at 8 o'clock at Cleverdale, Lake George, where he and his family were spending the summer. The deceased was fifty-three years of age and was born in this city, residing here until a few years ago, when business interests called him to New York.

Mr. Conkling was the son of the late Mr. and Mrs. Guerton Conkling, well known and highly respected citizens of this city. Mr. Conkling was born in this city in what was known as the Conkling residence, on which site the Home for Aged Women now stands.

On reaching his majority, he became associated with his father in business and the two conducted mines on Lyon Mountain and a gigantic stock farm just outside of what was then Sandy Hill.

Mr. Conkling had been in ill health for a long time and was forced to give up all business. He removed to Lake George a few weeks ago in the hope that the mountain air would improve his broken health, but the change did him no good. He grew gradually worse. He is survived by his widow; one son, Franklin Conkling; one daughter, Miss Gertrude Conkling, and one brother, John Conkling of New York. The funeral will be held Monday. The Rev. Oliver S. Newell will officiate. Interment will be in the Bay street cemetery.

NEW FEDERAL BUILDING FOR SARATOGA SPRINGS

May 22 1914

The United States federal building at Saratoga Springs, now nearing completion, is a beautiful structure of the most modern type. Its cost is approximately $80,000, with the site, $130,000. It is built of hard pressed terra cotta brick and West Virginia Sandstone. The interior is finished in Italian marble and quartered oak in the lobby. The main work room is finished in oak, with maple flooring. The main doors are of bronze, and are of massive construction. The sanitary arrangements are of the up-to-date type. A shower bath for clerks is a much appreciated improvement. The building is lighted throughout with drop ceiling lights, both gas and electricity being used. Steam is used for heating purposes.

The proposed federal building for Glens Falls will possibly be of this type differing, perhaps, in exterior construction. The Saratoga building was secured through the combined efforts of Postmaster W. W. Worden and Congressman C.

DEATH CLAIMS MANY

Grim Destroyer Invades Several Warrensburgh Homes.

ALSO IN OTHER NEAR-BY PLACES

Mrs. Sarah Thomas Called to Rest After Many Weary Weeks of Suffering— Veteran Warren County Teacher Dies in Corinth.

From its pain-racked tenement of clay Death released the soul of Mrs. Sarah Thomas at 1:30 o'clock Tuesday afternoon. The grim visitor, so universally dreaded, was welcomed by the weary sufferer, who was well prepared and longed for the eternal rest which the Master she had faithfully served has promised His servants. Mrs. Thomas was taken ill early in February and had been constantly growing worse. She was confined to her bed almost from the first. Her first trouble was pleurisy but other complications soon developed and she endured great suffering during the last weeks, which she bore with great patience and fortitude. The deceased was born in the town of Bolton, April 12, 1829, and was a daughter of Caleb Brown, who was born in the town of Warrensburgh in 1788 and died in 1876. His wife died at the age of eighty-nine. On July 15, 1849, the deceased was married to Miles Thomas, a prominent resident of this village, who left her a widow August 14, 1886. They had two sons Albert H. and Charles A. The latter died January 1, 1886, and Albert is the only surviving member of the family. His mother had lived with him since the death of his father. Mrs. Thomas also leaves one brother, Truman Brown, of this village. The funeral will be held from the house tomorrow afternoon at 2 o'clock and will be conducted by the Rev. Richard Abbott.

JUDGE RALEY'S FIRST TERM.

Warren County Court to Convene at Lake George Monday.

County Judge George S. Raley, of Glens Falls, will preside at his first term of court at Lake George next week. The session will convene Monday at 10 a. m. and continue until the calendar is disposed of.

There are five criminal cases and a few civil actions. Four of the cases are against Glens Falls men.

They would not want the ones they love,
To grieve for them today;
We must not say that they are dead,
For they are just away.

Away upon a journey
To a land that's bright and fair;
And though we all will miss them here,
We know they're happy there.

And memories of them will bring
New comfort every day
As we recall—they are not dead
For they are just away.
Adv.— *The Childre...*

BOLTON BOY WON CORNELL SCHOLARSHIP

ANDREW L. SMITH SUCCESSFUL IN EXAMINATIONS.

June 24 1911

RESULTS ANNOUNCED

Elsa C. Cornell of Cambridge Successful in Washington County—Theodore A. Knapp of Saratoga Spa gets Free Scholarship from Saratoga County—Other Successful Students.

Andrew L. Smith of Bolton Landing, a member of this year's class of the local high school was successful in the competitive examinations for the Cornell scholarship, according to an announcement made today by State Commissioner of Education Andrew S. Draper.

The winners in other counties in this part of the state are also announced as follows:

Washington, Elsa C. Cornell, Cambridge.

St. Lawrence, Ethel M. Southwick, Ogdensburg; Arthur Bilow, Gouverneur.

Saratoga, Theodore A. Knapp, Saratoga.

Schenectady, Francis E. Early, Schenectady.

Essex, Rena M. Bigelow, Port Henry.

Franklin, Ernest E. Elder, Malone.

Edward M. Shepard

July 13 1911

Reports from Earlowest, the Lake George summer home of Edward M. Shepard, last evening, were to the effect that the noted New York lawyer's condition remains about the same. Physicians and nurses are in constant attendance and his ultimate recovery is anticipated, although it will necessarily be some time before he regains his strength.

Alta P. MacDonald, Horseman, Dead

Star — July 12

ALBANY, July 11.—Alta P. MacDonald, known to turfmen the country over, died tonight at his home in Menands after several months illness. When fifteen years old he was a public trainer. Among the fastest horses he deloped are Major Delmar, bred in Glens Falls, 1.59 3-4, Sweet Marie, 2.02 and Dariel, 2.00 1-4. *1911*

DEATH OF MR. DEMUTH.

Mirror — July 1 1911.

Bolton Landing lost one of its prominent cottagers when on Monday of this week Mr. William C. Demuth of New York died at his summer home, Bay View, in that village. Mr. Demuth has been for many years one of the leading members of the summer colony and has always been heartily interested in anything that worked for the welfare of Lake George. Only last year he entirely rebuilt his beautiful summer home and had the grounds arranged so that the estate ranks easily with one of the finest on the lake. During the winter Mr. Demuth has been in poor health and came to Lake George about a month ago suffering from a complication of troubles, chief of which was a hardening of the arteries. Although it was known that his death might come at any moment, the end was quite unexpected as a result of an apoplectic stroke.

TRUE HEROISM.

All may be heroes. "The man who rules his spirit," saith the voice which cannot err, "is greater than the man who takes a city."—Mrs. S. J. Hale.

If hero means sincere man, why may not every one of us be a hero?—Carlyle.

'Tis as easy to be heroes as to
    sit the idle slaves
Of a legendary virtue carved
    upon our fathers' graves.
                        —Lowell.

Dream not helm and harness
The sign of valor true;
Peace hath higher tests of manhood
Than battle ever knew.
                        —Whittier.

Zera Frasier and family have moved to the Huddle.

Several school children are slightly ill of chicken pox.

Dr. E. L. Wilson made a visit to New York last week.

Walter E. Gates has recently sold a fine horse to a man from Poughkeepsie.

C. B. Maxim, who has been ill for a few days, of a severe cold, is improving.

Mrs. Fred Duell, of Shelving Rock, has moved into L. W. Boyce's tenant house.

Miss Pauline Nelson has been ill for some time with throat and stomach trouble.

Mrs. Mulaney, who has been visiting her parents, has returned to her home in Boston.

Miss Grace Plum, who has been working in Glens Falls, is home for the winter.

Theodore Sherman has leased Charles Davis' farm in New Vermont for the coming year.

Leigh Brown, who is attending the Albany Business college, was home over Sunday.

C. E. Ingraham, proprietor of the Wilson house, visited A. D. Roberts in Hartford last week.

Lawrence Ross, who is employed by Miss Pruyn, of Glens Falls, was a week-end guest of his parents.

The Bolton Light and Power company has been unable to furnish light lately, causing a great inconvenience.

Edward Lamb made a business visit to Glens Falls Friday. Curtis Lamb came home for over Sunday with his father.

Mrs. C. B. Maxim, who has been confined to the house for the past two weeks with muscular rheumatism, is able to be out again.

Mrs. Fred Duell, of Shelving Rock, has moved into L. W. Boyce's house on the schoolhouse hill, having sold her place to G. O. Knapp.

School was in session Monday in Miss Binan's room as she was making up for time lost by illness. The attendance continues good in spite of the severe cold.

Mr. and Mrs. Walter Gates, of Bolton, celebrated the tenth anniversary of their marriage Monday. A number of friends from this place were present.

Several basket ball fans from Lake George witnessed the game here Friday night in which the locals were defeated. A dance was held after the game which was enjoyed by all.

The Methodist Episcopal society is to hold a concert and entertainment in Navajo hall on the evening of March 3, for the benefit of the church. Judging from the program it will be well worth attending.

The Garnet show that was to appear Monday evening could not get through from Hague in time to give the evening performance on account of drifted and unbroken roads over Tongue Mountain.

Calumet Rebekah lodge gave a supper and dance at Navajo hall on Wednesday of last week. Music was furnished by J. W. Ward and Mrs. Duell. A good crowd was present and enjoyed both square and round dances.

Bolton

From the 9th of February to the 23rd, the average temperature here has b en fifteen and one-half degrees below zero. Fewer cases of colds and grip are reported than last winter when the mercury hardly ever reached the zero m rk. Still, it's costing something for coal and wood.

There was a spelling match in Miss Kelly's room Friday afternoon, participated in by the fourth, fifth, sixth, seventh and eighth grades, and Orlie Allen, a little boy in the fourth grade, beat everybody and stood up longest. Perhaps after this some in the higher grades may think it will look as well to study spelling more and flirting less.

Robert B. Gray, of New York, and George S. Noyes, Jr., of Port Chester, passed through here on the 17th inst., en route to their homes. They had with them a large dog that drew the sled on which was carried their sleeping and duffle bags. They came from Lake Champlain and camped for several days in the forest back of town.

Then and Now

In days of old, when knights were bold,
  What meant their lack of fears!
One got no start when auto cart
  Went whizzing past one's ears;
One's saddle horse kept on his course
  And calmly switched the fly,
No honking horn at night and morn
  Bade one to jump or die.

In days of old no bikes were sold
  With engines popping loud;
No cycling chap in leather cap
  Ploughed through a shrieking
    crowd;
No bags of sand shot to the land
  From gas bags o'er the scene;
Most any knave could be deemed
    brave,
  Ere age of gasolene.

Harriet Beecher Stowe

NEW YORK, June 5.—The centenary of the birth of Harriet Beecher Stowe will be celebrated in many sections of the country June 14. The relatives and admirers of the celebrated author of "Uncle Tom's Cabin" and other books will hold special memorial services in different cities. Particular attention will be given to honoring Mrs. Stowe's memory in cities where she spent periods of her long, active life, these being Andover, Mass.; Hartford, Conn.; Cincinnati, Litchfield, Conn., and Natick, Mass. Mrs. Stowe's son, Charles Edward Stowe, and her grandson, Lyman Beecher Stowe, have written a book entitled "Harriet Beecher Stowe—The Story of Her Life," which is being issued at this time in commemoration of her accomplishments. Charles Edward Stowe is a retired clergyman, and Lyman Beecher Stowe is one of the officials of the public service commission of New York. In the accompanying illustration is shown a scene at Bowdoin college, Brunswick, Me., where Mrs. Stowe resided when she wrote "Uncle Tom's Cabin." "Uncle Tom's Cabin" was begun as a serial in the National Era June 5, 1851, and completed April 1, 1852. Mrs. Stowe received the modest sum of $300 for her story. Before it was completed in the National Era she signed a contract with John P. Jewett, a young Boston publisher, to bring it out in book form. This contract was dated March 13, 1852, and the book was published March 20 of the same year. By the terms of this contract Mrs. Stowe was to receive a 10 per cent royalty on all copies sold. Her first royalty check was for $10,000. She might have had half profits, but the future of the book was considered so doubtful and the risk in its publication so great that her husband and other advisers urged her to accept the 10 per cent offer and incur no risk. Professor Stowe, her husband, is reported to have said: "It is a very unpopular subject, and I doubt if the book has a large sale. I shall be abundantly satisfied if you get enough out of it to buy a new silk dress." It has been estimated that over a million copies have been sold in the United States and over a million and a half in Great Britain and the colonies. It has been translated forty times, and we may safely estimate that in all 3,000,000 copies of the book have been sold. If Mrs. Stowe had received 1 cent per copy on this enormous circulation of her book she would have had a modest fortune, but she actually received but little.

A TYPICAL WINTER CAMP OF THE ARMY OF THE POTOMAC.

However hard may have been the soldiers' lot in battle, it was infinitely harder in time of enforced idleness, when by reason of impassable roads, heavy storms, and intense cold the armies were forced to go into winter quarters. During the heat of battle excitement and activity made a patriotic devotion to duty almost easy. But it was when the soldiers were in winter quarters, with nothing to look forward to but long weeks of cold and suffering and hunger, that their bravery and courage were tried. In the winter of 1864-5 the Confederate Army was reduced to a diet of corn bread in its winter quarters. Even coffee and tea could be had only in the hospital. Desertions took place on both sides with alarming frequency in winter, and the commanding officers of the armies were forced to show even greater resourcefulness when they were in charge of soldiers in winter quarters than when they were directing a battle; for their courage and spirit had to be depended on to keep up the esprit-de-corps of the men. The rude log cabins here shown made these soldiers' lot bearable, for they afforded greater protection against storm and cold than the canvas tents which in some cases were the armies' only protection, even in winter.

A CONTRIVANCE WHICH PLAYED AN IMPORTANT PART IN THE CIVIL WAR.

A CANVAS PONTOON, SUCH AS WAS USED FOR THE CONSTRUCTION OF TEMPORARY BRIDGES ACROSS RIVERS.

[Without the pontoon such a war as the civil war could never have been fought. Campaigns in territory where there are many rivers have failed simply because there was no way to transport the soldiers across the rivers. The engineering department of the United States Army had long advocated the use of pontoons, as they were used in France, Austria, and other countries, and as they had been used ever since the days when Xerxes crossed the Hellespont on them. But it was not until May 15, 1846, that Congress approved a bill organizing a pontoon department. This new division of the engineering department had a chance to do some work in the Mexican war. When the civil war opened, it was well organized, and a corps of well drilled pontooniers was ready to accompany the army to the front.

[The canvas pontoon boat, such as the one shown in the accompanying illustration, was found by far the best for general use in the civil war. Its weight was so light, as compared with the wood or copper pontoon, that it could be much more easily carried than the heavier boats. The wagons bearing these canvas pontoons could, in fact, keep pace with rapidly moving infantry, and so the soldiers were never kept waiting for their bridges.

[These boats, like all other pontoons, were fastened together stem and stern across the river. Beams were laid from one pontoon to the next, and across these beams plank roads were laid, strong enough to bear cavalry and supply wagons. The building of these pontoon bridges was fraught with great danger to the engineers who had the work in charge, for they were of course made the target, when possible, of the enemy's fire.

THE RUINS OF RICHMOND AFTER THE WAR.

HOW THE CONFEDERATE CAPITAL LOOKED AFTER THE GREAT FIRE WHICH FOLLOWED THE EVACUATION.

[During the mob rule that followed the evacuation of Richmond on April 2, 1865, an order from an unknown source was given to fire the four principal tobacco houses. From this start destruction spread throughout the entire business section of the city. On the morning of the fourth, when the fire had practically burned itself out, President Lincoln, accompanied by his young son, arrived on this scene of disaster. There, escorted by Admiral Porter, Capt. Bell and a few marines and Union sympathizers, he walked up the streets of the half burned city. The negroes and Unionists pressed about him to kiss his hands and hear his voice. A frightful sight met his gaze when he looked about. The streets were crowded with furniture and every description of wares dashed down and trampled in the mud or burned where they lay. All the Confederate government stores were thrown open and such supplies as could not be got off by the government were left to the people. Next to the river the destruction of property was frightfully complete. This part of the city was a waste of smoking ruins, blackened walls, and solitary chimneys. In the awful days that followed the burning of Richmond aristocratic southern women were often seen clinging to the few things they had managed to save from the ruins of their homes, begging rations from the Federal authorities. As is usual in such condition of devastation, suffering was increased because of the high prices charged by the few unscrupulous dealers who had managed to gain possession of food supplies.

SUMMER GUESTS AT THE OAKS, LAKE COSSAYUNA.

MAN SHOT IN THE LEG

Prowling Peddler Peppered With Charge of Buckshot.

MAKES SENSATION IN THURMAN

Leroy Tanner, of Warrensburgh, Was the Victim, Norman Russell the Alleged Assailant — There Is Said to Be Woman In the Case.

Leroy Tanner, a Warrensburgh tin peddler about forty years old, while prowling around a farm house in Kenyontown, Thurman, about 10 o'clock Saturday night, was shot in the leg with a charge of buckshot. Norman Russell, twenty-one years old, is said to have admitted that he did the shooting, and claims that Tanner's conduct justified the act.

Tanner had been drinking heavily for about two weeks, spending most of his time in various parts of the town of Thurman. On Wednesday of last week he left his horse and cart at the residence of Lewis Moon, in Kenyontown, and went to Athol to procure a fresh supply of booze material. He returned to the former locality Friday night or Saturday.

Saturday night he went to the Russell place and was poking about the house, peering in at the windows and rattling the blinds, when young Russell hearing the noise went out and ordered the intruder away. Three times he repeated the warning, but without effect. Then going into the house he procured his trusty shotgun, heavily loaded with buckshot, and returning blazed away at the shadowy form which he could dimly discern in the darkness. A yell of pain gave evidence that the shot had taken effect, but the rapid retreat of the unwelcome visitor gave evidence that it was not fatal.

Tanner, with three buckshots imbedded in the fleshy part of his right leg, and bleeding profusely from his wound, made his way to Lewis Moon's sugar camp, about half a mile away, and remained there until the following morning.

He was discovered at 9 a. m. Sunday by Lewis Moon, who took Tanner to his home and sent for Dr. J. E. Goodman, of this village, to attend him. The physician saw the man in the afternoon but the wound was then so badly swollen that the shot could not be located. He advised the patient's removal to the Glens Falls hospital.

Tanner was brought to this village Monday morning by Mr. Moon, Wallace Tucker and Norman Russell. The physician gave the wound temporary dressing and the patient was then placed on a trolley car and went to Glens Falls alone, arrangements having been made to have the hospital authorities meet him with the ambulance.

The wound would not have been particularly dangerous probably had it received prompt attention.

OLIVER C. LUCIA.

Oliver C. Lucia, proprietor of the Carpenter house, Lake George, died last night after an illness of about ten days. Death was caused by cerebral apoplexy, with which he was stricken while in his gasoline launch on Lake George on the evening of July 3. He was able to reach the dock before he collapsed and was removed to the hotel in a semi-conscious condition, in which he remained until his death at 7:45 o'clock last night. He was forty-five years old and leaves a widow and a son, Joseph Lucia, of Lake George; also three brothers, George W., of Warrensburgh, Antoine, of Randolph, Vt., and Alexander, of Burlington, Vt. The funeral will be held Saturday morning at the Church of the Sacred Heart, Lake George. The body will be brought to Warrensburgh for interment in St. Cecilia's cemetery.

Lake George Hotel Man Near Death.

Oliver C. Lucia, proprietor of the Carpenter house, Lake George, and a brother of George W. Lucia, of this village, had a stroke of apoplexy Monday evening and has since been unconscious. He is failing rapidly and there is but little hope of his recovery. Mr. Lucia was stricken while alone in his gasoline launch on the lake. Though his entire right side was paralyzed he managed to guide the boat to the dock before he lapsed into unconsciousness. His condition was observed and he was removed to the hotel, where he was attended by Dr. C. K. Burt.

News July 6, 1911

THURSDAY, JULY 13,

ANDRUS SENTENCED

Bakers Mills Murderer Sent to Prison for Life

FOR KILLING WILLIAM HOPKINS

Pleaded Guilty to Charge of Murder in Second Degree—May be Released in Twenty Years—The Story of His Terrible Crime.

For killing William Hopkins in a lonely farm house at Bakers Mills on the night of March 18, last, Charles Andrus was sentenced by Justice Joseph A. Kellogg Monday morning, at Lake George, to an indeterminate sentence in the state prison at Dannemora, the minimum of which shall be twenty years and the maximum life.

Andrus was indicted for murder. He saturated with kerosene oil, set fire to the building and fled from the scene.

To help him in his flight, the murderer took Hopkins' team. He drove them until they were exhausted and then deserted them. The horses found their way back to the home of a neighbor of Hopkins, James Piper, who upon trying to return them to the owner discovered the crime and a general alarm was sent throughout the county. Andrus was suspected from the first.

He was taken in custody on Monday, March 20, by Constable Charles Baker, at Northville, and in stopping over night at the Glens Falls jail confessed his crime to District Attorney Cunningham.

He first decided to enter a plea of self defense, but later upon the advice of friends and Edward M. Angell, his attorney, he decided to enter a plea of guilty of murder in the second degree.

MEMBERS OF THE UTOWANA FISH AND GAME CLUB AT THE SAGAMORE ON LAKE GEORGE.

JOHN O'LEARY IS CALLED FROM HIS EARTHLY LABORS

star July 31, 1911

John O'Leary, one of the best known and most highly respected business men of this city, passed away Saturday afternoon at five o'clock at his home 10 Center street, after an illness which had confined him to his home for the past ten weeks. He was born in Glens Falls, fifty nine years ago and had resided here during his whole life, forming numerous acquaintances who will greatly mourn his death. He was the son of Daniel O'Leary, a pioneer business man of Glens Falls, who for many years owned and conducted what is known as the Sherman stone quarry.

Mr. O'Leary started in the retail cigar manufacturing business in at small building on Exchange street in 1881. As his business increased he moved from Exchange street to Bay, Ridge, Glen streets and finally to South street, where he had been conducting wholesale and retail cigar manufacturing for the last six years.

Mr. O'Leary was a charter member of the local lodge of the Benevolent and Protective Order of Elks, the local council of the Knights of Columbus and the Exempt Firemen's association. He was a fourth degree member of the Knights of Columbus.

BE INDEPENDENT.

Stand close to all, but lean on none,
And if the crowd desert you
Stand just as fearlessly alone
As if a throng begirt you,
And learn what long the wise
have known—
Self flight alone can hurt you.
— William S. Shurtleff.

SECOND OLDEST UNITED STATES POST MASTER DIES AT SMITHS BASIN HOME

Star July 31 1911

George W. L. Smith, Appointed to Office During Administration of Abraham Lincoln, Passes Away at the Age of Seventy-Two.

George W. L. Smith died at his late residence at Smiths Basin, Washington county, Saturday evening at 6 o'clock. Mr. Smith was born October 25, 1839, and spent his whole life at Smiths Basin. He was educated in the public schools of his locality and spent several terms at Clinton Liberal Institute, then located at Clinton, N. Y.

Telegraph Operator

Ezekell Smith was first station agent at Smiths Basin and it was but natural that George W. L. Smith should take up telegraphy and he was the second operator on the Saratoga division of the Delaware and Hudson to take messages by sound.

Second Oldest Postmaster

In 1859 Mr. Smith was appointed postmaster under the administration of James Buchanan, and Montgomery Blair of President Lincoln's cabinet made him postmaster in 1861. He had held the office continuously ever since. In point of service he was the second oldest postmaster in the United States.

CONTENTMENT.

There is a jewel which no Indian mine can buy,
No chemic art can counterfeit;
It makes men rich in greatest poverty,
Makes water wine, turns wooden cup to gold,
The homely whistle to sweet music's strain;
Seldom it comes—to few from heaven sent—
That much in little—all in nought
—content.
—Wilbye.

A BIT OF LAKE GEORGE.

COL. GREEN GETS 6,242 PROPOSALS TO WED

news Sept 14

Hetty Green's Son Receiving Letters From Every Country.

1911

If Colonel Edward H. Green, son and heir to the major part of his good mother Hetty's many millions, were not an essential monogamist in principle he might find it easier to dig his way from under something like 6,000 proposals of marriage. The last total made by Colonel Green's secretary had it 6,242, and while the American girls were still very much on the job of landing the Texas Croesus, their alien sisters were represented by not fewer than 1,331 offers to love him.

The colonel has quietly admitted to his friends that his half jest and possibly half earnest declaration of some weeks ago that he was open for proposals had been better left unuttered.

That England has a money hunting, dollar searching contingent unknown until now to Americans is shown by the deluge of proposals to accept Colonel Green which every mail carries out of that tight little isle.

A woman of seeming breeding in Hampstead road, London, evidently caring nothing that Colonel Astor got an awful drubbing because at forty-six he wedded a girl under twenty, assures Colonel Green that he may have either of her two daughters, one fair, one very dark, both very much admired, each ready to prove that she can love him regardless of his money.

The same mail brings a queer letter from a parlor maid who assures him she quite appreciates how hard it was for him to earn his money and that she will take mighty good care of it. She asks God to bless the colonel and "your dear mother," and begs him not to let the fact that he is rich stand in the way. She will not mind it a bit.

PURCHASES HOTEL AT MAITLAND FLORIDA

Oct 11 1911 Star

Dr. J. Sutherland Stuart has purchased the Maitland Inn at Maitland Florida and will go to that place about the first of next month, where he will take possession of the hotel on December 1. The hotel is one of the most popular resorts in that section of Florida.

Dr. Stuart has been spending the summer at his hotel, Pearl Point, Lake George, and will return there May 1 next year. He will be accompanied south by Mrs. Stuart.

CHILD KILLED AT BOLTON.

July 20 1911

Run Down by Hudson Falls Automobile in Front of Hotel.

Doris Norton, the three and a half year-old daughter of Mr. and Mrs. F. R. Norton, of Bolton, was struck and almost instantly killed about 5 o'clock Saturday afternoon by a touring car, owned by B. J. Cloonan, of Hudson Falls, and driven by Patrick Cronin.

The child was playing in front of the Exchange hotel, conducted by the Nortons, and suddenly crossed the road directly in front of the approaching machine. The driver did all in his power to avoid the accident but could not do so.

As soon as the machine could be stopped Cronin picked up the almost lifeless body of the child, placed it in the car and hurried to the Sagamore hotel to seek medical aid, but the child expired before the hotel was reached. Cronin returned to the Exchange hotel and registered his name and number according to law.

The child sustained a deep cut on the head and the body was bruised in several places. The funeral was held Monday afternoon at 2 o'clock.

DIES AFTER BITE FROM WOODCHUCK

aug 26 1911.

Bitten by a woodchuck last evening, Isaac French of North Granville died in a few minutes, death being caused, it is believed, by heart failure. Mr. French had gone to the pasture to drive up his cows when he saw the woodchuck and killed it. In the fight the animal bit one of the fingers of his right hand. He went to his house and Mrs. French was in the act of bandaging the wound near the door, when Mr. French fell to the ground dead. Dr. Davies of Granville was summoned, but pronounced the man dead.

The physician was of the opinion that heart failure produced by the excitement was the cause of death, stating that death from tetanus could not have occurred so soon after the wound was inflicted. French was a highly respected resident of North Granville. He was sixty-six years old and a member of the local Methodist church and the North Granville Grange. In addition to his wife, the survivors are a brother, Albert French of Castleton, Vt., and a sister, Mrs. Levi Hatch of Whitehall.

GOES OVER NIAGARA IN A BARREL

Times July 26 1911

NIAGARA FALLS, N. Y., July 26.—Though badly battered in his barrel trip over the Horseshoe fall yesterday afternoon, Bobby Leach of Niagara Falls, Ont., was suffering no serious effects from the thrilling adventure. No bones were broken. However he will be confined to his bed for some days to come.

Asked this question if he would again attempt this feat, the cataract, Leach said—

"Let me tell you once is enough for any man; no more for Bobby. It may be though that I will some time try a parachute drop over the bloomin" big tumble.

Leach is through, too, with barrel trips through the whirlpool rapids and the whirlpool, which he has navigated four times. His doctor said today that it would be at least a week before Leach would be able to get about, for his legs are badly hurt.

70 YEARS ON THE LAKE.

Remarkable Record of the Veteran Commander of the Steamer Vermont

aug 15 1911.

(Burlington Free Press)

The old days on Lake Champlain, when hundreds of schooners and sloops plied its waters, when the lake furnished about the only means of communication between New York and Montreal, and when day and night boats made the runs from Whitehall to St. Johns, are recalled in all the details of the conditions of that time by Capt. E. B. Rockwell, now head of the Champlain Transportation company's fleet, who this year is spending his 70th year on board a ship on Lake Champlain. His history has never been equalled on this lake and perhaps never by a fresh-water sailor. The captain today is apparently as strong and alert as ever and does not even use glasses, his eyesight being far better than that of the average youth of 20. He attends to the duties connected with his office on the largest boat on the lake with a vigilance which cannot be surpassed.

Captain Rockwell was not old when he first took to the water, for in his eleventh year he shipped on board a sloop captained by his brother. He is now 81 years of age and has yet to miss a season. When he first shipped the British flag was seen on the lake as much as the American, for the trip was made from St. Johns to Whitehall and many Britishers and Canadians as well as people of the States had vessels.

JOHN O'LEARY DEAD.

Times July 29, 19

Well-Known Cigar Dealer Passes Away at Home on Center Street.

Glens Falls lost one of its best known business men Saturday afternoon at 5 o'clock when John O'Leary died at his home, 10 Center street, after an illness of ten weeks. Mr. O'Leary was fifty-nine years old. He was the son of Daniel O'Leary a pioneer business man of the village of Glens Falls, who for many years owned and conducted a stone quarry here.

Mr. O'Leary started in the retail cigar manufacturing business in a small building on Exchange street in 1881. As his business increased he moved from Exchange street to Bay, Ridge, Glen streets and finally to South street, where he had been conducting wholesale and retail cigar manufacturing for the last six years.

Mr. O'Leary was a charter member of the local lodge of the Benevolent and Protective Order of Elks, the local council of the Knights of Columbus and the Exempt Firemen's Association. He was a fourth degree member of the Knights of Columbus.

He is survived by three sisters, Mrs. Dennis McLaughlin, Mrs. John Feeney and Miss Mary O'Leary, and by two brothers, James O'Leary and Daniel O'Leary, all of this city. The funeral will be held tomorrow morning at 9:30 o'clock from St. Mary's church. Interment will be made in St. Mary's cemetery.

Members of the local lodge of Elks will meet tonight at 7:30 o'clock at the lodge rooms and will then go to the late home where the lodge of Sorrow will be held. All Elks are requested to attend.

"FIFTY YEARS AGO—AND NOW.

Aug. 1911

Mr. Russel Hulett of Ticonderoga in a recent conversation recalled his grandmother's prophecy, made fifty years ago, when Hulett's Landing was a little farm on the cove-level between the lake and its eastern hills, and when, occasionally, city-tired folks searching the lovely wooded shores of Lake George for a place of rest would stop at the farm house, and, for what would today be a small sum, enjoyed for a time its generous, if unpretentious hospitality.

This prophecy was that in a few more years there will stand "on this very spot," a large hotel and great numbers of people would come to it in the hot weather. Her children smiled. Her grand-children declared —"Grandmother thinks that one or two swallows are going to make a summer—by-and-by!," and laughed. But the old lady, nodding her wise head, said—"I won't live to see it but you will". And they did. Where the ancient farm-house then nestled under the maples now stands the Hulett House; where the apple orchard straggled, and the corn-rows stretched in pennon-fluttering ranks, twenty cottages are scattered over a grassy, tree-dotted plain; where grandmother Hulett used to sit knitting in the chimney-corner, tables are now laid in July and August for two hundred and more guests; where the clear waters of the lake, washing over the stones and lapping the sandy scimiter-shaped shore, once lulled the dear old woman to sleep under the mossy eaves now rocks a fleet of boats, and a fine pavilion tempts the votaries of Terpsichore to "trip the light fantastic.

GLENS FALLS-D

GEN. SICKLES IS NOW 86 YEARS OLD

Oct 25 1911

General Daniel E. Sickles, soldier and statesman, whose welfare is of more than ordinary interest to the older residents of Glens Falls and vicinity on account of his having been a resident of this city from 1831 to 1834, recently celebrated the eighty-sixth anniversary of his birth. The veteran warrior enjoys good health, and, according to one of his octogenarian friends, "is still able and ready for a fight or a frolic."

He was born in New York city, where he now resides, October 20, 1825, and besides achieving a fine record in the Civil War filled the following official positions: Elected to the New York State Assembly in 1847; New York State Senate 1856-7; United States Congress 1857-8-9-'61; United States Minister to Spain 1869. He was a division and corps commander and major general of the War of the Rebellion. The last time this distinguished gentleman visited this city, the home of his boyhood, he was accorded a public reception at the Rockwell House and addressed the citizens who assembled in great numbers to pay him the respect due a man of his years and reputation, speaking for some time from the hotel porch. General Sickles is a lifelong friend of Colonel J. L. Cunningham of this city.

WILL MEET IN BOLTON NEXT YEAR

Times — Sept 21

The sessions of the ninety-fourth annual meeting of the Lake George Baptist Association came to a close today in Warrensburg. The meeting will be held in Bolton next year. 1911

The closing sermon was delivered this morning at 11:30 by the Rev. G. N. Gates.

The following officers have been elected:

Moderator, Rev. E. H. Hovey of Thurman; clerk, Rev. B. S. Van Vleet of Chester; corresponding secretary, Rev. F. M. LaBarr of Minerva; treasurer, O. B. Ingraham of Adirondack.

The following committee was named: Missionary committee, Rev. F. M. LaBarr, Minerva; Rev. B. S. Van Vleet of Chester; Rev. T. J. Hunter of South Glens Falls.

"THE OLD WOODEN ROCKER."

There it stands in the corner with its
    back to the wall,
The old wooden rocker so stately and
    tall;
With naught to disturb it but the duster
    and broom,
For no one now uses the back parlor
    room,
O, how well I remember in the days long
    gone by,
When we stood by that rocker, my sister
    and I;
And we listened to the stories that our
    grandma would tell,
By that old wooden rocker we all loved
    so well.
                    —Chorus.

As she sat by the fire she would rock,
    rock, rock,
And we heard but the tick of the old
    brass clock;
Eighty years she had sat in that chair
    grim and tall,
The old wooden rocker that stood by the
    wall.

If this chair could but speak, O, the tales
    it could tell,
How poor aged grandpa in fierce battle
    fell,
'Neath the Stars and the Stripes he
    fought bravely and true.
He cherished his freedom, the red, white
    and blue.
He could tell of bright days and the
    dark ones beside,
Of the day when dear grandma stood
    forth as a bride.
This is why we all love it, this old chair
    grim and tall,
The old wooden rocker that stood by the
    wall.

But poor grandma is gone and her
    stories are done,
Her children have followed her, yes, one
    by one,
They have all gone to meet her in the
    sweet by and by,
And all that is left is dear sister and I.
Nevermore will we hide her gold specs
    on her cap;
Nevermore will we tease her while taking her nap;
Nevermore will she slumber in her chair
    grim and tall,
The old wooden rocker that stood by the
    wall.

The Real Thing.

Mabel—I am sure he must have loved her very dearly?

Maude—I should say so. He married her in spite of the fact that he had been out in the rain with her all one afternoon, was seasick with her, and saw her unexpectedly at home the morning after the dance.

"THREE PERISHED IN THE SNOW."

'Twas on one dark and stormy night,
    The snow was falling fast;
A mother and two little babes,
    Were wandering through the blasts.
Still clinging to their mother's breast,
    The little ones would cry,
"Please mamma won't you make us
    warm,
    Oh, mamma we will die."

"Oh darlings look up in my eyes,
    And say you will not die;
Poor mother's heart is breaking fast,
    And death to her is nigh."
Then wrapping up her little ones,
    She knelt down in the snow;
"Oh, God, in heaven take us home,
    We're ready now to go."

When morning dawned the sun came
    out,
    The snow was melting fast;
Three darling forms lay side by side,
    In one fond loving clasp.
A farmer heard the sad, sad news,
    Which made him weep to know;
That from his house not twenty rods,
    Three perished in the snow.

CHORUS.

Toll the village bells,
    Let all good people know;
'Twas on that dark and stormy night,
    Three perished in the snow.

EDWARD MORSE SHEPARD, NOTED NEW YORK LAWYER AND STATESMAN, DIES AT SUMMER HOME ON LAKE GEORGE

End Comes During Early Evening as Monastery Bell of St. Mary's-on-the Lake is Tolling the Hour of Six.

WAS UNCONSCIOUS DURING MOST OF DAY

July 29 1911 Star

Edward Morse Shepard

While the bell of the monastery of St. Mary's-on-the-Lake was tolling the hour of six, last night, the earthly career of Edward Morse Shepard was drawing to an end, and before the sound of the sixth tap of the bell had fallen upon the ears of those gathered in the sick chamber at Erlowest, the soul of one of New York's most gifted sons had taken flight to the world beyond.

Condition Becomes Alarming

In the early hours of yesterday morning Mr. Shepard's condition became alarmingly worse. At 7 o'clock he became unconscious, and shortly thereafter Dr. T. I. Henning, the attending physician, called Dr. G. H Butler of Brooklyn, a summer resident on Lake George, in consultation For one hour the physicians conferred, but finally decided that medical skill could bring about no relief and at 11:30 o'clock Dr. Henning gave out a bulletin to the effect that death was but the matter of a few hours.

Patient Rallies

About two o'clock in the afternoon the patient rallied, and, looking foward those about the bedside, murmured: "I know what you are here for ———," but before he had finished all that he tried to say, he had lapsed into unconsciousness, from which state he never awakened.

In the Sick Room

In the sick room, at the time of Mr. Shepard's death were the following relatives, most of whom own summer homes at the lake: Mr. and Mrs. Charles S. Shepard, Miss Edna Shepard, Mr. and Mrs. John F. B. Mitchell, Mrs. R. C. Leffingwell, Mrs. C. B Hewitt and Edward Shepard Hewitt.

—100—

church, is spending the summer at Lake George, and it is probable that he and the Rev. E. M. Parrot, rector of the Episcopal church at Lake George, will have charge of the service.

Will Arrive Today

Several of Mr. Shepard's close personal and professional friends will arrive at Lake George today, among them being R. C. Leffingwell, brother-in-law, and William Mason Smith, Mr. Shepard's law partner.

Honored and Respected

Mr. Shepard was a man beloved, honored and respected by all who were fortunate enough to know him. As a scholar, he ranked high; as a lawyer, he stood in the foremost ranks; as a politician, he stood for all that was best in his party and was never known to stoop to those tricks which lower men's standing with their fellow men, and as a man he represented the highest type of American citizenship.

Huppuch's Tribute

In speaking of his death last evening, Public Service Commissioner Winfield A. Huppuch, of Hudson Falls said: "I count it a very high honor to have known Mr. Shepard. His death means not only a great loss to the Democratic party but to the state at large. I considered him one of the foremost members of the party, a remarkably able and brilliant man. His death brings sorrow to me personally, for he possessed many characteristics which I greatly admired."

Mr. Shepard's Career

Mr. Shepard was born July 23, 1850, in New York city and last Tuesday celebrated his sixty-first birthday. He was educated in the public schools of New York and Brooklyn and spent one year in a preparatory school at Oberlin. *year later,* he became active in Democratic and reform politics.

First Public Office

He held his first public office in 1883, when he was appointed a civil service commissioner in the Borough of Brooklyn. He remained as civil service commissioner for two years at this time, and in 1888 was reappointed as chairman of the Board of Civil Service Commissioners, which position he retained until 1890. In 1884 and 1885 he was a member of the New York State Forestry Commission.

Candidate for Mayor

He was nominated by the Democrats as candidate for the office of mayor of New York in 1901, but was defeated. Since that time he had been prominently mentiond as a gubernatorial possibility and was a prominent figure in the recent Senatorial deadlock at Albany, having been a candidate for United States Senator.

As a Lawyer

As an attorney Mr Shepard was most successful and up to the time of his death was counsel for the Pennsylvania railroad. He served as director on a number of railroads and other corporations and was also chairman of the board of directors of the College of the City of New York. He was also a trustee of the Packer Collegiate Institute.

SHEPARD—On Friday, July 28th, 1911, at Erlowest, Lake George, N. Y., Edward Morse Shepard, in the sixty-second year of his age. Services at St. James' church, Lake George, on Tuesday morning, August 1, at 10 o'clock, and at the Church of the Holy Trinity, Montague and Trinity streets, Brooklyn, on Wednesday morning, August 2d, at 10 o'clock. Interment private. Please omit flowers.

The will of Edward M. Shepard was filed today for probate in the Surrogate's office, together with the petition of the executors, four in number, who are Charles S. Shepard, the brother; Agnes S. Hewitt, the sister; Edward S. Hewitt, the nephew and Russell C. Leffingwell, the nephew-in-law of the deceased.

No inkling of the amount of the estate is contained in the papers, save that in the affidavit, which states that both real and personal property amount to "above $10,000." With the will there is a brief codicile, dated July 6 last, relating to bequests contained in the will which the testator wished changed to some extent.

Lawyer William Mason Smith represented the executors in presenting the will for probate, and save for two affidavits, the document is really for probate. The will a very long one, minutely expresses the wishes of the testator as to the disposition of his estate, although in several places the wishes are not made absolute directions.

Erlowest goes to the sister, Mrs. Hewitt, the brother receiving the Paine farm adjacent and $25,000, which, the testator says, should equalize the value of the two gifts. There are many bequests to employees, and Holy Trinity church receives $5,000. The little St. James church at Lake George is given $1,000.

The residary estate is placed in trust for the brother, sister and the blood relatives.

Before arranging for the dividing of the income from the residuary estate, the testator provides for bequests to his nephews and nieces. The sister also is given the School House

Mr. Shepard's will is in manuscript and covers some twenty-seven pages, it is dated March 10, 1908. To show how carefully the testator expressed his preferences in the document, one paragraph says: "It is not my wish (but this is not a direction) that either my sister or brother or sister-in-law shall accumulate any substantial part of the income from principal which he or she shall enjoy under this will. The incomes are meant chiefly for their immediate and personal use and enjoyment and disposition, and not to accumulate for their old age or for others."

THE TERRIBLE AUTOMOBILE TRAGEDY AT SYRACUSE.

Racing car driven by Lee Oldfield and which was traveling at 75 miles an hour tearing through the crowd after leaving the track at the State Fair grounds. Eleven persons were killed and a score more injured. An account of the accident appears on the 12th page of the G l o b e.]

CALAMITY JANE.

DEADWOOD WOMAN WHO WAS A FRIEND OF WILD BILL.

Peculiar Female Character of Early Days Who Dressed as a Man and Could Shoot and Gamble With the Best of Them All.

THE Black Hills Pioneer Society are planning to erect a monument commemorative of the exploits of Calamity Jane, a famous character. Martha Cannary, or Calamity Jane as she was known throughout the northwest, died at Terry, S. D., in August, 1903, after having outlived to a certain extent her local fame. But she has not been forgotten in the flourishing town of Deadwood, in a little cemetery near which it is proposed to place a monument that the eventful career of this remarkable woman may be properly recognized and recorded. Locally, her fame is scarcely exceeded by that of "Wild Bill" Hickok, the man whom she most admired and whose grave is marked with an elaborate shaft while her grave alongside has only a little stone slab.

Not all the adventures of this remarkable woman are known to those best acquainted with her history, for she was extremely shy when it came to talking about her own affairs. No doubt she took part in many exploits in which her identity was not discovered and of which she never afterwards talked. It is known that she saw much of the fighting going on in the Black Hills during the Indian troubles. In the Sioux campaign of 1876 she drove team for a while in Gen. Crook's command, being dressed as a man, and her identity was not discovered for some time. She also did scout duty, carrying dispatches and assisting in gathering information about the Indians.

A DEVIL-MAY-CARE LIFE.

Calamity Jane was a familiar figure about Deadwood in the early days of that roaring gold town. So far as she had a home for the few years after the Deadwood rush in '75 it was there. She took to miner's boots as readily as she did to stirrups and as kindly to pick and shovel as to bridle reins. She took her share of wealth from the soil and spent it as the others spent it in the feverish recklessness of the time. Gambling was the chief recreation in a place where flour was $1 a pound and shoes $20 a pair. Jane gambled as every man gambled, and could back her busted flush with a marble face and a sack of hard-earned gold dust.

Most congenial to her were those occasions when border law gave swift justice, if such it was, to those foolhardy ones who gained property in ways not above questioning. The prominent details of these little ceremonies always required good management, and Calamity Jane liked the job. She was well qualified as a leader, too, and her popularity brought her forward as the best person to officiate at such times. Possibly those rough men of that region argued that a lynching more closely resembled the majesty of real law, when a woman presided. Even the culprits seemed to have a fitting sense of the honor conferred upon them when a woman condescended to direct summary proceedings looking to their hasty departure for the great beyond.

"Charming lady," said one scamp, as he stood on the barrel with the rope around his neck, "I kiss your hand. It shall never be said that I failed to observe the homage and respect due to one of your tender sex.

If anybody forgets he's a gent, or draws a gun and I hear of it" — Whereupon he nodded and was swung off into eternity with a smile on his lips.

WOMAN ONLY IN SEX.

Capt. George Bartlett, the famous scout and fighter of Indians and "bad men," who lived in Deadwoood at this time, knew Calamity Jane very well. Speaking of her he says:

"She was well known throughout the Black Hills camps, and although a singular character, traveling about alone and engaging in unfeminine enterprises, she was good and kind, always helping those in distress. An analysis of her character would be difficult, for I think there was never another quite like her.

"She was better looking than the average woman but took no pride in it. She was happiest when she could pass for a man. She was fond of sports, racing and hunting, and was always foremost at a jollification. In quiet times she was to be found about Deadwood, either attending a rough miners' dance or joking with a crowd of men.

"Whenever excitement was manifest Calamity Jane was to be found at the front. Whether it was an alarm of Indians or the lynching of a desperado she never failed to be present. On such occasions she always wore a man's suit of well made, neatly fitting buckskin and a broad brimmed hat, and she always rode a fine horse. Thus apparelled, with her long, glossy black hair tossing about with every motion of the animal, she was a striking figure. She would generally take the lead, would arrange the details of an execution and afterward superintend the funeral.

"Men would follow her into any danger. She could handle a rifle, revolver or knife with the skill of an expert, rode a vicious mustang and seemed utterly without the sense of fear. In short, she was a woman only in sex; a man in mind, heart, muscle and courage."

ADMIRED WILD BILL.

Probably the only man Calamity Jane ever really admired was "Wild Bill" Hickok, the most notorious of all western gun fighters. Tradition says that the woman was married three times, though little is known of this phase of her character. Matrimony was a trivial matter with her and she never allowed it to interfere with her love of adventure. By all accounts "Wild Bill" was a man to inspire admiration in such a woman. Aside from his honesty and kindness his record for being the most courageous in all the west is unequalled in border history.

"Wild Bill's" first great exploit needed the full confirmation it received to appear credible, so extravagantly melodramatic and sensational, so like a delirium of a Dumas, were its details. In single combat, armed with shotgun, revolvers and bowie knife, he killed outright eight members of the "Jake" McCandles band of outlaws who had attacked him, and mortally wounded the ninth. A stage full of passengers which drove up just after the fight furnished the witnesses, who certainly were necessary to establish such an affair on a basis of truth.

The country rang with the prowess of "Wild Bill," and from that time on the sole ambition of every "bad man" in the west was to kill him. There was no surer avenue to immediate fame than that offered by the murder of the great "gun fighter." As a result "Wild Bill," who always protested that he was the most peaceable of men and that he only desired to be left alone, had to earn the right to live day by day by frustrating the ambitious. He was shot at from ambush, in the street, in his home, while drinking, riding and card playing. Possibly there never was another man so quick on the trigger as he learned to be, and the notches on his gun numbered more than 40, each representing a fight that was forced upon him.

WILD BILL'S AVENGER.

As might be expected, such a man as this easily captured the masculine admiration and the remaining feminine susceptibilities of Calamity Jane. As the type of all that she had striven to be, she worshiped him, even her iron nerves fluttering whenever he reigned to give her a pleasant look or word. That is why she became his avenger with such passionate ardor.

"Jack" McCall, a little coward, brought death to the man so many more daring assassins had failed to do up. Through the crack of a gambling house door he shot "Wild Bill" in the back. The murderer was captured, but in the confusion and because of a division of opinion concerning the killing he managed to beg off under a promise that he would leave town at once and never return.

But if the citizens of Deadwood were willing to see the murderer go unpunished they was a citizen who had different views. The wrath of Calamity Jane knew no bounds when the news reached her,

---

9, 1911 *[handwritten: Nov?]*

FIRE AT LAKE GEORGE.

Summer Home of Charles Peabody Destroyed Saturday Afternoon.

The magnificent summer home of Charles J. Peabody, on the Bolton road about one mile from Lake George village, was completely destroyed by fire Saturday afternoon. All of the furniture on the first floor, and part of that on the second, was saved, but the house, built entirely of wood, was burned to the ground, entailing a loss of approximately $50,000.

As soon as the fire was discovered word was sent to the village and the church and town clock bells were rung and many men went to the scene of the conflagration. In spite of the persistent efforts by those gathered at the fire, the blaze resisted the water thrown on it by a hand pump and the handsome home was soon a mass of ruins.

The fire started near the roof and spread rapidly. Although the exact cause has not been ascertained, it is conjectured that the fire started from a blow torch used by plumbers, who were repairing the tin roof.

The house was built by Walter Price, of New York, who sold it to Mr. Peabody. The last owner is the brother of George Foster Peabody.

Mounted Panther Twice Saved From Fire.

Hotel Carson, at Schroon River, in the town of North Hudson, Essex county, which was destroyed by fire on October 12, stood on the site of Root's hotel, formerly conducted by Edward Owens, of this village, which was burned in the 90's. A mounted panther adorned the office of the old Root hotel and also that of Hotel Carson. Curiously enough this was saved from both buildings by Samuel Duntley, of North Hudson. It is the largest mounted specimen of the panther in the Adirondacks, if not in the state.

STEBBINS COTTAGE, LAKE GEORGE, OCCUPIED BY GOV. AND MRS. JOHN A. DIX THIS SEASON.

1911

RECEIVER FOR WABASH R.R. HAS RELATIVES HEREABOUTS

William A. Bixby, the ST. Louis *Dec 20* millionaire, who is a brother-in-law of the late William S. Tuttle, of this city, *1911* and Jay Tuttle, of Bolton, and an uncle of Mrs. Robert A. Braman, formerly Miss Edith Tuttle, who resides in East Sanford Street, this city, has been appointed one of the receivers for the Wabash Railroad in answer to a petition filed by the Westinghouse Air Brake company. The other receivers are F.A. Delano of Chicago, president of the Wabash and Edward B. Pruyn of St. Louis, vice-president of the road.

The claim in the petition is for $18,000. Each of the receivers is required to give bonds in the sum of $300,000 within ten days.

Mr. Bixby is the owner of a beautiful summer home, which is the old Mohican house rebuilt, at Bolton Landing on Lake George and, with His family passes his summers there. Supervisor Thomas, of Bolton, is a Brother-in-law of Mrs. Bixby, who was Born at Bolton Landing and was a sister of the late William S. Tuttle and Jay Tuttle.

BOLTON LANDING.

Walter Bentley and family moved from here on the 1st inst. on to Charles Davis' farm in New Vermont.

Mrs. George Vandenburg has so far recovered from her recent attack of appendicitis as to be out of doors again.

Mrs. A. G. Randall, of Glens Falls, is the guest of her brother, M. H. Tanner. Mrs. Randall will spend several weeks here.

Andrew Eddy and sister, Mrs. Martha Tanner, moved Wednesday to Hill View, where they have hired Charles Duell's house.

A. G. Randall, of Glens Falls, spent Sunday in town with relatives. Mr. Randall was accompanied by his granddaughter, Miss Dora Tripp.

Mr. and Mrs. E. J. Prescott and son, George, returned Tuesday morning from a visit of nearly a week with friends in South Glens Falls.

Miss Crandall and her niece, Miss Boss, and Miss Roxie G. Tuttle have recently sailed from New York for Italy, where they will spend the winter, returning to their homes here about May 1.

Mr. and Mrs. Joseph Barnes, of New York, are at Pine Grove cottage for Mr. Barnes's health. He has been very ill with pneumonia, but is growing stronger here. There's nothing like pure Lake George air for good health. *news Nov 9, 1911*

In spite of the pouring rain a party of our young people turned out and gave Mr. and Mrs. Benton a regular old-fashoined "horning" to help them to feel that their marriage, which took place Sunday, was properly celebrated. The bride was Miss Ethel Taber, daughter of Mr. and Mrs. John Taber, of this village. The groom has also been a resident of Bolton for several years and is well known here.

Florence, the fifteen-year-old daughter of Mr. and Mrs. Milan Weaver, died Thursday, at the home of her parents in New Vermont. The child attended school Monday, but was taken ill Tuesday; while she was not considered dangerously ill a doctor was called, but death came suddenly Thursday. She is survived by several younger sisters and one young brother. The funeral services were held Saturday afternoon at the Baptist church, the Rev. George Gates officiating. The little body was laid at rest in the Bolton cemetery.

RUSSELL STREETER.

Died Oct 28, 1912

Russell Streeter, a life-long resident of the town of Bolton, died in that place Saturday, at the home of Mrs. Harry Eldridge, lacking less than a month of being eighty years old. He was a veteran of the Civil War, having enlisted in 1861 in Company G, 93rd Regiment, under Captain Wilson, also of Bolton. In 1863 he was married to Mary A. Hill, of Granby, Oswego county, and in 1896 to Mrs. Claronda Traver of Glens Falls. Mr. Streeter is survived by one daughter, Mrs. Alec. Putney, of South Glens Falls; two sons, Eppie, of Putnam, and Orlan Philo, of Glens Falls; and two sisters, Mrs. George Green and Didama Streeter, of Bolton. The funeral was held Monday afternoon at 1 o'clock at his late home. Interment in the Huddle cemetery.

William S. Tuttle.

William S. Tuttle, who died yesterday morning at his home on East Sanford street, was one of the best known granite and marble men in the vicinity. Some of his work can be seen in the Glens Falls cemetery, where he erected the Fowler, Coolidge Goodman and Ordway monuments. One of his best pieces of work is the granite shaft in Crandall Park. *nov 14 1911*

Besides his widow, he is survived by one daughter, Mrs. Robert A. Braley; one son, Luther G. Tuttle; two brothers, Jay Tuttle of Bolton and Sidney W. Tuttle of Texas; three sisters, Miss Roxy G. Tuttle of Bolton, Mrs. W. K. Bixby of St. Louis and Mrs. George Cronkhite of East Lake George.

The funeral will be held Thursday afternoon at 2:30 o'clock from the home of his daughter, Mrs. Robert Seaman, on East Sanford street. Interment will be in the Glens Falls cemetery.

A GIRL WHO COST A KING HIS CROWN.

[Gaby Deslys, who comes here to entertain New Yorkers and who says she will receive $18,000 a week. It is probable that some of the $18,000 will be real money. Her presence on the American stage is a sad commentary on the state of the public taste.]

OBITUARY.

news Nov 2 1911

WARREN BEEBE.

Warren Beebe, a native of the town of Chester, and later for a number of years a prominent musician in Glens Falls, died on October 22, in Chicago, where he had resided about twenty-five years. He was sixty-three years old and leaves a widow and one daughter; also three sisters, Mrs. Charles E. Lavery, Mrs. M. J. Fitzpatrick, of Warrensburgh, and Mrs. James McGrath, of Boston. Death was caused by diabetes, and was preceded by a long illness. Mr. Beebe was a brilliant pianist and all-around musician. He was also a composer of merit and his music is very popular throughout the West. In his early days the deceased, with his sisters and M. J. Fitzpatrick, the veteran actor-musician, of this village, composed the Beebe Family Swiss Bell Ringers and traveled extensively throughout this and adjoining States.

---

new MRS. C. A. POTTER. *Dec 12 1911*

Mrs. Cynthia Cobb Potter, widow of the late Clark Potter, of Bolton Landing, died at that place Friday morning after only a few hours illness of neuralgia of the stomach. She was about eighty-six years old and is survived by one son, Frank L. Cobb, of Kansas City, Mo., and two step-sons, Highland and George Potter, of Bolton. The funeral was held Sunday morning at 9:30 o'clock, at the Baptist church in Bolton, in which the deceased was an active worker. The services were conducted by the pastor, the Rev. George Gates. The remains were brought to Warrensburgh for interment in the village cemetery.

Times WEDDINGS *Dec 26 1911*

Myers-Taylor.

George M. Taylor, proprietor of the Rockwell House, this morning announced the marriage of his daughter, Catherine Curtis Taylor, and Perit Colt Myers, Jr., which took place Wednesday, December 6, at Lake George.

Do Rich and Poor Alike Let Babies Die for Lack of Proper Care?

"Twenty-five per cent. of the children born to the rich of New York city die before the age of 5 because their mothers did not attend properly to their nourishment when they were infants. The children needed their mothers' milk and did not get it. Physicians, anxious to please the mothers,

Dec 9 1911 DR. ABRAHAM JACOBI. *Globe*

told them they need not stay away from bridge parties and matinees to nurse their babies, because cow's milk, properly prepared, would do as well.

"Fifty per cent. of the children in the tenements die in infancy because they are born into conditions of disease, malnutrition and neglect."

Such is the astounding presentation of conditions now existing in New York city, according to Dr. Abraham Jacobi, a physician of prominence in the metropolis. Continuing, he says:

"Our hospitals, insane asylums and penitentiaries are filled with the result of children brought into the world to swell families already too large for their means of support; or where their homes were too small; or where disease resulted from lack of ventilation and general uncleanliness, or the mother was either too busy, too careless or too ignorant to give the proper care to the child. Hence, in many cases there was no education. A puny, ill-nourished body went hand in hand with a puny, ill-nourished brain. Exit the subject into crime, disease and insanity.

"And this sorry stream emanates not alone from the poor, but from the rich as well; only the rich, because they are rich, are allowed to walk the streets.

"The State sees that people who commit crime are attended to so that the public good will be protected. The State takes charge of the people's mail. Why should it not take charge of the health of those same people?

"Fifty years ago, statistics showed, out of every 100 children born in the tenements 46 died before the age of 5. Now the mortality is 29 to every 100. That's a big improvement, but it has been slow making.

"We are endeavoring to take care of the babies. The various societies send nurses into the tenements to teach the mothers there how to keep the place clean and wholesome. They try to show the women that sewing the baby's clothes on for the winter is not wholesome. They educate them in the proper sterilization of milk bottles, how to warm the milk and dilute it with barley water and a bit of salt, perhaps.

Str. Sagamore and Her Record Breaking Crowd, Aug. 1906, Showing Tongue Mt. and Hundred Islands in the Distance, Lake George, N.Y.

The result of Tuesday's election in Warren county was, in the the main favorable to the Republicans. They elected their entire county ticket and many of their candidates in the various towns. Their greatest victory was in Warrensburgh, in the election of a Republican supervisor for the first time in

news Nov 9 1911

MILTON N. ELDRIDGE
First Republican Supervisor in the History of Warrensburgh.

DEATH'S SUDDEN STROKE.

Frank Jalet Dies of Heart Disease In New York—Well Known Here.

Frank Jalet, a native of Whitehall, thirty-seven years old, died suddenly of heart disease on Tuesday of last week, in New York. Mr. Jalet was a real estate commission broker and had taken two ladies in an automobile to inspect some lots which they contemplated purchasing, at Hastings-on-the-Hudson. Upon their return he stepped out of the machine and was about to assist the ladies when he reeled and fell to the walk unconscious. He was taken into the house and a physician was summoned, but before he arrived the young man was dead.

The story printed in a New York paper to the effect that Miss Belle Mitchell, one of the ladies who was with Mr. Jalet, was his fiancee, was not true, as the young lady was merely a client and her relations with the deceased were purely of a business nature.

Mr. Jalet was formerly a carpenter and contractor and with his father, the late John Jalet, of Whitehall, built the new Adirondack hotel in this village about 1896. He was well known here and was esteemed for his many excellent qualities. He is survived by a sister and three brothers. Mrs. David Asher, of Glens Falls; Fred Jalet, of Watervliet; John Jalet, of Troy, and Thomas Jalet, of Albany. The remains were taken to Whitehall and the funeral was held there in the Church Notre Dame des Victories.

news Jan 26 1912

Times Are Not So Bad.

During the first three weeks of December J. F. Holley, traveling salesman for a Glens Falls music dealer, traveled 194 miles by rail and 219 miles by stage and team, selling during that period eight pianos, one organ and two violin outfits. One day he drove sixteen miles and sold three pianos. Mr. Holley says he doesn't think times are so very hard as they are thought to be.

OBITUARY.

news Nov 16 1911.

DR. THOMAS McGANN.

Dr. Thomas McGann, a native of Warrensburgh, died on Wednesday night of last week, at 11:45 o'clock, at his home, 120 First avenue, Gloversville, of myocarditis. He had been in a critical condition for several weeks and his death was not unexpected. Last spring he had an attack of pneumonia and was at that time near death, but finally rallied and improved to such an extent that he was able to go to Lake Pleasant, where with Mrs. McGann he spent most of the summer at Morley's hotel. However, he did not entirely recover his health and heart trouble developed and caused his death. Dr. McGann was born in Warrensburgh in 1848, and was a son of the late Patrick and Mary McGann. He received his early education in the old Warrensburgh Academy and afterward graduated from Dartmouth college and the Albany Medical college. He began practicing his profession in 1871, at Wells, Hamilton county, where he remained for forty-seven years and became the leading citizen of the place. He represented the town on the county board of supervisors for many years and was then elected county judge and surrogate, which office he held for two or three terms. He was a member and had held various offices in the Medical Society of the State of New York, and also belonged to the Fulton county Medical society, and had many friends among the medical fraternity at home and abroad. He is survived by his widow, two brothers, John and James McGann, of this place, and one sister, Mrs. Margaret Conlin, of South Glens Falls.

An excellent program has been arranged by R. J. Bolton of Hague for the three days' racing to be held over the ice course at that place, commencing Tuesday, February 6. Purses aggregating about $650 will be put up for the events. *Feb 1912*

the history of the town. Some twenty years ago Warrensburgh was known as the "Gibraltar of Democracy" in this section. The efforts of the Republicans to elect any of their candidates for town offices were in vain. Later, however, they made substantial gains and for a number of years have secured a good share of the town offices, but never a supervisor until Milton N. Eldridge was elected Tuesday by forty-seven majortiy.

Mr. Eldridge is one of our most able and prominent business men. He is at the head of the Warrensburgh Woolen company, one of our most important industries, and is a young man of conspicuous ability. He is a "live wire" in everything he undertakes and is one of the few men who are born to lead.

news HUGH McCLOSKEY. *2 14*

Hugh McClosky, for many years a resident of Warren county, died suddenly on the 5th inst., at his home in Schroon Lake, after an illness of only a few days, aged eighty-four years. Death was due to complications incident to old age, and, although he was for a short time a great sufferer, the end came peacefully. The deceased was born in Devizes, near London, England, his parents returning soon after to Ireland, where he lived until he came to this country when he was twenty-one years old. He first located in New York city, but later, at the urgent request of his brother, came to Warren county, where he engaged successively in the mercantile and hotel business in the town of Horicon. Never physically strong he was early compelled to retire from active life, but he never ceased to regret leaving New York city with the golden opportunities of that time behind him. He is survived by his widow and four children—

THE STEAMSHIP IMPERATOR TO BE THE LARGEST VESSEL IN THE WORLD.

The new marine wonder, the steamship Imperator of the Hamburg-American Line, now building at the Vulcan ship yards at Stettin, Germany, will surpass all standards for size and luxury of equipment. The new ocean leviathan will be launched early in 1912 and will reach New York on its maiden voyage in the spring of 1913. The Imperator is 900 feet in length, ninety-six feet beam, and will be a vessel of 50,000 tonnage. This steamship will be a veritable floating skyscraper, having nine decks above the water line. A passenger list of 4,250 may be carried, in addition to a crew of 1,000. Among the features to be installed will be an elaborate Roman bath, gymnasium, squash court, sun parlor, rathskeller, and the like. The Imperator will be fitted with the Frahm anti-rolling tanks, which, with her great bulk, will counteract the motion of the roll.

Sup Troy Times Nov 10 1911

GEORGE H. BROWN,
Captain of the Citizens' Line steamer Trojan.

CHARLES H. BRUDER,
Captain of the Citizens' Line steamer Rensselaer.

ICE RACES AT THE LAKE.

News *Feb 1 1912*

Three Interesting Events Yesterday, Three More on Today.

A large crowd of enthusiastic horsemen enjoyed some fine sport at Lake George yesterday when three hotly contested races were trotted on the kite-shaped track in front of the Fort William Henry hotel.

Miss Bolton, owned by Supervisor Richard J. Bolton, of Hague, took first money in three straight heats, the best time being 2:29½. James Lamphier carried off the handsome silver cup offered to the winner of the gentlemen's driving race with his Gypsy Countess in three straight heats, the best time being 2:34½. In the 2:20 class for which there is a purse of $75, it was necessary to postpone the event until today owing to darkness after four heats had been held. Of the four heats Wilson's John O. had two first and George Russell's Hazelwood had the same. Charlie Baker's King Jim is the only other entry in the race.

Dick Baker announces that he will match his Bingen colt to race any three-year-old in the country over the Lake George course this week.

Today's events will include the free-for-all; purse, $100; 2:28 class, $50; and the 2:14 class, purse, $75.

A HORRIBLE DEATH

1911 *new*

Lawrence Murdock is Suffocated Under Seven Feet of Earth.

A SEWER DITCH CAVED IN

Was In Stooping Position Connecting Pipe When a Ton of Dirt Covered Him, Crushing Out His Life Without an Instant's Warning.

Lawrence Murdock, of this village, aged thirty-seven years, met a horrible death about 11 o'clock Monday forenoon when a ditch about seven feet deep, in which he was working, caved in, burying him alive.

Mr. Murdock with three other men were engaged in laying a sewer pipe on Lewis Thomson's property on upper Main street. The ditch was partially completed and Murdock was laying the pipe while the other men continued digging, being at work some distance away from him.

Murdock was in a stooping position adjusting the pipe at the bottom of the ditch when without the slightest warning the earth caved in from both sides burying the man so completely and suddenly that he could make no outcry. The sound of the falling earth faintly reached the other men and attracted their attention. They called to Murdock and receiving no response went to see if he was in trouble. The covered ditch told the story of his awful fate.

With frantic haste the three men began digging with a faint hope of rescuing their comrade before death had claimed him, but it was fully fifteen minutes before his body was taken out and life was then extinct. The body was found in a stooping position with hands clasping the pipe as he was at work, and there was no indication of a struggle for life, the earth having covered him so quickly and thoroughly that he was probably suffocated in a very short time.

In the meantime Dr. J. M. Griffin, coroner, had been summoned and was on the scene when the body was brought to the surface. A brief examination showed that there was no hope of resuscitation. There were no marks of any kind on the body and the coroner pronounced death accidental and caused by suffocation.

The body was taken to the home of Linsey Murdock, brother of the deceased, with whom he resided on the old Dr. Howard place, about a mile north of the village. Three other brothers survive him, Lewis, of Lake George; Henry, of Lake Pleasant, and George, of Buffalo; also one sister, Mrs. Everett Williams, of Saratoga Springs. He was unmarried.

Mr. Murdock was a faithful member of the Baptist church. He was converted during a series of revival meetings last winter,

COL. W. F. CODY (BUFFALO BILL).

Colonel Cody, a picturesque figure in American life, after twenty-eight years as a showman, preceded by many years in fighting Indians, hunting buffalo and other participation in frontier activities, retired to private life on November 1 and will spend his remaining years in the Wyoming Big Horn, where he helped make American history. His Western career began as a pony express rider, led him through more Indian battles than any other white man, and with the disappearance of the "wild and woolly" 'ed him into the show business, including annual trips throughout the United States and a notable tour in Europe. The sobriquet, "Buffalo Bill," he earned in the early sixties when he contracted to furnish buffalo meat to the laborers engaged in building the Kansas Pacific Railroad, and in less than eighteen months he killed 4,280 bison.

Nov 16 1911. Troy Times

SUMMER RESIDENT OF LAKE GEORGE DIES IN THE WEST

Dec 6/11   Times

George Barclay Moffat, special partner in the firm of White, Weld & Co., bankers at 5 Nassau street, died yesterday of a complication of diseases in Portland, Ore., in St. Vincent's hospital.

Mr. Moffat retired from active business a year ago because of ill health caused by gout and artery and heart trouble, withdrawing from the firm of Moffat & White bankers in which he and Alexander M. White of Brooklyn, his brother-in-law, were partners. The new firm was then organized to succeed it.

Mr. Moffat was 57 years old. He was born in Brooklyn, the son of Dr. Reuben C. Moffat. In 1875 he formed the firm of Carleton & Moffat as one of the partners and carried on a general importing and exporting business with the East Indies, China and Japan. Oil was extensively exported. Mr. Moffat made three or four trips around the world, combining business and pleasure. In 1892 he withdrew from the firm and became a partner in Spencer Trask & Co., going to London to open their English house, which was given up on account of the panic of 1893. The firm of Moffat & White was organized in 1895.

Mr. Moffat was a director in a number of railway and traction companies and was particularly interested in Portland in the Oregon Electric Railway Company and the Portland Coal and Coke Company, which he had organized. He went to Portland on a pleasure trip on October 12. Shortly after his arrival there he was taken with a severe attack which sent him to the hospital.

Mrs. Moffat who was Miss Frances White of Brooklyn, has been with him for the last month. Mr. Moffat is also survived by four children, two boys at Harvard, a third preparing at the Middlesex school, Concord, and a young daughter. His New York home was at East Seventieth street. He was a member of the Metropolitan Automobile and Downtown clubs and the Hamilton club of Brooklyn.—New York Sun.

Mr. Moffat's summer home was at Bolton. He was well known in this city.

The sort of weather we have been having is hard on the horses. The drivers of horses need to be reminded that as the weather is trying for them it is trying for the horse. The Elmira Star-Gazette lays down these rules for the owner and driver of horses to remember:

Keep him blanketed.
Keep him well shod.
Keep his stable warm.
Keep him protected from the wind when he must stand for some time.
Don't make him take into his mouth a frosty bit.

WATERSPOUTS.

Old Time Mariners Fought Them With Noise and Cannon.

In the waterspout the medieval mariner saw a malevolent living monster—a sea dragon. There were various means of combating them. Once all sailors carried black handled knives, which the monster was believed to hold in special abhorrence.

When a spout made its appearance these knives were produced and pointed in its direction, waved in the air so as to make the sign of the cross or, according to the recommendation of certain contemporary authorities, driven several times into the side of the ship. Certain passages from the gospel of St. John were recited as charms against waterspouts.

A loud noise of any kind was also believed to be efficacious against them—shouts, the clash of swords, the beating of drums and gongs, etc. The custom of firing cannon against water.

"My Star" Pacer Sold Again

My Star, formerly owned by C. J. Reardon of this city and handled by U. G. Smith for some time, was sold at auction at the Fastig-Tipton sale in New York city this week to D. F. Taylor of Utica for $180. A few years ago the horse paced a mile in 2.03 3-4, and was several times sold at fancy prices. Star Feb. 1912

"Mayor" Hayes Sells Livery to Dick Wood.

E. T. Hayes has sold his livery downtown to Dick Wood, of Saratoga Springs, who took possession Tuesday. Mr. Wood is an expert horseman and has been a trainer of trotting horses for many years. He was employed in that capacity by the late Capt. John L. Russell, in the palmy days of the Home Lawn Stock farm in this village. Michael Moynihan is employed by Mr. Wood in the livery. news Jan 18, 1912

HAGUE ICE RACES ARE INAUGURATED

TWO EXCELLENT EVENTS PULLED OFF ON FIRST DAY OF SERIES

Ideal winter weather marked the opening of the ice races over the course on the lake at Hague on Lake George yesterday afternoon. Two excellent events, the 2:20 class and the 2:38 class for a purse of $75 each, furnished plenty of sport for the many lovers of horse racing, who are gathered at Supervisor R. J. Bolton's hostelry at Hague for the racing, which will continue today and tomorow. Today's events will consist of the 2:14 and the 2:24 classes for a purse of $75 each. The track is in the best possible condition, and there are about twenty-five horses stabled at Hague, so that there can be no possibility of the various events not being well filled.

Both events of yesterday were won in three straight heats, Supervisor Bolton's "Miss Bolton" taking first money in the 2:20 class and Fletcher Dudley's "Red Wilkes" of Middlebury, Vt., carrying off first money in the 2:38 class. The best time made in the 2:20 class was 2:23 1-4 and in the 2:38 class the fastest heat was done in 2:27.

The results folow:

2:20 Class; Purse, $75

Miss Bolton (Bolton)	1	1	1
Al Harris (Mahoney)	2	2	2
Steve (Bailey)	3	3	3
King Jim (Baker & Wicker)	4	4	4

Time: 2:23, 2:23, 2:22 1-4.

2:38 Class; Purse, $75

Red Wilkes (Dudley)	1	1	1
The Goods (Wicker)	2	3	2
Barry B (Mosher)	4	2	3
Jed G (Baker)	3	4	4

Time: 2:27, 2:30, 2:30 1-4.

Road Builder Walker Buys Fine Team.

Thomas O'Connor, of the Adirondack hotel, Tuesday sold his fine team of fast bay pacers to Joseph F. Walker, who started with them yesterday morning to drive to Fort Plain. Mr. O'Connor raised the horses from colts. Mr. Walker is a road builder and has the contract for the Warrensburgh-Chestertown state highway, which he began in this village last fall. He says if the weather will permit he will resume operations here on April 1 with a force of at least 100 men. He has rented from Lewis Thomson the Bill Woodward place near the lime kiln on the Chester road, where he will make his headquarters next season. T. ?

David Farmer of North Bolton had his arm amputated just below the elbow at the Glens Falls hospital Thursday. The operation was necessary because of blood poisoning, which set in from a slight injury received a short time ago.

SATURDAY NIGHT THE COLDEST OF WINTER

IN THIS SECTION, THERMOMETERS INDICATING FROM 10 TO 36 DEGREES BELOW ZERO

Saturday night was without any question the coldest night, up to the present time, this winter. Persons who found it necessary to be out were glad to get within doors again to be near the warmth of a coal fire or a heater. Towards morning the thermometer indicated that there was to be a break in the cold spell and when the majority of people awoke there was every indication of an approaching snow storm, which will probably arrive shortly, and the thermometer was much warmer.

Warrensburg and places in that vicinity was undoubtedly the hardest hit by the cold snap, as the thermometer at the county home registered as low as thirty-three degrees below zero between Saturday night and Sunday morning. At the fair grounds, on the outskirts of the village, the mercury fell to thirty-two below and at the Wayside hotel it stood at thirty-four. Other places in this vicinity where the thermometers indicated the coldest of the season are as follows: Chestertown, thirty below; Schroon, thirty-one; Lake George, twenty-five; Wilton, twenty-eight; Fort Edward, thirty-six; Corinth, thirty-four; Saratoga, thirty-one; South Corinth, twenty-nine; Gansevoort, thirty-three; Moreau, twenty-nine; DeLong's brickyard, twenty-two; J. F. Hicks's farm, Ridge road, twenty-one; Albion hotel, Kattskill Bay on Lake George, twenty; Houghtaling's cottage, Glen Lake, twenty. Star Jan 15 1912

About the business section of the city the various thermometers showed from ten to twenty degrees below during Saturday night and on the outskirts of the city the mercury went even lower. A year ago the thermometers in the city stood at about twenty-six above at noon and there was rain during the day.

JOHN BROWN'S DAUGHTER

Globe June 20, 1912

Lives Alone in a Modest California Home, Near Mother's Grave.

Far separated are the remains of John Brown, of Osawatomie fame, and those of his second wife, who was the mother of 13 of his 20 children, his first wife having borne him seven, and who lived 25 years after his execution at Harper's Ferry. A huge boulder marks the resting place of John Brown in a rugged section of Essex county, N. Y., and his second wife, who shared the trials, sorrows and perils of his stormy career, sleeps in a little cemetery which nestles in the foothills of the mountains of California, near San Jose. While nearly the widest stretch of the American continent separates the graves of the husband and wife, it is worthy of note that there is a slight connecting link in the fact that the California cemetery in which is the grave of Mrs. Brown bears the title of Saratoga, the name of the famous New York State summer resort, not many miles from the grave of John Brown.

The last resting place of the militant abolitionist is unguarded by the watchfulness of relatives, for none lives near it, but the grave of the wife and mother is only a short distance from the home of one of her daughters, the favored child of John Brown, and the shadows of the same California mountain peaks stretch over both the grave of the mother and the home of the surviving daughter of one of the most picturesque characters in American history.

Perhaps the people don't know that a daughter of John Brown is living, for the lady is quiet and retiring and tries to avoid any form of publicity. She is Miss Sarah Brown, now 73 years old, with a strong, sweet face, showing traces of an earlier beauty, and hair now almost white. Her home is a modest cottage in the midst of five acres of prune trees, which she cares for herself, with the occasional aid of some Japanese, for she has devoted herself, during the past few years, to missionary work among these people who have come to California.

Miss Brown will not discuss the life of her father. She lives alone and wishes to be left alone. Despite her age, she is active and energetic. She is quite tall, walks erect, is well educated, refined, and shows the inheritance of much of her father's indomitable will power. Since 1881, when she went west with her mother and two sisters, she has resided in California. Her mother died in 1884.

THE DAUGHTER OF JOHN BROWN.

[Miss Sarah Brown, favored daughter of the famous abolitionist, as she appears to-day at the age of 73 at her home near San Jose, Cal.]

OBITUARY.

Feb 1. 1912

MRS. MARY A. MIDDLETON.

A correspondent of The News at Bolton Landing sends the following obituary notice of an old resident of that place whose death was briefly mentioned in our last issue:

Mary Ann Brown, daughter of John and Martha (Sherman) Brown, was born in the town of Queensbury November 20, 1824. When she was about eleven years old her parents removed to Shelving Rock, Lake George, where her father was engaged in lumbering for some time. A few years later he took up his residence at Riverbank on the farm now owned by J. H. Roberts. The deceased was married on February 16, 1839, to Benjamin Packer Middleton. They began housekeeping in the town of Chester. Four years later they removed to Riverbank and lived on the farm now owned by Sylvenus Smith. Forty-three years ago they removed to Bolton, where Mr. Middleton followed his trade of a stone mason. He died twenty-three years ago, and Mrs. Middleton then went to live with her son, Elisha B. Middleton, with whom she had since made her home. She was the mother of five children, two dying in infancy. Those surviving are the son already mentioned and two daughters, Mrs. George H. Allen, of Bolton, and Mrs. Sylvenus Smith, of Riverbank; also two grandchildren, Mrs. Jesse D. Starbuck and Frank P. Smith, and two great grandchildren. She departed from this life on January 18, after an illness of only five days' duration. She was highly respected by all who knew her.

PERMISSION GRANTED TO BUILD HIGHWAYS

WILL EXTEND FROM VILLAGE OF HILLVIEW, LAKE GEORGE TO THE LAKE SHORE

Star Feb 21 1912

An order was entered in the office of County Clerk Sisson yesterday confirming the report of a commission, allowing the construction of a highway from the village of Hillview on Lake George, to the lake shore, through lands formerly owned by the late General Henry E. Tremain. The matter has been in the courts for about four years and has three times been to the Appellate division. The death of General Tremain practically removed all opposition to the construction of the highway.

The highway will prove a great accommodation to the inhabitants of the village and of that vicinity, as it furnishes the only access to the lake shore, for a distance of about three miles, in either direction from Hillview.

The action was brought by Orville J. VanDusen to have the road constructed and he has been represented throughout the proceedings by Attorney James S. Riley, while the firm of Jenkins and Barker have appeared for the land owners. The commission, which allowed the construction of the highway, consisted of Attorney T. W. McArthur and Attorney H. Prior King of Glens Falls and Fred Vetter of Chestertown.

Feb 9. 1912

CAPT. M. NELSON DICKINSON.

Captain Dickinson of Warrensburgh, in point of membership, is the oldest living Mason in Warren County, having been raised in Glens Falls Lodge, No. 121, February 2, 1855, or fifty-seven years ago last Friday. He withdrew from that lodge February 5, 1857, to assist in the organization of Warrensburgh Lodge, 425, F. and A. M., and has occupied a prominent position in the Masonic order ever since. He is a member of Glens Falls Chapter, R. A. M.; Washington Commandery, 33, Knights Templar; Delta Lodge of Perfection; Albany Sovereign Consistory, Scottish Rites, thirty-second degree, and Oriental Temple, Nobles of the Mystic Shrine. Captain Dickinson was born at Bolton August 14, 1829, and has been a lifelong resident of Warren County. He served with distinction in the Civil War and was brevetted Captain for gallantry in battle. He was numbered among the early Republicans, having voted for Fremont in 1856, and has held several public offices in his home county. He retired from mercantile pursuits in 1891 and has traveled extensively throughout the United States and Canada.

PROMINENT TELEGRAPH MAN DEAD, ONCE LIVED HERE

Star Feb 19, 1912

Augustus C. Davis, a former resident of this city, and a cousin of Professor William Morse, the inventor of the telegraph, died last week at his home in Baltimore, where he had lived for a number of years. For sixty years Mr. Davis was engaged in the telegraph business, beginning his experience in Glens Falls while a boy. His first permanent position was obtained for him by his cousin, Professor Morse, in 1851. For several years he was superintendent of telegraph on the Grand Trunk lines, and the Baltimore and Ohio railroad. In the seventies he turned his attention to the development of the telephone, with which instrument he had much to do in perfecting. The survivors are his widow and one brother, Francis B. Davis, of Fort Edward.

NATICK COBBLER.

Centennial Honors for Great Man

Henry Wilson, Afterward United States Senator and Vice President Was a Farmer's Hired Hand at 10 and Tramped 100 Miles With His Worldly Possessions on His Back to Learn Shoemaking—Foe of Slavery and Friend of Lincoln.

THIS week in Farmington, N. H., where he was born, and at Natick, Mass., where he had lived, centennial honors were paid to the memory of the "Natick cobbler," Henry Wilson, who beginning life at the very bottom round of life's ladder climbed to a position of power and influence in the public affairs of the nation, (becoming a United States senator and Vice President of the republic), and died rich in his own sense of integrity and in the respect of Americans. He was a noted abolitionist and one of the steadfast supporters of the martyred Lincoln.

Wilson was born on February 16, 1812, in the pretty little town of Farmington, N. H., son of Winthrop Colbath, a workman in a lumber mill, and barism and contrary to the laws of the country."

IN CIVIL WAR DAYS.

During the civil war Wilson was chairman of the Military Committee of the Senate and a close adviser of Lincoln. He had previously served in the Massachusetts militia, and was commissioned a colonel of the volunteers. But he resigned his commission and continued his duties as a senator. After the war he took up the work of reconstruction. He toured the south, making speeches in which he urged southerners to continue loyal to the Union. In New Orleans an assassin's bullet passed his head and lodged in the wall behind him. He coolly continued his speech.

As chairman on military affairs he induced Congress to authorize the enlistment of 500,000 volunteers at the be-

Feb 12.1912   Globe.

THE CENTENNIAL OF A GREAT AMERICAN.

HENRY WILSON, THE "NATICK COBBLER," WHO BECAME A VICE PRESIDENT.

[Upper left is the stone marking his birthplace at Farmington, N. H.; right is a portrait of Mr. Wilson. Lower left shows him at the cobbler's bench and right is his residence at Natick.]

Abagail Wilson. When he was 21 he abandoned his father's name and took the maiden name of his mother as his lawful name.

His boyhood was full of poverty. He knew what it was to want for bread. When 10 years old he was apprenticed to a farmer until he should be 21. He performed the tasks common to boys on the farm, working from sunrise to sunset. He was given "schooling" by his master, as the terms of his indenture called for, and upon the completion ginning of the war and he remained at the head of this important committee until the close of the struggle. He entered the Senate of the United States in February, 1855, and when he resigned his seat on March 3, 1873, to assume the office of Vice President, to which he was elected on the ticket with Grant in 1872, he had served 18 years in the upper body of Congress. The same year he was stricken with paralysis and died November 22, 1875.

THE CRAMERS DISPLEASED AT MARRIAGE

Times Jan 27 1912

LeGrand C. Cramer, director in the United National bank of Troy, whose son's hasty marriage to Miss Marguerite S. Curley has stirred Troy society circles, denied last night that he would disinherit the young man. Besides saying that any rumor to that effect was maliciously false, the millionaire refused to discuss the romance except to say, "they are married now, and that is all there is to it. It is purely a family matter."

Friends of the family say the young man's family is greatly displeased at his action. The Cramer family was kept in ignorance of the romance and did not know of it, it is said, until the ceremony had been performed.

It is said that young Cramer visited the house after the wedding had been performed, although he did not confer with his father. The young folk have left the city and the members of both families claim not to know of their whereabouts.

The young bridegroom is heir to a fortune. The bride is a grandniece of John P. Stanton, millionaire brewer. When George H. Cramer died several years ago he left a comfortable fortune to his grandson, who was named for him. Valuable properties at Lake George also were left to the youth whose marriage has caused such a social stir.

MRS LUCINDA LATHAM.

Mrs. Lucinda Latham, aged seventy-two years and eight months, died Thursday, at Bolton Landing, where she lived with her daughter, Mrs. Mary Vandenburgh. Mrs. Latham was born in Granville and at different times lived in Glens Falls, Lake George and Warrensburgh. For several years she had made her home in Bolton. Besides the daughter mentioned she is survived by two grandsons, Rexford Whittemore, of Ridgewood, N. J., and John L. McElroy, of Bolton; also one brother, Mr. Gleason. The funeral was held in this village Saturday, at the Church of the Holy Cross, the Rev. G. H. Purdy officiating. Interment in the village cemetery.

Be proud of your blackened eye.
It isn't the fact that you're licked that counts,
It's how did you fight and try.

WINS FIRST MONEY IN ICE RACE AT LAKE

Purse $50—Steed Owned by James Dougrey—Fastest Time for Event, 2:23 1-2—Ten and Five Bushes of Oats are Prizes in Race

Star Feb 13, 1912

Large numbers of lovers of horse racing assembled at the head of Lake George yesterday to witness the matinee races held over the kite-shaped course under the auspices of the Lake George Driving association. The association officers are arranging for a three-day meeting to take place the last three days of this month. A number of excellent purses are to be offered and considerable interest is already being taken in the events.

The events yesterday consisted of two named races for purses of $50 each and a town race, with a prize of ten bushels of oats for first place and five for second. Four heats were necessary to decide the named races and five to decide the town race.

James Dougrey's "Putnam Jack" of Glens Falls took first money in the first event of the afternoon, securing first place in the first, second and fourth heats, and finishing second in the third, in which heat James Wilson's "John O" nosed Putnam Jack out at the wire. The fastest time for the event was 2.23 1-2, made in the second heat.

Star Feb 22 1912

GEN. MILES' BROTHER DROPS DEAD IN WASHINGTON D. C.

WASHINGTON, Feb. 22.—General Nelson A. Miles, retired, motoring along Pennsylvania avenue this afternoon saw a man suddenly fall dead in Lafayette park. Leaving his car, he found that the dead man was his own brother, Daniel C. Miles, of Westminster, Mass., who was in Washington visiting the General. Heart failure caused the death.

Star march 12

READ THIS, IF YOU DON'T KNOW WHAT NATURE FAKING IS

The Elizabethtown Post of Elizabethtown, Essex county, prints the following: "Sheriff Richards and Messrs Dudley and Brewster report that one day last week a dog belonging to William O'Donnell of Minerva chased a fox with a frozen tail so closely that Mr. O'Donnell has the fox tail as a trophy of the chase. Evidently as the dog jumped and caught the frozen tail the narrative snapped. Pretty cold Minerva weather is that which freezes tails on foxes, and in any event it is a smart dog that can come home with a frozen fox tail of his own getting, especially when he gets it right off the fox in full view of his owner, as was this case."

THE DEATH RECORD

Star march 7 1912

Mrs. Huldah Bartlett

Mrs. Huldah Bartlett, widow of the late Henry Bartlett, of Sabbath Day Point, died at the home of her daughter. Mrs. Adelbert Ward in Hague, March 1st, after a lingering and painful illness. She is survived by three sons, Erza and Gillette of Sabbath Day Point, and John Bartlett of Hague and two daughters, Mrs. Adelbert Ward of Hague and Mrs. James Adams of Silver Bay. Three brothers and two sisters also survive her: Edgar Sexton of Fort Ann, Jesse Sexton of Hudson Falls, and Hiram Sexton of Hague. The sisters are Mrs. David Cardle of Chestertown and Mrs. Janette Tobin of Horicon.

The Bartlett family first settled in Hague in 1875, at Silver Bay, and three years later moved to Sabbath Day Point. Mrs. Bartlett was an example of what may be accomplished by untiring industry, prudence and good judgment, and her family may well be proud of the record she has left, as a devoted wife, a loving mother and a successful home maker.

The funeral sevices were held at the church at Hague on March 3rd, and were conducted by Elder Dunn, assisted by Elder Wilson. The attendance was large. The interment was in Hague cemetery.

Model Wife
(Chicago News)

She will not care if I am late—
Kept at my office desk, you know;
If thus the dinner has to wait,
She'll think no doubt, 'tis better so.
She wont' object when I go out,
She will not scold when I come in;
She will not fail to be about
The calmest wife a man can win.

She will not ask for this and that,
And back it up with scowl and pout.
She will not need a brand new hat
But every other year—about.
She will not worry me with bills,
Nor ask for cash I haven't got;
My heart with love and longing thrills
For that sweet wife whom I have—
    not.

Oh, no! I am not wedded yet.
I simply try, as I may say,
To paint the wife I'd like to get
To be my very own some day.
Yet, hold! No self-respecting wife
Those things I've barred would fail
    to do;
And if she failed, to save my life
I could not love her much—could
    you?

The quarterly meeting

The quarterly meeting of the New York State Street Railway association was held at the Fort William Henry hotel, Lake George, Tuesday. Papers were read on the management of various departments and a dinner was served in the evening.

MRS. EMMA TAYLOR SUES.

news mar 21 1912

Injured In Accident Seeks to Recover Damages From Glens Falls Company.

Mrs. Emma L. Taylor, of Lake George and Albany, formerly Miss Emma Reoux, of Warrensburgh, has brought an action against the Glens Falls Automobile company to recover damages for personal injuries sustained in an automobile accident. The case will be tried at the next term of the Supreme court at Lake George.

The accident occurred last fall on the state road between Lake George and Glens Falls, at what is known as the Bloody Pond crossing. Mrs. Taylor and a party of five others had driven to Glens Falls early in the day and were returning to their home at Lake George in the evening. When they reached the Bloody Pond crossing the harness broke and the driver of the horses got down to the ground to repair the straps so as to be able to continue the journey home.

Mrs. Taylor and another woman, whose name was also Taylor, but who is no relative, remained in the wagon. They claimed that they looked up and saw an automobile driven by one of the Glens Falls Automobile company's chauffeurs coming down the state road toward Glens Falls at a fast rate of speed.

They sat in the wagon until, they claim, by the actions of the driver and the machine, they thought he was not going to turn out for them and both jumped to the ground and ran to the side of the road. According to their story, the automobile, when but a few feet from the rig, suddenly swerved to one side and went over to the embankment where they were standing knocking Mrs. Taylor down and running partly over her and inflicting serious personal injuries.

Chambers & Finn, of Glens Falls, are the attorneys for the plaintiff.

---

march 9 1912 news

Mrs. Huldah Bartlett, aged sixty-nine years, died Friday morning, at the home of her daughter, Mrs. Adelbert Ward, in this place. Besides Mrs Ward she is survived by one daughter and three sons—Mrs. James Adams, of Silver Bay; Ezra and Gillette Bartlett, of Sabbath Day Point; and John Bartlett, of this place; also by two sisters and three brothers, Mrs. Cardle, of Riparius; Mrs. Tobin, Horicon; Jesse Sexton, of Hudson Falls; Edgar Sexton, of Fort Ann, and Hiram Sexton, of this place. The funeral was held Sunday at the Baptist church, interment in the village cemetery. Mrs. Bartlett was a kind friend and neighbor, and was always ready to lend a helping hand.

—111—

COVERED BRIDGE WHICH COLLAPSED 22 YEARS AGO, CAUSING TWO DEATHS

Mar 19 1912

The above is a reproduction of the old wooden bridge connecting the towns of Queensbury and Moreau where the present river bridge between this city and South Glens Falls now stands. This bridge fell on March 15, 1890, twenty-two years ago last Friday, causing the death of Nelson Sansouci and Charles Carr, and also the injury of three others, who were on the bridge at the time.

Mr. Sansouci was assisting in the construction of the iron bridge, which had replaced one side of the old structure, and just as it was about completed, the old wooden bridge fell with a number of men on it. Mr. Sansouci and Mr. Carr, who was carrying mail from South Glens Falls to this city, were the only ones killed. Mr. Sansouci was dashed upon the rocks, at the foot of the stone abutment shown in the picture and rolled into the rapids, being carried away on the surface of the water. He was a brother of Charles Sansouci, a fireman at the South street station He was killed on Charles Sansouci's birthday.

WELL KNOWN PHYSICIAN DIES AT SILVER BAY

Star
Mar. 26 — 1912

Dr. D. S. Landon Passes Away at the Age of 86 Years—Funeral Was Held Sunday

Dr. D. S. Landon, a well known physician of Hague, died at his home at Silver Bay, March 22, after a long and painful illness, due to a complication of diseases and advanced age. He was born June 10, 1826. After completing his medical education, he practiced for some time in Chicago. On the breaking out of the war in 1861 he entered the army, becoming assistant surgeon, and later chief surgeon of the 104th regiment of New York Volunteers. His health failed in 1862 and he was honorably discharged and went to Troy to live. The late Judge J. M. Landon of that place, who died six years ago, was a brother.

Dr. Landon began the practice of medicine in Hague more than twenty-five years ago and about twenty years ago he bought a residence at Silver Bay and retired from practice. He lived there with his only daughter, Miss Ida Landon, who is the only near relative to survive him. The funeral services were held at the Methodist church at Hague, March 24, and the interment was at the cemetery at that place.

Chopped Off Finger in Feed Cutter.

Albert Beswick, the young son of Mr. and Mrs. Leonard Beswick, of West Bolton, one day last week cut off the first finger of his left hand at the second joint in a feed cutter. Dr. Goodman, of this village, dressed the wound. news. Feb 27

"DADDY'S LITTLE GIRL."

School time is over, 'round the old door,
The children gaily play.
One old maid, hair in a braid,
Starts homeward on her way;
A woman nearby, a tear in her eye,
Her heart beats wildly, too,
Says, "Tell me, dear, do you live near,
And whose little girl are you?"

CHORUS.

I'm daddy's little girlie,
I love him tenderly,
Long, long ago, my mamma, you know,
Was happy with daddy and me;
Now she is gone forever,
Down in the city's gay whirl.

BIG FIRES HERE MANY YEARS AGO

Times Mar. 29th 1912

MANY CONFLAGRATIONS OCCURRED IN GLENS FALLS.

FROM 1873 TO 1895

Interesting Facts About Fire Department Contained in History of Fire Department Published by F. A. Pike —Assistant Chief Discovered Fire During First Year in Department.

Some very interesting facts in regard to the Glens Falls fire department of former days have been gleaned from a history of the department published in 1895 by F. A. Pike. The most interesting feature of the book is a list of the great fires from 1873 to 1895.

The first great fire chronicled in this book is that which took place on August 1, 1873, when the Morgan barn on Park street was destroyed. It was in this year that William O. Capron, now assistant chief of the fire department, first joined the ranks of the fire fighters. At the time the big fire of 1873 broke out Mr. Capron was working in the old saw mill at the foot of Glen street hill; and he was the first of the force of men working there to discover this blaze. He gathered the men at that plant together and they rushed to the scene to aid the scant few who had already gathered there in fighting the blaze.

This fire was in one respect perhaps the worst that the city of Glens Falls has ever suffered, as the firemen were forced to battle with the flames, while they knew Mr. Morgan, the owner of the barn, was inside burning to death, while they could do nothing to aid him.

The list of fires as published in this old record are:

August 1, 1873—Morgan's barn, Park street.

February 9, 1874—Old Seminary building, Church street.

February 13, 1874—Carpenter's tannery, Lime street.

April 5, 1874—Felix Christian and a boy burned to death in a house on road leading from Plank road to Round pond.

July 17, 1874—Storehouse of Finch, Pruyn & Company on south bank of canal. Loss between $7,000 and $8,000.

February 15, 1876—Jointa Lime Company's storehouse. Loss $2,000.

January 17, 1878—Vermilia building, Warren street.

February 27, 1878—Straw shed of Glens Falls Paper Company. Loss, $4,000.

August 5, 1879—American House. Insurance allowed, $3,163.22.

June 4, 1880—Vanderheyden build-ing. Insurance allowed, $2,221.34.

January 16, 1881—G. G. Hawley building, Glen street.

August 4, 1881—Glens Falls Company's cooper shop.

July 29, 1882—Cooper shop of Glens Falls Company. Loss, $8,000.

August 20, 1882—B. B. Fowler's store. Loss, $2,000.

July 16, 1863—Glens Falls paper mill. Loss, $62,000.

November 9, 1883—Casavant building, Glen street. Loss, between $7,000 and $8,000.

April 28, 1884—Presbyterian church, M. B. Little opera house, Gildersleeve hall and Glens Falls opera house.

October 1, 1884—Sherman planing mill. Loss, $50,000.

November 26, 1884—Traphagen building, Ridge street. Loss, $15,000.

September 18, 1885—Freight depot and Glens Falls Paper Company's storehouse. Loss $20,000.

August 21, 1886—Glens Falls Company's cooper shop, kilns, storehouse and three sheds and the barn of the Transportation Company. Loss, $40,000.

October 22, 1886—Hub and Spoke factory. Loss, $5,700.

February 20, 1888—New Hall House, Glen street.

October 4, 1888—Hotel Elmwood.

July 20, 1890—Planing mill and factory of D. W. Sherman. Loss, $40,000.

February 15, 1891—Finch, Pruyn & Company's lime works, Canal street. Loss, $3,000.

February 25, 1894—A. S. Rugge's factory. Loss, $50,000.

May 11, 1894—Jointa and Glens Falls Lime Company's works. Loss, $15,000.

June 12, 1894—Kendrick's planing mill. Loss, $35,000.

November 26, 1894—Dr. Foster's residence (the third time).

February 13, 1895—Ferriss building, Glen street.

February 25, 1895—Holden building, Glen street.

STONY CREEK COUPLE ARE 101 YEARS OLD

the Times

april 1st 1912

The Albany Knickerbocker-Press today publishes the following:

Last Thursday Mr. and Mrs. Benjamin Harrington of West Stony Creek celebrated the one hundred and first anniversary of their birthday. They were both born March 28, 1811. One son was born to the couple, and he is the constant companion and caretaker of "Uncle Ben" and "Aunt Harriet," as they are known to all their friends.

Mr. Harrington helps about the farm and does all the barn chores. He milks ten cows twice a day. He has never been sick in bed. He served through the Civil war, and has many good stories to tell. His mind is clear, and his memory is as good as it was fifty years ago. 'I have always lived close to nature," he said yesterday, "and never used tobacco or whiskey, loved and respected God. He never questioned the ways of the creator. That's all I can tell you."

Mrs. Harrington works about the house and garden; makes her own clothes, has never worn glasses, and reads as readily as a school girl. She has monuments to her skill in needlework to exhibit to the admiring visitors, such as wonderful quilts and beautifully woven bedspreads.

He stood in a beautiful mansion,
Surrounded by riches untold,
And gazed at a beautiful picture
That hung in a frame of gold.
'Twas the picture of a lady,
So beautiful, young and fair;
With his eyes fixed upon the picture,
He murmured in sad despair:

CHORUS.

If those lips could only speak,
If those eyes could only see;
If those beautiful golden tresses,
Where they in reality.
Could I only take your hand,
As you did when you took my name;
But it's only a beautiful picture
In a beautiful golden frame.

With all his great power and his riches,
He knows he can never replace;
One thing in the mansion that's absent,
His wife's tender, smiling face.
Each time he looks at the picture,
These words you could hear him say:
"All my wealth I would freely forfeit
And toil for you night and day."

He sat there and gazed at the picture,
Then slumbered, forgetting all pain;
And there in the mansion he fancied
She stood by his side again.
Then his lips they softly murmured
The name of his once sweet bride;
Still with eyes fixed upon the picture,
He woke from his dream and cried.

Times

April 1st 1912

Mayor Griffing.

INAUGURATED AS THIRD MAYOR OF GLENS FALLS.

They called her frivolous Sal,
A peculiar sort of a gal,
With face that was mellow
And all round with fellow,
Was my old pal.
Her troubles, sorrows and care
She was always willing to share.
A wild sort of devil, but dead on level,
Was my gal Sal.

Glens Falls Insurance Building

The accompanying reproduction from a photograph shows the Glens Falls Insurance building after it had been placed upon rollers and prepared for its trip across Glen street. Large crowds congregate daily in Monument square to watch the progress of the work. The building has now been turned about twenty-five feet. The photograph from which the above cut was made was taken by Theron L. Winchip, Union street, who has been engaged as photographer for The Post-Star.

FRIDAY MORNING, MARCH 29, 1912.

HORICON LODGE IS TOTALLY WIPED OUT BY BLAZE OF UNKNOWN ORIGIN

Bucket Brigade Performs Heroic Work, Preventing Nearby Cottages From Catching Afire---Loss is Estimated to be Between $15,000 and $18,000

9/12

Fire of an unknown origin yesterday afternoon totally destroyed the Horicon lodge at Ripley's Point, one of the most popular hotels on Lake George. The loss is estimated at between $15,000 and $18,0000, which is partially covered by insurance.

Bucket-Brigade Handicapped

In addition to the building the contents consisting of furnishings and other material, were entirely consumed by the flames, the fire making such rapid progress that the thirty-five or forty men who formed a bucket brigade and carried water from the lake —a distance of a hundred feet or more —had their hands full preventing the nearby cottages on the Point from taking fire. No opportunity was afforded them to remove any of the furnishings of the hotel.

Steamer Landing at Horicon Lodge, Lake George.

— 114 —

The hotel was built twenty-seven years ago by the present owner, George A. Ferris, of Hudson Falls.

How Did it Start?

The only explanation which can be given for the fire is that rats or mice must have got into a box of matches, although it is said that great care was taken last fall to remove from the building all matches and other materials from which a fire might start.

Wind Saves Houses

A strong southeast wind which continued to blow while the fire was at its height, is all that saved every cottage on the Point from being destroyed. The wind carried the flames and sparks in an opposite direction. One of the cottages which stood in front of the hotel was in danger of taking fire several times and as there were a number of other cottages which would also have been lost in case the blaze was communicated. To this particular one the men devoted their efforts.

Had Gained Headway

The fire in the hotel had gained such headway when it was discovered that any attempt to extinguish it would have been futile.

Brayton Discovers Flames

From what information can be obtained, it is evident that the blaze was first discovered by the family of Fayette Jenkins, who live about a half mile from the hotel. Smoke was seen in the direction of the point and Richard Brayton, who was at the Jenkins home at the time, went to the Point to ascertain where the fire was. When he first obtained a view of the rear of the hotel he saw that flames were pouring out from the third floor near the roof.

Were Working at Dock

A number of men, including George Mickle and Melvin Bennett of this city, Nelson Landrie and Philip LaCrosse of Hudson Falls, and Buell Jenkins, Dan Harris, Fred Kollman, Adelbert and Abial Mattison, Cromwell Barber, James Harris and Seth Truesdale of Kattskill Bay and vicinity, were at work on the new dock, which is being constructed just north of the hotel. But, because of the fact that there were several cottages between the hotel and the place where they were working, they were not aware of the fire until Brayton informed them.

Not Due to Incendiary

Knowing that no one had been in the hotel they at once suspected that the fire had been set. In order to determine whether their suspicions had any foundation several of them walked around the hotel to see if there were any tracks in the snow, but no sign was found to indicate that any one had been near the place.

Work Strenuously

At first the men started to remove the furnishings from the burning hostelry, but after a few chairs had been taken out, it was seen that the cottage in front of the hotel was threatened. A bucket brigade was immediately formed, there being about thirty men, residents of the Point and vicinity who assisted the others in the work.

Caravanserie's History

The hotel stood in the midst of a pretty grove on the Point, five and one-half miles from Lake George, forty feet above the water, the grounds sloping gradually to the shore one hundred feet distant. The building was a commodious three-story structure, each floor opening upon a large wide piazza and accommodating one hundred guests. The lake could be seen from every window in the hostelry and the lake and mountain scenery was unsurpassed. Extensive improvements were completed on the hotel last year and the manager, G. W. Hart of Albany, who conducted the popular resort for twelve years, had completed arrangements for this season, which he expected would be one of the best ever experienced. Mr. Hart only recently received from the hands of the printers a handsome booklet describing the hotel and conveniences, many of which have already been mailed to patrons. The hotel was one of the most popular on the lake for Glens Falls and vicinity folk, largely because of the fact that many local people have cottages on the Point.

May Not Rebuild

Mr. Ferris, the owner, stated to a Post-Star reporter last night that he had not yet decided whether he will rebuild or not. In any event it is impossible to have a new hotel in readiness for the coming season.

Watch the Ruins

A force of men watched the smouldering ruins throughout the night to prevent any possibility of the cottages being ignited.

TRAGEDY RECALLED.

The Daily Times today received the following communication from F. A. J. Dunwick of Pulaski, a former resident of Glens Falls:

Henry Phillips, at one time a resident of Glens Falls, and who during the season of 1893 conducted a hotel at Lake George, was a visitor here this week. He seems to keep in touch with dear old Glens Falls. The terrible tragedy of the year mentioned is recalled by the fact that Phillips was conducting the hotel when his boat, The Rachel, went down and a dozen persons lost their lives. They were, as I remember it, on their way to a ball down the lake. But how time flies! That tragedy was two decades ago.

Times April 6 '12

REMOVING FROM VILLAGE.

J. R. Cady, who for years has been connected with the Union Bag & Paper Company has resigned his position and with Mrs. Cady will in a few days leave this village for Eddystone to make their home. Merch Cady, a former Hudson Falls boy and a son of Mr. and Mrs. Cady conducts a large pharmacy in that city. Mr. and Mrs. Cady have a large circle of friends in this village who regret their departure.

Times March 28 1912

ATTACKED BY WILD CAT.

Former Warrensburgh Man's Thrilling Adventure Near North River.

Louis Napoleon Beach, a former Warrensburgh man, who is now employed in Harry Raymond's livery stable at Riverside, while driving from North River to Hooper's Mines, late Friday afternoon, had a thrilling experience with a bob-cat which has been hanging around that section all winter.

Mr. Beach was driving a pair of horses, belonging to his employer, hitched to a light wagon, and as they passed under a large pine tree, about three miles from North River, he heard a noise in the branches, and down into the back of the wagon dropped the big cat. The horses became frightened and bolted, while the driver was struggling with the animal.

Mr. Beach attacked the cat with the butt of his horse whip, but this only served to enrage the fury of the creature and it clawed and bit, making several ugly wounds on the unfortunate man. The horses made a sudden jump to one side of the road which dislodged the cat from the wagon, and thoroughly maddened the team ran wildly toward the village of Garnet. As they came to the house of R. J. Bennett, they bolted into his barn yard, where they stopped so suddenly that Mr. Beach was thrown to the ground. *News April 18 1912*

After he was somewhat recovered he went into the house, where Mr. Bennett dressed the wounds inflicted by the cat. The attack has stirred up the people of that section. One of the horses, valued at $250, was badly injured, and will probably have to be shot.

CARE OF WARREN COUNTY ROADS

News April 1912

Liberal Appropriation Made by the State Highway Department.

The state highway department has appropriated $161,130 for the repair and maintenance of state roads in Warren county this year, together with $37,870 to be used for minor repairs and the pay of patrolmen, making a total of $199,000.

The money will be expended on the various roads as follows: Lake George-Bolton road, 9.74 miles, bituminous top; Glens Falls-Lake George road, 7.56 miles, bituminous top, $52,920; North Creek County Line road, 4.12 miles, oiling top, $3,500; Riverside-Chestertown road, 5.75 miles, bituminous top, $40,250.

The bituminous top dressing has been pronounced the best material yet discovered for the purpose. It was applied last year on the Loon Lake-Pottersville road and stood the test of hard service. The improvements and repairs will be made under the personal supervision of County Superintendent of Highways Bertram E. Murray.

FISH AND GAME BILL RECENTLY PASSED MAKES LAW MORE LUCID TO HUNTERS

All Measures Affecting Sportsmen are Virtually Uniform Now—Thirty Additional Protectors Provided for, Making Total of 125—New Superintendency

Apl 19. 1912

The fish and game bill signed by Governor John A. Dix fulfills the promise to make the law simpler, more uniform, more sensible and more understandable. Sportsmen, farmers, land owners and all others interested in this important branch of legislation were invited to give their views and lend their assistance in the formation and codification of this law which is calculated to give the people more hunting and fishing and more game and fish.

With the exception of Long Island, having climatic conditions differing from the rest of the state, the fish and game laws are now uniform. They have been simplified and conflicting features have been eliminated. It is not claimed that the new laws are perfect, but in view of the vast range of differences of opinion in various sections of the state and of interests which have a tendency to conflict, the Conservation commission and Governor Dix believe that a very gratifying result has been obtained for the general welfare of the entire state. The public has been taken into the confidence of the commission and the law makers in this great work, and the people who desire to see an increase of fish and game are cordially invited to lend their cooperation in the enforcement of the new laws. The operation thereof will be closely watched, both by the commission and by the people of the state, and all should work together to attain an ideal fish and game act. Any changes that may be deemed necessary to an improvement in fish and game conditions in the state can readily be attained by a crystalization and expression of public sentiment, as just illustrated in the many prominent improvements secured in the new laws. The conservation commission desires to thank the press, the sportsmen's clubs and all others who lent their valuable aid in the preparation of the codified laws.

Thirty additional game protectors are provided for, making a total of 125 in all. The office of superintendent of Inland Fisheries is created. Power has been reposed in the commission to give additional protection to fish and game localities where it is deemed necessary to do so. The commission is also empowered to grant licenses to take deleterius fish at all seasons of the year in any of the waters of the state, thus providing an efficient means of the more prominent changes on fish and game.

The Deer law provides that only two bucks having horns not less than three inches in length may be taken, from November 21 to January 1st, both inclusive, provided a license so to do is obtained from the commission, and deer and venison is tagged and marked under rules and regulation to be prescribed by the commission. No open season for wild moose, elk, caribou and antelope. Black and grey squirrels may be taken and possessed from September 16th to October 31st, both inclusive. The killing of squirrels within the corporate limits of cities and villiages is prohibited. A bag limit of five squirrels in one day. Varying hares may be taken and possessed from November 1st to January 31st, both inclusive. Cottontail rabbits may be taken and possessed from October 1st to December 31st, both inclusive. The use of ferrets is prohibited, but the owners or occupants of inclosed of occupied farms and lands or a persons duly authorized in writing by such owner or occupant may take in any manner at any time varying hares and cottontail rabbits which are injuring property. Hares and rabbits may be bought and sold during the open season. Beaver, no open season. Mink, raccoon, sable, open season, November 1st to March 1st, both inclusive. Skunks, open season November 1st to January 1st. Muskrat, November 1st to April 10th, open season. Ducks, geese and brant, season September 16th to January 10th. There is no open season for wood duck and swan. A bag limit of twenty-five water fowls in the aggregate of all kinds in one day or forty to a boat, blind or battery occupied by two or more persons. Rails, American coots, mud hens and gallinoles, open season September 16th to December 31st, bag limit of fifteen to a person, twenty to a boat or blind occupied by two or more persons. Quail and woodcock, open season from October 1st to November 15th. Six quails may be taken in one day and thirty-six in the open season.

Woodcock special on Long Island October 15th to November 30th. Grouse, open season October 1st to November 20th, both inclusive. Four grouse may be taken in one day and twenty in the open season.

The season on pheasants has been m... the ... and provides for the taking of pheasants on Thursdays in the month of October and possessed during the month of October. Only male pheasants may be taken and not more than three in the open season.

No open season for Hungarian or European gray-legged partridge. Quail, pheasants and grouse on Long Island from November 1st to December 31st. Six male pheasants may be taken in season September 18th to November 30. Fifteen shore birds in the aggregate of all kinds may be taken at one time.

The sale of all kinds of game except elk, deer, venison, mallard and black duck raised on private preserves and sold under a license issued by the commission, and such game must be sold from October 1st to March 1st, both inclusive. The unplucked carcasses of all species of Scotch grouse, European black game, European black plover, European red-legged partridge, Egyptian quail, and the carcasses of the European red deer, fallow deer, and roe buck may be imported from without the United States and sold therein at any time under a license issued by the commission.

Fish minnows may be taken by any person for his own use for bait without a license, but persons taking minnows for bait for sale are required to obtain a license from the commission. Black bass, size limit ten inches, open season June 16th to November 30th, not to exceed fifteen may be taken in one day, or twenty-five to a boat. Trout, open season from May 1st to August 31st, size limit six inches, except in Long Island where the open season is April 1 to August 31, for brook trout and April 16th to September 30th for rainbow trout, size limit fifteen inches of catch not to exceed ten pounds in one day. Lake trout, size limit fifteen inches, open season from April 1st to September 30th. Size of catch ten lake trout in one day to a person and fifteen to a boat. White fish, size limit twelve inches, open season June 1st to September 30th. Otsego white fish, size limit nine inches, open season June 1st to October 31st. In Lake Erie and Ontario lake trout, and white fish may be taken at any time.

Pike, perch; size limit twelve inches; open season May 1 to March 1, both inclusive. Pickerel and pike; open season May 1 to March 1. Size limit in St. Lawrence river not less than twenty inches in length. A person may take in one day not to exceed twelve great northern pike.

Shortnosed sturgeon; open season July 1 to April 30. Size limit twenty inches. Lake sturgeon; size limit thirty inches. Sea sturgeon not less than four feet may be taken at any time. Maskelonge; size limit twenty-four inches; open season June 16 to December 31. Striped bass; size limit twelve inches, may be taken at any time. Smelts or ice fish; size limit six inches, no closed season.

The sale of trout and black bass is at all times prohibited. This includes trout and black bass coming from without the state as well as those taken within the state. The sale of trout raised in private hatcheries is permitted, provided a license so to do is obtained from the commission, and all such trout marked and tagged; rules and regulations to be prescribed by the commission.

Tip-ups may be used, except in waters inhabited by trout, to take bullheads.

Set and trap lines. Set lines may be used except in waters inhabited by trout, to take white fish, bullheads, catfish, eels, perch, sunfish, carp, mullets and dog fish, provided a permit so to do is obtained from the commission. Under this provision a particular stream or body of water may be opened up for use of set lines under one permit.

Spearing. Under such a permit spears, grappling hooks, naked hooks and snatch hooks may be used, ex-

cept in waters inhabited by trout, to take white fish, mullets, carp, catfish, dogfish, bullheads, suckers and eels.

BOLTON LANDING
Times — apl 6 1912

Bolton Landing, April 3.—Captain and Mrs. C. E. Wilson have returned home from a visit with their son-in-law an daughter, Mr. and Mrs. Arthur Manning of Schenectady.

Miss Genevieve Kelly of the high school faculty is spending the week with her parents at Port Henry.

Miss Agnes Gates, teacher of physical culture at Tarrytown, N. Y., is home for the Easter vacation.

Miss Belinda Finkle of Greenwich and O. G. Finkle, Jr., of North Creek are spending the Easter vacation with their parents, Mr. and Mrs. O. G. Finkle, Sr.

News of the death of Mrs. Herbert Moon of Bridgeport, Conn., who was formerly Miss Faude Fish of this place, was received with sorrow by her many friends and acquaintances in this vicinity. Besides her husband, deceased leaves a mother, Mrs. Clarissa Fish, a brother, Judson Fish of this place and a sister.

Milo Weaver, a much respected resident of New Vermont, Bolton, died at his home Friday of pneumonia. He is survived by his wife and five children, his father, Jay Weaver, and three sisters, Mrs. Bert Monroe, Mrs. Allen Burch and Mrs. Eugene Coon. Funeral was held Sunday afternoon in the Baptist church at Bolton Landing. Interment was made in Huddle cemetery.

Mrs. James Anderson, a highly esteemed citizen of this place, died last Monday at her home. Deceased is survived by her husband, two brothers, John and James Cary, and a sister, Mrs. Alfred Bennett, all of Bolton. Funeral services were held at the residence Thursday morning. Interment was made in Huddle cemetery.

Mr. and Mrs. F. R. Norton have returned home from a visit with Mr. and Mrs. E. Reilly of Greenwich, Conn.

Members of the Bolton Landing club are rehearsing for a play which they expect to present in the Guild hall in the near future.

E. N. Lamb and sons, Cecil and Arthur Lamb, are visiting relatives in Vermont this week.

Paul Boyce, who is attending college at Worcester, Mass., is home for the Easter vacation.

William Moore died at his home last Wednesday of a disease of which he has long been a sufferer. He is survived by his widow and a brother, John Moore, of this place. Funeral services were held at his late home Saturday afternoon, Rev. George Gates officiating. Interment was in the Huddle cemetery.

LIGHTNING DESTROYS THE PRATT COTTAGE

apl 16 — 1912 Star

FIRE SETS IN AFTER BOLT STRIKES DWELLING AND DEMOLISHES STRUCTURE

A cottage on the Trout Lake road near the shores of Lake George about three miles north of Bolton Landing, owned and occupied by Eldridge Pratt and family, was struck by lightning and totally destroyed by the fire about 9:30 last night. The loss is estimated at $3,000 and is partially covered by insurance. Little of the furniture of the house was saved and because of the lack of fire fighting facilities it was impossible to combat with the conflagration.

Mr. and Mrs. Pratt, their infant child and Miss Putney, who was making her home with them, were cared for by neighbors.

The cottage was built only two years ago, and was rented by Mr. Pratt in the summer and occupied by his family in the winter.

The storm which visited Bolton Landing and vicinity last night lasted for a considerable length of time and was as severe as many of the storms of the warmer months.

"THE OLD RUSTIC BRIDGE BY THE MILL."

I am thinking to-night of the old rustic bridge,
  That bends o'er the murmuring stream;
'Twas there, Maggie dear, with our hearts full of cheer,
  We strayed 'neath the moon's gentle beam.
'Twas there I first met the sweet glance of your eye,
  That worked in my heart a sweet thrill;
Though now far away, my thoughts fondly stray
  To the old rustic bridge by the mill.

CHORUS
Beneath it a stream gently ripples,
  Around it the birds love to trill;
Though now far away, my thoughts fondly stray
  To the old rustic bridge by the mill.

'Twas there, dearest Maggie, as years passed away,
  And we plighted lovers became,
We wandered the path to the bridge day by day,
  The smiles of our love to regain.
But one day we parted in pain and regret,
  And our promise we could not fulfil;
But soon may we meet and our fond vows repeat
  At the old rustic bridge by the mill.

I'll keep in my memory our love of the past;
  To me it's as bright as of old;
Deep down in my heart it was planted to last,
  For in absence it never grows cold.
I think of you, darling, when lonely at night,
  When all 'round is silent and still;
My thoughts wander back in a dream of delight
  To the old rustic bridge by the mill.

OLD FLAG IS REPLACED BY NEW BANNER

Times apl 28 1912

The old flag that has floated on the top of the Masonic building since February 12, three days after the work was started on the removal of the building, has been torn to ribbons by the wind and has been replaced by a new flag.

The old flag was loaned by Colonel G. Frank Bryant to the Masonic Club on Lincoln's birthday. It had been owned by him since 1888, when he used it in the Benjamin Harrison campaign, which was conducted in this county by members of the Harrison-Morton Club, of which he was president. The flag has only twenty-five stars as there were but twenty-five states in the union at that time.

The scenes of activity of the Harrison-Morton Club in this county were around Lake George, where a log cabin was built by Colonel Bryant as the emblem of Harrison. This was the same emblem that his Grandfather William Henry Harrison had used in his presidential campaign when he

G. Frank Bryant.

became the ninth president of the United States.

Large numbers of people gathered at the lake when a public meeting of the club was held, and George A. Batcheller, one of the great orators of those days and later judge of the court in Egypt, was present and made a speech as the flag was raised over the log cabin. A short time later the same flag was used in a parade held by the club in this city.

The flag is now in the possession of Edward Durin of Washington, D. C.,

BROTHER RECOVERS LIFELESS BODY OF SISTER FROM WATERS OF LAKE GEORGE

Body of Grace Truesdale Found in Two Feet of Water Near Diamond Point --Suicide Theory is Advanced by Coroner

Apl 27 1912 ——————— *Star*

What is believed to have been a case of suicide occurred Thursday afternoon at Diamond Point on Lake George, when Miss Grace Truesdale, thirty-one years of age, daughter of Marvin Truesdale, a resident of Diamond Point, with whom the young woman resided, ended her life by drowning in two feet of water near a dock, located in a lonely spot just north of the Tremain place on the Bolton road.

Found by Brother

The lifeless body was found in the shallow water about 9 o'clock the same night by a brother, Fred E. Truesdale, who also lives at Diamond Point. The young woman was said to have been demented, having wandered away from home on another occasion, since the death of her mother, a year ago. It is said that she has been ill much of the time, which fact is thought to have led her to commit suicide, undoubtedly during a spell of despondency.

Of Mysterious Nature

The drowning was of a mysterious nature and Coroner Charles K. Burt of Lake George said last night that the case was undoubtedly one of suicide, although he had made no report. From what can be learned the girl left no word for relatives or other persons and no one could be found who saw her after she left the house to go for a walk to the home of a relative, about a mile distant.

Searching Party Formed

When darkness commenced to fall and the young woman had not returned home, her relatives became alarmed and telephoned to a number of neighbors, whom she was in the habit of visiting, but they were unable to learn of her whereabouts. Realizing that an accident must be detaining the girl, a searching party was formed and at 9 o'clock the body was found. Coroner Burt was summoned and, after viewing the body, gave permission for its removal to the father's home.

Besides the father, Miss Truesdale is survived by two brothers, Charles and Fred E. Truesdale of Diamond Point and three sisters, Mrs. Gordon Thompson of Brooklyn, Mrs. George M. Kinney and Miss Maud Truesdale of Diamond Point. The funeral arrangements have not been completed.

—/18—

CHICAGO MAN WRITES ON THE PROTECTION OF FISH

Times May 3 1912.

Chicago, April 30, 1912.

Editor Glens Falls Times:

I notice an interesting article in your issue of April 26 on the protection of fish. The most important point of all is wholly overlooked and will be better understood when the fishing conditions are made public that existed there sixty-five or seventy years ago. I speak of sixty-eight years ago.

In 1844 my father moved from Hartford, Washington county, N. Y., to Lake George on what was then known as the Smith Brook place, about four miles north of Caldwell village on the west shore of Lake George. I was then eight years old, being as poor as Job's turkey that leaned up against the barn to gobble. Fish was an important item. We would bind two logs together for a boat and with a long pole get outside of the rocky point east of the Diamond Point Hotel, the late Coolidge place: here or most anywhere else we could pole the raft. Either one or two people during the early months of summer could catch in less than one hour all the fish—black bass, perch and sun fish—a family could eat in two days.

As soon as we could buy an old boat we would follow the fish out on the grass ground, thirty-two to thirty-five feet of water, where in August and September we could catch black bass up to seven pounds and perch, bullheads and eels in any quantity desired.

In the spring all the brooks swarmed with suckers that run up the streams to spawn. In the fall, fall trout did the same, only in less numbers. With a long pole and line silver trout could be caught from shore at the outlet of the brooks during the summer months or early fall.

During those days rumors were afloat that some one had deposited a batch of young pickerel in Ripley's bay over on the other side of the lake. Another rumor I could or did not confirm was that some one stocked a pond in Bolton with pickerel and that it flowed into Lake George. Be this as it may, in 1854 or '55 I worked for Harvy C. Lowe, who kept the summer hotel on the east shore. One night I went out spearing and speared the first pickerel caught in Lake George. I killed him but I did not secure him. Two days later one of Orlin Brayton's boys found him washed up on the beach at the south end of the bay and displayed him through Harrisena. The fish weighed twenty-two and one-half pounds, a gigantic wonder in those days. I struck to kill just back of his gills. The fish floundered off the spear. The night was very foggy and dark and we lost him.

About three to five years later the lake swarmed with small pickerel ranging from one pound to five or seven pounds, yearly growing larger. Oh, but the cost was terrible! It was pickerel, pickerel, pickerel. Even in that pure water they proved to be strong and the poorest eating fish in the lake unless we except rock bass, commonly called sun fish or "Ring Eyed Jonathans."

A very few years later all fish seemed to disappear from the lake. The pickerel grew scarcer and all other fish vanished. I caught one pickerel weighing about three pounds and examined his stomach. I found one undigested perch, just swallowed, six inches long and several more partly digested. I continued the search until I identified one hundred heads of small fish in that pickerel's stomach. Then I knew why fishing was poor.

The pickerel first devoured the suckers, trout, bass and perch, and then ate themselves up. All this took place before the increase of fishing cut any great figure. Pickerel are the pirates of the lakes—sharks of the sea. Protect the fish and regulate the fishing except pickerel. Annihilate pickerel if you pay a bounty to do it. Each dead pickerel will restore annually many thousand smaller but better fish.

F. D. ORCUTT,
7348 Center avenue, Chicago, Ill.

A Statesman's Home

Star apr. 18. 1912

The Life of Edward M. Shepard at Lake George—His Official Estate—Personal Characteristics

(William Bruce Dowd in The Brooklyn Citizen)

Upon the breaking up of a conference held at the Trubee house, Buffalo, by representatives of delegates to the assembled Democratic convention, who were opposed to the nomination of Mr. Hearst for Governor in 1906, Edward M. Shepard, who had presided, turned to the table at which he had sat and said to a group of men who had paused to shake hands with him: "Gentlemen, I desire to draw your attention to the color of these flowers." He indicated a vase of purple asters on the desk. That was the only expression he gave of the thoughts going on within him. Others had spoken boldly, even bitterly, against the proposed nomination, but Mr. Shepard, when it came his turn to speak, said only a few words about the necessity of preserving party harmony and his hope that a way would be found to do it.

The emblem of mourning before him had sunk deep into his soul, however, and his parting remark was prophetic. It was also a perfect key to the mind and heart of this remarkable man. While he was practical, he was also an idealist. He filled to a fine degree Paul Leicester Ford's picture of a "practical idealist" in "The Honorable Peter Sterling," said to have been suggested by the career of Grover Cleveland.

Fulfilled Dream of Childhood

It is quite certain that Mr. Shepard resolved to have a summer or occasional home at Lake George in 1864, when he was only fourteen years of age. He himself had said it. In that year he went from New York to visit a friend in Vermont. This is his account of what happened on his way back:

"When I arrived at Ticonderoga I counted my pocket money to see if it were possible for me to return by way of Lake George. I found that I had just enough money to get home and buy my dinner if I went direct through to Whitehall. If I went by way of Lake George, I should have to go without my dinner. I decided to go without my dinner. As I passed through the lake I was so enraptured with it that I then resolved that at some time I would have a home on its shores."

A good many years elapsed before he realized his wish, but it became his habit during his maturing years to join in vacation some of his college chums in what was known as "Camp Manhattan," on Little Green Island, Kattskill Bay, in the lake.

He next took a lease of Westover (1891-2), and it was not until 1898 that he began his erection of the imposing and beautiful edifice known as Erlowest, in which he died. That name is worth a moment's consideration, for it shows Mr. Shepard's strong attachment to his belongings. He had formerly lived with his father's family at a place near Albany, named

places or people, the rule was the same; he was true to them all.

Thus when he became a proprietor at Lake George he engaged as superintendent of his property Smith H. Wood, who continued with him, through ever-increasing responsibilities, until Mr. Shepard died, July 23, 1911, a period of twenty years.

Loyal to Familiar Scenes

Mr. Shepard's intense love of his belongings, his firm attachment to friends and employes, his all-pervading sense of loyalty, came out forcibly in his life of "Martin Van Buren." From title page to finish, this book is saturated with the author's love of New York state, and it shows a most intimate knowledge of its history and people. One single passage from his analysis of Van Buren as a lawyer will illustrate the minuteness of the dissection of the subject's character and ability to reveal at the same time the innermost secret of Mr. Shepard's own personality. He says of Van Buren: "At an early age he became a successful and skillful advocate in arguments addressed to courts as distinguished from juries, a division of professional work in which no skill of readiness will supply deficiencies in professional equipment." It was this quality of thoroughness in Mr. Shepard himself to which Mayor Gaynor, in a statement made shortly after Mr. Shepard's death, attributed his great achievements.

Bearing in mind, then, the happy blending in Mr. Shepard's temperament of the practical and the poetical, his intense localism and love of country and his thoroughness in whatever he undertook, we shall be prepared to understand and appreciate what he did at and for Lake George.

It is worth while also to note that in locating there Mr. Shepard merely found his natural environment and adjusted himself to it. There is no other place in New York which was better suited to the tastes of such a man. Not only do Lake George and Lake Champlain form a natural art gallery of unsurpassed loveliness, but their shores are lined with historic monuments, their atmosphere is charged with stories of romance and wars and rumors of wars.

Champlain, Ethan Allen, Ticonderoga, Fort William Henry, King Hendrick, Fort Dieskau, Mohawks, Mohicans, J. Fenimore Cooper, Montcalm, Putnam, Howe, Burgoyne, Franklin even Washington himself! What an immense storehouse for the mind's delight is found in the history and fable of these lakes. It requires no effort to explain why Mr. Shepard was attracted to the place, assuming that his boyish fancy was not enough to fix him to it. That he thoroughly understood and appreciated its history is proved by a memorial window on the grand stairway of Erlowest.

There are separate panels in stained glass, bearing insignia of the names under which the lake has been known—Anditaracte, Du Saint Sacrament, Lake George and Horicon. The last was an invention of J. Fenimore Cooper, as stated in the preface to "The Last of the Mohicans," but it was taken from a tribe of Indians who lived near the lake in former times. Then, on still other panels, are the names and dates dominant in the lake's history to the time of the Revolution: Jogues (the priest who discovered it), 1642; Montcalm, 1757; Howe, 1758, and Schuyler, 1777. Last, at the bottom, are Erlowest, 1898. It tells the story of research and of artistic appreciation.

A Typical Home

Now it was by good chance that Erlowest was located where it was. In the winter of 1897-98 the superintendent wrote Mr. Shepard that a desirable place on the west bank of the lake, not far from Westover, which had been rented for some years, could be had at a reasonable price. Mr. Shepard answered that, from his recollection of the place, it would not suit him; but, being urged, he came up and bought the land, about twenty-five acres, and by February laborers were removing the snow, preparing the way for the edifice, which was begun, finished and furnished in that year. Mr. Shepard went to Europe that summer, and while there he bought much of the furniture, conspicuously a splendid Italian walnut dining-room set, and by the end of the year his house was in order and he was in it. The building, which is of stone, was made of rough fragments, resulting in the main from blasting a cut through a hill to make a suitable roadway to the premises. It was, from the beginning, a good-sized house, two stories and an attic, having spacious rooms, bathrooms, kitchen and a veranda on the lake side. It was located on the brow of a hill of gentle declivity and about 200 yards from the water, so that there is an expansive lawn in front of the mansion. In the winter time there is great tobogganing from the top of this hill over the lawn and far on the frozen surface of Lake George. Mr. Shepard used to delight in the sport, especially in the company of children. It was his habit to steal away from his work in New York city and come to Erlowest every winter, usually in February, for a few weeks' rest and recreation with his family and friends.

The word "family," however, needs explanation. Mr. Shepard was a bachelor. One of his intimate friends once asked him why he had not married, and his answer was "I have never had time." He was, however, essentially a domestic man. His home was the home of his sister, Mrs. Charles B. Hewitt, where her children, Mr. and Mrs. Leffingwell, their daughter, and Mr. and Mrs. Mitchell and Mr. and Mrs. Edward Shepard Hewitt and their children, often made long visits. With these and the family of his brother, Charles S. Shepard, who lived nearby, his friends, his books, his horse and dog, he was a neighborly man, for he was warmly attached to his neighbors, among whom, besides George Foster Peabody, were his brothers, Charles J. and Royal C. Peabody; Galoway C. Morris, first president of the First National bank of Lake George, which he and Mr. Shepard and some of their friends established in 1907, and the family of Edward Eggleston, the author, who lived almost dirctly across on the easterly side of the lake.

Moreover, Mr. Shepard was a sociable man. He entertained a great deal. He brought up small and large parties from New York city and elsewhere, and never grew tired of them. Indeed, as the years rolled on, he felt the need of more room, better room for himself and his family and friends. Therefore, about two years before he died, he began a large addition to his house, in which he was to enjoy an office and a second or retiring library, while his family and guests were to have ampler range and more freedom through the other parts of the commodious structure. Alas! the cozy office and the snug library were finished and a set of oak and leather furniture was placed in one—the old, old books and the old maps, old implements of literary labor were moved into the other—but the master came not. His working days and his leisure days were over.

It would be out of place to attempt an enumeration of all the attractive features of Erlowest, inside and out, but is worth while observing that the two libraries contain substantially all the standard works in history, fiction and travel, besides busts in bronze or marble of Dante, Cicero, Demosthenes, inter-alia and conspicuously a large collection of tomes, books and pamphlets on the subjects of the history and legends of Lake George. One of them also shows a collection of Bibles and prayer books (one of the last, 1814), and several volumes on Spanish and Italian literature. Mr. Shepard was an Episcopalian and a devoted, earnest worker in the church.

Then, too, it is interesting to know that Mr. Shepard was a musician. He not only loved music, but he played on the piano and sang with more than ordinary talent and enjoyment. So the music room of Erlowest is a feature, one may be sure.

Last comes the master's own bed chamber, a small, unpretentious room on the second floor, south side, in which the most conspicuous things are a small brass bed and a loving cup presented to Mr. Shepard by his co-trustees of the College of the City of New York, some years before he died.

Simplicity Marked Taste

It seems that the man of many talents, the lawyer, statesman, author, churchman, comrade and friend—when he was through with the day's work and play—preferred to return in simplicity and be alone with God. Mr. Shepard's out-of-door amusements were few. He loved horseback riding and kept it up until within a few years of the end of his life. He always had a good stable of the harness and saddle horses at Erlowest, and had six there at the time of his death. He never owned an automobile or a motorboat. He hired automobiles and motorboats for his guests, but himself was content with horses and rowboats. He was an oarsman and swimmer, but cared nothing for fishing or hunting. Had he cared more for sports it might have been better for him, for he was a small, frail man, and his nervous energy, which was great, consumed his bodily strength and called for constant replenishment. He died of pneumonia, the doctors said.

The grounds of Erlowest embrace a flower garden, a large fruit and vegetable garden, stable, smithy, grass tennis court—on which he sometimes played—and a very large variety of trees, plants and shrubs—doubtless the best on Lake George. In a conspicuous spot, near the dwelling, also, is an immense flagpole, from which the Stars and Stripes gave greeting of patriotism and good cheer to travelers on lake and land for miles around.

He was specially fond of dogs, and for several years he and Bruno, a beautiful collie, were inseparable while he was at Lake George. About the year 1909, however, Bruno met the fate of many noble dogs; he was killed by an automobile. There was mourning and lamentation at Erlowest.

Had 3,500 Acres

From the purchase of the small acreage which enabled Mr. Shepard to build his summer home (for he and his belongings were mostly in Brooklyn), he extended his holdings from time to time until he owned four separate tracts of land, comprising 3,500 acres. On each of these properties now stands a good dwelling-house, either of his building or of his remodeling. Each shows the marks of his genius as a man of practical affairs and of artistic taste. Together they comprise a considerable part of his comfortable fortune. One of these purchases, "The Old Mill" place, is conspicuously illustrative of Mr. Shepard's sagacity and refinement and will serve as a suitable subject for the conclusion of this brief sketch of his life as he appeared away from law and politics and the general strife of existence.

Some years ago a young man of Glens Falls, N. Y., inherited a fortune of something like $100,000. He came to Lake George, bought a few acres of ground by a rushing brook, just over the village line, and erected a great mill, in which he proposed to manufacture one thing or another. He built dams up the mountainside to hold the water in storage for the droughts of summer, but, firabile dictu!—he forgot about the freshets of spring—the snows melted, the dams were washed away, and the poor man's heart and pocket were both broken. So he failed and went away.

The mill was hushed and the property lay dormant for some years. Lake George had no such mill and needed none. The property was thrown upon the market and Mr. Shepard bought it. He went to work on the problem of changing it into a place of residence, and with the help of his nephew, Edward Shepard Merrill, the architect, he made it one of the showplaces of Lake George. He put his soul into every detail of the work, from the installation of the steam heating apparatus to the planting of the flowers in the boxes on the window sills. He laid out drives and walks and constructed a small harbor, bordered with masonry, at the foot of the lawn, for any tiny craft that might call or wish to find shelter in a storm. He furnished the house from top to bottom, going to the length of setting up a billiard table on the ground floor—and the premises were ready for occupancy when he died.

The general equipment of the place —though he intended only to rent it —its arrangement, elegance and fine appearance may be judged from the fact that the first person to take it was Mrs. Spencer Trask, widow of the banker, who left her magnificent home at Saratoga Springs to spend the winter there. Mr. Shepard did not live to know who the first person would be to enjoy the benefits of his remarkable work in remodeling the "Old Mill Place."

He knew and loved the people of Lake George. They knew and loved him. He was perhaps the greatest single benefactor that Lake George ever had. He was one of the pillars of the free library there, and it may be said of a truth that, in the twenty years of his all too short life (he died at sixty-one), which he spent partially as a visitor or resident at Lake George, no good work was ever brought to his attention to which he did not give a ready and helping hand.

July 25—1912

R. J. Brown to Assist in Historical Work.

R. J. Brown, of Bolton, has been appointed by the State Civil Service commission as temporary assistant in the history division, department of education. Mr. Brown is a civil engineer and surveyor of great ability and his long residence of at least fifty years in Bolton has given him a knowledge of local conditions which will make his services very valuable in the work to which he will be assigned—the collection of data in reference to the original trails and military roads used during the French and Indian war, covering the territory between Albany and Crown Point.

-120-

REV. PARROTT REPLIES TO J. B. SIMPSON

LAKE GEORGE CLERGYMAN ANSWERS HOTEL MAN.

Times — Sept 7 — 1912

2 ISSUES CONFUSED

Minister Says the Park and the Change of the Name of the Village Are Two Separate Questions and that the Former Is the More Important Issue.

The changing of the name of the village of Lake George to some other, which would be of more material benefit to the entire lake country, is uppermost in the minds of Lake George people. The recent letter sent to the Rev. Edward M. Parrott by John Boulton Simpson, in which Mr. Simpson refused to contribute to the Shepard Memorial Park fund so long as the village maintained its present name of Lake George called forth the following reply from Mr. Parrott:

Lake George, N. Y.,
Aug. 27, 1912.

Mr. John Boulton Simpson,
Sagamore, N. Y.

My dear Mr. Simpson:

I confess to a good deal of disappointment at your reply of August 16th to the appeal for the Edward M. Shepard Memorial Park.

Not so much because of your failure to contribute towards its purchase, which seems to be assured, as at what seems to me to be an unfortunate confusion of unconnected questions and at what can hardly help but retard the very change you so much desire.

When I recently discovered the strong sentiment down the lake in regard to the name of our postoffice and the inclination on the part of many of our neighbors to discriminate against this village in trade and general friendly intercourse, it seemed to me that there lay an appropriate field for the cultivation of Christian virtues for forebearance, patience and a willingness to give up what was cherished, to remove if possible a barrier toward that sort of fellowship which alone makes communities effective either as social opportunities for recreation or in commercial prosperity. I was willing to use such influence as I possessed toward removing stumbling blocks from the course of good will and neighborliness.

But the purchase of the lake front property for the public is another and much larger issue. Personally I am not here for a vacation, but to work, and I have not the least expectation of ever using the park for pleasure but unless the public does have free access to the shore at many points along the lake the whole development of this wonderfully beautiful country will be handicapped, a wide spread disaffection will be fostered and sooner or later at a much heavier cost and perhaps with much less chance of keeping the economic balance properly adjusted a free public lake front will be obtained. This may sound vague, but the land question in England just now may well give us a lesson in the possibility of turning a vague feeling of unrest into a revolutionizing political force.

And so I am sorry that the two issues are confused, and hope that in the settlement of each we may be able to bring dispassionate justice to bear and that the spirit of bargaining sentiment or justice for dollars may not be kept in the front.

May I again express to you my warm personal regard both for your courteous and frank treatment of this subject and the generous and farsighted way in which it is my great privilege to know that you exercise the stewardship bestowed upon you.

Cordially yours,
EDWARD M. PARROTT.

The Lake George Mirror this week publishes the following communication:

Editor Mirror:

I notice by means of the Mirror that the controversy as to the propriety of the name of "Lake George" for the honourable village formerly called Caldwell has not abated.

This is as it should be. The name seems incongruous. It conveys to anyone concerned with the content of words the idea that your village consists of an estimable body of citizens entirely surrounded by water. The name "Caldwell," I admit, is not particularly euphonious. That "d" is hard to pronounce, isn't it? Have you ever considered the name Fort William Henry for the village? It has the advantage of historicity, it is fully as widely known as Lake George, it associates your village with Fort Ticonderoga, Fort Edward and Fort Ann. Last but not least it would relieve your village of the odium of a Bull Moose egotism not relished by other dwellers on Lake George.

Yours sincerely,
J. D. KENNEDY.

Bolton, N. Y., Aug. 25, 1912.

GIRL ON LONG HIKE

Aug 7 1912

Miss Dora Rodrigues, a nineteen year old Dutch girl, who is walking through the United States and Europe, is expected to arrive in this city this afternoon en route to Montreal. During the past few days Miss Rodrigues has been lecturing at small theatres. It is probable she will give one of her lectures in this city.

COTTAGERS TAKE NEW RELIGION

Times Sept 3 — 1912

Regarding the change in the form of worship at what was the Union Methodist Episcopal church at Diamond Point, Lake George, and which was announced at the time in the Daily Times, a Lake George correspondent writes:

"If church doctrines are not in accord with your social inclinations, change the denomination of your church." Such is the belief of the 150 attendants of what was the Union Methodist Episcopal church at Diamond Point, Lake George, who at their annual meeting decided to change to the Episcopal form of worship.

The membership of the little church is composed largely of summer cottagers, who see no harm in social dances and card parties, but the Methodist Episcopal church places the ban on these forms of amusement, and the members decided that rather than forsake the festivities of the summer season they would forsake the teachings of the church.

Throughout the summer months dancing and card parties take place nightly at Diamond Point, and this summer they have proved more popular than ever, for the reason that a new religious faith has been adopted.

In accordance with the decision of the annual meeting, a petition was sent to Bishop William Croswell Doane of the diocese of Albany, asking that a rector be sent to Diamond Point. Bishop Doane turned the matter over to the Rev. Edward M. Parrott of Lake George, who is now in charge of the situation and who arranged for several rectors to supply the church until fall, when it is probable that a rector will be appointed.

Among those who have supplied the pulpit are the Rev. R. C. Hatch, rector of Christ church, Tarrytown, during July and the Rev. W. M. Gage, rector of St. Andrew's church, Albany, during August. Occasionally services have or will be conducted by the Rev. C. C. Harriman, rector of St. Peter's church, Albany, and the Rev. J. M. Melish, rector of Holy Trinity church, Brooklyn.

Star

COSSAYUNA LAKE HOTEL WILL BE ENLARGED

Sept 20 1912

The Oaks, on Cossayuna Lake, which closed Monday after one of the most successful seasons that the hotel has ever had, will be enlarged next season. A new kitchen, eight new sleeping rooms and three additional bathrooms will be added. The fishing this year was considered better than any previous year, due to the splendid protection the lake is receiving from the Fish and Game Commission.

BOY SCOUTS' LODGE BUILT AT HEAD OF LAKE GEORGE

Star Sept 25 1912

The above reproduction from a photograph shows the lodge erected by the Boy Scouts, Troop 4, of Christ church, at the head of Lake George. The lodge was erected at a cost of about $90 for material and the Scouts have already defrayed a large portion of the expense by giving entertainments of a varied nature. Throughout the summer the Scouts plan to spend their vacation at the lodge.

The lodge is provided with bunks for sleeping purposes and is equipped with a cook stove and such other appliances as are essential to scout life.

The World's Richest Man

Leading financial experts in New York have been quietly and carefully estimating the full wealth of the oil king, and have figured that John D. Rockefeller today is worth nine hundred million dollars.

Star Aug 6 1912

CHEF DIDN'T DROWN HAD HEART FAILURE

Autopsy Shows Smith Was Dead Before Falling into Lake George

Star Sept 20 1912

The remain of Walter J. Smith, the chef that was drowned between the Lake View house and the Algonquin on Lake George Tuesday, were removed to the home of the lad's parents, Mr. and Mrs. Albert Smith of Amsterdam, yesterday, and the funeral will be held from that city today.

The body was identified Wednesday by Frederick Smith of Syracuse, brother of the unfortunate man and Mrs. C. J. Gonala of Schenectady, a sister. Through them Smith's parents were located in Amsterdam.

It was first thought that death was brought on through a fit but an autopsy performed on the body after it was brought out of the water showed that he had died from heart failure. Later this was substantiated when it was found that the boy's people were sufferers from heart trouble and that their son had frequently complained of pains about his heart.

The autopsy further showed a mark on Smith's forehead. It is thought that when he fell out of the boat that he was unconscious as a short distance away two men had been fishing and they heard nothing until the boat was seen floating upside down. If Smith had made any outcry it would have been heard by the fishermen.

Another point that proves that the boy was either unconscious or dead when he fell from the canoe is the fact that he was found in nine feet of water and that he had made no effort to save himself.

Dr. Denning Victim of Serious Accident.

Mr. and Mrs. D. C. Remington, of this village, were informed Saturday of a serious accident which befel their son-in-law, Dr. G. W. Deming, on Wednesday afternoon of last week, at Topsham, Me. Dr. Deming, who is a skillful dentist, but owing to trouble with his eyes is spending a year on a farm, was riding on a lead of hay with two of his men and was facing the rear when as the rig passed under a tree he was swept off by a low hanging limb and one of his legs was broken between the knee and hip. He was resting as comfortably as could be expected when the letter was written. Mrs. Deming expected to visit her parents fair week, but the accident will, of course, change her plans. *Aug 3 1912*

THE MOUNTAINEER AND LAKE GEORGE VILLAGE. LAKE GEORGE, N. Y.

MOUNTAINEER WRECKED

MOUNTAINEER WRECKED

Star

Carrying 100 Passengers, D. and H.
Craft Runs Onto Rocks at
Kattskill Bay

aug 16 1912

(Special to Post-Star.)

LAKE GEORGE, Aug. 15.—The Mountaineer, owned by the Delaware and Hudson, a small boat which plies up and down the lake carrying excursionists, met with a mishap yesterday afternoon at 4.30 o'clock, when it ran onto the rocks at Kattskill bay. At the time of the accident, the craft was carrying in the neighborhood of a hundred passengers. The collision stove a hole in the Mountaineer above the water line and she was forced to put her passengers off at Rockhurst Landing, at Hotel Willard.

The boat steamed to the repair shop of Walter Harris and underwent repairs. It then went back to Rockhurst and picked up its passengers and brought them to the head of the lake. A high wind was blowing and it was raining in torrents.

The craft was making its regular trips last evening. A reporter called up the Delaware and Hudson station at the lake last night, but was refused any information on the subject.

AUTO OWNERS NABBED

Two Machine Proprietors, Hailed Before Enches for License Troubles Are Let Go

Star Aug 16 1912

Two automobile owners, Ernest Souci and H. C. Murray, were arraigned in city court yesterday before Judge Calhoun S. Enches on complaint of auto license inspectors from the office of the secretary of state. Murray was charged with having only one license number displayed on his car. He was allowed to go on promising to secure another number plate.

Souci purchased his car Wednesday and informed the court that the dealer of whom he secured it had given him two pasteboard numbers and told him they would answer the purpose of license numbers. He said he was unfamiliar with the automobile law. He was permitted to leave after he had signed an application for a state license and paid the fee.

The inspectors have been busy in this vicinity for some time and are determined to put a stop to autoists operating machines without licenses or with fake numbers.

BOLTON LANDING

aug 16 1912

Bolton Landing, Aug. 11.—Miss Bessie McCormick of New Jersey is the guest of Mr. and Mrs. M. O. Brown at Wilson's.

THE HORSE RACE, THE AEROPLANE AND THE CROWD AT THE CAMBRIDGE FAIR.

A reproduction from an unusual and striking photograph taken at a moment of intense interest at a typical country fair. The popular fair at Cambridge will be held for the twenty-third year on August 19 to 23. The late Col. Jerome B. Rice, who had been President of the fair since its inception, died on June 8 last and has been succeeded by John L. Hunt, an officer of the fair since the start.

RACE TRACK VETERAN HAS BEEN DRIVING 37 YEARS

Sept 24, 1912 Times

The following story about "Pop" Geers who was well known in Glens Falls in the days of the old Breeders' Meeting in this city will be of interest to local people.

Known as the "Silent man from Tennessee," Edward Geers is a hard man for a stranger to approach, and on and off the track he fulfills the import of his nom de guerre to the letter. Courteous, he answered questions put to him in monosyllables, and refrains from talking of his successes as much as possible. In a race, he never speaks loudly or harshly to his horse, and he seldom uses a whip. The sight of Geers appearing before the judges' stand to register a "kick" against any ruling or the driving of any of his opponents, is as rare a thing as could possibly be imagined. "Pop" as he is called by the talent from one end of the country to the other first saw the light of day in a little mountain home in the hills of Tennessee 61 years ago. When but a lad he showed a fondness for horses, and his natural instinct as a driver was early developed. He drove his first grand circuit race in 1875, which gives him a record of 37 years in the big show. For a number of years previous to driving in the big ring, "Pop" had held the ribbons over fast steppers on a number of half-mile tracks, and almost from the first attracted nationwide attention.

A clean liver, and honest and upright in all his dealings, Geers has always been respected both by his fellow horsemen and by the general public. "Lon" McDonald who has been associated with him longer than any other man in the game today pays him a high tribute when he says he doesn't believe there is money enough in the world today, or ever was, to buy "Pop" even for one heat. And to this trait, more than to anything else, Geers lays his success. Like all other veterans, he does not believe a man will make a success in the horse-racing game any more than he will in any other unless he is honest and above board.

It is to his cleanly habits all through life that "Pop" believes he owes his good health, for he is seldom ill a day. He is a man rather below medium height, and with the greater part of his weight above the waist line. He walks with a limp, and appears to a casual observer to be crippled with rheumatism. He never had the rheumatism in his life, he says, and his crippled condition is due to the many smashups he has had while driving horses. His legs have been broken four times and he has suffered with broken bones in his arms three times. And still, if he had his life to live over again, he believes he would again follow the racers. He "loves horses."

Despite his many accidents, "Pop," has never remained out of the game longer than was absolutely necessary, and on a number of occasions he has displayed almost superhuman pluck and endurance. No better illustration of his determination than two years ago this season at Detroit. Earlier in the year he had been thrown and was recovering from a broken leg. He had a pretty fair idea that his horse was good for a win, and yet he knew no one could drive the animal the way he could.

Appearing at the race track on crutches, his friends and hostlers had to assist him to his seat on the gig. Going around the track when every jounce of the wheels sent almost unbearable pain through his body, he drove The Abbe to a win in the two big stake events, the M. & M. and the Chamber of Commerce. It was the first and only time that the same horse has won both stakes, and Geers was the first and only driver to turn the trick. This is only one illustration of his great pluck. Many others of a like nature could be told of him. Skillful, crafty and wise, Geers is always ready to take advantage of the slightest error of judgment on the part of an opposing driver, and many a time he has brought a horse through a winner when but for these qualifications he would have been defeated. He is always considered a dangerous man behind any horse.

Geers will not talk about himself to any extent, except to his most intimate friends. When seen recently, he did not seem to feel very badly that he had not been one of the big winners on the circuit this season. "I have had my years," he said, "and will have them again. Someone has got to win, and it can't be the same driver always. My horses may not be quite so good, by a hair, perhaps, or may not be in form, and then there is always the luck to be considered. I don't care what the others may say, there is an element of luck in the racing game, just the same as there is in any other."

Mr. Geers has in his stable a horse by the name of Bergen, sired by Bingara, sire of Daden, winner of the Charter Oak trot this year. Bergen started in the event finishing third in the first heat, fifth in the second, sixth in the third, and being ruled out in the next. Many believe that Bergen is the best horse entered in the big stakes on the circuit this season, but the wise ones say that Bergen should have been only worked this season and started next. Mr. Geers will not discuss Bergen, other than to say that "he is a mighty good horse."

-124-

MIKE CRONIN WELL

Celebrity Recovers From Serious Mishap at Schenectady

Star

July 27 - 1912

Mike Cronin of Aiden Lair, driver on Roosevelt's famous dash to the bedside of the dying McKinley at Buffalo from Aiden Laire to North Creek, recovered from a fall he had in Schenectady about a month ago and returned to his home Saturday. Mr. Cronin fell over a trolley fender on a sidewalk on Albany street and taken to the Ellis hospital. His injuries which were, at first thought slight,

aug Sidney B. Irish. *5 - 1912*

Sidney B. Irish, aged 81 years died at his home at East Lake George Saturday. The funeral will be held tomorrow morning at the late home. Interment will be in the Seelye cemetery.

700 MOTORBOATS ON THE WATERS OF LAKE GEORGE

Aug 5 1912

YOUNG GIRL NEAR DEATH AT SAGAMORE

MISS WILSON OF NEW YORK SAVED FROM DROWNING.

BY JOSEPH DRUMM

Aug 12 1912

Girl in Bathing, Faints When She Cannot Touch Bottom—Sinks for Third Time, Before Her Rescuer Arrives—Rescurer Well Known Here in Social and Athletic Circles.

Miss Wilson, a New York girl, who is enjoying a sojourn at Sagamore on Lake George, had a narrow escape from drowning Friday afternoon, being saved from a watery grave by Joe Drumm of Troy, as she sank under the water for the third time.

Miss Wilson, who learned to swim some time ago, was bathing with a friend, Miss Middleton, near the dock in front of the Sagamore Hotel. The two young women had been in the water some time and both swam out a few feet. They turned and made for the dock, with the intention of leaving the water. When within a few feet of the dock Miss Wilson tried to place her feet on the bottom, but she was over a hole in the sand bottom at that time, and instead of touching, she sank under the water.

Frightened by her failure to touch the bottom, she fainted away and as she disappeared below the water, her companion's shrill shrieks for help were heard by Mr. Drumm and a companion, who were standing on the further end of the dock. Drumm ran with full speed to the end of the dock, reaching it just as the girl sank for the third time. With a dive he reached the spot where she had gone down, and swimming under the water, he came to her form and brought it above the surface. It was but a few feet to the dock and the unconscious form of the girl was taken from his hands by his companion on the dock.

The two men worked over her to bring about respiration and in a few moments, the young woman, was able to stand and make her way to the hotel. In a few hours, she was none the worse after her narrow escape.

Mr. Drumm felt no ill effects because of his plunge in the water. He is pitcher on the Glens Falls baseball team and was in perfect condition yesterday.

The Two Generals Grant

General Frederick Dent Grant, who died in New York, Thursday night, on the left, and his father, General U. S. Grant, on the right. The photographs show the striking resemblance between the late commander of the department of the East and his noted father. *Star apl 18 1912.*

Beats "How Old Is Ann?"

"How old are you?" asked the Municipal Court Judge Wednesday morning. "I don't rightly know, y'r honor," answered Ashtabula Aggie. "Can't you give the court some idea?" persisted the said court. "I sure can, y'r honor. You was a growed-up man when I was a little girl, and you are now sparkin' wid a lady what was a little girl when I was a growed-up woman." Sentence was suspended till His Honor could get a chance to figure it out.

LOUIS TOURNIER.

Louis Tournier died on Wednesday of last week, at his home in Starbuckville, in the town of Chester, after a short illness. The deceased was a French chef of great ability and in the 70s and 80s was employed in various summer hotels at Lake George, commanding a large salary. For the past twenty years or more he had been chef at the Chester house and the dishes he prepared have made that hotel famous for its table. He was probably about seventy years old. *July 11 1912*

OBITUARY

News July 11 1912

MRS ARTHUR BRADLEY

Mrs. Arthur Bradley, of Bolton Landing, died on Wednesday of last week after an illness of several weeks duration. She was given the benefit of the best medical skill and the tenderest care, but the hand of Death could not be staid and she was taken from her loving husband and daughters, Dorothy and Alice. She is also survived by her mother, Mrs. Philinda Fountain, of Moriah; four sisters and two brothers, Mrs. John Fairfield, of Schroon Lake; Mrs. Thurman Warren, of Far Rockaway, L. I.; Misses Pearl and Elizabeth Fountain, of Moriah; William Fountain, of Moriah, and Charles Fountain, of Watertown. The funeral was held at St. Sacrament church, Bolton Landing, Saturday morning at 10:30 o'clock.

MANKOWSKI WILL SMASH ALL RECORDS

COUNT'S NEW HYDROPLANE WILL BE SPEEDY.

Times July 9 1912

TO ENTER BIG RACES

Boat Will Compete for $1,000 Gold Challenge Cup on the St. Lawrence River—Has Speed of Forty-two to Forty-five Miles an Hour—Has Two 150 h. p. 8 Cylinder Motors.

This week's edition of the Lake George Mirror says:

To break the world's record and incidentally capture a few prizes, to bring to these waters some big events in motorboatdom, and generally set a new pace for Lake George sportsmen, are some of the modest motives that actuate Count Mankowski in his present enterprise, the creation of "Ankledeep," destined we hope to be known the world over as the fastest hydroplane ever built.

"Ankledeep,' gentle reader, is a beautiful creature of the feminine gender, and though she has not yet made her debut we may presume she will be as winning and captivating as her owner and skipper anticipates. She is now in construction—practically completed—in the shipyards of the Staten Island Ship Building Company and only awaits her motors, their installation and the preliminary trials before shipping to the St. Lawrence river where she will compete for the thousand dollar gold challenge cup.

For many years sportsmen on Lake George have desired that we could secure some of the big races of the country for these waters. How to get them? Why send out a boat and win some big challenge trophy and bring it here so the other fellows will have to come here and race for it. Count Cassimer S. Mankowski has been recently elected a member of the Lake George Regatta Association and that organization will shortly enter his new hydroplane, "Ankledeep" in the race for the gold challenge cup to be run August 1st.

Count Mankowski also hopes to qualify in the preliminaries for the International races to be held on Long Island Sound, the last of August, and it is possible that between these dates he will ship the boat west for the events at Chicago.

"Ankledeep of Lake George," will listen good to some of us who have hoped to see livelier times among the racing boats of this lake, and the guarantee of her builders makes the Count quite confident of success, barring accident or some unlooked for delay in completion.

"Ankledeep" is thirty-two feet over all and six feet beam, built of mahogany in two layers with canvass between. She has two 150 h. p. 8-cylinder motors built by the Sterling people of Buffalo. She has a complete double equipment of clutches, rudders, etc., and four gas tanks. When running at her speed of forty-two to forty-five miles per hour she burns forty gallons of gasoline every hour. Her motors are located in the stern and she has seating capacity—bucket auto seats—for four persons forward of her motors. She is finished in natural wood and is a beautiful creation. Her guaranteed speed is forty-two miles per hour, and since the contract under the guarantee was let some changes have been made which assure an increase in the estimated speed. She will be brought to Lake George either after the Thousand Island races or September 1st, so that we shall at least have a glimpse of her in these waters this season.

YOU NEVER CAN TELL.

He rocked the boat one summer day;
  The boat refused to tip.
He reached old age and passed away,
  A victim of the pip.

A fool there was who gazed into
  The muzzle of a gun;
His age was then but twenty-two—
  He died at eighty-one.

He skated where the ice was weak
  When he was but a lad.
And now he is an aged geek
  And grown men call him "dad."

Of dynamite he had a store;
  He placed it by the fire,
But it was twenty years before
  He played a golden lyre.

And then there was a careful guy
  Whose ways were wise and prim.
And from a cloudless summer sky,
  An airship fell on him.

LAKE GEORGE CLUB BUILDS DORMITORY

Times Aug 8 1912.

MANY IMPROVEMENTS NOTED AT ANNUAL MEETING SATURDAY.

OFFICERS REELECTED

Golf Links Are in Excellent Condition for the Annual Tournament for President's Cup to be Held August 15, 16 and 17—Finals Will Consist of Thirty-six Holes.

The annual meeting of the Lake George Club was held Saturday afternoon at the club rooms at Hill View. The various reports showed the club to be in a flourishing condition.

During the past year a dormitory has been erected at a cost of $5,000, which will be for the use of the superintendent and others.

The officers elected for the ensuing year are: President, W. K. Bixby; vice president, Antonio Knauth; treasurer, L. F. Hyde; secretary, H. W. Guernsey.

The board of directors was re-elected and are W. K. Bixby, Antonio Knauth, George O. Knapp, LeGrand C. Cramer, E. B. Warren, L. F. Hyde, Denny Brereton, H. B. Moore, Lawrence Jacob, J. B. Simpson, H. W. Watrous, W. F. Breyfogle, F. T. Gates, H. W. Hayden, W. E. Reis, Maurice Hoepes.

The golf links have been improved and are in excellent shape for the annual tournament for the president's cup, which will take place on August 15, 16, 17.

The qualifying round of eighteen holes will be played on Tuesday, August 15. All desiring to enter will please submit to the golf committee their three best scores on the links together with their rating at their house clubs. The competition will be match play on the basis of the respective handicaps assigned by the committee. The finals will consist of thirty-six holes and may be played under such conditions as may be agreed upon by the contestants named by the committee.

July 4 1912 PENFIELD-COOLIDGE. *News.*

Mrs. John B. Coolidge, of Diamond Point, announces the marriiage of her daughter, Anne to Charles E. Penfield which was solemnized on June 30, at Christ church, Glens Falls, by the Rev. Charles O. Judkins. After an auto trip in the Adirondacks Mr. and Mrs. Penfield will reside at their new home on Coolidge avenue, Glens Falls.

BIRTHDAY OUTING

J. Huyler White Celebrates 76th Birthday Anniversary at Mt. McGregor

Star June 28 1912

Together with his family and grandchildren, J. Huyler White enjoyed a picnic yesterday at Mt. McGregor, the occasion marking his seventy-sixth birthday anniversary. The trip to Mt. McGregor and return was made in Mr. White's Packard "6". The new macadam road leading from Wilton to the top of the mountain is fast nearing completion, it being possible for automobiles to travel within an eighth of a mile of the top. Mr. White describes the road as one of the finest in the country and says that the ascent was one of the most enjoyable experiences he has ever encountered.

Wants $1,500 Damages *May 28-1912*

The case of Mrs. Emma L. Taylor against the Glens Falls Automobile company, of which Milo J. Gray is president, was next taken up and will probably not be finished until late this afternoon. Mrs. Taylor is a resident of Bolton and seeks to collect $1,500 damages for injuries alleged to have been received when she was struck by an auto owned by the defendant company and driven by John P. Nugent, an employe. The accident occurred December 28, 1910, near the Bloody Pond crossing. Mrs. Taylor and a part of friends were returning to Lake George in a sleigh after a trip to Glens Falls and when just beyond the crossing the harness broke and the driver alighted to repair it. Mrs. Taylor and Mrs. Minnie Taylor left the sleigh and stood beside Howe's blacksmith shop at the junction of the state road and a highway leading toward Luzerne. Mrs. Taylor was struck by the car and thrown to the ground. The wheels did not pass over her but she alleges that she received severe and painful injuries, some of which, she claims, still cause her pain. The plaintiff is represented by Attorney Walter A. Chambers.

Attorneys J. Edward Singleton and Lyman Jenkins appear for the defendant and it is claimed by the company that Nugent did everything in his power to avoid an accident, and turned up the highway leading to Luzerne, so as not to hit the sleigh in which there were several children and another woman. It is further claimed that he sounded his horn when some distance from the scene of the accident but the occupants apparently failed to notice it, because they were all singing just before he got near the sleigh. The plaintiff alleges that no warning was sounded by Nugent.

TWO BURNED AT FIRE AT LAKE GEORGE

Times June 25 1912

Alexander H. Russell of Lake George, proprietor of the Parkside Inn, was badly burned about the hands and William Nason of this city was slightly burned in the same manner, when fire broke out early Sunday morning, in the awning in the rear of Mr. Russell's hotel.

This place, formerly the summer home of the Glens Falls club, is located on the shore of the lake and the fire was discovered by members of the Shuffler Club of this city, who were on the lake at the time. They hurried to the scene and aroused a number of Lake George people including Mr. Russell and a fight with water buckets and a garden hose was at once waged upon the flames.

An alarm of fire was sounded but before the fire company could respond the volunteers had extinguished the blaze. The fire had gained a great start before being discovered and only the absence of wind saved the building from total destruction.

MRS. GEORGE R. FISH. *May 29. 1912*

Mrs. Mary Ann Odell Fish, wife of George R. Fish, died Sunday evening at 6 o'clock, at her home at 134 Bay street, Glens Falls. Death was caused by paralysis, with which she was stricken about six weeks ago. Mrs. Fish was seventy-eight years old and lived the greater part of her life in the town of Bolton, from which place the family moved to Glens Falls last fall. She is survived by her husband and one daughter, Miss Irene B. Fish, both of Glens Falls; also by one sister, Mrs. Julius R. Burtt, of Queensbury.

GASOLENE GONDOLA.

New Craft In Service on Lake George —Owned by Capt. G. W. Bates.

Captain George W. Bates of Lake George is creating great interest among Lake George people as he plies back and forth on the waters of Lake George in a gasolene gondola. The boat is a beauty, built by Captain Bates himself along the Venetian lines and has been tried and found to be a most suitable craft. The gasolene engine, with which it is equipped, makes it an even more satisfactory craft than the Venetian gondola, which are propelled by hand.

The new water front at the Fort William Henry Hotel is nearly completed and as this is built along the Venetian plan, the gondola promises to fit in well with the decoration scheme at the head of the lake and without doubt its advent will be followed by more of a similar make.

OBITUARY.

Sept 19, 1912 News

MRS. MARTHA ROSS.

Mrs. Martha Ross died at the home of her daughter, Mrs. Lorenzo Hemenway, in Horicon, Saturday morning, September 14, aged eighty-four years. Mrs. Ross was the widow of Sylvester Ross, who died about fifteen years ago and had been a life-long resident of Horicon and Bolton. Her life had been associated with the early pioneer experiences of the section, her husband being for many years a lumberman, and she knew of the problems of life as they had to do with the earning of a livelihood fifty and seventy-five years ago. When a young girl she gave her heart to the Lord, and was baptized into the fellowship of the Horicon Baptist church. Possessing then the advantage of a genuine Christian experience, she was fortified for the hard struggle of those early days in facing the practical questions involved in the raising of a large family amid circumscribed conditions. Mrs. Ross was familiarly known as "Aunt Martha" by the people of Horicon and many interested friends besides, and was much loved and respected for her sterling worth, her marked common sense, and her unalloyed Christian integrity. Her departure removes one of the old landmarks from among the citizens of Horicon. She is survived by two sons, Joseph Ross, of Alaska, and Judson Ross, of Ticonderoga, and by five daughters—Mrs. L. S. Hemenway and Mrs. Ella Brownell, of Horicon; Mrs. Lura Wood, of Ticonderoga; Mrs. Betsey May, of Chestertown, and Mrs. Henry Rising, of Morrisville, N. Y. The funeral was held at the Horicon Baptist church Monday afternoon, and was conducted by the Rev. F. M. LaBar, who took for his text the words of Matthew 25:23; "Well done, good and faithful servant; thou hast been faithful over a few things, I will make thee ruler over many things; enter thou into the joy of thy Lord."

OBITUARY.

News June 27 1912

CLARENCE E. CRANNELL.

Clarence E. Crannell, aged sixty-two years, died Monday, at his home in Stony Creek. He had been in the employ of the Delaware and Hudson company for the past thirty years as station agent at Stony Creek and faithfully discharged his duties. He is survived by one son, Roscoe, and a daughter, Mrs. Harley Ormsby, both of Stony Creek. The funeral was held at his late home yesterday, the Rev. A. Murdock officiating; interment in the Dean cemetery.

—127—

DEATH CLAIMS OLD RESIDENT

Sudden Passing of George T. Lockwood Saturday Morning.

The jovial features of George T. Lockwood, which in pictured form look out upon our readers from this printed page, will never again be seen in life by his host of friends and acquaintances, for whom he ever had a word of cordial greeting. A week ago, apparently in good health, he was as usual busy about his place adjoining The News office; today, his cold and

June 27. 1912

Mrs. Amelia Gates, sister of the deceased and his housekeeper, heard him arise about 5 o'clock Saturday morning, and go to the barn. He soon returned and she heard him moving about his room a few minutes and then there was complete silence. Going to his door she called to him but received no response. Entering she found him lying lifeless on the bed, having apparently fallen backward while

sitting on the edge. His body was still warm though life was plainly extinct.

Dr. Goodman was called and expressed the opinion that death was caused by heart disease and was undoubtedly instantaneous.

Mr. Lockwood was a life-long resident of Warrensburgh, having been born here March 2, 1849, in the farmhouse on the West river now occupied by Benjamin Glynn. For many years he was engaged in the stage business, conducting a route between Warrensburgh and Glens Falls, and later between this village and Thurman. In this way he became widely known.

He is survived by one brother and two sisters, John H. Lockwood and Mrs. Amelia Gates, of this village, and Mrs. Caroline Jarvis, of Esterville, Iowa. The funeral was held at his late home Tuesday afternoon at 2 o'clock, the Rev. Richard Abbott officiating.

Bolton Horses Race on Fair Grounds.

A named race for a purse of $50, between horses owned by Bolton parties, was trotted on the fair grounds in this village Saturday afternoon. Dublin Dan, owned by P. O'Rourke, won the second, third and fifth heats and the race. Bay Tom (Ross) was second, Robert B. (Roberts) third and Daisy Armont (Gates) fourth. The time was 2:35, 2:34½, 2:35, 2:35 and 2:39. J. W. Wilson, of Lake George, was starter, J. A. Woodward and Seth Russell judges. — *Sept. 1912*

I remember, I remember
The girls I used to like,
They didn't run a motor car,
They didn't ride a bike.
They didn't play the game of bridge
Or rush to bargain sales.
They didn't go to problem plays
Or read eratic tales.
I remember, I remember
The girls I used to see;
I wouldn't want to see them now,
So out of date they'd be.
I'd be an old back number dub
To like them nowadays,
I much prefer the modern girl,
With all her modern ways.
—Judge.

GROUND IS BROKEN

July 9, 1912

Ground was broken yesterday at the rear of the Byrne property next to the Y. M. C. A. on Glen street for a new business block to be erected by Byron Lapham, president of the Glens Falls National bank, and Charles A. Hovey, who recently purchased the property. A new street, 20 feet in width will run along the lot next to the Y. M. C. A. The dirt being excavated will be used to grade the premises of Mr. Lapham on Maple street.

An Incident at Valley Forge.

To the Editor of "The Press."

Sir:—Your answer to the inquiry of John M. Mumford that the prayers of General Washington at Valley Forge were never printed, I think, was correct in connection with that inquiry. I desire to relate an incident which confirms my opinion that Washington did retire to some secluded place and there was seen in the act of prayer. The following incident was published a number of years ago in an art publication in the city of New York, and was verified as being true:—

General Washington had presented General Lafayette with a handsome horse, and on a Sunday morning General Lafayette invited General Muhlenberg to accompany him to the barn to see the horse. (Three years ago when I visited Valley Forge a portion of the stone foundation was still to be seen). As they entered the fodder room door they both saw in the extreme end of the room a man upon his knees in the act of prayer, and recognized him as Washington. They quietly withdrew, closed the door, joined arms and walked towards their headquarters. When General Muhlenberg broke the silence he said to General Lafayette: "I came down from the pulpit to defend my country, but this morning General Washington has gone up into the pulpit; and patriotism with religion must win."

FIRE AT LAKE VIEW.

mirror June 22 1912

One day last week fire was discovered on the roof of Lake View House at Bolton. The fire started from sparks out of the chimney from a wood fire in the fireplace. The rapid arrival of assistance from all quarters, the formation of an effective bucket brigade and the well-directed efforts of all concerned soon got the blaze under control and the big building was saved. The loss is considerable by reason damage by water but it will not interfere with the operation of the house this summer.

Volunteers quickly removed nearly all the furniture from the entire building, a monumental task, and it will be a little time before everything is restored, the building repaired and all traces of the fire removed.

DEATH OF MRS. BRADLEY.

Mrs. Gertrude Davis Bradley, wife of Arthur Bradley, of Bolton Landing, died on the third of July after a painful illness of peritonitis. The funeral was conducted by Rev. Edward M. Parrott of Lake George, the burial being in the Bolton Cemetery. Mr. and Mrs. Bradley have been very popular among the young married people of the village and her death brought universal sorrow to the community. Beside her husband two children are left to mourn her loss.

— *July 6 1912*

YOUNG JENKINS IS STRUCK BY AUTO

Star Nov. 9 1912

SON OF POLICE CHIEF HAS SMASH-UP WITH CAR NEAR MONUMENT SQUARE

Carl B. Jenkins, son of Chief of Police Fred G. Jenkins, was painfully injured near Monument Square Saturday afternoon, when he was struck by an automobile owned and driven by Fred B. Chapman. Jenkins was thrown from the bicycle which he was riding, his right hand was badly cut and his face bruised.

The wheel was demolished and the young man walked to the homes of three physicians before he found one at home. Five stitches were necessary to close the wound.

When the accident took place Jenkins was riding out of the Church of the Messiah Parish house onto Glen street, and his view of the approaching auto as well as that of Mr. Chapman, who was driving the car, was obstructed by the large pile of stone in front of the Masonic building, north of the Parish house, which was used in the moving of the structure from its former site. Mr. Chapman, who was operating his machine at a moderate rate of speed, brought the car to a stop as soon as possible, assisted the young man in bandaging the wound and assured him that he would pay for the doctors' bills and the damages to the bicycle.

STEAMER SAGA MORE APPROACHING HAGUE ON LAKE GEORGE.

TWO STEAMERS IN TROUBLE.

Sagamore and Horicon Strike Obstructions in Lake George.

The new steamer Horicon, carrying about 700 passengers on a moonlight excursion under the auspices of the Knights of Columbus, grazed a rock in the narrows of Lake George Monday night and barely escaped a serious accident. As it was, one of the paddle wheels was considerably damaged, part of the wheel-box was carried away and the hull was scraped. The boat was enabled, however, to reach Lake George under its own steam, and Tuesday was sent to Baldwin. It will be out of commission a week or ten days.

Saturday night the steamer Sagamore, with about 200 passengers aboard, ran on a sand bar opposite Hague village and was stranded for thirty-six hours. Word was sent to Lake George and the steamer Horicon, which was docked there, was rushed to the scene with all possible speed.

She pulled and tugged on the big boat for several hours, but to no avail, having moved the steamer only about three feet after breaking all her hawsers and anchor chains. She returned to Lake George and Sunday again took up the task with the result that the boat was freed from the sand. She was towed to the Hague dock and Monday afternoon resumed her trips with practically no damages except a badly scratched hull.

STEAMER HORICON ON LAKE GEORGE. N. Y.   4885-29

Saved Farm for Murdered Man's Widow.

News May 9, 1912

Mr. and Mrs. N. D. Ovitt, of Lamb hill, Bolton, have just completed the task of raising by personal solicitation the sum of $237 to pay off a mortgage on the farm of Mrs. William Hopkins, of Bakers Mills, whose husband was murdered about two years ago by Charles Andrus, leaving her with a family of children and little means. In order to save the farm for her Mr. and Mrs. Ovitt undertook to raise the amount due on a mortgage, with interest, by private subscriptions, and in this they have finally succeeded, for which they wish The News to state they thank God, and everyone who gave so liberally.

H. BROESEL DIES AFTER OPERATION

The funeral of Herman Broesel, Sr., the wealthy New York importer and commission merchant, was held this afternoon from his palatial home near Bolton Landing. Mr. Broesel died Wednesday afternoon at 4:30 o'clock, his death following an illness of about a year. It was decided that an operation must be performed and on Wednesday he was operated upon for intestinal trouble by Dr. Robert Abbe of New York, assisted by Dr. T. I. Henning of this city. Death resulted from the shock of the operation.

Mr. Broesel was about 54 years of age. He came to this country twenty-eight years ago from Germany. He located in New York, and for twenty-five years has been engaged in the importing and commission business. He was at one time president of the Jefferson Bank of New York and was financially interested in the Simplex Automobile Company, which is operated by his sons. He was also active in the wholesale dry goods business.

He was a prominent member of the German Club of New York and for twenty-two years, he and his family have spent the summer at Lake George. He spent much money on his estate at Lake George, which was generally regarded as one of the most beautiful of any on the shores of the lake.

He is survived by his widow, and two sons, Herman, Jr., and Carl.

H. BROESEL, SR. DEAD AT LAKE GEO.

...ATION PROVES FATAL TO ...Y. IMPORTER AND COMMISSION MERCHANT

MEMBER OF GERMAN CLUB

Was Former President of Jefferson Bank in New York City and Financially Interested in the Simplex Automobile Co.—Funeral Today

June 7 1912

Herman Broesel, Sr., a wealthy importer and commission merchant of New York city, died Wednesday afternoon at 4:30 o'clock at his palatial home on the Bolton road near Bolton Landing. Mr. Broesel had been ailing for about a year, and had been at his summer residence for some time. It was decided that an operation was necessary and Wednesday one was performed for the removal of an obstruction in the intestines, by Dr. Robert Abbe of New York city, assisted by Dr. T. I. Henning of this city. Death was caused by shock resulting from the operation.

The Survivors

Mr. Broesel is survived by his widow and two sons, Herman, Jr., and Carl. He was about fifty-four years of age and was born in Germany, coming to this country twenty-eight years ago. He located in New York city and for twenty-five years had been engaged in the importing and commission business. Mr. Broesel was at one time president of the Jefferson bank of New York city, was financially interested in the Simplex Automobile company, which is operated by his two sons and was also active in the wholesale dry goods business.

Member of German Club

In New York city, where he passed a part of his time, Mr. Broesel was prominent among the higher class of the German element and was a member of the German club in that city.

Home at Lake George

For twenty-two years Mr. Broesel and his family have been visiting Lake George, the beauties of which he never ceased to laud, and ten years ago he purchased his present home, which was formerly the Perlot estate. He expended considerable money and established one of the most beautiful estates on the shores of the lake. He always took great interest in the lake and all that pertained to its welfare and with his family passed several months of the year at his summer home. The funeral will be held this afternoon and interment will be made at Bolton Landing.

JEROME BONAPARTE RICE DEAD; FUNERAL TOMORROW

Star June 1 1912

Leading President of Cambridge and a Father of an Immense Seed Business Succumbs

ONCE HELD CAPTIVE IN LIBBY PRISON

The funeral of Jerome B. Rice, "the seedman" and the father of the Cambridge Valley Agricultural society, who died at his home in Cambridge Saturday, aged nearly seventy-one years will be held tomorrow afternoon at 2 o'clock from the late home. He had been a sufferer from rheumatism since the Civil War, when as a soldier he was confined in Libby Prison, and his malady increased with passing years. However, his mental activity until the end, and his remarkable achievements, in spite of physical handicaps, have been a source of wonder and admiration to all his friends and acquaintances.

Native of Washington County

Mr. Rice was a Washington county man. He was born and educated in the Salem schools, and was graduated from the Albany Business college at the age of nineteen. He worked on his father's farm in the town of Jackson, Washington county,

Growth of His Large Business

In 1868 he moved his business from Salem to Cambridge, occupying the second story of the old steam mill building on Main street.

July 19, 1877, Mr. Rice married Miss Laura Chandler.

MISS SARAH HADDEN, *1912*

Miss Sarah Hadden, a life-long resident of Warrensburgh, aged sixty-nine years, died Saturday afternoon at 5 o'clock, at the home of her brother, Fred O. Hadden, on Ridge street, where she had lived for many years. Death was caused by goitre. She had been afflicted with this trouble a long time but it had not assumed a serious phase until within a few months. She was confined to her bed only two weeks, during which time she was tenderly cared for by her niece, Miss Alice Hadden, a trained nurse, of Troy. Besides the brother mentioned Miss Hadden is survived by two sisters, Mrs. Henrietta Snyder, of Saratoga Springs, and Mrs. E. H. Hovey, of Hagadorn's Mills. The deceased was a dressmaker and in that capacity had served most of the families in town. She was highly esteemed by all. The funeral was held at the house Monday afternoon at 2 o'clock, and was conducted by the Rev. Richard Abbott, pastor of the Presbyterian church, of which the deceased had been a faithful member for nearly forty years. Interment was in the village cemetery.

The Bungalow
(Toronto Telegram)

The ants are in the butter dish, the
  flies are in the cream,
The only water we can get is carried
  from the stream;
The farmers will not sell their eggs;
  they say they salt them down;
And all their fruit and vegetables they
  send away to town.
The planks beneath our rugs are full
  of cracks both deep and wide,
And snails and slugs and crawling
  bugs come creeping up inside.
I found a caterpillar once encamped
  upon my toe,
But that is what you must expect
  when in a bungalow.
We cannot sit upon the porch, a hornet's nest is there,
At every sound they all come out with
  fierce and angry air;
The shingle roof is leaky, too, you
  wake and find the bed
Is soaking from the shower bath in
  action overhead.
My face and arms are all tattooed
  with raw mosquito bites,
And concerts by the owls and frogs
  make horrible the nights;
But when we write to city friends we
  say: "Why don't you go
Any buy an acre in the woods and
  build a bungalow?"

TEDDY'S BEST ASSETS

CHICAGO, June 17.—"The renomination of Taft has practically become impossible since the arrival of Roosevelt" This was the size up of ex-Senator Chauncey M. Depew, Taft delegate from New York, in an interview with a correspondent of a London paper whose stuff he had not counted on being given out here.

Of Judicial Mind

"Taft is of the judicial mind," asserted Depew, who is a real friend and supporter o fthe President. "But judicial decisions never won an election. His forces are under command of general principle and in the rough and tumble of a convention fight general principle is a poor leader.

Roosevelt's Best Asset

"Actions that would kill any other politician are precisely the best asset of Theodore Roosevelt. If Taft should come here it would kill his chances utterly but Roosevelt has come and they are shouting 'bully for Teddy, Where Roosevelt goes no man can stop him, for the devil is in him and the Lord doesn't seem to interpose. It's that damned charm of his as was said of the other woman in Barrie's 'What Every Woman Knows.'

Cause of Unrest

"All the unrest now pervading this country is due to its excessive prosperity. The workingmen all have good jobs and tremendous wages and they want still better jobs and higher wages. The radicalism so much talked of is artificial and somewhat harmless. Bryan tried to do the trick three times, but there is this distinction between Bryan and Roosevelt:

"Bryan always told you beforehand how he was going to do it and we were able therefore to pull his plan to pieces. In fact he proclaimed the ingredient of his own pill, but Roosevelt never gives the formula of his medicine."

Courtesy of Col. Lee Chamberlin, Troy.

NOTED GENERALS ON GETTYSBURGH BATTLEFIELD.

The recent action of the Confederate Veterans in annual encampment voting to accept the invitation of the Grand Army of the Republic to unite in the celebration of the fiftieth anniversary of the battle of Gettysburgh next year, recalls another occasion on which officers and soldiers of the North and the South met in a fraternal spirit on the same battlefield. This photograph, made on the field in 1886, shows a group of Generals who commanded opposing forces during the great battle of July 1, 2 and 3, 1863, together with a number of veterans and citizens. The group of Generals includes, from left to right, in front: Gen. Joshua L. Chamberlain of Maine, afterward Governor; Gen. Daniel Butterfield of New York; Gen. James A. Longstreet, commander of Confederate forces; General Hartranft of Pennsylvania; Gen. Daniel E. Sickles of New York; Gen. Joseph B. Carr of Troy, New York.

DESIGN OF CHAMPLAIN MONUMENT AT PLATTSBURGH.

A memorial to Samuel de Champlain, the discoverer of the lake bearing his name, now being erected at Plattsburgh.

POINTED PARAGRAPHS.

Quickly made friendships are quickly ended.

Life's most desirable pleasures cost the least.

Sorrows of life enable us to appreciate the joys thereof.

It's easy to talk philosophically if you are not personally interested.

Instead of trying to beat his record the average man should try to forget it.

Most of the things we learn from experience come under the head of compulsory education.

It has been observed that the average man is never so happy as when he is posing as a critic.

Don't forget that the brownstone front usually depends on a homely brick rear for support.

If sympathy could be converted into cash, it's doughnuts to fudge there wouldn't be so much of it wasted.—Chicago News.

A WEEK-END OUTING

Hon. L. W. Emerson Entertains House Party at Schroon Lake.

1912

BANQUET AT THE LELAND HOUSE

Directors of Manufacturers' National Bank, of Troy, and Other Guests, Enjoy Generous Hospitality of Their Esteemed Associate.

The Leland house, at Schroon Lake, famous for many years as one of the leading summer resorts of the Adirondack region, has been the scene of many brilliant gatherings, but never has there been assembled under its hospitable roof, at one time, a more distinguished body of business and professional men than was entertained there Saturday and Sunday at a house party given by the Hon. L. W. Emerson. The guests, twenty in number, were with a few exceptions, the directors of the Manufacturers' National bank, of Troy.

The party made the trip to Schroon Lake in automobiles and the gentlemen were thus given an opportunity to inspect and enjoy a portion of the Great International Highway, now in process of construction and rapidly approaching completion, which was secured largely through the efforts of their host's energetic brother and business partner, Senator James A. Emerson.

At Lake George a stop was made for luncheon at the Fort William Henry hotel and a stroll about the premises to view the many improvements which have been made there during the winter. Continuing the journey the party arrived at Schroon Lake early in the afternoon. It was a beautiful June day and they found the ride most delightful, but the greater pleasure began when they arrived at their destination. When the big machines glided up to the hotel piazza Senator "Jim" Emerson, who is personally in charge

Liqueurs, Brandy, 1849
Yellow Chartreuse   Russian Kumme

After this attractive layout had been properly attended to, and cigars had been lighted, "L. W." assumed the role of toastmaster and with appropriate and happy remarks called upon each guest in turn to say something, which each one did. Several extremely witty speeches were made and all were interesting.

After a late breakfast Sunday morning the party departed in their automobiles and motored to Lake George,

where they again stopped for luncheon at the Fort William Henry hotel still as guests of Mr. Emerson. They carried with them from the Leland house memories of an event which will mark June 1, 1912, as a red letter date in their calendar of social enjoyments for years to come.

Those present at the banquet were as follows, all but the last six being directors of the Manufacturers' bank: Ex-Congressman L. W. Emerson, Warrensburgh; F. E. Howe, president Manufacturers' National bank, Troy; C. S. Sims, vice president and general manager Delaware and Hudson company, Albany; Frank Gilbert, Troy; George Underwood, vice president International Paper company, New York; Dr. J. B. Harvie, Troy; A. M. Ide, delegate to the Republican national convention, Troy; C. N. Flack, Troy; J. W. Donnelly, Troy; W. A. Feathers, cashier Manufacturers' National bank, Troy; J. W. Gardner, Troy; William Bolton, of the Quandt Brewing company, Troy; D. M. Edwards, Syracuse; J. E. Connelly, secretary American Surety company, New York; C. L. Duval, president Manhattan Navigation company, New York; Albert Thieriot, Chestertown; J. W. Fleming, State Conservation commission; Senator James A. Emerson, **Warrensburgh;** Patrick Moynehan, president Post Publishing company, Glens Falls. To each of the guests was presented a silver lead pencil, bearing the recipient's name and the date of the banquet.

Of the hotel this season, was waiting to greet the guests and they were given every attention which the magnificent resources of the house permitted.

The real purpose of the gathering was a banquet which "L. W." had prepared for his friends and associates in the directorate of the Troy bank. This was served in the hotel dining room at 7:30 o'clock. Some idea of its quality may be gathered from the appended menu, but only those who partook of the delicious viands, etc., could fully appreciate their excellence. It would be difficult to prepare a more elaborate spread and it reflected much credit upon the resources of the Leland house. In working out the details the host was most ably assisted by his friend, Albert Thieriot, of New York and Chestertown. The dining room was beautifully decorated for the occasion with flowers and plants from the greenhouse of S. E. Prosser, in this village. The menu cards, which also served as place cards, and contained a fine half-tone portrait of the host and a picture of the hotel, were from The News press.

−132−

The menu was as follows:

HORS D'OEUVRES
Russian Caviar on Toast
Martini

SOUP
Olives   Consomme au Rie
Radishes   Salted Almonds
Manzanilla Sherry

FISH
Fried Brook Trout
Cucumber Salad   Sauce Vinaigrette
Potatoes Parisienne
Ch La Dame Blanch
From private family of Cruse and Fils

ENTREE
Pates au Sweetbreads
Chateau Lafite, 1902

ROAST
Spring Lamb, Mint Sauce

VEGETABLES
Fresh Green Peas
Asparagus, Sauce Hollandise
Chambertin, 1900

SHERBET
Au Kirsch

BROILED
Spring Chicken
Lettuce Salad,   French Dressing
Champagne V. C. Y. L.

CHEESE
Brie and Roquefort
Guava Jelly
Champagne V. C. Y. L.

DESSERT
Vanilla Ice Cream
Cakes   Strawberries   Bon Bons
Black Coffee
Segars, Hoyo de Monterrey Obsequios
Cigarettes, Pall Malls

"THE MOUNTAINEER"

1912

The Lake George Steamboat Co. have recently made a contract with Alexander McDonald, Staten Island, N. Y., for the construction of a gasolene, motor propelled, passenger launch, for service on Lake George.

The dimensions of the boat are, length over all 70 ft., beam, outside of guards, 13 ft; draught, 3 ft. 9 in. Fitted with cabins; the after cabin will be arranged something on the plan of a passenger coach having wicker work seats, capacity of each seat, two people, all facing forward; the forward cabin fitted with camp stools. Total accommodations of the boat about 75 people. Both cabins are enclosed, but the arrangement of the windows is such that in pleasant weather the sash will slide up into a pocket making the boat practically open.

The hull of the launch will be constructed of white ash and yellow pine; the cabin will be finished in mahogany. 125 horse power Standard gasolene engine will be the propelling machinery. The boat will have a speed of approximately 15 miles per hour.

She will be operated during July, August and early September, each year, for short trips of about an hour and a half duration, starting from Lake George at convenient hours, mornings, afternoons and evenings, making numerous landings which are not visited by the larger boats. The trips will alternate by running down the lake on the west shore to the Marion House, crossing to Kattskill Bay and returning by the east shore. The next trip will reverse that order. She will make about four trips a day, one in the morning, two in the afternoon and one in the evening and will augment the motor boat service established by the steamboat Company several years ago and which has each year been an added attraction to summer visitors along that part of the lake which is covered by this service.

The cost of the launch will be about $15,000 and it is expected to have her ready for service July 1st next.

Fort William Henry Hotel, Lake George, N. Y.

COPYRIGHT, S. R. STODDARD, GLENNS FALLS, N. Y.

THE LAKE GEORGE MIRROR

LANDING AT PARADISE BAY.

THE FOURTH AT BOLTON.

News July 11 1912

"Safe and Sane" Observance of Independence Day Over on the Lake.

The Bolton Landing committee entrusted with the task of arranging a suitable program for a "safe and sane" celebration of the Nation's one hundred and thirty-sixth birthday anniversary, on July 4, 1912, won the approval and thanks of their townsmen with the delightful entertainment they furnished. Beginning with the children's parade from the town hall to the Baptist church, at 11 a. m., and ending with the fine display of fireworks in the evening, the various events on the program moved along like a song under the direction of the committee.

The Rev. E. M. Parrott, rector of St. James' Episcopal church, of Lake George, read the Declaration of Independence, and the Rev. Francis Bates, pastor of the Bolton Landing Methodist Episcopal church, led the children in singing patriotic songs, and the Rev. George N. Gates, the Baptist pastor, invoked the Divine blessing upon the efforts of all.

There was much disappointment when it was learned that the Hon. George McAnenny was unable to be present, as had been planned, to give the oration of the day, he having been detained at the last minute by important business in New York city. But "When God shuts a door He opens a window," and on this occasion through it stepped the Rev. Dr. David Gregg, who gave a stirring address on the beauty of our flag and admonished the children to be loyal forever to the Stars and Stripes. Dr. Gregg brought to mind the fact that New York, being one of the thirteen original states, claimed the honor of a bar and a star. His address was liberally sprinked with humorous anecdotes.

A baseball game was on for the afternoon, but a welcome shower dispersed the crowd, while it laid the dust and cooled the air for the evening's enjoyment of fireworks. These were displayed from a barge in Bolton bay and included many really beautiful pieces. This feature was in charge of Henry Knoblauch.

At the conclusion of the program a tired but happy crowd of people wended their way home feeling that they had enjoyed the sanest, happiest and most glorious Fourth they had seen in many years.

STEAMSHIP IMPERATOR, LARGEST IN THE WORLD, WHICH WAS LAUNCHED LAST WEEK.

Scarcely has the largest steamship, the Titanic, settled to an untimely grave at the bottom of the ocean after collision with an iceberg on its ill-fated maiden voyage, than another greater and larger steamship, the Imperator of the Hamburg-American Line, is given its initial dip in the element which it is destined to conquer. Taking advantage of the sad experience of the great British liner the newer German vessel will be provided with every safety device, and will be equipped with life-boats in which room will be provided for every person carried, including passengers and crew. The life-boats will all be swung out board so they will be in readiness for launching at any moment. The newest ocean leviathan is 900 feet in length, ninety-six feet beam, with nine decks above the water line, and when finished will displace 52,000 tons. The Imperator will be fitted with the Frahm anti-rolling tanks, which, with her great bulk, will counteract the motion of the most violent sea. The steamship has a capacity for 4,250 passengers, in addition to a crew of 1,000. It is expected that the Imperator will reach New York on her maiden voyage in the spring of 1913.

4 DEATHS IN FAMILY IN A YEAR

1912

MISS AMY DEMUTH DIES OF PNEUMONIA AT BOLTON.

ILL ONLY ONE DAY

Father Died a Year Ago Tomorrow—Mother and Brother Passed Away During the Winter—One Brother Survives—Family One of Wealthiest Among Summer Colony.

For the fourth time in a year the family of the late William C. DeMuth has been visited by death, his daughter Amy DeMuth having died suddenly last evening at the cottage of John Mulligan, the family gardener, situated a short distance from the DeMuth home in the Bolton road.

Miss DeMuth left New York about a month ago going to Lake George to make preparations for the opening of the summer home. Sunday she was taken ill of pneumonia and after an illness of only one day succumbed to the disease.

The Mulligan family took her into their cottage and did everything they could to restore her to health but the grim hand of death which has been over the family for the past year, won out and she passed away within two days of the anniversary of the death of her father William C. DeMuth, which occurred June 26, 1911.

Last winter her mother and brother Louis DeMuth died in New York.

The death of Miss DeMuth leaves but one member of the family surviving Edgar DeMuth, a brother who resides in New York.

The surviving relatives arrived in Bolton today and made arrangements to have the remains taken to New York.

The DeMuth family is one of the wealthiest that summer at Lake George and the death of Miss DeMuth following so soon after her parents and brother's demise has cast a cloud of sorrow over the town of Bolton.

The young lady with her maid and footman had succeeded in getting everything in readiness for the opening of the home which would have occurred within a few days.

It is now believed that the DeMuth home will not be occupied this summer unless it is late in the season.

CAN'T FISH THRU LAKE GEORGE ICE

"OLD HORICON'S" WATERS WILL BE CLOSED TO ANGLERS IN THE WINTER.

Times Dec 18. 1912

Fishing through the ice on Lake George is a thing of the past under the new "uniform" fish and game law whose passage was secured by the conservation commission last winter. Heretofore an exception had been made in favor of those who wanted to fish for perch, of which the lake once boasted some of the finest in the country, and hundreds of pounds were taken out each winter and found ready market. Complaint was made by the cottagers that this form of fishing so cleaned up the lake that it was impossible to get a mess of yellow perch during several seasons past, although formerly they were one of the most plentiful of summer fishes.

The law positively prohibits fishing through the ice in waters that contain trout, and defines "trout" as either brook, brown, rainbow, or spotted trout as being the species which close a water to ice fishing. Brook trout were planted in Lake George many years ago by the former fish culturist, A. N. Cheney, who believed the lake had all the advantages that in the Rangeley lakes in Maine cause such a magnificent race of fish. In latter years also rainbow, red throat and brown trout have been planted in Lake George and have thrived and multiplied, and many of them have been running up the one or two large streams that empty into the lake during their spawning season.

The prohibition will of necessity force a change in the program of sports advertised for the winter at the Fort William Henry hotel, as this stated that "For those who enjoy fishing, holes have been cut in the ice and tipups set for ice fishing. In close proximity several firs huts have been erected, equipped with heaters for the comfost of the fishermen."

It is expected, however, that as a compensation for the far from comfortable ice fishing, the perch will in a fe wseasons be as plenty and as easily caught by the nunerous summer visitors as of yore.

Valuable Mare Probably Fatally Stricken.

A gray mare owned by Lewis Thomson, one of a well matched and valuable work team, was stricken suddenly with a paralyzing disease Monday, in the yard of the Warrensburgh planing mill, and was unable to arise. It is believed to be suffering from spinal trouble and its recovery is doubtful. The animal was moved with great effort to a nearby barn, where it is now under treatment.

BOLTON LUMBER CO. IN TROUBLE

Involuntary Petition in Bankruptcy Against Bolton Landing Lumber Co.

Dec 6 1912 Star

CLAIMS AGGREGATE $1,000

Glens Falls Men Are Interested —Concern Has Not Operated Its Plant During the Last Two Months

Four creditors, having claims of about $1,000 against the Bolton Landing Lumber company of Bolton Landing on Lake George, have filed an involuntary petition in bankruptcy against the concern. The creditors are Lamb Brothers, Edward Butler and William E. Norton of Bolton Landing and Horace Hubbell of Queensbury. The law firm of Chambers and Finn represent the petitioning creditors and others.

Manager H. A. Krumbholtz of the Sagamore hotel is president and Frank P. Shippey of this city is treasurer and secretary of the company. The amount of the liabilities of the concern is not known and it is possible the petition will be contested.

The company has not operated its mill since some time in October, when Sheriff Thomas J. Smith sold off the personal property to satisfy judgments, one of which was held by the law firm of Jenkins & Barker of this city.

The lumber company was the defendant in a negligence action brought by Byron Finkle, a Bolton Landing youth, who lost one hand while working in the mill, and the firm of Jenkins & Barker was employed to defend the case. The company won out but was apparently unable to pay the attorneys' fees and they secured a judgment.

At the time of the sale the judgments were assigned to President Krumbholtz, who purchased the stock of lumber.

It is believed the case will involve many important legal questions as it is claimed the personal property sold under the judgment was covered by a mortgage said to have been held by the Glens Falls Trust company.

When in operation the mill employed ten men and during busy seasons as many as seventeen were given work. For about three weeks Mr. Shippey has held a lease on the mill and done custom sawing.

FORT WILLIAM HENRY HOTEL

Having been shot at three times during the past three weeks by some person in ambush, Hollis I. Loveland, postmaster and D. & H. station agent at The Glen, has been forced to the conclusion that some unknown enemy, for some unknown reason, desires to remove him from the scene of his earthly activities.

The first attempt on his life was made about three weeks ago, about 8:30 o'clock one evening, when a shot was fired at the Loveland home, passing through the window dangerously close to Mrs. Loveland, and lodging in the ceiling. Though the direction taken by the bullet seemed to preclude the idea that it was a stray bullet, Mr. Loveland preferred to believe that it was such and paid no attention to it.

Monday evening, while going to his home Mr. Loveland was fired upon again, and later while he was sitting near a window in his home a sharp report sounded and another bullet whizzed by his head and with a spiteful spat buried itself in the wall. An investigation has now been started to discover the identity of the would-be assassin.

Mr. loveland is at a loss where to place his suspicion as he knows of no person who for any reason that he can imagine, could harbor such a grudge against him as to desire his death. His friends are indignant and will make a united effort to apprehend the cowardly miscreant.

A NEW RECORD ESTABLISHED BY COUNT MANKOWSKI'S "ANKLE DEEP"

Times Dec. 9, 19 12

Although the regular yachting and motor boat season ended two months ago, Count Casmir S. Mankowski had the Ankle Deep, the craft that had a lead of a mile and a quarter in the last race for the international trophy, out on Long Island Sound Saturday and put her over tht Glen Cove course at the rate of 51.3 statute miles an hour.

Several changes have been made in the Ankle Deep since she raced on Huntington Bay. The forward deck has been lengthened, thus placing the steersman's seat further aft and the angle of the planes has been lessened. A stiff south-southwesterly breeze blew across the sound when the Ankle Deep left the yards of Wood & McClure, at City Island, where the alterations have been made, under the supervision of Clinton A. Crane of Tams, Lemoine & Crane, her designers. On board were Count Mankowski, George W. Robinson and Frank J. Grenon. In an accompanying power yacht were C. A. Crane, Charles King and Oswald Bergen.

Whitecaps dotted the surface of the sound, and it was anything but placid as the Ankle Deep shot out from her anchorage, but planing beautifully, she shot over the troubled waters at a great rate and raised very little disturbance.

The changes in the angles of her planes have caused her to glide more evenly than she did last September, even when going at her best at that time, and she does not lift by the bow as she did. The fact that she was muffled did not appear to interfere with her speed, but gave the impression that she was going faster than really was the case—much the same as the Maple Leaf IV did.

The course over which the trials were made is on the outer part of Hempstead harbor and parallels the Castlegould estate.

Having concluded her trials the Ankle Deep sped back to City Island and in a few days will be shipped to Florida, where in a temperature more suited for the sport, she will contend for honors.

new Dec 9, 1912

Comrades in Camp and Battle.

The late Hiram Jebo, a native of Warrensburgh, whose death at Tupper Lake is annuonced in another column, was a tentmate of Benjamin Cilley, of this place, during their service together in the Civil War. The men enlisted on the same day and received their discharge at the same time. Mr. Cilley was much affected by the news of his old comrade's death, which he received Tuesday.

PAUL SMITH, NOTED AS ADIRONDACK GUIDE, DEAD

Dec 16 1912

Celebrated Sportsman and Hotel Proprietor Dies in Montreal Hospital.

Paul Smith, perhaps the most celebrated character of the Adirondack mountains, died yesterday in the Royal Victoria hospital, Montreal, Que., according to word received in Glens Falls this morning. Mr. Smith had been in the hospital several weeks and failed to recover from a serious operation. Disease had wasted his strength, and this, with his age of eighty-seven years, made him too weak to regain strength following the operation.

Beginning more than sixty years ago as a trapper in the Adirondacks, Mr. Smith was one of those who could see the future of the mountains. He invested all he could in lands and lakes and accumulated a very large fortune. He was the head of the Paul Smith Company and owned the town of Paul Smith's, on the lower St. Regis Lake, which for half a century has been the headquarters of wealthy men who annually go to the Adirondacks to fish and shoot game.

Born in the little town of Milton, Vt., in 1825, Mr. Smith celebrated his eighty-seventh birthday on August 20, when there was a gathering of notable men at Paul Smith's, all of whom had been friends of the pioneer trapper for many years. His father, a lumberman, lived until he was seventy-three, and his mother was ninety-five years old when she died.

Had Been Vermont Trapper.

In 1852 Paul Smith first went to the Adirondacks. In that year he found Loon Lake and there built a cabin, which he called Hunters' Home, and there he established the nucleus of what later became the wealthy clientele of the modern Paul Smith's.

In the cabins were partitions separating the cots in which men slept, and a large sitting room, the main feature of which was a great open fire. The next interesting feature was a barrel of whiskey. Whiskey was worth nineteen cents a gallon then and he always kept a barrel of it for those who stopped at Hunters' Home. There was a spigot in the barrel and a dipper. Men helped themselves, paying four cents for each drink.

In 1858 he and Dr. H. B. Loomis of New York were camping at the lower St. Regis Lake when he said he would like to have a hotel there. Dr. Loomis said he would finance it and Paul Smith spent the $300 he had saved for land and Dr. Loomis loaned $13,000 to him to build a hotel of seventeen rooms. That was the beginning of Paul Smith's.

This place attracted more wealthy men who were seeking sport, and when the Civil war broke out the first "big money" came to Paul Smith. Many influential men who had sent substitutes to the war, and others who did not care to go to the front, found the seclusion of Paul Smith's desirable, and throughout the war the owner of this resort had all he could do. He paid off the mortgage and had $50,000 in cash when the war ended.

With this money he purchased land. He continued acquiring Adirondack property until recently he owned more than thirty thousand acres of lands and lakes, without a dollar of mortgage on any of them.

In the days of Loon Lake he met the daughter of another pioneer in that region and they were married before the St. Regis Lake place was built. They had three children, all sons, of whom two survive. They are Paul Smith, Jr., and Phelps Stokes Smith. They are the managers of their father's estate.

Star Dec 18 1912

Bolton Man Buried.

BOLTON, Dec. 17.—The funeral of Judd S. Fish, who died Sunday aged thirty-eight years, took place at 2 o'clock this afternoon, Rev. E. M. Parrott officiating.

Boltonite Under the Knife.

Ralph Hill, son of Mr. and Mrs. Scott Hill, of Trout Lake, Bolton, was operated on for appendicitis at the Albany hospital on Wednesday of last week. *Dec 5 1912*

MRS. RICHARD J. BROWN. *1912*

Mrs. Richard J. Brown died at her home, the Lake View house, in Bolton, Tuesday morning at 8 o'clock, after a long illness. She is survived by her husband; also by a sister and brother, who reside in Brooklyn. The body was taken to Troy for burial yesterday afternoon.

To thine own self be true;
And it must follow, as the night the day,
Thou can'st not then be false to any
man. — Shakespeare.

$991,640 LEFT BY SHEPARD

times Oct 12 1912

The New York Herald today says:

Appraisal of the estate of the late Edward M. Shepard, the Brooklyn lawyer, who died on July 29, 1911, placed the gross value of his estate at $991,640.79, according to the report of John J. Bridges, state transfer tax appraiser, filed yesterday in the surrogate's office.

Deductions amounting to $53,982 for the cost of administrating the estate, commissions, debts and funeral expenses left the net value of the estate at $937,707.97. Mr. Shepard's personal effects at No. 44 Pierrepont street were appraised at $6,534. His real estate holdings are valued at $123,683.

Bonds and stocks are valued at $245,000.

The bulk of his estate is left to his sister, Mrs. Agnes S. Hewitt, of Lake George; his brother, Charles S. Shepard of No. 147 Columbia Heights, and sister-in-law, Mrs. Alice Shepard.

MAJOR CULVER DEAD

FORMER HUDSON FALLS MAN DIES IN PALO ALTO, CALIFORNIA.

times Dec 10 1912

Major John Oscar Culver died at his home in Palo Alto, Cal., Tuesday evening, December 3. Major, better known to old Sandy Hillers, as Oscar Culver, was born in Sandy Hill, now Hudson Falls, May 2, 1830, and was the last of eight sons of the late James and Kezia Lee Culver. Major Culver is survived by a widow, four sons and one daughter, who live in California and by a sister, Mrs. Eber Richards of Hudson Falls.

After graduating from the Albany Law school, Major Culver went to Madison, Wis., where he became a judge of one of the courts. At the breaking out of the Civil War he enlisted and was promoted to the rank of major. After the war he returned to Wisconsin and took up literary work and at one time was the publisher of a magazine. The last years of his life were passed in California.

I am beginning to suspect:
That all the world are partners, whatever their creed or sect:
That life is a kind of pilgrimage—a sort of Jericho road.
And kindness to one's fellows the sweetest law in the code.
      [Wallace Bruce.

SINGLEY DISPOSES OF BARBER SHOP

Star Oct 15, 1912

Long - Established Tonsorial Parlor Bought by George LaMere and Son

Bernard Singley, for thirty-eight years proprietor of one of Glens Falls' leading barber shops, located in the Holden block, has sold his business to George La Mere and son, formerly of Hudson Falls. The new proprietors took possession of the establishment yesterday.

In 1874 the shop, which was then occupying the store in the same building now occupied by Keefe's news-room, was purchased by Mr. Singley from George Loop. At that time there were three other barber shops in Glens Falls, which was then a village of about 3,500 population. Mr. Singley's recollection of Glens Falls at the time is vivid and he talks with apparent pleasure of the scenes of his early enterprise. Kerosene lamps were the only means of street lighting at that time. The streets themselves were not many and Glen, the main street of the village, had but two buildings beyond the present site of Fowler's store.

The one-time familiar lamplighter was an important figure here then and his duty was concluded at midnight when he carried about his ladder while extinguishing the oil burners. Gas succeeded the kerosene lighting system which also required the services of the lamplighter. The sidewalks were laid at infrequent intervals with flaggings and the roads were, of course, unpaved.

Mr. Singley has seen many barber shops open in the city since his career began in Glens Falls. Some of these have prospered, while others have long since suspended business. The Singley shop has been the school for a number of later proprietors of shops of their own. Two of these have opened places of business in the city and are now well known local barbers. One of these is Albert C. Sturtevant and the other is Michael Russell, now one of the firm of Russell & Dougherty.

Mr. and Mrs. Singley recently resided at 9 Coolidge avenue. He has sold his property and will leave with his wife for Mount Vernon, N. Y., where he has a son who is engaged in electrical work. Mr. Singley will devote his time to the sale of his hair tonic which he perfected at Glens Falls and which now has an established reputation on the market.

—137—

"UNCLE HENRY" CRANDALL IS OPPOSED TO MOVING SHAFT

Dec 14 1912.

"Uncle Henry" Crandall is very much opposed to the moving of the Soldiers' Monument from Monument Square. In an interview with a Daily Times reporter yesterday he forcibly expressed himself relative to the matter.

"Ever since the monument was erected I have looked after it and a few weeks ago because I was not able personally to look after it any longer."

Mr. Crandall told the reporter that the town of Queensbury owns the plot of ground on which the monument stands, and that when the shaft was erected it was one of the largest and handsomest monuments in the state.

He commented upon the seats arranged around the monument and

Soldiers' Monument.

kept it in repair," said he to the reporter, "and I firmly believe that it would be a rank injustice to disturb the memorial of the Civil war veterans at this late date.

"The monument is in bad need of repair, and it will take considerable money to place it in good condition. He gave up the care of the monument said that it was one of the most useful things ever promulgated in the city. He said it would be surprising if people knew just how many persons used the seats during the summer season.

"Uncle Henry" has a large easy chair placed in an upper bay window, fronting the square, and day in and day out views the busy scenes enacted in the square.

One of Glens Falls' Oldest and Most Prominent Citizen Passes Away at the Age of Eighty Years

Times
Dec 14 1912

FUNERAL WILL BE HELD MONDAY P.M.

Jonathan Miles Coolidge, one of the oldest and most prominent residents of this city, died yesterday afternoon at 5:30 o'clock at his home, 161 Glen street. He had been ill of bronchial pneumonia only five days.

Born in Bolton.

Mr. Coolidge was eighty years old. He was born in the Town of Bolton, March 3, 1832. His parents were Jonathan and Mary Opelia Coolidge. Mr. Coolidge lived with his parents in Bolton until 1866 when he came to this city and entered the mercantile business with his brother, Thomas S. Coolidge and George W. Lee, under the firm name of Coolidge, Lee & Company. He continued in this business until 1880 when the firm sold out to Haviland & Gilbert by whom it was continued for several years.

In Manufacturing World.

In the year 1879, with his brother, Thomas S. Coolidge, George W. Lee and William Wallace D. Jeffers, Mr. Coolidge engaged in the manufacture of wood pulp in the village of Ticonderoga and soon thereafter the business was merged with a paper mill in that place. The combined business of pulp and paper manufacturing was continued under the corporate name of the Lake George Pulp and Paper Company, until January 1, 1898, when the mills became one of the thirty properties sold to and taken over by the International Paper Company. Since that time Mr. Coolidge had not been active in any particular line, although he was interested in several local industries. At the time of his death he was a director in the Ticonderoga Pulp and Paper Company and vice president of the First National bank of this city. In Masonic circles he was prominent, being one of the oldest members of Warrensburg lodge, No. 425, F and A. M.

Noted Spy Is Buried In Queensbury

One of the greatest patriots, who did much for his country as a spy, was Moses Harris, who lies buried in the cemetery near the Stone church in Harrisena, town of Queensbury.

An imposing monument marks his grave. The monument was erected by his grandson, John J. Harris.

Moses Harris was one of the most trustworthy men employed by General Philip Schuyler to obtain knowledge of General Burgoyne's plans when the Burgoyne army was sweeping through this northern section during the Revolutionary war.

Mr. Harris is numbered among the great American spies. He carried Burgoyne's message to Schuyler before delivering them to a man in Albany who took them to General Clinton in New York. General Schuyler altered the messages so as to mislead General Clinton.

Harris professed to be an ardent Tory, converted to the cause by his uncle Gilbert Harris, a resident of Kingsbury, who recommended him to Burgoyne's officers as a man who would make a trusty messenger.

He carried a number of messages, all of which passed through Schuyler's hands before reaching Clinton, until Mr. Shepherd the man to whom they were delivered at Albany became suspicious and tried to poison Harris. This failed, but Harris was arrested shortly after and tortured by his captors in an attempt to extort a confession of treason. Three times he was strung up to a tree but was finally allowed to go, having given the Masonic sign of distress.

After this the enmity of his Whig neighbors was aroused against him. Jacob Benson, a patriot, lay in wait for him all one night declaring he would "put a ball through the cussed Tory," but being warned Harris took another route and escaped.

His adventures were many and full of danger. An account of them reads like one of Cooper's Leather Stocking Tales.

The last message with which he was entrusted by Burgoyne he carried to Washington with a commendatory letter from General Schuyler. He was offered a commission by Washington in the Southern army, but declined it.

He returned to Kingsbury saying "All the Tories this side of Hell shall not drive me from my home." Nor did they.

In 1787 he bought a large tract of land in Queensbury, Warren county where he lived until his death in 1838.

His descendants and those of his brothers who came with him still live in the settlement which is called Harrisena.

New Express Line at Bolton,
Oct 4 1912

Frank F. Merrill & company have established a freight and express route between Bolton Landing and Glens Falls and will make three round trips each week, on Tuesdays, Thursdays and Saturdays. They have a first-class equipment and are prepared to handle all business entrusted to them carefully and promptly.

MRS. JOHN FERRIS

Mrs. John Ferris died Friday at her home in North Chester, after an illness of several months' duration, during which she bore her sufferings with rare patience and fortitude. She is survived by her husband, whose faithful companion she had been.

-138-

APPEAL TO RESIDENTS OF BOLTON

INCREASE IN THE LIGHTING RATE IS NECESSARY.

oct 30 1/12

FROM 3 TO 5 MILES

Company Has Been Doing Business at a Loss and Will Have to Suspend About the First of the Year Unless Majority of the Residents Are in Favor of Increasing Rate.

The residents of Bolton Landing and of the lighting district in the town are being solicited by means of a petition to authorize the town board to increase the rate paid to the local lighting company to five mills on the assessable property of the district, the present rate being three mills on each dollar. It is stated that the reason for this course of action is that the company has been doing business at a loss since its organization and as its finances do not permit of a much longer continuation of this condition, it is necessary for it to increase its income by some means or give up the job which would mean quite a loss to the residents. The increase of income which would be derived from the source before mentioned would put the company in a much more favorable position, and, while not altogether giving it enough to assure any profits, would at least enable it to maintain its plant and distributing system in better condition, which in turn would stimulate more commercial lighting business. The petition in circulation makes two conditions, one that the candle power of the street lights be increased from twenty-five to thirty two and the other that when the gross income of the company shall exceed its total operating and fixed charges in any one year, this excess shall be deducted from the amount paid for street lighting, but that the total amount paid on this shall not be less than three mills.

The company has been giving service there for about two years and taking into consideration the facts that its power plant is of a type little understood heretofore, namely, produces gas, and that there is only one power unit, it has given excellent service. They have hardly any transmission troubles, the main causes for breaking downs and poor service being in the apparatus for generating the gas by which the engine is run and a good share of these troubles have been on account of the unfamiliarity of the proper operation and care of a gas producer. This type of plant, has, however, shown a wonderful fuel economy as the consumption of coal has only averaged 800 pounds daily and the plant has been run twenty-four hours a greater part of the time and has had, first and last, to supply a connected load of about 1,400 incandescent lamps. No other kind of power plant could better this except water power. The company's lines extend over a district about three miles long north and south it has about five miles of pole line, three of which is included in the lighting district. It is understood that an extension to the lighting district of about a mile and half on the southern end is being considered and if the present petition proves successful Bolton may have its main road lighted from the Huddle cemetery through to the northern boundary of the union school district about a mile north of the post-office at Bolton Landing, a length of three miles, in addition to the side streets in the village and other public roads amounting to another mile and a half. If, however, a majority of the residents are not in favor of the increased tax, the company will probably be obliged to shut down about the first of the year, or as soon as its business begins to drop off after the winter months, and wind up its affairs the best way it can. Moreover, it is doubtful whether or not another party would care to risk attempting the business in a place where a majority of the taxpayers should be so indifferent to such a decided improvement as not to be willing to sacrifice a little something to retain it and help it along Let us hope that this is not the case but that Bolton will prove itself equal and superior to its neighbors as it has done before.

WOMAN'S VERDICT FOR $900 SET ASIDE

Star — Jan 3 1913

Supreme Court Justice Henry T. Kellogg of Plattsburg has handed down a decision setting aside the judgment of $900 awarded by the jury to Mrs. Emma Taylor of Bolton Landing in her action against the Glens Falls Automobile company to recover for alleged injuries. Mrs. Taylor claims she was struck by a car owned by the defendant company on the Glens Falls-Lake George state road near the Bloody Pond crossing. At the first trial of the case last spring the jury returned a verdict of $500, which was set aside by Justice VanKirk. The case was retried in the fall and the jury returned the larger verdict.

SHERIFF BOLTON'S FATHER A DEPUTY

Star — Jan 3 1913

Sheriff Richard J. Bolton, Jr., who assumed the duties of his new office Wednesday, succeeding Sheriff Thomas J. Smith, has announced the appointment of his father, Richard J. Bolton, Sr., of Horicon as the last deputy sheriff with salary ($50 a year) to be named by him. Sheriff Bolton received more than 100 applications from Republicans in the northern towns, particularly Horicon and Chester and finally decided upon the selection of his father.

The special deputies, without salaries, who have been appointed by Sheriff Bolton are Alpha St. Claire of this city, Fred Case of Caldwell and Herbert Smith of Warrensburg.

THE DEATH RECORD.

Star Nov 28, 1912

John Harris.

John Harris died at his home at 35 Terra Cotta avenue Monday afternoon at 5.15 o'clock after a lingering illness. Beside his widow, he is survived by twelve children, Freda M. Harris of Clinton, Iowa; Mrs. William W. Cool of Denver, Colo., Mrs. Charles H. Barger of Hudson Falls, Stephen Harris of East Lake George, Mrs. Emery Hewitt of Johnsburg and Mrs. F. H. Jenkins, Mrs. J. L. Brown, Mrs. Westly Wildie, Washington, Fred and William of this city, twenty-four grandchildren and eight great-grandchildren.

Mr. Harris was born in the town of Queensbury, March 27, 1827. He married Lina Sherman September 23, 1847, Mrs. Harris dying in 1852. February 7, 1854, he again married, this time to Zelpha Sherman. Mr. Harris was a life-long resident of Queensbury and was respected by all who knew him.

The funeral was held from the late residence yesterday afternoon, the bearers being grandchildren of the deceased, Fred Brown of Lake George, Ira Hewitt of North Creek, Benjamin Harris of Queensbury and Washington Butler of this city.

Lake George.

The will of George S. Brayton, the Lake George recluse, who was found in a dying condition from exposure on a small island near Ripley's Point a few weeks ago, was admitted to probate yesterday by County Judge and Surrogate George S. Raley. The property possessed by Brayton at the time of his death is estimated at about $5,000. He leaves the entire estate, which consists of real estate on Lake George and a bank account, to his niece, Mrs. Sylvia Smith, who is named as executrix. A provision is made that in case either of his brothers, Wellington and Ira, or his sister, Mrs. Caroline Hitchcock, ever come to want they shall have their support out of the estate. *Morning Times Jan*

ELDRIDGE ENTERTAINS AT THE HALFWAY HOUSE

Dec 14. 1912

Supervisors, County Officials and News-paper-Men Guests of Honor.

The Halfway House was the scene of gay festivities last evening, the occasion being a banquet tendered by Supervisor Milton N. Eldridge, the youngest member of the county board, to observe the anniversary of his birth.

Mr. Eldridge's Guests.

Mr. Eldridge's guests were Chairman Fred R. Smith, Supervisors E. J. Worden, Fred Rogers, C. H. Baker, Beecher Glassbrook, Samuel C. Baker, Herbert J. Russell, Beecher VanDusen, Jesse F. Thurston, George A. Patterson, R. J. Bolton and Hon. Addison B. Colvin, Clerk Lolon R. Dunlop of the board, County Treasurer John Bazinet, County Attorney Loyal L. Davis, and representatives of the press.

An Excellent Feast.

Proprietor Arthur Lyle spread his usual excellent feast before the banqueters at 7 o'clock and three-quarters of an hour later, when the large number of hearty appetites had been appeased an extemporaneous post prandial program was observed.

Mr. Colvin's Address.

Hon. Addison B. Colvin was the first to be called on, responding to a toast, "What I Think of the Present County Board of Supervisors." After complimenting the board as a whole and individually, Mr. Colvin paid an excellent tribute to the late Taylor J. Eldridge, father of the host of the evening.

He recalled a banquet served in the Rockwell house in 1893, at which he and Taylor J. Eldridge, then assemblyman, were present. After wishing the host and the board success in all undertakings, Mr. Colvin closed by offering a silent toast to the memory of Jonathan M. Coolidge, who died Thursday afternoon at his home on Glen street. Mr. Coolidge was at one time a member of the board of supervisors.

Glassbrook Gets Hat.

One of the amusing features of the program was the presentation of a silk hat to Supervisor Beecher Glassbrook of Stony Creek. The presentation was made by County Attorney Loyal L. Davis. Mr. Glassbrook has gained much fame among his fellow supervisors as a collector of caps and hats, and it was thought the silk hat would prove a most desirable present. Mr. Glassbrook graciously accepted the hat, and agreed to wear it for the remainder of the session, but refused to appear within the limits of Stony Creek in such regalia.

Response by Baker.

Supervisor C. H. Baker responded to a toast, "Reminiscences," recalling the days when he and Taylor J. Eldridge were members of the board of supervisors in 1885 and 1886.

Other Responses.

E. J. Worden, "The Lake George Viewpoint;" Fred R. Smith, "Our Sightseeing Trip," Fred Rogers, "My Researches in Medicine;" Samuel C. Baker, "Horicon Nerve;" Jesse F. Thurston, "The National Pastime;" Beecher Van Dusen, "My Busy Day."

Supervisor G. A. Patterson read an interesting extract from a Florida newspaper and Supervisor Russell ended the program with a talk on "The Centennial."

At the conclusion of the banquet a rising vote of thanks was tendered Mr. Eldridge.

DEATH OF H. R. LEAVENS AFTER BRIEF ILLNESS

Star Jan 29. 1913

Henry R. Leavens, a lifelong and highly respected citizen of Warren county, died at 2.45 o'clock this morning in his home, 86 Warren street. Mr. Leavens was born in the town of Luzerne, sixty-eight years ago and came to this city in 1875. He engaged in the livery business immediately after locating in Glens Falls.

Mr. Leavens was taken suddenly ill Monday night but his condition was not regarded as serious until a few hours before his death. He is survived by two brothers, Thurlow C. Leavens and Daniel S. Leavens, both of this city. The funeral arrangements will be announced later.

Boating on Lake George.

Walter E. Harris made a trip through Lake George to Baldwin in a motorboat Sunday. This is a remarkable experience at this season of the year, as Lake George is generally icebound before the latter part of January. *Jan 28. 1913 Star*

Leaves Farm for Town.

news Jan 30

Clayton A. Barber, who has been in the employ of Dr. Nordstrom about two and a half years, has resigned his position and moved his family back to their home in Bolton Landing. *1913*

EMPIRE HOTEL CHANGES HANDS

MESSRS. CHAMPLIN AND ROBERTS BUY WELL KNOWN HARTFORD HOSTELRY.

Negotiations were closed late yesterday whereby the ownership of the Empire Hotel property at Hartford, Washington county is transferred from Levi Yarter, who has been the proprietor for a number of years to Burton Champlin of this city and Asa Roberts of Bolton. Messrs. Champlin and Roberts will take possession February 15. The hotel is a two-story frame building with twelve sleeping rooms. There is, in addition, a large horse barn and automobile garage. Numerous improvements are planned by the new owners. The purchase price was not made public.

Mr. Roberts has had considerable experience in the hotel business and until a year ago was proprietor of the Van Avery hotel in Northville, which was destroyed by fire. Since that time he has been connected with the Wilson House at Bolton Landing. Mr. Champlin is a young man of considerable ability. He was formerly secretary of the Glens Falls Dairy and is at present proprietor of an extensive freight transfer business. Mr. Champlin plans to continue his present business in this city. *Jan 22 1913*

LEONARD BIBBEY DIES AT HIS HOME IN FORT EDWARD

Knickerbocker Press

Pneumonia Proves Fatal to Widely Known Horseman and Senior Member of Brewing Firm.

Feb 1 1913

Special to The Knickerbocker Press.

GLENS FALLS, Jan. 31.—Leonard Bibbey died from pneumonia this afternoon at his home in Fort Edward. He was sixty years old and a native of England. He came to Glens Falls as a boy and later started a small bottling works out of which has grown the firm of Bibbey and Ferguson, brewers. He lived in Glens Falls until 1890 when, with several others, he went to Fort Edward and purchased the John R. Durkee Brewing company which since has been conducted under his personal direction.

Mr. Bibbey was a self-made man and charitably inclined. He was widely known as a horseman, having owned some of the best horses in the state. He was a member of Senate lodge, Free and Accepted Masons of Glens Falls, Royal Arcanum of Fort Edward and the Bibbey Hose company of Fort Edward was named in his honor. He is survived by his wife, one son, Walter, and a daughter, Mrs. W. L. R. Durkee.

SIX THOUSAND DOLLAR DINNER

Times Jan 4 1913

GEORGE F. UNDERWOOD ACTS AS HOST AT NEW YEAR'S DINNER FOR RELATIVES.

A $6,000 New Year's dinner was given at the Warren House, in Warrensburg Wednesday afternoon at 1 o'clock by George F. Underwood, of New York, to a party of relatives living in this locality. In the gathering were six first cousins of Mr. Underwood, to each of whom he presented during the dinner an envelope containing a registered bond bearing interest at 5 per cent.

The dinner was ordered at Christmas time and Landlord Maurice O'Connor was instructed to spare no effort or expense in its preparation. With the reputation Mr. O'Connor bears as a hotel man it is hardly necessary to say that it was most satisfactory to the host and his guests, among whom was the Hon. Louis W. Emerson, an intimate friend of Mr. Underwood, and the only guest who was not a relative by blood or marriage. Mr. and Mrs. Underwood who had been spending the holidays in Fort Edward, went to Warrensburg with their son and daughter, Mr. and Mrs. Adriance, and were met at the hotel by their relatives, the most of whom live in northern towns of the county. They were: Mr. and Mrs. Hiram Hemingway, Mr. and Mrs. Hiram Ross, Mr. and Mrs. Jeptha Bennett, Mr. and Mrs. George Smith, of Horicon; Mr. and Mrs. Lorenzo Hemingway, Miss Beatrice Hemingway of Chestertown; Mr. and Mrs. David Hemingway, of Hudson Falls and Mr. and Mrs. Maurice Wilson of Glens Falls. The recipients of the bonds were Hiram, Lorenzo and David Hemingway, Mrs. Ross, Mrs. Bennett and Mrs. Wilson.

Mr. Underwood was formerly a resident of Fort Edward. He was for many years a lumberman and is well known throughout this section. Some years ago he was made superintendent of woodlands for the International Paper Company and later became vice president of the company. His duties then called him to New York. He has a beautiful summer camp at Underwood where he entertains lavishly during the season. He has become very wealthy, but to his friends he is the same George Underwood he was in days of yore.

This Winter Like 1889.

Many of the older residents have been led by the mild weather this winter to rack their brains in an effort to recall similar conditions in years gone by. One old settler says that January, 1889, was about the same as this year and dust was blowing in the streets in the middle of the month. There was a great shortage of ice in the cities and large quantities were shipped from Lake George to Albany and New York. Two or three Warrensburgh men made a lot of money on ice that winter. *Jan 30 1913*

news

GIANTS EXPECT TO REPEAT.

McGraw Figures on His Team Being Stronger Than Last Year.

Manager McGraw, of the Giants, is one who is not given to boasting of what his team is going to do before the season opens, but it is pretty certain that the little Napoleon is confident that the Giants will land another pennant in the National League. McGraw will have the same line-up as he had last year, with possibly one or two changes. One of these will probably be in the outfield, where young George Burns is slated for a berth. There may also be a change in the infield. McGraw expects that his pitching staff this year will be better than it has been in years. He has several promising young twirlers to pick from and

Globe Jan 25 1913

BIG CHIEF MYERS.

some of the veterans are likely to do better work than they have in the last year or two. Behind the bat Chief Myers, the Indian backstop, will, of course, do the bulk of the catching. Myers did grand work for the pennant winners last season and all indications point to the Big Chief having another highly successful year in 1913.

Nov 28 1912 news

Jerome Is Settled for the Winter.

Jerome Jenkins, a well-known local character of bibulous habits, was taken to his winter quarters in the county jail at Lake George Tuesday by Constable Lon Sherman, having been committed by Justice George Hodgson. Jerome knows just where to hang his hat in the county hotel as he has been there several winters.

Mrs. M. N. Dickinson

Mar 25 1913

Betsey Coolidge, wife of Captain M. N. Dickinson of Warrensburg, died at 4 p. m., Sunday, aged seventy-six years. Besides her husband, she is survived by a daughter, Mrs. J. M. Somerville, and a son, L. C. Dickinson, both of Warrensburg. The funeral will be held Tuesday afternoon from the home at 2:30 o'clock, the Rev. Richard Abbott, pastor of the Warrensburg Presbyterian church, officiating. *Star*

JOHN HART, 106 YEARS OLD, DIES AT HIS HOME

Veteran of Two Wars Succumbs After Long Illness—Remembers War of 1812.

N. Press Feb 1 1913

John Hart, 106 years old, "Troy's grand old man," and probably the oldest resident of New York state, died yesterday morning at his home, 397 Fourth avenue, North Troy, after a long illness. Mr. Hart was a veteran of the Mexican and Civil wars, and even remembered incidents of the war of 1812. He received injuries in the Civil war and during his later years became childish, constantly telling of his wartime experiences. Because of his devotion to the flag which he defended in more than a dozen battles, he painted his cottage in North Troy, red, white and blue, and it was known for miles around as "the little red, white and blue house of Troy's grand old man."

Mr. Hart was born in New York city April 14, 1806, but after the Mexican war, during which he served under Taylor on his whirlwind campaign across the Rio Grande, he went to Schenectady in search of a daughter by his second wife, Virginia Hart. He finally located her in Troy nine years ago, and has since resided there with her. He received a double pension for his service in the Mexican and Civil wars and up to a couple of months ago, when he was confined to his bed, he did most of the housework. He enlisted in "A" company, Eighteenth regiment, New York volunteers, shortly after the fall of Fort Sumter, and was not mustered out until after Lee's surrender when he returned to Schenectady and resumed his trade as a carpenter.

ALBERT THIERIOT IN NEW POSITION

Jan 18, 1913.

Under His Management Bright Future is Assured the Fort William Henry Hotel

Under the new management of Albert Thieriot, the Fort William Henry hotel, is assured the brightest possible future. Mr. Thieriot was for many years in charge of Delmonico's restarant in New York and he is generally recognized as one of the leading men in his line in this or any other country.

His wide experience in providing for the wants of a fastidious public ably qualify him for his new position, and under his direction the noted Lake George hotel will spread its fame near and far.

Mr. Thieriot, who is a resident of Chestertown, is well known in Glens Falls and his many friends here will wish him every success in his new field. He was for many years executor and trustee of the Rosa Delmonico estate.

USEFUL LIFE ENDED

Feb 20 1913

Henry Crandall, Philanthropist, Goes to His Reward.

GRAND OLD MAN OF GLENS FALLS

Lived Ninety-two Years and Left Record of Many Noble Deeds—Started as Poor Boy and by Thrift and Industry Amassed a Fortune.

Henry Crandall, the grand old man of Glens Falls, widely known as a philanthropist and beloved by all who enjoyed his acquaintance, died yesterday morning at 6:15 o'clock, at his home in Crandall place, Monument Square, Glens Falls. He lived ninety-two years and left a record of many noble deeds for the benefit of his fellow men. Until with n a few months he was in remarkably good health for a man of his years and his mental faculties were unimpaired. About six months ago he began to fail and it soon became plain to his friends that his end was drawing near. He frequently expressed the desire to live until his ninety-second birthday anniversary and this boon was granted him, the date falling on February 13.

About two weeks ago Mr. Crandall had a slight shock of paralysis, followed last Saturday and Sunday by attacks of greater severity, which left him in an almost helpless condition. His throat and left side were paralyzed and Saturday he became unable to take nourishment of an kind. He then became unconscious and remained in that condition until his death.

Mr. Crandall's only surviving relative is his widow, who was Betsey Waters, of Horicon. They were married fifty-four years ago and she is now eighty years old. A well mated couple they lived happily together until separated by death.

Mr. Crandall was born February 13, 1821, at East Lake George, in the town of Caldwell. There he received a common district school education and while he was obliged to be away from school more or less, he succeeded in acquiring an education which stood him well in hand when he entered the business world. When but a small boy Mr. Crandall left home to work ten months in the hills for a compensation of from eleven to thirteen dollars a month. His ambition for successful business life was great and as a result of hard work and practicing the habit of saving, he had accumulated at the age of thirty years, the sum of $1,000.

He invested that money with John J. Harris and a man named Finch in a lumber tract in the Boreas River section and literally coined money. This was before and during the Civil War.

He is a large real estate holder, owning much property in Glens Falls and vicinity.

The deceased became a resident of Glens Falls in 1850 and had since resided there continuously. He took a great interest in the city and his beneficences for public purposes were large. About thirty years ago he bought the land now known as Crandall park, on upper Glen street, expending nearly $30,000 in the purchase, irrigation, grading and general improvement of this property, the free use of which was given to the city of Glens Falls and which will always be known and used as a park by the city. It is believed by some that the city may become the owner of the park, in which event it will be made one of the most modern and up-to-date parks in the country.

A smaller park in the rear of the Crandall residence, on Maple street, was also opened for public use. The deceased cared for the soldiers' monument for many years. In many other ways his philanthropy was felt, notably in the organization of the Boys' Saving club, one of the greatest philanthopic acts ever performed by a man of wealth in Northern New York. This club, formed more than two years ago, will be perpetuated, and if all rules are complied with one hundred boys, when they become of age, will have a good-sized bank account to their credit. Mr. Crandall gave each member of the club $25 with which to start a bank account. When they had added to this sum $37.50, making a total deposit of $62.50, Mr. Crandall added another gift to increase the amount to $100. This remains to the boy's credit until he reaches his majority when it will be placed at his command.

Besides his gifts and other good acts of which the public has known the deceased performed many acts of charity of which only the recipients knew. His whole life, in fact, was spent in doing good and he laid up treasures in heaven which he will now enjoy.

On a knoll situated almost in the center of the beautiful park bordering on upper Glen street, stands an imposing marble shaft, surmounted by a golden star and in the base of which are two compartments. The star is emblematic of the mark used by Mr. Crandall while engaged in the lumbering business and in one of the compartments, marked with the intials "H C," the body of Mr. Crandall will be laid to rest. In the other compartment appear Mrs. Crandall's initials, and it is here that she, when finally death claims its own, will be interred.

Funeral arrangements have not been completed but the obsequies will probably be tomorrow or Saturday, there being some delay owing to the necessity of procuring a special casket to go in the sepulcher in the base of the monument. It is expected that all business places in the city will close during the hour of the funeral.

-142-

MR. TAFT BECOMES A PRIVATE CITIZEN.

William Howard Taft has become again a private citizen. With a smile that was as genuine as his life he turned over the honors and the responsibilities of the presidential office to Woodrow Wilson, his successor, on Tuesday. He will take a few weeks of vacation in the South, and then go to New Haven, Conn., where he will get ready to become Professor Taft.

It is not the purpose of this article to review the work of the administration of President Taft, nor to fix its place in the history into which it has gone. It is simply to point out one or two things that are patent to all intelligent Americans.

Has anyone heard of Mr. Taft uttering a word of complaint over his defeat last November? Has anyone known of a sour look crossing his face over the fact that his party divided and let him down between the factions? On the contrary, Mr. Taft has been as great in his acceptance of the situation as he has been great in all his twenty-five years of service in an official capacity for his country. He has proved himself to be big brained, big hearted, generous, kind; and historians will write him down as one of our great presidents. He has gone out of office with the plaudits of men of all parties, without bitterness, without desire for revenge, but with a determination to devote himself, his wide experience and his great abilities to the good of his country.

FEBRUARY.

Though other months of fairer days
  Were well in line,
On February Fate bestowed
  Saint Valentine.

As though that gift was not enough
  When it was done,
She further gave the bobtailed month
  George Washington.

Not yet content, she deeper piled
  Her wreath so brave
And generous to little Feb.
  Great Lincoln gave.

Then jealously the months remarked:
  "How well it fits,
That adage old which teaches us
  'Them that has gits.'"
    —McLandsburg Wilson.

Jim Gates Settles in Hudson Falls.

James Gates, a well-known barber of Warrensburgh and Lake George, has settled permanently in Hudson Falls, where he has bought from M. B. Newman the three-chair shop at 37 Main street, known as the Terence Conway stand.

news Jan 9 1913

WARREN COUNTY'S OLDEST RESIDENT

Mrs. Mary Sage Will Tomorrow Celebrate Her One Hundred Third Anniversary

1. 1913,

HAS ALL HER FACULTIES

Mrs. Mary Sage, Warren county's oldest resident and probably the oldest woman in New York state, will tomorrow celebrate her one hundred and third birthday anniversary in her home in Darrowsville, a small hamlet of Chestertown. The occasion will be observed in a quiet manner and only a few relatives and near friends will be gathered about the aged woman.

Mrs. Sage, whose maiden name was Mary Prescott, was born in Sommersetshire, England, February 2, 1810. There she met and married Courtney Sage, who died several years ago. Mr. and Mrs. Sage and four children, among them her oldest surviving son, Courtney Sage of this city, came to America in 1849 and after one year in New York, removed to Darrowsville, where she has since resided.

Mrs. Sage was the mother of twelve children, five of whom are now living and residing in this county. Courtney Sage, who lives in South street, this city, is the eldest, being seventy-five years of age and a veteran of the Civil war. Next in order are John Sage of Miller Hill, William Sage of Darrowsville, Mrs. Mary Hastings of Warrensburg and Frank Sage of Darrowsville. Frank is the youngest of all the children born to Mrs. Sage, and is fifty years old.

Mrs. Sage is a descendant of a family of longevity, her father having lived until within one or two years of the century mark. She was one of fifteen children, all of whom, with the exception of two who met accidental deaths, lived to be over seventy years of age. She has a brother, the youngest of her immediate family, living in England. While she does not know his exact age, she thinks he is nearly ninety years old.

Mrs. Sage was recently a guest of her son, Courtney, and while here she stated it was her first visit to Glens Falls in twenty-five years. She repeatedly expressed her wonder at the many great changes that had taken place in the city and admitted that she did not recall a single familiar sight. On her way to this city she saw and rode on a trolley car for the first time in her life, and while here was treated to her first view of animated pictures. She also had her first ride in an automobile.

Mrs. Sage is enjoying good health and performs all the arduous duties of the housewoman in her Darrowsville home, washing and ironing once a week.

BARBER'S BAY FIRE DESTROYS COTTAGE

Star Feb 8. 1913

Building Owned By O. J. Mason Goes Up in Smoke— Losses $4,500

A fire, discovered at 7.30 o'clock last evening and believed to have originated from a wood fire in the dining room, destroyed the cottage at Barber's Bay, two miles north of Katskill may, on Lake George. The building was owned by Orlando J. Mason of Harrisena and was conducted last year by Alfred Starks of this city as a summer boarding house. Mr. Starks was at the lake yesterday making preparations for the opening of the house this season and after dark went to the McCabe cottage nearby.

Some time later he saw the blaze at a distance and with neighbors rushed to the scene to save whatever property possible. The building was a mass of flames when they arrived and only a dress suit case and a few small pieces of furniture on the ground floor could be saved.

The cottage had accommodations for about fifty boarders. It was a wooden structure, valued at $3,500 and was nearly entirely covered by insurance. Mr. Starks had $500 insurance on the contents, which were valued at $1,000.

Navigation Records Broken.

Navigation records of eighty years standing have been broken on the Hudson river. On Wednesday of last week the trips of the river boats from Albany to New York marked the 288th day of the season and broke the record of thirty years. The trip Monday night shattered the eighty-year record and the boats are still running. Last year the closing date was January 3.
news Jan 16/1913

"Jack" Smith Settled in New Home.

Mr. and Mrs. John G. Smith have moved into their new residence at the corner of Hudson street and Woodward avenue. The building has been in course of construction for more than two years, and is unquestionably the finest house in Warrensburgh. The greater part of the lumber in it was personally selected by Mr. Smith and much of it he sawed himself from the logs. The fittings are of the finest and no pains were spared with the workmanship. It would be difficult, indeed to build a more perfect house than is this in every respect. *Star Feb 20 1913*

TO SEARCH EUROPE FOR BROOD MARES

Star Feb 12. 1913

Representatives of Adirondack Farms Will Sail Tomorrow On Important Trip

Two representatives of the Adirondack Farms will leave this morning for New York from which port they will sail tomorrow for an extended business visit in Europe. While away they will visit many foreign countries, inspecting and purchasing the best obtainable heavy and registered mares, to be shipped for breeding purposes to the Adirondack Farm at the mile track.

A consignment of mares reached this city yesterday and the animals were at once taken to the Mile track stables and placed in their winter quarters. There were eighteen in number, the majority being the Belgian-breed. They were purchased in Indiana and each weighs from 1,400 to 1,800 pounds.

Fire at Edgecomb Pond.

Jamon McDonald's house on the shore of Edgecomb pond, in the town of Bolton, caught fire Sunday afternoon and was considerably damaged before the flames were extinguished by a bucket brigade composed of neighbors who promptly responded to an alarm. The blaze, which started in the upper story, was probably caused by an overheated stovepipe or a defective chimney. Mr. McDonald and Mr. and Mrs. Alexander Burch, who live with him, are at present staying at the home of F. G. Palmer.

BOTH MEN HAPPY

Dr. M. D. Smith appeared yesterday on the streets with his new five passenger Carter touring car, which he purchased from the Glens Falls Automobile company. The machine of the 1913 model, is a self starter and equipped by electric lights and friction drive, the latter eliminating all gears. It should be added the physician is just as happy as M. J. Gray of the selling company. *Star Apl 5-1913*

IGERNA. *Dec 4 1913*

Walter E. Gates, of Bolton Landing, drove to this place Monday.

Watson Hammond is moving his household goods from the Prosser place into Myron Clark's house.

Mr. and Mrs. Joseph Kenne, of Newcomb, spent Thanksgiving day here with Mrs. Kenne's parents. Mr. and Mrs. Louis Wood.

EDWIN J. WORDEN HAS NARROW ESCAPE

In Race His Boat "Zero" Hits Thin Ice and Injures Owner

Star Feb 5 - 1913

THIGH BADLY LACERATED

(Special to The Post-Star.)

LAKE GEORGE, Feb. 4.—Edwin J. Worden, proprietor of the local Arlington hotel, miraculously escaped serious injury this afternoon on Lake George, while sailing in his iceboat, "Zero," which he was racing against his boat "Jack," and which was handled by August Wilson. He was taking all possible advantage of the high wind and in pursuing as direct a course to the goal as possible, he sailed so close to where the lake was not frozen the forward runners of his boat broke through the thin ice.

As the boat was travelling at nearly a mile a minute, Mr. Worden was thrown with great force against the stearing wheel and one of his thighs was lacerated badly, a four inch incision being inflicted. "Zero" came out of the accident uninjured and, with the assistance of some spectators standing near, Mr. Worden fastened rope to the forward part of the craft and hauled it onto the thicker ice.

Although suffering considerable pain, Mr. Worden resumed the sailing. The "Zero" is a graceful boat and spectators to the afternoon's sport rejoiced that it was not materially damaged and that the owner had escaped more serious injury. Besides the two boats belonging to Mr. Worden, the Fort William Henry hotel had two other fast ones on the ice.

The ice races, which were to have been held yesterday, today and tomorrow, were postponed until February 18, 19 and 20, owing to the thinness of the ice.

MAKES BED QUILT IN 86TH YEAR

Times Feb 12. 1913

Mrs. Stokes Ellsworth, who resides at 7 Basin street and who celebrated her eighty-sixth birthday last October, has just completed a bed quilt which she cut and sewed together without help. The aged woman has been at her task for the past two months and is highly elated over her prowess with the scissors and needle. The quilt contains 1,050 pieces.

LEONARD BIBBEY TAKEN BY DEATH

Well Known Man Succumbs in His Home in Fort Edward

Feb 1. 1913

PNEUMONIA ATTACK FATAL

The Grim Reaper took one of the best known men in northern New York at 4 o'clock yesterday afternoon when Leonard Bibbey, of the firm of Bibbey & Ferguson of this city, died at his home in Fort Edward. He had been ill of pneumonia for some time and for the last week his condition was regarded as extremely critical.

Mr. Bibbey was born in England fifty-nine years ago and came to the United States at an early age. With G. Fred Ferguson he established the firm of Bibbey & Ferguson in 1881. He resided here until 1890 when he moved to Fort Edward, where he established the brewing company of Bibbey & McNaughton, with which he was actively engaged at the time of his death. The high esteem in which he was held by his fellow townsmen was indicated by the fact that the Bibbey Hose company was named after him.

Harry Bolton Buys "Bill" Swan's Farm.

Harry Bolton has bought William H. Swan's farm, formerly known as the Truman Everts place, on the river road some distance above the county home. There is about 200 acres of fertile land, much of it heavily timbered. The purchase price is understood to be about $5,000. The farm is considered one of the best in this section. Mr. Bolton, who retired from the hotel business last fall, moved on to the place yesterday.

HURT AT LAKE GEORGE, VICTIM DIES IN ALBANY

Star Feb 6 1913

LAKE GEORGE, Feb. 5.—Information was received here today of the death this morning in the home of his father in Albany, of Samuel D. Emery, son of John W. Emery. The young man's death was due to injuries which resulted from a fall while he was riding horseback at his father's camp at Lake George last July. Since then he had made a hard but hopeless fight for recovery.

He was twenty-five years of age, and a graduate of William college.

—144—

ABRAHAM LINCOLN.

Feb 28. 1913

Star Apl 8 1913

Bolton Landing, April 6—Chief Engineer John W. Moore, U. S. N., retired, who died at his home in Ridgewood, N. J., March 30, was born in New York in 1832, and entered the navy as a third assistant engineer in 1853. He was on the Niagara in the Atlantic cable expedition in 1857. From 1861 to 1863 he served in the West Gulf Blocading squadron, and later, in New York, as superintendent of ironclads. He was on the frigate Franklin as fleet engineer on the staff of Admiral Farragut in 1867. Later he served on the old Hartford, and was retired in May, 1894. Chief Engineer Moore had the rank of Rear Admiral on the retired list of the navy. Mr. Moore originated the method of vessels of Farragut's fleet in the Civil war, protecting their side with chain cable. He also was the first to cover vessels with a muddy paint, to make them less conspicuous targets. He fought at the capture of Forts Jackson and St. Philip, at the capture of Vicksburg and New Orleans, and took part in the action against the Confederate ram, Arkansas. Rear Admiral Moore was a member of the Massachusetts Society of the Cincinnati and the Military Order of the Loyal Legion. He was commander of the California branch of the Order of the Loyal Legion and a member of George Washington Post, G. A. R., the Veteran Corps of Artillery, a society dating from the war of 1812, and the Sons of the American Revolution. Admiral Moore had made his home in Bolton Landing for the past twenty years or more. He was much respected and well liked by all. A widow, three daughters and one son survive him. Funeral services were held at his late residence, Park Slope, Ridgewood, N. J., and later services were here in St. Sacrament church. Interment was made in Bolton Landing.

SCORES HAVE A NARROW ESCAPE FROM WATERY GRAVE WHEN BIG SUSPENSION BRIDGE FALLS INTO RAGING HUDSON

G.F. Times Mar 1 28

1913

With a crash that struck terror to the hearts of pedestrians, the big steel suspension bridge which spans the Hudson at the foot of Glen street hill, was washed away at 9:55 o'clock last night, and as the huge structure tumbled into the raging torrents below a cry of horror went up from onlookers, scores of whom had barely escaped a watery grave.

Narrow Escapes.

Maurice Roach, a resident of Saranac Lake, who is visiting his sister, Mrs. Charles Bennett, in South Glens Falls, had reached the archway near the South Glens Falls end of the bridge when he heard the noise of twisting steel. Looking back he saw the huge structure swaying and hastening his steps had barely reached a place of safety when the crash came. Not twenty feet in front of him was Clarence MacMaster of South Glens Falls, homeward bound from a visit in this city.

Brilliant Electrical Display.

As the bridge went tumbling into the river scores of electric wires were cut asunder and for a few moments there was a brilliant electrical display which made the place as light as day. Then came darkness and with it increased horror until it became definitely known that the two pedestrians who but a minute or so before had taken their lives in their hands had passed safely over.

Women Escape Death.

Among those who narrowly escaped death are Mrs. Jane Welcome of this city and Mrs. James Davidson of Warrensburg, both of whom had gone to the river to view the high water. It was their intention to cross over to South Glens Falls but when within about fifteen feet of the bridge the structure gave way. Almost overcome with fright the two women beat a hurried retreat and today have not fully recovered from the excitement.

Good Work by Police.

Like wildfire the report spread throughout the city that the bridge had gone and within ten minutes after the catastrophie occurred hundreds of sight-seers were working their way down the river hill only to be halted near the junction of Berry street by the police who were quick to take the situation in hand and who are deserving of unlimited praise for the masterly manner in which they handled a most persistent crowd.

A Vivid Description.

Henry W. Batterson, a commercial traveler from Springfield, Mass., was an eye witness to the falling of the bridge and when the crash came was less than twenty feet away, having just passed over from South Glens Falls. In an interview today Mr. Batterson gave a vivid description of the sweeping away of the bridge, speaking as follows:

"A few seconds before the bridge fell I had crossed over from South Glens Falls, and all the way I could feel the swaying of the structure. Hardly had I left the bridge when I heard a creaking noise. Looking backward I saw the big bridge heave upward in the middle and drop into the river below, taking with it dozens of electric light wires which, when short-circuited, made the place as light as day. Fearing that I might come in contact with some of the fallen wires, I stood still probably for three or four minutes until a watchman with a lantern piloted me to a place of safety."

Wrecked Structure Located.

A few minutes after the bridge collapsed a searchlight was brought into play in an effort to locate the fallen structure, but it was not until this morning that sections of the steel work were located around the bend, 150 yards down the river.

Traffic Prohibited.

Since early morning yesterday it was generally believed that the bridge was doomed, and shortly before noon all unnecessary traffic was stopped. At 8 o'clock the impending danger had increased to an extent such that only pedestrians were allowed to pass, and then not without being warned of the danger which confronted them. Gradually the bridge assumed more distorted proportions, and at 6 o'clock its destruction was looked upon as a matter of only a few hours at the longest.

Since early morning thousands of sightseers have visited the scene of the catastrophe, and employes of the various telephone and electric companies have been busily engaged making repairs.

SEEKING HERE FOR DEAD MAN'S RELATIVES

Star Mar 21, 1913.

A Mr. Waddell of Johnsburg was in this village yesterday seeking relatives of a William Pettys, whose body is believed to have been picked up Sunday in the Hudson river near New Baltimore. The body corresponds in many respects to that of a William Pettys, who at one time resided in this vicinity. One eye was gone and there was a scar on the forehead, identical to the one possessed by Mr. Pettys. In the dead man's pockets were two letters, one addressed to Mr. Waddell and the other to Mr. Pettys. George Podvin is a nephew of the Mr. Pettys referred to, but he was unable to direct Mr. Waddell to any nearer relatives.

ROOT BURIED TODAY

March 2 1913 G Times

Masons to Conduct Funeral of Prominent Glens Falls Man.

Special to The Knickerbocker Press.

GLENS FALLS, March 1.—Funeral services for Adelbert F. Root, Sr., who died Friday, will take place at his home in Church street tomorrow afternoon. Mr. Root fell on a slippery sidewalk Thursday, bursting a blood vessel at the base of the brain. The funeral will be conducted by Senate lodge 456, F. and A. M., of which Mr. Root was a prominent member.

Corinth Hotel Has New Proprietor.

The Central hotel at Corinth has been sold by Alfred T. Mallory to William Johnston, of Horicon, who took possession last week. Mr. Johnston is an experienced hotel man, having successfully conducted the Central house at Horicon for a number of years. *news April 18, 1913.*

New York, April 7.

To Farmer Smith, the silver-tongued orator and scientific soil-tickler, greeting. May his shadow never grow less and may he live to eat the hen that scratches over his grave.

GEORGE M'DONALD IS EIGHTY YEARS OLD

Made "Log Drives" With Henry Crandall More Than Half Century Ago

"LAST LEFT OF OLD CROWD"

Star Feb 22 1910

While the remains of Henry Crandall lay cold in death, yesterday his life long friend and companion of the river drives of long ago, George Mac-Donald, celebrated the eightieth anniversary of his birth in quiet fashion in his Third street home.

Over fifty years ago Mr. MacDonald began to "make log drives" down the river from the north woods and for fourteen years Henry Crandall was a member of the party and Mr. MacDonald's companion. On one of the drives, which was over ten days in duration, the two men camped together, sleeping side by side in a tent during the long nights, preparing their meals together over a camp fire during the day and passing practically every minute in each other's company.

The last meeting of the two took place during the latter part of last summer near Mr. Crandall's residence. The aged men chatted over an hour, the principal topic of their conversation being the old days of the river drives. "George, we are about the last of the old crowd that are left," said Mr. Crandall.

After fourteen years "driving" down the river, Mr. MacDonald took up lumbering with Charles Gilchrist at Shelving Rock. He remained there until about fifteen years ago, when he purchased a farm in Corinth, from which place he moved to this city a year ago yesterday, taking up his residence in the home he purchased and now occupies in Third street.

Mr. MacDonald is in excellent health. His wife, who is seventy-eight years of age, is his sole companion. Both are active and able to work about the house. Mr MacDonald did considerable work of an agricultural nature last summer and is planning the planting and care of four acres of land this season in addition to the planting and care of four gardens about the city.

• A wealthy American girl was attending a social function at a country house in England.

"You American girls have not such healthy complexions as we have," said an English duchess to the girl. "I always wonder why our noblemen take a fancy to your white faces."

"It isn't our white faces that attracts them,' responded the American; "it's our green backs."

Local Men Attend Costly Banquet.

The Hon. L. W. Emerson, of Warrensburgh, and Manager Albert Thieriot, of the Fort William Henry hotel, Lake George, on Wednesday evening of last week attended an elaborate banquet of the second panel of sheriff's jury, held at the Hotel Knickerbocker, New York, at which the assessment was sixty dollars a plate. Among the other prominent men of Northern New York present were Clifford S. Sims, vice president of the Delaware and Hudson company; George F. Underwood, of the International Paper company, and Louis C. Duval, president of the Manhattan Steamboat Line. The total number of guests was more than 450. The banquet was served on the famous solid gold service of the Hotel Knickerbocker.

GEORGE W. SISSON DIES IN POTSDAM

Feb 4 1918 Star

(Continued from page 1.)

In Glen street on the site of Veile's drug store. This building was destroyed in the big fire in 1864. He conducted a drug business here until 1867 when he sold out to Havilands & Ferriss.

He then went to Potsdam, where he became engaged in the lumber business. He became associated with Augustus Sherman of this city under the firm name of A. Sherman Lumber company. Later he purchased Mr. Sherman's interest and continued the business with his five sons. In 1889 he organized the Racquette River Paper company.

Five Lads Have Saved $37.50 to Which Late Philanthropist Added $63.50 as Gift.

Special to The Knickerbocker Press.
GLENS FALLS, March 1.—Joseph R. Duell, manager of the Crandall Boys' Savings club has made the first report of the standing of the members of the organization which is in a flourishing condition. Five members of the club have succeeded in obtaining the required $37.50 to which amount Mr. Crandall added the remainder to bring the total up to $100 which will become their own to do with as they see fit when they attain their majority. The report as submitted by Mr. Duell follows:

The Crandall Boys' Savings club was organized January 1, 1911, with one hundred members and there have been twenty-eight changes in the club up to date. One boy left to join the boy scouts, two withdrew on account of moving out of the city and four left without giving any reason; one was instantly killed by an automobile on Miller Hill and twenty were dropped because they failed to live up to the rules of the club.

The vacancies have been filled with other boys with the exception of James Clements who has moved away. His place will be given to another boy as there are many boys waiting to become members of the club.

MILES BAKER GETS LIFE PENSION

Post Star April 18th 1913

Swift & Company Reward Long and Faithful Service of Local Man

IN HARNESS THIRTY YEARS

Veteran of Civil War Engaged Since Boyhood in Meat Business—Honorably Retires On Half Pay

Swift & Company have rewarded the faithful service of Miles Baker of this city, who the last thirty years has been connected with the firm's local station in a managerial capacity, by honorably discharging him from active labor and granting him a pension at half pay during the remainder of his life.

AUTOIST RIDES DOWN MR. BULL

April 7 1918

The police have been asked to find the automobile driver, who early last evening ran down and wrecked a bicycle ridden by G. N. Bull of this city. The latter was on his way home from work and was spilled from his bike almost in front of the Belvedere restaurant, Glen street. Eye witnesses say the auto was steered by its only occupant, a young man who apparently made no effort to prevent the machine running upon Mr. Bull. The bicycle's rear wheel was demolished and as it was drawn to one side, the car was speeded up and was quickly out of sight. That the driver made no effort to ascertain the extent of the damage he caused, greatly incensed several spectators. The license plate on the car is thought to have been issued in Massachusetts and it carries the figure number 2461. Mr. Bull made a complaint at police headquarters.

Mar 20 1918 News

JOHN A. STEVENS.

John A. Stevens, for many years one of the proprietors of the Stevens house, at Lake Placid, and one of the most prominent hotel men in the Adirondacks, died at his home on Tuesday evening of last week of pneumonia. He was about sixty-five years old

WILL END WORK HERE THIS WEEK

County Sealer Pasco to Pass About Three Days More in This City

WILL THEN GO UP-COUNTY

Finds Surprisingly Small Number of Weights and Measures Not Up to Standard in Glens Falls

Clayton L. Pasco, county sealer of weights and measures, will this week complete the work of inspecting the weights and measures in Glens Falls. He started on his semi-annual round of local stores about a month ago and has about three more days' work ahead of him in this city. After leaving here, Mr. Pasco, and his assistant, Ira Chase, will go up the county, visiting Lake George, Warrensburg, Bolton, Chestertown and other places.

Mr. Pasco in his trip around to the different stores in Glens Falls, found surprisingly few of weights and measures which were not up to standard. One man was arrested for having a container with a false bottom, but aside from this one case, the stores generally were found to be free of short weighs or measures. In one instance, however, Mr. Pasco found a pair of scales, the mechanism of which had been injured so that the proprietor was giving overweight.

Mr. Pasco expects to find the conditions about the same up the county as in Glens Falls.

The work of the sealer is no easy matter. It requires considerable time in one store, the visits in some establishments often lasting as long as three hours. No store, no matter how large or small, is ignored and each receives a visit from the official.

Times Mar 19, 1913

BOLTON LANDING HAS MOVING PICTURE SHOW

Paul Fosmer and Robert Duell of Bolton Landing have purchased a Powers' moving picture machine from Joe Miller and have opened a moving picture theatre in their home village. The theatre has been named the "Navajo," and will feature none but the best pictures obtainable. The venture is meeting with unexpected success.

WM. H. BURNETT IS CLAIMED BY DEATH

State Game Protector Dies at His Home at French Mountain of Heart Trouble

State Game Protector William H. Burnett of Lake George died this morning at 6:30 o'clock at his home at French Mountain. He had not been feeling well during the past few days. During the night he had trouble with his heart and this morning expired.

Mr. Burnett was seventy-three years old and had been engaged as a game protector since 1875, when he was appointed protector for the town of Queensbury.

He was appointed special state protector when the state conservation commission was organized and since the Lake George Protective association was organized in 1885 he has been active in protecting the game of this part of the state. He had charge of the protectors employed by the organization. In point of service Mr. Burnett was one of the oldest protectors in the state.

About two months ago Chief Game Protector Llewellyn Legge of the conservation commission advanced Mr. Burnett to the first grade of protectors.

THURSDAY, APRIL 10 *1913*

LIFE LOST IN A FIRE

William Merrill Perishes in Store Building at Bakers Mills

CHARRED BODY FOUND IN RUINS

Blaze Probably Started from Lantern Man Was Carrying About While Intoxicated — Rumors of Arson and Suicide are Discredited

William Merrill, for many years a prominent business man and leading citizen of the little hamlet of Bakers Mills, in the town of Johnsburgh, was burned to death shortly after 1 o'clock Tuesday morning in a fire which destroyed his store and residence building and the barn a few feet in the rear. Mrs. Merrill and her nephew, Edgar Cole, who were asleep in the upper story, barely escaped with their lives.

Mr. Merrill had been sleeping for some time in the store and it was there the fire started. It is believed to have caught from a lantern the man was carrying about the building during the night while he was intoxicated.

BODY FOUND IN RIVER.

The body of a man supposed to be William Petteys, at one time a resident of Warrensburg, was found recently in the Hudson river near New Baltimore. Two letters in a pocket one addressed to Mr. Petteys and the other to a Mr. Waddell, one eye gone and a scar on the forehead are the identifications. Mr. Waddell has been trying to locate the man's family. William Petteys married Hattie Morrison at Wells, Hamilton county, and they had two children, Willie and Mabel. Mr. Petteys worked in Warrensburg in the factory about twelve years ago, making his home with his sister, the late Mrs. L. N. Beach. *11/9/18*

JOSEPH LA FLURE DIES WHILE SEATED IN CHAIR

Mar 28, 1913

Joseph LaFlure, one of the best and most widely known lumbermen in Northern New York, died at 8:30 o'clock last night while seated in a chair in his home in Chester. He was talking to his daughter, Mrs. C. W. Kittenbach, when he suddenly threw up his hands and fell backward, dead. Mr. LaFlure was seventy-three years old and had lived in the town of Chester thirty-two years. He was born in Canada in 1840. While a resident of Chester established for himself an enviable reputation as a business man.

FIGHTING FOR LICENSE

Star — Apl 19, 1913

Attorney Beecher S. Clother, acting in the interests of Mrs. Sarah A. Streeter, owner of the Phoenix hotel, Hague, has served notice on County Treasurer Sprague and State Commissioner of Excise Farley that application has been made by him to County Judge Raley for a writ of certiorari to compel the county treasurer to issue a liquor license to Mrs. Streeter. The matter is returnable April 22 before Judge Raley. County Attorney Davis will appear for Mr. Sprague.

News Feb 27, 1913

Large Purchase of Timberland.

The Finch-Pruyn company, of Glens Falls, has added a large tract of timberland to its holdings in the Adirondacks by the purchase of 63,000 acres from the McIntyre Iron company in Essex county. The company will cut only trees eight inches or more in diameter, thus leaving a continued growth and certain seed trees will also be left standing. The logs will supply the timber for the company's new steam saw mill. The company now controls 250,000 acres of timber land

STEEL BRIDGE IN SERVICE 23 YRS

G. F. Sweetser 28

HUGE STRUCTURE WAS CONSTRUCTED AT A COST OF 9,000 DOLARS.

1913

NEVER GAVE SATISFACTION

IRON TRUSSES ADDED SOME YEARS AGO, EXTENDING NEARLY TO ROCKS BELOW—HAD SWAYED FOR YEARS.

The big steel bridge, which for twenty-three years has spanned the river between this city and South Glens Falls and which unable to stand the pressure of the high water and rushing logs, collapsed last night, was built at a cost of $9,000.

From the time the bridge was built it had never given complete satisfaction, owing to the fact that the people did not consider it sufficiently strong. The structure was built by the Berlin Iron Bridge Company of East Berlin, Conn.

At the time the bridge contract was awarded the company, there was considerable opposition brought to bear against the company, on the ground that the bridge, when completed, would not give satisfaction. As a result the bridge has been considered weak and a few years ago it was strengthened and later with a view to making it still stronger, several iron trusses were placed underneath the bridge, reaching almost to the rocks below.

The bridge was never strong enough for the large amount of traffic that it was called upon to carry. For years it sagged and swayed when persons crossed at it the same time cars were going over it.

The building of the steel bridge, which was completed during the month of March, 1890, was considered a very important event, as it replaced an old lattice-covered bridge which for years had been an eyesore to the traveling public.

A. J. Robinson was highway commissioner of the town of Moreau at the time the bridge was built and the commissioners of the town of Queensbury were George Connery, George Ashton and Andrew Moore.

BODY OF HENRY CRANDALL PLACED IN FAMILY CRYPT

Feb 22 1913

Fully 2,000 Friends View Remains at the Late Home in Glen Street.

Encased in a solid copper casket, the remains of Henry Crandall were placed in the family crypt in the base of the gigantic monument in Crandall Park this afternoon. The committal services were attended by several hundred persons, who accompanied the remains from the home in Glen street. As soon as the body had been placed in the crypt taps were sounded by Stuart Crandall Mason, bugler of the Crandall Boys' Saving Club. The funeral services at the house were of a private character, with the Rev. Oliver S. Newell, rector of the Church of the Messiah officiating.

Many View Remains.

During the hours that the body lay in state, from 11 to 1 o'clock, fully 2,000 persons passed through the house and viewed the remains. Among this large number of friends and admirers of Mr. Crandall were large delegations representing E. M. Wing Post, G. A. R., the Woman's Relief Corps, Sons of Veterans, Spanish War Veterans and a host of business men and city officials.

As soon as the casket was borne from the house to the hearse the Crandall Boys' Saving Club with its fife and drum corps assumed the position of escort and led the way to the park.

Honorary Bearers.

The honorary bearers were Dr. Sherman Williams, Colonel John L. Cunningham, Thomas S. Coolidge, Louis M. Brown, Charles F. Everest, Charles W. Minahan, Henry E. Nichols, Louis P. Juvet and George Leggett.

The burial place of Mr. Crandall is perhaps one of the most unique ever devised. The crypt is arranged for one other body, and that is the aged widow. It was Mr. Crandall's wish in life that they lie side by side after life's journey had been completed. For fifty-four years they had traveled together and in arranging the crypt it was planned that both caskets should be side by side after Mrs. Crandall joins her husband in death.

Design of Casket.

The casket in which Mr. Crandall's remains are encased is covered with the finest black broadcloth. The interior is of heavy plain satin, and the mountings are of oxydized silver. The design of the casket is square with ornate corners.

The monument which marks the resting place of Mr. Crandall was erected in 1899. The shaft is nearly forty feet high and is of pentagonal shape. It is surmounted by a five-pointed bronze star, which is recognized as the log mark used by Mr. Crandall in his lumber operations nearly fifty years ago. Each point of the star is studded with an incandescent light which at night will illuminate the last resting place of the "Grand Old Man of Glens Falls."

MRS. RICHARDS' SISTER DAYTON FLOOD PRISONER

P Slander 2 1913

Mrs. Frederick B. Richards is just in receipt of a letter from a sister who was marooned three days in the third story of a hotel in Dayton, Ohio. As the water was up to the second story, the food supply was necessarily scanty and like the rhyme of the Ancient Mariner, there was "water, water everywhere, and not a drop to drink" except what rain water they could catch or by melting the snow on the roof. With this they made tea and cocoa over an alcohol lamp which one of the party happened to have. When the flood subsided, a dead horse was found to have floated into the bar-room of the hotel.

SAM GINSBERG TO MARRY NEXT WEEK

1913

Manager of Park Theatre to Wed Fair Daughter of Oil City, Pa.

Samuel Ginsberg, the popular manager of the Park theatre, will leave today for Oil City, Pa., where next Tuesday night he will be united in marriage to Miss Minnie Cohen. The ceremony will be performed in the Jewish Temple at 6:30 o'clock and a reception will follow in a large hall. The ceremonies will be attended by many friends of the young couple.

-148-

THURMAN TEAMSTER INJURED.

news Mar 13, 1913

George Dow Caught Between Logs and Tree Has Four Ribs Broken.

George Dow, a Thurman teamster, employed by Watson Everts, had four ribs broken and sustained internal injuries in an accident which occurred at that place Monday morning

Dow was drawing a heavy load of logs on a wagon from the Alvin Harris place in Athol to the Hudson river. Reaching an icy place where the road inclined toward a sloping bank he whipped up his horses and succeeded in getting the front wheels over the dangerous place, but the rear ones slewed and carried the wagon over the bank.

The load tipped over and Dow was pinned between the heavy logs and a tree. Mr. Everts, who was near by, went to his assistance and removed the logs from the unconscious man. He was taken to the home of Thomas Coyle the nearest residence, where he was attended by Dr. J. M. Griffin, of this place.

One of the man's ribs was torn loose from the backbone and another was broken in two places. Though he was also injured internally nothing serious of that nature has yet developed and his recovery is expected.

FORMER RESIDENT DROWNED.

news Mar 22 1913

Body of William Petteys Found In Hudson River Near New Baltimore.

William Petteys, a former resident of Warrensburgh, about fifty-five years old, was drowned in the Hudson river some time ago and his body was found last week near New Baltimore.

In a pocket of the dead man's coat there was two letters, one addressed to William Petteys and the other to Jabez Waddell, of Johnsburgh. Mr. Waddell was notified and his son, Delbert Waddell, went to New Baltimore and viewed the body. By means of a scar on the forehead and a missing eye, as well as the general appearance, and also by the letters in his possession the body was positively identified by Mr. Waddell as that of Mr. Petteys who formerly resided in Johnsburgh and was well known to the Waddells. The body had evidently been in the water several weeks and how it got there is a mystery which cannot be solved.

Petteys married Hattie Morrison, of Wills, Hamilton county, and they had two children, Willie and Mabel. Mr. Waddell has been endeavoring to locate the family, but is unable to do so.

It was about ten years ago that Petteys lived in Warrensburgh. He was employed in the shirt factory and made his home with his sister, the late Mrs. L. N. Beach.

MISS JANE NICHOLS.

Miss Jane Nichols, seventy-five years old and a life-long resident of Lake George, was found dead in bed at her home on Canada street about 4:30 o'clock Monday afternoon. She had been ill more than a year. Three sisters and three brothers survive her— Miss Lorene Nichols, Mrs. Eliza Brown, Miss Eva Nichols, Sidney and Melvin Nichols, of Lake George, and Henry E. Nichols, of Glens Falls and Shelving Rock, Lake George; also two nieces, Mrs. Charles Martindale, of Lake George, and Mrs. George Caswell, of Cohoes, B. C.

The Fortune He Left.

New York, April 1.—Estimates of the fortune left by J. P. Morgan, as made in the financial district to-day, range from $75,000,000 to $300,000,000, this sum including his art collections. It is understood that the financier's will is of comparatively recent date, but no intimation has been made as to when it will be given to the public. Mr. Morgan's personal counsel declines to discuss the matter.

GEORGE STREETER.

news May 8

George Streeter, proprietor of the Phoenix hotel, at Hague, died Saturday evening after an illness extending over several years. He was about forty-five years old. The surviving relatives are his widow, one sister, of Hague, and three brothers, Eugene, Scott and Robert Streeter. The funeral was held Tuesday morning at 10 o'clock. *1913*

A GENTLEMAN.

I knew him for a gentleman
   By signs that never fail;
His coat was rough and rather worn,
   His cheeks were thin and pale—
A lad who had his way to make,
   With little time to play;
I knew him for a gentleman
   By certain signs today.

He met his mother on the street,
   Off came his little cap,
My door was shut, he waited there
   Until I heard a rap,
He took the bundle from my hand;
   And when I dropped my pen
He sprang to pick it up for me,
   This gentleman of ten.

He does not push or crowd along,
   His voice is gently pitched;
He does not fling his looks about
   As if he were bewitched,
He stands aside to let you pass;
   He always shuts the door,
He runs on errands willingly
   To forge and mill and store.

He thinks of you before himself,
   He serves you if he can;
In whatever company
   The manners make the man.
At ten or forty—'tis the same.
   The manners tell the tale,
And I discern the gentleman
   By signs that never fail.
          —The Christian Instructor.

HENRY CRANDALL.

The pioneer Adirondack lumberman and philanthropist of Glens Falls, who died last week Wednesday at his home in Glens Falls a few days after his ninety-second birthday. Mr. Crandall was born at East Lake George February 13, 1821, and his early life was marked by hard work on farms and in the open. He was thrifty, however, and at thirty-one years of age accomplished his ambition to some time "have a thousand dollars." He invested that amount with John J. Harris and a Mr. Finch in a lumber tract in the Boreas River section of the Adirondacks and retired soon after the Civil War a wealthy man. At the time of his death he was a large holder of real estate and his wealth was estimated at from $1,000,000 to $2,000,000. His public and private benefactions were large, and he was noted for his philanthropy, though his giving was usually most unostentatious. He was most generous to the village of Glens Falls, giving Crandall Park and another smaller park to the municipality and he also cared for the soldiers' monument in the town of Queensbury. His wife, who was Miss Hattie Waters of Horicon and whom he married fifty-four years ago, survives. Mr. Crandall was buried in one of the two compartments under an imposing marble shaft which he had erected in Crandall Park. The shaft is surmounted by a star, the emblem used by Mr. Crandall as a lumber mark. The above portrait of Mr. Crandall was photographed on his ninetieth birthday.

WILLIAM O. TERRY.

news May 1. 1913

William O. Terry, lessee and landlord of the Bolton house, on lower Main street, died Sunday evening shortly after 9 o'clock after only two hours illness of cerebral hemorrhage. He was apparently in good health until about 7 o'clock in the evening when he complained of severe pains in his head. Two physicians were at once summoned, but could afford no relief. The Rev. Father Livingstone was also called from Lake George and administered the last sacraments of the Catholic church. Mr. Terry was forty-one,

LINCOLN'S ASSASSIN

nem Smar 13, 1913

Story of Pursuit and Capture of John Wilkes Booth

TOLD BY ONE OF HIS PURSUERS

Private John W. Millington, Who Enlisted at
Chestertown, Gives Graphic Descrip-
tion of His Part In Historic
Affair and Other Details.

John W. Millington, a native of
Chestertown, but now a resident of
Portland, O. e., who served two terms
of enlistment in the Union army during the Civil War, and was a member
of the party that pursued and captured
John Wilkes Booth after his assassination of President Lincoln, has written
the following graphic description of his
part in the historic affair, with other
details, which, through the courtesy of
of the writer's brother, Robert Millington, of this village, we are permitted
to publish, as follows:

I do not write this to make any
claim that I did more than others who
did their duty as soldiers, but to give
to those who are interested the facts as
they occur to me, as near as I can in
the hunt and capture of John Wilkes
Booth and Harold, also a short history
of myself and my service.

I was born in Chestertown, N. Y., in
1843. I enlisted in Company E, 93rd
N. Y. Vol. Inft., December 3, 1861;
was with McClellan in '62 on the Pen-
insular campaign, was taken with typhoid fever in April, was sent to a
New York hospital then furloughed
home I returned to my regiment at
Hampton, Va., which was then sent to
Washington and then to Antietam, and
afterward marched on toward Fredericksburg. I got as far as Warrinton
and as I was too weak and sick to go
further, was sent to the hospital there.
Then I was sent to the Washington
hospital, Trinity church, corner of C
and Third street, then again I was
sent to Philadelphia, where I returned
to convalescent camp near Alexandria,
Va., was examined and discharged on
the 27th day of February, 1863. I
went to my home in Chestertown to
recover and on the 21st of July re-enlisted in Company H, 16th N. Y.
Cav., at Plattsburgh, Clinton county,
N. Y. The company was sent to
Washington to serve as scouts and patrols in the country between Washington and the Army of the Potomac. We
had a good many scraps with Mosby's guerillas. Sometimes we were
in Sheridan's command. In the winter of 1864-65 we were camped at
Vienna, Va., where we were in camp
until the 15th of April. The morning
of the 15th, '65 I was on camp guard
when an orderly from division headquarters rode into camp with an order for the regiment to report immediately to form a cordon to guard and
try and keep the assassins of the
President from escaping from the vicinity of Washington, as the President had been shot at Ford's Theatre
and was dead. They were a gloomy
set of men, but determined to do their
best That evening the regiment returned. It had been a rainy day and

the ride as they were deployed
through the brush was not very
cheering to their low spirits. In a
few days we were ordered to Washington as escort to the funeral from the
White House to the Capitol.

After the funeral we were detained
in Washington at the Eighth street
barracks and were then sent in squads
to patrol the vicinity in order to get on
the track of the conspirators. On the
24th of April I had been on patrol and
had returned to the barracks and fed
my horse. Leaving him saddled at
the stable I went to the barracks to
get something to eat myself, when
"Boots and Saddles" was sounded and
there was a rush for the stables. The
order was given to fall in as fast as
we led out, and not to mind company
formation. As my saddle was already on my horse I slipped on the
bridle, led out and mounted. There
was one sergeant at the head. He
stopped and I was next on the left.
Others came immediately. Orders were
to count off in fours by right forward
trot march. We went to Pennsylvania
avenue out to Fourteenth street, about
opposite to the old Willard hotel and
halted before the office of Colonel Baker, chief of the government detectives and scouts. Lieutenant Dogerty reported and in a few minutes he
and two detectives, Lieutenants Conger and Baker, came out and mounted
their horses, and we were ordered

"forward trot march" which we continued to the wharf of the navy yard
on east branch of the Potomac or the
Anacestin river, where we took the little steamer John S. Ide and started
down the Potomac river. Lieutenant
Dogerty showed us a photograph of
John Wilkes Booth and told us that
they had some trace of his crossing the
Potomac near Port Tobacco. We went
down to Aqua creek and landed about
10 o'clock that night. We then started
through the country, searching all
houses and buildings, routing out the
inmates and overlooking nothing.

Next morning we met some men who
had been fishing and stopped them.
They said that a closed hack had passed
through there a few days previous with
two men in it. A rebel captain was in
charge. They asked for some water,
but the men were not allowed to go
near the carriage, though they caught
a glimpse of the inmates and thought
they resembled the description and
the photograph which we had. They
were on the road leading to the Rappahanock river, at Port Conway. We
followed on, still making diligent
search in all the places along the route
till we came to Port Conway about 2
o'clock, then we deployed out to different places to get something to eat, as
we had had nothing since leaving
Washington. When the party I was
with returned—there were about five
of us—some of the others were crossing the river in a scow boat, which was
about twenty feet long by eight feet
wide, which could hold about ten men
and horses at a time. After we had
crossed we learned that Mr. Rawlens,
the owner of the ferry, had carried the
party we were seeking, a few days
previous, across and knew the Rebel
captain as Captain Jett, formerly of
Mosby's command, and that we would
be likely to find him at Bowling Green,
situated about fifteen miles from Port
Royal and he volunteered to pilot us
there. We started out as soon as we
were all across, it being then about 4

p. m. About three miles on the way
and near Garrett farm we came on a
man on horseback and he fled down the
road. Some of the men pursued him,
but he escaped in the young pines, and
as it was nearly dusk we did not follow further but took up our way to
Bowling Green, where we arrived
about 11 o'clock that night. Leaving
our horses with every fourth man outside the town we surrounded the hotel
and a search revealed Captain Jett.
After some forcible persuasions he
agreed to show us where he had left
the two men he had in the chase when
he crossed the Rappahanock river a
few days before, but he claimed that
he did not know their identity. They,
he said, claimed to be returning Confederate soldiers who had got into
trouble in Maryland and wanted to
keep in hiding till it had blown over
and was settled. He led us back on
the road we had just come on to within three miles of Port Royal, to a
house that stood some distance from
the main road. There was a lane and
a gate which was opened carefully so
as not to wake the inmates and make
them aware of our approach. We surrounded the house and old man Garrett
came to the door and was questioned
where the two men were. He denied
that there was anyone there, and was
thereupon threatened with hanging if
he did not tell, and the officer called
for a picket rope to execute the job.
Just then a young man came running
in from the direction of the outbuildings and wanted to know what was
wanted. He was told the men that
were stopping there and he said
they were in the barn. Part of the
men were ordered to surround the barn,
but enough were left to watch the
house, as it might be a ruse to let
them escape. As the barn was surrounded a movement and some talking was heard inside. The lieutenant
called on the inmates to come out and
surrender. Booth wanted to know
who we were. The answer was "it
makes no difference, we know who
you are" so to come out. He said he
would not, but said if we would draw
off thirty rods he would come out and
fight the whole squad. When he was
informed that we would not consider
the proposition we heard some talking and heard Booth accuse Harold of
cowardice and deserting him. He
called out and said that the other
man would surrender. He was told
to pass out his arms and come out
Booth said that Harold had no arms
as they all belonged to him. Harold
was told to come to the door, which he
did, the door was opened and Lieutenant Dogerty took hold of him and
pulled him out and tied him to a locust
tree and put me to guard him. Harold
talked quite freely with me. I asked
him if it was Booth that was with him,
he said it was but denied that he had
intended to allow President Lincoln to
be killed; he was only to be kid-
napped. Then I said "why did you
help Booth to escape?" He replied
that he did not dare to leave him as
Booth had threatened to kill him too.
He also said that they left Washington
immediately after Booth came out of
the rear of the theatre and went from
there to Dr. Mud's, where Booth's leg
was set They then went down near
Port Tobacco and hid there all the next
day. That night they found an old
fisherman and compelled him to take
them over into Virginia It was so
windy the fisherman did not want to

cross till it was calmer, but he was made to go by threats of being shot and it was so wild that the waves dashed into the boat and Harold said he had to keep bailing it out to keep it from sinking. After they crossed they stopped a few days in the low-land, then they became uneasy and started out and happened on Captain Jett, who helped them to the Garrett place. They saw us as we passed there the evening before and had hid in the barn for fear of being found, and had hopes of making their es-cape. Soon after the officer came around and forbade me to converse with him, I being relieved soon after. I could hear all that was going on at the barn, it being but a short distance away and being a few minutes after Harold's capture till Booth was shot. Booth was given five minutes to sur-render in, or the barn would be fired. He said they might prepare a litter as he would not surrender alive. Detec-tive Conger passed around to the oppo-site side of the barn and set a match to some loose straw under the sill and im-mediately I heard a shot and saw the door open. They brought Booth and carried him to the house and put him on the porch to the left of the door as one enters. Then a soldier started for Port Royal for a docter who came as soon as possible, about one and one-half to two hours after Booth was shot. It was then day and we could see our surroundings. The barn had burned down and some were hunting in the ruins for the relics. There were some revolvers, two I think. One of the boys had grabbed the carbine when they got Booth. I do not know what became of it. The revolvers were spoiled by the fire. They and the cart-ridges made quite a popping when the fire reached them. Booth lived about three hours. He was rolled in a government blanket and after we got breakfast was placed in an old wagon and an old horse driven by a negro started with us to take him to the place where we had left the boat at Aqua creek, which we reached about dusk that evening. When we were all aboard I was placed in one of the cabins with Harold to guard him and a guard outside the door also. Harold lay down on the floor and was soon asleep. I was relieved after a while and lay down near a boiler, as it was chilly and I had no overcoat. When I awoke we were near one of the monitors at Washington near where we started from, and after we were made fast Lieutenant Dogerty ordered me to go down on deck of the moni-tors and help with Booth's body, which we laid on deck. There were two or three sailors I remember stand-ing there when we landed at the dock I think Harold was left on the monitor, I will not be sure. I was anxious to get to my quarters for some rest and something to eat, having eaten only three times and being very weary. After stabling my horse I went to my bunk and when I awoke about 10 o'clock the papers had been published and there was a great deal of excitement over the capture.

When Booth was carried to the house he was unconscious and when he came to he said to tell his mother that what he did was for the good of the country, and when the doctor tried to give him some medicine he said it was useless. All this was in a low whisper, as he could not speak loudly. Garrett's two sons were taken to Washington

with us. There was quite a tearful scene with one of them and his young wife. The two sons had just returned from the Confederate Mosby's com-mand. Jett got away, I think that was part of the agreement with him if he showed us where he had left Booth.

In writing this, it being my first at-tempt to write for publication, I am like Mike Leon, an Irishman in my company. He was awkward and slow to learn the manual of arms and when the drill officer rebuked him, he said: "Don't hurry me now, how should I know when I never did it before?" Finally one night our picket reserve was attacked and part of them cap-tured. Some hid and I heard the fol-lowing conversation with a Reb. and Mike. "Surrender you d——n Yar-kee," demanded Johnny Reb. "Don't hurry me now," says Mike, "how should I know when I never did it be-fore?"
JOHN W. MILLINGTON.

KID MILLIONAIRE

P. Star Feb. 21st 1913

NEWPORT, R. I., Feb. 20.—John Nicholas Brown, one of the wealthiest boys in America, son of Mrs. John Nicholas Brown of this city, will cele-brate his thirteenth birthday anniver-sary tomorrow. When an infant in arms young Brown inherited the $2,-000,000 estate of his father, the late John Nicholas Brown of Providence and Newport. About a week after the death of his father he inherited also the estate of his uncle, valued at an equal amount. Still later he fell heir to one half of the $35,000,000 fortune left by his grandmother, Mrs. John Carter Brown.

News New Plumbing Shop. June 19

Orrin Tubbs will open a plumbing shop on the 25th inst. in D. E. Pasco's building on River street, ad-joining E L. Patrick's barber shop, and will estimate on and accept contracts for all work in that line, tinning, steam, hot water and hot air heating, etc. Mr. Tubbs is an exper-ienced workman and will guarantee satisfaction in every respect. 1912

MADE BRIDE HIS SLAVE.

Life With Bossy Husband Too Strenu-ous for Western Girl.

Ralph M. Harrington, a wealthy ranch-er of Hartzell, Col., soon after marry-ing Viva Harrington, a country school-teacher, threw her on the floor and held her until she admitted that he was boss. Then he forced flypaper into her mouth to close it. She was granted a divorce and alimony after telling her story

---

EDITOR RAPPED BY C. A. PERRIN

Star May 9, 1913

Scored for His Attitude Toward Upper Jay-Lake Placid Bill

The following communication has been received by The Post-Star from Charles A. Perrin of Upper Jay, a for-mer resident of Glens Falls:

Editor, Post-Star: "O wad some power the giftie gie us to see ourselves as ithers see us." This is from the brilliant pen of Robert Burns and we commend it to the receptive mind of another Robert—Robert P. McKee.

McKee, who edits an Essex county weekly, went on a tirade the other day against the Upper Jay-Lake Placid highway measure He wanted to do something unusual—and he did. At-tacking the proposed route to the fa-mous summer report, and attacking it blindly and without reason, he has found himself "a man apart." The bill, favored by nearly every news-paper in the state, fostered by gen-eral good will and appealing to the legislature as the logical route, has passed both houses and is up to the governor for his signature. While the intelligent press of northern New York was battling in its favor, Bob could not see the light and groped about in vain.

After a hard fight by Assemblyman Prime, the measure was reported out of committee, and it passed the assem-bly on Wednesday, April 23; but the fact finds no mention in Bob's paper of Friday, April 25. He is content to dispute the assertion that the bill was on the calendar Monday, April 21, and wrangles over the carefully qualified statement that the fate of the measure would probably be determined on that date.

In connection with this sketch I must not forget to mention that Bob has found a section of the Adirondacks that is "not supposed to be populated." The section in question lies along the proposed route to Placid, and we want to know if it is a dictate of Fate that this particular portion of the earth is destined to be uninhabited. Bob, we suggest that you see ex-King Theodore, of whom you were such an enthusiastic supporter, and get all the light you can.

Yours very truly,
CHARLES A. PERRIN.

-151-

Weston, at 75, Off On Another Walk

Gil. June 8
9/13

WESTON STARTING FROM NEW YORK.

Edward Payson Weston, now 75 years old, the man who astonished the world in 1910 by walking from ocean to ocean in 76 days, is on another hike, this time to Minneapolis, Minn. He left New York city this week, making the campus at the College of the City of New York his starting place. There, amid the cheers of the student body, he declared he is in better condition than he was ten years ago and that, while he does not expect to try for a record, he will be in Minneapolis by Aug. 2, when he is scheduled to lay the cornerstone of the Minneapolis Athletic club's $4,000,000 home.

Weston will follow the Erie railroad through New Jersey, Pennsylvania, New York, Ohio, Indiana, Illinois, and Wisconsin, as the most direct route to Chicago, where he expects to arrive July 2. From that point he will follow the Northwestern road to Minneapolis. On his journey he will be accompanied by an automobile and two attendants who will provide for his safety and look after his comfort.

Weston declares his only purpose in undertaking the long walk is to demonstrate to the public that more men are killed by lack of exercise than by it, and that the man who takes regular exercise and eats moderately will live longer and be able to do at 75 feats that would tax the strength of the average man of 50.

SELL LIVERY STOCK AT AUCTION SALE

Many Exceptional Bargains Secured at the Griffing & Leland Stable

May 1—1913 Star

LARGE CROWD ATTRACTED

One of the largest auction sales ever held in Glens Falls or vicinity was that held yesterday by the Griffing & Leland company. The sale began at 10 o'clock and lasted all day. At 6 o'clock Auctioneer Frasier announced the sale would be continued today, beginning at 10 o'clock.

The sale was held on the Griffing & Leland property. A large number of buyers was present from out of town and many good bargains were secured by the bidders. The sales totaled $5,000. There still remains about $20,000 worth of stock, and the auction will be continued until all is disposed of.

Two matched pairs of coach horses were sold to out of town parties. A handsome pair of gray horses were sold to Lake Placid club for $495 and W. M. Stone of Saratoga secured a handsome pair of gray cobs for $470. Two demi-coaches were sold, one to Charles W. Seeley, the Exchange street liveryman, for $485, and one to a Mr. Pattridge of Schuylerville for $415.

Nine more demi-coaches of the highest class still remain, as does also the livery and repository stock. The horses, wagons, coaches, harness, etc., are going at slaughter prices, and many a man who travelled a long distance to attend the sale was well repaid by securing an excellent bargain.

Mayor Griffing stated last night that everything will be sold. After passing over thirty years in the business, Mayor Griffing is to retire and with his retirement one of the most prosperous and most widely known liveries in this section of the state will pass out of existence.

News May 29

Myron Lamb is causing the board of education some little trouble by refusing to send his children to school. His only reason for acting so seems to be that he has nothing else on hand to stir up a strife about. *1913*

We are having a regular epidemic of measles here; measles of all varieties too, some have the German and get off quite easy, while some have the genuine old-fashioned variety of red measles.

A. B. Bouthillier, a New York architect, will arrive in this city today to locate the foundation walls and make other necessary arrangements for the construction work of the Glens Falls Country club. The contract for the erection of the club house has been awarded to Hartman and West, who have stated the building will be ready for use by August 1. *Star April 28, 1913*

COMMENTS ON THE ROOSEVELT TRIAL

"Getting Drunk" is Discussed in Editorial by Henry Watterson.

May 29 1913

LOUISVILLE Ky., May 29.—In a long editorial on "Getting Drunk," Henry Watterson makes the following remarks about the Roosevelt trial in the Louisville Courier:

"History and literature are so studded with the hobnails of vinous hilarity, all the way from Noah and onward through aeons of notable persons who are not commonly represented as examples of strict sobriety, that it would seem a much ado about nothing in Col. Roosevelt to seek to fix by legal inquiry and affirmation the various kinds of intoxicants he has never used and which he actually detests and the precise number of drinks he has not had for breakfast.

"With what purpose is he proceeding and to what end. Whether he drinks wine or beer, or cocktails or mint julips or does not drink at all may be said in a sense to be nobody's business but his own, assuredly nobody's concern except the immediate circle about him.

"Surely a man who has lived in the world three and fifty years, in the limelight thirty of them, the head of a happy and prosperous household, a good husband and father, a prodigiously hard worker, could afford to let tongues wag as they will about his exites and his entrances, his food and his drink and his intimate personality.. It must be to most self-respecting Americans a humiliation to have the most world-famous of their living countrymen, an ex-president of the United States, engaged in what appears so trivial and needless a task as that which has taken him to the Michigan village. It seems a kind of fools errand. It will change no man's opinion, good or ill, certainly not the opinion of just and thoughtful men."

---

news May 13

Horse Dies at Great Age. *1913*

"Old Roscoe," a faithful work horse that had attained the extreme age of thirty-five, after passing his declining years in peace and comfort on Dr. C. S. Merrill's farm in this place, passed to his reward last Thursday and was given a good burial by Dr. Merrills' efficient overseer, James Harrison, who was greatly attached to the animal.

PROMINENT LAWYER DIES AT THE LAKE

G. F. Star May 15th 1913

Charles M. Parsons Passes Away After Lingering Illness —Funeral Saturday

Charles M. Parsons died yesterday afternoon at 4 o'clock at Lake George, after a lingering illness. He was the husband of Dr. Eleanor Parsons of Lake George. He was a prominent attorney of New York city and was a member of the New York City Bar association and the Warren County Bar association.

Mrs. J. L. Russell and son, William H. Russell, have-arrived in town from Troy and have settled down at Bonnie Brae villa with announced intention of making it their permanent home. The house has been wired for electric lights by Seymour G. Taylor, of Glens Falls, and many other improveents have been made about the place. Mrs. Russell is at present entertaining her friend, Mrs. Paine, of Troy, and her granddaughter, Miss Mary Louise Archibald, of New York. *News 1913 June 19*

YOU MAY LEAD A HORSE TO WATER

Judge.

You may lead a horse to water,
But you can't make him drink;
You may send a boy to college,
But you can't make him think.

You may preach some men a sermon,
But you'll never change their way;
They will go right on tomorrow
As they've started out today.
You may tell them to be banking,
But they'll never save a cent;
You may urge them to be building,
But they'll keep on paying rent.

You may write a lot of verses
That you'll never see in print;
You may tell a bore you're busy,
But he'll never take the hint.

You may lead some men to business,
But they'll never make a start;
You may show some men their duty,
But they'll never do their part.
You may dress some folks in satin,
But you'll never change their looks;
You may give some folks a bookstore,
But they'll never read the books.

You may lead a horse to water,
But you'll find this true, I think,
That unless the horse is thirsty,
There's no way to make him drink.

'BURG IS PROMISED EXCITING HORSE RACE

May 29 Star 1913

WARRENSBURG, May 26.—What promises to be one of the most exciting horse races ever staged in Warren county will be held Memorial day at the Warrensburg fair grounds. The horses which are entered are the same which met in what proved to be one of the best races on the tracks in the season of 1912. A fifth heat was necessary to determine the winner in the first race, Daniel R. finally winning the event.

The horses entered are Daniel R., owned by Daniel O'Rourke; Robert R., owned by Robert Roberts; Bay Tom, owned by Ernest Ross and Inola, owned by L. T. West.

WORK IS PROGRESSING AT THE COUNTRY CLUB

Times May 27

Notwithstanding the inclement weather, work is progressing satisfactorily at the Country club. The architect, Addison B. Le Boutillier of Boston, has been spending two or three days in this city, going over the work carefully with the contractors. He will return again at the end of the week. Major D. J. Hogan today received the contract for plumbing and starts on the work tomorrow. The rain is doing wonders for the greens, and grass is growing well. The number of visitors at the club-house property increases daily. **1913**

GENERAL SICKLES IS NOT AFRAID OF FIRE

Times May 27 1913

NEW YORK, May 27.—When a small blaze in a coal vault beneath the house occupied by General Daniel E. Sickles filled the place with smoke yesterday and drove three other families into the street, the general became peevish when he was aroused by the firemen; went back to bed and told the fire fighters they could notify him if the blaze got any worse. Informed that the house was full of smoke, the general said:

"What do I care? I love smoke. I eat it. I don't want to be disturbed at this hour of the morning. If the flames come up into the house you can notify me."

News May 25 1913

George La Salle to Manage Algonquin House

The Algonquin hotel, one of the most popular summer hotels on Lake George, situated at Bolton, will be under the management the coming season of George LaSalle, formerly secretary of the Glens Falls club. The Algonquin has been successfully conducted for several years by E. G. Penfield.

May 29 1913

BIG BUSINESS DEAL

Empire Shirt Co. Forms Alliance With Great Collar Concern

FOR SALE OF ENTIRE OUTPUT

Twenty-five Salesmen, Covering Whole Country, Will Sell Goods of Both Factories—Means Great Prosperity for Warrensburgh.

A big business deal has just been completed by the Empire Shirt company, of Warrensburgh, with one of the largest collar manufacturing concerns in Troy, which provides for the sale of the entire output of the local factory, with its present capacity doubled.

The Troy concern, which manufactures collars and cuffs exclusively, has twenty-five salesmen on the road, covering the entire country, and each one of these men will carry a complete line of the Empire Shirt company's samples. With their collar trade firmly established, the selling company will introduce to their customers the superior shirts manufactured by the local concern. This will positively assure a ready market for all the goods that can possibly be made here.

As the men are now selling for the fall trade work on their orders will not be started for sometime. In the meantime the capacity of the local factory will be greatly enlarged and when the fall business begins there will be a great demand for operators. Steady and renumerative employment will be furnished all who apply and the present force will be increased, if possible, by at least 200. The laundry, in which men are mostly employed, will also share in the boom.

This means much to Warrensburgh. With plenty of work for everybody the old days of prosperity will return. The empty houses, of which there are at present not a few, will all be filled and property values will rise again.

Families in surrounding towns who desire steady work need not hesitate to make arrangements to come to Warrensburgh in the fall for they will find here pleasant homes and many advantages not enjoyed in the rural communities and many of the smaller villages.

Warrensburgh business men, in all lines of trade, will share in the benefits of the coming boom and all should put their shoulders to the wheel, wherever they can find an opening, and help it along.

SITE FOR HOSPITAL

News May 15th

Wyatt Ellsworth Farm Choice of Supervisors' Committee

1913

PROPERTY NEAR GLENS FALLS

Five Miles From City on Bay Road—Possesses All Requirements Demanded by State for Tuberculosis Sanatorium—Probable Cost.

The special committee appointed by the Warren county board of supervisors to select a site for the proposed county hospital for the treatment of tuberculosis, has after inspecting various properties unanimously selected the Wyatt Ellsworth farm of 160 acres, situated in the town of Queensbury, on the Bay road, six and a half miles from the city of Glens Falls. The committee, which is composed of Supervisors E. J. Worden, John E. Collins, Fred R. Smith, Beecher Glassbrook and Fred Rogers, inspected this site last week and at the same time visited the Mack farm and the Patrick Breen property, both also in Queensbury. All of the committee took part in the inspection excepting Supervisor Rogers, who was unable to join them.

After a careful survey of the three properties, it was unanimously decided by the committee that the Ellsworth farm was by far the most desirable and they voted to recommend its purchase by the county for $7,000, the price put upon it by the owner.

On the place is a house, built no more than six years ago, which would serve as a home for the caretaker of the institution, and there is also an excellent barn which would prove useful. The hospital building will cost, according to a careful estimate, about $10,000, making a total expenditure of $7,000 for the institution.

It is expected there will be a revenue of at least $1,000 a year from the fruit and vegetable output of the farm. There is a large orchard of young apple trees, the trunks of each now being not more than six inches in circumference, which promises to increase in the amount of its product for many years to come. Last year the trees bore sixty-five barrels of apples and this season they will probably produce a hundred and in 1914 125 barrels. There are also cherry trees, which last year bore fifty bushels of fruit; plum trees, which bore sixty bushels, and a large number of pear trees. There are sixty acres of tillable land, on which large quantities of potatoes and other marketable products may be grown. There are also a great many raspberry and currant bushes, and it is hoped strawberry plants may be cultivated in large numbers. The work of caring for the trees, bushes and vegetables may easily be carried on by the male patients in the institution.

Anyone who has tuberculosis who have not the means to pay for care in the institution would be taken as readily as any other, and the fact that he or she has not paid will be a matter that will be kept secret, made public only on the reports of the institution, and then by the numbers of such patients and not by the individual names.

E. L. Nelbach, of the State Charities Aid association, is expected to visit Glens Falls within the next few days to inspect the site and give the state's approval before the committee makes its report to the board of supervisors. His requirements were known to the committee before they started on their tour of inspection and have been complied with in every detail. One of the requirements, with which the state is very strict, is met with more fully on this site, perhaps, than in any other such institution in the state. That is the water facilities. There are several springs on the farm and in addition, two separate brooks run within its boundaries.

The committee will report to the board of supervisors at the regular quarterly meeting in July and it is likely that their recommendations will then be accepted and the property purchased. In that case the work of preparing plans, letting contracts and completing other necessary details will be done next fall and winter so that construction work may be started early the following spring and the building made ready for occupancy as early as possible in the summer of 1914.

MRS. TRASK'S STRONG ARRAIGNMENT OF WAR

May 12 1913 — Enine

One of the strongest, most logical and most convincing arguments against war and in favor of peace and arbitration is the little book "In the Vanguard" by Katrina Trask of Saratoga, recently issued from the press of The MacMillan Co., of New York, says the Albany Times-Union.

The argument is presented in the form a playlet, the hero of which is a young lawyer-soldier, who abruptly quits fighting at the end of his enlistment period, on the field of battle and when a commission of captaincy is offered him for extraordinary valor, after his eyes were opened to the real meaning of the war being waged.

There is a love romance running through the poetic classic like a golden thread in a silken flag, the heroine of which is a hero-worshipper a lover of war and valorous deeds. It is for love of her, as much as for love of country, that the hero goes to war.

Both come to a realization of the real meaning of war, the horrors of the murderous man-to-man battles, at about the same time and the ending is a happy one for the reunited and reawakened lovers.

1913 May 29

News

CRANDALL WILL CONTEST.

Heirs of Late Glens Falls Philanthropist Start Litigation.

Several persons who claim to be heirs of the late Henry Crandall, of Glens Falls, have taken steps to contest the aged philanthropist's will. These heirs are Harvey S. Crandall, of Lake George, Henry Crandall Durkee, Anna Wickes and Anna M. Lawlor.

When the matter of probate of the will was taken up in Surrogate's court in Glens Falls Tuesday morning Beecher S. Clother, appearing as attorney for Harvey S. Crandall, filed several objections to the will. The chief objections are that the will is not the last will; that it is invalid to pass real and personal property, and also that the trust intended to be created under and by the provisions of the alleged will are unlawful and void.

The late Mr. Crandall died about two months ago, leaving his entire estate, estimated at $1,000,000, in trust for the city of Glens Falls. Most of the estate is real property, part of which is a park of several thousand acres.

DUNLOP & RIDDELL GET TELEPHONE CO.

Times May 22

Purchase Property and all the Rights of the North Creek Concern.

1913.

An important transaction in telephone property in Warren county was completed yesterday when Solon R. Dunlop of Stony Creek, clerk of the county board of superiors, and M. B. Riddell of Luzerne purchased the interests, consisting of forty miles of poles and lines and all rights and franchises of the North Creek Telephone Company within the limits of the Town of Stony Creek. Messrs. Dunlop and Riddell will take possession of the properties June 1, and after that date it will be known as the Luzerne Telephone Company.

The new owners will make extensive improvements to the system, in which there are at present fifty subscribers. The present telephones will be returned and new instruments installed. A girl is to be engaged for the exchange, which is located in the Stony Creek office, where a new switchboard has been installed.

BURGLAR'S LAST JOB

Hudson Falls Man Killed While Robbing House at Hague

SHOT BY ARTIST HARRY WATROUS

Frank Cardinal Fatally Wounded by Two Bullets from Colt Automatic—His Brother Escapes Uninjured But Is Captured and Jailed.

Harry W. Watrous, a New York artist, at 2 o'clock Monday morning discovered Frank and Joseph Cardinal, of Hudson Falls, engaged in burglarizing his summer home at Hague and opened fire on them with a Colt Automatic revolver. Two bullets struck Frank Cardinal in the abdomen, inflicting wounds which caused his death in the Moses hospital in Ticonderoga at 3 o'clock in the afternoon. The brother jumped through a window and escaped He was pursued by Sheriff Richard Bolton, and was captured at 10 a. m. and lodged in the county jail at Lake George.

Mr. and Mrs. Watrous occupied a room in the second story of the cottage and the latter was first awakened by the noise the men made in their operations. She aroused her husband, who took an electric flashlight and a revolver and went to investigate the cause of the noise. Entering the dining room, clad only in his night robe, Mr. Watrous flashed his light and its rays fell directly upon the crouching figure of a man. Not knowing whether the intruder was armed Mr. Watrous fired at him and at the same instant his thumb slipped from the button on the flashlight, leaving the room in darkness. Again he flashed the light and saw what he thought might be a different man, so aimed a shot at him. The man fell to the floor with a groan and at the same time a crash of glass was heard as the other man plunged through a window in another room and fled in the darkness.

NEW YORK, May 16.—Levi P. Morton, former vice president of the United States and for nearly half a century a leading figure in American banking and financial circles, entered upon his ninetieth year today, having been born May 16, 1824. There was no observance of the anniversary, owing to the state of Mr. Morton's health. For many weeks past the venerable banker has been confined to his bed and for days his condition was reported to be extremely critical.

---

news May 9

A writer in the Troy Times, in the Wayside Whispers column, in Monday evening's issue "wrote up" one of the best known residents of this place. As many readers of The News would not otherwise see the article I take the liberty of reproducing it herewith, as follows: " 'Uncle Jed' Smith is certainly some character in the neighborhood of Horicon. He has the well earned reputation of knowing Brant Lake better than any other bass fisherman in the world. He is also the town's tooth extractor, also he is an authority on bee culture, also he is the town telephone repair gang, also he is one of the best story tellers in the woods, being gifted with more than his share of that mixture of native philosophy and original use of words that is characteristic of men who have communed with nature all their lives. Jed has had a long and varied career and some real adventures. Jed was the thirteenth child of fourteen children, so anyone can see with half an eye that the author of Jed's particular brand of the Smith family had to hustle to keep things going, and incidentally to keep things from going, too. He did both pretty successfully and the elder Smith left his family grown up and with a goodly inheritance. The elder Smith, as can be imagined, did not have much time in all this hustling to pay strict attention to family details, like minor accidents to his children. One day when Jed was eleven years old a fine big buck deer was seen swimming across Brant Lake. Young Jed hustled into a boat and rounded up the deer in the water. The deer fought. Young Jed said he pulled out his jackknife 'to meller him;' the deer's hoof hit the knife and sent it through the air. The knife cut young Jed's wrist and then sank into the bow of the boat. Young Jed used a white ash oar to complete the 'mellering,' and after the smoke of battle had cleared away and the deer had been towed ashore Jed displayed the trophy of his skill with pardonable pride to his father and then called attention to the bad long cut that lay open bleeding in his wrist. He expected sympathy, for the wound was a painful if not a dangerous one. His father looked at the extended wrist. For a moment he said nothing. Jed imagined the words of sympathy 'the old man' was framing up in his mind. At last the father spoke. List to the words of sympathy: 'Well, that'll heal up some time. Now, go to work.' Jed is called 'Uncle Jed' advisedly. 'I'm really uncle to most all this town. You'd be surprised to know how many nephews and nieces I have 'bout here.' Then he explained that almost all of his brothers and sisters had grown up and had married and most of them had large families, so Jed is really 'the town uncle.' "

1912

Big Log Jam In the Hudson.

The largest jam of logs ever known by rivermen in the Hudson river has been lodged the past week between Thurman and Stony Creek. It extends up the river four and a half miles, a solid mass of spruce pulp logs. Great difficulty is being experienced in breaking it up. *1918*

news April 24

E. M. SHEPARD LEFT $924,642 ESTATE

Star May 1, 1918

Accounting Filed By Executors in Office of Surrogate in Brooklyn

PROPERTY WORTH $71,000

Deceased Had Mexican Mining Stocks Valued at $93,490— Part of Assets Held to Be Sold to Advantage

---

THURMAN YOUTH DROWNED.

news June 1918

Hiland Wescott Loses Life While Swimming In River at Newcomb.

While swimming in the Boreas river at Newcomb, Monday afternoon, Hiland Wescott, of Thurman, nineteen years old, was seized with a cramp and before help could reach him sank to the bottom and was drowned.

Young Wescott was employed on the state road work near Newcomb and after his day's labor was done went to the river to seek relief from the intense heat by a refreshing bath in the cool waters. He was a good swimmer and did not hesitate to venture into deep water, but when the cramp paralyzed his limbs he was unable to help himself. Other men were near but were unable to reach him in time.

The body was brought to his home in Thurman yesterday and the funeral will be held there this afternoon at 2 o'clock. He is survived by his parents, Mr. and Mrs. Albert Wescott, three sisters, Misses Myra, Francis and Lulu, and a brother, Linwood Wescott.

"ANKLE DEEP" TO RACE.

June 16 — June 16

Count Cassimer Mankowski of Bolton will enter his hydroplane, "Ankle Deep," in the races off Long Island to be conducted by the Motor Boat Club of America, July 7, 8 and 9, to decide which three American boats shall represent America as challengers for the British international trophy known as the Harmsworth cup. *1913*

MRS. LYDIA A. ARMSTRONG.

Mrs. Lydia A. Armstrong, an old resident of Johnsburgh, died at her home Sunday in her eighty-eighth year. She is survived by one son, William H. Armstrong, and a daughter, Miss Elizabeth Armstrong, with whom she made her home

UNUSUAL RECORD OF CAPT. ROCKWELL

1918

E. F. Tracy
June 2nd, 29W

Begins Seventy-second Year of Service on Lake Champlain.

A FAMILY OF SAILORS.

Veteran Navigator Tells How Lack of Morphine Caused Loss of Steamer Vermont Back in the Year 1878.

Seventy-one years on Lake Champlain is the record of Capt. Eli B. Rockwell, the oldest inland water captain in years of service in all probability in the world. Captain Rockwell began Saturday his seventy-second year. He belongs to a family of sailors. At present there is only one of the Champlain passenger boats afloat that does not number at least one Rockwell among the officers or crew, while two of the boats have three Rockwells. Captain Rockwell's father followed the lake, his five sons have made it their life work and their sons in turn have many of them' followed the water. Captain Rockwell was born in North Hero in February, 1830, one of a family of twelve children. January 22, 1856, Captain Rockwell married Miss Lucy A. McElroy of Sandy Hill, N. Y. She died November 19, 1901. Of seven children born to them six are now living. Captain Rockwell began his Lake Champlain career as the cabin boy aboard the schooner Cynthia at St. Johns P. Q., when he was less than twelve years old. The schooner ran from St. Johns to Whitehall, N. Y. His eldest brother, J. G. Rockwell, was captain. When Eli B. Rockwell was seventeen years old he was captain of a schooner. For two years Mr. Rockwell was captain of the Cynthia before a promotion to The Frances. From that boat he went to the Merchants' Lake Boat Line as commander of the sloop Columbia. Later he was pilot of the steamer Clifton. In 1853 he was at work finishing the steamer Canada at Whitehall and came up on her as first mate under Captain Foster. In 1854 he was captain of the sloop Mike, in '55 and '56 of the schooner General Scott and in '57 pilot of the steamer America with his brother, J. G. Rockwell, under Capt. William H. Flagg. He remained as pilot under Flagg fifteen years, changing from the America to the Canada. Mr. Rockwell was captain of the tug Glen Iris, the freight steamer Ethan Allen and the freight propeller James H. Hooker; the last two being the property of The Northern Transportation Company of Whitehall. From the Hooker, Captain Rockwell became pilot on the Adirondack under Captain Flagg and from that to the United States under Capt. George Rushlow. In 1871 he

was transferred to the Vermont, 2d, and came out with that boat on her trial trip.

Lost on Account of Morphine.

He remained on the Vermont until in 1878 the steamer was lost one beautiful night about eighteen minutes after leaving Westport Landing, northbound. Captain Rockwell says the cause of the accident was the lack of morphine. He explains this somewhat astonishing statement by saying that after the accident a detective was placed on the track of John Eldridge, the associate pilot, and it was found that he was the victim of the morphine habit and during the trip ran out of the drug. Morphine contracts the optic nerve, and as Eldridge had become accustomed to the use of the drug, when he was without it the expanding back of the optic nerve threw his range of vision out of focus. The steamer went on Split Rock Mountain and was split in two. No one was seriously injured. After passing two years at his home in Alburgh Captain Rockwell superintended the building of the Reindeer and the boat was launched in 1881. It required a week to launch it. When Captain Rockwell left the Reindeer he built the schooner Hiram Walker at Champlain, N. Y. He was later captain of the steamer Coquette built at Newburgh, N. Y., and made the first trip with the boat. T. M. Leonard of New York, manufacturer of Valveline oil, who had a summer home at Rouse's Point, N. Y., was the owner of the Coquette. Captain Rockwell left the Coquette to become pilot of the Chateaugay, being later transferred to the new Ticonderoga. He succeeded Captain Baldwin on the Vermont, 3d, and for ten years has been captain of that, the most luxurious boat on Lake Champlain. Captain Rockwell has had many distinguished guests in the pilot house. Among them he recalls Gen. Phil. Sheridan, President Ulysses S. Grant, Justice David J. Brewer, President William H. Taft, Ambassador James Bryce and Ambassador Jusserand.

EDWIN HADLEY LAWRENCE.

may 24 IN MEMORIAM *1913*

Edwin Hadley Lawrence was born July 8, 1870, and died March 30, 1912. His early life was spent in the village of Luzerne, where as a child he assisted his father, James Hadley Lawrence, in his store and later in the postoffice. At the age of seventeen he went into business for himself remaining until 1893.

He left Luzerne in 1894, going to Albany, where he had a responsible position with C. H. and W. J. Sutherland. In 1895 he left Albany for Hartford, Conn., and by his wonderful energy soon rose to a high position with the Pope Manufacturing company.

After several years with this company he accepted a position as traveling salesman for a bicycle house in Philadelphia. During the years of employment as a salesman he traveled over the greater part of the United States.

MRS. BRERETON RECOVERS.

Wife of Warren County Assemblyman Restored to Health After Long Illness.

The Hon. H. E. H. Brereton arrived at his home on the Bolton road on Lake George last Thursday accompanied by Mrs. Brereton, who has fully recovered from the serious illness which for many months has afflicted her. Several years ago Mrs. Brereton underwent a severe illness which culminated in surgical treatment. Since that time she has been in poor health and her nervous system greatly prostrated. During last summer a marked change for the worse made it necessary for her removal to a sanitarium, where she has since remained under the care of specialists. During the past two months Mrs. Brereton has been on the road to complete convalescence and now she is returned to enjoy the early summer months with her husband at their beautiful new home on the shores of Lake George. As soon as the special session of the legislature has closed in Albany this summer Hon. and Mrs. Brereton will go abroad, where they will spend several months in the great art centers of Europe.

Mrs. Brereton is a daughter of the late Mrs. Loop, of Saratoga Springs, and inherits from both parents a strong artistic temperament, coupled with great ability, both as a musician and painter During the past two years Mr. Brereton has had under construction a summer residence on his estate, the sole motif of its design being to surround Mrs. Brereton with the conveniences and luxuries which she would particularly appreciate. Among its many pleasing attributes are the pipe organ and big studio. The extensive sweep of lawn to the lake shore is now being terraced and about the house an army of masons are rushing the completion of the beautiful wall which marks the first terrace. Inside, the big, inviting rooms are nearly complete and the home now only waits the last artistic touches of femininity which its fair mistress can so effectively administer.

A host of friends of Hon. and Mrs. Brereton in Warren and Saratoga counties will rejoice to learn of the recovery of Mrs. Brereton and of her return to assist in the completion of the de-

lightful home which they had both planned for so many years.

Mrs. Elizabeth A. Worden, aged sixty-nine years, died Sunday morning at her home in the town of Caldwell, about one mile north of the village of Lake George. She is survived by four sons—

FIRST BRIDGE OVER RIVER
UNLIKE ONE NOW PLANNED

Star May 3 1918

Old Wooden Structure Was Just Wide Enough for One Team to Pass Over—Toll House on Span

Bridge Across River at Glens Falls in 1825.

The above is a reproduction of an engraving made by a French artist in 1825—and the wooden bridge which spanned the river at that time was probably the first ever built across the river. The engraving is in the possession of C. H. Sherman, Bay street, and is on exhibition in the show windows of the B. B. Fowler company's store.

The engraving was made by an artist from France who made a series from places along the Hudson from Hadley south to Newburg. W. Rockwell of Luzerne has several pictures of scenes at that place and Fred Howland of Hudson Falls also has an engraving made of Hudson Falls, or Sandy Hill as it was known then.

The old wooden bridge shown in the above picture was just wide enough for a team to pass over. The date of its erection could not be learned last night, as nobody could be found who even remembers the structure. The bridge was a cheaply constructed affair, the abutments being built of logs, but it served its purpose in those days,

nearly a century ago when automobiles and trolley cars were inventions of which the good people of that time never dreamed. The structure was probably built for a small sum of money. Today the people want a bridge that will cost $150,000.

In the old days the banks on both sides of the falls were lined by trees. The site of the plant of the International Paper company was a forest and there was a large number of trees where Finch, Pruyn & company's mill stands. There were a few houses in the vicinity, as will be seen from the above cut, but they were very few. A mill is shown on the South Glens Falls side of the river, but just what kind of a mill it was is not known by the owner of the engraving, although it is believed to have been either a saw mill or grist mill. The structure was a toll bridge, the toll house being plainly seen in the middle of the span. The picture is the first engraving of Glens Falls ever seen by Mr. Sherman and it is therefore quite rare.

POTTERSVILLE FAIR
BIGGER THAN EVER

Horse Racing Will Be Feature and Good Purses Have Been Offered.

Special to The Knickerbocker Press.

GLENS FALLS, April 19.—At a meeting of the directors of the Pottersville Fair association Tuesday preliminary plans were made for this year's fair which will open September 9. The fair will be of four days' duration and horse racing will be featured on the last three days, the program being as follows:

Wednesday—2:20 class, purse, $100; peg race; slow race.

APPLICATION THROWN
OUT BY CO. JUDGE

LIQUOR LICENSE CRUSADE GIVEN JOLT BY RALEY'S DECISION.

Times April 22 1913

County Judge George S. Raley today dismissed the application of Mrs. Sarah Streeter, proprietor of the Phoenix Hotel in the Town of Hague, through her attorney, Beecher S. Clother, for a writ of certiorari to compel County Treasurer Beecher W. Sprague to show cause why he should not issue a liquor license for use at her hotel

—157—

MORE STATE ROADS
IN WARREN COUNTY

Times ap 25

SENATOR EMERSON SAYS HIS BILL WILL BE PASSED BY LEGISLATURE MONDAY.

1913

Unless all signs fail Senator Emerson's bill authorizing the appropriation of $460,000 for State road construction in Warren and $418,000 in Essex counties, will be passed by the legislature next Monday night and when signed by Governor Sulzer will give to Warren and Essex counties the only appropriations authorized for road work by the present legislature.

Senator Emerson, who is first last and all the time, looking after the interests of his constituents, has been busily engaged piloting this bill through the many legislative channels and despite the fact that he has met with stubborn opposition, led by Minority Leader Brown, he announced today that the bill was sure of passing.

In opposing Senator Emerson's request for an appropriation of $878,000, the opposition contended that two years ago the Warren County Senator acquired $2,100,000 for road work and that a new appropriation should not be granted, but when "Senator Jim" starts on the war path he usually gets what he goes after.

With this new appropriation the following roads will be constructed: Warren county—Glens Falls to East Lake George, Stony Creek station to Stony Creek village, Thurman station to Athol and North Creek to Wells, connecting with the road to Utica and opening up a direct route from western cities to the Adirondacks; Essex county—Lake Placid to Upper Jay, Westport to Elizabethtown, Ticonderoga to Schroon Lake.

GRANGER SAYS HE
HAS ONLY $1.43

Star apl 24 1913

UTICA, April 23.—Claude C. Granger, a summer hotel man at Kattskill Bay, has filed a petition in voluntary bankruptcy in the United States court here. In it Granger made an affidavit that the only property he possesses is $1.43 in cash, that he did not have means with which to pay the required fees to go through bankruptcy, and that he has forty creditors with claims amounting to $4,305. Granger says that Solomon W. Russell of Glens Falls has a claim for $1,200 which is covered by a chattel mortgage on property owned by his wife. Granger also holds a lease of the Grove hotel at Lake George. His creditors are all located in Warren county, Albany and New York.

CLARENCE WEAVER FATALLY INJURED

Times — Aug 16

Neck Was Broken While at Work on the Glen Dale Farm Yesterday. *1913*

Clarence Weaver, for a number of years an employe on the Alfred Sweet farm in the Town of Queensbury, was fatally injured yesterday afternoon when his neck was broken as the result of his being thrown from a wagon. The accident occurred at the Glen Dale farm shortly before 2 o'clock and at 5:30 the injured man was removed to the hospital.

The physician in charge of the injured man says that it is a matter of only a short time before he will die, as the injuries are fatal. It may be that the injured man will survive several days and possibly weeks, it all depending upon his vitality.

Mr. Weaver and Mr. Sweet were drawing hay from the barns to a freight car on a siding near the farm. Mr. Sweet was driving the horse, while Weaver sat on one of the wagon boxes. As the wagon turned from the field into the highway the wheels were cramped so that the wagon box was suddenly raised up and Mr. Weaver was thrown backward, striking his head and shoulders on the ground. Mr. Sweet went to Mr. Weaver's assistance and finding him in a serious condition, helped him into the house. Dr. Fred B. Streeter was summoned.

The injured man remained unconscious throughout the afternoon and night and today was resting as comfortably as conditions would permit.

LOCAL MAN DROPS DEAD AT GLEN LAKE

Times — Aug 12

Ernest Hovey Succumbs to Apoplexy While Waiting for Hudson Valley Car *1913*

Ernest Hovey, aged fifty-four years and a resident of Glenwood avenue, dropped dead shortly after two o'clock this afternoon while waiting for a Hudson Valley car at White's station, Glen Lake. It is believed that he succumbed to apoplexy.

Information was telephoned to Hudson Valley Dispatcher Bartlett by a conductor and Mr. Bartlett, in turn, sent word to relatives of the men in this city, but at the hour of going to press the body had not been removed, owing to the fact that Acting Coroner Dever could not be located.

Besides his widow and several children, Mr. Hovey is survived by a brother, C. A. Hovey and a sister Mrs. Henry Webster, of this city

OLD TRUNK REVEALS FORTUNE IN JEWELS

June 17 June 17 1913

Late Dr. Albert H. Phelps Finds Treasure Left By His Grandmother

---

KEPT STORY FROM PUBLIC

Dr. Albert H. Phelps, whose funeral will be held this afternoon from the family residence in Ridge street, left no will according to a statement made by a member of the family and the entire estate will pass into the hands of his sons, Guy M. Phlps of Troy and Leroy G. Phedps of Bridgeport, Conn.

Among the may valuable possessions left by the late physician is a collection of rare gems, containing many diamonds, rubies, sapphires and other valuable gems which was found about a year ago by the deceased in an old trunk, which had been the property of his grandmother and which had been placed in a store room in the rear of the house and left unopened for years.

A reporter for The Post-Star learned of the physician's find a short time after it was made and on interviewing him was told the details

BOLTON LANDING

New ... May 15 1913

Miss Rose Taylor was a visitor in Glens Falls on Wednesday of last week.

Addison B. Comstock, of Glens Falls, was a business visitor in town last week.

James Dearstyne, who has been ill for some time, is somewhat improved at present.

Miss Lizzie Lenox and John Lenox, of French Mountain, were called here by the death of their aunt, Miss Stewart.

State Historian James A. Holden, of Glens Falls, was a guest of Mr. and Mrs. H. E. Nichols, at Shelving Rock, Sunday.

Mr. and Mrs. George Gurney and Mr. and Mrs. James Williamson and daughter, Hessier, of Glens Falls, were in town last week, called here by the death of Miss Stewart.

Bishop Nelson, of Albany, made an official visitation to St. Sarcament church Sunday morning at 11 o'clock, preaching a very able sermon and confirming a class composed of the following members: Mr. and Mrs. J. R. Stickney, Dr. E. L. Wilson, Mrs. Haskins, Hulda Barber, Vivian Palmer, Calvin Monroe and Bernard Baker.

Miss Susan Stewart, daughter of Deacon Robert Stewart, formerly of French Mountain, died at the home of Mrs. Andrew Lenox Friday, May 9, of paralysis, aged seventy-four years.

The largest fish ever caught in Lake George, except one, was taken in yesterday morning by William Taylor of Bolton and G. O. Eddy of Bristol, R. I, It was a pickerel and weighed 25 3-4 pounds. *July 19 1913*

BOY SHOOTS COMPANION WITH AN AIR RIFLE

Sept 16 — 1913

While playing with an air gun a few days ago at his home in Warrensburg, Thompson Rice, the young son of Mr. and Mrs. Philip Rice, shot Harold Wilsey, son of Mr. and Mrs. O. R. Wilsey of that village, in the cheek an inch or two below the left eye. The shot penetrated the flesh for an inch and a half and it was some time before Dr. C. B. Cunningham could remove it.

Young Rice did not know that the air rifle was loaded when he pointed it at the Wilsey boy and pulled the trigger. His parents were away from home and had told his grandmother let him have the air rifle

ONLY SIX ABOVE FREEZING POINT

Jack Frost Sends Mercury Scurrying Down to Thirty-Eight *1913*

Star Sept 15

ALL HUMANITY SHIVERS

Overcoats Much in Evidence and Fires Are Started in Many Buildings—Sunny Side of Street is Most Popular

---

With the mercury volplaning at rapid speed, shivering humanity last night turned its thoughts to overcoats, heavier 'uns and coal bills. Jack Frost, at the same time the friend and foe of Dick O'Brien, ice man and bathing beach proprietor, blew into town on the crest of a cold wave and sent his natural enemy, Mr. Mercury scurrying for the bottom of the thermometer until at 2.30 o'clock this morning it registered thirty-eight degrees, the lowest mark of the fall.

The usual comments about the man with the overcoat and straw hat were heard, and the automobilists wore heavy coats and furs. Pedestrians kept close to the buildings to escape the cool breeze which sent its message of warning to those who got their exercise at the furnace after the lawn mower has been put away for the winter. Clothing and dry goods dealers are anticipating a boom in the heavy clothing trade today.

ANKLE DEEP GOES TO THE ISLANDS

times July 19

Count Mankowski Renounces High Honors to Stick by Lake George. 1913

The Lake George Mirror of today says:

Lake Georgians will be jubilant when they are advised of the fact that Count Cassimer Mankowski has wired to New York to have the Ankle Deep shipped by express Monday night to the St. Lawrence where she will be the entrant of the Lake George Regatta Association for the Gold Challenge Cup in the international races to be held there July 31, August 1 and 2.

Count Mankowski has just returned from New York and Long Island Sound, where the Ankle Deep has been the only contestant to qualify as the American challenger for the Harmsworth trophy. The Count has been sorely tempted to go to England with his boat, especially in face of the flattering inducements offered him both in the sporting and in the social world. It was only his loyalty to Lake George which prevented him from going to the Solent where it is almost certain that the Ankle Deep could have carried off the honors and won world-wide fame. Great credit is due the count for his unswerving loyalty to Lake George, which he so ardently admires. When asked this morning what he would do about making a choice between being the Lake George contestant at the Thousand Islands and the American challenger at the races on the Solent, he said:

"I feel that I owe it to Lake George to keep faith with the Lake George Regatta Association. I am deeply interested in the promotion of motor boat racing here, and it was for that purpose that I built the Ankle Deep. To abandon the races at the Thousand Islands for the honor of being the American challenger would not be good sportsmanship and would seem like deserting Lake George, therefore, I have this morning wired my regrets to Commodore H. H. Melville of the Motor Boat club of America and instructed that the Ankle Deep be shipped by express to the Thousand Islands."

Count Mankowski further stated that he had offered to go to England after the races at the Thousand Islands in case a postponement of the event could be had. There is some talk of such a postponement, but the Count seemed to think it very doubtful if it could be had.

Commodore A. Graham Mills, who has charge of the Thousand Island races and is the owner of the P. D. Q. III, a contestant for the trophy, in a telephone conversation with the Count this morning, begged him not to forsake the Thousand Island races, for he concedes that it is quite likely that the cup will go to New York unless the Ankle Deep intervenes, and the

Commodore is frankly in favor of the Lake George entrant as against the New Yorkers, as he is desirous of keeping the sport out of the professional class.

And inducements such as these, besides many flattering offers the Count is too modest to make public, are what he has turned down in order that he may bring if possible the big international races to Lake George another year. We take off our hats to him for his sportsmanship and his magnificent display of loyalty to Lake George.

Countess Mankowski has been ill for the greater part of the past year with pleurisy and rheumatism and was unable to witness the races last year on the Sound. She has taken a deep interest in the success of the Ankle Deep and was very anxious that the Count enter the races in England; however, she acquiesces in his decision to go to the Thousand Islands and her great regret is that she will be unable to attend.

LAKE GEORGE VETERAN FOUND

news July 16, 1913

George W. Bates, Reported Missing at Gettysburg, Located in Hospital.

George W. Bates, a Lake George veteran, and a member of Latham post, G. A. R., of that place, who accompanied sixteen of his comrades to the Gettysburg reunion and mysteriously disappeared from his tent in the encampment on Sunday, June 29, was finally located in one of the hospitals of the camp and was brought home Saturday.

Mr. Bates, who is seventy years old and has been in poor health for several years, in explanation of his sudden disappearance said he was overcome by the heat and wandered about the battlefield for some time. He entered a tent some distance from his own quarters and lying down upon a cot became nearly unconscious. He was found by a boy scout, but was unable to tell his name and there was nothing about him to give a clue to his identity. The boy reported the case and the veteran was taken to the third ward of the field hospital. For several days his memory remained clouded and nothing could be learned about him.

The strange case was reported to Washington with the hope of thus learning the man's identity. Before the war department could be heard from, however, Mr. Bates fully recovered his memory and was able to supply the much wanted information.

Col. G. F. Bryant, of Glens Falls, whose son married Mr. Bates' daughter, was naturally much interested in the case and was assiduous in his search for the missing man, and when he was found brought him to his home, where he was met by his son-in-law, John Bryant, with an automobile, and conveyed to his Lake George home.

TO GO TO BOLTON CHURCH

June 30 1913 Star

WATERVLIET, June 29.—Rev. H. E. Martin preached his farewell sermon in Trinity Episcopal church tonight. This week Rev. and Mrs. Martin and family will leave for Homer, Mr. Martin's home. Shortly Mr. Martin will take charge of St. Sacrament church, Bolton Landing, for the summer.

BIG HERD OF JERSEY CATTLE BRINGS $14,490

POTSDAM, June 29.—Eighty head of Jersey cattle brought $14,490 at a sale on the farm of George W. Sisson, Jr., of Racquette River Paper company, one mile east of Potsdam. The highest price paid for one animal was $800. Two others were sold for $600 each. May Irwin, the actress, purchased one animal.

Star June 30 1915

Mr. Sisson is a brother of Mrs. E. R. Safford of this city.

BOLTON LANDING.

R. J. Brown suffered a slight shock of paralysis about a week ago.

Mr. and Mrs. Hosea Barber and little daughter are visiting relatives in Hudson Falls. *news July 10, 1913*

Rumor has it that our enterprising young merchant, Harry Ward, was recently married to Miss Clara Holleran, who has been one of the faculty of the local school the past year.

Mrs. William Frasier, of North Bolton, died of measles Monday. She is survived by her husband and two young children; her parents, Mr. and Mrs Jacob Norton, one sister and two brothers, all of Bolton.

The Ladies' Guild of St. Sacrament church held a strawberry and ice cream festival on F. W. Allen's lawn the evening of July 3 and realized about $20 from their efforts. These ladies are of the enterprising sort and never do things by halves.

Rev. and Mrs. E. J. Prescott and son, George, of Blue Mountain Lake, are guests of friends here. Both Mr. and Mrs. Prescott have been in the Glens Falls hospital for treatment lately and as soon as they recover their strength will return to their charge at Blue Mountain Lake.

James Dearstyne, aged about sixty years, died Saturday morning at his home here. Most of Mr. Dearstyne's relatives live in Troy and Albany. He is survived by his wife, who was formerly Miss Anna Lennox, of this place. The funeral services were held at his late home Monday afternoon, the Rev. E. M. Parrott, of Lake George officiating. Interment was made in Bolton cemetery. About eighteen masons from this place and Warrensburgh conducted services at the grave.

It is with pride that we notice the number of young people from our small village who have been for several years past attending the higher institutions of learning. Last year has to its credit at least fourteen.

SPEECH-MAKING MARKS THE FORMAL OPENING OF CENTENNIAL CELEBRATION

Addresses of Welcome Are Followed by Glittering Tributes from Sons of "Little Warren," Here to Pay Honor to the Home County.

The formal opening of the celebration marking the Centennial anniversary of the founding of Warren County was attended by a good sized audience in the Empire theatre yesterday afternoon. The theatre was handsomely decorated for the occasion with flags and bunting and Pond's orchestra furnished an excellent musical program.

Success is Assured.

The celebration was declared open by Hon. Addison B. Colvin, presiding as chairman of the Centennial committee, and the success with which the opening exercises were attended is assurance that the entire week's program will be one of the most successful events ever carried out in Warren county.

Addresses Delivered.

Addresses were delivered by City Attorney Singleton representing Mayor W. Irving Griffing, General Daniel E. Sickles, Hon. George Foster Peabody, and Jeremiah A. O'Leary, of New York and a son of Daniel O'Leary of this city. Mr. O'Leary is one of the prominent young lawyers of New York and in fact is a leading member of the New York bar association. Miss Helen Safford read the poem as announced and published in The Times last evening owing to a severe throat difficulty of the Rev. Obediah Cyrus Auringer, its author, who was seated on the stage with the other speakers.

Speakers Introduced.

Mr. Colvin, in introducing each speaker, did so in a complimentary manner bestowing words of appreciation and commendation on each. He briefly outlined the success each of the speakers had attained, especially Mr. O'Leary and General Sickles, former Glens Falls boys.

Previous to the speaking the Rev. F. X. King, assistant pastor of St. Mary's church gave the invocation, after which Mr. Colvin, in calling attention to the occasion, said that Glens Falls, the city beautiful and always hospitable, is always ready to welcome strangers within its gates, and that now in her holiday attire, in celebrating the one hundredth anniversary of the founding of the county, she takes great pride in extending felicitations to the returning sons and daughters of "Little Warren."

Singleton's Address.

The first speaker was J. Edward Singleton and he extended a cordial welcome to every home coming native of Warren county. He gave a brief review of the progress of the county from its founding to the present day.

"This week we are celebrating the one hundredth anniversary of its birth," said he, "and, as we gaze back, a feeling of gratitude steals over us. One hundred years ago this section was a wilderness and inhabited by the savage. Hostile feet trod the roads and bloody engagements took place. Its mountains have re-echoed with the shrill war-whoop of the savage and its waters have been reddened with the blood of their victims. The war whoop gave place to the settler's axe to pave the way for civilization.

"From a small beginning, Warren county has advanced from a wilderness to a prosperous community, all within a hundred years, which alone is short, the span of one man's life. Many of her sons and daughters have gone abroad and have won success in new fields and becoming celebrated statesmen and soldiers have reflected credit upon the county and us who have remained at home.

"They came back to Little Warren on this occasion and I say you are all welcome. We are glad to have you with us, to recall scenes of childhood days and we hope that your visit will be filled with pleasure and with joy."

Poem Is Read.

Following Mr. Singleton's address of welcome, Miss Safford read the centennial poem. Miss Safford is possessed of considerable elocutionary ability and consequently the reading of the poem was received with deep appreciation.

Address by Sickles.

The next speaker was General Daniel E. Sickles and his address was remarkable, owing to his great age of ninety-three years. He was pushed in his wheel chair to the front of the stage by his special attendant, Henry Lord. It appears that Mr. Lord did not get him as close to the audience as he wanted to be and in asking to be put nearer he said: "I want to get close to my friends, as well as to my enemies."

Chairman Colvin, in presenting the aged general to the audience, dwelt to a considerable extent upon the Battle of Gettysburg, in which General Sickles won distinction and said that of all the brigade generals in that great and decisive battle, only one was left to relate the story as it was enacted and he had come back to the home of his youth, a gallant defender of his flag, to tell his home people of the great struggle.

Chairman Colvin said that it thrilled him with pride to introduce this son of "Little Warren," as one of the most pleasing features of the entire celebration, a conspicuous fighter bereft of his limb, in defending the flag, and a man who had won distinction in other walks of the nation's life.

When General Sickles was moved to the front of the stage he was greeted with a burst of applause.

"I must first express my thanks to the chairman in presenting me to you" said General Sickles. "I am afraid that he has led you to expect more than you will receive. It is true that I did take part in the struggle at Gettysburg and in other important battles at Chancellorsville, Fredericksburg and other important points. I suffered my only wound of the battles and that was the one which resulted in the loss of my limb. Of course we all take chances and we surely did on that battlefield. If you had seen the bullets and cannon balls rushing through the air, you would wonder how any of us survived. It was indeed a great battle, one of the greatest in history.

"There was never a battle fought on which so much depended. If the battle has been lost by the North, England and France would have intervened and that would have been the end of the union. So firmly was President Lincoln impressed with this thought that he prayed to the Almighty God to help him as upon the success of this battle depended the preservation of the nation.

"My friends," continued the general, "our country has been greatly helped by Divine Providence. He has been our friend and saviour from the darkest days of the Revolution to the suppression of the rebellion.

"I am glad to come back to my old home in Glens Falls, a beautiful city, made so by your chairman, Mr. Colvin and by his enterprising associates. No man can visit Glens Falls and not be deeply and favorably impressed with the commercial and progressive spirit evidenced on all sides, as well as with the beautiful homes and streets."

The general then gave a description of his visit to Glens Falls in 1863 and went into detail regarding the reception accorded him.

"I have always had a fondness for Glens Falls. My early boyhood was spent here where my father had large business interests. I always felt that this was my early home and when I received an invitation to attend the Centennial celebration, I availed myself of the opportunity to visit Warren county, with alacrity and pleasure. I have enjoyed myself every minute since I have been here and the cordial reception I received on my arrival and the ovation given me at the hotel last night overwhelmed me with gratitude.

"Now, ladies and gentlemen, you owe a great deal to Mr. Colvin and other gentlemen of enterprise for what they have done for Glens Falls. I don't know of any other city that is so attractive.

"I wish you well, one and all, and

progress and growth. I hope to be spared to come here once more during my life time. Of course I have reached that stage in life where one is uncertain of what will take place.".

O'Leary Next Speaker.

Following General Sickles, Attorney O'Leary spoke and his address was a masterpiece and reflected credit upon the city of Glens Falls and Warren county.

Chairman Colvin, in presenting him, to the audience, said that he was one of the young men who had gone to New York and had done what he had been told to do and kept his mouth shut. Mr. Colvin told of the success that Mr. O'Leary had attained and of how he was feared by many corporations who were willing to pay him a retainer of $500. He is one of the boys of Glens Falls who has made good.

Mr. O'Leary in acknowledging the introduction told the audience that Mr. Colvin wanted him to say that everything he had succeeded in getting he got from Glens Falls and that he would admit that it was so." It is a real pleasure and a proud privilege to come back home and talk to you and congratulate you on an occasion of this kind," said Mr. O'Leary. "To you who have lived here in the city of Glens Falls and the rugged county probably it seems humdrum and monotonous but to one who is away this simple life is ideal. It is almost twenty years since my departure. But the place of my birth, like that of all men, is deep in my affection. It takes me back to days free from care. When a man away from home meets a person from the home town, it seems as if life had begun anew for him. In this way I can safely say that the Warren county colony has become known to every former resident of the county in all parts of the country. The county has made good in every way. It has given two of its native sons to govern the state, in the person of ex-Governors Hughes and Dix. It is not the first time that native sons have been honored with state offices. I can remember when Mr. Colvin was state treasurer. I then was a growing boy. Then there is Mr. Holden, now state historian. Such, you see, are the possibilities of a county like Warren.

"The county has been endowed with nature's choicest blessings. They are in abundance. In fact every thing great and essential belongs to this community."

Here Mr. O'Leary paid a tribute to the schools, the beautiful homes of the city, the conservative banking institutions and the well stocked stores.

"Well, it is that you have cause to compare the present with a hundred years ago. It is pardonable to anticipate the future of the coming generations, as they cannot but be impressed with this celebration.

"They must be taught to have a common cause and that they must do their share in carrying out the ideals that may add to the lustre and glory of the county.

"Looking back a century, which is swept with a single glance, one readily sees what has been done. What human genius worked such a change? We are indeed the same people. What did our forefathers find that wrought such a change?, Was it the virgin forests, the skulking savage? Such things only increased their determination to go ahead. Look in the Declaration of the Independence, search the

cruel snows of Valley Forge, the fields of Saratoga and Gettysburg. All men are created with an equal right and in governing it is the right of every man to exercise his freedom. This spirit of freedom put hope in the breast of 30,000,000 persons with the result that the nation is unparalleled in the world. Wise men were Washington, Jefferson and the rest to build our government on the wisdom of the ages.

"What a wonderful spectacle it is as we glance back over the government of the county grown from a wilderness. Let us not forget our benefactors and Giver of all our blessings that this county may continue to triumphant for another century.

"Finally, let us hope that this county and our glorious country shall continue for another century and forever to propagate the immortal heritage of our fathers, the great principles of democracy and freedom which give power to the dynamos of our industries and spring hope eternal in the human breast, not only in this county and country but throughout the world."

Speech by Peabody.

Hon. George Foster Peabody, spoke last and said that it was a privilege to represent not only the natives of Warren county but all people who find that the mountains and lakes in Warren county are a source of restoration for fatigue and for those in ill health.

"Warren county has been wise in conserving these resources which are fountains of blessings, as is evidenced in General Sickles' remarkable vitality. In speaking of government he said that a county is a method of governing for local purposes. I am impressed at the beginning of the century with the new problems facing the county.

"Now in a county such as Warren, young men are to be trained so as to apply the liberties of the past to the future. They will go forth far and wide and in New York will become leaders. So I venture to go from this place to rejoice that the young men and women will be so trained in the school system as to conserve your resources."

WARREN COUNTY IN HISTORY
Aug. 5 1913

Among the graves of Revolutionary soldiers to be marked by Chepontuc Chapter, D. A. R., in connection with the Centennial celebration this week are those of Jonathan Coolidge, William Robards, Anson Comstock and James Stevenson.

William Robards was born in Canaan, Conn., February 10, 1749. He became a resident of Queensbury patent and died August 9, 1802. He is buried in the Oneida cemetery. He saw service with the Albany county militia, 13th regiment.

Anson Comstock was born in 1763 and died September 14, 1841. Little is known of his history aside from the inscription on the tombstone at his grave in the Glens Falls cemetery, Bay street, which says, "Pensioner of the Revolutionary War."

James Stevenson was born 1754 and died October 22, 1820. He saw service with the Albany county militia, 17th regiment. He is buried in the Oneida cemetery.

Jonathan Coolidge, (Contributed.)

At this centennial season when much thought is being given to the names of the early settlers of our county, as some are of record or can be recalled, or more especially of those herein settled a full hundred years ago, the writer has been reminded and would make mention of one Jonathan Coolidge who with his wife and their two children, removed to, and was settled in the town of Bolton in this county from about the year 1804.

My informant and friend, who is likewise a friend of one of the younger descendents of Mr. Coolidge has told me that Jonathan was a descendant in the fi'q generation of John Coolidge. The emigrant ancestor, who came hither from Cambridgeshire, England, in or about the year 1630, bringing with him it is said the frame of a house that right away erected in Watertown, Mass., and which he thereafter occupied so long as he lived.

He, Jonathan, was born in the town of Ashburnham, Mass., on September 6. 1760, being the fourth of eleven children born to Elisha and Sarah Coolidge, who were thereat settled from the year 1752, having removed thither in that year, from the town of Cambridge, Mass., a suburb of Boston.

The brothers of Jonathan were John,, Elisha and Flavel, while the names of his sisters were Catherine, Sarah, Permelia, Judith, Elizabeth, Relief and Lucy.

Of his life in youth, or prior to his first enlistment in the Revolutionary war, we find on record, yet of Elisha, his father who appears to have been an Inn holder, and likewise interested in lands and mills during those years, much is told in the history of Ashburnham as compiled and published of said town more than one hundred years after his decease.

Our first record of Jonathan bears te of May 5th, 1777, when at the early age of sixteen years and eight months we find him enlisted in Captain Sargent's company of Colonel Josiah Whitney's regiment, serving therein for a period of sixty-eight days in defense of Rhode Island.

Again the same year or in September, 1777, we find him enlisted in Captain Nathaniel Carter's Company, Colonel Job Cushing's regiment, in the war being despatched to the rally to the Hudson, there to join the Americans, mostly under General Gates, who has more recently succeeded General ___ fallen in its command, and was at the time encamped on Bemis Heights, while awaiting the arrival of reinforcements that were being enlisted and sent him from every direction, before attempting to surround or force the enemy to retreat.

He had already intercepted and was holding in check the further advance of such army, five thousand strong under command of General Burgoyne—same encamped on the plains of Saratoga, but a few miles to the northward and where the following month or on about October 17th, 1777 of General Burgoyne surrendered unto him his whole army.

Jonathan's discharge from that enlistment bears date October 23, or but six days after Burgoyne's surrender.

His next enlistment appears to have been in Captain John Putnam's company of Colonel Wade's regiment, that marched from his (Worcester) county on June 30th, 1778 to join General Sullivan at Providence. Such service covered only a period of twenty-six days and thus endeth his record as a soldier.

So far as we have consulted those from him descended no one, if ever told seems to remember how long thereafter he remained in New England with his people or how he happened to leave his home town and come hither alone to the town of Easton in Washington county, but it is presumed that the impressions of the locality when he came hither as a soldier was the attraction.

It was there we next hear of him and where on April 15th, 1797 he married Anna, daughter of John and Mary (Jewett) Burdick whose home was near a farm he had previously purchased and where they thereafter lived, till as first stated they removed to and settled in the town of Bolton in this county as did many other New England people about that time, such settlement having begun about twelve years previous to his time.

Of their children ten, three were born in the town of Easton and the others in Bolton.

The names of their children, and the order of birth were, Anna, Sarah, Jonathan, Eunice, John B., Elizabeth Anna, Mary, Flavel B. and Laura. All of the foregoing or second generation had died prior to the year 1900

The lands in Bolton, about 250 acres, to which they moved were mostly in timber which in part only was cleared and cultivated prior to his death on September 25, 1822 where his wife lived on till July 9th, 1860, when she died and was buried beside him in the Huddle cemetery.

Of the third generation from him there are but six living at this time same being Mrs. E. W. Goodman and Thomas S. Coolidge, children of the late Jonathan and Mary Ophelia Coolidge who are residents of Glens Falls, Mrs. A. G. Goodman, daughter of Walter and Elizabeth Pritchard, who resides in Bolton, also Mrs. Aaron Randall, Morgan H. Tanner and Mrs. William H. Griffin, children of Harvey and Laura Tanner, the former is residing in Glens Falls, while Mrs. Tanner and Mrs. Griffin are still residents of Bolton.

Those belonging to the fourth and fifth generation are many and too numerous to mention.

For a number of years the graves of General Warren Ferriss and Anson Comstock, both soldiers of the Revolutionary war, have remained unnoticed but the work of the members of Chepontuc Chapter will bring tardy recognition to these men, who fought for their country in her early struggles. The remains of these two soldiers with those of many other persons were removed from the old burying ground in West Street to the rear of the Glens Falls cemetery in Bay street near the vault, where they are buried in a double row close together.

HISTORICAL DAY FOR QUEENSBURY

Exercises Held This Afternoon in the First Presbyterian Church.

A good sized audience attended the historical exercises for the Town of Queensbury held this afternoon in the Presbyterian church with the Elbert W. Griffith, superintendent of schools, presiding. The invocation was given the Rev. Herbert E. Martin, of Watervliet, chaplain of the Second regiment, in camp at Miller Hill.

The principal address was delivered by State Historian James A. Holden and appears in full in another part of this paper.

Frederick B. Richards presented the memorial markers in behalf of Che-

State Historian James A. Holden.

pontuc Chapter, Daughters of the American Revolution. Mrs. J. W. Walters spoke briefly in behalf of Jane McCrea Chapter, Daughters of the American Revolution.

General Daniel E. Sickles delivered interesting remarks and the Centennial ode, written by the Rev. Obediah C. Auringer, was read by the poet.

An excellent musical program was rendered throughout the program. J. O. D. de Bondy presided at the organ. The decorations were in keeping with the occasion.

JULY 8, 1913

U. S. Grant

LOS ANGELES, July 7.—A pretty little romance will culminate within the next two weeks in the marriage of Mrs. American Will, of this city, and Ulysses S. Grant, jr., son and namesake of the former president of the United States. Although he has passed his 61st birthday Mr. L. Grant is enjoying robust health and he asserts he is just in the prime of life. Mrs. Will is thirty-three. The couple met two years ago on a Pullman car of a westward bound train. Both were in mourning for their recently deceased first mates. The two met as fellow passengers do, and their friendship grew. Soon after Mr. Grant arrived at his home in San Diego he wrote to Mrs. Will, who has settled at the home of her mother, here. He later visited the beautiful widow at her home. As his visits became more regular their were rumors among friends of the couple of an engagement. Mrs. Will has verified the report with Mr. Grant's sanction. They will enjoy their honeymoon in Europe.

news July 14 1913

MRS. JOHN REIRDEN.

Mrs. John Reirden, aged seventy-six years, died Friday morning at 10 o'clock, at her home on Schroon avenue. She had been ill a long time with a complication of diseases. Mrs. Reirden was born in Ireland and came to this country with her parents at an early age. They settled in Granville, where the deceased was married in 1846 to John Reirden, then a resident of that place. Forty-seven years ago they removed to Warrensburgh and settled on a farm on Harrington hill, where they resided until about a year ago, when they came to their place in the village to spend their declining years. Besides her husband Mrs. Reirden is survived by one daughter, Mrs. Fra H. Worden, of Lake George. The funeral was held at the house Sunday afternoon at 4 o'clock, and was conducted by the Rev. T. J. Hunter, pastor of the Baptist church. Interment in the village cemetery.

JOHN ANDERSON, SR.

John Anderson, Sr., the venerable father of John Anderson, Jr., the well known Adirondack lumberman, hotel man and merchant, died Monday at his home in Newcomb, after an illness of only one week of diseases incident to old age. Mr. Anderson was born in Canada eighty-seven years ago. For many years he lived on a farm in Wevertown, leaving there about eight years ago to make his home in Newcomb. He was a man of sterling character and was highly esteemed wherever he was known. He was married fifty-six years ago in Glens Falls and his wife preceded him to the grave only four weeks ago. They are now lying side by side in the Catholic cemetery at North Creek. Mr. Anderson's funeral was held yesterday morning at St. John's church, in Newcomb, and was conducted by the Rev. Father Desmet. news aug 7

E. J. WORDEN HAS AN EXCITING TIME

July 8 — 1913

Tossed About On Lake George Five Hours in Small Motorboat

DURING HEAVY WINDSTORM

Gasolene Tank "Runs Dry" When Craft is in the Middle of the Lake—Passes the Night On the Water

Supervisor Edwin J. Worden yesterday passed one of the "quietest" days of his career in an endeavor to recuperate from his harrowing experiences of early yesterday morning and Sunday night, when for five hours he was tossed about on the surface of Lake George in a small motor boat at the complete mercy of the waves in the terrific storm.

Mr. Worden went out on the lake shortly after 9 o'clock Sunday night, taking a number of men to the east shore to fight the fire which raged on the mountains there. After passing a little more than an hour on that side, he started to return to the village after more men. When he reached a point near the center of the lake, the gasolene tank "ran dry" and he was left stranded without an oar of any kind. The high wind quickly turned his boat about so that it lay in the trough of the waves, the water dashing high over the sides of the boat, soaking its interior as well as the clothes of its occupant, who in desperation had torn up a part of the flooring of the boat in an unsuccessful endeavor to paddle to shore.

About 1 o'clock yesterday morning the terror stricken residents of the east side of the lake tried to get into communication with the supervisor in the Hotel Worden, when it was learned he had left the east shore more than two hours before and that he had not reached the hotel. Genuine alarm was felt in the hotel for its owner's safety and a search was started for him but the rescuing party confined its efforts to the upper portion of the head of the lake, while the supervisor and his boat were floating toward shore fully a mile below.

Meanwhile Mr. Worden wrapped himself in a blanket and braved the elements in one end of the boat until daylight when he found himself about 100 feet from shore, near what is now known as Menzies Point. His boat was hurled into the shore but with the aid of the piece of wood he had ripped from the bottom of the boat, he managed to prevent the vessel from dashing on the rocks. He alighted on shore and hurrying to the Menzies cottage, borrowed a quantity of gasolene and embarked on his homeward journey, arriving at the hotel in less than an hour.

In addition to the forest fire and his nerve racking experience of yesterday, Mr. Worden is also confronted by serious difficulty because of the condition of the water reservoirs of the village of Lake George. Residents of the place have been given orders to discontinue the use of garden hose, as the supply of water in the two reservoirs now in use is growing so small the condition is somewhat threatening.

There are two other reservoirs for use by the village, but both are unfit for use at the present time because of accidents. One of the accidents effects the piping of a reservoir and is of recent date while the other, a minor one, dates back to the high water of early spring. A large gang of men is being worked on the reservoirs and it is hoped to have both connected with the supply pipes within three days.

Add to the above mentioned cares, his duties as proprietor of one of the most popular hotels on Lake George, as owner and manager of the Worden garage and as a member of the board of supervisors now in quarterly session, and it may be said Mr. Worden spent a "quiet" day yesterday.

MRS. ELIZABETH HARRIS.

Mrs. Elizabeth Harris, aged seventy-six years and for more than half a century a highly respected resident of Lake George, died Monday morning at 2 o'clock at the home of her son, Walter P. Harris, with whom she had resided since the death of her husband, Capt. E. S. Harris, December 19, 1906 At that time Mrs. Harris suffered a nervous breakdown and had since been in failing health. During the last year her decline had been very rapid. Besides the son mentioned she is survived by another son, George B. Harris, of Bolton Landing, and two sisters, Miss Matilda Fisher and Mrs. S. C. Johnson, of Luzerne. The funeral was held yesterday afternoon, at the Presbyterian church, the Rev. Randolph Rock officiating. Interment in the Lake George union cemetery. The bearers were Supervisor E. J. Worden, R. E. Archibald, H. W. Sisson, R. Cutler Bradley, F. F. Hawley and Arthur F. West. *news July 19 1913*

One Little Boy

A Poem Replete with Human Love

By heaven's first law my house was kept,
  The brass was polished bright,
Each room was dusted well and swept,
  It was a pleasant sight.
But now mud-tracks are on the floor,
  And with them many a toy,
And finger-marks upon the door
  Tell of one little boy.

Once quiet reigned, or silvery sounds
  Of music filled the air;
Now tramp of many feet resounds,
  And, clanging up the stair,
March martial bands, with fife and drum,
  All flushed with pride and joy,
Behold at "double-quick" they come
  Led by one little boy.

Time was I pondered Browning's verse
  And Walter Pater read;
Of Ibsen I could once converse,
  But now—a tired head
Is cuddled close at "story time"
  When evening shadows fall,
And I am wise in nursery rhyme
  And fable, that is all.

Once, when I tucked him into bed,
  He hugged me tight, and then
"What would you sell me for?" he said—
  I kissed him once again
And answered, "Not for diamonds, pearls,
  Nor gold without alloy;
Nor all the wealth of all the worlds
  Would buy one little boy."

Delegate to Peace Conference.

Mrs. Inez Rice Keller, of New York, who was at the Fort William Henry hotel, Lake George, for several weeks, and recently visited her friend, Mrs. Daniel L. March, in this village, sailed from New York Saturday, on the Hamburg-American steamer Imperator, for Holland. Mrs. Keller is a delegate to the International Peace Congress which will meet at The Hague in September. *news Aug 13 1913*

Schroon River Very Low.

The Schroon river is now but little more than a big brook, the water having fallen nearly as low as in any dry period of previous years. Water in the reservoir of the village waterworks system is nearly exhausted and unless the protracted drought is broken soon there will surely be a water famine.

GIRL IS KILLED IN AN AUTO ACCIDENT

Times July 12 1913

Miss Gertrude Mordecai of Charleston Dies on Way to Hospital.

FIVE HAVE NARROW ESCAPE

Accident Occurs on the Bolton Road When Tire Bursts, Sending Machine Crashing Into Tree.

In an automobile accident which occurred about 2 o'lock this afternoon near the George Foster Peabody residence on Bolton Road, Gertrude Mordecai, aged 19, of Charleston, S. C., was fatally injured, Cornelia Mordecai, aged 16, her sister and Owen Starr, the chauffeur, were painfully injured and Mrs. T. M. Mordecai, mother of the girls, Hanna Folk, a guest and Henry Schermerhorn narrowly escaped being hurled to their death.

At the time of the accident the Mordecai machine was headed toward Bolton. In turning out for an approaching car a tire burst and without a moment's warning the machine crashed into a tree, throwing the occupants with terrific force to the ground.

Gertrude Mordecai was rendered unconscious, and bleeding profusely she was picked up and placed in an automobile driven by Royal Peabody, who with all possible haste hurried to the Glens Falls hospital, but on the way death overtook the young woman. In the car also were Mrs. Mordecai and Cornelia, the latter of whom is not believed to be seriously hurt.

Miss Folk sustained a broken arm. The party had been in Glens Falls on a shopping tour and was homeward bound' at the time of the accident.

Miss Mordecai's skull was fractured and the brain was lacerated. The remains will be taken to Charleston tonight, leaving on the sleeper.

The Mordecai family arrived at Lake George about eight weeks ago and was spending the summer in a cottage owned by James W. Lockhart, until such a time as their new home on Bolton road was completed. Mr. Mordecai is a prominent Charleston attorney.

It is said that the chauffeur was in no way at fault for the accident, as he did all in his power to avoid crashing into the tree.

JOHN G. HARRIS.

John G. Harris, a native of Warrensburgh, who left here about fifty years ago and made his home in Johnstown, where he engaged in glovemaking, died Sunday night after a year's illness from a complication of diseases.

CHARLES J. PEABODY IS A GLENS FALLS VISITOR

In Interview Financier Says Financial Conditions Are Threatening.

Charles J. Peabody, Lake George and New York city, was in town this morning with his family, having driven down for trading purposes and diversion. Mr. Peabody is now domiciled for the summer months in the beautiful new home built on Bolton Road, and certainly has every convenience, facility and advantage that advanced architectural talent can produce. Not one of the modern and costly homes of the large colony on this celebrated thoroughfare is more pretentious.

Interviewed with reference to the financial situation, Mr. Peabody, who is a man of large financial interests, said: "There will be no large sums of money floating about looking for borrowers in the future. Conservative users, who make legitimate disbursements and operate along safe and sane lines, will no doubt obtain reasonable requirements. No trying experiences or nerveracking periods are in sight, according to my best judgment. The concensus of opinion among bankers and large financial men in the money centers is that financial conditions are so threatening all should conserve their resources and keep a steady hand on the pilot wheel, and carefully watch ahead for breakers."

'Lavery Store to Open Saturday.

Charles E. Lavery will reopen his store at the foot of Elm street, opposite the Osborne bridge, Saturday, with a full stock of general merchandise, specializing on shoes. Mr. Lavery formerly conducted the store but went out of business several years ago and rented the building to another merchant. It has now been closed about three years and it will be a pleasant sight to see its doors again swing open to the public with Mr. Lavery's smiling face and courteous attention extending a welcome to all who come. It is announced that the store will be closed on Wednesday and Friday evenings at 6:45 o'clock. *News*

Aug 23 1913

OBITUARY

Times Aug 1913

Edgar Wetmore

Edgar Wetmore, proprietor of the Grove House at East Lake George, died last evening at 8:30 o'clock at the home of his daughter, Mrs. W. R. Root, 42 Grant avenue. He was eighty-three years old and was known throughout Northern New York as one of the best hotel men. Death followed a stroke of apoplexy. Mr. Wetmore attended the Centennial celebration in this city last Wednesday, and it is believed that the excitement was too great for him.

OLD ENOUGH TO KNOW OWN MINDS

Star Sept 19 1913

Syracuse Woman, 83, Travels 250 Miles to Wed Man, 81

ACQUAINTED FIFTY YEARS

Ceremony Starts Isaac Worden On Third Matrimonial Voyage —To Reside in Lake George —Cupid is Busy

LAKE GEORGE, Sept. 18.—After having traveled 250 miles by rail, a Mrs. Wright of Syracuse alighted from the 7:20 o'clock train Tuesday evening in the Lake George station and, linking her arm in that of Isaac Worden made her way to the home of Rev. Randolph Rock, where a ceremony was performed which made the couple man and wife. The bride is eighty-three years of age and the groom is two years her junior.

The marriage was the culmination of a pretty romance brought about through correspondence and the aid of relatives, although the pair is said to have met about fifty years ago when Mrs. Wright was here with her husband, who was then employed on the construction of the old Fort William Henry hotel.

Mr. and Mrs. Worden are as happy and enthusiastic as any newlyweds who sought the shores of historic Lake George to while away the blissful hours of their honeymoon. They have leased rooms in a residence owned by Fred Selleck and plan to begin light housekeeping within a short time. Both are surprisingly active and look forward to a long period of domestic happiness. The present Mrs. Worden is the third wife of her aged husband.

Cupid's work of Tuesday evening was not completed with the marriage of Mr. and Mrs. Worden and in less than half an hour after Mr. Rock had wished the aged couple the best in life, another pair of lovers found their way to his residence to be made man and wife. They were Miss Bertha Marton of Gansevoort, who was employed as a domestic in the home of Dr. C. K. Burt, and Forrest Wallace of Glens Falls, who worked in the Howe restaurant during the summer season. Mr. and Mrs. Wallace plan to go to Warrensburg next week where they will make their future home.

—164—

MYSTERY SOLVED BY OLD LETTERS

Isaac Morris Tells Why Liberty Bell Carried Famous Inscription.

PHILADELPHIA, July 1.—The great mystery of the Liberty Bell, the manner in which the famous inscription, "Proclaim Liberty Throughout All the Land Unto All the Inhabitants Thereof," came to be cast in the bell, and the reason for it, which has baffled the historian for half a century, has at last been solved. With the finding a few days ago of letters written by Isaac Morris, who was superintendent of the old State House when the bell was ordered, in 1751, Wilfred Jordan, curator of Independence Hall, has been able to supply the long sought explanation.

According to the papers which have disclosed the secret, the inscription was placed on the bell in England when it was made, in 1751. The object was to dedicate the bell as a memorial on the fiftieth anniversary of the granting of the charter to the City of Philadelphia by William Penn. The words were suggested by Morris, who was a profound Biblical student, and they were taken from the tenth verse of the twenty-fifth chapter of Leviticus.

This intelligence is contained in letters addressed to members of the Assembly by Morris when the plans for the bell were under consideration. It had been planned to celebrate the anniversary of the city's semi-centennial, and as the small bell used in the State House had proved insufficient, it was suggested that a mammoth memorial bell be made to replace it, which would be the largest in British America.

The bell is a copy of the famous "Big Ben," the largest of the bells in Westminster Abbey, London. The firm which cast the bell at Whitechapel, which at that time was outside the limits of the City of London, was that of Thomas Lester, which is still doing business.

One of the letters written by Morris states that when the bell was recast in this country to improve the sound, Pass and Stow, the mechanics, made a better job of the inscription than the makers in London, the letters being more legible and more artistic.

The recasting of the bell was made necessary because of a crack which occurred within a year after its arrival in this country. Two colonists who were given the job of recasting it added one and one-half ounces of copper to every pound of the bell metal, which they believed, would not only make the bell tougher, but add to its sound.

The result however, was to give the bell so muffled a tone as to render it unfit for use, and the two men who recast it were subjected to so much ridicule that they begged for permission to do the job over.

This was granted, and after the copper had been reduced to a lesser proportion the bell was replaced in the tower, finer than ever, where it hung until thirty-six years after it had been cracked the second time. This last break, which is the one which is now seen in the bell, occurred at the funeral of Chief Justice John Marshall, on July 4, 1835, and not on July 4, 1776, when the Declaration of Independence was proclaimed.

One of the letters written by Morris, dated March 10, 1753, after the bell had broken the first time, is in part as follows:

"It was cracked by the stroke of the clapper, without any other violence, as it was hung up to try the sound; though this was not very agreeable to us, we concluded to send it back to London by Captain Budden, but he could not take it aboard, upon which two ingenious workmen undertook to cast it here. I am just now informed that they have this day opened the mould and have got a good bell, which, I confess, pleases me very much that we should first venture upon and succeed in the greatest bell cast, for aught I know, in England and America. The mould was finished in a very masterly manner, and the letters, I am told, are better than on the old one."

SMITH M. WEED IS IN ALBANY

Times June 8 1913

OLD-TIME POLITICIAN RECALLS HAPPENINGS OF TWENTY-FIVE YEARS AGO.

(Albany Journal.)

Smith M. Weed, the veteran Democratic politician from northern New York, has been spending several days in town. He came principally to pay his respects to Governor Sulzer. He met a few old time friends about the capitol and some others at the Ten Eyck. He has enjoyed their company and delighted to talk over the times when he was in Albany in an official capacity.

Warrensburgh-Lake George Road Opened.

The new state road between Warrensburgh and Lake George, which has been in course of construction for two years, was opened for travel Saturday by order of the state highway department. The road is not yet entirely completed, but the top dressing will be applied while it is in use. The road is pronounced by motorists one of the best in this section. The last three miles of the Chestertown road will be finished in about ten days and a long stretch of improved highway will then be completed between Albany and Westport, Essex county.

HORSE KILLED BY HUDSON VALLEY CAR

Wagon is Demolished, But the Driver Escapes With Only Slight Injuries.

MAN HAD FALLEN ASLEEP

Horse Driven by Dennis Pratt Strays Onto the Tracks and Meets Death Near Batesville.

Times Sept 22 1713

One of the most miraculous escapes from instant death was experienced by Dennis Pratt of Bolton, shortly after 8 o'clock Saturday evening on the tracks of the Hudson Valley Railway Company, just south of the Batesville crossing, near Lake George. The horse Pratt was driving was instantly killed and the wagon in which he was riding asleep was carried 100 feet with him in it, the wagon being demolished. Pratt was found beside the tracks still sitting in the detached wagon seat, in which he was riding just before the horse and rig were struck. Pratt escaped with a cut over his left eye and bruises about his legs. The man, horse and wagon were on the company's right of way at the time of the accident.

Pratt was on his way home and is claimed to have been in an intoxicated condition. He fell asleep in the open rig in which he was riding alone and when the horse got to the Hudson Valley tracks, leading from the county clerk's office around toward Batesville, it followed the tracks. The animal hauled the wagon with its unconscious load bumping over the ties to within 700 feet south of the Batesville crossing, when the southbound car, in charge of Motorman William H. LaPoint and Conductor Ross Taylor struck it.

According to a statement made by Motorman William H. LaPoint, his car left Warrensburg at 8:10 p. m. The car was going at about forty miles an hour, just before he rounded a curve beyond the Batesville crossing, when he slowed down. As the curve was rounded LaPoint says he saw the horse and wagon with the man in the seat, apparently asleep coming up the track. They were then about four poles distant from the front of the car. The powerful arc light on the front of the car showed the man and outfit very plainly. LaPoint said that he applied the air and put on the reverse but being on considerable of a down grade was unable to bring his car to a stop in time to avoid a collision.

The front end of the car first hit the horse and killed it almost instantly. The body of the animal was thrown to the left side of the track and the wagon was then struck.

—165—

WORKING TO THE TOP

news Sept 25

Warrensburgh Boy Winning Wide Fame as Trombone Soloist

1913

OFFERED CHAIR IN SOUSA'S BAND

"Dick" Whitby, Who Learned to Toot a Horn In Local Band, Is Now Star Performer and Shining Light In the Musical World.

"Dick" Whitby, who as a boy in Warrensburgh learned to toot a horn in a brass band, has since he left here some fifteen years ago become a professional musician and has by sheer ability risen so rapidly in the musical world that he is now in the front rank of instrumentalists and is considered one of the few great slide trombone soloists in the country. Such is his ability that he has recently been offered the second chair in the trombone section of John Philip Sousa's celebrated concert band, with a promised promotion to the first chair upon the retirement of a veteran musician who now occupies that position.

STARBUCK'S AUTO DAMAGES BICYCLE

Saratoga Man Immediately Proves He is Unlike Most Motorists

1913

Star Sept. 25

CAR DRIVER NOT AT FAULT

Edgar Starbuck of Saratoga demonstrated a little after 5 o'clock yesterday afternoon before a large crowd in front of Dolan's drug store that he greatly differs from the average autoist. Mr. Starbuck was coming down Glen street in his large touring car and in Bank square the machine struck and damaged the rear wheel of a bicycle ridden by an elderly man, whose name was not learned. Calling to his chauffeur to stop, the Saratoga man alighted and tendered the victim a ten dollar bill, asking as he did so:

"Will this cover the damage?"

The scowl faded instanter from the cyclist's features and was replaced by a broad smile which for a time threatened to split the face from ear to ear as the man yelled:

"You bet, that covers the entire damage."

Mr. Starbuck reentered his auto and proceeded on his way, followed by prolonged cheers from the spectators. In the opinion of the cyclist and several eye witnesses Mr. Starbuck's driver was entirely blameless. As the owner trundled the damaged bike away he was heard to murmur: "I hope that man's car hits my wheel every week day and twice on Sundays."

A LAKE GEORGE ISSUE.

Nov 7 1913

The Summer Hotels Win an Interesting and Important Controversy.

The township of Bolton, on Lake George, is unique among rural towns in the extent of its summer business, owing to the fact that some of the best-known hotels on Lake George, and therefore in America, are within the borders of the town. These hotels are directly or indirectly the chief source of revenue for the people of the lake shore villages, and are also of great importance in supplementing the social life of the owners of large private estates on the west shore of Lake George. These hotels, of course, find their patronage benefited by a liberal policy with regard to license, not because of any important results in the sale of liquors but very largely because of the prejudice existing among the traveling public against those hotels which are distinctly known as "temperance hotels," in "temperance towns." That is a condition and not a theory. Therefore, as a measure of importance to the prosperity and even to the continuance of these hotels on any scale of magnitude, their proprietors have always opposed such action as would exclude them from a license privilege. As in all rural towns, there are in Bolton advocates of a no-license policy, and the subject was made an issue at the town meeting Tuesday of this week. The arguments that if the town were to retain the summer business which is its chief source of revenue it must avoid a narrow and exclusive policy finally prevailed, and the prohibitory forces were defeated.

This decision affected no less than seven hotels in Bolton, composing on the whole the largest property interest in the town—by far the largest when the private estates whose owners are also opposed to a no-license policy are included. An important result of this tolerant action is shown in preparations made, now that the question has been disposed of, to enlarge and improve the hotel accommodations along the lake front.

For instance, the Sagamore, which is one of the leading summer hotels of the country, is about to expend in preparation for next season $10,000 in improvements to the house and grounds. This money would not have been expended if the no-license policy had been adopted, and the management had under serious consideration in that event discontinuing the location of the hotel at that point. The improvements will include a complete fire-escape system

---

Oct 30 MRS. DAVID FOSMER. *1913*

Mrs. David Fosmer died very suddenly of heart trouble Friday morning, at her home in Bolton. Besides her husband she is survived by two sons, Paul and Earl, and a sister, Pauline Fuller, all of Bolton. The funeral was held Sunday afternoon at 2 o'clock, at the house.

HE HELD HIS GROUND.

He didn't "own the country,"
But as he looked around
He found a joy in living
And held his little ground.

He didn't gain the far heights
Where Fortune's friends are crowned,
But Love strewed roses where he held
Love's title to his ground.

---

news cut

MRS WILLIAM COON *1913*

Mrs. William Coon, of Bolton Landing, died Sunday after a long illness resulting from an attack of measles last spring.

LEVI OGDEN IS CLAIMED BY DEATH

Had Been in Failing Health During the Past Week.

times Oct 30 1913

IS TAKEN VIOLENTLY ILL

Had Been in the Transportation Business on the Champlain Canal—Was a Progressive Citizen

Levi Ogden, one of the oldest and best known residents of this city, died this morning at 3 o'clock at his home, 61 Bay street. He had been in failing health during the past week, but was not confined to the house until yesterday afternoon, having been taken violently ill while eating diner. During the morning he enjoyed a drive about the city in company with Mrs. Sharp, an aunt of his wife, and appeared to be in usual health. On returning to his home he ate a good dinner, but on rising from the table complained of terible pains in his abdomen and a physician was summoned. Hypodermics were administered and between 8 and 9 o'clock he rested. During the night he suffered intensely and at 3 o'clock this morning the end came.

Mr. Ogden was a native of this city and from early manhood had been engaged in the transportation business on the Champlain canal. He also conducted a horse business. In the transportation business he was known all along the canal from New York to Rouses Point on Lake Champlain. He was one of the old-time boatmen when boating was at its height. During late years he had owned a fleet of boats which plied the canal from Glens Falls to New York.

In 1899 he was elected village trustee of the old village of Glens Falls by the Republicans. He was always progressive and did much to promote the interests of the city.

Mrs. Frances Ross, aged nearly seventy years, died in Bolton Wednesday night, September 24, at the home of her son, Ernest Ross, with whom she resided. Mrs. Ross had been a great worker all her life until within the last year. She is survived by five sons, George, Forest, Jay, Edward and Ernest, all of Bolton; one sister, Mrs. Eliza Remington, of Chester; two brothers, Wellington and Forester Bentley, of Bolton, and several grandchildren. The funeral was held at the Bolton Baptist church Sunday afternoon and was conducted by the pastor, the Rev. George N. Gates. Interment in the Huddle cemetery.

PINNED UNDER AUTO BUT ONLY BRUISED

Orville C. Smith, On Bicycle, Struck By Machine Owned By Robert Gibson

HAS MIRACULOUS ESCAPE

Star Sept 30 1913

Grocer Riding Up Bay Street Thought Autoist Was Going to Turn Into Maple—Head-on Collision Results

Pinned under an automobile in such a manner it had to be propped up to release him, but sustaining only bruises, Orville C. Smith had a miraculous escape from death, fatal or serious injury last evening. A machine owned and driven by Robert Gibson struck a bicycle Mr. Smith was riding from his store to his home at 122 Bay street, and threw him under the wheels of the car.

Mr. Smith left the store about 6:30 o'clock and was proceeding up Bay street. Mr. Gibson was coming down the street. When the former neared the corner of Maple street he thought Mr. Gibson intended to turn down that street, and in order to avoid the auto he turned to the left. The autoist, however, had no intention of going down Maple and turned to the right. The result was the automobile and bicycle met in a head-on collision.

Mr. Smith was thrown under the machine. The car was going slowly and the driver soon brought it to a stop. With the aid of several bystanders he went to the grocer's assistance, but the latter was pinned under the car in such a manner that it required no little effort to release him. The car was lifted off the ground and Mr. Smith was placed in the machine and taken to the office of Dr. T. I. Henning, where he was treated, after which he was removed to his home. No bones were broken, but he was badly bruised and complained of lameness in his back.

Both Mr. Gibson and Mr. Smith each declared the other was not at fault, and at the latter's home it was stated Mr. Gibson had done everything possible to aid the injured man.

LAMB-DENNO.

Merritt L. Lamb and Miss Ellen Denno, both of Bolton, were married on September 24, by the Rev. George N. Gates, at the Baptist parsonage in that place.

Post Oct 2 1913

DEATHBED WEDDING OBSERVED SATURDAY

Times

Bolton Girl in Presence of Dying Father Weds Glens Falls Youth.

Oct 3 1913

Complying with a request made by her father, Stephen M. Pratt, an aged resident of the town of Bolton, who died yesterday afternoon, Miss Elizabeth Pratt, his youngest daughter and Lester Duell, a former Glens Falls boy, were married at the bedside of the dying father, Saturday night, shortly before nine o'clock. Tuesday Mr. Pratt, who was seventy-one years old, was stricken for the third time with a shock of paralysis and realizing that the end was near he called his daughter to his bedside and told her that he would be pleased to see her married, so long as the wedding had been arranged for this fall. The daughter at once agreed to the request and at once sent word to her fiance. Saturday night the Rev George Gates pastor of the Baptist church, was called in and in the presence of the dying father, the two young people were married. Only immediate relatives were present.

From that time until yesterday afternoon at 4:30 o'clock the old man continued failing.

Mr. Pratt was a veteran of the Civil war, and was also a member of the Odd Fellows' lodge.

AGED RESIDENT IS CLAIMED BY DEATH

Times Oct 22 1913

Edwin Roberts, Eighty-two Years Old, Succumbs to Paralytic Shock.

Edwin Roberts, one of the oldest residents of Warren county passed away at his late home, 43 West street at nine o'clock last night. He was in his usual health up to two weeks ago, when he suffered a stroke of paralysis, from which he did not rally. He was born in Dorset, Vt., January 6, 1831, and was 82 years old. When about thirty years old he removed to Brant Lake, where he spent the greater part of his life, engaged in farming and the fur business. Always a Bible student, his greatest pleasure was in discussing and reading the Bible.

In the year 1863 he married Ann Eliza Leach, who died June 11, 1906.

STEPHEN M. PRATT.

Stephen M. Pratt, one of Bolton's oldest and most respected citizens, died of paralysis Sunday afternoon, after only a few days' illness, aged seventy-one years. He was a veteran of the Civil War and was well known throughout the northern part of the county.

IMPORTANT REAL ESTATE TRADE

Star Sept 30 1913

McMullen & Leavens Shirt Co. and Edward McSweeney Exchange Properties

One of the most important real estate transactions of the year was completed yesterday when officials of the McMullen & Leavens Shirt company and Edward McSweeney, proprietor of the McSweeney house, reached an agreement which provided an exchange of properties on diagonally opposite corners of Lawrence and Cooper streets.

The trade is regarded as most advantageous to both the contracting parties. The McSweeney house will be moved from its present site to the opposite corner within a short time, when it will be in an even more suitable place than at present. It will be on the side of Lawrence street which is most extensively traveled by pedestrians from the D. & H. station.

Their newly acquired lot will give McMullen & Leavens a frontage of about 250 feet on both Lawrence and Cooper streets, the large factory of the company forming an L.

PREFERRED TO TAKE CHANCES

Star Oct 10 1913

Man of Millions Who Conducted His Business as a Game of Chance

The late John W. Gates was always ready and willing to make a wager on every question that came up at any time or place. He was familiarly known to his intimate acquaintances as 'Bet-a-Million' Gates. A friend once referred to him as a born gambler. "Yes, I am," said Mr. Gates, "and so long as I win at least fifty-one per-cent. of the time I'm going to continue to gamble.'" He made many millions of dollars in his various business enterprises and it is said that he always referred to them as games of chance.

ELLA ACCUSED OF BIGAMY

Oct 1 1913 *Star*

Ella Baker of Hague has been held to await the action of the grand jury on a charge of bigamy, it being alleged she married within New York state after her first husband, Clarence Baker, of Hague, secured a divorce from her. Bail has been fixed at $500.

"LUMBERMAN LEW."

news nov 6 1913

A Story of Warren County Politics and a Warrensburgh Man.

"Lumberman Lew," a book recently issued from the press of the Glens Falls Publishing company, has as its principal character a man whose identity the reader will have no difficulty in guessing. Though he is mentioned by no other name than that from which the book takes its title, and the name of the town in which most of the scenes are laid is given as "Warrensville," there can be no mistake in assuming that the happenings recorded in the tale, real and imaginary, took place in Warrensburgh, and the hero is none other than L. W.—well, as the author has not disclosed the full name, we won't. Anyhow, we all know him, and so do thousands of people in the big world outside, and know that too much that is good cannot be said about his ability as a political leader, financier, manufacturer and a man of high distinction in the various walks of life he has entered.

MRS. ELIZA VANDERBURGH

Mrs. Eilza Vandenburgh, aged seventy-seven years, died of paralysis Thursday night, at her home in Bolton, after an illness of less than three weeks. She was the widow of Jacob Vandenburgh, who died about eight years ago, and is survived by two sons and five daughters, George and Edward Vandenburgh, Mrs. Fred Wilcox, Mrs. Jay Ross, Mrs. Theodore Braley and Miss Carrie Vandenburgh, of Bolton, and Mrs. Lorenzo Kent, of Glens Falls. Mrs. Vandenburgh was a native of Edinburgh, Saratoga county, and is survived by many relatives in that vicinity, including one brother; also by a brother in Wisconsin. The funeral was held at her late home Saturday afternoon and was largely attended. The service was conducted by the Rev. George N. Gates, pastor of the Baptist church. Interment was made in the Bolton cemetery. *Oct 16 1913*

JOHN FERRIS.

John Ferris, of North Chester, died Monday night. Though seventy-two years of age, he was until last Friday in excellent health. During the day he was taken ill and from the first there seemed little hope of his recovery, as his whole system seemed to give way. He had been a life-long resident in the Gore section, marrying in early life Miss Mary Jane Hammond, who died a year ago this month. Since her death he has made his home with John E. Cole, where he was cared for to the last. The funeral was held at the North Chester Baptist church, the Rev. Bert S. Van Vleet officiating. Interment in the cemetery on Federal flats.

AGED LADY'S NARROW ESCAPE.

news nov 13, 1913

Mrs. Margaret Morgan Overcome by Coal Gas at Diamond Point.

Mrs. Margaret Morgan, an aged lady of Diamond Point, was found by one of her neighbors unconscious on the floor of her home early Sunday morning nearly dead from asphyxiation by coal gas. A physician was summoned and she was revived with much difficulty.

Mrs. Morgan had been visiting relatives in Glens Falls and returned home Saturday. She built coal fires in her kitchen range and parlor heater and when she retired closed the draughts. Alone in the house she awoke in the night or early in the morning suffering extreme distress from nausea. She arose and made an effort to reach a window, but fell to the floor beofre she could do so. She became unconscious and how long she remained in that condition before she was found she could not tell. Fortunately a window had been raised about two inches and the fresh air thus admitted diluted the deadly gas sufficiently to make its action slower so that Mrs. Morgan was able to withstand its effect for a longer period. However, it would surely have caused her death had not assistance reached her as it did.

Mrs. W. H. Straight, of this village, who is a niece of Mrs. Morgan, received a telephone message about 8 o'clock Sunday morning informing her of the accident and immediately started tor Diamond Point to care for her relative. Mrs. Morgan has now almost entirely recovered

---

A Holiday Hint.

Anyone interested in having photographs taken for Christmas presents for their friends will do well to call at once at A. L. Mix's gallery, and make arrangements for the same. He has a good line of card mounts to order from.

You'll see his sign above the door,
A pleasant, warm retreat,
Just opposite to John G. Smith's,
North side of Hudson street.

Walter Gates, of Bolton Landing, was called to this place last week Wednesday to attend the funeral of his uncle, John Ferris. *news nov 20 1913*

DEATH RECORD *1913*

Post Star nov 27

News was received here yesterday of the death of Daniel Sprague, a former resident of this city, which occurred Monday night in the St. Louis home of his son, Charles B. Sprague. Mr. Sprague was a well known resident of Bolton and came here a few years ago to reside with his son, who was at that time foreman of the ironing department of the Yorke Shirt company.

FORMER LOCAL BOY GUARDS ROOSEVELT

Erwin J. Smith in Charge of Detective at Testimonial Dinner.

AN ENVIABLE REPUTATION

Apprehends Butler Who Recently Robbed the Colonel's Home of Jewels Valued at $5,000.

Erwin J. Smith, a former Glens Falls boy, who some years ago left here to win fame and fortune, and who for some time has been manager of the New York office of the W J. Burns Detective Agency, is fast establishing for himself an enviable reputation in the detective world.

At the dinner to be tendered Col. Roosevelt tonight in New York by the National and State Progressive service, Mr. Smith will have charge of a squad of Burns men. The sleuths will be garbed in evening dress and will be so seated as to command a view of the entire assemblage.

Tomorrow Mr. Smith will have charge of a squad of Burns men, who will accompany the Colonel to the steamer Van Dyke, on which he will take passage for South America.

These precautions are taken not at the request of Colonel Roosevelt, but in response to demands by his friends that he be given all possible protection.

It was Smith who apprehended the butler who recently robbed the Roosevelt home at Oyster Bay of jewels valued at $5,000. There now hangs in Mr. Smith's office a highly prized photograph of the Former President, bearing the appended inscription: "To E. J. Smith, Esq. With the best wishes of Theodore Roosevelt."

W. W. Brown Takes Another Hotel.

W. W. Brown, formerly of Glens Falls and Lake George, has taken the management of the Aspinwall hotel at Lenox, Mass., for next season. Mr. Brown will continue as proprietor of the Granliden hotel, Lake Sunapee, N. H., also the Dewey hotel, Washington, D. C. Mr. Brown is a son of Myron O. Brown, the first manager of the famous Sagamore hotel, at Bolton and therefore is a hotel man by birth as well as training. *Dec 18 1913*
news

CRANDALL BOYS' SAVINGS CLUB, MEMBERS OF WHICH LED FUNERAL PROCESSION OF HENRY CRANDALL, GLENS FALLS PIONEER LUMBERMAN AND PHILANTHROPIST

NEW YEAR'S PARTY AT THE ROCKWELL HOUSE

Glens Falls Times

Thankful beyond the power of expression,
Mine Host George Taylor has planned a session,
To watch the flight of the dying year,
And welcome the new with abundant cheer. *Dec 30, 1913*

At the Rockwell House tomorrow night,
He'll set 'em up in a style that's right;
There'll be fodder and drink and music, too,
But of course you'll pay for whatever you do.

The fodder, as usual, will be dished out free.
For a nickel or more you may sip of tea;
If the tea is too weak, jingle your tin,
Whisper your order and take it in.

Ring out the old, ring in the new.
George'll be there and Charley, too;
The latter is booked to stand the treats.
To even up for Georgie's eats.

And when at last the year has flown,
And the old brass rail stands all alone,
With the glasses empty and the dishes clear—
Why, how do you do? Happy New year!

USE OF PARKS AND LIBRARY GIVEN TO CITY IN HENRY CRANDALL'S WILL

Perpetual Corporation Is Named to Control Institutions---Entire Estate Left to Widow Who Is Made Executrix---Savings Club Provided For

Star Feb 23 1913

F. R. SMITH GETS JOB

Glens Falls Times

Chairman of Warren County Supervisors is Named Chief Doorkeeper. *Jan 7 1914*

DEFEATS NEW YORKER

Chairman Fred R Smith of the County Board of Supervisors was last night elected chief door keeper of the assembly chamber in the capitol building in Albany, at a salary of seven dollars per day for the session of the legislature. Mr. Smith is a resident of Bolton Landing. His name was presented for the place by Assemblyman H. E. H. Brereton, and he won out by 53 to 26 over Michael E. Kehoe of New York city, who was backed by the Greater New York members.

OBITUARY *Times*

Jan 30 1914

George S. Gates.

George S. Gates of the firm of Gates Bros. & Co., Bolton, died Jan. 24. He was born in Bolton, where he had always resided. He is survived by his wife, Sarah Gates; a daughter, Miss Agnes, and a son, Rupert Gates, and two brothers, Jonathan S. and Dodge S. all of Bolton. The funeral was held from his late home on Tuesday and interment was in the Huddle cemetery.

RACE ON LAKE GEORGE

Star Jan 22 1914

A named race for a purse of $50 will take place Saturday on Lake George. The following horses will compete: Lady Bon Bon, owned by J. B. Cooper, Captain Greason, owned by George Russell; Lydia Pinkham, owned by Bert Waddell; Ada McGregor, owned by W. J. Hall; Jersey Lightning, owned by Joe Mallory; John Henry, owned by E. J. Worden, and Helen K., owned by William O'Connor.

MYSTERY IN SUIT AGAINST BRERETON

Says He Does Not Know Woman Whose Action Involves His Property

Stur nov 10 1913

PAPERS FILED IN NEW YORK

Assemblyman Refuses to Discuss Details of the Case—Says it is One of Several and There is Nothing Unusual

Glens Falls people showed considerable interest in the article in the New York papers Saturday morning stating that Assemblyman H. E. H. Brereton had been sued by Mary Cahoon of New York and that the nature of the action had not been disclosed.

In an interview with a reporter for The Post-Star, Mr. Brereton said that the action involved property he owns in the metropolis, but would not discuss the details of the suit. He said there was nothing unusual about the case, and that it was only one of several which had been started against him in various places. The action is to recover damages, but further than that Mr. Brereton would not disclose the facts.

Mr. Brereton said he does not know the plaintiff and that he never heard of her. He said all his property is managed by his agent in New York and that the latter will look after the case. The summons was filed in the New York county clerk's office by Edward J. Flynn, an attorney of 17 Battery place. The New York papers claim the complaint was served upon the defendant in his home in Bolton, but Mr. Brereton declares he has not seen any of the papers in the case.

THIRD SMALLPOX DEATH

Knickerbocker Press

Coal Passer Added to Plague's Victims on Battleship Ohio. *1914*

CHARLESTON, S. C., Jan. 7.—The third death from smallpox among men exposed on the battleship Ohio during the recent Mediterranean cruise, was recorded here today. It was that of a coal passer, Rae Hardy Ackerman. He died in quarantine.

Ackerman was a native of Hague, N. Y., and had been in the navy since 1912.

Jan 8 '14

J. E. SAWYER & CO. PURCHASE BUILDING

Buy Old Griffing & Leland Stable From Mayor W. Irving Griffing

CONSIDERATION . $35,000

Purchasers Will Take Possession Next Week and Will Move Gradually as Changes Are Made to Structure

The biggest real estate deal which has taken place here in some time was consummated Saturday when J. E. Sawyer & Company purchased from Mayor W. Irving Griffing the three story brick building on Glen street hill formerly occupied by the Griffing & Leland Company as a livery stable and later by Mr. Griffing until his retirement from business last spring. The consideration was not announced, but it is said to have been in the neighborhood of $35,000.

Negotiations have been going on for some time by Sawyer & Co. for a new location, their business having greatly outgrown their present quarters and improved facilities for handling their rapidly increasing trade. This firm enjoys the distinction of being one of the largest and most progressive concerns in its line of business in New York State. The new business will at once commence a general improvement of the property so as to conform with handling of their stock with the least possible expense.

As soon as complete equipment has been put in, they will move into their new building which will be probably about March 1.

J. E. Sawyer & Company have been in business thirty years, having first established a harness and horse goods establishment in 1883 near the Jointa Lime company's property in Lower Warren street. Later they moved to the store now occupied by R. E. Burger. Eight years later they moved to Park and Glen streets and seventeen years ago moved to their present site at 30 Warren street. The company occupies the three floors at No. 36 also the loft over the National Express company's office and has a large store shed in the rear.

HISTORY OF A TOWN

Indian Lake, a Beautiful Village of the Adirondacks

SKETCH BY HIGH SCHOOL PUPIL

Miss Gretchen Houghton, Age Thirteen Prepares Paper of Great Excellence and Wins Contest Participated In by Schoolmates.

For the purpose of procuring a history of Indian Lake to be printed in catalogue for the village union school soon to be published, Principal J. W McCormack recently inaugurated a contest among his pupils and several excellent papers were prepared and submitted to a committee appointed to judge of their merits. After a careful examination the effort of Miss Gretchen Houghton, aged thirteen years was selected as the best. For the information of our many readers in Indian Lake, and other Adirondack towns, we are pleased to reproduce the paper in its entirety, as follows:

The village of Indian Lake is situated in the heart of those beautiful mountains, the Adirondacks, 1750 feet above sea level. The town is composed of Indian Lake village, Sabael, Big Brook, Cedar River, and Blue Mountain Lake village. This beautiful little place, the Matumbla of the Indians, and their legendary burying ground, is situated on the shores of Blue Mountain Lake, a famous summer resort. Indian Lake, from which the town derives its name, is three miles south of the village.

One day about the year 1765, a lone Indian left the Province of Quebec and journeying through the Canadian woods came at last to the shores of Lake Champlain. There he probably fashioned a canoe of birch bark and launching it sailed up that beautiful sheet of water. We have no history to tell us the hardships he suffered nor the steps he made while on his way, but we have a legend that when reaching the southern end of the lake, he left it and plunged into the vast deep forests on the New York side. He journeyed through these pathless forests on the lookout for moose because for this purpose he had made his journey.

One day, breaking through a covert of underbrush, he stood on the shore of a little lake, the first human being ever known to gaze on those waters which were named by the early settlers, Indian Lake, after the Indians. The lake at this time was about three miles long, but at its middle point was separated almost into two lakes by the narrows which had been formed by sediment brought down by a little mountain brook, which now bears the name, Squaw Brook. This Indian was Sabael Benedict, a Banakee. John Mitchell, a resident of this town, and the grandson of Sabael, is the only living member of this tribe in this part of the country.

MRS LAURA GILMORE

Glens Falls Times
Jan. 7, 1914

Recalls Interesting Incidents in Notable Career of Her Late Husband.

LIVES AT 7 PINE STREET

One of the most remarkable old women residing in Northern New York is Mrs. Laura Gilmore, widow of James R. Gilmore, author and one of the peace envoys sent by President Abraham Lincoln during the Civil war to urge Jefferson Davis, president of the Confederates states, to terminate the war in a peaceful way.

Mrs. Gilmore, who is eighty-two years old, bright and active for her advanced age, resides at 7 Pine street where a Times reporter found her yesterday afternoon.

Mrs. Gilmore was in a reminiscent mood relative to the great work done by her late husband and by her father, Judge J. W. Edmonds, who years ago was one of the most prominent supreme court justices in the State of New York.

Mr. Gilmore was an interesting writer. Among the books written by him were "On the Border," "Among the Guerrillas," "A Campaign Life of James A. Garfield in 1880," "Rear Guard of the Revolution," "Advance Guard of the Western Civilization," "John Sevier as a Commonwealth Builder," "Among The Pines," "My Southern Friends," "Down In Tennessee" and various other books and poems. Mrs. Gilmore proudly exhibited several of the books written by him. The book, "Among the Pines," brought Mr. Gilmore or "Edmond Kirke" into the lime light. At the time the story was written, Mr. Gilmore was employed as a writer on the New York Tribune. The story, instead of being published in the Tribune, appeared in the Continental Monthly, of which Mr. Gilmore was one of the founders. When the story appeared Horace Greeley, owner of the Tribune, at once set out to secure some of the writer's work, although he did not know who the author was. He went to the Continental office and begged for the name of the author.

journey after a pause at the Halfway House, French Mountain. Such scenes were common s to Lake George.

D ALL   GLENS FALLS, FRIDAY, DECEMBER 5, 1913

Home of the Glens Falls Country Club at Round Pond

Above is reproduced a picture of the Glens Falls Country Club house, near Round Pond, which will be formally opened Monday evening. Two special Hudson Valley cars will leave Bank Square at 8 p. m. for the accommodation of members.

THREATENS TO SHOOT DR. LEMON THOMSON

West Mountain Man, Ejected From Bungalow, Returns With Gun

Star
Nov 15 1913

PARTY'S UNINVITED GUEST

Arrested Saturday Morning By Deputy Sheriff O'Connell On Charge of Attempting to Commit Assault

Charged with threatening to shoot Dr. Lemon Thomson, Orville Hull was arrested Saturday morning in his home at West Mountain by Deputy Sheriff Philip O'Connell. He was arraigned before Justice Prentiss Gifford and as County Judge Raley was out of town and could not be found to fix the bail for holding the prisoner for the grand jury, he was locked up here in police headquarters.

Dr. Thomson recently built a bungalow at the foot of the mountain, where he often entertains. Last Thursday evening a party was given there. Hull, who had not been invited, appeared during the evening under the influence of liquor and made himself obnoxious. The result was that he was thrown out of the building by Dr. Thomson. It is said he went to his home about two miles distant and returned with a gun with which, Dr. Thomson says, Hull intended to shoot him.

The man was overpowered and the gun taken from him.

-171-

VERMONT MINISTER OLDEST IN WORLD

East Middlebury Has Man Who at Age of 104 Still Preaches

HAS HAD 22 PASTORATES

Star Dec 16 1918

RUTLAND, Vt., Dec. 15.—Rev. Sedgwick W. Bidwell of East Middlebury, Vt., has just celebrated his one hundred and fourth birthday. He is believed to be the oldest minister in the world. Both physically and mentally he is as alert as many men of 60. His appetite is fine and he seldom misses his four meals a day.

He shaves himself and can read and write without the aid of glasses. Until he was 100 years old Mr. Bidwell preached regularly at the Middlebury Methodist church, and still preaches on occasions.

When he was 102 years old he delivered a vigorous sermon to a large congregation, and it was published in many cities and towns in Vermont.

Mr. Bidwell was born in Starksboro, Vt., and his father was the first settler in that section. He has had pastorates in twenty-two towns in Vermont and New York, and now makes his home with his son, Frederick H. Bidwell, at East Middlebury. He has a remarkable memory and has a large and interesting store of anecdotes gathered by experience in his long career.

Courtesy of J. L. Cunningham, President Glens Falls Insurance Company.

VIEW OF GLENS FALLS AS IT APPEARED IN 1825.

This reproduction of an old painting is most interesting as it shows the historic falls at Glens Falls as they appeared nearly a century ago, with what was probably the first bridge across the Hudson River in that vicinity.

EXTREME LOW WATER IN HUDSON RIVER AT GLENS FALLS.

A view showing the falls and river bed before the bridge had been swept away by last spring's flood, for comparison with the view above from nearly the same point a century ago.

LAKE HIGHWAY TO BE LIGHTED

Times Nov 29, 1918

Work Toward Installing Electric System Between Bolton and Lake George Nearly Done.

The complete electrification of the ten miles of lake shore between the village of Lake George and the village of Bolton is nearing completion. Captain Wood, lessee of the Bolton-Lake George Road Light Company, has put up poles from the northern end of this line as far north as the Lake George Country Club house, and the Bolton Light and Power Company has extended its line of poles south as far as the Marion House.

Captain Wood draws his supply of current from the Adirondack Electric Power Corporation at the village line of Lake George, and it is understood that he has made it an object to the Bolton Light and Power Company to take its supply of current from the end of his line and to discontinue the operations of its plant, although the change-over will mean a considerable loss to the latter company, owing to the fact that the current is of a different cyclage and voltage and new transformers will have to be installed in place of those now in use.

It is expected that the business of the Bolton company will materially increase as the supply of current is practically unlimited for its purpose and closer regulation and dependability will be obtained. The change will be welcomed by many and it is hoped that both the customers and investors of the Bolton company will be benefited.

Troy Times Dec 17 1912

PAUL SMITH.

The Grand Old Man of the Adirondacks Whose Death Was Announced Yesterday With Sorrow.

OLD GLENS FALLS RECALLED
BY AGED RESIDENT

Glens Falls Times Jan. 3, 1914

There are many people residing in Glens Falls who vividly recall old Glens Falls, especially at that period of its history when the lower part of Glen street hill was the principal part of the city while several dwellings crowned the top of the hill. Of all the buildings in existence in that time only one now stands, and that is the wagon shop building occupied by the La-Salle carriage business.

This is practically the last landmark of the real old Glens Falls. It is a real old-fashioned building, with gable roof and style of architecture quite popular seventy or eighty years ago.

A large part of old Glens Falls has been firmly impressed upon some of the older people of the city today by stories and information handed down to them.

From a prominent person now in the seventies, who frequently heard his father talk of the early days of Glens Falls, the appended review of those days is given:

In 1828 the village had not more than 300 or 400 inhabitants, but it was a lively and busy place, especially that portion lying "under the hill." Let us here state that the localities in Glens Falls were known as "the top of the hill" and "under the hill." If you inquired for the residence of Colonel Morgan you would be told that it was on "top of the hill," and if for Spencer's tavern you would be told that "it was under the hill."

In that portion of the village "under the hill," from the canal bridge to the river, were located Reuben Putnam's (Rube Put's) trip hammer and edge tool factory, Williams' woolen mill, Hyman J. Cool's cabinet and chair factory, Gardner's ark mill, Arms' grist mill, George Put's (Putnam) wagon shop, Easterbrook's store and Spencer's tavern. That was the busy part of the village.

The stores and dwellings were mostly "on top of the hill." On the east side of the road leading up the hill was a deep ravine, covered comparatively with a heavy growth of pine, hemlock and spruce trees, leaving but a narrow path for a walk, and east of the road as far as the junction of what are now Warren and Canal streets were woods of cedar and yellow pine. "On top of the hill," from Elm street to the mountain, and north to Lake George, were dense woods of yellow pine, with here and there an opening. The streets in those days were called roads, and were cared for by the town. If used for pleasure grounds by the public no complaint was made.

May was the opening time for baseball. All citizens, old and young, participated. The game was played in the street in front of Threehouse's tavern. The "ketcher" stood where the fountain now is; the "field" was south; the "goals" were marked by stones, placed about thirty feet apart, in a circle extending back to the "ketcher." The umpire, with a stick and knife in hand, recorded the "ins" made, and when the game was concluded the defeated party paid the wager in egg cider, which was drank on the ground. No complaints were made because the streets were occupied, as the merchants could both play in the game and "tend store." Any customer would wait until the end of the game to be waited on by the merchant.

Glens Falls was well supplied with "taverns" at this early period, but had no saloons. Liquor was sold by the glass at the taverns, and by the pint or measure at the stores. There were five stores "on top of the hill" at the time mentioned—three general stores and two drug stores. Let us recall the names of some of the prominent citizens then living in Glens Falls: Judge Buell, Judge Geer, Judge White, Judge Roberts, Judge Hay, John L. Cortenius, Ira A. Paddock, William McDonald, Abraham Wing, Keyes P. Cool, Hyman J. Cool, Elnathan Parsons, Parsons Ranger, Samuel Ranger, Daniel and Herman Peck, James Sisson, Elias and George G. Hawley, John A. Ferris, Bethuel Peck, Dr. Rugge, Judge Spencer, Lewis L. Pixley, Enoch Ellis, Alonzo W. Morgan, Delavan Gardner, Peter D. Threehouse, Frederick Cortenius, Ira A. Paddock, James Burnham, Alex. McGregor, Mr. Sewell and Mr. Storer.

Lyman Arms died in 1826. John and Cyrus Burnham came to Glens Falls in 1832; Orlin Mead and Lewis Numan a little later; E. H. Rosekrans, Daniel H. Cowles and Jonathan W. Freeman a year or two later.

Good progress was made in business in the years 1830-31-32, and there were many additions to the population. About this time came John L. Kenworthy and his two slasters to work in the cotton mill in South Glens Falls; and a little later came Jones Ordway, whose first employment was chopping wood for fifty cents a cord. The pluck and industry displayed by Mr. Ordway were the foundation stones of his great wealth. About the same time came George G. Sickles and family from New York, representing the owners of the Glens Falls company's property, now owned by Finch & Pruyn.

There were no side streets on the Sandy Hill road from the McDonald residence to the Threehouse tavern in 1832. The first street (Center) was opened by Alonzo W. Morgan, who later opened Maple street and built the house now owned by Emmet T. Johnson. Where is now the opera house block was Daniel Peck's residence, and where the Fennel and Lee residences stand on Warren street were Ellis' livery stables and resi-dence. The present site of St. Mary's Catholic church was occupied by James Palmeter's wagon shop. There was but one church edifice in 1832—the old white Presbyterian church Later the Methodist society erected a stone church building on the brow of the hill on Church street, on the lot now occupied by St. Mary's academy.

The bear garden is not, as many suppose, of modern growth. It originated as early as 1832 in the sitting room of Threehouse's tavern. The garden was never without a quorum in the evening, but there was a better system then of soothing the bears and dispersing them to their homes at the proper time. The village employed a "bell ringer," whose services were paid for by subscription. It was his business to ring the bell of the Presbyterian church at 6 a. m., at noon and at nine o'clock in the evening. The last bell was a warning for the bears to depart to their homes.

The Threehouse tavern was a famous hostelry. Visitors to Lake George came by stage from Saratoga, stopping at the tavern for dinner. When the stage reached the toll gate on the island it was immediately surrounded by bright youngsters, eager to show the visitors (for a fee) the caverns, the "catamount on the rock" and the "big tree" on the opposite bank of the river, where Hawkeye shot the Indian, as related by the novelist, Cooper. The very spot where he planted his foot to "take aim" at the unfortunate Indian was minutely described, so that the visitor, for a six-pence of ready money, would know it all.

All sorts of devices to amuse the citizens in the long winter evenings were resorted to. A dramatic club called "The Thespian Association" was formed by the young men and received good encouragement from the older ones. The theatre was in the "Montonial" school building on Ridge street. There are those now living who will recall the names of many of the young members. There were "Link" Ferris, "Dodd" Spencer, "Dott" Hay and "Dan" Sickles, all of whom became distinguished citizens later in life. "Link" (Orange) Ferris was judge of the county and member of congress; "Dodd" (George) Spencer was a graduate of Union college and writer of books of great merit; "Dot" (DeWitt) Hay was an engineer, and became a partner in the house of Wraden, Wright, Hatch & Co., of New York; "Dan" (Daniel) Sickles was minister to Spain, and a noted general in the late war. He is still living, and the only surviving member of the ancient "Thespian Association" of Glens Falls.

THE DISTRICT SCHOOL.
MRS. E. F. BELER.

I've a pleasant recollection
Of a quiet farming section
In a certain valley that I used to know,
Where with slow but sure gradation
I began my education
In the land of Far-away and Long-ago.

Those were days of "yes, ma'am," "no, ma'am,"
"Please may I speak?" and "May I go, ma'am?"
And when classes to recite stood in a row
Then if rules should be unheeded
And punishment be needed
That was what the teacher hastened to bestow.

NEW BANK BUILDING FOR FIRST NATIONAL

Etein

Directors Decide to Purchase the Byrne Property in Glen Street

HAVE SECURED AN OPTION

Work On Structure Will Be Started During the Summer or Fall—Several Styles of Architecture Considered

The directors of the First National bank have decided to purchase the Byrne property at the corner of Glen street and Park avenue as the site for the magnificent new building which is being planned by the officers of the institution. An option has been secured on the property and it is assured the necessary details toward a purchase will be consumated within the near future.

ANOTHER PROMINENT MAN PASSES AWAY

Star Jan 15 1914

Daniel O'Leary, Jr., Dies in His Home in Grove Avenue, After Long Illness

WAS LIFELONG RESIDENT

Glens Falls yesterday lost another prominent resident, the second within a few days, when Daniel O'Leary, jr., one of the best known citizens of the city, died in his home, 21 Grove avenue. His condition had been serious several weeks and yesterday morning he experienced a sinking spell from which he never rallied.

Mr. O'Leary was born in Glens Falls sixty-nine years ago and was the son of Daniel and Mary Mellen O'Leary, who came here in 1834. He had always lived here. January 10, 1872, he married Miss Mary Leavy. Mr. O'Leary was at one time engaged in the manufacture of cigars, but for many years past has been in the real estate and insurance business. He held many offices, including village collector, village president, excise commissioner, member of the board of education and postmaster. He was also chairman of the city charter committee.

TRAFFIC DELAYED AT RIVER BRIDGE

Times Feb 5 14

Cars Obliged to Haul Loaded Sleighs Across the "Great Divide."

Hudson Valley traffic between this city and South Glens Falls was badly tied up this afternoon, shortly after one o'clock, when several sleigh loads of furniture became stuck on the river bridge and on the railway tracks leading down to the bridge.

Before the cars could operate, it was necessary to pull each load across the bridge by fastening a chain to the sleigh. When Conductor Traver of the cross-town car thought he had the way cleared so that the car could be run up the hill into Bank Square, another sleigh load was pulled onto the tracks, the driver being determined that he too, should be pulled across the bridge by the car.

In the meantime the car from Saratoga was waiting at the other end of the bridge and at the canal bridge the car bound for Saratoga was waiting, as well as a South Glens Falls car.

There is no snow on the tracks from the canal bridge to River street in South Glens Falls, and it is almost impossible for some horses with loads behind them to get across the bridge. It is a difficult task for horses attached to light rigs to travel the thoroughfare.

Just as long as sleighs are used there will be more or less interruption with traffic between this city and South Glens Falls.

Examination for Bolton Landing Postmaster

Aspirants for the position of postmaster at Bolton Landing, a fourth-class office, will be given an examination by the U. S. Civil Service commission on March 14, in Glens Falls. The late George S. Gates, who died January 24, held the position several years and since his death his son, Rupert Gates, has been in charge of the office. The compensation of the postmaster for the last fiscal year, was $962. News March 5 1914

HIS LEG BROKEN AS RESULT OF KICK BY A STALLION

John Francis Beckwith, Author and Naturalist Painfully Injured at Riverbank.

DISPLAYS GREAT NERVE AFTER THE ACCIDENT

Has Been Engaged in Writing of Moving Picture Plays and was to Have Directed Taking of Pictures by Universal Company This Week.

Times Jan 21

John Francis Beckwith, author and naturalist, who makes his home at Riverbank, sustained a fracture of the right leg Sunday, when he was kicked by a stallion, which had been left in a stall in Beckwith's stable. Beckwith had a number of guests for dinner, including Stewart MacFarland, Ledwith Dowd and George Doty of this city. The local men drove to Riverbank from Warrensburg and their horses were also placed in the Beckwith stable. During the afternoon Beckwith went to the stable to give the horses some hay and as he was walking in back of the stallion, which was owned by one of his guests, named Smith, who lives in that vicinity, the animal kicked him in the leg.

Displays Great Nerve.

Beckwith displayed great nerve and managed to crawl from back of the enraged steed's heels to the outside of the stable. He then called for aid and his guests assisted him into the house. Dr. J. E. Goodman of Warrensburg was summoned and attended the injured man. His friends endeavored to induce him to allow them to bring him to the Glens Falls hospital, but he refused to make the trip. Mr. Beckwith will be confined to his bed for some time.

Writes Picture Play.

In addition to his short story writing and naturalist work, Mr. Beckwith of late has engaged in writing moving picture plays at the rate of one each week. Representatives of the Universal Film company were to have visited his home this week for the purpose of securing pictures of a play to be acted in that vicinity, under the direction of Mr. Beckwith.

COLLECTION OF INDIAN RELICS

Feb 2 1944

Many Valuable Curios Possessed by Mrs. Laura Gilmore, Pine Street.

One of the rarest and most interesting collections of Indian relics to be found in the state or in fact in the country is that owned by Mrs. Laura Gilmore, an aged woman who resides in Pine street, this city. The relics were given to her by her father, the late Judge J. W. Esmond of New York, who was an Indian commissioner in 1835. It was on his visits to the Indians at that time that he succeeded in getting together one of the finest collections of Indian made articles including domestic and warfare.

A large number of these relics of the old Indian day are hung in Mrs. Gilmore's sitting room where every one who visits her has an opportunity to see them. In the collection are genuine tomahawks besmeared with blood, war clubs carved in an ornamental way, bows and arrows with flint heads fastened in the end and Indian pipes more than three feet long, together with moccasins and leggins all covered with Indian bead work and porcupine quills. The pipes are long, slender and flat and were used mostly by the Indians when the pipe of peace was smoked.

She also has a war club used by the Mexicans which was given to her father by General Worth.

Another interesting relic is a copy of Sir Walter Scott's "Lady of the Lake," bound in wood covers the wood being taken from a tree that grew on Sir Walter Scott's homestead.

She also has an old-time chair, probably one hundred years old. This chair is an extremely comfortable one and many dignitaries have used it when writing law, fiction, sermons and poetry. Mrs. Gilmore is extremely proud of the chair, and says that it should inspire everyone who sits in it. Her father wrote law in the chair and her husband, known to the literary world as Edmund Kirk, and one of the original peace commissioners sent by Abraham Lincoln to interview Jefferson Davis at Richmond, Va., with a view of having the Civil war brought to a close without any great bloodshed, wrote his novels and poetry in it and a few years ago William Dean Howells, the great American author, was visiting Lake George he finished one of his novels in it and Father Hector of New York, one of the Paulist fathers, who annually visits Lake George, wrote sermons while sitting in it.

Jan 8 1914

Miss Blanche E. Sanderson, who recently completed her training course in the Glens Falls hospital school for nurses, has accepted a position as district nurse in Bolton and Lake George.

MRS. BETSY WATERS CRANDALL FOLLOWS HUSBAND TO GRAVE

Passes Away Eight Hours After Sustaining Shock of Paralysis—Found Unconscious in Her Room

Star Jan 19 1914

Betsy Waters Crandall, widow of the alte Henry Crandall died at 6 o'clock yesterday morning in her Glen street home as the result of a paralytic shock which she suffered at 10 o'clock Saturday night while preparing to retire. News of her death came as a sudden blow to her many friends, only a few of whom had learned of her illness.

Mrs. Crandall was in her eighty-first year and had passed Saturday in her usual good health. She passed the afternoon and evening paying social and business calls about the city and reached her home shortly after 9 o'clock. She was found at 10 o'clock by her maid lying unconscious on the floor of her room on the second floor of the building. Dr. M. D. Smith, the family physician and Dr. S. A. Rowe were summoned to the home and although they took advantage of every means known to medical science, it was impossible to restore her to consciousness before the end came eight hours later.

Mrs. Crandall was born in Bolton, the daughter of Howard and Laura Waters. She was married to Mr. Crandall in 1858, coming with him to Glens Falls immediately after the ceremony. She was not only his wife but his advisor, his constant companion, with him on all his extensive travels and during his hours of business, always planning for his comfort and welfare.

Her sole ambition was to make him happy during life and in his waning hours she proved her fidelity to the admiration of those who were privileged to know the details of their private life. At his bedside at all times, she waited patiently for same slight expression which might intimate a wish and having secured the same she did not rest until the wish was fulfilled.

After his death, which lacks a month of being a year ago, she has faithfully tried to carry out his plans. The Crandall Free library, the Boys' Savings club and the other philanthropic institutions which stand as monuments to the memory of Mr. Crandall have been continued by her along the lines which he desired.

Mrs. Crandall was among the last of her generation in Glens Falls, the city which she loved so dearly. Among her greatest pleasures were the many hours she passed in conversation with younger folk, describing the changes in the place she made her home for nearly three score years. Kindness and generosity were her main virtues and her cheerful face and pleasant manner will long be cherished by those who were fortunate by having known her.

She is survived by a brother, Almen Waters of Bath, and three sisters, Mrs. C. H. Faxon and Mrs. Almira W. Myers of Chester and Mrs. Mary A. Beach of Oshkosh, Wis.

Mrs. Myers an a niece, Mrs. John B. Brown of New York, arrived at the Crandall homestead yesterday in response to telegrams announcing the news of her death and have assumed charge of the household affairs. The funeral arrangements will be completed today. The remains will be placed beside those of her husband at the base of the great granite shaft in Crandall park.

Near Death's Dark Portal.

Mrs. Alice Gates is ill with a complication of diseases and is in a critical condition.

Bolton Supervisor Gets Assembly Job.

Fred R. Smith, of Bolton Landing, chairman of the Warren county board of supervisors, Tuesday night was elected chief door keeper of the assembly chamber in the capitol building in Albany, at a salary of seven dollars per day for the session of the legislature. Assemblyman H. E. H. Brereton backed Mr. Smith for the position and secured his election by a vote of 53 to 26 over Michael E. Kehoe, of New York city, who was backed by the Greater New York members.

ARTHUR W. LANFAIR.

Arthur W. Lanfair died on the 3rd inst., at West Belton, in his sixty-ninth year. He leaves two daughters, Mrs. Cora Reirden, of Warrensburgh, and Mrs. Leonard Beswick, of Diamond Point, and one son, Melvin Lanfair, with whom he made his home. The funeral was held at the house Thursday afternoon at 2 o'clock, and was conducted by the Rev. C. S. Agan, of this village. Interment in the Warrensburgh cemetery. The bearers were Edward Turner, George Wilcox, Warren Wood and Stewart Fuller.

—175—

THREE HATLESS MEN

Each Unknown to the Other and Widely Separated

Mar 11 1914

ATTRACT ATTENTION OF CURIOUS

Charles T. Smock, of Chestertown, Has Scorned Headgear Many Years—Men In New York City and Ballston Claim Like Distinction.

"Why not go hatless?" is the query propounded to the editor of the New York Times in a communication from a city reader, published in that paper as follows:

Is headgear necessary? Why so?

You are not, Mr. F. L., the only one. Warren county has a man who has not worn a hat for going on twenty years. His name is Charles T. Smock and he is a prominent and highly respected resident of Chestertown, though his home was formerly in your own city.

That Mr. Smock has found the practice beneficial to his health is evidenced by his robust appearance. He is frequently seen in Warrensburgh and is the picture of health.

Never since he has lived in Chestertown has Mr. Smock worn a hat, or head covering of any kind, excepting that provided by nature, a heavy growth of hair, now iron gray. In a rainstorm or on an excessively hot day he sometimes uses the protection of an umbrella, but further than that his head is freely exposed winter and summer. Cold weather has no terrors for him. It is not unusual for the thermometer to register thirty and forty degrees below zero in Chestertown, but that is not too frigid for his head. It is the same in the summer when the mercury climbs up to ninety or above in the shade.

Mr. Smock is by no means eccentric. On the contrary, he is well educated and refined, a cultured gentleman. He is possessed of sufficient means to lead a life of leisure and devotes a great deal of time to public interests in the town he has chosen for his home. Particularly useful has he made himself in connection with the village library, which he established and through his personal efforts maintains, though he is assisted by the ladies, among whom he is very popular. He is a bachelor, by the way, and apparently immune to matrimony.

Naturally, in the earlier years of his residence in Chestertown he was the subject of considerable wonderment. The local gossip wondered why he came there, how long he was going to stay and what he was going to do. They wondered if some girl would capture him and they wondered who it would be. They're wondering yet and the subject of their cu-

rosity is pursuing the even tenor of his way, happy and hatless.

For several years he has held the appointment of court crier of Warren county and at every session of court at Lake George may be seen at his post of duty. Going about in that place and Glens Falls where he is not so well known, he attracts a great deal of attention because of his bare head, but this bothers him not a bit and his dignity is never ruffled by the stares and remarks of the rude and curious.

Ballston Spa has also has a hatless man, who sometime ago was written up by the Amsterdam Recorder-Democrat as follows:

Ballston Spa has the distinction of having the only bonafide hatless man known in the state, and probably in the country. Fred Armer is his name, and he has not donned a lid for several years, or, at least, since doctors advised him to go barebeaded.

LOCAL FIRMS ARE AMONG CREDITORS

G. B. McIntosh Files Voluntary Petition in Bankruptcy in

March 4 1914. Utica.

Among the large number of creditors of G. B. McIntosh, the Warren street grocer, who yesterday filed a voluntary petition in bankruptcy in United States Court in Utica through his attorney, James S. Kiley, are the appended, who are engaged in business in this city: Glens Falls Publishing Company, advertising, $102; Harry H. P. Waite, garden truck, $25; C. M. Wilmarth, rent of store, $324; Post Publishing Company, advertising, $171; Armour & Company, meats, $188; Finch-Pruyn Company, grain, $47; Glens Falls Gas Company, lights, $72; Little & Loomis, insurance, $31; Lapham & Parks, grain, $135; National Biscuit Company, $464; Swift & Company, meats, $187; Red Line Fruit Company, $133; Varney Brothers, grain, $63; Glens Falls Auto Company, $131; Speery & Hutchinson, green stamps, $150; Pearsall & Gray, cigars, $131; Hovey Fruit and Ice Company, two claims, one of $273 and the second of $650; National Bank of Glens Falls, $150, and Finch-Pruyn Company, $193.

Isaac Van Vechten of Esperance is a creditor for $1,000 and $245 additional, representing interest for the past four years.

The schedules filed by McIntosh show:

Liabilities, secured, $324; unsecured, $16,542; accommodation paper, $145. Total, $17,013.

Assets — Cash, $8; stock, $3,680; household goods, $425; carriages, delivery wagons and sleighs, $1,220; store fixtures, $1,402; debts due, $3,045. Total, $9,782.

The matter has been referred to Referee in Bankruptcy James A. Leary of Saratoga Springs to call a meeting of the creditors.

WORK OF VISITING NURSES.

Supervisors' Resolution Ineffective—Rev. E. M. Parrott Offers a Suggestion.

Following is a copy of a self-explanatory letter addressed to Supervisor E J. Worden, of the town of Caldwell, by the Rev. E. M. Parrott, rector of St. James' Episcopal church of Lake George·

St. James Parish House.

news Lake George. N. Y.
March 10, 1914.

Mr. E. J. Worden, *Mar 11 1914*
Supervisor Town of Caldwell.

My Dear Mr. Worden:—I learn from a conversation with the superintendent of the poor. Edward W. Griggs. that the recent action of the board of supervisors in appropriating $200 each of the towns of Queensbury, Caldwell and Bolton, to help in the work of visiting nurses, will be ineffective owing to its failure to comply with certain state laws.

May it not be that this is a good time before the April meeting of the board for a more general discussion of the possible usefulness of visiting nurses

It hardly seems fair to taxpayers of the whole county to vote county money to work in three townships only, and to put expenditure of county money in the hands of irresponsible individuals or societies.

If a commissioner of charities were appointed under the authority of the board to supervise county nurses who would go wherever needed inside the county, it might be better, but best of all Superintendent Griggs might effectively direct activities of county nurses who should be able to help him when the need required at the county home.

The nursing work in which I have been interested has demonstrated its value again and again. I keenly appreciate the action of the board in contributing towards nursing in towns in which I am most interested and I am sure that no better investment can be made with county money than preventing the progress of disease in the many isolated homes where it might soon cripple or destroy life.

There is no reason why such county nurses might not work in co-operation with health inspectors in the schools and in so doing give as useful oversight to health in rural districts as is now given in large cities.

Yours very truly,
EDWARD M. PARROT.

Walter E. Gates has recently sold a fine horse to a man from Poughkeepsie.

C. B. Maxim, who has been ill for a few days, of a severe cold, is improving. *news Feb 25 1914.*

Mr. and Mrs. Walter Gates, of Bolton, celebrated the tenth anniversary of their marriage Monday. A number of friends from this place were present. *news Feb 26 1914*

Rourke-Robinson.

The marriage of Miss Ada Belle Robinson, of Bolton Landing, with Daniel Rourk, of the same place, was solemnized Monday by the Rev. E. D. White. Miss Nettie G. Harris was the bride's attendant, and Eldu Pratt acted as best man. Mr. and Mrs. Rourk went to Albany for a short visit, and upon their return will reside in Bolton Landing

LUDICROUS ANSWERS

Culled from Regents' Papers Reviewed in Albany.

BONA FIDE BITS OF RARE HUMOR

Students of Public Schools Offer Ingenious Solutions of Many Problems and Shed Light Upon Mysteries of Mind and Matter.

The drudgery of correcting answer papers after school examinations is sometimes lessened for the teachers by the ludicrous answers received, says Principal J. W. McCormack, of the Indian Lake high school. Recently in his school, Mr. McCormack states, the stomach was located south of the chest. That answers as strange as this are quite common is shown by the following, collected from Regents' papers by Principal McCormack's brother, who spent part of last summer reviewing papers at the State Education department in Albany:

A vacuum is a large empty space where the pope lives.

When Cicero delivered this oration he was a prefix.

Feminine gender of friar—toastress.

Climate is caused by the emotion of the earth.

Guerilla warfare is where the soldiers rode on guerillas

Typhoid fever can be prevented by fascination.

The main provision of the Mayflower Compact was potatoes.

The people on the coast of South America are subject to earthquakes.

Shad go up the river to spoon.

Navigation without people is unusual.

A useful mammal—the oyster.

An insect—the frog.

One of the functions of the stomach is to hold up the petticoats.

Lakes may be destroyed by the bottom dropping out.

The salmon fisheries in the Columbia river and Pacific Oceans are canned.

The finished products from cotton are oleomargarine, benzine and linseed oil.

The cause of the salt in the ocean is the salt fish in it.

If the soil is too dry for raising corn, good navigation should be introduced.

Two compounds of personal pronouns are "he-goat" and "she-devil."

Pompeii was destroyed by an eruption of saliva from the vatican.

The plural of ox is oxygen.

Elaine gave Launcelot an omelet before he departed for the tournament.

Oysters are packed in fresh salt water.

Philadelphia is noted for its steel mines.

Some wheat is made into oatmeal.

James is the subject of a fine-eyed verb.

Harper's Ferry is the ferry that runs between New York and Hoboken.

A volcano may fill up a lake as it passes over it.

Tuberculosis may be caught by sleeping with him.

Four animals belong to the cat family—father cat, mother cat and two little kittens.

The chamois is valuable for its feathers, the whale for its kerosene oil.

Qualification of a voter at a school meeting—he must be father of a child for eight weeks.

To prevent the spread of tuberculosis kill all the people who have it.

The chief nutrient present in grapes is water. This is used to make bone tissue.

To resuscitate an unconscious drowning person—Loosen tight clothing, such as corsets, etc., and give him cold water to sip to keep him from fainting.

Alcohol weakens the capillaries of the skin so that they cannot drive bacteria out of the blood. They fall over each other like drunken people.

The invention of the steamboat caused canals and rivers to spring up all over the country.

Definition of a mineral—A mineral is composed of nothing. It is simply found in the earth

Animals go down in the earth and bring up the surface.

Warm waters of the Gulf Stream have been successfully tried both for commerce and pleasure trips.

The bodies of the solar system may often be seen without the aid of a microscope.

A useful insect—the potato bug, because it kills insects that are harmful to the plant.

Practical suggestions for the care of the eyes—You shouldn't pick flies out of your eyes with a lead pencil, use a handkerchief.

A mountain pass is a pass given by the railroads to its employees so that they can spend their vacations in the mountains.

Animals are an agent of erosion because they gnaw at the ground and sometimes eat. Animals gnaw the rocks.

Birmingham, Ala., is located in the cotton and fruit districts. Therefore it raises a great deal of cotton and fruit. It is also located near the Gulf of Mexico and connects the Atlantic Ocean and will connect the Pacific as soon as the Panama Canal is finished. It connects it now but it is farther around South America. It is also located near the St. Lawrence river.

THE GIRL I LEFT BEHIND ME.

The dames of France are fond and free,
  And Flemish lips are willing,
And soft the maids of Italy
  And Spanish eyes are thrilling;
Still, though I bask beneath their smile,
  Their charms they fail to bind me,
And my heart falls back to Erin's Isle,
  To the girl I left behind me.

For she's as fair as Shannon's side,
  And purer than its water,
But she refused to be my bride
  Though many a year I sought her;
Yet, since to France I sailed away,
  Her letters oft remind me,
That I promised never to gainsay
  The girl I left behind me.

She says "My own dear love, come home,
  My friends are rich and many,
Or else, abroad with you I'll roam,
  A soldier stout as any;
If you'll not come, nor let me go,
  I'll think you have resigned me."
My heart nigh broke when I answered "No,"
  To the girl I left behind me.

For never shall my true love brave
  A life of war and toiling,
And never as a skulking slave
  I'll tread my native soil on;
But, were it free or to be freed,
  The battle's close would find me
To Ireland bound, nor message need
  From the girl I left behind me.

FISH HATCHERY IN WARRENSBURG

Star Dec. 6 1913

Lockwood Farm Selected as the Site—Twenty Thousand Dollars Appropriated

WARRENSBURG, Dec. 5. — The state fish hatchery in Warrensburg provided for by Senator James A. Emerson's bills passed during the legislative session of 1910-11, and for the erection of which $20,000 was appropriated, is soon to become a reality.

For a long time the matter was held in suspension by the difficulty of finding a site to meet the requirements of the fish commission. Several inspections were made of proposed sites, but all were rejected until the old Lockwood farm, on the Hudson river, in the western part of the town was examined by the state officials and pronounced an ideal site.

LINA SAD AS SHE SAILS WITH SECOND HUSBAND

"Girls Ought to Wait Until They are 44 Before They Marry,"

Sighs Noted Songstress.

NEW YORK, April 9.—Lina Cavalieri and her new husband, Monsieur Muratore, sailed for Paris on the steamer France. The famous singer and beauty was in a melancholy mood when approached by interviewers.

Her utterances were most pessimistic, particularly those pertaining to marriage. M. Muratore understands but little of English and strove vainly to understand his wife's words.

Said Lina when asked what she thought of married life: "Married life is not so good. Girls ought to wait until they are forty-four before they marry. Then they should have one child. I have had more than 800 proposals of marriage. I think that international marriages are very good.

"My advice to girls is to marry for love if you can, but never fail to have an eye for convenience. Sweet words and kisses won't pay the chauffeur. New York girls should never marry. They are too frivolous; too fond of dancing. They make poor wives."

Hollis I. Loveland Promoted by D. & H.

Hollis I. Loveland, who has been station agent for the Delaware and Hudson company at The Glen about twelve years, has been transferred to Hydeville, Vt., a larger station. He left for that place Monday. His family will remain at The Glen for the present, probably until fall. L. M. Holland will be transferred to The Glen from Corinth and will begin his duties Monday. The grain store conducted by Mr. Loveland, near the station, has been taken over by C. M. Collins, of North Creek.

—177—

MICHAEL CRONIN ADJUDGED INSANE

Proprietor of Aiden Lair Taken to the Ogdensburg Asylum

WAS TREATED IN SARATOGA

Star April 20 1914

Former Resident of Glens Falls Made Famous By Trip With Colonel Roosevelt After President McKinley Was Shot

Michael Cronin, proprietor of Aiden Lair and famed for the famous trip he made across the mountains to North Creek with Former President Roosevelt the morning after President McKinley's death, is insane. He was taken Saturday morning to the St. Lawrence Insane asylum in Ogdensburg, after receiving treatment several weeks in the Saratoga Cure and infirmary.

Mike Cronin, as he is familiarly known throughout the Adirondacks, is a former resident of Glens Falls, being a son of James Cronin, who lived in William street until he moved to Pittsfield, Mass., a few years ago. Cronin enjoyed a wide acquaintance. He is known from one end of the Adirondacks to the other and is intimately acquainted with many men of note, including the Mighty Hunter, who have visited Aiden Lair lodge.

Cronin first leaped into fame after the famous Roosevelt ride and there is hardly an acquaintance of the former who does not know the story of that wild dash over the rugged mountains with the colonel. Mike liked to tell about the trip and to dwell upon his friendship with Teddy. Several years ago Cronin tried to force his way through a crowd to greet Roosevelt when the chief Bull Moose was president, but was intercepted by secret service men. When Roosevelt, glancing over the heads of the thousands of persons at the meeting, saw his friend Mike, struggling with two or three secret service men, he immediately ordered them to release him and a minute later he and Mike were shaking hands and talking about their night ride through the Adirondacks.

Cronin first showed signs of mental disorder about six or seven years after some trouble over land near Aiden Lair. During his last visit to Glens Falls he appeared to be in good condition and his friends believed he was permanently cured.

Michael Cronin

LABELED JOKES

And now we have the county fair
  With pickles on display
And quilted goods and willow ware
  And hominy and hay.

The massive porker in his pen
  Now makes his owner proud,
While aunty 'Dominicker" hen
  Attracts a goodly crowd.

The trotting race in many heats
  Might well excite a claim;
And father takes a prize with beets
  And mother with her jam.

Prize butter and the biggest squash,
  And other things are there.
There is no better fun, by gosh,
  Than going to the fair.

FRENCH-BAKER.

Charles French and Miss Cordel'a Baker, both of Bolton Landing, were married in that place Thursday evening by the Rev. S. J. Liberty, at the Methodist Episcopal parsonage. The witnesses were Miss Gertrude French and Mrs. Liberty. After the knot was tied a good-sized crowd of friends assembled outside the parsonage and gave a serenade, after which the bridegroom produced a box of cigars and everybody went their way with a cloud of smoke rolling over their backs and wishing the young couple a long life together and much happiness. The happy couple left by automobile for Glens Falls, where they will make their home. Mr. Ripley is a conductor on the Hudson Valley railway.

Bolton Fishermen Caught Napping.

Four Bolton fishermen while angling for pickerel through the ice in Northwest bay, on Lake George, Saturday, were caught red handed by Game Protector D. N. Bump, of Lake George, and arrested for violation of the game law in fishing out of season. They were given a hearing before Justice Tabor, at Bolton Landing, Tuesday. Oscar Belden was discharged as there was not sufficient evidence to hold him. Charles Belden and Byron Frazier paid the fines imposed upon them, and Hiram Fraizer, lacking sufficient funds to settle, was committed to the county jail at Lake George for eleven days.

AN UPWARD LOOK

THE CONVERSION OF SILAS

Of all the fossels in our town,
  Si Haskins was the boss.
He said the autymobile never
  Would replace the hoss.
He always used to sneer and snort
  Whenever one went by,
And when he'd see one busted down,
  He'd laugh until he'd cry.

He said the owners all were fools
  To go and spend their dough
For them gol ding contrivances
  That never seemed to go.
Them devil wagons got his goat,
  He'd never fall for one,
Of all the gol-dum foolishness,
  Gas wagons took the bun.

One day a nephew died and left
  An old one-lung machine
A-standing out in old Si's barn,
  Si got some gasoline
And poured it in the gosh durned
    thing to see if it would start,
He cranked her up and thought he'd
    try
  To drive the old gas cart.

He drove it down the road all right,
  Forgettin' all his care,
And rode around till almost night
  And visited everywhere.
Next morning bright and early he
  Was poundin' down the street,
He scared the hosses right and left
  And knocked folks off their feet.

A week from then he bought a car.
  It was of high hoss-power.
He didn't take time off to eat,
  But drove it every hour.
He raced with everybody who
  Showed up within a mile
He said you might as well be dead
  As not to be in style.

His whiskers blew out in the breeze,
  As down the road he flew,
He said, "I'll show those gol-ding
    boobs
  A fancy trick or tew."
He spent all his waking hours
  In showing them new tricks;
Four cylinders became too tame,
  And so he bought a six.

He's been arrested nineteen times
  For speedin', so they say,
He got his whiskers all shaved off,
  For they got in his way,
He talks of touring cars all day
  And dreams of them at night.
And nowadays whene'er he sees
  A piece of horseflesh pass
He sort of chuckles, sneering like,
  And hollers out: "No Class!"
    —Topeka (Kan.) State Capital.

TRASK ESTATE SUSTAINS $35,000 LOSS BY FIRE

Times Aug 21. 1918

Blaze Caused by Steamer Pocahontas Which Goes Up in Smoke---Mrs. Trask in Critical Condition

Fire, presumed to have been caused by the steamer Pocahontas, caused damage estimated at nearly $35,000 early this morning, when the north island of the Triuna group, formerly known as Three Brothers Islands, and owned by Mrs. Katrina Trask, was swept by a blaze which refused to cease its work of devastation until about everything on the island had been reduced to ashes.

As a result of excitement, Mrs. Trask, who has been critically ill for a number of weeks, but who was on the road to recovery, is today in a critical condition and grave fear is felt that she may be unable to withstand the shock.

Early this morning she was removed to Abenia, the summer home of George Foster Peabody, and should her health permit later, she will be removed to her beautiful home, Yaddo, Saratoga.

Dr. Glentowrth Butler of New York, the family physician, has been summoned from his summer home in the Catskills and is expected to arrive tonight or tomorrow morning.

Although in an extremely weakened state, Mrs. Trask this afternoon stated that she wished, through the press, to extend her thanks to all who assisted during the fire, and to say that she rejoiced in the thought that there was no loss of life.

Property Destroyed.

Included in the property destroyed was the following: The steamer Pocahontas, three motor boats, five row boats, the docks, boat houses, storage gasoline tank, coal bunkers, and the servants' quarters, a big building in which was located the laundry.

Boat Is Ignited.

When the Pocahontas tied up at her dock last night the fires were banked as usual, but it is thought that the pan became dry and that the hold of the boat became ignited. Gradually the fire communicated with the docks and it was not long before the island was enveloped in flames.

Explosion Gives Alarm.

Although it is thought the fire had been burning an hour or more, it was not until four o'clock that a general alarm was sounded by the explosion of a gas tank in one of the motor boats. The explosion was heard by one of the maids who immediately awoke the care taker. As quickly as possible the entire servant force was fighting the flames and with the successive explosions and the flames shooting heavenward cottagers for miles around were awakened and hastened to the scene of the conflagration in boats and automobiles.

For a time it was feared the entire estate would go up in smoke, but luckily the wind shifted and with the combined efforts of scores of cottagers and their employes the buildings on two of the islands were saved.

A Unique Resort.

The Trask summer home at Bolton is one of the most unique resorts of its kind in the Adirondacks. The three islands are connected by stone causeways and collectively form a villa which has been and is the admiration of all who have seen it.

In this morning's fire the contents of the buildings were destroyed and the servants lost virtually all of their personal effects. The housekeeper was slightly burned while returning to her room to get some personal property.

Memorial Window for John T. Rice.
Philip E. Rice and mother, of Warrensburgh, have sent $30.00 to the pastor of the Presbyterian church, the Rev. Fred A. Gates, for a memorial window for the late John T. Rice, who was an elder in the church at the time of his death.—The Corinthian.

SAGAMORE HOTEL TOTALLY DESTROYED BY FIRE BELIEVED TO BE INCENDIARY

Blaze Said to Have Started From Outside of Building Spreads Rapidly Through Structure, Causing Loss of About $250,000— Insurance is $150,000—Impression is Hotel Won't be Rebuilt

Star Apl 13 1917

The Sagamore Hotel at Bolton, the largest summer hotel on Lake George and one of the largest in the Adirondacks, was destroyed by fire early yesterday morning with a loss estimated at approximately $250,000, and the impression prevails in Bolton that it was of incendiary origin. It is said that the fire started from the outside and near the dining room on the southeast side of the building, although this could not be definitely learned yesterday.

The fire was discovered about 2:40 o'clock by J. W. Ward, and the building was practically destroyed within forty minutes. Mr. Ward notified the telephone operator who aroused all the men in the village. A bucket brigade was formed, but the flames had gained such a great start that it was impossible to save the building or any of the contents. The fire spread rapidly from the middle of the structure and at 4 o'clock all that was left of the once famous hostelry were the smouldering embers. The laundry and the boiler room were saved, as were also the six cottages on the hotel grounds.

The engineer had been in the boiler room Saturday but so far as could be learned nobody was in the hotel Saturday night. S. G. Finkle, the caretaker, was in Schenectady Saturday night and he could offer no explanation as to the probable cause of the conflagration. The fire was a spectacular one, throwing a reflection into the sky which could plainly be seen in Glens Falls.

The Sagamore was a three story wooden building and contained 350 rooms. Many improvements had been made during the winter. About $800 was spent to repaint the structure and about $2,000 were expended on the dock. Fire escapes were also installed and other improvements were made.

The hotel, which was built twenty-one years ago to replace the old Sagamore hotel, was one of the most popular on the "Queen of American Lakes"

and was generally filled to capacity during the season.

The hotel was owned by the Green Island Improvement company. John Boulton Simpson of New York is the heaviest stockholder. E. Burgess Warren and the estate of the late George Burnham of Philadelphia are also interested. The hotel was managed by T. Edmund Krumbholz, who is now in Camden, S. C., where he conducts the Kirkwood. He and his staff generally arrived in Bolton about May 1 to get the hotel in readiness for the opening about the first of June.

Owing to the fact that none of the owners was in Bolton yesterday it could not be learned whether the hotel will be rebuilt, but residents of Bolton expressed the opinion that the Hotel Sagamore has passed out of existence for all time. Mr. Simpson is expected today in Bolton.

The loss is covered by insurance to the extent of $150,000, through the agency of Charles W. Cool. The furniture destroyed included furniture owned by persons who passed the summer in the hotel.

East View of the Sagamore on Lake George, Sagamore, N. Y.

VIOLATES ORDER, GETS SIX MONTHS

Star May 13 1914

Ezra Cilley of Bolton is in Jail for Contempt of Court

County Judge Raley has imposed a fine of $160 or imprisonment of six months in the county jail on Ezra Cilley of Bolton for contempt of court. Cilley was unable to pay the fine and is now serving the prison sentence.

A judgment was recently taken against Cilley by J. E. Sawyer & company and supplementary proceedings were started before Referee Archie C. Taylor to learn whether the man owned any proprty. It was found Cilley had a large equity in a piece of woodland in the town of Bolton, which he had bought on a contract and which was almost paid for. Referee Taylor ordered him not to dispose of any property owned by him and it is claimed that later the man disposed of the contract and his equity to the person from whom he purchased the same, the consideration being, it is claimed, the release of Cilley from the remaining amount due on the contract.

Attorney Charles R. Patterson appeared for Sawyer & company in the supplementary proceedings and brought the matter to the attention of the court after the transaction was made on the contract in violation of the referee's order.

THIS MAN IS TWENTY-TWO YEARS BEHIND TIMES

There is at least one resident of Warren county, Emerson Lloyd of Hill View in the Town of Bolton who is just 22 years behind the times, if his letter addressed to County Clerk Van Cott received today by County Clerk E. C. Sisson is any indication.

Lloyd was drawn as a juror for the term of County Court which today was convened at Lake George. Several months ago Lloyd suffered an attack of nervous prostration and although he is able to be out, he is not well enough to attend court. In his letter to County Clerk Van Cott the Hill View man enclosed a doctor's certificate certifying that his health could not permit him to attend the term.

William H. Van Cott to whom the letter was addressed, a late Glens Falls resident, completed his occupancy of the office of county clerk December 31, 1892, about 22 years ago and died several years later. Mr. Van Cott was also proprietor of the Van Cott hotel in South street, now the Hotel Madden, and was a one time postmaster of the Glens Falls postoffice.

SUICIDE AT BOLTON HOTEL

New May 14 1914

New York Woman Hangs Herself With Strap Tied to Bedpost.

Miss Nellie Gunn, of New York, committed suicide yesterday afternoon, at the Wilson house, Bolton Landing, by hanging herself in her room. She tied her trunk strap tightly about her neck and fastened the other end to a bedpost. Then throwing herself prostrate against the strap she slowly strangled to death. Miss Gunn had been boarding at the hotel about three weeks. Her actions were somewhat eccentric, but not sufficiently so to arouse the suspicion that her mind was unbalanced. She retired to her room yesterday shortly after the noon meal and was not seen again during the afternoon. When she did not appear at supper time the proprietor, C. E. Ingraham, rapped on her door but received no response. Some time later he repeated the summon with the same result. Trying the door he found it locked. Suspecting that something was wrong he forced the door open and was confronted by the gruesome spectacle of the dead woman with face contorted by the horrible agony of her death throes.

Dr. D. L. Rogers was summoned and after an examination stated that the woman had been dead several hours. Coroner Charles K. Burt, of Lake George, was notified and after a brief investigation officially announced that death was caused by strangulation by voluntary act of the deceased.

Miss Gunn was apparently about forty years old and was of refined manners and appearance. She had a sister in Bolton, Mrs. McElroy, who is employed as cook at the Fenimore hotel.

Col. John L. Cunningham, who yesterday resigned as President of The Glens Falls Fire Insurance Company after forty-seven years in the service of the company, was born in Hudson April 5, 1840. In 1861 he was graduated from the Albany Law School. He practiced at Essex in Essex County for a time and then enlisted in the One Hundred and Eighteenth Regiment of New York Volunteers and saw much service, returning with the rank of Major and Brevet Lieutenant Colonel. After the war he was appointed Collector of Internal Revenue for what was the Sixteenth Congressional District of New York, resigning in 1868 to take charge of the field work of the insurance company, with which he has since been associated. He became President in 1892 succeeding Russell M. Little, who died the year previous.

Post Apr 30 1914

BOLTON

Star Apr 30 '14

BOLTON, April 29.—Miss Sarah Griffith died Saturday morning in her home in North Bolton, following a long illness. The deceased is survived by one sister, Mrs. H. Barber, and one brother, Delbert, both of Bolton. The funeral took place at 1 o'clock Monday afternoon from the late home and interment was in Bolton cemetery.

MAN, 91, SWIMS ASHORE WHEN BOAT CAPSIZES

Star

Captain Crandall Has Narrow Escape, But Says Its "Just An Accident"

June 6 1914

LAKE GEORGE, June 5.—One of the oldest inhabitants of Lake George village, and well known to hundreds of summer residents as Captain Crandall, experienced today what many a younger man would have called a narrow escape from drowning, but which the captain termed "just a little accident."

Shoving off the dock in a small boat for a fishing trip, Mr. Crandall, ninety-one years old, but still hale and hearty, tripped over an oar which lay in the bottom of the boat and plunged head foremost into the icy waters.

In spite of the fact that he was weighed down by a heavy sweater and coat, the captain, who in his day was an expert swimmer and has saved many from drowning, showed that he had not forgotten the art, by striking out for the shore and reaching it in record time. Undaunted by his experience, he secured another boat and again ventured forth, this time bringing in his capsized craft.

After putting on dry clothes, the captain found he was none the worse for his cold bath, and in fact, seemed rather proud to have been one of the first this season to have a dip in the lake, which he described as invigorating.

MIKE CRONIN IS DEAD

News June 1 1914

Well Known Adirondack Hotel Man Passed Away Yesterday in Ogdensburgh.

Michael F. Cronin, of Aiden Lair, died yesterday morning at the St. Lawrence State hospital in Ogdensburgh, where he was taken early in April for treatment. Previous to that time he had been for some time in a Saratoga sanatarium, but with little benefit.

Mr. Cronin was born in Glens Falls fifty years ago, and was educated in the local schools and the Fort Edward Collegiate Institute. After graduation he entered the law office of the late Judge Rosekrans and studied law. Becoming afflicted with rheumatism about twenty-five years ago he was advised by his physician to go into the north woods. It was then he settled at Aiden Lair, where he later engaged in the hotel business as proprietor of Aiden Lair Lodge, which was recently destroyed by fire.

"Mike" won considerable fame by driving Theodore Roosevelt from Aiden Lair to North Creek when President-McKinley was shot while Roosevelt was on a hunting trip in the woods. The drive was made in record time and Mike and T. R. on the trip formed a friendship which had since endured.

Mr. Cronin leaves a widow, one son, Arthur Cronin; eight daughters.

Spt 2 8 1914

Made Use of It to Relieve Many Tense Situations.

(From The Youth's Companion.)

Did Lincoln laugh? He made others laugh, told perpetual, inimitable stories that neither tears nor anger could resist; but he himself was neither a loud nor a riotous nor an inappropriate laugher.

To him laughter was a solvent of the difficulties of life—a gentle, universal balm to soothe the blows and rubs and stings that even the stoutest shoulders must receive from the buffeting of common toil, and, above all, from the immense effort to set right the tangled tissues and the unhinged framework of this everlastingly imperfect world in which we live. To Lincoln laughter was not a gesture; it was a point of view.

It was something exquisite and necessary as an antidote to tears. How would the great President have borne his unequaled load of pain if he had not been able to relieve it by the smile that comes from seeing the pettiness of all evil as compared with the goodness of God?

But it was not merely for comic relief that Lincoln made use of laughter. He gave it a richer function. For relaxing tense situations he knew that there is nothing like it. A man cannot knock you down, or even insult you, if you make him laugh. The burly Stanton, the aggressive Chase, the fiery Seward went to Cabinet meetings each with a chip on his shoulder. Lincoln told a story, and they laughed, one and all, until the chip fell off. Then he could mold them to his purposes.

The rarity of such humor in statesmen of Lincoln's rank has never been sufficiently noticed. Where was it in Cromwell or Napoleon? Take the long list of great Americans—Jefferson, the Adamses, Jackson, Webster, Sumner; how much more attractive some of them would have been if they had had it! Take even Washington; great as he is, he stands above us and apart from us, on a cold pedestal. But Lincoln we can touch—

Concerning Patrick Henry.

One of the Columbia professors recently delivered an interesting lecture on Patrick Henry, whose patriotism is so deserving of our admiration. There is, however, another side to his public life, and that is his bitter and invincible opposition to the present national Constitution. During my early days I once met an aged Virginia gentleman who told me that he attended a public meeting where Patrick Henry denounced the acceptance of the Constitution as one of the greatest calamities which could befall the nation. Virginia, however, accepted it, this being due to the influence of Madison and Washington, whose better views prevailed. It is a striking illustration of the errors of great men that George Clinton, who was then our Governor, was equally opposed to the Constitution, and thus one sees how such men are divinely overruled for national welfare. Governor Clinton, however, was opposed by such broad-minded patriots as Hamilton and John Jay, and under their influence New York entered the Union. May 9 1914 of times

---

June 11 1914

Misfortune of Well-Known Bolton Man.

R. J. Brown, proprietor of the Lake View house, one of the oldest and most popular summer hotels at Bolton-on-Lake George, recently lost the sight of his left eye through paralysis.

His right eye has become impaired through the strain caused by his work for years past with the transit and level in his operations as a surveyor. Mr. Brown was at one time Warren county engineer. In spite of his affliction Mr. Brown will carry on his hotel business the present season and has made extensive improvements to his property in anticipation of a record-breaking season. news

---

They Will Not Return

From 'round the curve of the one-half world,
  Far over the Western main.
With tattered banners of battle furled,
  Our boys have come home again
From out of the wars to the dear old shores
    Of the land that they love so well.
And our hearts are full of gratitude
    And gladness we can not tell.
But our joy is stilled and our eyes grow dim,
    We think of the hearts that yearn
For the boys who were left on the battle-
  field—
    For the boys who will not return.

NEW KATTSKILL HOUSE WILL BE ERECTED

times

Promoters of "Bungalowtown" Will Build and Operate New Hotel.

Aug 25 - 1913.

It is definitely announced by McCourt Brothers of New York who have had a considerable experience with resort business, that they will build a new and modern hotel on the site of the Kattskill House which was destroyed by fire in the summer of 1908. This site is one of the finest on the lake, and the new owners are to be congratulated on their enterprise which will no doubt be to them a source of profit. It is understood that Claude Granger will be the resident manager of the new hotel, and that it will be ready for opening early in 1914.

The McCourt Brothers, have for some years been engaged in the business of building and leasing bungalows at watering places, one of their chief ventures being "Bungalowtown" on Staten Island. They have for some time had an eye on Lake George with this idea in mind, and while they will probably for the first year confine their operations largely to the hotel proper they announce that they also will provide bungalows or tents on short notice for those who desire them.

TERRIFYING TREMOR

Feb 12 1914

Earth Quivers Like Ball of Jelly for Thirty Seconds

ALL EASTERN STATES AFFECTED

Disturbance Extends Along Line of "the Logan Fault" from Montreal to Philadelphia—Warrensburgh Felt Full Force of the Shock

"The Logan fault," which geologists tell us is a split in the lower rock stratum of the earth extending along the Atlantic seaboard from Canada to Florida, made another slip Tuesday which at 1:34 p. m. caused a severe, earthquake shock extending from Montreal to Washington, D. C., and as far West as St. Louis. It continued from twenty to thirty seconds and while it lasted the earth quivered like a big ball of jelly, with a terrifying tremor which spread consternation wherever it was felt.

In Warrensburgh the shock was felt in its full severity. For the first two or three seconds it was the general impression that there had been a heavy explosion somewhere nearby, and many people had the idea that snow or ice had fallen from their house and caused the jar, but as the tremors continued it became evident to all that it was something more than a merely local disturbance. Then the first thought was to get from under buildings that might fall and in all parts of the village people were seen rushing from their homes into the open. Most of those who were already outside did not feel the quake.

In the local factories the jar of the machinery covered up the jar of the quake and it was therefore not observed.

No damage is reported in this vicinity, nor elsewhere for that matter. In several Warrensburgh homes dishes were shaken from tables and in one place a valuable ornament was tipped from a pedestal in the parlor and shattered to pieces on the floor. Pictures swayed on the walls and the vibration made metal things jingle. Though it seemed like a long time it was really all over about as soon as it began, leaving only the dread of another shock.

From all towns in this section and from cities in the eastern states comes the same story of rocking houses, rattling dishes and frightened people.

LEVI. P. MORTON IS NINETY YEARS OLD

Former Governor and Vice President Celebrates Birthday Anniversary.

HEALTH IS MUCH IMPROVED

Physicians Predict That Energetic Old Man Will Live at Least Until He Reaches Century Mark.

NEW YORK, May 15.—Levi Parsons Morton, former governor of New York and one of the four men living who have been vice presidents of the United States, will celebrate his ninetieth birthday today at his summer home, Rhinecliff on the Hudson.

DICK SMITH TO RETIRE.

news April 30 1914

South Horicon Merchant Sells Business and Will Remove to Pottersville.

Richard P. Smith, who has for many years conducted a general store at South Horicon, and is the leading citizen of that community, has sold his store building and stock of goods and his handsome residence near by to Fred B. Duell and on June 1 will retire from business and remove to Pottersville, where he will make his future home.

Mr. Smith has been a life-long resident of Horicon and his departure from the town will be regretted by every resident.

FRIDAY AFTERNOON, MARCH 27, 1914.

The Telephone.

(Ethel M. Kelley in St. Nicholas.)

Whenever Mother telephones
   She talks about a lot of things,
So Father only sits and groans,
   Whenever anybody rings.
"The season's earlier this year."
   "I haven't got my new straw hat."
"I can't, because my child is here."
   "What did her husband say to that?"

And Father only says, "Hello!"
   And takes the 'phone up in his hand.
"Is that you, Hawkins? This is Snow.
   I wired Chicago. Understand?
I think our man intends to fight,
   But we can best him if we try.
You'd better do so then, to-night.
   See you to-morrow. Well, good-by."

And Sister says, "Oh, is that you?"
   And then she fixes up her hair,
'S if anybody could see through.
   "Oh, I don't know. Oh, I don't care."
"I think I can, if you insist."
   "And wasn't yesterday a dream?"
"There's seven on the waiting list."
   "I do love strawberry ice cream!"

But what I do is just to say
   To Annabel, or Lucy White,
"Can you come over here and play?"
   And then they answer me: "All right!"
Perhaps when I am really grown—
   I'm only seven and a half—
I'll get my friends upon the 'phone,
   And talk and talk, and laugh and laugh!

GIRL KILLED ON BOLTON ROAD

Her

Miss Gertrude Mordecai, of Charleston, S. C., Victim of Auto Accident.

Miss Gertrude Mordecai, daughter of Judge T. M. Mordecai, of Charleston, S. C., was killed Saturday afternoon when her father's automobile, in which she was riding with four other persons, was wrecked on the Bolton road while running about fifty miles an hour. Her skull was crushed and she was injured internally. She died at the Glens Falls hospital an hour after the accident. *July 19, 1913*

With Miss Mordecai in the automobile were her sister, Miss Cornelia Mordecai; Miss Hannah Falk, of Savannah, Ga.; Henry A. Schermerhorn, of Schenectady, N. Y., and Olin Starr, the chauffeur. One of Miss Falk's arms was broken and she suffered minor injuries, but her condition is not serious. Mr. Schermerhorn, Miss Cornelia Mordecai and the chauffeur were only bruised.

The accident happened while the young people were going to get Mrs. Mordecai, who was at the grounds where a large summer home is being built for the Mordecai family. Not very far from the grounds Starr turned to one side of the road to pass another automobile, and as he did so the right front tire on the Mordecai automobile exploded.

The car then skidded and crashed into a big tree in front of the home of George Foster Peabody. It was wrecked and its occupants were caught in the twisted mass of steel and wood.

Immediately after the accident occurred a number of people gathered to assist the unfortunate victims and R. C. Peabody's car was used to take Miss Gertrude and her mother to the Glens Falls hospital. Dr. Burt, of Lake George, and Dr. Griffin, of Warrensburgh, were summoned and were shortly on the scene, Dr. Burt arriving before Miss Gertrude was taken to the hospital. Mrs. Mordecai was sent for at the new place a mile north of the scene of the accident and upon her arrival went with Miss Gertrude to the hospital, where they were met by Dr. T. H. Cunningham, of Glens Falls, who cared for the young lady until her death at about 3 o'clock.

The Mordecai family came to Lake George eight weeks ago to spend the summer at the Lockhart cottage on Montcalm street. The body of Miss Mordecai was prepared for burial Saturday evening and the family left with the remains on the midnight train for Charleston.

O. W. Sheldon, one of Fort Ann's most prominent business men, passed away today, Oct. 27. Mr. Sheldon was 87 years of age and had been a life-long resident of Fort Ann. He is survived by one daughter, Miss Helen Sheldon of Chicago, and five grandchildren — Winfred, Edward, Margaret and Carol of this place, and Mrs. Florence Downs of Massachusetts. *Oct 20 1914 Liz*

SAGAMORE TO RISE FROM RUINS

Lake George Hotel, Recently Destroyed by Fire, to be Rebuilt This Summer.

The stockholders of the Green Island Improvement company, owners of the Sagamore hotel, at Bolton Landing, which was destroyed by fire on Easter Sunday, at a recent meeting in New York decided to rebuild the structure during the present summer.

It is learned from an authoritive source that the hotel company is to be reorganized, this time to be headed by Dr. William Meyer and H. H. Judson, of New York. These, with a number of other directors from New York and Philadelphia, were at Bolton Sunday looking over the ground and their presence is regarded as a significant indication of an early start of building activities.

Preparations have already been begun by the management to provide for as many people as possible this season. The dormitory connected with the hotel, but which escaped the flames, is being remodeled into a kitchen and dining room to be used in connection with the cottages located on the hotel property. The electric lighting plant has again been put in commission.

RUN DOWN BY STAGE AUTO.

news June 1 19

Orson Wilsey Victim of Chauffeur's Carelessness on Lake George Road.

O. R. Wilsey while enjoying a spin in his Maxwell touring car on the Glens Falls-Lake George road Friday afternoon, accompanied by his wife and little son, Charles, was run into by Miller Brothers' Glens Falls and Bolton automobile stage. Nobody was hurt and neither machine was seriously damaged, but Orson had the scare of his life.

Mr. Wilsey states that he was coming toward home and just before he rounded the turn near the intersection of the Luzerne road stopped by the roadside for a minute. While his machine was standing still, as far out of the road as a railing would permit, the heavy auto stage, well loaded with passengers, rounded the turn bound in the opposite direction. Being on an up grade, fortunately, the big machine was going slow. The chauffeur, Mr. Wilsey asserts, was giving his attention to a woman sitting beside him and was not looking at the road, consequently did not see the auto ahead of him. He was equally oblivious to the frantic toots of Mr. Wilsey's horn and stentorian shouts until he was close upon him. It was then too late to entirely avoid a collision, though a quick turn prevented a head-on contact.

The Wilsey machine was considerably damaged though the owner was able to run it home. The blame was clearly upon the Glens Falls chauffeur, but all the satisfaction he gave was the remark, roughly framed, that the touring car should have been out of the road. Mr. Wilsey is justly indignant and there may be more to the story later.

A LAKE GEORGE VETERAN.

Mar 26 1914

Capt. Lee Harris, Old Steamboatman and Guide, Visits Warrensburgh.

Capt. Lee Harris, of East Lake George, a veteran steamboatman of the Queen of American Lakes, now retired, was a welcome caller at The News office Tuesday and related many interesting reminiscences of the old days on Lake George when he was a prominent figure as a steamboat captain and guide for many prominent visitors of that time.

Captain Harris, who confesses to eighty-two years, but doesn't look it, is a fine example of the value of right living. With a sturdy body, an honest heart and a kind and genial disposition which during his long life has endeared him to a host of friends, he is a remarkably fine specimen of the well preserved octogenarian.

Almost the first steam yacht that plied the waters of Lake George, the Owl, was commanded by Captain Harris, who ran the boat for excursion parties in connection with the Fort William Henry hotel's boat livery. At that time there were only three or four power boats on the lake.

MAC SMITH MAY LOSE SIGHT OF EYE

march 14 1914

LAKE GEORGE, March 13.—It is feared Under-Sheriff Mac R. Smith has permanently lost the sight of his left eye. The cause of his affliction is entirely unknown. Mr. Smith retired last evening apparently with perfect sight. When he awakened this morning it was impossible for him to see out of the left eye.

He hurried to Glens Falls to consult Dr. Sherwood LeFevre who stated it was too early to determine whether the blindness would be permanent or whether it would eventually affect both eyes. *Star*

THE CONNECTICUT "BLUE LAWS."

These statutes were enacted by the people of the "Dominion of New Haven," and being printed on blue paper, came to be generally known as Blue Laws:

No one shall run on the Sabbath day, or walk in his garden, or elsewhere, except reverently to and from meeting.

No food or lodgings shall be offered to Quaker, Adamite or heretic.

No one shall travel, cook victuals, make beds, sweep houses, cut hair or shave on the Sabbath day.

No one shall kiss her children on Sabbath or fasting days.

No one shall read common prayer books, keep Christmas or set days, eat mince pies, dance, play cards or play on any instrument of music except the drum, trumpet and Jew's harp.

Married persons must live together or be imprisoned.

NEAR-DROWNING AT LAKE GEORGE

news May 24 1914

Brave Youth Saves Veteran Steamboatman from Watery Grave.

Capt. Harvey Crandall, of Lake George, a veteran steamboat man, who is said to be near the age of ninety, while fishing from a round-bottom boat near the Fort William Henry hotel dock Thursday afternoon, leaned too far to one side to bait his hook and in an instant was in the water clinging to an overturned boat which was sinking rapidly under his weight, and crying lustily for help.

Arthur Finkle, a Lake George youth, standing with a companion on the D. & H. steamboat wharf, and watching the Mohican round the bend at Assembly Point, heard the old man's cries and without an instant's hesitation, only to remove his coat and shoes, plunged into the lake and swam to the rescue. Being an expert swimmer he covered the distance quickly and after five minutes' hard work, succeeded in completing his brave act by getting the old man to shore, undoubtedly saving him from a watery grave.

Captain Crandall was the owner and captain of the first steam yacht placed on Lake George, the Julia, which was brought to the lake from New York and was then—about forty years ago—one of three steamers on the lake, the others being the Minnehaha, a side-wheeler, and the Ganouski, a propeller. There are now more than 700 power boats on the lake.

Taylor House Property Sold.

The hotel property at Schroon Lake, consisting of a main building, and fifteen cottages, with one mile of lake front and a large tract of woodland, known as Taylors-on-Schroon, was sold at public auction at Lake George Thursday to Charles G. Eddy, of Troy, who bid $9,000. The sale was for the purpose of satisfying a mortgage of $12,000 held by the Mechanics Savings bank of Cohoes. Mr. Eddy is one of the directors of the Taylor House association. *news May 24 1914*

THURSDAY AFTERNOON, MAY 28, 1914.

An Old Melody.—The Bluebird's Song.

(Prize poem in St. Nicholas by Lucille H. Quarry [aged sixteen].)

A melody of the springtime!
  A tune of the April sky!
A music like vocal sunshine,
  As a flash of blue skims by.

Blue are the sky and the river,
  And the music the Lord hath made
Is held in the throat of a songster
  That gleams with the same bright shade.

And we know that spring is coming,
  When we see the bird of blue,
And hear his song in the orchard—
  A melody old, yet new.

For it seems that the bird is a spirit
  Whose summons sweet will bring
Over the river the dawning,
  And over the hills the spring!   ?

MRS. ALICE GATES.

Mrs. Alice Gates died Sunday afternoon, at her home on River street, Lewisville, aged seventy-four years. Death was caused by a complication of diseases. She is survived by a son, James, and a daughter, Miss Minnie Gates, both of this village. The funeral was held at the house Tuesday afternoon, the Rev. C. S. Agan officiating. The bearers were Walter Pasco, Sr., D. E. Pasco, Andrew Magee and Truman Brown. Interment in the village cemetery.

Golf Links or No New Sagamore.

It is reported in Bolton that the rebuilding of the Sagamore hotel depends upon the success of the owners in finding a suitable site for golf links and if this cannot be found the hotel will not be rebuilt. The report lacks confirmation, but if it is true it is high time for Bolton people to join in a search for the desired site which, it would seem, could be easily found.

REMEMBERS NAPOLEON

Star Aug 23 1913

PARIS, Aug. 22.—Probably the only person now living who has a clear personal recollection of the great Napoleon is M. Pierre Schamel-Roy, who on Monday next will celebrate his 106th birthday anniversary at his home at Neuilly. M. Schamel-Roy, as a boy of 12 saw the fallen emperor in exile at St. Helena, where he was taken to visit his father, who was a faithful follower and servant of Napoleon until the latter's death.

OBITUARY.

news May 24 1914

FREDERICK O. HADDEN.

Frederick O. Hadden, born in Warrensburgh September 30, 1854, and during his entire life a resident of this village, died at his home on Ridge street Sunday morning at 2:30 o'clock, after a brief illness of pneumonia.

The editor of The Whitehall Times is a discerning person. He recognizes enterprise when he sees it, hence the following comment on the activity of the Hon. James A. Emerson:

About twenty-five Great Meadow prison inmates are repairing roads in Warrensburgh, the bailiwick of the Honorable James Alwaysonthejob Emerson. There are plenty of roads in this county for the Great Meadow prison men to repair, but as Washington county's alertness is not particularly conspicuous and Jim's is, the activity of the state's wards on the boulevards of Emersonburg at the cost of board is easily accounted for, while Superintendent Riley or Warden Homer can not be blamed for complying with requests.

Comstock inmates have begun work on the piece of road between Comstock village and Whitehall and will rebuild the Comstock-Fort Ann road. A gang of prisoners will be sent to Saratoga county to do state road work.

—184—

DETECTIVE SMITH LANDS SILK SHIRTS

Former Local Boy Engineers Successful Crusade to Recover Stolen Property.

The New York World publishes the appended interesting story, in which Ervin J. Smith, a former Glens Falls boy, figures:

E. J. Smith, assistant manager of the New York office of the W. J. Burns International Detective Agency, didn't disguise himself or his operatives with false beards or anything like that when he was asked to find stolen silk shirts valued at $10,000. Smith and seven of his detectives simply wore the same brand of shirts that had been stolen and went around town trying to find something like them—cheap.

The shirts—200 dozen of them—had been stolen from the loft of the Expert Laundry Company, No. 30 Howard street, on March 19. They had been sent there to be laundered by S. Liebovitz & Son, No. 75-77 Leonard street.

As a result of the shopping tour of the silk-shirted detective Harry Bayer, twenty-six, of No. 2 West One Hundred and Eleventh street; John J. Menching, forty-seven, an expressman, of No. 307 Bowery, and David Goldstine, thirty-six, a cafe proprietor, of No. 3 Hamilton Place, were arrested by Detective Edward Costano of the Mulberry street police station. Bayer, Menching and Goldstein will be arraigned in the Tombs Police court on a charge of receiving stolen goods.

Bayer runs one of these "marked-down" shops at One Hundred and Thirty-seventh street and Third avenue. He said that the three dozen shirts which he had on sale at $1.25 each, had been purchased from Menching. Menching said he had bought a suitcase full of shirts from a stranger.

But the police have express company records to show that Menching shipped three trunks full of shirts to "J. Kaplan, care of Blustein," Savannah, Ga. The Savannah police are awaiting the arrival of the trunks.

Proprietors of two music stores of the Bowery will also be asked to explain more carefully how they happened to have so many fine silk shirts mixed up with the latest popular songs on their sale shelves. Other small merchant too have been questioned along the same lines by Assistant District Attorney Van Rennsaler. They will be questioned again.

"The way we got on the trail of the silk shirts," said the Burns detectives, "was by cutting our hair close back of the ears in a sort of diagonal slant downwards, with a soup-bowl effect behind. That made us look like east side gamblers, and we figured that whoever had the shirts would be willing to give us a chance, especially after we winked and pointed to the ones we were wearing."

MISTAKE MAY BE FATAL

Mrs. Richard A. Lane Takes Mercury Tablet for Headache Cure.

news May 21 1914

Suffering from a severe headache Sunday morning Mrs. Richard A. Lane, of 9 Jefferson street, Glens Falls, went to a medicine cabinet to obtain a remedy. In separate envelopes of similar appearance were headache tablets and a bichloride of mercury tablet which had been procured to be used as a disinfectant for a wound on her hand. By mistake she took the poison. In a short time her husband noticed that she was very pale and called her attention to it. She then told him that her stomach seemed to be burning and she was afraid she had taken the wrong tablet. Before going for a physician he called in a neighbor who promptly gave Mrs. Lane the white of an egg as an antidote. If her life is saved she will owe it to this simple remedy, which may have absorbed the deadly poison before it entered her system.

Mercury poisoning acts in two ways, according to the medical profession. By its corrosive action it sometimes causes death within a few hours, while in other cases it acts upon the kidneys and has a slower action, proving fatal generally in about two weeks. There is no known cure after the poison enters the system. The only hope is in the prompt administration of an antidote which will prevent this.

The physician attending Mrs. Lane says she has a chance for recovery owing to the fact that the antidote was administered in fairly good time. While she has passed the first danger point she will be in a critical condition for two or three weeks.

Mrs. Lane's husband, Prof. Richard A. Lane, is a music teacher well known in this and adjoining towns. He has had piano pupils here for several years. Many friends will sympathize with him in his terrible trouble.

$4,000 FIRE AT BOLTON LANDING

Star Nov 24 1914

Flames of Unknown Origin Destroy Boat House and Three Craft

(Special to The Post-Star)

BOLTON LANDING, Nov. 23.—Fire, which broke out about 7:30 o'clock this evening in what is called the J. B. Simpson boat house, situated on Green Island, destroyed the structure and three boats that were in it, entailing a loss estimated at $4,000, partly covered by insurance.

The Katrina, owned by C. E. Wilson, jr., the Calypso, belonging to J. B. Simpson, both steam craft, and a gasoline launch, the property of John Traver, were practically consumed by the flames. The origin of the fire is not known.

CAPTURED LINCOLN'S ASSASSIN

1914

Johnsburgh Soldier Who Played Important Part in War Dies in Portland, Ore.

John W. Millington, a Civil War veteran who enlisted in Johnsburgh, December 3, 1861, and served with distinction throughout the war, died on November 11, at the home of his son, John E. Millington, in Portland, Ore.

The deceased was one of a detail of soldiers sent out from Washington. D. C., on the night of April 14, 1865, in pursuit of John Wilkes Booth, the assassin of President Lincoln, and the story of his thrilling experience on that memorable night, which resulted in the capture and death of Booth, was told in the columns of The News a few years ago.

Mr. Millington was mustered out of the service at Washington, October 5, 1865, and went to Sioux City, Iowa, and lived there until about eleven years ago, when he took up his residence in Portland with his son. During his first two years in the army Mr. Millington was a member of Company E, 93d Infantry, N. Y. Vols., but in July, 1863, he was transferred with others to the 16th regiment New York Volunteer cavalry in which he served until the end of the war.

BOLTON LANDING.

times Oct 30 1914

Bolton Landing, Oct. 28.—Mr. and Mrs. E. O. Ormsby are visiting the latter's brother and sister, Mr. and Mrs. Fred West of Binghamton.

Herbert Moon and sister, Mrs. Marion Scribner of Bridgeport, Conn., were recent visitors of friends and relatives in town.

Mr. and Mrs. E. M. Vandenburg and Mr. and Mrs. T. J. Ormsby returned yesterday from a motor trip to Ausable Chasm.

L. A. Persons has established an express route between Bolton Landing and Glens Falls, making two trips a week, Tuesdays and Fridays.

Dr. E. L. Wilson has returned from a business trip to Baltimore.

Mr. and Mrs. J. L. Maranville have returned home from a visit of two weeks with relatives and friends in Rutland, Vt.

Mr. and Mrs. L. A. Persons have moved into the Baptist parsonage.

Mrs. Helen Burbank, who has been ill for some time, died Sunday night at the home of her son, Frank Burbank. The funeral was held Tuesday afternoon. The body was taken to Schroon Lake Wednesday morning for interment.

"Dick" Smith to Locate in Chestertown.

Richard P. Smith, Jr., who last spring sold his store and residence property at South Horicon and removed to Pottersville, is soon to make another change and become a resident of Chestertown, having recently purchased "Greyhurst," the summer home of Mrs. S. Benton, of Memphis, Tenn., at that place.

-185-

WAR DAYS RECALLED

Mar 19 1914

Warrensburgh's Part in the Great Rebellion of 1861-65

REPORT OF THE WAR COMMITTEE

Just Published by Town Board In Book Form —Record of Strenuous Efforts to Supply Quotas of Men Called for by President Lincoln.

In a book of forty-five pages, published by the town board of Warrensburgh and recently issued from The News Press, is given a complete report of the proceedings of the War Committee of 1861-65 in its work of supplying the quotas of men required from the town by the several calls of President Lincoln, to suppress the Rebellion and preserve the Union. It is a record of strenuous effort and duty faithfully performed. Its publication in this form was made possible by the foresight of Henry Griffing, who preserved the minutes of the committee's meetings and compiled them for this purpose for their permanent preservation and the information of those who may find them of interest.

The expense of the publication was provided for by an appropriation from the town funds voted by the town board of 1913, composed of Milton N. Eldridge, supervisor; Herbert C. Smith, town clerk; George Hodgson, J. Freeman Cameron, John Brown and Don H. Heath justices.

The War Committee was appointed at a meeting of citizens of the town of Warrensburgh on August 18, 1862, held at the Academy building and called for the purpose of raising money to pay bounties to fifty-two volunteers, the town's quota under President Lincoln's call for 600,000 men. Joseph Woodward was chairman of the meeting and James Fuller secretary. Thomas Cunningham was then supervisor of the town and by virtue of his office was made chairman of the War Committee. The other members named were Fred O. Burhans, Stephen Griffing, 2d, George Richards and Hiram McNutt. Mr. Burhans was made treasurer.

In response to President Lincoln's first two calls for volunteers, on April 15, 1861, and May 5, 1861, twenty-two Warrensburgh men enlisted for two years' service without bounty. The next call, in July of the same year, was for 500,000 men for three years and 25,000 of this number was required from New York state. Thirty-eight Warrensburgh men responded to this call without bounty.

The following year Warren county paid a bounty of $50 per man and forty-three more Warrensburgh patriots went to the front. The county bounty having been expended it became necessary for the town to pay $50 each to twenty-five men required to fill the town's quota. Eighteen volunteers were secured at an expense of $900

On July 8, 1863, a draft was made for 300,000 men, and Warrensburgh's quota was eleven. Four soldiers were secured here and seven men paid $300 each and were exempted from the draft.

As the war advanced bounties increased and the committee had considerable difficulty in raising funds to meet the demands. In 1863 the price went up to $300 a man and the following year volunteers were receiving in some cases $1,000 each. On August 9, 1864, a special town meeting was held to raise $8,000 for bounties and the appropriation was carried by a vote of sixty-three to twelve. A committee composed of Thomas Cuningham, Fred O. Burhans, Hiram McNutt, Samuel T. Richards and Henry Herrick, was appointed to raise the sum named on the credit of the town, to fix the amount of bounties to be paid and to make all proper effort to fill the town's quota.

Neighboring towns and counties were raising their bounties, offering from $500 to $900. The time for the approaching draft was drawing near and many young men showed a strong desire to trave', with Canada as their objective point. Feeling that they were unable to pay more than $300 and being unable to secure volunteers at that figure the committee caused another special town meeting to be held and $12,000 was voted. Twenty-one men were then enlisted at $800 each and three at $900.

On the list of men enrolled in the town, liable to military duty, there were 228 names. The report of the War Committee shows that of this number 130 volunteered and served from one to four years.

Mentioned in the book for distinguished service are Col. Charles O. Gray, who was killed in action at the Battle of Kingston, North Carolina, December 14, 1862, falling at the head of his regiment while bravely and splendidly leading it to a successful charge. Major Charles H. Burhans recruited Company I, 96th N. Y. Vols., at his own personal expense, and was commended by his colonel for his gallantry and fidelity as a soldier and for bravery in the face of the enemy at the Battle of Fair Oaks. Capt. M. Nelson Dickinson enlisted as a private August 1, 1862, and won promotion by successive stages. He was wounded and captured in action October 27, 1864, at Fair Oaks, Virginia, paroled and discharged for wounds May 3, 1865. March 6, 1866, brevet captain. Samuel T. Richards was colonel of the 118th Regiment, N. Y. Vol. Inft., and was discharged for disability July 8, 1863.

The report will be of especial interest to veterans of the war and their descendants. The edition was small and the books will therefore be judiciously distributed. One copy has been placed in the Richards Library for circulation and another has been placed on the reference shelves.

CIVIL WAR VETERAN ANSWERS LAST CALL

Edward H. Gates Dies at Home in Third Street—Funeral Tomorrow.

aug 20 1914 time

Edward H. Gates, a veteran of the Civil war, died yesterday at his home in Third street. He had been ill several months. Mr. Gates was seventy-four years old and had resided in this city thirty-four years, having come here from Saratoga.

Mr. Gates for a number of years was a well known contractor and builder in Glens Falls. His military record for three years in the Civil war reflects great honors upon him. He enlisted in Saratoga on August 27, 1862 in Company D, 77th New York Volunteer Infantry and on October 1, 1863, he was detailed to service in the Third New York Independent Battery of Volunteer Artillery. He was promoted to the rank of Corporal, July 12, 1862 and as such was wounded in the Battle of Petersburg, Va., November 5, 1864. He was promoted to sergeant May 1, 1865, and was mustered out of service June 24, 1865.

Mr. Gates was a member of Glens Falls lodge, No. 121, F. and A. M, and during twenty-five years had been a member of E. M. Wing post, G. A. R. During that time he had filled nearly every office with which his comrades could honor him.

He is survived by his widow, a son, B. E. Gates, of Boston, and a sister, Mrs. Mary J. Brown. The funeral will be held at 2:30 o'clock tomorrow afternoon from his late home.

OBITUARY.

nov 2 D 1914 news

JOHN VANDENBURGH.

John Vandenburgh, during his entire life of ninety years a resident of the town of Bolton, and one of its most prominent and highly respected citizens, died at his home Saturday after an illness of about two months duration. He is survived by four sons and a daughter, Lewis, William, Swenson and Orlin Vandenburgh, of Bolton Landing, and Mrs. Lowell D. Waters, of Horicon. The funeral was held at his late home Tuesday afternoon at 1 o'clock and was conducted by the Rev. E. M. Parrott, of Lake George. Interment in the Bolton cemetery by the side of his wife, who died several years ago.

Kingsley.

John M. Cronkhite of Kattskill Bay, Lake George, died yesterday afternoon at the home of her daughter, Mrs. Farley B. Jenkins, at Harrisena. Besides the daughter mentioned she is survived by two sons, Charles D. of Harrisena and George H. of Kattskill Bay, and a sister, Mrs. George Abrams of Wellsboro, Penn.

THREE BROTHERS DROWN IN BROOK

Star Aug 13 1913

While Going to Pasture for Cows, Little Tots Meet Death in Stream in Ticonderoga

Special to The Post-Star.)
TICONDEROGA, Aug. 18.—In the parlor in the home of John Fleming tonight were three coffins, containing the last mortal remains of his three children, whose bodies were found in Trout brook, a short distance from the place where three brothers named LaRose met their death in a similar manner five years ago. The little fellows ranged in age from five to nine years. They were bright lads and great favorites in the section of the village where they lived. Their death cast a pall of gloom over the friends of the family, but this pales into insignificance compared with the grief in the little home where a heartbroken father and mother mourn for the three children who were taken with one stroke by the Grim Reaper.

The boys were sent out Sunday afternoon to drive the cows in for the night and in order to make a short cut to the field where the animals were pastured they had to cross a log which spanned the brook. When they failed to return their parents instituted a search and within a short time a large crowd was scouring the nearby woods while others dragged the stream.

The fact that the log was gone caused the theory that the lads had been drowned and after a short search, the bodies were found near each other a short distance from the place where the log had spanned the stream. The parents, who had anxiously watched the searchers, broke down when the little bodies were taken from the stream and laid on the banks until the arrival of the coroner.

Many theories as to the manner in which the boys met their death are advanced, but the most plausible is that one of the lads fell into the water while crossing the log and his brothers went to his assistance and they too drowned.

The fatality recalls the drowning of the three LaRose brothers five years ago. One of the boys fell into the mill pond and the other two tried to rescue him with the result they too went down to their death.

DEATH RECORD 1914

Post Star Dec 1

The remains of Mrs. Ethel Barnum of Naugatuck, Conn., a granddaughter of the late Selah Morgan of Glens Falls, will today be brought here for interment in the family plot in the Glens Falls cemetery. Mrs. Barnum, who was 21 years old, died Sunday in the Saratoga hospital. She was formerly Miss Ethel Giles and was born in Saratoga.

She is survived by her husband; two brothers, Louis Giles of the United States ship Louisiana, and Vinton Giles of New York. Her mother will be well remembered by Glens Falls residents, she having been Miss Hattie Morgan before her marriage. The funeral services will be held at 12 o'clock noon today, privately, from the home of her aunt, Mrs. E. M. Kenyon, 513 Broadway, Saratoga.

From Larimore, N. D., comes the sad intelligence of the death of Julius H. Smith, who expired while engaged in work about his barn in that town. Mr. Smith was born in Schroon Lake, December 25, 1850. He went to North Dakota in 1884. His only near survivor is his widow, who is a sister of George W. Crawford of this city. Mr. Smith was a prominent member of the Masonic order, and his funeral was conducted by the Larimore lodge.

Jeremiah Green, a life long resident of West Fort Ann, died yesterday morning in his home following a short illness. He was born December 6, 1837. In July, 1861, he enlisted in Company B, One Hundred and Twenty-third regiment, New York Volunteers, in which he served creditably throughout the Civil war, taking part in many of the important battles.

He is survived by his widow; three daughters, Mrs. George Hughes of Hudson Falls, Mrs. George Keach of West Fort Ann and Mrs. Sumner Steves of South Bay; three sons, Fred, Willis and Elmer Green of West Fort Ann, and two brothers, Jerome Green of West Fort Ann and Frelon Green of Pattens Mills. The funeral will be held at 1 o'clock Thursday afternoon from his late home, Rev. George Webster of Pattens Mills officiating. Interment will be made in West Fort Ann.

DISPUTE OVER DEBT LANDS MAN IN JAIL

Times Oct 13 1914

Ezra Cilley of Bolton and Sawyer Company of Glens Falls Contending Forces.

What was originally a dispute over a claim of fifty dollars has led to the incarceration of Ezra Cilley of Bolton in the county jail at Lake George, the filing of a petition in bankruptcy, the increase of the claim, by the addition of court costs, until it now amounts to about $160, and many more interesting proceedings are promised.

Upon the application of Attorney Walter A. Chambers of the law firm of Chambers & Finn, Judge Ray of the United States District court has granted an order restraining the firm of J. E. Sawyer & company, James M. Patterson, Attorney Charles R. Patterson and others from disposing or interfering with Cilley's property, including that levied up to satisfy the claim of the Sawyer company.

Several months ago the Sawyer company through its attorney, Chas. R. Patterson, attempted to collect about fifty dollars, alleged by the concern to be due it from Cilley. Supplementary proceedings were commenced for the purpose of determining whether Cilley had any property upon which a levy could be made. Attorney Taylor was appointed referee by Judge Raley in County court and an order directing him not to dispose of any of his property was served on Cilley.

After the proceedings were opened, it was discovered that Cilley had disposed of his interest in a piece of woodland to a relative. The matter was brought to the attention of County Judge Raley by Attorney Patterson and the judge directed Cilley's arrest and confinement in the county jail until such a time as he should satisfy the claim.

Napoleon and Tobacco.

Napoleon, who tried to smoke once and then with dire results, instituted the French tobacco monopoly, which the German government now proposes to adopt so far as cigarettes are concerned. At a court function held early in 1810 the emperor remarked a lady wearing jewels of such magnificence that he inquired how her husband made his money. "He is a tobacco merchant", was the reply, which led him to seek further information as to such a profitable business. Before the year expired Napoleon issued a decree restricting the sale and manufacture of tobacco exclusively to the state. It has remained a monopoly ever since and for many years past has brought in an annual revenue of over $80,000,000.

GLENS FALLS FEARS HOPE OF BRIDGE IS DASHED

Temporary Structure Now Going Up Over Hudson May Be Only One For Long Time, is Apprehension.

Special to The Knickerbocker Press.

GLENS FALLS, May 24.—With a temporary wooden foot bridge spanning the Hudson, the Hudson Valley Railway company building a temporary steel structure above, which may be completed within another month or so and nothing being done toward calling a special election to vote on propositions for a permanent structure, residents of this city and of South Glens Falls are beginning to express the fear that the day when a permanent structure will become a reality is far distant.

Fear is expressed that when finally the special election is called the proposition to raise $160,000 for the construction of a permanent concrete viaduct will be defeated in this city and that a repetition of joint meetings of the common council of this city and of the town board of Moreau will be in order and may continue indefinitely.

A large number of Glens Falls and South Glens Falls residents are expressing indignation over the action of the common council and the town board in appropriating taxpayers' money and the $2,000 secured by popular subscription for the construction of a temporary bridge by the Hudson Valley railway company, which it develops will be large enough only for street car traffic with automobilists and horse-drawn vehicles sandwiching in between cars crossing the structure eight times per hour.

The Hudson Valley railway company, it is said, will have right of way and will station men at either end for the regulation of traffic. Congestion of automobile and vehicle traffic at both ends of the bridge is to be expected.

TEMPORARY WOODEN FOOT BRIDGE OVER THE HUDSON AT GLENS FALLS WHICH MAY HAVE TO SERVE YEARS

YOUTH KILLED ON RETURN FROM HUNT

1914

Wellington Brayton Places Gun On Dock Near His Assembly Point Home---Weapon Accidentally Discharged. Shot Pierces Lad's Side and He Expires Within Five Minutes---Victim Brother of Iselin Brayton of Glens Falls

(Special to The Post-Star.)

LAKE GEORGE, Nov. 10.—The first fatal hunting accident of the season occured this afternoon at Assembly Point, when Wellington Brayton, 16 years old, son of Mr. and Mrs. Fred Brayton, was almost instantly killed by the accidental discharge of his shotgun. The shot entered his right side and he died within five minutes. The accident occurred at the dock near the youth's home.

Brayton and Harvey Mead of Glens Falls had passed the afternoon hunting muskrats from a rowboat in the vicinity of Dunham's Bay and were returning home. They rowed their boat up to the dock which is only a short distance from the Brayton home. Brayton placed his gun on the dock with his left hand and in some unaccountable manner it was discharged, the full charge striking him in the side. He fell back into the boat.

A number of persons attracted by the shot ran to the scene and with the aid of Mead lifted the unfortunate youth out onto the dock. A call was sent to Glens Falls for physicians,

and Drs. Floyd M. Palmer and Alexander McKee arrived at Assembly Point before 3 o'clock, but not until after the youth had expired.

Brayton was popular in this section. Besides his parents, he is survived by one sister, Mrs. Charles Dickinson of Assembly Point and two brothers, Lee Brayton of Assembly Point and Iselin Brayton of Glens Falls.

NELSON-BARBER
June 11 1914

George W. Nelson and Miss Lucille Barber, both of Bolton, were married at 4 o'clock Tuesday afternoon, by the Rev. E. M. Parrott, at St. James' Episcopal church, Lake George. The attendants and witnesses were Miss Jessie A. Barber, Miss Pauline Nelson and Miss Matilda Veach. Miss Helen Weaver played the wedding march. The bridal party left Bolton about noon, by automobile, and after the nuptial knot was tied returned to the home of the bridegroom's parents, where a reception was held. They will reside there until fall when Mr. Nelson will build a house. Both of the young people are very popular in Bolton and have the best wishes of many friends

---

Bolton Boy With U. S. Army at Vera Cruz.
June 1914

Mrs. Ernest Wood, of Bolton Landing, has recently received a letter from her son, Percy Wood, who is a soldier in the United States army and is now stationed with his regiment at Vera Cruz, Mexico. He sent a picture of his company and says that he is very much pleased with army life.

PENCIL THRUSTS.

Good Dope.

If you want to live in the kind of a town
Like the kind of a town you like,
You needn't slip your clothes in a grip
And start on a long, long hike,
You'll only find what you left behind,
For there's nothing that's really new.
It's a knock at yourself when you knock your town.
It isn't your town—it's you.
Real towns are not made by men afraid
Lest somebody else gets ahead.
When everyone works and nobody shirks
You can raise a town from the dead.
And if while you make your personal stake
Your neighbor can make one, too,
Your town will be what you want to see.
It isn't your town—it's you.

FORMER LOCAL BOY SOLVES MYSTERY

Aug 50 1914

Erwin J. Smith Secures Confession from Man Who Stole $150,000 from Bank.

Ervin J. Smith, a former Glens Falls boy, now assistant manager of the New York office of the William J. Burns Detective agency, recently brought additional fame to himself by locating and obtaining from Thomas Piptone, a confession which solved the mystery surrounding the disappearance of $150,000 from the banking house of Redmond & Co., 30 Pine street, New York.

Piptone, for five years, had been in charge of the foreign exchange department of the bank by which he was employed, which is a private institution and therefore not under federal supervision.

Mr. Smith began work on the case at one o'clock in the afternoon of Monday, August 3 and at three o'clock he had located his man.

In his confession Piptone stated that he had lost all of the $150,000 in the stock market. It is possible that the exchanges through which he did business may be prosecuted, as the acceptance of money from a person employed by a bank is strictly prohibited.

After his arrest Piptone made an unsuccessful attempt at suicide.

Mr. Smith is now devoting much of his time to a study of the finger print system with a view to becoming an expert in this line of work. He had planned to study abroad, but the European war compelled him to change.

Oct 9 1914 Star

APPOINTED FLAGMAN.

J. R. Fish has been appointed flagman at the Platt street crossing of the Delaware and Hudson railroad.

CONCRETE WORK IS NEARLY FINISHED

times Oct 13 1914

Ornamental Work on New Hudson River Viaduct is Now in Progress.

Very little concrete work remains to be done in connection with the building of the viaduct between this city and South Glens Falls. All of the arches and main foundation work is completed and from now on all that is to be done is to put in the concrete foundation for paving and the building of the parapet wall.

Workmen are engaged moulding fourteen concrete lamp posts which will be placed in the parapet wall. Each post will stand 21 1-2 feet above the sidewalks. Concrete sidewalks are to be laid and with the building of the spiral stairway down to Cooper's Cave the concrete work will be completed and the bridge, as soon as the paving is done, will be thrown open to the public.

The contractors will compete the work first on the western part of the bridge and will continue to advance to the eastern part of the bridge which is now being used by the public. In a few days the present roadway will be narrowed and work started by the Hudson Valley Railway company toward laying its permanent tracks in the center of the viaduct. The present temporary tracks will be used until the permanent tracks are laid. In the meantime traffic will be regulated across the bridge. When the roadway is narrowed it will be impossible for two autos or carriages to pass.

The large tower at the northern end of the bridge, which has been used in conveying concrete and timbers, has been removed to the lot west of the northern end of the bridge and from now on it will be used in cleaning up under the viaduct.

At the south end of the viaduct earth filling has been placed in position for some distance which gives to the passerby a good idea of the width of the bridge.

LAKE GEORGE ASSN. TO SUE SMITH LUMBER CO.

Aug 22 1914

At a recent meeting of the Lake George association the navigation committee was empowered to engage counsel and commence action against the Smith Lumber company of Ticonderoga for an alleged violation of the law prohibiting the rafting of logs through Lake George after July 1. Motorboats on several occasions have crashed into the rafts in the dark, and stray logs floating about the lake are also a continual source of danger to motor craft. Officers of the association for the ensuing year were elected as follows: President, Harry W. Hayden; vice presidents, William K. Bixby and Dr. Charles O. Kimball; treasurer, Albert L. Judson; secretary, Edward A. Knight.

Sept 2 1914

Russell-Duell.

Miss Ida Duell of Hill View, Lake George and Attorney Harry L. Russell of the law firm of VanNess and Russell of Greenwich, a former resident of this city, will be married tomorrow at noon in the Episcopal church at Hill View. Mr. Russell is a graduate of the local High school and the Albany Law school. He is a brother of Attorney J. Ward Russell and George Russell of the firm of Russell and Wait of this city and a son of Bloomfield W. Russell of Moreau. Among those who will attend are Mr. and Mrs. George Russell and son, Morris, and daughter, Bessie, Attorney and Mrs. J. Ward Russell and daughter, Julie S., of this city, Miss Isabelle Long of Cambridge, Bloomfield W. Russell and Mr. and Mrs. Rufus Henderson of Moreau.

Funeral services were read yesterday over the remains of Mrs. Edwin J. Worden, by Rev. E. M. Parrott, a private service being held at 3 o'clock in the Hotel Worden and one open to friends at 3:30 in the Episcopal church of Lake George. The latter service was largely attended.

VILLAGE OF BOLTON-ON-LAKE GEORGE

SAGAMORE IN ASHES

Palatial Lake George Hotel Burned Early Sunday Morning.

LOSS ESTIMATED AT $300,000

Property Was Insured for $150,000 and Nothing in Building Was Saved—Origin of Fire Unknown Probably Incendiary—Will be Rebuilt.

The palatial Sagamore hotel, at Bolton Landing, the largest and finest summer resort on Lake George, was completely destroyed by fire at an early hour Sunday morning. The loss is estimated at $300,000 and the insurance was $150,000. The origin of the fire is unknown, but from the fact that it started on the outside of the building incendiarism is strongly suspected.

The fire was discovered at 2:50 o'clock by J. Wilson Ward and in less than an hour the magnificent hotel was but a mass of smouldering ruins. Mr. Ward aroused the central telephone operator and she summoned to the scene as many men as could be reached. When the crowd arrived at the burning structure, on Green Island, a short distance from the village, the flames had gained such headway that nothing could be done to check them. Neither was it possible to gain entrance to the building, therefore none of its contents could be saved. The nearest outbuildings, the engine and boiler house and the laundry, were saved with little effort as they were of brick and steel construction. Of the six cottages on the hotel grounds only two were at any time threatened. These were owned by E. Burgess Warren and the George Burnham estate, both of Philadelphia. The stables being a considerable distance from the hotel were not endangered.

Engineer, B. C. Green, was working in the engine room Saturday, as far as could be learned, nobody was in the hotel. The caretaker, Sheridan G. Finkle, was in Schenectady Saturday night and expected to remain there over Sunday, but was called home on account of the fire. He could offer no explanation as to the probable cause of the conflagration. The big building made a spectacular fire and threw a reflection upon the sky which was plainly visible in this place.

The Sagamore was a three-story wooden building with about 350 rooms. Last fall it was painted at a cost of $1,000 and many improvements had been made during the winter, including several fire escapes which were erected at a large expense. About $1,500 was also expended for improvements on the deck.

The hotel was built twenty-one years ago to replace the old Sagamore which was also destroyed by fire. It was owned by the Green Island Improvement company, of which John Boulton Simpson, of New York, is president and the heaviest stockholder. E. Burgess Warren and the estate of the late George Burnham, of Philadelphia, are also stockholders. The house enjoyed a large patronage under the management of T. Edmund Krumbholz, who has been in charge of it since 1907. The buildings were situated on a beautiful point of land, surrounded by great pine trees, and each season attracted the attention of thousands of tourists going through the lake because of its magnificent appearance.

Mr. Simpson visited Bolton Monday and stated that the hotel will be rebuilt and on a much more up-to-date scale. Work will be started on the new structure as soon as insurance adjusters have finished their work. Plans will be prepared at once by S. G. Slocum, a New York architect, and the new building will be fire proof, being constructed of reinforced concrete. It will be about the same size as the old one and will accommodate upwards of 300 guests.

In addition to the building of the new structure Mr. Simpson states that the company will also erect several cottages along the lake shore, making it, in reality a pretty lake colony. It is hardly probable that the new hotel will be in readiness for opening before the season of 1915.

The Troy Times

The Sea of Life.

(A Hymn).

BY (REV.) JOSEPH C. BOOTH.
Written for The Troy Times.

On the Sea of Life I sail,
  To a mystic land unseen;
Hope, my anchor, in the veil
  By mine eye of faith is seen;
When the rising billows roll,
Jesus, lead my anxious soul!

On the Sea of Life, in storm,
  Lashed by sin's destructive sweep,
Let me see Thy welcome form
  Walking on the angry deep;
When the boiling billows roll,
Jesus, lead my helpless soul.

On the Sea of Life, my bark
  Driven by the friendly gale
Threatening wave nor dangerous shark
  Can against my soul prevail;
When the billows cease to roll,
Jesus, lead my trustful soul.

When the Sea of Life shall end
  And my ship at anchor lies,
At the Customs be my friend,
  With my Passport let me rise;
Where no billows ever roll,
Jesus, lead my blissful soul.

ADIRONDACK FARMS

Enterprise of Eugene L. Ashley Highly Commended by Glens Falls Post-Star.

The Adirondack Farms, established by Eugene L. Ashley, at Glens Falls, was the subject of a highly commendatory editorial in a recent issue of the Glens Falls Post-Star, from which we reproduce the following paragraphs:

"Eugene L. Ashley has set a splendid example to the farmers of this state. With his brains and money he has developed, incidentally with his greater affairs, a business of horse breeding and farming, interdependent and inseparable, which contains the vital germ of a distinctive and permanent system in agricultural tactics. No economist can fail to perceive that he has laid the foundation of a very broad and profitable enterprise.

"The magnificent results Mr. Ashley has attained on his Adirondack Farms emphasize the supremacy of his ideas in the affairs of men. They afford a vision of unmeasured power and possibility of business enterprise in agricultural pursuits which under closest analysis cannot fail to energize hope and faith and ambition among all progressive men who are engaged in that honorable calling. And by this improvement of stock throughout New York and New England he is conferring a lasting benefit upon mankind.

"It is a noteworthy fact that Glens Falls is the seat of the large importing and breeding establishment in the east. Here is being conserved and distributed the pure blood of the world's champion draft and saddle horses. Adirondack Farms consist of 1,700 acres under cultivation and 250 horses, and the passport of this institution to public favor is its great record of prize winnings. At seven fairs last fall its registered draft horses alone won $3,000 in prizes and 204 ribbons, which is perhaps the greatest record of winnings ever achieved by any one exhibitor of draft horses in America.

"The costs of production and maintenance of horses on these farms have been reduced scientifically to what is claimed to be the lowest minimum per pound in the history of American breeding. The horses are self supporting through the work they do on the farms. The value of crops maintains them. Upon this economic basis are administered the affairs of Adirondack Farms, and the message its example conveys to agriculturists everywhere is hopeful, encouraging, stimulating. It is a far-reaching message that draws to Glens Falls the attention of many men interested in farming and stock raising from Maine to Florida—and occasionally from such distant world corners as South Africa, as evidenced Thursday by a visiting delegation of Boers. All of which is a matter of real local pride."

Mrs. Daisy Morehouse, aged about twenty-three, died last Thursday at her home at the Huddle, of Bright's disease. The funeral was held at her late home Sunday afternoon, the Rev. S. J. Liberty officiating. Mrs. Morehouse is survived by her husband and young son, her father, Anthony Dagles, and several brothers and sisters. Interment in the Bolton cemetery.

MAN DROWNS IN THE HUDSON RIVER

Times Aug 3 1914

Garfield Brice, Aged Thirty, Goes to Watery Grave— Body Recovered.

While bathing in the river about three-fourths of a mile above the fifth platform, late yesterday afternoon, Garfield Brice, thirty years of age, who resided with his mother, Mrs. Miller, at 95 Saratoga avenue, South Glens Falls, was drowned. The body was recovered at 10:30 o'clock last night in five feet of water, about thirty feet from the shore, by Herbert Cossey. It is believed that Brice either waded beyond his depth, as it is said he could not swim, or was siezed with cramps. The young man was alone at the time.

Brice left his home shortly after 2 o'clock yesterday afternoon and an hour later he was seen in the water by Mrs. Wesley Lewis, who has a camp in that vicinity.

About 3 o'clock a passerby found the young man's clothing and a towel and soap, but saw no evidence of the owner. He then went to the Miller home and asked if Brice had returned. The man was informed that he had not yet returned.

Early last evening a searching party was formed and at 10:30 o'clock the body was recovered. Coroners' Physician J. S. White gave permission for the removal of the body to the Miller home. Brice was a collector of antiques and a young man of good habits.

TOWN OF IGERNA IS WITHOUT POSTOFFICE

Times Aug 22 1914

Acting upon orders from the postoffice department in Washington, Postmaster Andrew Loveland of Igerna Saturday closed his office permanently and retired from the government service. The little hamlet in the northern part of the town of Chester is now without a postoffice and the residents must arrange to get their mail at the office most convenient for them. Olmstedville will probably accommodate the greater number, while others will go to North Creek.

Some time ago a movement was started by some of the residents to secure a rural free delivery route from the Igerna office. A petition was forwarded to Washington and in due time an inspector was sent to investigate. As a result of his inquiries the application was denied.

There is much indignation among the farmers and other residents who are inconvenienced by the drastic order and a strong effort will be made to have the matter righted.

—191—

TRAFFIC TIED UP AND BUSINESS SUSPENDED AS A RESULT OF BIZZARD

Official Weather Observer Reports Total Downfall of Thirty Inches at Three O'clock This Afternoon

Sun Feb 14. 1914

CHIEF MACK WARNS AGAINST FIRES

With traffic completely tied up, many business places and manufacturing institutions closed, curbs piled shoulder-high with snow and the streets virtually forsaken, Glens Falls is today in the grip of the most severe storm since the memorable blizzard of 1888.

For the first time in many years Northern New York is experiencing a real old-fashioned winter. The storm started with a light downfall of snow shortly before midnight, increasing in furors throughout the night until dawn brought an almost blinding sheet of white. So heavy was the fall that pedestrians this morning found it impossible to distinguish acquaintances less than twenty-five yards away.

At three o'clock this afternoon a fall of thirty inches was reported by Weather Observer Williams and the storm was still raging, with no promise of relief.

Operations on Hudson Valley lines have been abandoned, so far as passenger traffic is concerned; service on the Delaware and Hudson is at a standstill; cabmen long before noon sent their rigs to the stables and noon found the city without means of transportation.

Virtually every store in the city suspended operations this afternoon, allowing the major portion of employes to go to their homes.

Reports from Warrensburg and the North state that the storm, while the most severe of recent years, is not as great as in this city.

A Hudson Valley car leaving Warrensburg at 12 o'clock this noon and preceded by a snow plow reached Glens Falls at 3 o'clock.

Alarm is felt in some sections because of the danger of possible fires. Chief Mack requests that property owners and tenants lose no time in removing snow from hydrants. He also suggests that care be exercised in the operation of furnaces and stoves.

Reports from out-lying districts state that in many sections a strong wind is blowing. Houses and outbuildings are fast being buried and roads have been made impassable. Should the wind continue many families will be without means of securing provisions, especially those in rural districts.

THOUSANDS HEAR PLEA FOR PEACE

Europe's War Threatens the Framework of Civilization Declares Governor Glynn

Star — Sept. 21

VICE PRESIDENT SPEAKS

1914

Champ Clark, at Big New York Meeting, Says We Should Lead in Plan to Disarm By Percentage

NEW YORK, Sept. 20.—An audience of many thousands filled the Sixty-ninth Regiment armory tonight and heard the cause of peace urged by Vice President Marshall, Speaker Clark, Governor Glynn and others. Elbert H. Gary, chairman of the United States Steel Corporation, opened the meeting and introduced Governor Glynn as permanent chairman. Several thousands were unable to crowd their way into the armory.

"The framework of the civilization upon which the American commonwealth is built is in danger today because of the most horrible war in history being waged in Europe," said Governor Glynn, "and there is no nation that can with equal good grace offer its mediation as can the United States.

"We can offer to help France, because France helped us when in Revolutionary days she gave us the sword of Lafayette and the troops of Rochambeau.

"We can offer help to Germany, because Germany gave us the sword of Siegel and the brains of Carl Schurz.

"We can offer help to England because England gave us the greatest man of English lineage that ever walked on this side of the Atlantic—the immortal George Washington.

"Our aid for mediation is offered not to one nation but to every nation in order that the tears of women and children shall cease to mingle with the blood of men slain on the battlefield. And when the time comes for our great president, Woodrow Wilson, to offer the assistance of this country in mediation every man in the country will be found aiding him."

When the governor mentioned the name of the president cheers echoed throughout the hall.

HAROLD COOL DIES IN AUTO ACCIDENT

Aug. 28 — 1914

Local Boy and Two Companions Instantly Killed Near Hartford, Conn.

CAR SKIDS AND HITS POLE

Victims Employed By Insurance Company in Hartford—Owner of Machine Escapes Injury— Held for Reckless Driving

C. Harold Cool, son of Former Mayor Charles W. Cool, and two companions were instantly killed Wednesday night at Windsor, Conn., about seven miles from Hartford, Conn. when high powered roadster in which they were riding skidded and sideswiped a telegraph pole, crushing the left side of the car where the three killed were sitting. News of the accident reached Glens Falls yesterday morning and Former Mayor Cool immediately left for Hartford. The three youths who lost their lives were Mr. Cool, Allan F. Sisson, formerly of Baltimore and James D. Orne, formerly of New York. They were all employed in the home office of the Hartford Accident and Indemnity company.

The car was owned and driven by H. Wickoff Mills of Hartford and the quartet were returning to Hartford from a hotel where they had dined. The car had seats for only two persons. Mills was at the wheel with Sisson sitting beside him. Cool sat on the floor at Sisson's feet and Orne was on the running board. The tragedy occurred on the Hartford-Springfield highway and according to passengers on a trolley car which the auto passed, the machine was going at a fast clip when it struck the pole. The bodies of the victims were found about 20 feet from the pole. Each had sustained a fractured skull.

Mills was unable to give a connected story of the accident other than to say the steering gear failed to work properly. He escaped injury and the machine was only slightly damaged. Mills was held under $1,000 bonds on a charge of reckless driving and will be given a hearing this evening.

Mr. Cool, who was 22 years old, had been employed in Hartford since last April. He enjoyed a wide popularity in Glens Falls and had many friends in Hartford. Besides his father and mother, he is survived by one brother, J. Gilbert Cool.

THOMAS EDISON

Star — 1914

The inventor, who has been invited by Secretary of the Navy Daniels to take a trip under the sea on a U. S. Navy submarine. This will be the first time Mr. Edison has even been aboard a submarine, although he understands the mechanism of the craft thoroughly. Photographers will not be permitted to take pictures of the starting because no photographs for publication have ever been made of U. S. submarines.

H. E. Nichols Estate Valued at $73,000

Appraisers of the estate of the late Henry E. Nichols of Glens Falls have fixed the value of the estate at $73,000.

The report has been filed with Judge Raley in surrogate's court and the inheritance tax has been fixed at about $875 to be paid by Mrs. Jessie B. Nichols, the widow who is the sole beneficiary, under the will. The deceased was a native of Lake George, and was for many years superintendent of George O. Knapp's estate at Shelving Rock. *Sept. 24*

Krazy Kat a Double Winner.

Krazy Kat, the fast little boat owned by George C. Reiss, a Sagamore cottager, won the Fort William Henry loving cup for the second time in the feature race of the Iroquois regatta at Lake George last week and thus gained permanent possession of the trophy. Mr. Reiss also won The Mirror Cup for traveling over the course faster than any other small boat on Lake George except those which competed recently in Bolton for the championship of North America. The time was equivalent to thirty-two miles an hour. *Sept. 3, 1914*

ANKLE DEEP WILL NEVER RACE AGAIN

Times

Famous Boat Which Brought Glory to Lake George Out of Commission.

1914

Farewell to the Ankle Deep! How those words pull at the heart strings of the sporting populace of Glens Falls and vicinity, for the people of northern New York have learned to admire the big speed boat, which has won for Warren county a high place in the sport of motordom throughout the world. Count Casimer S. Mankowski's Ankle Deep is no more. No such tidings since the death of Ellsworth has caused such remorse in this vicinity. The mahogany craft, which won such high honors on the water, will never be put in commission again to race for trophies against the speed demons of the world.

In the races at Buffalo during the first part of the month, the Ankle Deep was so badly burned by reason of the rupture of the gasoline feed pipe that she is practically a total loss to Count Mankowski, as no insurance can be carried on boats of her character. By reason of this fact, the famous Ankle Deep will never again sail over the clear waters of Old Horicon either to capture or defend trophies held in high esteem by motor boat enthusiasts.

Whether there will be another boat to succeed this famous racer is very much a matter of doubt. Countess Mankowski, though rejoicing in the victories which were won by the Ankle Deep, was ever in constant fear for the safety of the count, so much so that when she got the wire that the Ankle Deep was practically destroyed and the count and his mechanician safe that she said:

"Thank God that the boat is gone and no one is hurt; and now I can have my husband back again." In an interview a few days ago the countess said: "I am glad the Ankle Deep is gone— I am the happiest woman in the world, and I hope the count will never build another racing boat."

Nevertheless, the count is a mighty good sport; he has been bitten deep by the racing bug, and it is a fairly safe wager that another season will see him in the game again with another world beater. Whether or not he is again the master of a speed boat, he has won a niche in motor boating fame that can never be denied him. From the time that the Dixie boats began to win world wide recognition up until 1912 there had been no marked advance in the development of reliable racing boats. There had been freaks and boats capable of short fast spurts, but the Ankle Deep was the first great long distance racer in several years to break all records and set an entirely new standard for the speed craft of the future.

To Count Mankowski and the Ankle Deep belong the honor of creating a new epoch in motorboatdom, and no matter how fast the boats may go in years to come, Lake George and Warren county will always remember with pride the name of the beautiful queen that carried her flag to victory on the St. Lawrence, and will ever delight to honor the loveable unassuming man who could laugh at defeat with a whole heart.

EMERSON HARRINGTON KILLED.

Former Warrensburgh Man Meets Death in Accident at Hoosick Falls.

Emerson C. Harrington, a former resident of Warrensburgh and Bolton, was killed Saturday in an accident at Hoosick Falls. He was struck by a train while walking on the track of the Boston and Maine railroad and sustained injuries which caused his death a short time later in a Troy hospital.

Accompanied by his uncle, a Mr. Lloyd, Mr. Harrington walked in the morning to a lumber camp some distance from the city in search of employment. Their quest was fruitless and in the afternoon they started homeward somewhat disheartened. Walking together on the railroad track they heard two trains whistle, but being engaged in conversation failed to notice that they were close at hand. When one train was almost upon them both sprang from the track on opposite sides. Harrington stepped directly in front of the other train, traveling in the opposite direction, and was struck and hurled several feet to the side of the track. *Sept 10 1914*

The train, which was bound for Troy, was stopped at once and the unconscious victim was taken to that city and to a hospital. One leg and an arm were broken and his skull fractured. He died about half an hour after reaching the hospital without regaining consciousness. The body was brought to this place Monday and the funeral was held at 5 p. m., at the Baptist church, the Rev. T. J. Hunter officiating.

The deceased was born in Warrensburgh and lived here until he moved to Bolton some years ago. From that place he went to Hoosick Falls. He leaves a widow and six children. His aged father, Theophilus Harrington, survives him, also one brother, Samuel Harrington, of this village, and four sisters, Mrs. Orlin Pratt and Mrs. Alfred Duell, of Bolton; Mrs. Lillian Hayes, of Chestertown, and Mrs. William Fuller, of Warrensburgh.

Oct 29 1914

Frank Smith's Automobile Burned.

Frank W. Smith's five-passenger Cadillac automobile was destroyed by fire yesterday afternoon near the county home while Mr. Smith, accompanied by his wife, was on his way to Bolton. The fire is supposed to have started from a leaky gas pipe. Mr. Smith tried to extinguish the flames with dirt, but was unable to do so. The loss is covered by insurance.

Lincoln's Double.

Elmer Loomis, of Girard, Kans., bears the distinction of being the "double" of Abraham Lincoln, and has since he was a young boy. He is 80 years old now and a veteran of the Civil war. During the closing days of that conflict he was detailed as a nurse to Douglas hospital at Washington, and here Lincoln saw him often and spoke to him and smiled in his slow way, but never mentioned the similarity which was so apparent. Just before the close of the war Lincoln took Loomis to the White House for luncheon. The affair was brief, but nevertheless a fact, and Loomis bears that honor and memory as his most precious possession.

Mr. Loomis wears garments of "Lincoln style," and appears in them at na-

ELMER LOOMIS.

tional G. A. R. encampments. During the war he was a member of the One Hundred and Seventy-Seventh Ohio infantry. Now he is a retired farmer and is known to his neighbors affectionately as "Uncle Abe."

Aug 2 1914

ROBERT T. LINCOLN

Robert T. Lincoln, eldest son of the late President Lincoln, was born in Springfield, Ill., Aug. 1, 1843. He graduated from Harvard in 1864 and then took up the study of law. Near the close of the Civil War he served on the staff of Gen. Grant. After the war he completed his law studies and engaged in practice in Chicago. He became Secretary of War under President Garfield in 1881 and remained in that position under President Arthur. Under President Harrison he served as United States minister to Great Britain. After his retirement from the diplomatic service, Mr. Lincoln became general counsel of the Pullman Company and later succeeded George M. Pullman as president of the company.

OUR NATIONAL HYMN

The Star Spangled Banner Composed Hundred Years Ago.

ANNIVERSARY ON SEPTEMBER 14

State Department of Education Recommends That Event Be Appropriately Celebrated In Public Schools— Story of Great Anthem

The State Education Department, in a communication to city, village and district superintendents, under date of September 2, calls attention to the fact that The Star Spangled Banner, which is now our national hymn, was written on September 14, 1814, and suggests that a very fitting way of celebrating the centennial anniversary of this event will be to have the hymn sung in all the schools of the United States, public and private, at noon on September 14 of this year. The department recommends that the superintendents bring this matter to the attention of all their teachers and that the press be asked to give publicity to the request and to publish the words of the hymn with the following brief sketch of the circumstances under which it was written:

In the latter part of August, 1814, when the United States was at war with England, Dr. William Beanes, an old resident of Upper Marlborough, Maryland, was captured by General Ross of the English army and held on the admiral's flag ship, the "Surprise."

When Francis Scott Key, a young lawyer of Baltimore, heard that his friend, the old doctor, had been captured, he hastened to apply to the government to secure his release. A vessel which was used as a flag of truce for the exchange of prisoners, was placed at Key's disposal.

The young American was courteously received by an officer of the English fleet and the release of Dr. Beanes was promised by General Ross, provided the three Americans, John S. Skinner, who had charge of the vessel, Key and Dr. Beanes, would remain on board the "Surprise" until the impending attack on Fort McHenry, near Baltimore, had been accomplished.

All during the tragic night of September 13th the great guns of the English fleet sent their merciless shafts of shot and shell upon the staunch American fortress. On the deck of the enemy's ship Key and his two companions watched with breathless anxiety the progress of the battle. Could the fort hold her own? Would "Old Glory" be torn aside by the enemy? Despair mingled with hope as the "bombs bursting in air" thrilled Key's frame with terror and again offered the consolation that "gave proof through the night that our flag was still there." At intervals, by the "rockets' red glare," Key, whose eager eyes penetrated the smoke of the conflict, caught a glimpse of the stars and stripes. His heart grew great with thankfulness.

All night he kept watch and dawn found him zealously straining his eyes to see the fort through the mists which clouded his vision. The supreme moment came and there, above the ramparts, bravely floated the Star Spangled Banner over her gallant defenders. The attack had failed. No wonder that Key's poetic talent crystallized and that his heart poured forth in his wonderful apostrophe to the flag, our national anthem.

The young hero knew not how many lives had been lost; whether his relatives, defenders of the fort, had been spared. He knew "that our flag was still there," and his pent up emotion burst into sudden joy. Taking an old envelope from his pocket he wrote the first stanza, beginning: "O say can you see by the dawn's early light." The day after the bombardment Key and his companions were taken ashore. On the boat he composed the remaining verses of the song. That night in a Baltimore hotel he revised the lines, leaving them substantially as we sing them today.

Instantly the song was taken up by the public. Its sentiment is so genuine that everyone who wishes to voice his love and allegiance to the flag naturally falls into the lines and finds that they abundantly express his admiration, devotion and consecration to the country for which it stands.

THE STAR-SPANGLED BANNER.

O say can you see by the dawn's early light.
What so proudly we hailed at the twilight's last gleaming?
Whose broad stripes and bright stars, through the perilous fight.
O'er the ramparts we watched were so gallantly streaming.
And the rocket's red glare, the bombs bursting in air,
Gave proof through the night, that our flag was still there:
O say, does that star spangled banner yet wave,
O'er the land of the free and the home of the brave?

On the shore, dimly seen through the mists of the deep,
Where the foe's haughty host in dread silence reposes,
What is that which the breeze, o'er the towering steep.
As it fitfully blows now conceals now *discloses?*
Now it catches the gleam of the morning's first beam,
In full glory reflected now shines on the stream:
Tis the star spangled banner, O long may it wave
O'er the land of the free and the home of the brave.

And where is the band who so vauntingly swore
That the havoc of war and the battles confusion
A home and a country should leave us no more?
Their blood has washed out their foul footsteps' pollution.
No refuge could save the hireling and slave
From the terror of flight and the gloom of the grave
And the star spangled banner in triumph doth wave
O'er the land of the free and the home of the brave.

Oh thus be it ever, when freemen shall stand

Between their loved homes and the war's desolation.
Blest with victory and peace, may the heaven rescued land
Praise the Power that hath made and preserved us a nation.
Then conquer we must, for our cause it is just,
And this be our motto: "In God is our trust";
And the star spangled banner in triumph shall wave
O'er the land of the free and the home of the brave.

News July 30 1914

DARING FEAT DISASTROUS.

Young Man Paralyzed After High Dive Into Lake George at Hague.

Glorying in his daring, George Sexton, twenty-one years old, Tuesday dove from the roof of the boat house of the Mohican hotel, at Uncas, into Lake George, a distance of about eight feet. The water where he made the plunge was only about five feet deep and he struck the bottom with great force.

Though he was not rendered unconscious by the shock young Sexton's body was completely paralyzed from the shoulders down and he was unable to rise to the surface. His brother, Howard Sexton, who with several other youths, was a member of the bathing party, went to the rescue and carried him ashore. He was taken to his room in the hotel, where he was attended by Dr. C. K. Burt, of Lake George, and Dr. Cummings, of Ticonderoga. Though free from pain his condition has remained unchanged since the accident and there is but little hope of his recovery.

IGERNA POSTOFFICE CLOSED

Aug 29 1914

Mail Privileges Withdrawn from North Chester Hamlet.

Acting upon orders from the postoffice department in Washington Postmaster Andrew Loveland, of Igerna, Saturday closed his office permanently and retired from the government service. The little hamlet in the northern part of the town of Chester is now without a postoffice and the residents must arrange to get their mail at the office most convenient for them. Olmstedville will probably accommodate the greater number, while others will go to North Creek. *News*

Sometime ago a movement was started by some of the residents to secure a rural free delivery route from the Igerna office. A petition was forwarded to Washington and in due time an inspector was sent to investigate. As a result of his inquiries the application was denied and the privileges already enjoyed by the people were taken from them.

There is much indignation among the farmers and other residents who are inconvenienced by the drastic order and a strong effort will be made to have the matter righted.

COUNT MANKOWSKI NOW COMMODORE

Star Sept 10 1913

Iroquois Regatta Association Honors Owner of Hydroplane Ankle Deep

---

E. A. KNIGHT IS REELECTED

Organization to Be Incorporated and Seek Membership in American Power Boat Association

---

LAKE GEORGE, Sept. 9.—Count Cassimer S. Mankowski, owner of Ankle Deep, the hydroplane which recently won the American Power Boat association gold challenge cup raced for on the St. Lawrence river, was elected commodore of the Iroquois Regatta association at a meeting of the yacht club held here this afternoon. O. J. Stephens of New York was elected vice commodore and LeGrand C. Cramer was named as rear-commodore. E. A. Knight of Lake George was reelected secretary and treasurer.

The meeting was most enthusiastic and after hearing a report of the treasurer on the regatta held two weeks ago, which showed a surplus in the treasury, considerable business of importance was transacted. A committee composed of LeGrand C. Cramer, E. J. Worden and E. A. Knight was appointed to have charge of the incorporation of the organization as the Iroquois Regatta association and further to make application for membership in the American Power Boat association.

Upon the suggestion of E. A. Knight it was decided that the Iroquois association would conduct a series of Saturday afternoon races during next summer, the events to terminate in the annual regatta of the association which will be held at Lake George village Thursday and Friday, August 27 and 28, 1914. These races will be held under the A. P. B. A. rules and will be a source of attraction to hotel guests and cottagers, especially the week-end visitors.

E. J. Worden was named as chairman of the committee that will lay out a measured course for the races of the regatta next season. The work will be done on the ice during the winter and buoys will be anchored eight feet below the surface of the lake to mark the course. The buoys will be raised during the races.

Following incorporation which will be done at once, a permanent judges' stand will be erected on the shore of the lake and an outlay of money will be made for the purchase of regatta equipment and a complete modern numbering system as well.

SIMPLEX XV SAID TO BE SPEED KING

Boat Owned By J. P. Randerson Has Figured in Many Regattas

TO RENAME CRAFT DART II

LAKE GEORGE, Sept. 9.—J. P. Randerson of 755 Madison avenue, Albany, is now owner of Simplex XV, three years ago and possibly now the fastest automobile power boat on Lake George. The boat was specially built for the late Herman Broesel and was bought from the Broesel estate. It was not put into the water this summer and will not be launched by Mr. Randerson until next spring.

The Simplex XV has always been looked upon as one of the most luxurious as well as speediest boats which have sailed the waters of Lake George. She is 39 feet, six inches in length and has a beam of 4 feet, 7 inches. A 75 horse power Sterling engine, making 1,110 revolutions a minute sends the mahogany craft through the water at a speed better than 27 miles an hour.

The Simplex XV has figured in many of the regattas on Lake George the last four years and in the fall of 1908, the year of her launching here for the first time, she won the championship of the lake in an endurance run in competition with Le Grand C. Cramer's Wininish through the length of Lake George and return. The course complete measured 62 miles and overcoming a handicap allowed the Wininish of 4 minutes and 14 second the Simplex XV finished 2 minutes and 32 seconds in the lead. The average speed of the winner was 26 1-2 miles over the course.

In 1908 the Simplex XV won a leg of the LeGrand C. Cramer cup which was offered in the Glens Falls Club regatta and in 1911 the craft took the race for the Fort William Henry cup, thereby winning a leg of this cup. The Fort William Henry cup is still to be raced for as no boat has won the race twice, the condition of claiming the trophy for permanent ownership. The Carol II, owned by G. W. Stebbins of New York, and the Mignon, owned by

George Reis of New York, also have won a leg of the cup. The Simplex XV will race for the cup next summer.

Mr. Randerson is the owner of an estate on the fashionable Bolton road six miles north of Lake George village, property which he bought about two years ago. Last spring he purchased a speed boat from Captain O. M. Smith which did not develop the power that he wished and the Simplex XV was consequently purchased. Mr. Randerson's sons, John E. H. and Howard, will enter the boat in future races on Lake George. The boat will be re-christened Dart II.

MRS. WORDEN DIES AFTER LONG ILLNESS

aug 1 1914 Star

Wedded to Caldwell Supervisor Twenty Years Ago at Lake George

Harriet White Worden, wife of Edwin J. Worden, supervisor of Caldwell, died at 12 o'clock yesterday noon in the Hotel Worden, Lake George, where she had been ailing during the last several years. Mrs. Worden was beloved by an unusually large circle of friends and her death came as a sudden blow.

Mr. and Mrs. Worden were married in Lake George, June 6, 1894, a few days after he had assumed the management of what are known as the Worden and Arlington hotels. During her husband's successful career as a hotel proprietor, she was his principle assistant, his inspiration and aid in the launching of each new and successful idea. Unusual business ability for a woman, a kindly heart and great generoity were the more prominent traits of her nature.

Mrs. Worden was 43 years old and was a granddaughter of the late Captain Edward White, pilot of the Lily M. Price, one of the big Lake George boats which was in use until 20 years ago. She was in her youth a member of the Presbyterian church but in later years she attended services in the Episcopal church of Lake George. Her husband, her father, Alonzo White, and a sister, Miss Mae White, are her near survivors. The funeral services will be held at 3:30 o'clock Sunday afternoon from the Episcopal church, Lake George, Rev. E. M. Parrott officiating. Interment will be made in the Lake George cemetery.

Friends of Charles Carey, of Trout Lake, Bolton, and Mrs. Fannie Persens, of this place, have been interested to learn of their marriage, which took place last week. News

—195—

COOPER'S CAVE MAY BE MADE MORE ACCESSIBLE TO TOURISTS

May 27, 1914 Times

International Paper Company Writes State Historian Holden That it Will Leave Land to a Responsible Organization.

For the past sixty years or more, Cooper's cave, which is situated on the island in the Hudson River at the foot of Glen street hill between this city and the Town of Moreau, has been a mecca for thousands of tourists. This cave, made famous by J. Fenimore Cooper's "Last of the Mohicans" has done much toward advertising Glens Falls throughout the nation.

In the past, wooden stairs led from the bridge to the rocks in which the cave is situated, but with the carrying away of the bridge last year, these stairs were swept into the torrent. With the erection of the new concrete viaduct there will be no provision made for the stairs being replaced nor will there be any method provided for tourists reaching the cave.

Although the cave possesses nothing of historical interest, Cooper has made it famous the world over, and to the end that something may be done toward providing access to the cave. State Historian James A. Holden took the matter up with the International Paper Company, which owns the island on which the cave is situated. Mr. Holden asked that the company provide a method for tourists to reach the cave, but Mr. Parks gave several reasons why the company did not feel like undertaking to carry out the idea. Mr. Parks stated, however, that he would take the matter up with the president of the company, and Mr. Holden is in receipt of a communication from Chester W. Lyman, assistant to the president, which states practically what Mr. Parks had stated before.

However, Mr. Lyman, in the communication, states that the company would be glad to see the cave made accessible to the public. He further states that the company will place the property at the disposal of any responsible organization or association, giving such a body a lease, for a purely nominal sum, for a long term, the company reserving the right to modify the lease or restrict or cancel it in case the height of the dam or any other change in the development of the local plant, would cause such a change to be necessary. In that case, Mr. Lyman stated that the company would be willing to provide that any reasonable expenditure which had been made in fitting up the island, would be reimbursed by the company.

Now, it is up to the citizens of Glens Falls and the Town of Moreau to take advantage of the offer of the company, and see that this public spirited purpose is accomplished. Subscriptions might be raised to install stairs leading from the bridge to the rocks below. If such a thing is decided upon by any organization or association in this vicinity, it will have to be done in the near future, as it might be a difficult matter to have the stairs placed in position after the new bridge is completed.

Killed by Horse's Kick.

Byron Merrill, of Bolton, residing in the northern part of the town, in the locality known as Padanarum, died Monday morning from the effects of injuries sustained when he was kicked by a horse Saturday afternoon. He was driving home alone from Horicon when the accident occurred and was found unconscious in the road and taken home by a passer-by. He leaves a widow and two small children; his parents, Mr. and Mrs. Edward Merrill, and one brother, Marion Merrill.

1914

STRUCK BY ENGINE AND FATALLY HURT

Hoosick Falls Resident a Victim of the Practice of Walking on Railroad Track.

SKULL, SPINE AND ARM FRACTURED

Unfortunate Man Was Taken to Troy, Where He Died in the Hospital Ambulance.

Emerson C. Harrington, a resident of Hoosick Falls, was struck and fatally injured by a westbound passenger train while walking on the track near Maple Grove cemetery Friday afternoon.

Harrington, who for the past two years had been employed by the Walter A. Wood company, but had been out of work some weeks, went to Hoosick on Friday in search of employment. He was accompanied by his wife's uncle, William Lloyd of Glens Falls. They went to a lumber camp near Hoosick, where Harrington secured a job and was to have gone to work Monday morning.

A Fatal Walk.

Harrington and Lloyd decided to walk back to Hoosick Falls and took the railroad track. They had reached a point near Maple Grove cemetery when their attention was attracted by an eastbound train on the lower track. So engrossed were they in watching the eastbound train that they failed to notice the approach of a train behind them. Lloyd jumped aside and escaped injury, but Harrington was struck and fatally hurt, an arm, his spine and skull being fractured. The train halted and Harrington was brought to the Hoosick Falls station, where Dr. McGrath examined him and advised his removal to the Troy hospital.

Died in Ambulance.

Harrington was placed on a cot and taken in the baggage car to Troy, where the hospital ambulance awaited the train. He was lifted into the ambulance, but despite the fact that doctors worked over him he died before the hospital was reached. Harrington's body was brought to this village and taken to his late home on Dolin avenue. Monday morning the remains were taken to Warrensburgh, where the funeral was held yesterday.

The deceased, who was 39 years old, was born on what is known as Harrington Hill in Warrensburgh, his parents being Samuel and Martha Bassett Harrington. He is survived by his wife and six young children, his parents, a brother, Samuel Harrington, Jr., and four sisters, Mrs. Alfred Duell and Mrs. Orville Platt of Bolton, Mrs. William Fuller of Warrensburgh and Mrs. Lilian Hayes of Caldwell.

The Fanita—owned by John Bolton Simpson, of New York and Bolton Landing, Lake George
Published by L. E. Taylor, Bolton Landing, N. Y.

BABY RELIANCE BREAKS RECORD

Ankle Deep Finishes Poor Fifth in Opening Race at Bolton

Star — July 31

HAWK EYE DISAPPOINTS

1914

BOLTON, July 30.—A new world's record for forty-foot motorboats over a 30-mile surveyed course was made today when the Baby Reliance V., owned by J. Stuart Blackington of the Atlantic Yacht club, finished first in 32.81 minutes. The cup defender, Ankle Deep, was a poor fifth, partly owing to a bad start.

One of the largest crowds that ever attended such an event thronged the shores of Lake George while many spectators occupied small craft in a space roped off on the lake. The grandstand and boxes on the Sagamore grounds were taxed to their capacity. Weather conditions were ideal and when the race was started at 5:15 o'clock there was a fair sky and only a slight wind.

The Baby Speed Demon II., owned by Mrs. Paula H. Blackington, wife of the owner of the winner, took second place. The others finished in the order named: Buffalo Enquirer, owned by W. J. Conners of the Buffalo Yacht club; P. D. Q., V., owned by Alfred G. Milyes of the Thousand Island Yacht club; Ankle Deep, owned by Count Casimir S. Mankowski; Tech, jr., owned by Coleman du Pont of Cape May; P. D. Q., IV., owned by J. J. Harty of the Kingston, (Ont.,) Yacht club; Hawk Eye, the entry of the Lake George Syndicate.

The race was practically a trial heat of the endurance contest which will be continued tomorrow and Saturday and while general disappointment is felt here because of the poor showing of the Ankle Deep and Hawk Eye it is predicted great changes will be made in the finishes. Boats which were considered inferior to the Ankle Deep and Hawk Eye made a far better showing today and local enthusiasts are confident that the two boats will "come back" with a vengeance.

A bad start for several of the entrants slightly marred the races. This, however, cannot be blamed upon the officials but rather on the crews who had a tendency to lie back for the start. On the first shot for the get away, Peter Pan got an excellent start, the next boat being the Buffalo Enquirer which was at least three lengths in the rear. Baby Reliance the winner, took sixth position, while Ankle Deep and Hawk Eye drew out from the rear. All were spread out in such a manner as would make it appear that it was anybody's event and the majority held their relatives positions until nearly the end of the first lap. It was then that some of the boats changed places. The winner secured the first berth and was never overtaken, the nearest craft being Baby Speed Demon V. which captured second honors.

Plenty of excitement was furnished in the third lap the Ankle Deep drew up from fifth place and nosed out the Buffalo Enquirer and when later Hawk Eye showed a burst of speed and crept up from the rear. By this time there was one boat missing, Peter Pan having been ruled out owing to trouble with the engine. The crew of the craft was forced over to the sidelines. After this lap, however, there were no close sprints of any description and the boats maintained their positions until the finish not any with the exception of the leader appearing to try to "open up."

Toward the final lap Baby Reliance V. tripped its best time and got across the finishing line quite a distance ahead of Baby Speed Demon II. owned by Mrs. Blackton. Enquirer took third honors and P. D. Q., V., ran a good fourth. The other boats finished a short distance apart Ankle Deep, the favorite holding down fifth place and Hawk Eye, the other boat of which a great deal was expected, coming in last.

Owing to the postponement of the races Wednesday, the second "heat" will be run tomorrow morning at about 10 o'clock. Another race will be held tomorrow afternoon and this will practically complete this endurance event. It is tomorrow that enthusiasts expect that the best form will be shown and a great deal of confidence is placed in Ankle Deep, especially if the day is windy at all. The mile speed race will not be held until Saturday morning and this event, which is expected that some of the boats will make record time for a short distance, will bring the season to a close.

WILLSON'S AUTO CROSSES VIADUCT

august 1914

One-half of the Glens Falls-South Glens Falls viaduct was opened to traffic at 4 o'clock yesterday afternoon, the first vehicle to cross being the automobile owned by L. Gyle Willson, superintendent of the South Glens Falls International Paper company's plant. The passengers were Mr. and Mrs. Willson, K. Hodge, N. J. Rabideau, H. W. Lang, A. L. George and E. Burton, the last four named being employes of the Callanan & Prescott company.

The bridge will be temporarily closed at 1 o'clock Monday morning to all traffic except pedestrians. It is expected that by noon the structure may be used by all kinds of vehicles. It is hoped to be ready for trolley car traffic by Tuesday afternoon. During Monday and Tuesday it will be necessary for the Hudson Valley company *to walk passengers over* the bridge.

QUITS POTTERSVILLE FAIR.

Edward F. Irish Resigns as President and Sells Stock in Association.

Edward F. Irish, of Glens Falls, has resigned as president of the Pottersville Fair Association, and having sold his three shares of stock has entirely severed his connection with the enterprise. For this action he gives as his reason that the last exhibition in August was not conducted along the lines he had laid down and he therefore refused to be longer identified with it. *news Oct 1 1914*

Mr. Irish was elected president of the association in 1910, just after it had been re-organized, and by his vigorous and resourceful management has placed it in the front rank of town fairs of the state. Every year it has paid dividends to the stockholders besides the expenditure of $2,000 in improvements. This is a record which has probably been equalled by few if any independent associations in the same period. It has been accomplished mainly by advertising. As a press agent Mr. Irish particularly excels. He has secured for the fair special articles in the New York Sunday papers, Troy and Albany papers, and in the local press, which money could not buy. Thousands of souvenir programs and other literature have been distributed with little expense to the association, the cost of publication being met by the revenue from advertising the programs contained. Publicity has been the keynote of the energetic president's efforts and the result is a tribute not alone to his talent, but also to the wonderful efficacy of printer's ink.

The stockholders expressed their regret at Mr. Irish's retirement by adopting resolutions in which they fully recognized the value of his work. This action was taken at the annual meeting. Dr. Lee Somerville, of North Creek, was then elected president to fill the vacancy. Other officers elected were: Vice president, Sterling F. Higley, of Glens Falls; secretary, W. B. Leonard, of Glens Falls; treasurer, Harry S. Downs, of Chestertown. Mr. Irish sold his stock to Sterling F. Higley, who now controls six shares.

SCHROON LAKE HOTEL BURNED.

Leland House, Episcopal Church, Three Cottages and an Electric Light Plant Destroyed Early Yesterday— Sawmill at Lake George Burned— Saturday Night Fires at Glens Falls— Other Halloween Conflagrations.

The Leland House, three cottages and a small electrict light plant, connected with the hotel at Schroon Lake village, which were destroyed by fire early yesterday morning, proved the largest loss among a number of fires Saturday night and yesterday, which had to do in part at least with Halloween. The other fires included William F. Worden's sawmill at Lake George, which

It had been owned the last twenty-one years by Senator James A. Emerson and L. W. Emerson, of Warrensburgh, who conducted it as a summer hotel. On account of its location on the through state highway it had enjoyed a very large automobile patronage in the last few years. Three small cottages and a small electric light plant, all owned by the hotel, were also totaaly destroyed by the flames. The hotel was valued at about $100,000 and is well insured. It was too early to state whether or not it would be rebuilt, but it was stated that without doubt some kind of a hostelry would take its place.

The Annex Saved.

An annex to the hotel, formerly the Lake House, was saved. This was situated just across the street from the

LELAND HOUSE, SCHROON LAKE.

was burned yesterday with a loss of $6,000 partly insured; dwelling house at Glens Falls owned by Timothy Breen, burned Saturday night, with a loss of about $2,500. partly insured, and a barn at Glens Falls owned by H. H. Pruyn and burned Saturday night, causing a loss of $1,000, partly insured. Saturday afternoon there was a fire near Ballston Spa, when the farm buildings and stone residence of Philip Riley were detroyed.

The Leland House Blaze.

The Leland House blaze is thought to have started from a cigarette or cigar stub tossed carelessly among leaves between one of the cottages and the hotel. The Halloween roisterers had been especially active, and during the evening had rung the church bells. As a result, when the fire started about 12:40 o'clock and the bells were rung nobody thought of a fire. The result was that the blaze was humming before anyone appeared to fight it. The hotel was a three-story frame building, erected forty-three years ago by W. G. Leland.

burned hotel and on the edge of the lake. The Leland had a capacity for 300 guests and was the largest hotel in the lower tier of the Adirondacks. I had a frontage of 162 feet. During the last two years more than $20,000 had been expended in additions and repairs.

The Episcopal Church.

The Episcopal church was also a frame structure and burned like tinder. The church was insured, but not for its full value.

Fire Near Ballston Spa.

The house and all the farm buildings on the Philip Riley place, two miles east of Ballston Spa, were destroyed by fire Saturday afternoon. The fire started in one of the barns and spread rapidly from one building to another. The house being built of stone it was hoped could be saved, but sparks and the heat set fire to the wooden portions and it was gutted. The loss will amount to several thousand dollars.

Native American Centenarian.

After living to the ripe old age of 104 years, John Camp, a full-blooded Maine Indian, yesterday joined his tribesmen on the Happy Hunting Grounds. Camp,

who migrated to Lake George upwards of seventy years ago from the Maine woods, had since lived in a hovel in Virgin Hollow, near Lake George village. Troy times Dec 18 14

DESTITUTION IN 1914 PITIFUL PHASE

Destitute Family is Found Living Seven Miles Out of Spier Falls.

One of the most pitiful cases of destitution which has ever been found in Saratoga county has been reported to Humane Society Officer Robert S. Rimington of Saratoga Springs. Mr. Rimington spent Thursday investigating the case and yesterday made a public report. He found the family seven miles out of Spier Falls in the Town of Moreau.

There were six children in the family; a boy seventeen years old was an idiot; the three next eldest 8, 11 and 14 years respectively were in school; and there were two children 5 and 6 years old who were at home. These two had no shoes or stockings and what little clothing they did wear was of the summer quality, so thin as to be useless in keeping out the winter cold.

The older boy who is idiotic caused considerable trouble. Often he would play out-doors until his feet, which were unclothed bled from the cold. His parents said that they had to coax him to do anything because he had a violent temper.

Officer Rimington said that in the kitchen, there was a stove, one chair which had no back, a cot beside the stove which was evidently used as a seat for the children to warm themselves. One side of the cot had no legs. The only covering was a robe which probably had been taken from a sleigh. This was in fact the only article which would give real warmth in the house. When he pressed the button which held the door open into the bed room, Mr. Rimington stated that the door toppled over on him.

In the bedroom was one bed which was as black as the floor and which contained an old dilapidated mattress. Under the bed were corn stalks which were no doubt used by the children as their sleeping places.

There was one other room off the kitchen where the snow was deeper than it was out-doors. In the upstairs the windows had no panes so that the cold came in freely.

The only food which could be found in the house was a pot of potatoes which were cooking on the stove. Outside the door, Mr. Rimington found some yellow corn which had been partly parched and was half eaten. There was no pantry and no dishes save the ones in the kitchen which were left just as they were used at the last meal.

Superintendent Rimington today stated that the condition of the family was in the largest measure due to drunkenness.

REPORT PRAISES THE COUNTY JAIL

Dec 21 1914

Padded Cell Recommended for County Bastile—Jail Labor Urged.

Copies of the report of the recent inspection of the Warren county jail have been distributed in this city by the State Prison Association. The inspection was made November 7, 1914, by E. R. Cass. The report is appended:

The sheriff of the county is R. J. Bolton. The jail is under the supervision of the under-sheriff, M. R. Smith. There is a salaried male cook, and Mrs. Bolton acts as matron, and receives $1.50 when women are detained.

The total population at the time of the inspection was ten, classified as follows:

Adult males held for the grand jury, 1; adult males serving sentence, 9.

The population of this jail at the time of other inspections has been comparatively small. It was stated that, including grand jury prisoners, a fair average would be 15, and without grand jury prisoners, 12.

The jail is a small structure. There are satisfactory facilities for the proper classification of prisoners, with a small population. The complete toilet and bathing equipment which was installed in the early part of this year, is well taken care of and a satisfactory condition of cleanliness existed in all parts of the jail, with the exception of one side, which is reserved for grand jury prisoners. This section was occupied by one prisoner, who should be made to exercise a little more care in the arrangement and cleanliness of his particular section.

The jail was well heated, and the prisoners expressed satisfaction as to the quantity and quality of the food and treatment accorded to them.

A new heating boiler has been installed since the last inspection.

While the average population of the jail is small the possibilities of undertaking a large scheme for employing the prisoners is not feasible, but, nevertheless, much has been done to make use of jail labor. First of all, three or four prisoners are always employed in the jail cleaning, etc., and also in the county buildings.

Through the co-operation of the village president, Dr. C. K. Burt, the prisoners have been worked extensively on the village highways in the following ways: Cleaning, curbing and widening. Men have also been employed in laying cement walks. The cost of material for this work is defrayed one-half by the village and the other half by the owner of the property in front of which the work is being done.

The prisoners work within the corporate limits, under the supervision of a man hired by the village. The prisoners have been rewarded for this work by some extra rations, and in cases where clothing has been necessary the cost of the same has been defrayed by the village. This scheme is a good one if sufficient work can be found to keep the small population of the jail busy. It was said that men will be used this winter to keep the street walks and the roads clear of snow.

The local authorities are to be commended for their desire to make use of the jail labor. The county supervisors are authorized by section ninety-three of the county law to make use of jail labor. This statute should be made use of in order to extend such labor in some of the towns adjacent to the county seat. The county and town highway superintendents should be called upon to co-operate with the board of supervisors to make as much use of such labor as possible.

EMERSON'S ACTION STIRS SCHROON LAKE VILLAGE

"Indignation Meetings" Follow the Tearing Down of Old Bandstand

Stat July 9

LAKE GEORGE, July 8.—Residents of Schroon Lake village are up in arms over the action of Senator Emerson, proprietor of the Leland hotel, who, incensed at the delay of the village board in removing a band-stand which he claimed obscured the entrance to his hotel, took matters in his own hands, and with a crew of helpers from Warrensburg, tore down the offending structure.

The bandstand was built twenty-three years ago, but of late had fallen into disuse. In answer to the senator's demand that it be removed a meeting of the village board was called to consider the matter, but a quorum failing to appear, action was deferred until the next regular meeting, two weeks later. 1914

Although before its destruction, residents of the village had no particular love for the band-stand, the senator's tactics caused a reversion of feeling in many and in consequence "indignation meetings' 'are of daily occurrence with the end not yet in sight.

SISSON PURCHASES LAKE GEORGE GARAGE

1914

Deputy County Clerk H. W. Sisson, who with Fred L. Brown has conducted the B. and S. garage at Lake George, has purchased Mr. Brown's interest in the business, and will conduct it in his own name in the future. Mr. Sisson will not be actively engaged in the business, but has secured a competent manager to look after it.

Times d 19

TRIBUTE PAID TO MEMORY OF TRASK

Memorial Fountain Erected by Saratogians Unveiled at Spa Today.

Times July 14 1914

GOVERNOR GLYNN SPEAKS

Veil Released by Miss Frederica Mitchell, a Niece of Mr. Trask—Governor Entertained at Luncheon.

SARATOGA SPRINGS, July 14.—With an oration by Governor Martin H. Glynn, a memorial fountain erected by the citizens of this village in memory of the late Spencer Trask, the first chairman of the New York State Reservation commission, was dedicated here today. The governor, who spent the night at Yaddo, Mrs. Trask's home, was escorted by Company L, Second Infantry, to Convention hall, where the services were held.

Governor Pays Tribute.

Governor Glynn paid a tribute to Mr. Trask, and in the course of his address declared that wealth and power have come not only to the captains of industry but to the people generally through their efforts. Former Surrogate Charles C. Lester also delivered an address.

Unveiling Ceremony.

The ceremony of unveiling the memorial took place in the new quarter of a million dollar village park system which has just been completed. Miss Frederica Mitchell, a niece of Mr. Trask, pulled the string which released the veil, and George Foster Peabody, chairman of the reservation commission, spoke briefly.

Following the ceremonies the governor was entertained at luncheon in the Casino. He will leave for Albany late this afternoon.

Several thousand spectators attended the dedication ceremonies.

NORTH BOLTON.

Times Dec 20 1914

North Bolton, Dec. 19.—Mrs. Betsey Rose, who suffered a shock of paralysis about three weeks ago, died at the home of her daughter, Mrs. William Sherman, Saturday night at 11 o'clock. She is survived by five children, Mrs. Erastus French, Mrs. Arthur Coon, Chauncey Ross and Clennie Ross, besides the one mentioned and a brother at Schroon, Frank Stowell. The funeral will be held at the home Tuesday forenoon at 10:30 o'clock. Interment will be made in the New Vermont cemetery.

GLIMPSES AT LAKE GEORGE.

Interest Centres on the Approaching Motorboat Races—Great Things Expected of the Hawk-Eye in the Races.—Some Other Incidents in the Vicinity—Spinning Wheels and Mail Carriers. *July 23 1914*

Special Correspondence of The Troy Times.

Lake George, July 23.—The summer populace is devoting much attention to the motorboat races, which are to take place at the Sagamore course next week, but there are scores of visitors at the lake that are interested in the nearby residents and historical facts of the lake. Not a few acquaintances are made each season by guests and hosts at Lake George, which become permanent and enjoyable. *T. Times*

The Syndicate's Boat.

The syndicate's boat, the Hawk-Eye, designed to be the fastest racing hydroplane in the world, was built by The John L. Hacker Boat Company with a guaranteed speed of fifty miles an hour, and the company's sales manager states that it has exceeded that speed on a straightaway course by ten per cent. The boat is powered with a 300 horsepower Van Blerck motor, and a speed approaching the mile a minute seems assured.

Carrying the Mails.

It is more than ten miles from the Lake George Postoffice by wagon road along the shore of the lake to Bolton Landing, and over this two stages carry the mails—one in the morning and another in the afternoon. One team is driven by Charles Davis, who purchased the stage line last spring, and he employs Marlon Merrill to drive the second stage. Winter and summer for many years the mails go through, sometimes with the snow up to the horses' backs, and again with the thermometer many degrees below zero. Along the stage route are hotels and many dwellings and camps, and the stage driver stops to pick up mail which is placed in home-made clothes-bags and hung out on a nail, where the stage man can get it without leaving his seat. On the return trip the bags containing incoming mail are replaced where the driver found them. At several places en route watering troughs are found. They are fed from springs up in the mountainside and led in pipes to barrels by the side of the road.

The Ancient Spinning Wheel.

The making of hand-knitted mittens and stockings still occupies the attention of a few of the all-year-around residents of the Lake George section. On a recent visit The Times reporter met Mr. and Mrs. Caleb Baker of Bolton Landing, and Mrs. Baker proudly exhibited the ancient spinning wheel that has been in the family for 100 years. Wool from sheep raised nearby is secured by the Bakers, washed and then sent to Warrensburgh, where it is carded and returned, after which Mrs. Baker with the aid of the spinning wheel turns it into yarn used in the manufacture of sox and mitts so much desired in winter by residents of the colder regions. The yarns are doubled and twisted into fine strains of thread, a process **that adds to** the wearing quality of the stockings and mittens.

BOLTON MAN HAS NARROW ESCAPE

Frantic From Burns, He Falls From Blazing Boat Into Lake George

Star July 16 1914

CRAFT SINKS TO BOTTOM

(Special to The Post-Star)

BOLTON, July 12.—Asa Hastings had a narrow escape from fatal injury at 7 o'clock this evening in a motorboat accident which resulted in the complete destruction of the "Rob Roy," a 30-foot craft owned by Rev. Ernest M. Stires, D. D., pastor of the St. Thomas Episcopal church, New York, who is passing the summer at his cottage on North West Bay.

Mr. Hastings was out alone in the boat when the engine suddenly exploded as the result of a back fire. A sheet of flame enveloped him and frantic from the burns on his face and hands he leaped back and fell into the water.

Although an excellent swimmer, he found he was unable to take care of himself properly. The boat was then like a roaring furnace and he remained almost stationary, treading water until picked up by Royal Boon, a local boy, who was in a row boat.

Row boats and small motor craft hurried up to the "Rob Roy" within a few minutes and every possible attempt was made to extinguish the blaze by throwing water upon it. The efforts were without avail and after completely destroying the bow and stern the ruins of the craft sank to the bottom in about fifteen feet of water. The boat was four years old and was valued at about $1,800.

CAPT. W. A. ALLEN CLAIMED BY DEATH

Feb 1 1915 Star

Aged Civil War Veteran Had Resided Here Full Seventy Years

WAS NATIVE OF LUZERNE

Captain Warren A. Allen, a highly respected resident of Glens Falls during the last 70 years, died at 4:45 o'clock Saturday afternoon in his home, 28 Washington street. He was born in Luzerne 86 years ago and came to Glens Falls when he was between 15 and 16 years old. He enlisted November 5, 1861 in Company E of the Twenty-second Regiment of New York Infantry volunteers and within a few days was raised to the rank of a corporal. During the campaign he made steady progress up the military ladder and during the last seven months of the war commanded his own company with the rank of captain. He was one of six brothers to serve in the war.

He was wounded three times during the war and suffered serious injuries to his spine while before Fredericksburg by being crushed under a pontoon boat. Returning to Glens Falls he passed 16 years as an officer of the law either as a deputy sheriff or constable of Queensbury.

Mr. Allen is survived by a son, T. D. Allen of Glens Falls, and a sister, Mrs. Esther Jackson of Three Rivers, Mich.

THIRTY DEGREES BELOW ZERO IN WARRENSBURG

Henry Griffin of Warrensburg, one of the substantial residents of the northern metropolis of the county, was in this city today. He took the trolley at 8 o'clock when the thermometer registered thirty degrees below zero. Mr. Griffin said from all indications the "Johnsburg thaw" would continue indefinitely.

Dec 26, 1914

GREAT EXPECTATIONS—SQUAW BROOK, NEAR INDIAN LAKE.

FIRST NATIONAL TO HAVE MODEL HOME

Ground Broken for Structure of Classic Colonial Architecture to be Erected for Glens Falls Banking Institution —Modern Inventions to Protect Against Burglarious Attacks and Electrically Illuminate the Interior

New Building for the First National Bank of Glens Falls.

Ground has been broken and Glens Falls will soon be able to claim the honor of having one of the finest and most complete exclusive bank buildings in the state of New York—certainly the finest for many miles around.

The new structure as above illustrated will be located directly opposite the new Y. M. C. A. building and will embody the acme of architectural skill in design, being of the Georgian period of classic Colonial architecture, a dignified one story structure, having an imposing entranceway on the front and four large arched window openings on the side.

In 1853 the First National bank was organized as the Commercial bank, a state institution, and in 1865 it was re-organized under its present title as a National bank.

Its officers and directors are men of the highest and most conservative standing, and the management has strongly intrenched the institution in public favor.

The First National bank's record of wondrful prosperity in the past promises well and even greater in the future, and the service which it has always afforded to its patrons, it will continue to maintain, as one of the important reasons for its success.

Abraham Lincoln's Church.
(Joe Mitchell Chapple in National Magazine.)

Sunday in Washington is always a delight to the tourist. It is never too long a day, for although the departments are closed the churches are open, the Zoo is open, and the parks seem more alluring than on week days. Besides, Sunday is just the day to revel among historic scenes. Near the throbbing centre of business activities on Fourteenth Street is the New York Avenue Presbyterian Church, which President Lincoln attended, and I dropped into the historic edifice late one Sunday evening. As, amid the echo of the clanging street-car bells, I passed up the winding stone steps into the sanctuary, I felt as if the scenes of fifty years ago were again before me. The galleries extend around the full length of the auditorium, and a glass partition between the door and the auditorium is about the only change that has been made since Lincoln's time. Dr. Wallace Radcliff was delivering a Sunday address on "Peter Waldo and the Waldensians," which seemed an appropriate setting for the memories that came surging back to many in the congregation. The elderly man sitting beside me recalled having seen the tall form of Lincoln, as he worshiped there, and pointed out the Lincoln pew, well down the centre of the church, on the right. This pew is distinguished by the black wood in the back of the seat, contrasting sharply with the lighter wood of modern church benches. There was a very abbreviated back to the pew, not more than eighteen inches, a Calvinistic protest against the snug and exclusive high-back pews of more fashionable churches. In the Lincoln pew there could have been no sleeping—the auditor was fairly compelled to sit up and take notice. On the arm of the pew is a silver plate, simply inscribed with the name "Abraham Lincoln."

After the benediction a group of strangers gathered about this pew, where from the great heart of Lincoln went up many outspoken prayers. To sit in the very place where Lincoln worshiped is a privilege sought by young and old, and the respect accorded the memory of Abraham Lincoln in the church where he worshiped is most impressive.

This is a Presbyterian Church of the North; President Wilson, born in Virginia, attends the Central Presbyterian Church. While the people and the nation are reunited and have obliterated memories of the great civil conflict, the resultant division of various churches, North and South, is still maintained—about the only reminder to the public of the sectional dissensions of the American people.

MANKOWSKI ORDERS NEW RACING BOAT

feb 2 1914 times

Will be 26 Feet Long, Horse-Power 500 and Speed Mile a Minute.

Word has been received in this city that Count Casimir S. Mankowski of Lake George and New York, is having a motor boat built which he expects will make a reality of the dream of motor boat racing enthusiasts—the mile-a-minute boat. The new craft is to be twenty-six feet long and will be equipped with two engines of 250-horse power each. Fred Chase of the firm of Tams, Lemoyne and Crane, is the designer. The boat will be ready to participate in all the motor boat regattas at Chicago, Thousand Islands and Lake George.

Count Mankowski came into the limelight three years ago with his boat the Ankle Deep which burned at Buffalo last fall. With the Ankle Deep he raced for the Harmsworth trophy in Huntington Bay and won the Gold challenge cup at the Thousand Islands two years ago, only to lose it at Lake George last summer.

The new boat will be named Ankle Deep Too. The old Ankle Deep was thirty-two feet long and contained one engine of 300-horse power. It will be seen by the dimensions of the new craft that Count Mankowski is making a radical change, not only in the length of the boat but in the engine. The new boat will be six feet shorter and will be greater by 200-horse power.

COUNTY'S OLDEST RESIDENT.

Mrs. Mary Sage, of Darrowsville, Observes 105th Birthday Tuesday. *Feb 2*

news

Mrs. Mary Sage, of Darrowsville, near Chestertown, on Tuesday celebrated the 105th anniversary of her birth. Mrs. Sage, in spite of her advanced age, is enjoying good health and her mental faculties are but slightly impaired. *1915*

The aged woman was born in Sommersetshire, England, February 2, 1810.

With her husband and four children she came to this country in 1849, settling at Darrowsville. Her husband has been dead many years.

M s. Sage is the mother of twelve children, five of whom are now living in this country. The oldest, Courtney Sage, a Civil War veteran, has reached the age of seventy-seven years, while the youngest, Frank Sage, of Darrowsville, is fifty-one years old. Mrs. Rufus Hastings, of this village, is a daughter of Mrs. Sage. The latter visited here for some time last summer.

FOUND DEAD IN BARN.

news Feb 2 1913

Alonzo D. McKinstry Stricken With Heart Disease While Stabling Team.

Alonzo D. McKinstry, proprietor and driver of the Warrensburgh-Horicon mail route and stage line, died suddenly of heart disease yesterday in Fred W. King's barn, where he stabled his horses while on his daily trips to this village.

Mr. McKinstry arrived here as usual about 11 o'clock yesterday morning. After attending to some errands around the village he drove to the barn and unhitching his horses placed them in their stalls. He had just completed this task when he was evidently seized with the fatal attack. His body was found lying just behind one of the horses where, he fell when leaving the stall.

Mr. King made the grewsome discovery. Working in the yard, near the barn, about 2:30 p. m., he noticed that the barn door was open and the stage sleigh was standing in the yard, though it was past the usual time for its departure on the return trip to Horicon. Fearing that something was wrong he entered the barn and found the body of Mr. McKinstry cold in death.

Coroner J. E. Goodman was immediately summoned and pronounced heart disease the cause of death. The body was removed to Woodward's undertaking rooms and in the evening was taken to the home of the deceased in Horicon.

Mr. McKinstry was fifty-six years old. He leaves a widow, one son, Elwaine, and a daughter, Miss Elsie, both of Horicon, also several brothers and a sister. The funeral arrangements have not been completed.

GARAGE AT LAKE DESTROYED BY FIRE

Cadillac Automobile Burned in Blaze Which Caused

July 27 1914

$5,000 Loss.

(Special to The Post-Star.)

LAKE GEORGE, July 26.—A large and well equipped garage in the rear of Alexander Backus' summer home on the Lake George-Bolton road was completely destroyed by fire at 2 o'clock this afternoon as a result of what is thought to have been spontaneous combustion.

A 1914 Cadillac automobile and all other contents were destroyed with the building. The fire was not discovered until it had gained considerable headway and a fight against the flames was made impossible.

Mr. Backus stated tonight he could not accurately estimate the damage, but he thought it would be about $5,000.

---

news Jan 21 1915

EDWARD MERRILL

Edward Merrill, of Bolton Landing, aged about eighty years and a veteran of the Civil War, died at his home on the 10th inst. For many years Mr. Merrill had lived in the northern part of Bolton in the locality known as Padan Aram and was one of the most prosperous and best known of Bolton's farmers. Several years a sufferer from rheumatism and quite feeble, his death was not unexpected. He is survived by his widow; one son, Marlow; a sister, Mrs. Elliott Fish, and two brothers, Maroni and Nephi Merrill. The funeral was held at his late home on the 13th inst., the Rev. S. J. Liberty officiating. Interment in Bolton cemetery.

BUFFALO BILL IS THROUGH WITH SHOW

Col. William F. Cody Retires to Private Life After Eventfull Career *1915*

Star Aug 22

CIRCUS IS BANKRUPT

DENVER, Colo., Aug. 21.—Col. William F. Cody ("Buffalo Bill"), announces that he has definitely retired from public life.

It was when he was chief of scouts under Gen. Crook that he won fame by killing in single combat the Indian chief, Yellow Hand, knife against tomahawk.

In 1867 he won his title of Buffalo Bill. It was then that a gang of 1,200 men were laying the tracks of the Kansas-Pacific across the plains and were famishing for fresh meat. Cody volunteered to furnish the meat and in 18 months, with his horse Brigham and his favorite breach-loader, "Lucretia Borgia," he killed 4,280 bison.

In the '70's Col. Cody tried acting in a melodrama of the west and it was the success of this which led to the formation of the "Wild West" show, with which his name has been linked for thirty years. The big show was launched in earnest in 1883. The first performance was given in Madison Square Garden, New York city, when Henry Ward Beecher introduced the famous plainsman and scout to the public. On the first presentation of the show in Washington a few weeks later Gen. Philip Sheridan acted as master of ceremonies, riding in the Deadwood stage coach (in which he had traveled to the Black Hills), accompanied by President Arthur. The army officers attended, and the speaker of the house found it necessary to adjourn on account of a lack of a quorum.

When Buffalo Bill first launched his show the experienced men in the business laughed at him and said that it was a wild scheme, but in less than six months he was making more money than Barnum. The show toured Europe several times and was as successful there as on this side of the water.

Just how much Col. Cody has left of the millions of dollars he has earned in the show business is problematical. Of late years the profits have not been so large as formerly. It is said that the famous old scout has lost considerable sums in poor investments. But those who are in the best position to know declare that the personal fortune of Buffalo Bill is unimpaired by the disasters that have overtaken the show that bears his name. It is generally believed that he is well fixed financially and in no danger of coming to want in his old age.

In talking over his future plans, Buaffo Bill says: I expect to spend my remaining days in the west. Every cent that I have made in the show business I have invested in this section in developing the arid plains that are now fine home lands, peopled with happy American families. I was the first to undertake and successfully accomplish results under the Carey Arid Land Act through irrigation, the locality being in the Big Horn Basin. Once I spent $700,000 in digging an irrigation canal before I got a cent returned.

LARGEST VESSEL AFLOAT, THE VATERLAND, WHICH JUST COMPLETED ITS FIRST VOYAGE.

This giant trans-Atlantic steamship of the Hamburg-American Line, the largest in the world, has just completed its first round trip from Europe to America and return. The first voyage across the Atlantic from Cherbourg to the Ambrose Channel Lightship was made in exactly five days and seventeen hours, or at the remarkable speed of 23.2 nautical miles an hour. The great floating city, for such it really is, is 950 feet or nearly one-fifth of a mile in length, with 100 feet beam. It has a gross tonnage of 58,000, and requires 1,100 tons of coal a day to develop the required 93,000 horsepower. It carried 1,747 passengers on its first trip, with 400 stewards and 100 cooks, butchers and bakers to provide for their comfort, to say nothing of the balance of the big crew. The immense size of the steamship created considerable commotion even in the harbor of New York, the city of big things, and found some difficulty in maneuvring in and out of its berth at Hoboken. The ship provides almost every known comfort and convenience, including many not provided in the greatest hotels, especial interest being taken in the large swimming pool and in the magnificent ballroom.

DEATH FROM NAIL IN SHOE.

Patrick Burke Succumbs to Lockjaw Caused by Wound in Foot.

Patrick Burke, aged forty-nine years, and a life-long resident of Warrensburgh, died of blood poisoning and lockjaw Monday morning at 8 o'clock, at the home of his sister, Mrs. John Lynch, 16 South street, South Glens Falls. Jan 14 1915

Mr. Burke's trouble started from a seemingly insignificant wound in his right foot caused by a nail in his shoe. He paid little attention to it until a severe pain shot up his leg and he then called Dr. J. E. Goodman, who found his condition serious. The spread of the poison could not be checked and the physician decided that amputation of the foot would be necessary to save his life and advised his removal to the Albany hospital for the operation. The patient started from here Saturday morning, accompanied by Dr. Goodman, but when he reached Glens Falls had become so weak that it was deemed advisable for him to stop for a time at the home of his sister. During the day a priest was summoned from St. Mary's church and administered to him the last sacraments of the Catholic church.

Early in the evening the patient's jaws began to set and in a short time they became tightly locked. Dr. J. S. White and Dr. M. M. Dolan were summoned but could afford no relief.

PICKEREL KING IS CAUGHT IN HUDSON

Jan 14 1915 - Star

"Oh! the gallant fisher's life
It is the best of any;
'T is full of pleasure, void of strife,
And 't is beloved by many."
—The Angler.

This is not a fish story. It is a fish fact. Listen—

Fred B. Sprague, a piscatory friend, yesterday exhibited in the office of The Post-Star a pickerel that dazzled the eyes of the members of the staff and made their mouths water. The fish weighed 13 pounds, was 3 feet long and had a diameter of 7 inches.

The catch was made in the Hudson River. Mr. Pickerel came out of what is known as the Junction, not far from Big Bay.

Fire Destroys Loveland Building at Igerna.

A large two story frame building at Igerna, owned by Andrew J. Loveland, was destroyed by fire yesterday morning. The fire was caused by an overheated stove in A. G. Snyder's store on the first floor of the building and had gained such headway when discovered that it was impossible to check the flames. The second story was used as a dwelling but was not occupied at the time of the fire. The loss is estimated at $3,000 and is covered by insurance. Jan 28 1915 - News

BOLTON LANDING

Jan 28 1915 news

Henry W. Barber, who has been visiting relatives in Glens Falls, returned last week.

Miss Edith Finkle, who is attending the Glens Falls high school, was home over Sunday.

Miss Gertrude French, of North Bolton, was a guest of Miss Eva Morehouse last week.

Jay Ross, who has been drawing logs for Charles Carey at Minerva, is home, the job being completed.

Charles Davis sprained his ankle Thursday and was obliged to give up his trip on the stage line. Calvin Monroe takes his place.

J. L. Maranville has several teams drawing dirt for filling on Clay Island. The dirt is taken from the George P. Fish place at the Huddle.

The fifteen-cent supper given at the St. Sacrament rectory Thursday was a great success. The net proceeds were about $25.00. There was a large attendance and everybody had a good time.

Sergeant J. T. McElroy, Company D, 10th U. S. Infantry, Camp E. S. Otis, Lascascadas, Panama Canal Zone, who has been here on a furlough, left Saturday for Ridgewood, N. J., for a week's visit with his brother before rejoining his company. He enlisted about two years ago and was promoted to the rank of corporal eight months afterwards and soon after to sergeant. He has just finished his furlough of two months. Soon after he joined he was taken sick with malaria and was confined to the hospital about a month.

TOM O'CONNOR WINS RACE.

"Teddy Roosevelt" Scoops Seventy-Five Bushels of Oats for Next Postmaster.

News Jan 14

"It's better to be born lucky than rich," is a common saying. In Warrensburgh Tom O'Connor's luck is proverbial.

It's a matter of general knowledge that everything comes his way. Not that it's all luck, though, for he has a habit of going after things he wants—and getting them. Incidentally, it may be said that he has distanced all competitors for the postmastership of Warrensburgh and it is conceded that he will step into Postmaster Robert Murray's nice soft job when the latter's term expires on February 8, or as soon thereafter as the Democratic machinery in Washington can grind out the appointment, said machinery being just at present a little bit obstructed by the disagreement between President Wilson and the senators regarding the distribution of patronage *1915*

Tom's most recent stroke of good fortune materialized Saturday afternoon when his speed roadster, Teddy Roosevelt, beat D. J. Brown's Refer Greenback in a four-heat race on the ice at Lake George and scooped the prize of seventy-five bushels of oats, which will help some in feeding him (Teddy) the remainder of the winter.

This was the second race of the afternoon, the first being between Sheriff Richard J. Bolton's Miss Bolton and Supervisor E. J. Worden's Wardmore, for a purse of $150. It was a close race, bitterly contested, and was won by the sheriff's entry in three straight heats.

The racing brought out a crowd of at least 800 people. The conditions were ideal, the weather being clear and not too cold, and the ice as smooth as glass. Many of the spectators were on skates and between times indulged in the exhilarating sport.

ELDERLY LAKE GEORGE COTTAGER IS DEAD

Mrs. Elizabeth Goodliffe Horn, Dies at the Age of Eighty-five.

July 20 1915 Times

Mrs. Elizabeth Goodliffe Horn, aged eighty-five years, who had spent fifty-seven summers at Lake George, died this forenoon at 9:45 o'clock in her cottage opposite the Fort William Henry hotel. Mrs. Horn was one of the oldest residents of Lake George and was a descendant of a family who was among the early settlers of that place. She was greatly interested in Lake George village and the beautiful lake annd regularly every summer for more than a half century she had visited the lake. Her winters were spent in New York. She is survived by a son, Dr. Charles F. W. Horn of New York, and a daughter, Dr. Eleanor I. Parsons, of Lake George. The funeral will be held Wednesday afternoon at 3 o'clock from St. James Episcopal church. The Rev. F. M. Parrott will officiate. The burial will be in the Lake George cemetery.

GEORGE FOSTER PEABODY DISPOSES OF PALATIAL HOME AT LAKE GEORGE

Jan 19 1915 Times

Acquires Title to Hotel Princeton Property in Boston—Many Believe That New Summer Hotel is to be Built on Bolton Road in the Near Future.

George Foster Peabody of Saratoga Springs, governor of the Reserve bank for the district of New York, this week figured in two gigantic real estate deals involving a change in ownership of valuable Lake George and Boston, Mass., properties.

Mr. Peabody has disposed of his palatial summer residence on the Bolton road near the head of Lake George together with the stables, green houses, boat houses and fifty acres of land, including 400 feet of shore front, to J. Sumner Draper and Temple Dowling of Boston. The consideration is reported to be $150,000.

Title was taken this week by Mr. Peabody to the Hotel Princeton property in Boston and the Boston Globe yesterday printed the following story concerning the transaction:

"One of the largest transactions closed in Alston for a number of months involves the sale of the well-known Hotel Princeton, 1277 Commonwealth avenue. The purchaser was George Foster Peabody of Saratoga, N. Y., governor of the Reserve bank for the district of New York. The transaction was effected through the office of W. J. McDonald, 95 Milk street, who represented the grantor, W. Stanley Tripp, while James F. Bailey, 60 State street, acted for the purchaser.

"The Princeton is one of the most complete houses of its kind in the city. It was finished about four years ago from plans by John C. Spofford, architect, contains forty-eight modern suites of two and three rooms with bath, one-half of the suites has all the facilities for housekeeping.

"It is constructed in the Italian style of architecture, with granite and sandstone trimmings, and has a coping of Arabian red tile. There are three entrances, one from Commonwealth avenue, leading directly to the office, cafe, private dining-room, etc., the other two from Spofford road and Glenville avenue to the apartments. There are large reception rooms and immense roof garden.

"It was erected for Mrs. Fannie L. Randall, has been under her personal management ever since its completion and will continue so under the ownership of Mr. Peabody.

"The consideration was for a large figure in excess of the total rating of $271,900. There is 16,230 square feet of land taxed for $21,900. The frontage on Commonwealth and Glenville avenues is seventy-seven feet, while that on Spofford road is 210 feet.

"The final papers have been placed to record at the Suffolk registry of deeds."

In addition to the Lake George property sold to the Boston parties, Mr. Peabody owns more than fifty acres additional, and it is stated on good authority that he intends to spend some time each year at the lake as he has done for many years.

The question of what relation the transactions bear to each other is causing considerable wonderment locally. Attorney John H. Barker of the firm of Jenkins & Barker, who represented Mr. Draper in investigating the title of the property, is authority for the statement that the Princeton hotel property, which has been acquired by Mr. Peabody, is a part of the deal between himself and the Boston gentleman. Mr. Barker also stated that it is the intention of Mr. Draper to use the Lake George property as a summer home, but there are many who believe that a new summer hotel is to be erected on the place.

Fortune Found in Old Trunk.

Feb 12 1912 news

When Horace Taber, cashier at Greenwich, and Philip Kahn, appointed appraisers of the estate of the late Willard Harrington, of Archdale, town of Easton, Washington county, made an examination of the personal property of the deceased at his late home last week, they found $18,000 in bills tucked away in the top lid of an old trunk. The money was so hidden that the appraisers almost passed it by.

OBITUARY.

C. L. ROCKWELL.

Gray 13 1915

C. L. Rockwell, a native of Luzerne, who in his early manhood, in partnership with his father, the late George T. Rockwell, conducted the old Rockwell house in that village, and who later, in the early seventies, established the Rockwell house in Glens Falls, died Saturday morning at Clifton Springs, where he had been under treatment at a sanitarium for several months. He was sixty-six years old and leaves a widow, two daughters, Mrs. F. N. Sanborn, of Brooklyn, and Mrs. H. Hamilton Lewis, of Louisville, Ky.; one son, George T. Rockwell, and a brother, George H. Rock-

"STAR SPANGLED BANNER" IS OLD ENGLISH DRINKING SONG

Players Are to Give Composer's Name in Solving Song Pictures—Catalog is Official List.

Where did the United States get her national airs? Who were the authors and composers of the inspiring songs that have fired thousands of men to perform deeds of bravery on our battle fields?

Most of us know the words and tunes to the songs that are commonly known as "National Airs." Most of us think we know the origin and composers of these famous songs. But do we?

It seems a shame to say it, but the United States has no "National Song." That is strictly speaking, for none of our patriotic songs are of American origin. We have borrowed from other countries. Our poets have fitted words to airs and melodies composed by Englishmen, Frenchmen and Germans, and we have accepted them as real examples of "American National Airs."

Not even that grand, inspiring "Star Spangled Banner" belongs to us. It was stolen bodily from the British. Most of us think that Francis Scott Key was the originator. This idea is quite generally accepted, and when the suggestion sheets and the catalog in "The Game of Song and Story" were put out, the Song and Story Editor of The Times was kept busy telling participants that these lists were correct, and that "Arnold" really did compose the music to "The Star Spangled Banner" and that Francis Scott Key was only the author of the words.

As a matter of interest to the players in "The Game of Song and Story," the following authentic history of the "Star Spangled Banner" is here given:

The music to this world famous piece was composed by an Englishman, Samuel Arnold. It was a jolly drinking song and the composer also wrote the words and entitled the piece "To Anacreon in Heaven." This song was written and composed while America was still a loyal colony of Great Britain. It became immensely popular in the public houses and tap rooms of England and finally drifted to the Colonies.

Key was not even the first to use it as an American patriotic air One, Samuel Treat Payne, Jr., set verses to it and called it "Adams and Liberty." This was many years before Key wrote his words.

The song as we now know it sprang into nation-wide favor during the war of 1812. During the British invasion in 1814, while Ft. Henry was being bombarded by the British fleet in Baltimore Bay, Francis Scott Key wrote the immortal words:

"Oh, say can you see by the dawn's early light."

He was watching the British frigates pouring shells into the American fort. All through the night he watched the flame of battle, and when morning broke his first thought was, "Is the flag still there." Through the powder, smoke and the early morning mists he saw that "It still waved over the home of the free and the land of the brave." The British had not succeeded in lowering "The Stars and Stripes."

Francis Scott Key was born in Maryland in 1780. He was a lawyer of some note, practicing in Washington and Baltimore. He died in 1843. A book of his poems was published in 1857.

"Yankee Doodle" is another English "steal." It had been introduced into Boston by the red coats ten years before the Revolution, and was used with various doggerel verses to make fun of the pious Puritans on Sunday. While the British troops were marching to Lexington, April 19, 1775, they played "Yankee Doodle" in derision. On the British retreat from Lexington, the Minute Men whistled "Yankee Doodle" to hurry the flying British regulars into Boston town. When Lord Cornwallis surrendered at Yorktown and ended the Revolution, his army passed before the Continental army, whose bands were playing "Yankee Doodle." Thus an English air was used by the Americans for the opening of the war and for the grand finale.

FISHING IN WHITE LILY LAKE

Jan 8 1915

Isaac J. Davis Establishes His Right to Guard Waters from Trespass.

White Lily lake, in the town of Thurman, formerly known by the less euphonious name of Bear Swamp pond, has been a bone of contention among certain residents of the neighborhood for some years and the cause of considerable expensive litigation.

Isaac J. Davis, who acquired by purchase the land upon which the lake is situated, has been forced to establish his title and has done so by decision of a competent court.

Failing in their efforts to wrest from him his legal rights, certain people, Mr. Davis asserts, have sought to cause him annoyance by trying to establish their right to fish in the lake because, they have maintained, its waters were stocked by the state.

Mr. Davis has for some time been in correspondence with the State Conservation Commission and now has letters signed by State Fish Culturist Tarleton H. Bean stating that there are no records in his office to show that the lake has ever been stocked with fish by the state, as there would be had this been done. Mr. Bean writes that Patterson creek, which has its source in White Lily lake and empties into the Hudson river, in the town of Thurman, has twice been stocked with fish by the state upon application of Thomas E. Goodman, of The Glen, while he was supervisor of the town of Thurman. This, however, Mr. Bean states, gives no person the right to trespass upon Mr. Davis' private property and does not, by any means, open the pond to public fishing.

Mr. Davis firmly believes that he has been persecuted by some of his neighbors and now that his rights have been clearly defined and established by competent authority he intends to maintain them at all hazards.

July 13 1916 BOLTON LANDING. news

The Rev. D. J. Griffith, student pastor of the Baptist church, of this place, was ordained in the church Friday evening, June 30. He is a graduate of Hamilton Theological Seminary, entering that institution three years ago upon coming from Wales, his native land. He contemplates returning to Colgate for post graduate work this fall at the close of his third summer's work here. The Bolton Landing church invited eighteen neighboring Baptist churches to send their pastor and two delegates to sit in council with them. Thirty-two delegates responded. The ladies of the local church entertained the visiting clergy and delegates at a chicken dinner, served in the town hall.

BERT S. VAN VLEET.

—205—

PLATTSBURG WOMAN KIDDED BRITISHERS

July 13—1914

"Aunt Esther" McCreedy's Historic Home Remains Practically Unchanged

ENEMIES' QUARTERS IN 1814

PLATTSBURG, July 14.—One of the historic houses of Platsburg is the McCreedy homestead on the Beekmantown road now owned and accupied by D. A. Merrihew.

Built prior to 1800, the main part, which is of wood, stands today practical'y the same as when erected by Thomas McCreedy, who came from New England to settle in the little new village at the north. In 1823 he added the stone wing.

Saying the house is unchanged means the exterior. The interior was remodelled and the chimney removed. This was one of the huge affairs of the time when the hearthstone was literally the heart of the home. They built the fire equipment first and then joined on the rooms as it happened.

Thomas McCreedy's chimney was twelve feet square, starting with stone at the base, and it kept the dimension to a height of twelve feet with exception of the slope for two fireplaces. The one in the living room allowed for an eight-foot log, and the mantel was a little over five feet up. The other fireplace was somewhat smaller.

The British when they landed in here in 1814 naturally found the McCreedy place a pleasant one for location. The beautiful, says the Plattsburg Star, was in the glory of early September, and the pleasant house offered inviting quarters to the invaders.

James McCreedy, who died in 1874, was ten years old at the time of the battle and well remembered the events of the time, telling them to his children.

Mrs. McCreedy, his mother, was one of the bright, expansive, every-ready people who are everybody's friend, and equipped to take the whole universe by adoption. "Aunt Esther," (pronouuced Eester) was her familiar name in the township, and the British officers picked it up. Ardent patriot as she was, it is impossible to think of her absolutely frigid to even the lord of the shades himself if he made claim on her hospitality and kindness, and no doubt she met the enemy accordingly.

WILL OF THE LATE CORNELIA WING FERRISS IS ADMITTED TO PROBATE

July 9 1914 Times

Three Trust Funds Are Created, Two of Which Are for $30,000 Each—Numerous Bequests Are Made to Public Institutions —Estate Worth About One Hundred Thousand Dollars.

Two trust funds of $30,000 each and one, the amount of which is not given, are created by the will of the late Cornelia Wing Ferriss, widow of Orange Ferriss, whicn was admitted to probate today by Judge Raley in Surrogate's court. The value of the estate is not mentioned in the will, which covers thirteen typewritten pages and which was drawn November 25, 1913, but it is estimated to be worth more than $100,000. In the will Mrs. Ferriss named Attorney Louis M. Brown and Maurice Hoopes as executors. The witnesses to the instrument were City Judge Edwin R. Safford and Julia A. Taylor.

The petition for the probate of the will was made today by Louis D. Ferriss, a son of the beneficiary, through his attorney, James McPhillips. Judge Raley issued letters testamentary to the executors.

The trust funds of $30,000 each are created for the benefit of Antoinette C. Higby, a sister of the deceased, and Helen M. Ferriss, a daughter-in-law and wife of Louis D. Ferriss. Each is to receive the sum of $1,200 per year from the income and if in any year the income is insufficient to pay this amount, the deficiency is to be made up out of the principal.

The trust fund created for the son, Louis D. Ferriss, consists of the remainder of the entire estate, after the two funds of $30,000 each are set aside. Mrs. Ferriss provided in her will that the executors are to use the income of the trust fund, created for the son, for his maintenance and in case of his recovery, both mentally and physically, they are to turn over to him. the fund or such portions as they deem prudent.

One paragraph of much interest is included in the will. In this Mrs. Ferriss bequeaths the sum of $1,000 to a county tuberculosis hospital for Warren county, provided one is incorporated and established before the death of her sister. The clause is appended:

"If before the decease of my sister, Antoinette C. Higby, or if she shall not survive me, then in such case if before my decease a county tuberculosis hospital be incorporated and established in Warren county, then in such case I give and bequeath to such hospital the sum of $1,000 and I request (without intending to impose any obligation which the authorities of such hospital will be legally bound to observe), that said legacy be used if practicable to equip and maintain a room or bed in such hospital in memory of my daughter, Millie Ferriss. such room or bed to be known as the "Millie Ferriss Memorial Room or Bed."

Under the clause by which the trust fund for the benefit of the sister, Antoinette C. Higby is created, it is provided that at her death the following sums be paid:

To the rector, church wardens and vestrymen of the Church of the Messiah of Glens Falls the sum of $11,000. Of this amount Mrs. Ferriss directed that $1,000 be used for the work of the Parish house.

To the Glens Falls hospital the sum of $1,000.

To the Glens Falls Home for Aged Women. the sum of $1,000.

To the Protestant Episcopal church of the Epiphany of Washington, D. C. the sum of $1,000 to become part of the church's endowment fund.

To the Men's Mission of the said Church of Epiphany the sum of $1,000.

To the Protestant Episcopal Church of St. Sacrament in the village of Bolton, the sum of $1,000.

It is under this same clause that the bequest is made to the tuberculosis hospital.

"Aunt Esther," said one cf the officers, "we have always been curious to know what that famous 'Yankee hasty pudding' was like. Won't you make us some?"

Of course Aunt Esther acquisced and turned out a dish of superfine quality. The visitors tasted and re-tasted, partook sparingly and finally owned they didn't like it very much.

"Well," said Aunt Esther, "if you don't look out, before you are through you'll get a dish of Yankee hasty pudding you'll like less than you do this."

The McCreedy orchard yielded cider of the gold and amber variety sung by poets and swigged in joy by plain man. The gastronomics under the red coats were no proof against the nectar, and the barrels in the McCreedy cellar were on steady tap by the Britishers. One little sentry especially couldn't get enough, and on the morning of the engagement as he hurried away, he told Aunt Esther after they had finished the Yankees he would come back for the rest of the cider.

The cellar door opened from the front hall, and when the sentry returned after the show was over he made a dive for it and out the bulkhead blew.

"Why don't you get the cider?" called Aunt Esther, but the pad of retreating feet was all the answer she received.

—206—

AUGUST 29, 1913.

MADAME HOMER
BUYS PROPERTY

Oct 11 1916 Times

Plans to Erect Summer Residence on Ninety Acre Tract Near Bolton.

MADAME HOMER BUYS PROPERTY

Madame Homer, the famous Metropolitan opera star, who with her family has spent several seasons at Lake George, has purchased a fine tract of land of approximately ninety acres near Bolton on the lake shore back of the Trask islands. Madame Homer acquired the property from William K. Bixby of St. Louis, Mo., who also has other valuable property which he occupies during the summer.

The property purchased by Madame Homer is known as Bixby's Point and is one of the most splendidly undeveloped tracts of land along the Bolton shore. There are no buildings on the property and it is Madame Homer's intention to erect a large summer residence on the place.

Madame Homer has six children, and both she and her husband are great admirers of Lake George, where they have a large acquaintance.

GEORGE FOSTER PEABODY.

George Foster Peabody, banker, reformer and philanthropist, who lives in summer at Lake George and during the winter in Brooklyn, is a big figure in many of the important public affairs of the state. He is chairman of the Saratoga Springs state park commission and has been identified with the anti-Murphy movement of recent years. Mr. Peabody was born in Columbus, Ga., July 27, 1852. He was educated in private schools, Washington and Lee university and the University of Georgia. He is vice president of the Mexican Northern railroad company, Potosi and Rio Verde railway company, Mexican Coal and Coke company, Alvarez Land and Timber company, Campania Metallurgica Mexicana, and the Montezuma Lead company. He is a director of the Mexican Mineral railway company, Conquista Coal railway company, and the Southern Improvement company of New York. He was treasurer of the Democratic national committee from 1895 to 1905. He was vice president of the National Civic Federation in 1905. He is a member of many New York clubs and has offices at 2 Rector street, New York.

A Corinth Inventor.

The auto fender safety lamp, an invention of Thomas Derby, formerly of Round Lake, now a resident of Corinth, is about to be placed on the market. The lamp is lighted by gas or electricity and is attached to the fender of the automobile, where at night it marks the clearance space between cars going in either direction. A company has been formed by C. A. Tyre and John H. and W. J. Pitkin to exploit the lamp and Mr. Derby will go on the road for the new concern.

Times July 29 1914

BOLTON MAN HEADS MEDICAL SOCIETY

Oct 2 1916 Star

Dr. E. L. Wilson Elected President During Meeting in City Hall

The Medical Society of the county of Warren last evening in City Hall elected the following officers:

President, Dr. E. L. Wilson, Bolton; vice president, Dr. B. J. Singleton, Glens Falls; secretary and treasurer, Dr. Morris Maslon, Glens Falls.

A resolution was adopted endorsing the proposition to be submitted at the November election to appropriate $50,000 for the establishment of a county hospital. A splendid address was delivered by Dr. Oswald Lowsley of Belleview hospital. Following the meeting, Dr. M. L. Haviland entertained the members in his home in Ridge street.

LIBRARY IN RUINS

Fire Wrecked Magnificent Stone Structure Tuesday Afternoon.

PART OF VALUABLE CONTENTS SAVED

Property Loss About $18,000, Insurance $5,000—Dense Smoke Blocked Efforts of Firefighters to Locate and Extinguish Blaze—Only Walls and Chimney Left Standing—Building Erected in 1900.

The Richards Library building is in ruins, wrecked Monday afternoon by a fire which probably started from the furnace or an overheated pipe in the basement.

Only the outer walls of stone and the chimney are left standing. The newly organized Hackensack Hose company made a brave and determined fight to save the building, but the dense smoke which filled every room made entrance impossible and blocked their efforts to locate and extinguish the blaze.

Part of the valuable contents were saved, but many of the books taken out were damaged by smoke and water. The total loss is estimated at $18,000 The building, which was supposed to be practically fireproof, was insured for $3,500 and the contents for $1,500.

The fire broke out while the janitor, Thomas W. Smith, was at dinner. He left the building at 11:30 o'clock, just after he had coaled the furnace and adjusted the drafts, according to his usual custom. The librarian, Miss Mary S. Crandall, and Miss Clark, left at 12 and locked the doors About 12:45 Seth A. Reed while passing the library noticed an unusual amount of heavy black smoke issuing from the chimney. Suspecting something wrong he went up the walk and peering through the glass door discovered that the interior of the building was filled with smoke. He immediately informed Principal Chilson, of the high school, and a fire alarm was rung on the school bell. William Hadden, chief of the fire department, was notified by telephone at the shirt factory and Lewis E. Crandall, the uptown captain, was called out with his men and apparatus. The response was prompt, but the roads were drifted with snow and it was probably twenty or thirty minutes before a line of hose could be strung from the hydrant near the residence of Dr. J. E. Goodman, fully 1000 feet distant from the burning building. In the meantime several chemical fire extinguishers were procured, but were of little use as the source of the fire could not be reached on account of the smoke. For this reason the fire hose also was of little avail.

For a considerable time the fire smouldered with no sign of a blaze. It could be seen, however, that the flames were feeding on the woodwork in the roof. Local builders express the opinion that the fire started in the cellar and ran all over the building, through the air spaces between the stone outer wall and the inside lining, thus reaching the ceiling and roof. Finally little tongues of flame began to appear around the cornice and when a hole was chopped in the roof the blaze found vent and made a rapid advance. It was checked in places by streams from the hose, but was too widespread to be brought under control.

A violent gale of wind which blew nearly all day Monday was at its height while the fire was in progress and this would have made it almost impossible to save the building had other conditions been more favorable.

While the hopeless fight to save the building was being waged by the firemen, other brave workers turned their attention to saving the contents. This was dangerous work on account of the smoke, but many willing helpers persevered and entering the building brought out armfuls of books, furniture and other fittings. Most of the records were thus saved, also the card catalogue and borrowers' cards upon which were charged the books in circulation.

Seth A. Reed, knowing the value of the many rare curios in the museum, rallied a force around him to save them. Though the task was a difficult one it was successfully accomplished, nearly every article, including many pieces of delicate and fragile china, being removed intact and carried to a place of safety. The ancient Korean chest, a gift of the late Mrs. Cordelia Allen, of Honolulu, Hawaiian Islands, as were many other valuable curios, was removed undamaged and placed in the school building for safe keeping. Most of the books saved were also stored there for the present. The museum, besides Mrs. Allen's contributions, contained also many valuable and interesting articles gathered by Miss Richards and Mrs. Kellogg on their travels in foreign lands. In his rescue work Mr. Reed had the valuable assistance of Charles F. Burhans, J. E. Johnson, William Hadden, Earl Herrick, Maurice Ashe, and others. As a result of inhaling so much smoke Seth is now speaking with a deep bass voice several tones lower than his normal key. Professor Chilson dismissed the high school and with his boys did valiant service.

It is perhaps unfair to single out these men for special mention when so many others also did their best, but no invidious distinction is intended. All who assisted in any way are entitled to much credit for their work in the face of many difficulties. Those who entered the building took desperate chances in braving the smoke and the danger from falling timbers.

With even better facilities it is doubtful if the building could have been saved owing to the difficulty of reaching the source of the fire. The firemen, under the circumstances, did remarkably well. With competent instruction, drills and discipline, they will make efficient firefighters.

The burned building was a one-story structure of handsome design, as shown by the picture accompanying this article. It was built of native granite quarried on the farm of James Hammond, in North Caldwell. Construction was begun in 1900 by Contractor Jonah Hess, of Johnstown, who during the preceding year built the high school building. The contract price was about $9,000 and Mr. Hess completed his work in December of that year. The library was opened in the new building on August 13, 1901. In 1911 an addition was built which nearly doubled the capacity. This involved an additional outlay of nearly $5,000. With the furniture, fittings and books the value of the property was approximately $18,000. The entire expense of erecting the building and supplying the contents was borne by Miss Clara Richards, of this village, and Mrs. Mary Richards Kellogg, of Elizabethtown, with the exception of $100 a year which for several years has been contributed by the town to be devoted to the purchase of new books.

The library upon its organization in 1901,

THE RICHARDS FREE PUBLIC LIBRARY *Warrensburgh*

INDIAN CENTENARIAN DEAD.

John Camp, of Lake George, Called to Happy Hunting Grounds.

John Camp, a full-blooded Indian of the Abanakois tribe, said to be more than 100 years old, died at Lake George last Thursday, at the home of his step-daughter, Mrs. Asa Hastings. He had lived in that place upwards of seventy years, coming with others of his tribe from Maine. He leaves several sons and daughters and one of the sons is about seventy years old. His wife died about thirty years ago. The father of the deceased was a chief of his tribe and died at Lake George at the age of 106 years. On his 100th birthday anniversary, which came in January, 1878, he went skating on the lake. John Camp's funeral was held at the Methodist Episcopal church, Lake George, Saturday afternoon at 2 o'clock. The large number of citizens in attendance, including most of the prominent men of the village, attested the esteem in which the deceased was held by all. Interment was in the village cemete

FAMOUS SON OF JOHNSBURGH

Eben E. Rexford, Distinguished Author, Dies in Wisconsin.

Eben E. Rexford, a native of the town of Johnsburgh, died on the 18 h inst., in a hospital in Green Bay, Wis., after a three weeks' illness of typhoid fever. Mr. Rexford won national fame as a poet and song writer, being best known as the author of "Silver Threads Among the Gold," a ballad that will never die. Other of his well-known pieces are "Grandmother's Garden" and "Brother and Lover." The deceased was born in Johnsburgh July 16 1848 and his parents removed to Wisconsin when he was a boy. He never came back to the scenes of his youth. Mr. Rexford was a cousin of R. B. Kenyon, of this village. *news Oct 21*

GATES-TRIPP.

Myron J. Gates, of Warrensburgh, and Miss Mary Tripp, daughter of Fester B. Tripp, of Landon Hill, Chester, were married Monday by the Rev. W. F. Hassel, at the home of the bride. Immediately after the ceremony they left for Garnet Lake, where they will enjoy the first week of their honeymoon in a rented cottage. They will go to Florida for the winter, where Mr. Gates will be employed as a barber.

IGERNA BUILDING DESTROYED BY FIRE

June 27 1915

Two-story Frame Structure is Consumed With Loss of About $3,000. *Times*

Fire, which broke out shortly after eight o'clock this morning in the general store of A. G. Snyder in Igerna, completely destroyed the two-story frame building with a loss of about $3,000, which is covered by insurance. The building was not a new structure and for a time the upper story was used as a dwelling by Andrew J. Loveland, the owner of the building. At the time of the fire, however, the second story of the building was not inhabited.

It is thought that the fire was caused by an overheated stove. As near as could be learned this afternoon Mr. Snyder had started a fire in the store when he opened it for business this morning. He evidently forgot to check the drafts and the stove or pipe got so hot that the partitions became ignited. Once the flames got under headway, the building burned like tinder. All efforts to save the structure were without avail.

LARGEST HOTEL IN ALL THE WORLD

Fifteen Million Dollar Hostelry in Big City to Have 2,500 Rooms

TIMES SQUARE'S HONOR

Aug 30 1916

NEW YORK, Aug. 25.—The greatest transient city on the globe, even in times of peace, is neither London nor Paris but New York. The 200,000 visitors who come to New York every day would swamp the hotel facilities of either the English or French metropolis. But the New York visitor, according to the New York American, remains in the city on an average of four and one-half days, making an average of nearly 1,000,000 visitors in New York most of the time. It is this vast and rapidly growing army of visitors that makes it almost impossible for New York to keep its hotel facilities up to the demand.

The Hotel Commonwealth, the $15,000,000 monster which is to be located in the Times Square district, is New York's latest expedient for taking care of visitors. With its 2,500 rooms, a number that would have been staggering a few years ago, it will be the largest hotel in the world.

"New York city ever has been a great bonanza for hotelkeepers," says a local paper. "Its hotels and their bonifaces long have been famous throughout the world.

"The average of passenger traffic in and out of the city is daily 493,000 persons and 2,340 trains.

"There is the boat and automobile traffic, for which figures are not available. These classes of traffic are constantly increasing.

"Approximately 150,000 commuters come in and go out of the city on week days.

"The out-of-town visitors, it is estimated, average 200,000 persons. The average out-of-town visitor's stay in in town is estimated as four and one-half days. The expenditures of the visiting 200,000 average during a day $1,200,000.

"Thus the average visiting individual spends close to $10 a day—not all, of course, in hotels.

"The city has 215 hotels with fifty or more bedrooms.

"Statisticians have figured that the 200,000 guests, whose visits average four and one-half days in town, spend $2,120,000. For their dinners they spend $250,000 a day. Daily they pay $800,000 for lodgings and other meals. Their shopping tours use up $320,000 per diem. The theatres get from them $200,000 a day. In all kinds of side trips they spend about $280,000 a day.

"It is significant that the three newest large hotels, the McAlpine, the Belmont and the Biltmore are all paying handsome dividends. The Belmont is said to earn forty percent upon its stock, and the Biltmore a smaller return on much larger capital."

The figures given are conservative. For instance, at the Grand Central of 280,000 people arrive and as many more depart

LONG TRIP IN AUTOMOBILE.

Mr. and Mrs. James Scripture Will Motor 2,300 Miles to New Home in South.

James Scripter, going on seventy years of age and a life-long resident of Warrensburgh, has departed from our midst to make a new home for himself and wife way down South in Mississippi. They started Monday in a Maxwell touring car, recently purchased from Edson Granger, of the Warrensburgh Garage, and intend to make the entire trip in the machine, a distance of 2,300 miles. Mr. Granger accompanied them as chauffeur and expects to complete the journey in about ten days, barring accidents.

Mrs. B. F. Glynn, a niece of the Scripters, accompanied them on the trip and Mr. Granger's wife and son, Gordon, went with him to Philadelphia, from which point they will go to Valois, N. Y., their former home, to await his return. After landing his passengers at Bond, Miss., their future home. Mr. Granger will return by train, as will also Mrs. Glynn.

The manufacturers of the Maxwell automobile are greatly interested in the long trip as they consider it a severe test of their car, and a good advertisement of its durability, for they are confident it will cover the distance without a skip. They have instructed Mr. Granger to report to them daily, by telegraph, at their factory in Detroit, and the record of each day's run will be published at the completion of the trip. *Feb 25 7915*

Mr. Scripter has a fine place in Mississippi which he purchased about a year ago. A comfortable house has been built on the property which will be ready for immediate occupancy when they arrive there, as their household goods have been shipped by rail and will be placed in the house by a man who accompanied them. Mr. Scripter's favorite horse also went in the car. On the place there is a large fig orchard from which our former townsman expects to derive a large revenue. He anticipates also an improvement in his health as a result of the change of climate. *news*

President Wilson, His Son-in-Law and Grandson

This is the first picture of the latest White House baby, Francis Sayre, Jr., who made his bow to the world at the Executive mansion a few weeks ago. The boy is the son of Mr. and Mrs. Francis Sayre, the latter formerly Miss Jessie Wilson, the second daughter of the President of the United States. The photograph shows the highly-pleased grandfather, the more-than-tickled father, and the patient-and-enduring youngster in their first public pose.

Store Visitor Tumbles Into Cellar.

Amasa Griffin after drinking a glass of water from the faucet in D. E. Cameron's store in Lewisville Tuesday evening stepped backward into an open trap door way and fell to the bottom of the cellar. One arm was broken and his legs and body were severely bruised. He was carried to his home nearby, where Dr. J. E. Goodman attended him. *Aug 13 1915*

GLENS FALLS. *June 25 1915*

Damage estimated at $150 was caused yesterday afternoon in Isador Yaffee's tailor shop, when a pressing table took fire from a hot iron which had been left on the table.

Daniel Allen, jr., suffered a fracture of his right arm in a fall in the Young Men's Christian Association gymnasium yesterday.

ADIRONDACK MAN MEETS WITH SERIOUS INJURY
Feb 17 1915 times

Horton Ross, of Adirondack, met with a painful, if not fatal accident yesterday while unloading logs onto a skidway at the Phelps mill in Pottersville. Mr. Ross was struck in the head by a log and rendered unconscious. He was taken to the Wells house where he was attended by Dr. George Bibby. This morning he was removed to his home in Adirondack. This afternoon he had not regained consciousness and it is feared that internal injuries may develop. Mr. Ross is thirty-three years of age and has a wife and three children. He was in the employ of W. L. Porter as a teamster.

Bolton Youth Drowned. *Aug 13 1915*

Douglass Morehouse, nineteen years old, was drowned in Lake George Tuesday afternoon while bathing at Bolton Landing. He was hanging to the stern of a rowboat and losing his grip sank to the bottom. The body was quickly brought to the surface but all efforts at resuscitation failed. He is survived by his parents, Mr. and Mrs. James Morehouse, a brother, Floren and a sister, Eva, all of Bolton.

Lee "Spot" Parks and Jay Weaver are in the act of ascending Prospect Mountain at Lake George. Messrs. Parks and Weaver for three weeks past have been making daily trips for the purpose of reducing their weight. That Mr. Parks, at least, is meeting with success is evidence by the fact that the other evening while sitting in Hotel Ruliff he unconsciously crossed his legs above the knee and for the first time in twenty years saw his foot.

GREAT EXTENSION SALE!

Jan 18 1913

O. R. Howe, for years Hudson Falls' leading dry goods merchant, has extended his great emergency sale six days more. W. R. Darcy & Co. of Boston, Mass., conducted one of the largest sales that was ever held in this vicinity and in going over my stock I find a few things such as remnants in piece goods, etc., that a sale such as this one is bound to leave on hand. Every day our store has been jammed to the doors and at times were forced to close the doors so great were the crowds. I also wish to announce the reason of this great sale and also to stop some foolish rumors going around town. Being heavily overstocked I was fortunate in closing a deal with this great concern to conduct a special 10 days' sale for me. W. R. Darcy & Co. conduct such sales all over the United States for merchants in every line of merchandise. Some people thought they brought goods with them for this sale but every article sold was from my own stock and was sold under my guarantee of perfect satisfaction or money cheerfully refunded. Next Saturday night when I close this sale I will not have an odd piece of goods or anything in odds and ends in the store. Opening up Monday, January 25th, with a complete line of new up-to-date merchandise and you can feel confident that in buying goods here you will be shown only the newest styles the market produces.

I wish to thank the general public for their generous patronage during this great sale and anticipating your future good will, I am,

Most respectfully yours,

O. R. HOWE

Hudson Fall,   N. Y

---

news Feb 1913

SOUTH HORICON STORE BURNED.

Fred H. Duell & Son Put Out of Business by Early Morning Fire.

Fred H. Duell & Son's general store at South Horicon, was burned to the ground this morning at 2 o'clock. The origin of the fire is unknown. The total loss is about $4,000. The stock was insured for $2,000 and fixtures for $200 through the Warrensburgh agency of Thomas & Reoux.

The store was an old landmark in Horicon. It was conducted for many years by Richard P. Smith, Jr., and his father before him. Mr. Smith sold the building and business, together with his handsome residence property nearby, to the Duells last spring and it had since been conducted by them. The fire was well advanced when discovered. An alarm brought many willing workers to the scene but with meagre facilities at hand little could be done to check the flames. Goods to the value of about $500 were removed from the back part of the building.

The stand is one of the best in that section and the store will undoubtedly be rebuilt.

The South Horicon postoffice was located in the store.

"EDDIE" WORDEN A MAGIC NAME

march 8 1915

"Dick" Smith and Others Tell of Wonderful Powers of Mysterious Words.

Few men are possessed of a name qualified to be substituted for the words of magic, "Open Sesame" but Supervisor Edwin J. Worden of Lake George is one of the few, if the tales related by "Dick" Smith and other men of the northern part of the county are to be given credence. Mr. Smith is authority for the statement that if a lone tourist from the wilds of "Little Warren" finds himself stranded in New York with nothing but a bundle of postoffice money orders or uncertified checks, all he has to do is to step into the postoffice or nearest bank without somebody to identify him and in responding to the rapid-fire questions from behind the counter, drop the name of "Eddie" Worden and the long green is flashed across before he realizes it.

How much faith can be placed in the stories of the marvelous occurrences of having checks and money orders cashed and securing credit in New York establishments by mentioning the genial Caldwell Democratic State committeeman, supervisor, hotelman, horseman and all-round good fellow is left for the discretion of the reader, but Chairman Fred R. Smith of the Board of Supervisors, who is spending the winter in Albany, holding down the job of second assistant assembly door keeper, insists that "Eddie's" name has the same magical effect in the Capital city.

DR. AND MRS. WILSON ENTERTAIN BY CARDS

Feb 11 1915 Star

BOLTON LANDING, Feb. 10—The pretty home of Dr. and Mrs. E. L. Wilson was the scene of a pleasant gathering Monday evening. Twelve couples indulged in progressive card playing, the spirit of competition waxing high. When the final game was played it was found that Mrs. Theodore Ormsby was winner of the ladies' first prize and C. E. Wilson, jr., the gentlemen's first. For gentlemen's consolation, a draw resulted in Arthur Lamb's being presented a pack of cards with the injunction to practice a little. The same advice was given Miss Genevieve Kelley, winner of the ladies' consolation.

Refreshments were served, following which the guests departed for their several homes all assuring their charming host and hostess that their hospitality would be long and pleasantly remembered.

LAKE GEORGE RACE MEET IS FINISHED

Star Feb 12 1916

Six Trials Are Necessary Before Baker's Orvis Wins Named Event

JAY POINTER A WINNER

LAKE GEORGE, Feb. 11.—The annual Lake George winter ice race meet was brought to a close this afternoon with the most interesting program of the week. Six heats were necessary to decide the first event and four to choose a winner in the second race. The summary follows:

Named Race—Purse $75.

Orvis (Baker)	4 3 1 1 2 1
Robert R. (Roberts)	1 1 4 4 3 3
Lady Bonboy (Worden)	3 2 2 2 1 2
Edna Wilkes (West)	2 4 3 3 3 .

Time—2:30 1-4, 2:27 1-4, 2:20, 2:34 1-2, 2:31 3-4, 2:29 1-4.

Named Race—Purse $75.

Jay Pointer (Sommerville)	1 1 4 1
Wardmore (Worden)	2 4 1 2
Frazzle (McAuley)	3 2 3 3
Blackford (White)	4 3 2 4

Time—2:29, 2:30, 2:26, 2:25 1-4.

At the close of the meet, arrangements were made for a day's racing next Tuesday when a matched contest will be staged between E. J. Worden's Wardmore and J. B. White's Blackbird. A named race also will be staged.

TO ABOLISH TAX COLLECTORS.

March 4 1915 news

Proposed Bill of Assemblyman Brereton Approved by Supervisors.

The Warren county board of supervisors has approved of a bill Assemblyman Brereton is about to introduce in the assembly providing for a change in the system of collecting taxes in this county, which it is believed will produce better results and effect a large saving for the taxpayers.

At a meeting of the board, held at Lake George Monday, Attorney Daniel F. Imrie appeared in behalf of Assemblyman Brereton and explained the provisions of the measure. He stated that the bill is not as revolutionary as is believed by many, but is in line with what is being done in other counties and cuts down the already too long list of appointive officers in towns.

If the bill becomes a law it will abolish the town offices of school district and town collectors in the eleven towns of Warren county, numbering nearly 200, and place the duties upon the town clerk of each town. The bill provides that the clerk shall receive a salary to be fixed by the town board in lieu of all other compensation fixed by law, but he shall receive allowances for necessary disbursements.

HALL ICE CREAM COMPANY IS NOW LOCATED IN NORTHERN NEW YORK'S MOST MODERN INSTITUTION

Steady and Sure Development of Ice Cream Business Well Illustrated by Growth of Local Concern Whose New Plant is a model of Sanitary Perfection—Business Started in 1899 by Byron E. Hall.

New Plant of the Hall Ice Cream Company.

The steady and sure development of the ice cream business is no better illustrated than by the way the Hall Ice Cream company, by hard work and close application to business, built up a trade that made it necessary for the concern to erect a new factory, which has just been completed and is now in operation.

Mr. Hall started in the ice cream business in 1899 with a hand freezer and with a mallet crushed the ice used in freezing the cream. Later he put in a power freezer and crusher.

In 1907 P. J. Smith became associated with Mr. Hall in the business, new machinery was installed and after two years it was necessary to have larger quarters.

The property at 2 Maple street was then bought and alterations and additions were made to the building. More new equipment was obtained to enable them to be able to give to their customers a product made in a clean and sanitary manner.

Success has been theirs and last fall it was deemed advisable to provide for "a greater output which brought about the erection of the present factory.

The building now located at 4 Maple street, on the site of the old Ide property, is a two-story brick structure, 45x70, with drive-way entirely around the building and a loading platform in the rear.

The entire building is used in the manufacture of ice cream and the handling of soda fountain supplies.

The Maple street entrance opens into a commodious reception or waiting room, from which the public may be served with package or brick cream. This is a handsome room with tiled floor, and oak wainscoting with marble base. Glass partitions on the right and left allow the customer to view the interior of the factory from this room.

The freezing room is in the southwest corner of the building, facing Maple street. It is light and airy, and has a tiled floor and side walks. The whole front being of plate glass, the 2 40-quart Miller freezers may be plainly seen when in operation by passersby.

Back of the freezing room is the hardening room which are divided into two compartments with ante rooms at either end, so that the cream may be put through a revolving door from the freezing room into the ante room and then into the hardening rooms and out from the opposite end to the shipping platform.

Ice and salt used for shipping is close by, the salt reaching the platform from the second floor by means of a gravity system, where it is crushed and conveyed through the partition to the same platform.

The hardening rooms are heavily insulated with sheet cork and lined with cement plaster. Special Stevenson refrigerating doors are used in the rooms and also in the ante room entrance.

The temperature, which is carried at around zero, is furnished by an eleven ton York refrigerating plant, which produces this temperature in the bunker lofts, from which it is forced to the hardening room by means of a five horsepower fan which keeps the cool air continually in circulation.

The ammonia compressor is driven by a twenty horse power General Electric motor and is directly in front of the plate glass window on the opposite side of the building from the freezing room.

In the rear of the compressor is located a 10 horse power, high pressure boiler, which furnishes the building not only with heat during the winter months but with hot water and steam for washing and sterilizing purposes.

The mechanical washer of the Manning type is used for washing packing cans which is the last thing to be done to insure a sanitary packing can, as this machine not only washes and rinses the can, but sterilizes it as well.

Two drive wells furnish water to the condensers by means of a Gould suction pump which delivers approximately twenty-four gallons per minute. The condensers are also connected with city water so that either may be used.

The brine used in freezing the cream is stored in a combination cold storage vat, and short order box, attached to the hardening rooms where it is cooled by means of the Ammonia compressor, then circulated through the brine system to the freezer by means of a five horse power motor.

All supplies are taken to a large and commodious store room on the second floor by means of a power elevator.

Raw cream and milk are placed in

a cooling room, prepared especially for their reception, which opens direct to the mixing room where are installed a mechanical mixer, steam kettle, gas dissolver and other apparatus used in the making of sanitary ice cream.

The fruit and extract room also opens into the mixing room, as it is here where the delicacies made by the Hall company are prepared.

The mixing room is directly over the freezing room and the mixture, when prepared, is delivered to the freezer by means of a gravity system, through sanitary pipes.

The offices and hall are located on the second floor, front, finished in oak and are reached by a broad stairway, leading from the main entrance.

The building is arranged so that materials used in manufacturing moves continuously from the time they enter the building at the back platform until they return to the same platform to be shipped a finished product, and is the result of numerous trips of inspection by Messrs. Hall and Smith to other cities where refrigerating plants had previously been installed.

The detailed plans for the building were made by the Ice cream Construction company of New York city

FISH SMOTHERED

march 13, 1917.

At Mud Lake, near Redwood, in the Adirondacks, ice in this shallow lake is 30 inches deep and as a result the fish in the lake are being rapidly smothered out of existence. They have come down in swarms onto the racks of the grist mill at Redwood and Game Protector John Dollinger has been busy taking them out.

In the last few days Mr. Dollinger has taken out 3,000 pickerel and has transferred them to Butterfield Lake. There are many perch being taken from the lake

---

MR. BIXBY REPLIES TO MR. BOYER.

August 25, 1915.

Lake George Mirror,

Referring to your issues of the 21st., mention is made of fast running boats and you print a letter from Mr. Boyer of Uncas evidently referring to one of my boats. I have written Mr. Boyer stating the facts in the case and only wish to say that there is no more careful and prudent pilot on the lake than the one who was running the boat at the time mentioned. He was never run into or injured anyonee and is not likely to. He heard no reply to his signal and changed his course while he could do so without running ashore or on a reef and coming into close proximity with another boat. No one is more opposed to reckless running of fast boats or automobiles than I am; and no one who knows Capt. George Harris would for a moment accuse him of reckless running.

W. K. Bixby.

New Postmaster Learning the Ropes.

Scott B. Smith, recently appointed postmaster of Warrensburgh, will take possession of the office on July 1. He is now familiarizing himself with the work under the guidance of Postmaster Robert Murray and his assistants, Arthur Irish and Miss Edna Harrington.

July 10 1915

CHARLES COLE DIES AT LAKE GEORGE

April 26 1915

Cold Contracted While Automobiling, Develops Fatal Attack of Pneumonia

LAKE GEORGE, April 25.—Charles Cole, during many years a prominent resident of Glens Falls, died at 4:30 o'clock yesterday morning in his home in Lake George, where he was engaged in the feed and grain business as a member of the firm of Selleck & Cole. Mr. Cole contracted a cold a week ago yesterday while on an automobile ride along the river road. During Wednesday he became seriously ill, and pneumonia developed.

Mr. Cole was the only descendant of Charles and Anna Thompson Cole and was born in Hudson Falls a little more than 53 years ago. After passing all his early life in Glens Falls and Hudson Falls at the age of 32 years he removed to Oshkosh, Wis., where he remained during 15 years, conducting a large and prosperous business. He returned to this vicinity seven years ago and three years later purchased a half interest in what is now the Selleck & Cole firm of Lake George.

The funeral services will be conducted at 2 o'clock Tuesday afternoon from his late home, Dr. Mills officiating. Interment will be made in Union cemetery, Hudson Falls.

ISAAC WORDEN

Isaac Worden, aged eighty-two years and the greater part of his life a resident of Lake George, died in that place Monday morning at 11:30 o'clock, at the home of his son, Frank H. Worden. Besides this son he leaves a widow, his second wife, one daughter, Mrs. Stewart D. Brown, of Albany, and a sister, Mrs. Jennie Patten, of Fort Edward. For many years Mr. Worden was a prominent contractor and builder and was also caretaker of the old Fort William Henry hotel when it was owned by T. Roessle & Son. The funeral was held at his son's home Saturday afternoon at 2:30 o'clock, the Rev. E. L. Miller, D. D., officiating. Burial in the Lake George Union cemetery.

INEXORABLE DEATH

Ends Activities of Albert Thieriot, D. & H. Hotel Manager.

WON SUCCESS IN CHOSEN FIELD

Formerly Conducted Delmonico's, World-Famous New York Restaurant— End Came Friday, at Home in Chestertown.

Aug 1 1915

A victim of indomitable energy, which prompted him to efforts beyond his strength, Albert Thieriot, manager of the Delaware and Hudson Company's hotel properties and dining car service, died Tuesday afternoon at 3 o'clock, at his home in Chestertown. His illness dated from last winter, when he suffered a severe attack of pneumonia at the Fort William Henry hotel, Lake George, where he was then stationed as resident manager. Though he recovered from the disease itself the after effects greatly impaired his vitality and after a time brought on a relapse of an old stomach trouble which gradually grew worse. However, he refused to heed the earnest advice of his physician, Dr. John M.

ALBERT THIERIOT.

Griffin, to take the rest he so greatly needed, allowing himself only a two weeks' respite from business cares at Atlantic City just before the opening of the Hotel Champlain at Bluff Point, on June 23, when he went there to assume the active management of that popular resort. From that point he also directed his subordinates in all details relating to the conduct of other D. & H. affairs under his supervision. In his weakened condition he was physically unequal to the self-imposed strain and last week he collapsed. His condition at once became serious.

GRAPHIC REPRODUCTION OF AUTO FIRE TRUCK PURCHASED BY CITY OF GLENS FALLS

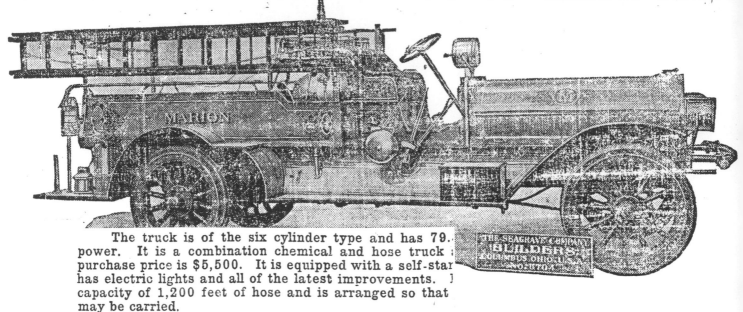

The truck is of the six cylinder type and has 79. power. It is a combination chemical and hose truck purchase price is $5,500. It is equipped with a self-star has electric lights and all of the latest improvements. capacity of 1,200 feet of hose and is arranged so that may be carried.

MRS. ELIZA J. PRUYN CLAIMED BY DEATH

Dies at Home in Elm street at the age of eighty-one years.

Mrs. Eliza J. Pruyn, widow of the late Samuel Pruyn, died this morning at 2 o'clock at her home, 20 Elm street. Mrs. Pruyn had been in failing health since last March but up to that time she was enjoying excellent health for a woman of her advanced age.

Mrs. Pruyn was born May 28, 1834 in Cambridge, Washington county. She was a daughter of the late Mr. and Mrs. James Baldwin In 1860 she was united in marriage to Samuel Pruyn who died in 1908. Mr. Pruyn was one of the original founders of the Finch, Pruyn and company. Since their marriage Mrs. Pruyn had resided in Glens Falls and forty years of her residence were passed in the home where she died. She was an estimable woman and her loss will be felt by the older residents of the community.

She is survived by three daughters, Mrs. Louis F. Hyde, Mrs. Maurice Hoopes and Miss Nellie K. Pruyn. A son, John Knickerbocker died in infancy.

The funeral services will be held Monday afternoon at 2:30 o'clock from the late residence in Elm street. The Rev. Dr. John Lyon Caughey will officiate. The remains will be placed in the family vault in the Glens Falls cemetery.

JOHNSBURG IS A TOWN OF BRIDGES

Has 164 Structures of Span from 20 to 50 Feet—Four to be Erected in Spring.

With a total of 163 miles of highway within its boundaries, the town of Johnsburg has 164 bridges of a span of from twenty to fifty feet or better than one for every mile of highway, to say nothing of hundreds of smaller bridges and culverts.

Plans have been completed for the erection this spring of four steel bridges in the town. One will have a span of forty-nine feet and will be erected across Mill creek. The other with a span of forty-five feet will be put in place across the North creek at Bert Straight's place. The other two bridges have a span of twenty feet each. The total cost of erecting the new structures, which will be modern in every way, including concrete floors, will be about $7,000.

Being located in the Adirondack watershed, the town has hundreds of streams, large and small, and it can boast of having more bridges than any other town in the state. The cost of the maintenace of bridges is no small item as has been found by Supervisor Fred Rogers and the other town officials and the expense has become an increased burden of late because of the heavy traffic brought about by automobiles, which necessitates close attention to the condition of the bridges.

SUMMER RESORT BUSINESS BOOMING

Big Demand for Hotel and Cottage Accommodations Forecasts a Busy Season.

Hon. L. W. Emerson yesterday during a business visit at Lake George, stated that the new Leland house at Schroon Lake is to be opened for Memorial day. The Emersons have undoubtedly hung up a new record in hotel construction in the brief space of time occupied in the erection of this modern summer hotel.

Mr. Emerson stated that the demand for cottages throughout the Adirondacks this spring is unprecedented and he looks for one of the best seasons in the history of Adirondack summer resorts. All cottages along the Bolton road at Lake George with the exception of several renting for $3,000 to $5,000 for the season, have been taken, and Deputy County Clerk Henry W. Sisson, who is interested in the Lake George real estate business, is authority for the statement that it is a hard matter to secure enough cottages to supply the demands that are daily being received.

DIES IN SOLDIERS' HOME.

County Treasurer Beecher W. Sprague has received notice from the Soldiers' Home at Bath of the death on February 15 of Charles Lamb, a former resident of Warrensburg. Burial was made at Bath. Lamb has relatives residing in Bolton and other parts of Warren county.

MRS. COFFIN DIES IN SCHUYLERVILLE

July 19 1915

Widow of Sanford Coffin Passes Away in Eighty-Eighth Year

Mrs. Catherine Wing Coffin died Saturday afternoon in the Schuylerville home of her granddaughter, Mrs. Edward C. Gow.

Mrs. Coffin was in her 88th year and was the daughter of Richard and Sally Newcomb Wing and had always resided in Glens Falls or in its immediate vicinity. Her father was a descendant of Abraham Wing, the founder of this community. In 1852, she was married to Sanford Coffin by Rev. A. J. Fennel, the pastor for so many years of the First Presbyterian church of Glens Falls.

The more than forty years of her married life were filled with loving endeavors for the best interests of her husband, her children and her home. After the death of her husband in 1893 she bravely took up the burdens and responsibilities of life, always insisting upon maintaining her own home where she could welcome her own family and her friends.

Although always frail in body, she was possessed of a well ordered mind. Perhaps her three strongest characteristics were her love, her sense of duty and her thrift; loyal sympathetic love for her family and friends, a sense of duty that never deviated to save herself and thrift that was self-sacrificing that others might benefit. Her family and friends well know and will always remember her keen sympathy with the plans and ambitions of the younger generation and her sincere interest in the advancement of all worthy causes; her abrupt manner of expressing her point of view, her original observations and the fact that her advice always had a kindly objective. Her staunch orthodox religious beliefs were powerful factors in her life as was also her patriotic love of country.

BE KIND TO THE LOVED ONES AT HOME.

Be kind to thy father, for when thou wast young
Who loved thee so fondly as he?
He caught the first accents that fell from thy tongue
And joined in thy innocent glee.
Be kind to thy father, for now he is old,
His locks intermingled with gray,
His footsteps are feeble, once fearless and bold—
Thy father is passing away.

Be kind to thy mother, for lo! on her brow
May traces of sorrow be seen.
Ah, well mayst thou cherish and comfort her now,
For loving and kind she hath been.
Remember thy mother, for you will she pray
As long as God giveth her breath.
With accents of kindness then cheer her lone way,
E'en to the dark valley of death.

MAY 20, 1915
SAGAMORE HOTEL WILL BE SMALLER

To Rebuild Hostelry With 155 Rooms and Surround it With 12 Cottages

TO OPEN FOR 1916 SEASON

Site of Old Hotel to Have Semi-Fireproof Building—Simpson Predicts Prosperous Future for American Hotels

A smaller but a more modern Sagamore hotel is to be rebuilt at Bolton and will be ready to open at the beginning of the 1916 season. Announcement to that effect was made last night to a reporter for The Post-Star by John B. Simpson of the Sagamore company, who is passing a few days in this vicinity and who tomorrow will go to Bolton with his guest, W. F. Reynolds of New York.

Plans for the hotel, revised only a few days ago by Mr. Simpson, call for the erection of a semi-fireproof four story building constructed of timbers and stucco with 155 rooms for guests. The old Sagamore hotel contained nearly 300 rooms. The decision not to have an absolutely fireproof building was reached after considerable investigation had revealed to the satisfaction of the management that a fireproof hotel on the shores of a lake could not help being damp, especially on being reopened after the winter and spring closed seasons.

The hotel will be constructed on the site of the hostelry and will be surrounded by about 12 well appointed and elaborately furnished bungalows. The latter will be for the accommodation of families who desire to pass an entire summer at Lake George. These people will dine in the main hotel and enjoy all its privileges, but will be allowed the added privilege of living by themselves separated if they so choose from the guests who remain only a short time at the hotel.

Mr. Simpson last evening expressed the opinion that the summer hotel trade of the future will be made up almost entirely of people who do not stay more than two or three days. The automobile has made it possible for persons to travel in luxury and east from point to point in the Adirondacks and Mr. Simpson is strong in the belief that a great majority of the summer visitors are better pleased with that plan than by the old one of staying continually at the one place.

Mr. Simpson said that 1915 was sure to be a good year for the summer hotels, but that 1916, 1917 and the four or five years to follow would be even better. In his opinion there will be practically no people leaving America during the next several years to travel in Europe, because of the ruin the war has brought and that not only will Americans remain at home but their wealthy neighbors of Europe will come here to pass the summers.

DROWNED IN LAKE GEORGE

Two New York Physicians Meet Death While Canoeing Near Tongue Mountain.

Dr. David B. Anderson and Dr. Morris Kusch, two young physicians recently made internes at Mt. Sinai hospital, in New York city, were drowned Thursday afternoon in Lake George, at Montcalm Point. Each was about twenty-five years of age.

The two young men arrived at Bolton Landing a week ago Sunday, to pass their vacation there at the T. P. Braley cottage. Thursday afternoon they set out for a canoe trip. While near Turtle Island they were advised by Erasmus C. Smith, a resident of the island, to discontinue their trip and remain with him over night, as the lake was extremely rough. The young men refused to listen to his advice and decided on paddling home, going down the west shore of the lake to Tongue Mountain. It is believed that as the canoeists reached Montcalm Point, at the end of Tongue Mountain, the heavy northwest wind caused their frail craft to capsize. The water at this point is very deep.

Because of the failure of the young men to put in an appearance at their boarding place, searching parties were organized, and worked all that night, but without success. Friday morning, however, the canoe was found three miles south of Tongue Mountain.

Dr. Kusch's father and Dr. E. Boas, of Columbia University, arrived at Bolton Friday, the latter offering a reward of fifty dollars each for the recovery of the bodies. They have not yet been found, however, and the grief-stricken father and friend have returned to the city.

COLE, CIRCUS MAN, LEAVES $5,000,000

Part Owner in Barnum and Bailey Show—Widow His Only Near Kin.

William Washington Cole, at one time a member of Cole Brothers' circus and later a part owner in the Barnum and Bailey shows, left an estate valued at $5,000,000, according to his will, which was filed with Surrogate Daniel Noble of Queens county last week. Mr. Cole died in Whitestone, L. I., on March 10. He left no children, brothers or sisters and beyond his widow, his next of kin are collateral relatives. Some are in England and in Scotland and it is said that some are in Africa.

TO CONSTRUCT HOTEL ON SAGAMORE SITE

Neither of New Building's Three Floors Will Have Any Corridors

July 24 1915

OTHER NOVEL FEATURES

BOLTON, July 23—It is expected that within the next month work will be started on the contract providing for the erection of a modern hotel on the site of the far famed Sagamore Hotel, which last spring was destroyed by fire.

A novel feature of the design lines in the fact that there will be no corridors, all rooms opening direct on large porches, which will encircle the building on all three floors, insuring a maximum of light and air and freedom from fire danger. There will be no private baths, but the equipment of the hotel in all respects will be thoroughly modern. The rates will be reasonable with a special dollar-a-day rate for long periods.

The hotel will stand on an eminence commanding a view of one of the most beautiful parts of the lake and will have ample shore frontage. It will be easily accessible by the Bolton state road, along which the "Millionaire Cottage Row" extends.

The company which is behind the project is entirely separate from The Sagamore Company and consists of Jules A. Thatcher, Walter Gates, Jerome Robinson, Louis and George Vandenburgh and several others.

MOTORCYCLIST BADLY INJURED.

news July 24

John L. Morehouse Forced to Take Fence by Careless Truck Driver.

9 15

John L. Morehouse, Horicon avenue, while returning from Bolton Landing about 7 o'clock Sunday night, on his Indian motorcycle, met a big motor truck running on the wrong side of the road and was forced to "take the fence" or be crushed by the big machine. He chose the first alternative and as a result had his right leg broken in two places, four toes fractured on his left foot, second finger and thumb of his left hand broken and a deep cut on his forehead. The occupants of the truck did not stop to ascertain the extent of his injuries or offer him any assistance. He was brought home by his father-in-law, who lives near the scene of the accident, and he was attended at his home by Dr. J. E. Goodman. His motorcycle was not greatly damaged.

OBITUARY.

news July 29 1916

JOHN D. HARRIS.

Having lived six years beyond man's allotted span of three score years and ten John D. Harris Monday morning laid down the burden of life and entered into rest eternal. He was ill little more than a week and death was caused by Bright's disease. A native of Thurman he left that town twenty-six years ago and came to Warrensburgh to make his home. For the past fifteen years he had been engaged in buying wool for the Warrensburgh Woolen company and he had a large circle of friends and acquaintances throughout the northern section by all of whom he was highly esteemed. He was the owner of the Harris block in which he occupied a suite of rooms.

Aaron Gates Randall.

Aaron Gates Randall died yesterday morning at 4 o'clock at his late home, 130 Bay street, aged seventy-six years. Mr. Randall had been in failing health for some months, yet he was confined to his room and bed scarcely two weeks, when he died from acute brights disease.

He was born in North Bolton on August 20, 1838, and lived there continually until the year 1900. Save three years spent in the 118 Regiment, N. Y. S, serving as adjutant in Captain Dennis Stone's company. In the year 1900, he and Mrs. Randall removed to to this city, where they have since lived with their daughter and son-in-law, Mr. and Mrs Isaac Tripp.

---

aug 12 1915

Small Boy Drowns in Lake George.

Donald Fenn, of Cambridge, Mass., while standing on the dock of the cottage of William Emerson, of Stillwater, on Lake George, was horrified, upon gazing into the water, to see the body of five-year-old James Frothingham, who a short time previous had been playing near the shore and dock. The body lay in six feet of water. Mr. Fenn jumped in and securing the body carried it to the dock. All efforts to restore life by means of artificial respiration failed. The boy was a son of City Judge and Mrs. E. V. Frothingham, of New York City.

A. T. KELLOGG DEAD; ILL THREE MONTHS

aug 23 1915

Superintendent of Hudson River Drive Dies In Bay Street Home

LIVED HERE SEVEN YEARS

Born in Minerva July 26, 1861, and Formerly Conducted Hotels at That Place and Warrensburg—Funeral Tomorrow

Ashley T. Kellogg, one of the best known men in Northern New York, and for many years in charge of the Hudson river log drive, died at 3:30 o'clock yesterday morning in his home, 84 Bay street, following an illness which extended from last May. Mr. Kellogg was a director of the Glens Falls Trust company, but had retired from active business, with the exception of his activities on the river each spring.

Mr. Kellogg was born in Minerva July 26, 1861, and, after receiving a common education in the schools of that place, opened a hotel which he conducted successfully until 17 years ago when he removed to Warrensburg where he took over the management of the Warren house. Seven years ago he came to Glens Falls and had since resided here. By thrift and close application to business, Mr. Kellogg amassed considerable money and with his removal to this city he retired from active business. He made countless friends during the years he was in the hotel business and was admired by all for his honesty and integrity.

Mrs. Kellogg died February 1, last. Mr. Kellogg was stricken ill May 13, and later underwent an operation in the Glens Falls hospital.

Algonquin Hotel, Bolton Landing, Lake George, N. Y.

RIVER VIADUCT IS NEARLY COMPLETED

Will be Inspected in Near Future by City and Town Officials.

Within two weeks the Hudson river viaduct between this city and South Glens Falls will be inspected by Mayor Griffing and the members of the Common Council and the Town Board of Moreau, preparatory to accepting the bridge from the contractors, Callanan and Prescott and the Concrete-Steel Engineering company of New York.

Bronze tablets, about two feet wide and three feet long bearing names of the city and town officials, as well as the contractors and engineering company who had charge of building the bridge are being placed at either end of the bridge. Two tablets will be placed at either end of the bridge. They are being placed in the arch of each pylon. On two tablets is the following inscription: "Hudson River bridge, designed by and erected under the direction of the Concrete-Steel Engineering company, consulting engineers of New York city. William Mueser, supervising engineer and Ernest H. Harder resident engineer. Built by Callanan and Prescott Inc., contractors of Albany. Moses J. Rabideau, superintendent of construction.

On the other two tablets is the following inscription:

"Hudson River Bridge, erected 1913-1915. City of Glens Falls. Common Council 1913-1914—W. Irving Griffing, mayor; Dennis McLaughlin, president; councilmen, Joseph P. Bickley, Powell J. Smith, Henry G. Taylor, James Williamson, Thomas Goundry, Loren F. Goodson, clerk; 1914-1915, John Reilley, president; J. Fred Acker, councilman."

"Town of Moreau, town board of Moreau 1913-1914. Austin L. Reynolds, supervisor; Frank J. Keenan, clerk; Justices, Edward R. Varney, John Blackburn, Henry C. Reynolds, R. S. Sherman, A. E. Sweet, superintendent of highways; John E. Hodgman, county superintendent of highways; 1914-1915, C. M. Cronin, supervisor; D. V. Newton, clerk; Justices, George H. Skym, William E. Washburn; W. E. Whipple, superintendent of highways."

In a few days the bronze railing for the spiral stairway leading down to Cooper's cave will be placed in position as well as a bronze tablet at the head of the stairway calling attention to the historic spot made famous by James Fenimore Cooper in his "Last of the Mohicans."

BRERETON AND WIFE AGREE TO SEPARATE

Star

Assemblyman Provides Annual Income for Support of Mrs. Helen Loop Brereton

It was learned yesterday from an authentic source that a separation has been affected between Assemblyman H. E. H. Brereton and his wife, Mrs. Helen Loop Brereton who during many years made their home at Diamond Point. There was no contest, the Republican Assemblyman making arrangements whereby his wife will receive an annual income which should more than supply her needs. This income is in part secured by a mortgage of $20,000 with interest payable at six per cent.

Mrs. Brereton is at present in the Diamond Point residence and refuses to discuss the separation. Mr. Brereton is performing his duties as a member of the finance committee of the Assembly and could not be reached last night by telephone.

It is understood that Mr. Brereton will retain his home in Diamond Point and will continue to make his permanent residence in Warren county. Mrs. Brereton will, according to rumor, reside in the vicinity of Lake George during the summer months of each year but will pass her winters either in California or Florida.

15/1915

Commodore Harrison B. Moore.

Commodore Harrison B. Moore of New York, who had a beautiful summer home near Baldwin-on-Lake George, died last week in his winter residence in Miami, Florida. Death was due to apoplexy, following Bright's disease. Commodore Moore was seventy-four years old, and besides his wife is survived by two sons and one daughter. He was well known in this city and throughout this section of the state, particularly at Lake George, where he ever took an active part in all undertakings having for their purpose the betterment of Old Horicon.

AGED ACCIDENT VICTIM RESTING COMFORTABLY

Andrew Eddy, 84 Years Old, of Lake George, Struck By Motorcycle

Times

Andrew Eddy, 84, Lake George, who yesterday suffered a fracture of his left leg when he was run down by a motorcycle in that village, was resting comfortably last night in the Glens Falls hospital. The aged man, it is said, stepped in front of the motorcycle while trying to dodge an automobile near the southern part of the village. The motorcycle was ridden by Ralph Casey of Schenectady and Albert Butler of Rotterdam Junction. They were arrested, but were released by Justice Bryant of Lake George in custody of their counsel, Walter A. Chambers.

HIT BY MOTORCYCLE, DIES IN HOSPITAL

June 10 1915

Andrew Eddy of Lake George died at 1 o'clock yesterday afternoon in the Glens Falls Hospital as the result of injuries sustained June 2 when he was struck by a motorcycle as he attempted to cross the highway a short distance north of the Lake George Court House. He was 79 years old. His remains this morning will be removed to his late home in Lake George.

ORVILLE BRANCH

Orville Branch, a successful farmer of Diamond Point, and a veteran of the Civil War, died Thursday morning, September 23, at his home in that community, after years of illness of Bright's disease.

THE NARROWS AND ISLANDS, LAKE GEORGE.

FIVE MEMBERS OF FAMILY DIE TRAIN HITS AUTO

Five members of a Whitehall family were killed and a sixth seriously injured at 3:30 o'clock Sunday afternoon when a northbound D. & H. train, traveling at 50 miles an hour, struck an automobile, driven by a deaf man, at the Bay street crossing.

His father, mother, sister, wife and baby dead, John Norton, 28 years old, the sole survivor of the ill-fated party lies on a cot in the Glens Falls hospital unaware that most of his family was wiped out by the catastrophe. To his repeated entreaties regarding his wife, the physicians and nurses only reply: "She's alive."

The dead are Mr. and Mrs. Nelson Norton, each about 65 years old; their daughter, Miss May Norton, 19 years old; their daughter-in-law, Mrs. John Norton, 30 years old, and the latter's daughter, Edith, five years old.

The deafness of Nelson Norton and a clump of trees which obstructed the view of the tracks were responsible for the accident.

Engineer King blew the whistle and, according to eye witnesses, the automobile swerved, as if the driver made an attempt to ditch it, and then took the road onto the tracks directly in the path of the onrushing train of 3 cars. John Nelson was thrown from the car at the crossing, his wife and baby were carried a distance of about 100 yards, and his father, mother and sister were carried on the pilot of the locomotive about 400 yards until the train was brought to a stop.

Persons who were on the scene immediately following the accident will never forget the sight. Strong men wept and tears were in the eyes of the members of the crew.

Mrs. John Norton was alive when bystanders reached her side. Opening her eyes, she asked in her dying breath:

"Where is my baby?"

A minute later she joined her baby and the other three victims in death.

The car, a Ford, was purchased by Nelson Norton about a month ago. Sunday morning the six victims left Whitehall to visit Mr. and Mrs. Nelson Norton's daughter, Mrs. Schuyler Crandall at Lake George. After passing the day there, the six started for home by way of Glens Falls. They drove down Bay road. The father and son were in the front seat and the three women and baby in the rear seat. When the car reached a point about 10 feet from the crossing, one of the occupants probably called the attention of the driver to the fact that a train was approaching as he swerved the auto toward the ditch and then righting it into the road drove onto the track.

The big engine, No. 444, struck the car squarely in the middle. John Norton was thrown to the ditch on the west side of the road and south of the tracks. The automobile was carried on the pilot. About 200 yards from the crossing, the rear seat became detached and fell to the side of the tracks and near this place Mrs. John Norton and her baby's body were found.

Chief of Police Fred G. Jenkins secured most of the possessions of the victims. The automobile was demolished, and souvenir seekers, or persons with dishonest motives yesterday removed most of the different parts of the car.

The clump of trees makes the Bay street crossing one of the most dangerous in this vicinity. It is about 100 yards outside the city, and consequently the Common Council has no authority over it. Walter K. Sumner, secretary of the Chamber of Commerce yesterday said an effort had been made last autumn to induce a Mr. Knoz who own the property to cut down the trees, but that the efforts was fruitless. R. E. Burger had a bill board there, but removed it on request from the Chamber of Commerce. The bill board, however, was of no consequence compared with the trees. Last winter a pair of sleighs stalled on the crossing and the driver barely had time to unhitch the horses before a train struck the sleigh. Three weeks ago, a train struck an automobile at the Ridge street crossing. The car was wrecked, but the driver escaped.

TWO SERIOUS FIRES

apl 15 1915

Bolton Landing Visited by Disastrous Conflagrations.

SUSPICION OF MANY AROUSED

Bungalow on Knauth Estate Burns Saturday Night—Residence Owned by Mrs. Sheridan Finkle Destroyed Monday.

Saturday night and Monday morning proved to be disastrous for the village of Bolton Landing, as fire on these occasions destroyed two dwellings, one being a bungalow built during the past winter on the Knauth state, and the other a house owned by Mrs. Sheridan Finkle and occupied by Dr. C. S. Wilson.

The first fire broke out about midnight Saturday, and before anything could be done to combat the flames, the structure was a mass of ruins. The bungalow, which was to be occupied by John Tabor on May 1, was erected during the past winter. The loss, partly covered by insurance, will amount to about $2,000. Mr. Tabor had moved a small portion of his furniture into the building, all of which was lost. It is thought by some that the fire was caused by an overheated furnace.

The rapid ringing of the Baptist and Methodist church bells awakened the Bolton villagers for the second time about 3 o'clock Monday morning, when they found, to their horror, that another fire was raging in their midst. The house owned by Mrs. Sheridan Finkle, and occupied by Dr. F. L. Wilson, was discovered to be on fire by Nelson Ormsby, who promptly aroused the neighbors. Dr. Wilson was alone in his room upstairs, his wife being away on a visit with her parents in Baltimore, when he discovered the presence of smoke, and in attempting to go down stairs, found it so dense as to render his passage out impossible. Returning to his room, the doctor pulled the bedstead up to the window, knotted the sheets into a rope, threw one of his two cats out of the window, and carrying the other in his arm, slid down to the ground in safety. The doctor was but partly dressed, but had managed to throw a suit of clothes out of the window. His desk, piano, and three or four chairs were taken from the lower rooms, the other furnishings being lapped up by the hungry flames. The house, practically a new one, was totally destroyed, entailing a loss of about $7,500, partially covered by a $3,000 insurance policy. Dr. Wilson's loss amounts to about $1,500.

At the time the conflagration was discovered, there were no electric lights turned on and no wind was blowing. The fire is said to have started in the bay window of the dining room, away from any stove or furnace. There was a small coal fire in the furnace, but not enough to do any harm. As this is the fourth fire within two weeks at Bolton, the villagers have become nervous, lest something may be wrong in their community. The first fire broke out at Elisha Middleton's farm house, from a defective chimney; another destroyed a house in North Bolton, owned by Charles Belden, the third and fourth being the ones mentioned above.

THE DOG.

I've never known a dog to wag
  His tail in glee he didn't feel.
Nor quit his old-time friend, to tag
  At some more influential heel.
The yellowest cur I ever knew
  Was, to the boy who loved him, true.

I've never known a dog to show
  Half-way devotion to his friend;
To seek a kinder man to know.
  Or richer, but unto the end
The humblest dog I ever knew
  Was, to the man who loved him, true.

I've never known a dog to fake
  Affection for a present gain—
A false display of love to make,
  Some little favor to attain.
I've never known a Prince or Spot
  That seemed to be what he was not.

But I have known a dog to fight
  With all his strength to shield a friend,
And, whether wrong or whether right,
  To stick with him until the end.
And I have known a dog to lick
  The hand of him that men would kick.

And I have known a dog to bear
  Starvation's pangs from day to day
With him who had been glad to share
  His bread and meat along the way.
No dog, however mean or rude,
  Is guilty of ingratitude.

The dog is listed with the dumb.
  No voice he has to speak his creed.
His messages to human come
  By faithful conduct; and by creed
He shows, as seldom mortals do.
  A high ideal of being true.

ERVIN J. SMITH NATIONAL DETECTIVE AGENCY INCORPORATED IN NEW YORK

Former Glens Falls Boy, for Several Years Assistant Manager of the William J. Burns Agency's New York Office, President of Newly Incorporated Concern With Prominent Associates

Another Glens Falls boy, Ervin J. Smith, who left this city a few years ago to seek fame and fortune, has made good—at least so far as fame is concerned and there is every reason to believe that fortune, if it can be secured through faithful, efficient and honest service, will be forthcoming.

The Ervin J. Smith National Detective Agency, with headquarters at 13-21 Park Row, has been incorporated and has been chartered to do business.

Associated with Mr. Smith, who has been elected president, are Hoey E. Hennessy, son of John A. Hennessy, secretary and treasurer; Louis A. Sarecky, secretary to Former Governor William Sulzer and William J. Ellis, all New York men.

The agency is incorporated for $6,000 and has mapped out a program of activities which is bound to gain for it wide-spread recognition in its particular field of endeavor.

Ervin J. Smith.
President Ervin J. Smith, National Detective Agency.

For fifteen years Mr. Smith has been engaged in investigation and research work in New York city, having been associated with the William J. Burns International Detective Agency, as assistant manager of the New York office. Possessed of almost indominable energy and never resting until he has accomplished whatever task he has in hand, Mr. Smith carefully considered plans which he had for some time had in mind, and, spurred on by the advice of staunch friends of national and international reputation, finally resigned his position with the Burns agency, and immediately set about organizing an agency of his own.

Mr. Smith has learned the detective business from the ground up and is thoroughly familiar with all its branches. As an operator he has few equals and no superiors; as a manager, his efficiency has long been recognized. To recount the important cases which have been successfully handled under the personal direction of this detective genius would require columns. Suffice to say that Erving J. Smith has never yet failed to render service which elicited grateful praise from clients and has made the name of Smith synonymous with efficiency.

One of Mr. Smith's warmest friends is Former President Theodore Roosevelt, for whom this youthful Sherlock has performed many an important task. Hanging in Mr. Smith's office is a large autographed photograph of Col. Roosevelt, presented to Mr. Smith some months ago after he had accomplished a most difficult task entrusted to him by the Former President.

"Work hard and be true to every trust reposed in you and success will be yours." This is the motto which Young Smith adopted when he set out to carve his name in the Hall of Fame. That motto he has kept ever before him and he has succeeded.

No more significant tribute can be paid Mr. Smith, than is contained in the following excerpt from a letter written recently by a prominent New York business man, who is one of the country's most noted men:

"Smith is going into business for himself, and I feel sure that before many years have rolled by he will have established for himself an agency which will be in a class by itself. I have employed him on several different occasions and always I have found him to be honest, efficient and absolutely to be trusted in every spot and place. Professionally, he is one of the leaders in his profession, and his private life, I know, is above reproach. He is young and ambitious, but he never allows ambition to lead him astray. He has set out to win and those who know him best have no hesitancy in acclaiming their confidence in his ability to accomplish whatever he sets out to accomplishing and coming through with a clean record."

The operators employed by the Erving J. Smith agency include some of the best men in the business and all of them have been chosen solely because of their ability and honesty of purpose.

In a few words, it will be the aim of the Ervin J. Smith National Detective Agency to render efficient and honest service to clients.

Dwelling House Burned at Bolton.

Elisha Middleton's farm house on Bolton Hill, about a mile from Bolton Landing, was destroyed by fire at 9:30 o'clock Tuesday morning. The loss is about $1,500 with no insurance. The fire started from a defective chimney and was discovered by Clarence Monroe, who was passing the house. With no fire-fighting facilities whatever nothing could be done to check the flames. Mr. and Mrs. Clarence Putney occupied the house and the owner boarded with them. Most of the furniture belonged to Mr. Middleton and only part of that on the ground floor was saved. The house was a two-story frame building. *news Apl 3/1913*

Mrs. Lucinda Harris and Mrs. Walter Gates and children, Ferris and Zilpha, of Bolton Landing, were in camp on the fair grounds last week, with Mrs. Harris' son, Daniel Harris, of Queensbury, who had charge of a fine exhibit of cattle from the farm of H. H. Hubbell.

The watch fires kindled on these hills
Were lighted not in vain,
But burned to beacon victory
On Yorktown's classic plains.

FIVE BUILDINGS DESTROYED; 50 THREATENED BY FLAMES

Losses Mount to $50,000 as Fierce Forest Fire Rages On Carpenter Mountain as Result of Blaze Which Starts in Ice House at Riverside---Bottling Works, Barn and Two Houses Consumed---Cottages On Camp Grounds Saved

Post aStar 7/9/13

(Special to The Post-Star)

RIVERSIDE, April 26.—Five buildings are in ashes and a fierce forest fire is spreading over Carpenter Mountain tonight as the result of a blaze which started at 3 o'clock this afternoon in an ice house owned by the Riverside bottling company. Fifty cottages on the famous Methodist camp meeting grounds were threatened, but it was believed tonight that danger of their destruction had passed. The total loss to the buildings is about $50,000, but owing to the fact that the fire is still spreading rapidly through the forests it is impossible to estimate the total loss.

A few minutes after the woods caught fire rain began to fall, but stopped within two minutes. Residents paid little attention to the forest fire, directing their attention toward the protection of the cottages and consequently the fire raged unchecked until it assumed such proportions that it was impossible to stop it. The Conservation Commission was notified late this afternoon.

The origin of the fire is unknown, but it was said there was no suspicion of incendiarism. From the ice house the flames spread to a large barn also owned by the company and then to the bottling works, a large two story structure. There was no fire fighting apparatus in the hamlet and the few men here forced to fight the fire with the aid of buckets. Most of the furniture had been removed from the residences of the McCarthy brothers, but it caught fire after being taken to what was considered a place of safety and was totally destroyed. The houses also were soon in ashes. A sharp wind which preceded the shower carried sparks across the Hudson river onto the mountains and within a few minutes several fires were burning in the woods. Meantime the volunteer fire fighters were busy saving the Standard Oil Company's plant and the grain store of T. J. Smith & Son.

Only one of the 50 cottages on the camp grounds was occupied and the occupant, Henry Raymond, moved out. The Hudson River at that point is about 300 feet wide and the grounds are on its bank. It was feared that the fire only 300 feet distant would communicate to the cottages.

The bottling works was owned by McCarthy Brothers and Joseph Martin.

THE OAKS BURNED.

Well-Known Cossayuna Lake Hotel Eaten Up by Flames—A Defective Chimney Caused the Blaze.

The Oaks Hotel at Cossayuna Lake was completely destroyed by fire this morning, with a loss of more than $20,000, which is partly covered by insur-

July 2 1910

the blaze spread with startling rapidity. There was no fire protection. The wind, which soon accomplished the destruction of the hotel, also kept the blaze away from the cottages nearby, so that the main building was the only one touched. The fire originated in the attic, and is believed to have been caused by a defective chimney. Many guests were expected to arrive to-day and to-morrow. Bookings in advance made it likely that the hotel would be well filled before the

THE OAKS HOTEL AT COSSAYUNA LAKE.

Widely Known and Popular Hotel at Cossayuna Lake That Was Destroyed By Fire This Morning With Loss of $20,000—Season Had Just Opened.

ance. The hotel was owned by John Liddle, who was its proprietor until this year, when it was leased to Derrick & Buck. The season was just opened, and it was said that the first patrons arrived while the fire was in progress. The fire started about 9 o'clock this morning, and, fanned by a strong east wind,

Fourth of July. The hotel was located on a wooded promontory extending out nearly to the centre of the lake. Its location gave it full command of all the natural beauties of the lake and shore. The Oaks accommodated about 100 guests. It was a well built, handsome structure, practically surrounded by wide, double decked piazzas.

FIRE AT RIVERSIDE

1915

Bottling Works of Riverside Distributing Company Destroyed.

SPARKS START A FOREST FIRE

Three Buildings of Plant and Homes of Two Proprietors Wiped Out With All Contents--Stanley Timber Lot Swept.

9/29 news

A spark from the smokestack of the Riverside Distributing Company's bottling house at Riverside, lodging in the shingle roof of an adjoining building belonging to the plant, Monday afternoon started a fire which destroyed five buildings and practically all of their contents, including the main building of the works, the large barn and ice house and the homes of William J and Jerry T. McCarthy, who, with Joseph Martin, comprise the membership of the corporation. The loss will aggregate about $25,000, partially covered by insurance in the C. W. Cool agency, of Glens Falls. The plant was entirely wiped out.

Carried by a high wind, sparks from the burning buildings set fire to the forest on the camp-meeting grounds of the Riverside Grove Association, across the river, and the flames swept through the dry leaves with such rapidity that Carpenter Mountain, in the rear of the camp-meeting grounds, was soon a mass of flames. About fifty cottages in the Riverside grove were greatly endangered, but were saved through the exertions of a large body of firefighters who had come from all directions in response to the alarm and telephone calls for aid.

Forest Ranger R. T. Armstrong, of Johnsburgh, took charge of the fight on the forest lads and had a force of about thirty-five men to assist him. About 350 acres of valuable timber lands were swept by the fire, owned mostly by H. F. Stanley, of Riverside.

Mrs. Calista Gates *true*

Mrs. Calista Gates, widow of Franklin Gates, for many years a well known hotel man at Lake George, died this afternoon at 12:12 o'clock at the home of her son, Milford R. Gates, 12 William street. Mrs. Gates was eighty-one years old. During the past few months she had been quite ill and owing to her advanced age was unable to withstand the illness. Mrs. Gates was born in Vaughn's Corners. She was, before marriage, Calista Vaughn, daughter of Russell and Betsey Vaughn. For more than twenty-five years she and her husband managed the East Lake George hotel at Kattskill Bay. About nine years ago they came to Glens Falls to reside. About seven years ago Mr. Gates died. The surviving relatives are one son and four daughters, Milford R. Gates, Mrs. G. W. Jones, Mrs. Belle Brayman, Mrs. Frank Herald and Mrs. Warren Smith of this city. The funeral arrangements have not been completed. *Oct 8 1914*

PARENTS MOSTLY TO BLAME

A pastor in one of the large Vermont churches preached a splendid sermon last Sunday on human sympathy; its application or want of application to present day conditions. The sermon so impressed one of the congregation that he took occasion to express himself through the public press and draw lessons therefrom. The judge, for such he was, makes allusion to two lads whom he but a short time ago sentenced to imprisonment for violation of the law. Shortly after their release, one of them was again brought before the magistrate, and the heartbroken mother pleaded for her boy, saying she did not know he was going with bad boys.

The judge then asks: "Why didn't she know? No good reason can be given why she did not know. It was her duty to know what company her boy was keeping, and why he was out roaming the city at all hours of the night. What are the fathers and mothers in this city thinking of? Why don't they know that their boys are out nights consorting with vile women on the streets? Why don't they know that their girls, eleven, twelve and fourteen years of age, are almost nightly at the postoffice and other places keeping clandestine appointments with the boys, and many of them vile boys of the city!"

The judge then sounds a note of warning to fathers and mothers of children of impressionable age. Live closer to your children, keep your eye on them, teach them that their proper place evenings is by the family fireside. Know that they are not mingling with vile associates.

REMEMBERS TITANIC

It was on the tenth of April, three
years ago today,
In that busy town of South Hampton,
I stood upon the quay.
There were thousands there beside
me, a delightful sight to see,
For that mighty ship, "Titantic" was
to sail across the sea.
I stood and watched, and wondered
as the passengers went by,
For no one thought of danger, as they
said their last good bye.

Off she sailed, in mystic splendor—
What could hurt this mighty
queen?
Fifteen thousand tons of steel work
and greatest ever seen,
Yet 'twas but a few days later, all on
board were gay and bright,
When a crash was heard, like thunder, in the stillness of the night.
"All hands on deck" was shouted;
willingly did all obey,
While a wireless they were sending,
full two hundred miles away.
"We have struck a mighty iceberg"
was the message that was passed,
"And need assistance badly, for we
are sinking fast."
Alas, the cry was answered, "We are
coming right away."

"Launch the life boats, boys, do your
duty nobly, too;
Then none can call us cowards, if we
do what Britons do;
First the women, then the children,
and we can hopeful be,"
While the band was sweetly playing
"Nearer My God, to thee."
                    MISS SUSIE McMAHON.

HEAVY FROST DOES THOUSANDS OF DOLLARS' DAMAGE TO GROWING CROPS

Times May 22 1915

Ice Varying in Thickness from an Eighth to a Quarter of an Inch Forms in Many Sections—Temperature Hovers Between Twenty and Thirty.

Jack Frost put in an appearance last night and before sunrise this morning had succeeded in doing thousands of dollars worth of damage to growing crops in this vicinity.

From many sections of Warren, Washington and Saratoga counties came reports today that ice had formed, varying from an eighth to a quarter of an inch in thickness and the temperature hovered between twenty and thirty degrees.

At Harry Waite's Hill View farm, north of the Brickyard, it was said today that upwards of three acres of green peas had been destroyed. It was planned to have these peas in the market not later than June 10 but now that replanting has been made necessary home grown green peas from the Waite farm will not be procurable before the latter part of July. Tomatoes and sweet corn in big quantities, were destroyed and potatoes were given a setback, but it is believed that they will resprout.

At the Wing farm in Kingsbury it was stated that peas were unharmed but that string beans and sweet corn were badly damaged. Wing Brothers had set out 4,000 tomato plants and of these fully one-half were destroyed. Cucumbers, squashes and pumpkins were destroyed and from present indications there will be only about a half-crop of strawberries.

Glens Falls gardeners were hard hit by the frost putting the quietus on many a "Breaks Record for Early Peas" story.

That the frost was general throughout the state is indicated by dispatches received today by The Times.

BOLTON'S BOOSTERS

Most interesting has been the work in the school gardens. They have extended from the Huddle far up on the hills to Edgecomb pond and North Bolton. Little children of seven and eight years, as well as the older ones, have toiled over their little plots most conscientiously. Two girls have the highes marks for plots free from weeds. The North Bolton school district again has been awarded the prize for the best average of gardens and therefore will keep the silver cup won last year. The fine display of the children's vegetables at the flower show was one of the best features of the exhibition.

A noticeable improvement along our highroad is that the offensive dump of last year has been made beautiful by a fine growth of squash vines.

A condition of the highroad that does not improve is that of Finkle hill and northwards with its bumps, hollows and inequalities.

Two lectures were arranged for the association during the spring and summer at the Navaho theatre. The first, on May 26, was by Miss Lona Minns, instructor at Cornell, on "Gardens and Gardening." with many fine slides. There was a large attendance and the lecture was of much value to the prospective gardeners, with its many suggestions for color and arrangement.

The other lecture, on July 26, was by Dr. Tarleton H. Bean, fish culturist of the State Conservation commission, who gave his services and all expenses. Dr. Bean gave a most instructive talk, with many slides of the fish hatcheries and different varieties of fish of the state and their distribution through its lakes, showing the great increase of food thereby provided by the state. A new hatchery has been established at Warrensburgh which will be the source of supply for Lake George.

In consequence of a sad accident at the lake this summer, a lungmotor has been purchased by a number of members of the association to be kept at the service of the community for use in cases of drowning or suffocating. It will be kept at the central telephone office for use in emergencies.

The greatest need of the Bolton association now is for a larger membership of the all-the-year-round people. With the increasing expenses for cash prizes, etc., the yearly dues do not meet the demand and a reserve is drawn upon each year. It is therefore urged that each member bring in a new member for the coming year.

MRS. MARY H. LOINES,
President.

"Dick" Whitby to Join Sousa's Band.

Richard A. Whitby, a former Warrensburgh boy, has signed an eight months contract with Sousa's band, beginning April 1. Mr. Whitby has for some time been engaged in orchestral work at the Palace theatre, in New York. Mar 11 1915

ROB MURRAY DOUBLES.

Two Men at Large Exact Duplicates of Warrensburgh Traveling Man.

It is said that every man has a double somewhere in the world. So seldom do they come together, however, that when they do it occasions wonder and remark. Not once in seven million times though will there be found within a radius of 200 miles three men, not related in any way, who are almost exact duplicates of each other, looking so nearly alike that each will pass for the others among their friends and acquaintances.

Former Postmaster Robert Murray, of Warrensburgh, now a traveling salesman for a wholesale carpet house, is one of such a set of triplets who live within two hundred miles of each other in this section of the Empire state. The others are James D. Keating, of Fort Edward, traveling salesman for the Troy Paper company, and James Dolan, of Canton, district attorney of St. Lawrence county.

Fortunately, all of these gentlemen are law abiding citizens, well settled down and not given to cutting up any kind of didos which might get the others into trouble or place them in embarrassing positions. "Jim" Keating, before he made his present business connection, was for twenty years or more a printer, and this, in the eyes of a member of the craft, is a sufficient guarantee that he's all right. Attorney Dolan, occupying the position he does, is, of course, beyond suspicion, while everybody in this vicinity is sure that Rob Murray always goes straight.

Every little while someone will drop into a seat on a train and sit down by Mr. Murray and begin to talk as he thinks to Mr. Keating, and Keating is constantly meeting and being greeted by Murray's friends and acquaintances who think he is Murray. Murray had heard for a long time of Keating and Keating had heard of Murray, but they had not met each other until one day last summer in a Plattsburgh hotel when they came face to face.

Keating was ushered into the dining room by a waitress who sat him at a table; another girl came in and said, "Don't put Mr. Murray there as he likes to sit at that table over there." As the girls were talking another man entering the room caught their eyes and they stood as though petrified, for there was Murray being seated at the table that Murray liked to sit at.

Later, in the office of the hotel, Keating went up to Murray and said "I am very glad to meet you Mr. Keating," and then Murray dropped to the fact that he was face to face with the double he had heard so much about.

Mr. Murray has never met District Attorney Dolan, of Canton, but, Mr. Keating has had some amusing experiences in being taken for him.

---

news Apl 29 1915

Hollis Persons Bolton Highway Patrolman.

Hollis Persons was appointed state road patrolman in Bolton, instead of Leslie Persons, as stated in our last issue.

THE "HAWKEYE," A ONE-STEP HYDROPLANE ON LAKE GEORGE.

This is a twenty-six-foot hydroplane with a twelve-cylinder Van Blerck motor, built by The Hacker Boat Company of Watervliet and owned by a syndicate of Lake George men, with A. L. Judson as Chairman. It was built for the Gold Cup Races on Lake George last summer, but failed to win because of breakdowns. The chain drive, where the break occurred, has been replaced with a gear drive and the Hawkeye is expected to give an account of itself in racing this summer. It has a guaranteed speed of fifty miles per hour.

Troy Times May 8, 1915

BOLTON LANDING.

Elmer Dickinson is having a bath room built in his house.

Isaac Stafford is improving the appearance of his house by giving it a new coat of paint.

Bert Lamb spent Saturday and Sunday in Saratoga Springs at the meeting of the Troy conference.

Miss Eloise Cummings, of Glens Falls, spent her Easter vacation here as the guest of her father.

Our warm and delightful weather and the recent rains have started the grass up finely, but it is yet quite dry.

Leslie Persons' new motor truck came last week and is now in use as an express between here and Glens Falls. *Apl 15 1915 news*

On Easter Sunday, Leah Vandenburgh and Ursula Smith were baptized in the Methodist church. In the evening a program of recitations and musical selections was rendered.

The masquerade ball given last week by the local lodge of Rebekahs was a great success. It was held in Navajo hall, music by Mrs. Elizabeth Duell and Mr. Ward. Over $30 was taken by the Rebekahs.

Gordon Jones, who has been living in Montreal, Canada, several years, is now in Schenectady, where he has a fine position repairing automobiles. Mrs. Jones and their little daughter, visiting here, have now joined him in the electrical city.

M. H. Tanner's pet horse, old Jack, suffered several days last week from lock jaw, caused by getting a nail in his foot. Everything possible was done to relieve his distress and for a time he seemed likely to recover, but grew worse and died Saturday night.

The Rev. S. J. Liberty was in Saratoga the past week in attendance at the Troy conference, of which he is a member. He is to be stationed the coming year at Lyon Mountain, in the Saranac Lake region. The townspeople in general will miss him and his family very much.

Mrs. Sarah Gates has rented her living rooms to Dr. and Mrs. E. L. Wilson, who have now moved in.

We are having unusually warm weather for April and vegetation is showing the effects of it, even though the ground is very dry.

The Rev. S. J. Liberty officiated at the marriage of George S. Middleton and Miss Daisy Scripter, both of Bolton, on the evening of the 5th inst.

Rev. and Mrs. J. S. Prudom, formerly of Lyon Mountain, took up their residence in the Methodist Episcopal parsonage Friday, the church here and the one at North Bolton being Mr. Prudom's charge. *news*

Mr. and Mrs. L. D. Waters, of Horicon, motored here in their new car one day last week. They expect to reside here this summer, Mrs. Waters having recently purchased a house and lot of her brother, Swenson Van Denburgh.

BOLTON LANDING

BOLTON LANDING, May 26—Samuel T. Harrington, sr., 87, died May 16 in the home of his son, Samuel, in Warrensburg. He is survived by five children, Mrs. Alfred Duell and Mrs. Orlin Pratt of Bolton, Mrs. Jack Morehouse of Chester, and Mrs. William Fuller of Warrensburg, besides the son mentioned; also by twenty-three grandchildren and eight great grandchildren.

A daughter recently was born to Mr. and Mrs. Henry Baker.

Miss Marian Miller of Wardboro has entered the Union school here for the remainder of the term.

Rev. D. J. Griffith, a student from Hamilton college, who supplied the pulpit of the local Baptist church last summer and was well liked, will be here the coming season. He will preach his first sermon next Sunday morning. Mr. Griffith also will preach at the new Vermont schoolhouse the same as last year. Mrs. A. Duell and Mrs. S. P. Dudley recently started the Sunday school there and will continue it during the summer. *May 2? 1916*

BOLTON.

Mrs. Mary L. Vandenburgh of Bolton yesterday in Surrogate's Court turned the tables upon her brother-in-law, Lewis Vandenburgh, who was endeavoring to secure letters of administration on the estate of Mrs. Vandenburgh's husband, the late F. Swenson Vandenburgh. Lewis Vandenburgh made application for letters Tuesday and citations were issued, returnable June 1. Upon receiving her citation the widow consulted her attorney and yesterday applied for letters in her own behalf. Because of the widow's legal right of priority to administer the affairs of her husband's estate Judge Raley granted her the letters. The estate consists of $8,000 personal property and $5,000 real estate. *Mau 22 1915*

C. J. PROWSE PURCHASES BUILDING AT 92 GLEN

Times ? May 3, 1916

Charles J. Prowse has purchased of H. McKie Wing the building at 92 Glen street, occupied on the ground floor by J. C. White's cigar store. The adjoining building, in which Mr. Prowse's restaurant is located, is also owned by Mr. Prowse. In the near future, the new owner is planning on removing the ground floor partition between the two stores and enlarging his restaurant. A single front entrance will be made with an upstairs entrance at the side. When completed, the new restaurant will be one of the best, if not the best and most up-to-date restaurants in this part of the state.

Troy Times may 22, 1915

From painting in DeWitt Clinton High School, New York, copyrighted by C. Y. Turner.

OPENING OF THE ERIE CANAL, OCTOBER 26, 1825.

The formal opening of the eastern section of the new Barge Canal west from Troy by Governor Whitman and state officials last Saturday recalls the historic event ninety years ago of the formal opening of the original Erie Canal. Governor Clinton worked for years to get the Erie Canal and it was opened while he was Governor, being a great achievement for that day before the railroads were built and meant much for the commercial development of New York state, a development which the Barge Canal is expected to enhance. The scene, depicted by the painting, represents the packet boat, decked with garlands, in which Governor Clinton and a party of friends made the first trip from Buffalo to Troy and thence down the Hudson River to Albany and New York. The other pictures of the group were not intended for portraits, but curiously enough the woman seated in the picture is said to resemble Miss Catherine Smith, who afterward became the second wife of Governor Clinton, who was a widower at the time of the opening of the canal.

THE STATE CENSUS

Field Work to Begin June 1 and Continue Two Weeks.

WARREN COUNTY ENUMERATORS

Appointments for Various Towns Announced by Secretary of State— P. H. Haselton, of Glens Falls, Supervisor.

Every five years the state of New York counts the people within it's borders and through the agents who procure the names secure also other data useful for statistical purposes. The last count was made in 1910 in connection with the United States census. Another is therefore due this year and the field work will be commenced, it is expected, about June i. Enumerators for Warren county have been appointed by Secretary of State Hugo, with Philemon H. Haselton, of Glens Falls, as supervisor. The enumerators for the various towns, one in each election district, are as follows:

Bolton—Rupert Gates.
Caldwell—S. Gordon Gill.
Chester—District 1, Louis Young, of Chestertown; district 2, Clayton Russell, of Pottersville.
Glens Falls—First Ward, District 1, Henry Gurney; District 2, Henry Buckley; Second Ward, District 1, Joseph Thieriot; District 2, C. L. Wagner; Third Ward, District 1, S. M. Shapera; District 2, B. F. Cowles; Fourth Ward, Earl F. Hall; Fifth Ward, District 1, William Carpenter; District 2, William Wood.
Hague—Noble Waters.
Horicon—Henry W. Smith.
Johnsburgh—District 1, George M. Waddell; District 2, Earl Rogers; District 3, Harry E. Bentley.
Luzerne—Clarence W. Hall.
Queensbury—District 1, James Riley; District 2, Charles Coffin; District 3, Homer Hewitt; District 4, Harry Gleason.
Stony Creek - Hartwell Austin.
Thurman—James A. Lillibridge.
Warrensburgh—District 1, Milon U. Brown; District 2, Carroll E. Harrington.

Maps of each election district are now being made at the census office in Albany for the use of the enumerators. The map of each district is being photographed and a set of three prepared in each case. One of these is placed in the portfolio, which contains the field sheets of the enumerators, with a description of the district. Another is filed with the secretary of state, and the third will be filed with the supervisor in each county.

The instruction book for enumerator is also being prepared. In addition to counting the people of the state, which is the primary object of the state census, the enumerators will be expected to obtain more additional data that has ever been asked before. They will be required to set down the residence, relationship to the head of the family, color,

---

JOKE APPRECIATED BY ASSEMBLYMAN

Ezra Cilley of Bolton Gets One Vote for Member of
Sept 30 1912 — *Times*
Assembly.

One vote cast in the Republican primaries Tuesday for Ezra Cilley of Bolton for the nomination of member of assembly afforded much amusement to Assemblyman Brereton, though the significance of the vote cannot be appreciated by but few unless they know the reason for the vote being cast and the assemblyman has no objection of letting the reason be told.

Several years ago a local concern, one of whose members resides in the Third ward, and who has a wide reputation as a humorist, secured a judgment against Cilley for goods sold. Supplementary proceedings were commenced and during the time they were pending Cilly is alleged to have disposed of his interest in a wood lot in Bolton. Charges of contempt of court were preferred against Cilley and he was sentenced to the county jail for six months. This was in the summer, when Cilley's time was required on his farm, there being nobody there but his wife and little children to care for the cattle and crops.

Assemblyman Brereton became interested in the matter because of the pitiful conditions at the Cilley home, and Cilley being unable to pay up his indebtedness as long as he was kept in jail, the assemblyman used his influence to secure his release from jail, which was brought about a month after he was sentenced.

Some time later the assemblyman mailed some campaign literature to the member of the local firm, who is a resident of the Third ward and a few days later it was returned to him with the inscription "You had better give this to Cilley." Assemblyman Brereton, therefore, is not at a loss to know who cast the vote for Cilley and enjoyed a hearty laugh today in the office of the Board of Elections when his attention was called to the fact.

---

9 1915

Miss Daisy Burbank of Bolton and Adelbert Stiles of Fort Ann were united in marriage at 7 o'clock last evening by Rev. O. S. Newell in the home of Mr. and Mrs. Charles Mahoney, 29 Davis street.

The bride was attended by her sister, Miss Rose Burbank and John Stiles acted as best man for his brother, the groom. After a brief wedding trip, Mr. and Mrs. Stiles will go to Shelving Rock where they will make their home during the summer.

BARTLETT-BOLTON.

William Bartlett, of Graphite, and Miss Nora Bolton, of Horicon, were married on the 16th inst., at Horicon. They will reside in Graphite.

grt May 30 1915

AGED CHIPPEWA CHIEF.

cently when Minneapolis entertained this tried and true friend of the pale-face as an honor guest. Though it was not his first visit to Minneapolis it was the first time anybody now living in the Northwestern city had seen him, for Minneapolis was only a fort garrisoned by a company of Revolutionary soldiers when, as a boy, the surviving chieftain of the once powerful Chippewa nation watched the men of his tribe smoke the peace pipe with strangers who came up the river to hold council near the Falls of St. Anthony. Wonderful changes were noted with stoical calm, but there was satisfaction in the breast of Wa-be-na-gwe-wes. His life-long faith in the white man was justified by the marvels he saw and experienced.

One hundred and twenty-nine years old by his own reckoning, and his existence as a youth vouched for by the government records of 116 years ago, the Chippewa chieftain seems to have been forgotten by death. Winter storms and summer suns have wrinkled his face and withered his body almost beyond belief, but the flame of life burns brightly in the depths of the keen-seeing eyes which first opened to the light before Washington became president, when the Indian roamed at will through all the wilderness empire west of the Mississippi river.

A clergyman tells an amusing story, as reported in a London paper, of a worthy vicar in a rural parish who had waxed eloquent in the interest of foreign missions one Sunday and was surprised on entering the village shop during the week to be greeted with marked coldness by the old dame who kept it. On asking the cause the good woman produced a half-crown from a drawer and, throwing it down before him, said: "I marked that coin and put it on the plate last Sunday, and here it is back in my shop. I knowed well them poor Africans never got the money."—New York Globe.

8,000 HEAR ADDRESS BY WHITMAN IN BANK SQUARE

Governor Pays Tribute to Prosperity of Glens Falls, the Success of Its Industries and the Fine Appearance of Its Buildings---Praises Work of Agricultural, Health, Highway and Educational Departments --- Three Thousand School Children Wave Flags as Executive's Car Passes Them

Glens Falls yesterday extended a hearty welcome to Governor Charles S. Whitman, who delivered an address at noon in Bank Square, in connection with Merchants' and Farmers' Week. Eight thousand people, including 3,000 school children, heard the address, which was brief and mostly upon the state and different state departments.

Governor Whitman was met at the river viaduct by the reception committee in about 40 cars, and the guest of honor and his hosts made a short parade before stopping in Bank Square. The school children had been lined up on both sides of the street through which the parade passed, and as the governor's car passed them, they waved small American flags. The governor was deeply impressed. He smiled and doffed his hat to the kiddies and the grown-ups who cheered him. The students from St. Mary's Academy carried large banners, bearing such inscriptions as St. Mary's Academy," "Interscholastic Champs," etc.

The blowing of whistles was the signal to those in Bank Square that the procession was approaching. The band, stationed on the Rockwell House piazza, played national airs. Daylight fireworks were exploded.

Governor Whitman rode in Byron Lapham's car. The other occupants of the machine were the governor's military secretary, J. Augustus Kellogg, and George E. Goodson, chairman of the executive committee of the Merchants' and Farmers' Week organization.

A platform had been erected on the sidewalk in front of the Rockwell House and the appearance of the governor on the platform was the sign for an outburst of applause. Members of the reception committee also occupied seats on the platform.

Mr. Kellogg introduced the governor, and referred to the fact that two of his predecessors were natives of Glens Falls.

The "Show Me III," owned by W. K. Bixby of St. Louis, and used at his beautiful home at Bolton Landing. The six-cylinder engine drives the boat better than thirty-two miles per hour straightaway, and in a fifteen-mile race with six hairpin turns the elapsed time was twenty-nine minutes.

Tho' you're thrown with the crowd, work above them,
   Do more than your share; it will pay.
Someone will see and remember the man
   Who does well the tasks of each day.
There's always a bigger job waiting,
   If you work with a willing grace.
Somebody's taking your measure—
      Are you FIT for a larger place?

Helen P. Metzger.

ATTEMPT MADE TO ROB BRERETON HOME

Five Shots Fired at Fleeing Man By Special Deputy Sheriff Sylvester Brown

Star —

ON WATCH FOR PROWLERS

May 14 1913

LAKE GEORGE, May 12.—Sheriff Bolton's deputies are maintaining a close watch for prowlers in this vicinity, following the attempt made Monday night to burglarize the home of Assemblyman H. E. H. Brereton at Hillview. The man escaped but it was not the fault of Special Deputy Sylvester Palmer, Mr. Brereton's chauffeur, who fired five shots from a revolver at the fugitive.

The attempt to loot the home was made at 9:30 o'clock when Mr. Brereton, the only occupant of the house, was in his study. It is thought the thief remained in hiding until he had seen Mr. Brereton and all the servants leave the building and then, believing Mr. Brereton to be in Albany, the fellow entered the house. That he was very quiet in his movements is evidenced by the fact that he did not attract the attention of Mr. Brereton.

Mrs. Brereton returning from a walk with two maids discovered the man on the top floor of the residence. Her attention was attracted by the small light which darted to and fro, flickering on and off. She realized that Mr. Brereton would not be in that part of the house and sending one of the maids to Mr. Palmer's cottage a short distance away, she and the other maid ran into the study where Mr. Brereton was reading.

Informed of his wife's discovery, Mr. Brereton armed himself with a revolver and led the two women up the stairs. They hade made considerable noise and the thief thus warned managed to elude them. He was seen slunking in the shadows of the house by Mr. Palmer, who called on the stranger to throw up his hands.

The stranger's only answer was a growl and a dash for liberty. Palmer fired five shots but missed the mark each time.

The man evidently had been in the house only a few minutes before Mrs. Brereton discovered him as few articles had been disturbed.

FERNDALE FARM HOUSE STRUCK BY LIGHTNING

During the electrical storm this afternoon lightning struck the house on Ferndale farm, located between Ridge and Bay streets. A hole was torn in the roof but not much other damage was done. Mrs. William Withington and Wilfred Putney were in the house and received slight shocks. The farm is owned by the Jointa Lime company. *Times* June 26 1911

May 8 1915

MOTORBOAT FOR VINCENT ASTOR MADE IN WATERVLIET.

This view shows the launching slip at the south end of the shop of The Hacker Boat Company in Watervliet, and the speedy motorboat, the Mystery, built last year for the young multimillionaire. A second boat of the same type, the Mystery II, for Mr. Astor was launched last week, preparatory to its trial on the Hudson River at this city. It is not generally known, however, in this vicinity, that an industry of such fame in the motorboat world exists here. The Hacker Boat Company of Detroit decided to open a plant at the head of navigation on the Hudson River last year and the conditions have been found so favorable here that a large addition to the shop in Watervliet will be erected next fall and the Detroit plant will be abandoned. Only the best type of motorboats, capable of attaining a speed of thirty-five to fifty or more miles an hour and built with the perfection of the automobile, together with racing hydroplanes of the kind represented in the Lake George international regatta last summer, are to be made here. The company is now engaged in building six other boats, two for use on Lake George, one a thirty-two-foot, eight-cylinder, eight passenger motorboat for George Foster Peabody and another for W. E. Ogilvie, President of the Cuban Railroad, who has a summer home at the lake. A novel feature as showing the perfection attained in motorboat construction is a commission received for building five matched boats during next winter to be placed on Lake George in the 1916 season. All the boats are of one type—the pleasure runabout—and will be used for "one design" racing, a new departure in sport which is receiving the favorable attention of its devotees.

Auto Club

"The rules of the road ought to be taught in the public schools," declared Secretary of State Francis M. Hugo last evening, during the Glens Falls Automobile club's banquet in the Rockwell house. "This would do much to prevent accidents and too much loss of life. The accidents can be and ought to be prevented. The automobile owners have no right to take advantage of the pedestrian. I feel sympathetic toward the man who has to use his legs in opposition—if you please—to the man who uses a car."

The good roads question was thoroughly discussed during the banquet and if any of the 175 persons who attended the affair were unaware of the fact that there are at least a few improved highways in the Thirty-third senatorial district, before they attended, they were considerably wiser before the toastmaster said "amen."

Adult Dies of Measles.

N. Lester Beswick, forty-five years old, died yesterday at his home in Dimmick's Corners, south of Glens Falls, after a week's illness of measles. The members of his family, except one son, are ill of the disease and are unable to leave their beds. Mrs. Beswick and her oldest son Reynolds, of South Glens Falls, are very ill, while two smaller children are quite ill. Delbert Beswick, another son, thus far has escaped the disease, being at school in South Glens Falls.

HORSE SEVERELY BITES MAN'S ARM

John H. Moynihan of Queensbury Injury By Animal Owned By H. Hubbell

1915

John H. Moynihan of Queensbury suffered a severe injury to the muscles of his right forearm at 5 o'clock yesterday afternoon when bitten by one of the horses of a team owned and driven by Harry Hubbell. The latter was on his way home and stopped in front of the Moynihan residence.

Mr. Moynihan, after inviting Mr. Hubbell to come in, grasped the headstall of one of the horses and started to lead the team up the driveway. One of the horses snapped at him, catching his right forearm and injuring it as above stated. Dr. John J. Dever was summoned to the family home and ordered the injured man's removal to the Glens Falls hospital. Last night it was stated that the patient was suffering great pain and that it would be necessary to sew the torn muscle together.

Bolton House Sold to Mrs. Wm. Drake.

Mrs. William Drake has purchased the Bolton house on lower Main street, from Harry Bolton. The price is reported to be about $4,000. The lessee, Mrs. William Terry, will remain in posession until October 1.

news apl 8 1915

MILLION DOLLAR HOTEL FOR SARATOGA SPRINGS

New York Men Forming Syndicate to Utilize Woodlawn Park Property.

Aug 21 1916 Times

SARATOGA, Aug. 21.—Several wealthy New York men are forming a syndicate to build a million dollar hotel in Woodlawn Park, which was purchased Friday by George W. Loft of New York for $112,000. It is said that Charles W. Morse, who has large shipping interests is a part purchaser of the property.

According to present plans the hotel will be modern in every way and will be so built that a third of it can be kept open all winter. It is said that Leland Sterry may be the manager of the new hotel.

Remarkable Shot of Bolton Octogenarian.

Selah Fuller, of West Bolton, aged eighty-one years, the other day took down his seventy-year-old gun—a muzzle-loading shot gun—and with the natural sight of his eyes, shot and killed a squirrel on the top of a building, at the first shot. Few men who have arrived at this age can equal this remarkable feat of steady nerve and skill.

SIMPSON TO BUILD A MODERN HOTEL

Apl 13 1915

Will be Erected on the Sagamore Property at the Landing. *Star*

A local business man, who has recently returned from a trip to New York city, advises The Times that John Boulton Simpson, who owns a controlling interest in the Sagamore property at Green Island, Lake George, has decided on plans as to re-building.

A modern, fireproof hotel, with one hundred and fifty rooms will be erected, and it is the hope and belief of Mr. Simpson the same will be in readiness for the season of 1915. Possibly the construction cannot be satisfactorily arranged so that guests will be accommodated although it is the hope of the owners and others interested that it will be opened some time during the season.

The above mentioned means much to this city and Warren county. In the past many wealthy summer residents have been attracted to Bolton Landing and locality through the Sagamore hotel. They are among the most liberal people who visit our city for purposes of trading. They give life and activity to the entire Lake George section. The unfortunate experience of hotel owners on all parts of the lake in the past has been discouraging to investors. Nevertheless, a fireproof hotel, new and supplied with every facility and advantage, cannot prove other than profitable, and all should encourage the construction and maintenance of the same in every way possible. We take it for granted the hotel will be built so that additions can be made if business warrants subsequent outlay.

BOLTON LANDING *Star*

BOLTON LANDING, April 27.— Rev. S. J. Liberty officiated April 15 at the marriage of George S. Middleton and Miss Daisy Scripter, both of Bolton.

Rev. Mr. and Mrs. J. S. Prudon, formerly of Lyon Mountain have taken up their residence in the Methodist parsonage, the church here and the one at North Bolton being Mr. Prudon's charge.

Mrs. Jane A. Burge, Mrs. Stephen Burge and Miles Burge of Chestertown, recently were here calling on relatives and friends. They motored here on the State roads.

Dr. and Mrs. E. L. Wilson are occupying rooms adjoining Gates store and formerly occupied by Mrs. Sarah Gates and family.

ROCKWELL DIES IN CLIFTON SPRINGS

May 14 times

Well Known Hotel Man Succumbs in Sanatorium—Funeral Thursday. *1915*

C. L. Rockwell, founder and owner of the Rockwell house, died this morning at 10 o'clock in Clifton Springs. Mr. Rockwell had been in ill health some time, and several months ago he entered the sanitorium at Clifton Springs. Mr. Rockwell was born in Luzerne about sixty-six years ago and when a young man engaged in the hotel business with his father, George T. Rockwell, in that village. For a number of years they managed the old Rockwell house in Luzerne. In the early seventies Mr. Rockwell came to Glens Falls and opened the Rockwell house, which he managed several years. A few years ago he disposed of the management to Myron Brown, who was succeeded by George M. Taylor, the present landlord.

The remains will be brought to the home of Mrs. Jerome Lapham in this city tomorrow afternoon. The funeral will be held Thursday morning at 11 o'clock from the home of Mrs. Lapham. The burial will be in the Glens Falls cemetery. The Rev. Dr. John Lyon Caughey will officiate.

Besides his wife he is survived by two daughters, Mrs. F. N. Sanborn of Brooklyn and Mrs. H. Hamilton Lewis of Louisville, Ky.; a son, George T. Rockwell, and a brother, George H. Rockwell, of Luzerne.

EARTHQUAKE IS FELT UP-COUNTY

New Jan 6 1916

Shock at 9:10 A. M. Confined to Comparatively Small Area

Warren county and a part of Essex county was shaken by an earthquake shortly after 9 o'clock yesterday morning, but although a few persons declare they felt the shock in this city, it is not believed Glens Falls was affected. In some of the places up-county there was little doubt as to whether it was an earthquake. In Pottersville houses shook and windows rattled. One house about five miles north of Bolton was so severely shaken that the occupants were almost panic stricken.

The earthquake occurred about 9 o'clock and seemed to have been confined to a section a few miles wide extending from the town of Queens-

VETERAN BOATMAN *Times* IS INTERVIEWED

Oct 2 1915

David Walker Observes Fiftieth Anniversary of Entering Transportation Business.

David Walker, a veteran Lake George boatman, who resides in Leonard street, is celebrating the fiftieth anniversary of his entering the transportation business on the lake. Mr. Walker began boating on Lake George at the age of eighteen years. He is now sixty-eigth years old. For many years Mr. Walker resided at Bolton, but during the past fourteen years he has made Glens Falls his home.

A reporter met Mr. Walker at the D. and H. station yesterday and as he was in a reminiscent mood the reporter learned considerable relative to boating on the lake fifty years ago.

The largest excursion boat in those days carried less than 200 hundred passengers. It was no unusual sight to see a boat on the lake with a brick smoke stack. According to Mr. Walker the first real excursion boat to make its appearance on the lake was the John J., owned by John J. Harris. Later several boats appeared, among them being the Lilly M. Price, the Mountaineer and the Minnehaha. From time to time other and larger boats appeared until the time came for the launching of some of the big boats.

Mr. Walker was a fireman on the Lilly M. Price and at times he did pilot work under Captain Edward White. He also followed the rafting business, using the Lilly M. Price to tow rafts to saw mills.

Mr. Walker told a reporter that in various parts of the lake one today may see the hulks and ribs of many of the old-day steamboats. For instance, the ribs of the Lilly M. Price are sunk near Lake George village and the old Minnehaha may be seen protruding above the water in the vicinity of Black Mountain.

Cow Swallowed Wire Nail and Died.

news apl 3 1916

A new milch cow owned by Byron Duell, of Bolton Landing, died Thursday night under peculiar circumstances. The animal had been sick about a week, apparently of distemper, and finally died in great pain. A post mortem examination disclosed the fact that a wire nail, no doubt swallowed by the cow with her food, had caused her death.

bury to North Hudson, Essex county. Distinct shocks were felt at Lake George, Warrensburg, Chester, Pottersville, Schroon Lake, Schroon River and North Hudson, but the tremor seems to have extended no farther than North Hudson. It was not felt in Keene, Elizabethtown, Ticonderoga, Port Henry or Whitehall.

The shock was more severe in Chestertown than in Pottersville, although the two towns are only six miles apart.

BURLESQUE CIRCUS PROVES A HUMMER

Prof. Holcomb and "Owner" Charles Allen Outdo Sautelle, McMullen, Ringling

MORE THAN 5,000 SEE SHOW

Parade Stops Traffic—Features Galore in Line and at Place of Exhibition — Boy Scouts Aid Police

Al Ringling in his palmiest days had nothing on Allen when it comes to depicting the dignity of the circus owner. Mr. Allen seated behind a milk white horse rode at the head of the procession. His companion was David Wells, better known as "Bison Bill, the Kid Karson of the Adirondacks," and who owns the wild west department of the circus.

The parade had difficulty in passing through many streets owing to the immense crowds. Hudson Valley trolley and automobile traffice was completely blocked at times. Only good work on the part of the police prevented an accident.

Immediately behind Mr. Allen came the main band f the show under the leadership of Mr. Holcomb. Then came a group of horse riders who were scheduled to do fancy bare back riding stunts in the big show. The negro band rode in an old stage coach steam was furnished by footpower. The calíope was furnished by Cluett & Sons' local store.

The parade ended at the Rockwell House and Professor Edward Cheritree, the celebrated magician, who performed in the side show as well as doing the announcing. In the free exhibition a young woman (a doll), made the dizzy dazzling descension of 500 feet (from the roof of the Rockwell House), while hanging by her hair to a wire (thread.)

Then came the sideshow with music by the negro band. Banners painted and donated by George Roby depicted the stoutest man on earth (and he did not resemble John Cashion), the bearded lady, the armless wonder, the largest snake in captivity, and the smallest man in the world.

Then came the big show, the ni ic for which was appropriate opening as do most circuses with a William Tell overture. Then came the fancy riding acts, during which Charles Briggs worked overtime snapping the whip and keeping things lively. Mr. Briggs also rang the jingle bells during the elephant act and did much to keep the concert "circussy."

After a number of acts, came Mr. Cheritree's announcement of the concert and it was in the concert that many of the real features were staged. Arthur Brunelle, never was in better voice. *Music was* provided by the Glens Falls City band.

DR. HALL BUYS DIX MANSION

Located in Ridge Street—Birthplace of Former Governor John A. Dix.

July 7th 1916.

The Dix mansion in Ridge street has been purchased by Dr. D. M. Hall. Dr. Hall has not yet determined as to what use he will put the property and may not make any decision for a week or two.

In the large brick house, known throughout this section as the Dix homestead, former Governor John A. Dix was born and lived for a number of years.

The house is located well back from the street on a lot which extends back from Ridge street along Lawton avenue for a distance of 300 feet and with a frontage of 140 feet on Ridge street. The grounds are well shaded and there is an abundance of fruit trees, and spacious lawns on all sides.

Dr. Hall intends to keep the grounds in better condition than they have been for several years and make the place more attractive.

The house is in excellent condition, a large sum of money said to amount to $4,000 having been expended on repairs by John R. Morrison, who some time ago went through bankruptcy.

Occupying a splendid location the house and grounds when kept up have been one of the show places of the city.

HAGUE HAS COSTLY FIRE.

Feb 15 1917

McClanathan Building Destroyed, Probably by Torch of Incendiary.

The village of Hague was threatened with total destruction by fire ea ly yesterday morning when the John McClanathan building was burned, together with most of its contents. Only the absence of wind prevented the fire from making a clean sweep of everything in its pathway. The villagers made a hard fight to save the structure, but handicapped by the lack of water and apparatus their efforts were of no avail. They did succeed, however, in confining the fire to the building in which it started. The building was owned by Mr. McClanathan and was occupied by Fred Hart on the second floor as a barber shop, the first floor being used as a bowling alley. Only Mr. Hart's shop outfit was saved. A storehouse in the rear of the building was also destroyed. *News*

Jesse Sexton dicsovered the fire as he was passing the building about 2 o'clock in the morning on his return from a trip to Ticonderoga He noticed flames in the stairway leading to the barber shop and gave an alarm by firing several shots with a revolver. A crowd quickly gathered but the fire had then gained such headway that it was impossible to stop it with the facilities at hand. The fire is believed to have been of incendiary origin, as it evidently started in the hallway where there was nothing for it to catch from. The loss is estimated at about $2,500 partially covered by insurance.

THE MOST VALUABLE HEN IN THE WORLD

This is Lady Eglantine, holder of the world's record, 314 eggs in a year, valued at $100,000, and the only hen that has travelled in a private Pullman car. Her owner, A. A. Christian of Philadelphia, brought her to New York in a private car. An automobile took her to a prominent hotel where she was installed in a luxurious suite. From day to day she is taken to the poultry show to be exhibited.

COUNTY POPULATION

Little Warren Shows Gain of 774 in Past Five Years.

REPORT FROM RECENT CENSUS

Figures Show Gains and Losses in Various Towns—Glens Falls Has Drawn from Smaller Places, Warrensburgh Loses.

Albany, No. 15—Having made a gain in population of 774 during the past five years, Warren county now numbers 32,997 residents including 174 permanent inmates of its institutions. The county has an alien population of but 1,301. In 1900 Warren county had a population of 29,943 which increased to 31,335 by 1905 and to 32,223 in 1910. In the fifteen years past the county's gain in population amounts to 3,054.

Glens Falls, the only city in Warren county, has increased its residents by 1,080 during the last five years and has a present population of 16,323, made up of 836 aliens and 15,487 citizens. Lake George village has grown from 632 when the Federal census was taken in 1910 to 750 last June.

The final tabulation of many of the counties of the state has now been completed. By means of the sojourners' blanks, residents who were temporarily absent from their home last June, have been duly credited to the places where they rightfully belong.

Secretary of State Francis M. Hugo will make his official report on the last census to the legislature next January. Embodied in it will be the following figures for Warren county:

Towns	Aliens	Citizens	Total	1910
Bolton	22	1375	1397	1518
Caldwell	12	1612	1624	1482
Chester	33	1597	1630	1721
City Glens Falls	836	15487	16323	15243
Hague	90	853	943	1043
Horicon	83	973	1056	1001
Johnsburgh	51	2307	2358	2315
Luzerne		1070	1070	1185
Queensbury	156	2565	2721	2667
Stony Creek	5	714	719	858
Thurman	1	806	807	805
Warrensburgh	10	2234	2244	2385
	1301	31676	32977	32223
Village Lake George	4	746	750	632

Aged Bolton Lady Knits for Foreign Soldiers

Mrs. Arvilla Watson, of Bolton Landing, who on May 15 celebrated her eighty-sixth birthday anniversary, has since January knitted six pairs of socks and ten pairs of long wristlets for the Red Cross society. The product of the aged lady's industry goes to the soldiers fighting in the European war. *June 2 1915*

ROCKY KNOLL FARM BUILDINGS BURNED

Thomas Place in Bay Road, Owned By Van Hyning, is Scene of $20,000 Fire

Dec 27-1915

ONLY $6,000 INSURANCE

One Horse, Seven Head of Cattle and Practically All the Farm Implements, Wagons, Grain, Hay, Etc., Consumed

A spectacular fire which lighted up the countryside for miles, Saturday night destroyed four buildings on the old Stephen Thomas farm in the Bay road a mile outside the city, owned by C. H. Van Hyning of this city, causing a loss of more than $20,000. The loss was covered by insurance only to the extent of $6,000, Mr. Van Hyning a year or two ago having reduced the amount of the policy $4,000. The residence and stable which were under one roof and which made one of the largest farm buildings in this vicinity, a shop, an ice house and a creamery were destroyed as were also a horse, seven head of cattle, and practically all the farm implements, wagons, grain, hay, and a Marion automobile.

Royal Bullion and William Decker, employes of Mr. Van Hyning, resided on the farm, but were downtown Saturday night. About 10 o'clock, Mrs. Washington Harris who occupies a house across the road from the Van Hyning farm discovered the fire in the hay loft and a few minutes later the roof caved in. Neighbors fearing Bullion and Decker were in the building broke in the doors and searched through the living apartments and, discovering the two were away, devoted their efforts to saving the stock. Seven horses and 20 head of cattle were removed and the implements in the dairy were saved, but everything else, including a thoroughbred Holstein bull was burned. Robert Smith's hands were badly burned while he was engaged in the work of rescuing the cattle.

While the fire was at its height some person turned in an alarm from box 46, Ridge and Sanford streets, but realizing they could do nothing out in the country without water the firemen returned to quarters.

The farm was one of the best known places in Queensbury, and was known as the Rocky Knoll farm. The large building was 50 feet wide, 218 feet long and two stories high. One hundred head of cattle, in addition to the wagons, farm implements, hay, grain, etc, could be housed in the stable.

Mr. Van Hyning will continue his milk business from his residence, 1 Lincoln avenue.

GIRL LOSES $1,100 ON PREACHER'S TIP

George Foster Peabody One of Defendants in Suit Brought Yesterday

Nov 38 1915 Times

NEW YORK, Nov. 30.—George Foster Peabody, who as trustee of the estate of the late Spencer Trask is a special partner in the banking firm of Spencer Trask & Co., is one of the defendants in a suit brought yesterday by Miss Cecile Taylor, a stenographer, to recover about $1,100 of her savings. This money represents an investment, Miss Taylor alleges, the banking firm made from $3,000, all the money she possessed, in stock of a company which later went into the hands of receivers.

Miss Taylor explains in her Supreme court action how she came to intrust her money to the Trask concern. Ill and without any source of income, she took the advice of a clergyman, whom she mentions as Dr. Alsop, and turned her life savings over to the banking firm. Mr. Peabody being represented by Dr. Alsop as a "good, charitable man."

Empire Theatre—The management of the Empire theatre announces many big vaudeville headline acts for the spring season. Glens Falls theatregoers having expressed a preference for the always-enjoyable vaudeville form of amusement, Manager Corr has made arrangements whereby they will have the best.

Twelve big acts have been booked, starting with this week. Four acts will be offered each day, the bills changing in their entirety three times weekly—on Monday, Wednesday and Friday. The admission will be ten and fifteen cents for all matinee performances and ten, fifteen and twenty-five cents for all evening performances. Ladies will be admitted in the afternoon to balcony and orchestra for ten cents. The last three rows in the orchestra and the entire balcony will be fifteen cents at night. The ten-cent seats at night will be in the second balcony. The orchestra seats, except the last three rows, will be twenty-five cents. This scale of prices will allow everybody to attend and will also allow the theatre management to present very fine vaudeville entertainments. A feature photoplay will be offered as an added attraction with each bill.

Park Theatre—Mrs. Vernon Castle, who is known as the best-dressed woman in America, will make her first appearance in a multiple reel motion picture at the Park theatre today.

In the above reproduction from a photograph is represented the Glen and Bay street property which will be converted into a city park provided the proposed park project is voted favorably upon at the special election to be held March 20. The proposed park, if it becomes a reality, will start at the junction of Bay and Maple streets erty along Bay and Glen streets to the Coolidge National Bank building and along Maple street avenue.

Lon Fosmer a Warrensburgh Visitor.

News Jan 13 1916

W. A. Fosmer, proprietor of the Rising house, Chestertown, was a Warrensburgh visitor Tuesday. Mr. Fosmer is to retire from the hotel on February 1, having sold the property to Mr McConnell, of New York, who will take possession on that date. Mr. Fosmer will continue to make his home in Chestertown having become greatly attached to the place during his residence there, which has extended over a period of about twenty years. He informed a News man that he is not retiring from business because of depressed conditions in Chestertown, as has been stated, but solely on account of his health, which has not been good for some time, and which he expects will be greatly improved by relief from business cares.

GLENS FALLS SEES FIRST MOTOR SLED

Feb 17 1915 Times

R. J. Scoville and Arthur Pike have the distinction of introducing the first "motor sled" in Glens Falls. A motor such as is used on bicycles was attached to bob sleds and last night the young men drove through the streets, attracting considerable attention. A motorcycle lamp was at the front of the conveyance and the chugging of the motor as the bobs skimmed over the snow caused many persons to gaze in wonder upon the conveyance.

"Times do move," remarked one elderly man, "when the boys can coast uphill as well as down."

By John Kendrick Bangs

THE LITTLE BIRD

"Peep!" said a little bird one morn
When I was feeling quite forlorn.
I took a "peep" and saw arrayed
In loveliness the world displayed.

"Cheep!" said the little bird, and I
The truth of it could not deny,
For all earth's lavish beauty spent
On me had cost me not a cent.

ATTEMPT TO BURN HARTFORD HOTEL

Nov 16 Star 1915

HARTFORD, Nov. 15—The Empire House yesterday was damaged to the extent of about $1,000 by fire believed to have been of incendiary origin. It is said the floors, walls and some of the furniture were saturated with kerosene and that the fires were started in three different parts of the building. Owing to a lack of draft, the fire burned itself out after the walls and woodwork had been blistered. The hotel is owned by Asa Roberts of Bolton Landing who conducted it until a short time ago when it was closed after the town had voted against licenses.

Ox Teams Scarce in Chestertown.

Jan 6 1916

But five ox teams are driven hereabouts now. These few are under control of David Wallace, Emery McKinstry, Charles Fish, Artemus Frazier and Charles W. Fish. A small band of reputable farmers these, who represent an estimable farming element. Genial, honest Charles Noxon, who has shod more oxen than all other local blacksmiths combined, in the period covered by his career, says: "Thirty-five years ago, when Putnam & Whitney, drovers, in coming here made Weatherhead's, now Downs' hotel, headquarters, they had no difficulty in purchasing from twenty-five to thirty yoke of trained oxen, which were driven to Westchester county at one time to be used for farming purposes. Martin Ingraham, of Horicon, in former days kept from fifty to sixty head of cattle and cut 100 tons of hay, and if more hay was wanted 100 tons could be purchased any day from his neighbors at $10 a ton."

STEPHEN S. HARRIS SHOOTS LARGE DEER

Nov 11 1915 Star

Animal Weighing 268 Pounds Brought Down By Hunter at Northwest Bay

Stephen S. Harris of 28 Terra Cotta avenue yesterday shot one of the largest deer that has been taken out of the Adirondacks, bringing down a 268 pound buck on the Frank Dagles property at North West Bay on Lake George. The animal possessed a beautiful head, its antlers having 13 prongs.

According to Mr. Harris, the animal ran up to within 10 feet of him before he shot. When he first caught sight of the buck it was about six rods away from him and he took aim at it but refrained from shooting as long as the animal was coming toward him. The buck started to whirl around when it was 10 feet from Mr. Harris and he fired, the first shot passing through the deer's neck and out of its left ear. It required four men to tow the animal's body a mile.

Mr. Harris brought the deers head to this city last evening and it is now on exhibition in Homer Dailey's cigar store show window.

JURY DISAGREES IN GAME VIOLATION CASE AT BOLTON

Jan 12 1916 times

Hiram Frasier of Graphite, who was arrested January 7 by Game Protector Bump of Lake George on a charge of having in his possession a woodpecker the killing of which is prohibited by the Conservation law, yesterday stood trial before Justice of the Peace Taber in Bolton and the jury disagreed. The matter was adjourned until Tuesday of next week, when it is expected Frasier will again stand trial. The penalty imposed by the Conservation law for the offense of which Frasier is accused is a fine of sixty dollars for violation of the law and twenty-five dollars for each bird taken.

CITY WILL AGAIN SUE WARREN CO.

Dec 10, 1915

City Attorney Singleton Will Institute Certiorari Proceedings Agst. Supervisors.

Within the next four months City Attorney Singleton acting upon instruction from the Common Council will institute certiorari proceedings against the Warren County Board of Supervisors for the purpose of compelling that body to audit the city's claims against the county which were incurred by the building of the viaduct across the Hudson river between this city and South Glens Falls. The original claims was about $20,000 but interests and costs have made an additional claim of approximately $5,200. The supervisors recently rejected the claim and decided to take an appeal from the decision of the Appellate division of the Supreme court which was in favor of the city.

This action on the part of the city was taken at a meeting of the Common Council last evening for the sole purpose of protecting the rights of the city. It is necessary that the city take legal proceedings within four months. Mr. Singleton, in discussing the matter last evening, said that he was of the opinion that the supervisors wanted to postpone paying the city's claim on the ground that they were short of funds.

Further Hearings in Bolton Road Case.

news Jan 12, 1916

County Judge George S. Raley has denied the motion of Attorney Frank Hurley, of Glens Falls, for the affirming of an order made by a commission to alter a highway in the town of Bolton upon the application of Myron J. Lamb. County Attorney Loyal L. Davis, in behalf of the town of Bolton, raised a question as to the legality of the notice given of the hearings held in 1913, claiming that the taxpayers of the town were not given sufficient opportunity to be heard in opposition to the application.

SECOND ATTEMPT TO BURN HOTEL

Star Nov 22 1915

Two Hartford Women Frustrate Efforts of Firebugs in Automobile

LITTLE DAMAGE IS DONE

(Special to The Post-Star)

HARTFORD, Nov. 21.—A second attempt to burn the Empire House exactly one week after it was first fired, was frustrated early this morning by two women who from the window of their home, saw a man throw kerosene on the porch of the hotel and then apply a match to it. They gave the alarm and the fire was quickly extinguished. The residents of the town are thoroughly aroused over the second bold attempt to destroy the hotel which is a two story structure and contains about 30 rooms.

About 1:30 o'clock a car containing three men drove into the village from the south and when it reach a point in front of the hotel one of the occupants alighted and took a position near the porch of the building. The car then went about half a mile up the road and about that time a young man who resides here drove into the village. The firebug evidently saw him and feared to set the fire at that time. Meantime the car returned to the village, turned about and went up the Granville road about a mile and a half.

The man who stood near the hotel threw something, believed to be kerosene, on the porch and applied a match. As the fire started the car returned and the stranger jumped into the machine which soon disappeared along the road to the south. The two women who saw the man set the fire immediately gave the alarm and the flames were extinguished. The porch and lattice work were slightly damaged.

CAUGHT BY GAME PROTECTORS.

news Dec 26, 1915

Pottersville Man Pays Dearly for Selling Venison and Partridges.

For selling venison and partridges in violation of the law Harley P. Brace, a Pottersville merchant, has just paid into the state coffers $1,025. He got off easy at that, for had the full fine been imposed he would have been compelled to pay $1,425.

Local game protectors had for some time been aware that someone in that vicinity was acting as a go between for hunters in the sale of wild game. They were unable, however, to secure sufficient evidence upon which to act, owing to their being so well known. Two special protectors were therefore sent into the field by the state department to work up the case. Posing as wealthy sportsmen these men procured dinner at a vicinity hotel, called for and were served with the contraband game and birds. Gaining the confidence of the landlord they expressed a desire to obtain a supply of the forbidden luxuries to carry with them to their homes in the city. They were told confidentially that the goods could be procured at Mr. Brace's store in Pottersville. With their trap baited with an apparent willingness to pay a fancy price to satisfy their desires, the merchant was easily caught. When he realized his predicament he showed no desire to fight the case, but simply went to Albany and made the best terms he could for settlement. When the fine was fixed he paid it without a murmur.

It is believed that Brace had been carrying on the business for some time.

REQUESTS CHANGE IN BOLTON ROAD

Star Dec 1, 1915

County Judge Raley Receives Petition of Myron J. Lamb to Change Highway

Attorney Frank Hurley yesterday appeared before County Judge Raley and filed an application in behalf of Myron J. Lamb to alter the highway leading from Bolton Landing to Edgerton Pond in the town of Bolton, so that the road would extend in the direction of Mr. Lamb's farm. The application is made following a favorable report on the matter by a commission composed of Robert F. Imrie, Fred Truesdale and Herbert Miller. The commission was appointed by County Judge Raley.

The question as to who shall pay the damages of constructing such a road remains open and Attorney L. M. Pulver, who appeared in behalf of the town of Bolton, opposed the charging of such damages to the town. On Mr. Pulver's application, the hearing was adjourned until Tuesday December 14.

NEW SANFORD STREET SCHOOL
BUILDING HIGHLY COMMENDED

Jan 4 1916 Times

New Sanford Street School Building.

FREEZE TO DEATH IN CABIN

Last Letters to Mother Found Beside Bodies of Two Montana Homesteaders

Dispatch Feb 4 1916

Realizing they slowly were freezing to death in their remote homestead cabin east of Havre, in Northern Montana, two school teachers wrote letters to their mother in Ohio, telling of the bitter cold and bidding farewell to the folks at home.

The story was brought to Butte Tuesday by Cliff Meed, a traveling man, who was in a neighboring village when the frozen bodies were brought in. Their names were Misses Moore. The nearest inhabitant was nine miles away and a trip through the fierce blizzard was hopeless.

The two girls took up a homestead a year ago. They resided with a rancher and his wife, at first, but when their funds ran low they decided to live on their own place to cut expenses. The rancher took them to their little home, and it was after he had driven out of sight they realized they had no matches.

That night the mercury dropped 40 degrees in an hour. By morning it was 60 degrees below. The girls had few blankets. Realizing they were freezing to death, the sisters each wrote a letter to their mother. Their frozen bodies were found Saturday wrapped in blankets. The letters which lay on the table with "Good-by" written by frozen fingers.

Dec 10 1915

Merrill Hartson, who for quite a number of years has occupied one of the flats over Gates Brothers' store, moved Monday into Mrs. M. Finkle's rooms. Jacob Sucman and family moved from the Finkle rooms to the flat vacated by Mr. Hartson. Times

Antoine Knauth, of New York, aged about sixty years, died December 3, at his summer home here. Mr. Knauth was not well when he came here last spring and had been ill ever since. He is survived by his widow, three daughters and two sons. The body was taken to New York for interment.

GRANGERS BUY HARTFORD HOTEL

Times Jan 15

Empire Hotel Property That Wouldn't Burn Will be Converted Into a Hall. 1916

The Grange at Hartford is the latest of the Washington county granges to acquire a piece of real estate and prepare to establish itself in a home of its own. The Hartford grangers have just purchased the Empire hotel property in that village and will make such changes in the building as are necessary to make it suitable for their use. Several other Washington county granges already own their buildings. The Argyle grange has just moved into a new hall secured by making extensive changes to a church building, which they purchased a year or two ago.

The Empire hotel, which was formerly owned by Asa Roberts of Bolton, has been closed since Hartford has been "dry," something over a year. On November 11, at an early hour in the morning smoke was seen issuing from the building, and it was found that kerosene had been liberally spread about the building and a fire set, but it failed to burn. Just a week later a second attempt was made to destroy the building. During the night an automobile stopped near the hotel, kerosene was thrown on the porch and a match applied. Neighbors saw the fire and it was extinguished before serious damage was done.

NORTH CREEK
HOTEL BURNS;
BANK SAVED

Jan. 18

Fire Destroys the Adirondack House and Adjoining Barn and Scorches Window Sill of Bank

TOTAL LOSS MAY REACH $50,000

NORTH CREEK, Jan. 17—Fire to night destroyed the Adirondack House, the hotel barn and threatened the North Creek National Bank. The loss is probably between $40,000 and $50,000.

The fire started between 6:30 and 7 o'clock, presumably from an overheated chimney. It was first discovered in the vicinity of the hotel kitchen and the flames made such rapid headway it was impossible to check their progress. Only a few articles of furniture were saved.

From the hotel, the flames quickly communicated to the barn which also was soon a roaring furnace. The bank building was saved only by the diligent work of the members of the bucket brigade. The heat caused the windows to break and the window sills were scorched, but the damage to the bank building was slight.

The hotel was owned by Patrick Moynehan of Glens Falls and John Anderson Jr., of Newcomb. It was three stories high and had accomodations for 100 guests. 1916.

CHESTERTOWN HOTEL SOLD.

New York Man Purchases Rising House From W. A. Fosmer.

W. A. Fosmer, for nineteen years proprietor and landlord of the Rising house, one of Chestertown's two popular year-around hotels, has sold the property to John O'Connor, of New York, who is expected to take possession this week. Mr. O'Conner is a son-in-law of Cornelius Murphy, proprietor of the popular summer resort, Hotel Atateka, at Friends Lake. Our correspondent writes that the departure of Mr. Fosmer, generally known as "Happy Lon," and his family, will be regretted by all of the people of the town and this statement, he says, cannot be too strongly emphasized. Our correspondent adds: "Mr Fosmer states that he can see no prospective betterment of financial interests in Chestertown and this primarily is the real basis for his decision to dispose of his interests here."

CAPT. ELI B. ROCKWELL.

The well-known commanding officer of the steamer "Vermont" on Lake Champlain, who enjoys the distinction of being the oldest active steamboat captain in years of service in the United States, if not in the world. Captain Rockwell comes of stalwart stock of Norman origin, the family leading back in direct line to 860. His grandfather and great-grandfather on both sides took part in the Revolutionary War, and his father, Merritt Rockwell, was in the battle of Plattsburgh in the War of 1812. Captain Rockwell was born in North Hero, Vt., in 1830 and has been in continuous service on Lake Champlain from the time he began as a cabin-boy on a sloop at the age of twelve years to the close of the present season, when he was in command of the queenly ship "Vermont the Third." He has served on the steamers "Chefton," "Canada," "America," "Adirondack," "Champlain," "United States," "Coquette," "Reindeer," "Chateaguay," "Vermont, the Second," "Ticonderoga" and is known to thousands who have sailed with him. Captain Rockwell voted for Franklin Pierce for President in 1852, has voted for every Republican candidate for President since and says he hopes to cast his ballot in 1916 for Charles E. Hughes, who as Governor was a guest on board the "Ticonderoga" during the three hundredth anniversary of the discovery of Lake Champlain. Captain Rockwell is a walking storehouse of knowledge concerning historic facts and very entertaining when his modesty can be overcome and he is induced to talk. He is also a baseball fan and although eighty-five years of age he keeps young in spirit, attending the recent World Series, rooting enthusiastically for the Boston "Red Socks." He is active, sturdy, enjoys the best of health, and looks forward to sailing the waters of Lake Champlain for many seasons to come.

SOLDIER'S WIDOW SENDS SAD LETTER

Informs His Mother of His Death On European Battlefield

Jan 14 1915

RELATIVE OF LOCAL MAN

Joseph Capone has received word of the death of his nephew, Isadore Cervone of Formicola, Italy, who was killed while fighting with the Italian troops in the European war. Mr. Capone also has received a copy of a letter sent by the young man's widow to his mother in Boston. The letter, which was interpreted by Nicholas Capone for The Post-Star follows:

"Dear Mother:—

"After a long silence I give you note of my misfortune. Dear mamma, I don't know what to write, but the supreme strength of which little is left encourages me to write a few lines to let you know of my misfortune. I cannot tell you else, for I cry for our beloved Isadore.

"After two months without a word from him, I decided to telegraph to the Pope in Rome, and His Highness answered by wire, stating Isadore Cervone has passed beyond to the other world. All I do now is cry, cry, cry. Tell all his cousins in the United States of his misfortune, for my heart is gone since his life is no more. Oh, mamma, the world for me is at an end and my tears flood me day and night, and yes, to think, three more little children left fatherless.

"I would have been satisfied to have him home, a cripple of any kind, rather than have it end as it has. Oh, Lord, why did you take him away from me?

"Let us all be embraced with the impulse of courage. I cannot write more, my strength is gone and my tears are covering this letter. I kiss you and remain your unfortunate daughter-in-law."

Times Jan 15, 1916

COTTAGE BURNED.

The cottage at Ballston Lake owned by Charles E. Massey of Ballston was totally destroyed by fire about 3 o'clock yesterday morning. As the cottage had not been occupied in some time, it is believed to have been of incendiary origin. It was one of the most substantial cottages on the lake shore and was well furnished. It is particularly unfortunate that it should happen at this time while Mr. Massey is seriously ill. It is believed that the loss is only partly covered by insurance.

BURNS ARE FATAL TO WARRENSBURG LADY

Nov 19 1915 Times

Miss Sarah E. Farlin, Injured a Week Ago, Succumbs— Was 68 Years Old.

Miss Sarah E. Farlin, who was badly burned about three weeks ago while burning leaves in her yard in Warrensburg, died this noon at her home in that place. Miss Farlin was sixty-eight years old, and it was due to her advanced age that she was unable to withstand the shock and effects of the burns.

At the time Miss Farlin met with the fatal burns she was cleaning up her yard and burning the leaves. In leaning over the flames her apron caught fire and before she was aware of it she was enveloped in flames. She was painfully burned about the body. Dr. C. V. Cunningham of Warrensburg attended her.

Miss Farlin had resided in Warrenburg for a period of forty-five years, going to that place from Glens Falls. She lived alone. There are no near surviving relatives.

CENSUS FIGURES FOR WARREN CO.

Times Feb 18

Total Population 32,977, According to Figures Furnished by Secretary Hugo.

1916

Secretary of State Hugo has filed with County Clerk E. C. Sisson a certificate giving the official figures of the census enumeration made in Warren county in 1915. The total population of the county is given at 32,977 of which 31,676 are citizens and 1,301 aliens. The number of inhabitants of the City of Glens Falls is given at 16,323 of which 15,487 are citizens and 836 aliens. The Village of Lake George has 750 inhabitants of which 746 are citizens and four are aliens. Luzerne is the only town in the county which has no aliens among its inhabitants. The Town of Thurman is next lowest with but one alien. Queensbury has 186 aliens, the largest number of any of the towns.

The population of the towns of the county is as follows:

	Citizens	Aliens	Inhab.
Bolton	1,375	22	1,397
Caldwell	1,629	13	1,642
Chester	1,597	33	1,630
Hague	853	90	943
Horicon	973	83	1,056
Johnsburg	2,307	51	2,385
Luzerne	1,070	..	1,070
Queensbury	2,565	156	2,721
Stony Creek	714	5	719
Thurman	806	1	807
Warrensburg	2,300	11	2,311

WILLIAMS' CLAIM AGAIN REVIVED

Times — Jan 24

Was Missionary the Lost Dauphin Left When a Boy With Lake George Indian?

1916

Whether the Rev. Eleazar Williams was the lost dauphin of France has never been decided, although reams have been written to prove and disprove his theory.

That the man who first addressed the Onondagas on March 31, 1816, was really Louis XVII, the lost prince, probably was believed by the man himself, and, from the evidence produced he had good reasons to believe it, but there are other just as good authorities to contend that Williams was only a very intelligent half-breed Indian.

Whether the Indian missionary was a son of the ill-fated Louis XVI and Marie Antoinette probably never will be definitely known. Anyway, France now seems to be an established republic, and has other troubles to keep it busy. Louis Charles, the lost dauphin, was born in 1785. His mother and father were beheaded in 1793, and from Aug. 13, 1792, until June 8, 1795, the prince was kept a prisoner in the tower.

Many claim that the child who died in the tower was not the prince, that the dauphin was carried away by royalist sympathizers and hidden in America. Stories of the treatment given him in the tower show that he had become a mental wreck because of abuse, and that when he was last seen there knew no one.

Next in support of the Williams theory is told the story of a family called De Jardin, which arrived in Albany from France in 1795, having with them a very beautiful boy and girl, the boy known as Monsieur Louis. The couple was well supplied with money and had many articles, including gold plate, belonging to the dead king and queen. They later disappeared.

The same year a French boy was left with a half-breed Iroquois chief Thomas Williams, near Lake George. The boy seemed to be of unsound mind until one day when he fell from a rock and cut his head. Afterward he appeared normal, but had no recollections of his former existence. Williams in later years said he could remember nothing before seeing the hills and forests around Lake George, although there were visions of a hideous face, supposed to have been Simon, the prince's torturer of the tower. "All else is chaotic confusion," the account states, "in which Indians roasting chestnuts around a fire are mixed with dream-like and vague images, which elude the effort to grasp them, as realities, of splen

did architecture, of troops exercising in a garden, of being in a room where there were persons magnificently dressed and of lying on the carpet with his head against the silk dress of a lady."

Then there is the story of the Frenchman, with the ruffled shirt and the powered hair who visited the Indian family in the woods, kissed and wept over the boy, and how, soon afterward, in 1890 young Eleazar was sent to Massachusetts to be educated by Nathaniel Ely. The great difference in appearance of Eleazar and his supposed Indian brothers was subejct of much remark then. He had blue eyes, light hair and every appearance of being French, it was said.

The change was remarkable. From a wild Indian lad he soon became a bright student and quickly adapted to the prevailing customs. Later he went to Canada, and was received with much consideration. During the war of 1812, he served the American government in secret service work, his knowledge of Indian dialects and customs being very valuable.

Then began his work in the Episcopal church, which in 1816 brought him to what is now Syracuse and to the Onondaga Indians. He was not ordained, however, until 1826. In 1821 he acted for the government in getting the Wisconsin reservation at Green Bay for the Oneida Indians.

Williams claimed that in 1841 the Prince de Joinville, representing the king of France, tried to induce him to sign a renouncement of his right and title to the throne, but he refused. The prince denied this story. M. Bellanger, a portrait painter, is known to have been one of the few who last saw the prince in the tower. A Frenchman named Bellanger, who died in New Orleans in 1848, confessed on his death bed that he brought the dauphin from France and placed him with Indians in northern New York. Williams' Indian mother, Mary Ann Williams (Konwatewenteta) made an affidavit that she adopted him.

After remaining with the Oneidas in Wisconsin 30 years, Killiams returned to New York state and died at Hoganeburg in 1858. Nothing ever came of his claim. He was only one of many so-called pretenders to the throne of France, the lost dauphin, about whose mysterious disappearance numerous romances have been written.

GRANT COTTAGE HOUSES THREE WAR TELEGRAMS

SARATOGA, Jan. 13—The daughters of the late Dr. William Blakee of Utica have presented to Colonel O. P. Clarke, custodian of the Grant cottage on Mt. McGregor, three telegrams which were sent by General U. S. Grant during the Civil war.

Dr. Blakee made a collection of the original telegrams sent by General Grant and the physician's daughters had three of them framed for the Grant cottage. *Jan 14 1916*

T. C. LUTHER CUTS ELM 720 YEARS OLD

Times Feb 3 1916

Stood Within Sight of Historic Fort Ticonderoga — Will Make 5,600 Board Feet.

On one of his lumber jobs in the town of Putnam, Washington county, and within sight of the historic Fort Ticonderoga, T. C. Luther of Saratoga Lake, has had cut and drawn to his sawmill, located on the shore of Lake Champlain, an elm tree that will make 5,600 board feet of lumber.

The trunk of the tree measures 68 feet to the limbs, is 60 inches in diameter at the butt and 27 inches at the top, which by Scribner's log rule will cut 5,100 feet, and some of the limbs which are as large as good sized trees will cut 500 more feet, making a total of 5,600 feet.

There was so little taper to the tree that the first two 12 foot logs will cut 1334 feet each. A rare thing in a tree of this size is that it is perfectly sound and without a check or blemish on the surface the entire length of the trunk.

The rings of the tree indicate it is 720 years old, which shows it started long before the discovery of America. On account of its enormous size, the ordinary sawmills that are in common use now cannot manufacture it into lumber, and Mr. Luther is now making special arrangements for manufacturing this and some other extremely large logs he has in stock.

Foresters and lumbermen who have seen this tree in the mill yard, pronounce it the finest and largest specimen of the elm they have ever seen.

HOLLIS I. LOVELAND PROMOTED

Young Railroad Man Rising Rapidly in Service of the D. & H.

feb 1916

Hollis I. Loveland, formerly station agent at The Glen, on the Adirondack division of the Delaware and Hudson railroad, from which post he was promoted two years ago to Hydeville, Vt., and the summer agency of the company's leading summer resort, Bluff Point and Hotel Champlain, has recently received a second promotion to the permanent agency at West Rutland, Vt., made vacant by the death of James Leamy, the oldest station agent in the employ of the company. West Rutland is the center of the great marble industry of Vermont, is served by three railroads and is one of the most important stations of the D. & H. The appointment of a man so comparatively young in the service as is Mr. Loveland is a very distinct recognition of his character and efficiency.

FEDERAL BUILDING READY ON APRIL 1

TRIPP GETS CARTAGE JOB

Contractor Held Up in Work By Delay in Arrival of Material

United States Inspector Charles R. Marsh in Glens Falls Yesterday—Civil Service Room Provided

The new federal building, Warren and Jay streets, is completed, with the exception of the placing of marble in the main lobby, some wood work on the lower floor, the laying of floors throughout and the hanging of doors. The total cost of the building to the government will be in the neighborhood of $100,000 and Superintendent Bemish of the Hills Construction company of New York is confident he will be able to turn the building over to the Glens Falls postmaster April 1, the date stipulated in the contract.

At present, the contractors are losing time because of being held up for lack of marble and woodwork. Telegrams received yesterday stated the shipments were on the way. It will require from four to five weeks for the marble setters to complete their work which is confined entirely to the lobby of the building.

EPIGRAMS BY PRESIDENTS.

Not Many Deathless Sentences Have Been Handed Down to Us.

How very few things which any of our presidents said can anybody recall offhand!

Washington's most frequently quoted phrase is, "In time of peace prepare for war."

John Adams talked all day and wrote diaries all night, but perhaps "Independence forever"—his toast for the very Fourth of July on which he died—is more widely known than any other one thought.

"Few die and none resign," heads Jefferson's list of deathless sentences, although parts of the Declaration of Independence are known to millions.

The doctrine keeps Monroe's name forever to the front, but his state papers, speeches and letters, like those of Madison, John Quincy Adams, McKinley, Taft and many other men long and honorably in public life, are devoid of handles—nothing to take hold of.

Rutherford B. Hayes gave us one very fine thought, "He serves his party best who serves the country best."

Jackson was forever saying "By the eternal!" but what else?

"With malice toward none" and "a government of the people," etc., are Lincoln's master strokes. However, his letters and papers are full of unique thoughts.

PRESENT TENANTS HAVE FIRST CLAIM

Joe Miller, sole owner of the property corner Warren and Glen street, familiarly known as the Holden block, which includes the wooden business building and brick block on Glen street abutting the property has notified all tenants they will have the first claim upon such quarters as they now occupy. Rents, which have been much lower than the new owner feels certain he will be able to secure, are raised and terms made uniform.

In the event of any tenant not feeling disposed to pay the new scale thirty days will be given such tenant to find new quarters. Out of town concerns including tobacco drugs, restaurant and other lines of business are applicants. With the new arrangement of these properties, improvements and furnishings, location considered the highest rents in the city will maintain.

Attractive electric light advertising will cover the entire top of the wooden building illuminating the sidewalk and street in front of the property bright as day.

"LON" FOSMER GIVES A DINNER.

News' Jan 20 1916

Retiring Proprietor of Chestertown Hotel Entertains Some of His Cronies.

Our Chestertown correspondent sends the following details of a recent social event in that village:

One of the social events of the current season was a dinner given by Alonzo Fosmer, on Tuesday evening, to a few of his many friends. The dinner was in no sense as a farewell occasion, as Mr. Fosmer though transferring title of the Rising house to other interest on February 1, will continue to reside in the west end of our village.

Mr. Fosmer proved to be a delightful host as his guests were all made to feel that each was in a measure a host in himself. The fact remains that in the years of continuously serving the public all guests have been uniformly well protected when under the hospitality of "genial Lon," a title Mr. Fosmer has earned without effort, as he is by nature endowed with a sense of fair treatment, and is by instinct a gentleman. To the passing guest, the invisible value, force and industrious assistance extended at all times by Mrs. Fosmer has been a dominating factor in the accomplishment of Mr. Fosmer's success, as Mrs. Fosmer has assumed the responsibility of managing departments, not in the avenue of public gaze, but nevertheless her influence and industry is conceded as most important in maintaining the hotel organization on a profitable and harmonious basis

The Rising house as conducted by Mr. Fosmer has not only been a business plant, but a refined home for the Fosmer family, a protection and comfort to the traveling public, and a restful meeting place for citizens to congregate at their convenience and pleasure.

TO MARK COTTAGE WHERE GRANT DIED

Sons of Veterans Will Make Plans During Albany Meeting February 27

LOCAL MEN ON COMMITTEE

Bronze Tablet May Be Placed Next Spring On Mount McGregor House, as Suggested By Glens Falls Camp

Pursuant to instructions given at the 1915 division encampment last June in Albany, a special committee of the Sons of Veterans, U. S. A., will meet in Albany Sunday, February 27, for the purpose of making further arrangements for marking with a bronze tablet the cottage on Mount McGregor Saratoga county, where General Grant died about thirty years ago, and of also placing a marker at the railroad station at Wilton and other places along the highway leading from there to the crest of Mount McGregor.

OBITUARY

Mrs. Fanny C. Simpson 1916

News has been received in this city of the death of Mrs. Fanny C. Simpson, wife of John Bolton Simpson, which occurred Wednesday, March 29 at Bretton Hall, New York. Mrs. Simpson was a prominent summer resident at Lake George, where Mr. Simpson was interested in the hotel business at Bolton. Mrs. Simpson was well known throughout the Lake George region, and also had numerous friends in this city who will mourn her loss. She was a very estimable woman. The funeral services were held Friday. Mrs. Simpson was an active church worker and was a member of St. Andrew's Guild of which she had been president for twenty-eight years.

---

150 SNAKES IN NEST.

News Feb 10 1916

Southport (Conn.) Man Found Them While Digging Cellar.

A nest of snakes in which there were estimated to be not less than 150 was discovered by S. Maiewsky of Southport, Conn., while excavating for a cellar. The second shovelful brought up snakes and the succeeding ones still more. The snakes, which were of the common striped variety, were dormant and averaged about eighteen inches in length.

PALMER JENKINS, WELL KNOWN RESIDENT OF QUEENSBURY FOUND DEAD IN WOODS

Was Brother of Hon. Lyman Jenkins of This City Who Was Conducting Proceedings in Surrogate's Court When Sad News Was Brought to Him.

Palmer Jenkins, a well known resident of the Town of Queensbury, was found dead in the mountains back of Kattskill Bay about noon today, by his wife and daughter, Minnie, who, fearing that harm had befallen him, started a search.

Early this morning Mr. Jenkins hitched up a team of horses and drove into the mountains for a load of wood. When he failed to return Mrs. Jenkins thought it time for him, she became alarmed and as time went by and he failed to appear, she called her daughter and both went into the woods in search of him.

After walking some distance they came across the team of horses and near the team, which was standing in a wood road, was the lifeless body of Mr. Jenkins. Believing that life was not extinct and that he probably had been overcome with the extreme cold weather, they succeeded in placing him on the sleigh and brought him home. Arriving at their home the mother and daughter learned the worse that Mr. Jenkins was dead and had been dead for some time.

Relatives and friends were notified shortly after noon and among them was Hon. Lyman Jenkins, who received the sad message of his brother's death while conducting a proceeding in Surrogate's court before Judge Raley. Mr. Jenkins immediately asked to be excused and hurried to the home of his brother.

The dead man was fifty-eight years old. The only near survivors are the wife, daughter and brother.

Dr. Floyd Palmer arrived at the house shortly before 3 o'clock but as life was extinct he was unable to be of any assistance.

Relatives of the dead man attribute the cause of death to heart trouble as for some time Mr. Jenkins had been complaining of a difficulty with

---

THURSDAY, FEBRUARY 17, 1916.

BRERETON BUNGLED.

Henry E H. Brereton, member of assembly and would be Republican leader of Warren county, will soon be able to write finis to the history of his political career. At the end of his present term he'll be through—unless he has the good grace to resign at once and thus relieve his party of the odium his continuance in office will cast upon it. The proceedings of the Assembly committee on privileges and elections, of which Mr. Brereton is chairman, and the record of its reckless and well-nigh criminal expenditures of state moneys will be viewed with contempt by all except those who are committed to the principles of graft.

Mr. Brereton in his effort to build up a political machine in Warren county which he would direct to the end that he might overwhelm and supplant the sagacious leaders whose supremacy has been justified in many a hard fought battle, very evidently figured to have the state pay the expenses of construction rather than deplete his millions for that purpose, and thereby he bungled. His own party condemns him and some of its adherents pronounces him politically dead.

There is said to be two sides to every story. One side is told in the article printed on another page giving details of the Brereton committee's artistic work. Mr. Brereton's side is yet to be heard. So far as we can learn he has not yet offered any defense.

THURSDAY, JUNE 1, 1916.

WHAT BILL DID.

Bill Turner was a farmer, he labored all his life. He didn't have no schoolin' and neither had his wife. But Bill was built for business and made the wheels go round, and left a healthy fortune when they put him under ground. He was always taking chances, paid a hundred for a bull. His neighbors called him crazy, but he left a stable full of cows that broke the record, making butter by the top, an' Bill had his picture printed in the Squeedunk Weekly Sun. He had newfangled notions of making farming pay. He even bought a fool machine to help him load his hay. The neighbors fairly snorted when they saw the bloomin' thing; said Bill would never make it work. It wasn't worth a ding. Bill didn't say a single word, an' didn't care a darn 'bout what they said, fer slick as grease, his hay went in the barn an hour before a thunder storm came sailin' out that way and caught his neighbors in a pinch and spoiled their new mown hay. Bill's neighbors put their milk in cans, and set 'em in a tank. Bill skimmed his milk with a machine and turned it with a crank. Smith chops his firewood with an ax. Bill used some gasoline and saws a hundred cords a day with another blame machine. Today Bill's wife rides in a car and dresses up in silk. Smith's wife rides in a wagon and keeps on skimming milk.—Taylor County, Ky., Enquirer.

---

news May 4

Richard J. Brown, proprietor of the Lake View house, Bolton, motored to Warrensburgh Sunday, accompanied by his nurse, Mrs. Mary Vandenburgh, and housekeeper, Mrs Veach. Mr. Brown has been in poor health several years. About a month ago he suffered a second shock of paralysis and for some time his condition was critical, but he rallied sufficiently to get about again and his many friends hope for his continued improvement.

R. J. Brown Has Third Shock.

Richard J. Brown, of Bolton, recently suffered a third shock of paralysis and is now in a critical condition at his home. Mr. Brown has been a wonderfully versatile man, having achieved success in several lines of activity. He has been for many years one of the most expert civil engineers and surveyors in this section, was an accomplished violinist and a skillful telegraph operator and for more than twenty-five years has successfully conducted the Lake View house, a popular summer resort on Lake George. He held several town offices and is highly esteemed in the town where he has passed the greater part of his long life.

SUFFERS ANOTHER SHOCK.

Richard J. Brown, one of the most prominent residents of Warren county, is critically ill in his home in Bolton suffering from a third shock. Since suffering from the first shock several years ago Mr. Brown has been more or less confined to his home. For many years he was one of the most expert civil engineers and surveyors in the country and conducted the Algonquin hotel at Bolton. June 4 1916

LAKE GEORGE FIRE LOSSES ARE $7,300

Hammond Building Destroyed, But Firemen Prevent Blaze From Spreading

Mar 28 1916 Star

LAKE GEORGE, March 27—The Canada street building owned by the Charles Hammond estate, was destroyed by fire early this morning. The fire started in the cellar of Pharmer's market and was discovered by Reuben Hammond. The total loss was $7,300 on which there was $3,800 insurance.

The building was about 100 feet north of the Hotel Worden on the state road. Good work by the fire fighters under the leadership of H. J. Gabb kept the flames from spreading

The loss on the building itself said to be $5,000, on which there was an insurance of $3,000. The Hammond family, which occupied one part of the structure, lost $1,000 in cash and furniture, on which they had $300 insurance. Mr. Pharmer's loss was $800 and he carried $500 insurance. E. J. Worden leased some rooms in the building as sleeping quarters for his help in the summer and he lost all his furniture said to be valued at about $500. He had no insurance.

TROUT LAKE, BOLTON.

Leonard Beswick has tapped Mrs. Anna Young's sugar camp again this year.

Mr. and Mrs. B. C. Dickinson, of North Caldwell, were Sunday guests of Mr. and Mrs. B. C. Putney.

Mrs. Bertha Traver, of Glens Falls, and her brother, Forest Kenyon, of Fort Edward, made a business trip to this place Saturday.

Judd Pratt's barn, with a quantity of fodder, and a flock of twenty hens, was destroyed by fire Friday evening of last week. There was no insurance. *march 30, 1916*

Jim Putney has secured employment with Dr. C. J. Nordstrom for the summer, and has moved his family from Glens Falls into the doctor's little stone cottage.

Billy Sunday Sizes 'Em Up.

Billy Sunday says many a man prays when he is up against it, but when he can stick his thumbs in his armholes and take a pair of scissors and cut his coupons, it is "Good-bye God, I'll see you later."

new TROUT LAKE, BOLTON. *916*

Milo Cardle has moved his family into the Frank Cheney house.

Whooping cough has attacked a number of children in this place. *1916*

Judson Pratt and Robert Whitcomb, of Wilton, visited Bert Pratt one day last week.

Robert Wilcox, of Bolton Landing, will move his family into the house vacated by Milo Cardle.

may 2 1916
CALF WITHOUT LEGS.

A calf without hind legs has been purchased by Sam Swyer from a Cossayuna farmer. The animal is four weeks old and crawls along the ground dragging its body, making it a fit subject for investigation by the Humane *Society.*

Bolton Teacher Closes School in Johnsburg

Miss Bertha Loveland has closed her school in district No. 10, Johnsburgh, and has returned to Bolton to pass the summer with her mother, Mrs. Charles Loveland. *news June 22, 1916*

At Home.

Are you at home when you're home,
   Or are you still down at your den,
Figuring and fighting it out
   There in your world of men?
Are you at home when you're home,
   Or are you way off somewhere—
Oh, how one's thoughts will roam
   Back to their toil and care!

When you come home do you bring
   The office along, old man,
Or the store, or the shop, or the thing
   That you're struggling to perfect
      and plan?
When you come home, do you leave
   All worry and trouble behind,
With nothing but wife and the babes
   And the sweet home life on your
      mind?

Tidmarsh-Nichols Wedding Tonight.

The marriage of Elmer A. Tidmarsh, of Glens Falls, and Miss Louise Knapp Nichols, of Shelving Rock, Lake George, will be solemnized this evening at Christ Church, Methodist Episcopal. The Rev. C. O. Judkins will officiate. A large number of invitations have been issued and the wedding will be an important social event. Mr. Tidmarsh has a large class of piano pupils in this place and many of these will witness the ceremony.
news nov 2 1916

Horace Greeley died in November, 1872. Soon after his death a movement was started by Whitelaw Reid, William W. Niles and other friends and associates of Mr. Greely to erect a public statue to his memory. A committee of sixty-five well known citizens from different parts of the country was selected, in whose name an appeal for subscriptions was made. The panic of 1873 interfered with the raising of a sufficient amount at that time. Some time later, however, Mr. Reid and The Tribune association carried the undertaking through.

Dancing Pavilion to Open July 4.

B. J. Green, of Lake George, announces the opening on July 4 of a large open-air dancing pavilion he has just completed on his property at Snug Harbor, just north of the county court house, in that village. Two dances will be given on the Fourth, afternoon and evening, and similar entertainments will be given twice weekly during the summer until Labor Day. Tierney's orchestra, of Glens Falls, has been engaged to furnish the music for the season. *news June 22, 1916*

TO WORK FOR BOARD TO STUDY POULTRY

Leonard Baker of Bolton, one of the Farm Boys that have been in camp at Loomis' Chestnut Ridge farm, has become so enthusiastic over George F. Bayle's chicken farm that he has arranged with Mr. Bayle to work on the farm for a month for his board. Baker has 40 chickens on his fathers' farm. Mr. Bayle has about 3,000 laying hens. *June 28 1916 Star*

STATE ROAD PATROLMAN DIES AT LAKE GEORGE

July 21 1916 Times

Charles Manchester, employed as a state road patrolman at Lake George, died yesterday afternoon as a result of injuries sustained about ten days ago when he fell and injured his stomach. He was 54 years old. Besides his wife he is survived by a son, Leonard; his mother, Mrs. Ephriam Manchester; two sisters, Mrs. Paul Reubents and Mrs. Bert Dewey, of this city. The funeral will be held tomorrow afternoon at 2 o'clock from the late home. The Rev. E. M. Parrott will officiate.

TAFT CHUCKLES OVER SITUATION
albany Journal

Speaks in Highest Terms of Hughes But is Silent When Roosevelt is Mentioned. *June 12 1916*

New York, June 13.—Smiling broadly and evidently at peace with all the world, William Howard Taft arrived in New York from New Haven, Conn., last night. Mr. Taft lagged behind the other passengers, and entering a taxicab unobserved was driven to the McAlpin hotel. A reporter asked him what he had to say regarding the nomination of Mr. Hughes and the defeat of Theodore Roosevelt, and the latter's declaration that he had retired from politics for good and aye.

"I think I said all I have to say on the nomination of Mr. Hughes when I was in Philadelphia last Saturday," he replied with an audible chuckle. "I at that time said he was the highest type of American, and you may repeat that statement. He is a scholar, a statesman and the proper man for the office of President. I said that then and you may repeat it for me. His nomination is a testimonial to his patriotism, his statesmanship, his character and personality. All this you may repeat for me."

"How about Mr. Roosevelt?"

Mr. Taft chuckled more audibly and cheerfully than before. "I'm going to get up early in the morning," he replied, as he entered an elevator. "You see, I'm to deliver a lecture at Georgetown."

"Do you believe Mr. Roosevelt will take the stump for Mr. Hughes?" asked the reporter.

"Good night," chuckled Mr. Taft, as the elevator door slammed and he was wafted upward.

BOLTON LANDING

BOLTON LANDING, March 23—Mr. and Mrs. Sewell P. Braley of North Bolton are moving to the village. They will reside with their son-in-law, William Norton.

George Allen, who has lived for many years near Edgecomb Pond, about two miles west of this village, was found dead in bed Sunday morning by his son. Mr. Allen was over eighty years of age and had been in ill health for about a year. His death was due to old age.

Sarah, wife of Alvah Hier, died Saturday morning. She was sixty-four years of age. She is survived by her husband and six children, Edward N. Lamb and B. W. Lamb of this place; Mrs. Duncan Murch of Ticonderoga, Mrs. Gordon Bennett of Glens Falls; Mrs. Charles Hayes and Mrs. Harry Wright of North Bolton; one brother, Frank Turrell of this village. The funeral was held Monday afternoon from her late home on Federal Hill. Tuesday the body was taken to Shoreham, Vt., to be placed by the side of her first husband.

MADAM HOMER IS TO GIVE BENEFIT RECITAL HERE

MADAM HOMER

The advance sale of tickets for the concert to be given Thursday evening in Christ church by Madam Homer indicates a large attendance.

Madam Homer will give the recital for the benefit of the Tri-County Association of the Blind and has promised a program which will please the audience. A resident of Lake George in Bolton, she believes in the work of the blind association and voluntarily offered to sing here for the organization's benefit.

As a songster, Madam Homer needs no introduction to the music lovers of Glens Falls. For years she has been among the leaders in the ranks of the world's great singers and her appearance here will be a big event in local musical circles.

BUY LIVERY BUSINESS

April 15, 1916

Purchase Made from Leavens Estate—Conduct Enterprise Along Modern Lines.

Times

Thurlow C. Leavens and George Roberts have purchased from the Leavens estate the livery, saddlery and wagon business in Ridge street and have also leased the stables and sales rooms, taking possession at noon today. Messrs. Leavens and Roberts will continue the business, and it is their aim to make it the most up-to-date enterprise of its kind in Northern New York.

Mr. Leavens is an experienced liveryman and Mr. Roberts has long been identified with business enterprises in Glens Falls. Both are well and favorably known and undoubtedly will meet with marked success.

It is the intention of the new firm to operate at least two automobile cabs. Their livery is centrally located and well adapted to the plans.

-238-

GEN. JAMES LEE DIES AT HAGUE

July 28 1916

Was Eighty Years Old and Served in Civil and Spanish Wars

HAGUE, July 27—Brigadier General James G. C. Lee, U. S. A., retired is dead at his local home. He was eighty years old and was in the United States army from April 1863 until 1904 He joined the colors during the Civil War, rating as a captain and quartermaster. He was born in Hamilton, Ont., and during the Spanish-American War had charge of the preparations for the landing of the United States forces in Cuba.

General Lee lived in a beautiful mansion just north of the settlement of Hague and was widely known and highly respected throughout the community. His remains have been taken to Washington, D. C., where funeral services will be conducted Saturday.

Ervin J. Smith, president and general manager of the Ervin J. Smith Detective Agency, Inc., of New York, was a week-end guest of Charles F. Burhans, in this village. Mr. Smith is a former Glens Falls boy and has been enjoying a brief visit in his old home the past week. *Mar 9, 1916*

Leaving Glens Falls about twelve years ago, filled with ambition, Mr. Smith by dint of perseverance and the energy characteristic of red headed people, in which class he belongs, worked his way into the United States secret service under former Chief Drummond. After three years he resigned from the force to enter the employ of William J. Burns, the famous New York detective, with whom he remained about eight years, becoming assistant general manager of the New York office. Last year Mr. Smith organized the agency of which he is now the head, and which is already recognized as one of the best in the country. At the present time Mr. Smith is arranging a lecture tour which will embrace many of the larger cities in the United States. The particular subject with which he will deal is "Criminology—Crime and Its Causes."

SILAS DISCUSSES HALF-HOSE.

Said Silas McGuggin, in Peeweeple's store: "Well, socks don't belong to the men any more. The women have grabbed 'em. They call 'em half-hose. Each year brings us men a whole lot of new woes. They've gobbled our shirts and they've gobbled our hats. They're wearin' our collars, our cuff and cravats. I'll bet you our wives and our daughters and aunts won't stop till they rob us pore men of our pants. This mornin' my daughter says: 'Mother, to-day I'll get some half-hose. They're so cool, the girls say.' I started to tell her it never would do, when up spoke my wife sayin': 'Get me some, too.' The anger I felt wus too deep to describe. I told 'em I'd wear all the socks for our tribe. My wife gave a sneer and she laughed as she said: 'Don't mind him, my dear. Father's out of his head.' If women wear socks at my house, I declare I'll pack up my baggage and get out of there. I don't know of nothin' I'd hate quite as much as females in socks and short dresses and such. The world's goin' backwards a heap all the time. The way we are slippin' is shorely a crime. Half-hose for the women are awful, say I, and them who refutes this are tellin' a lie." Just then there appeared in the door Alec Knox. Said he: "Gosh, there's Minnie McGinn wearin' socks!" Si ran to the door and he said: "Holy Smoke! I wish my field glasses had never got broke." Jed Peeweeple grinned and he said: "Pore old Si! He hates them half-hose like a school boy hates pie or like a young lady hates chockerlate drops." Si frowned and began a discussion of crops.

(Copyright, 1916, Otis F. Wood)

LAKE GEORGE DUE FOR BIG SEASON

Cottages and Summer Homes in Greater Demand Than Formerly

Star

BOLTON ROAD HOMES TAKEN

Apl 6/1916

LAKE GEORGE, April 5.—Lake George men expect the summer of 1916 will prove one of the most successful the lake has ever known, despite the fact that it is a presidential year. In support of this belief, they point to the fact that a cottage or home along the Bolton road cannot be rented at any price at the present time and that there are only four or five large places on the entire lake which are open for lease.

One prominent New York man recently authorized a Glens Falls real estate dealer to secure a Bolton road place for him at any cost. An offer of $1,000 a month has been made and refused and he is ready to go higher than that. As far as can be learned $5,000 for four months is the highest rental price that has been paid on Lake George within recent years.

Bungalows and small cottages about the lake are in great demand and there are only a few unleased. This is regarded as unusual by persons who deal in Lake George real estate.

TROUT LAKE, BOLTON.

Judd Pratt, of Wilton, visited relatives here Sunday.

Leonard Beswick is doing farm work for Mrs. Anna Young.

One of the recent high winds blew down D. S. Gates' partially completed garage.

Superintendent of Highways Bradley and a crew of men are repairing the roads in this vicinity.

Mrs. George Wilcox is ill of inflammatory rheumatism. Dr. Goodman, of Warrensburgh, is attending her.

Fred Branch bought a horse of J. H. Sturdevan, of Warrensburgh, last week. He also purchased two cows recently.

Wedding bells are expected to ring here in the near future. Rosell Putney and Miss Georgiana Thebo are the contracting parties. *May 26 1916*

Soldier Feared Seasickness.

Gen. John C. Fremont, at the close of one of his most important trips to California, is said to have traveled home overland through an extremely dangerous and Indian-ridden tract of country because he feared seasickness if he went by the Isthmus of Panama.

WHITE CAP METHODS

Warrensburgh Men Decisively Discourage Wrongdoing.

GIVE YOUNG MAN GOOD DRUBBING

Despoiler of Workingman's Home Gets Drastic Dose of Law of Home-Made Brand, Which Scorns Appeal or Delay.

Going back to the methods of "the good old times," twenty years ago, when the White Caps flourished and took it upon themselves to regulate the morals of various communities, a party of Warrensburgh men, ten or twelve in number, Monday night took the law into their own hands and punished severely a young man whose evil actions had for some time merited the reprobation of all decent people.

No effort was made at disguise, the self constituted vigilance committee going about the business they had set out to do with no attempt to conceal their identity. The young man who had invaded the home of a hardworking man of family, who has been employed out of town, was found with his guilty partner in misdoing, the mother of three children, at her home in the village, near the Warren county fair grounds. While all but one of the party hid behind a convenient woodpile, he went to the door of the house and rapped for admittance. There was a scurrying about within but the door did not open. The watchers, however, saw their man slip from a back door and make a dash to put a wide distance between himself and the visitors whose unfriendly intentions he suspected.

A spirited chase ensued but the quarry unwisely sought to escape through the fields with the result that he floundered in the snow and was easily overtaken. Each member of the regulating committee was supplied with a stout whip and proceeded to apply it where he thought it would be most effective. The victim howled with pain and promised exemplary behavior in future if he were allowed to go. But not until he had received a severe drubbing was he allowed to depart and then he went on a run vowing that he would never be caught there again.

The woman was not molested, though she deserves perhaps more censure than the man. Her husband and children have been betrayed and the morals of the latter corrupted. The husband, who has recently completed an extended term of employment in the lumber woods, has gone to another place to look for work and if he is successful will move his family where he goes.

The male culprit is of a notoriously bad character, having done his "bit" in a state prison. He has been so badly frightened that he will very likely be shy about further misdoing in this community.

DR. RALPH J. HOWE DIES IN HOSPITAL

Mar 22. 1916

Had Been Ill of Heart Trouble But Not Seriously Until Last Week

Times

Dr. Ralph J. Howe, son of Mr. and Mrs. D. S. Howe, Glen street, and one of the most highly respected members of the younger set of this city, died this morning at 8:30 o'clock at Willard, N. Y., to which place he went last Thursday to accept a position in a State hospital there. For some time past, Dr. Howe had not been in the best of health, suffering from heart trouble, which caused his death, but it was only a few days ago that his condition became alarming. His father left yesterday for Willard, and was with his son when he passed away.

Dr. Howe was well and widely known in this city. He was a graduate of the Glens Falls High school in the class of 1910, and took an intense interest in his school life in this city. Upon his graduation from the local institution of learning, he entered the New York university, graduating from that institution in 1914. At this time he was given an appointment to the City hospital on Blackwell's island, New York, relinquishing this position last fall to accept another position in a State institution. He was at his home in this city until last Thursday, leaving then for a visit with his brother, Clinton, in Utica, before taking up his new duties in Willard.

IN CUPID'S REALM

Owen K. Maranville of Bolton Landing, well known in this city, and Miss Hazel Frances Walrath were married recently in Maryland, the native village of the bride. Appended is an article on the wedding, published in the Oneonta Star:

A pretty home wedding was solemnized at noon Monday, February 12, at the home of Mr. and Mrs. A. L. Walrath of Maryland, when their daughter Hazel Frances, was united in marriage with Owen K. Maranville of Bolton Landing, in the presence of about 40 of the immediate relatives and most intimate friends of the bride and groom. The ceremony was performed by Dr. E. J. Farley of Oneonta.

The bride is a graduate of Oneonta State Normal school, class of 1910, and has successfully taught in Babylon for six years. She is a young lady with a charming personality, and musical talent and has a wide circle of friends who will extend their heartiest congratulations.

The groom, a former student of Colgate is one of the foremost young business men of Bolton Landing.

Miss Henrietta Miller, for the last twenty years housekeeper of the Chester house, died in the hotel last Thursday morning at 7 o'clock. She was born in Ticonderoga October 3, 1841, and was therefore seventy-five years old. She will be remembered by guests and staff of the Chester house as a generous, whole-souled woman who was always on the alert to look after the comfort of guests.

Use More Milk

Chemists tell us that one quart of milk is equal in food value to any one of the following animal foods:

3-4 pound lean beef at 20 cents....	15c
8 eggs at 36 cents per doz.........	24c
3 pounds fresh codfish at 12 cents..	36c
2 pounds chicken at 20 cents......	40c
4-5 pound pork loin at 15 cents....	12c
3-5 pound ham at 20 cents........	12c
1 pint oysters at 20 cents.........	20c
Average	22c

Any price expended for a quart of milk buys the same food value that averages to cost 22 cents in the above list. Milk also has a greater digestibility and a nearer perfect balance between its various ingredients.

SMOCK IS OUT FOR GOOD TIME

May 2 1916 Times

One of Chestertown's Notables "Takes in" Local Vaudeville and Picture Shows.

Justice of the Peace Charles T. Smock of Chestertown, who is also official court crier for the terms of County and Supreme courts, is in the city making the rounds of the picture and vaudeville shows. Charlie says nothing ever hits Chestertown that can compare with the local entertainment houses, with the possible exception of the Chestertown correspondence in the Warrensburg News. But that appears only once each week.

While the court crier and justice of the peace is well contented in the summer months with hundreds of tourists visiting the pretty little hamlet he becomes decidedly restless during the other seasons. How very listless life becomes in Chestertown in the winter is evidenced by Charlie's tale of a native of the place having dropped dead on the postoffice steps and not being found until three days later. Even then it was not discovered by anyone going to the postoffice for mail but by the janitor who was making his weekly visit to oil the hinges and lock of the door to make sure they did not become set.

70 YEARS OLD MAN STRUCK BY AUTO

May ₂₁ 1916

Mark Brown of Warrensburg Will Recover From Slight Concussion of Brain

TWO SUNDAY ACCIDENTS

WARRENSBURG, May 21.—Mark Brown, 70 years old, yesterday was knocked down by an automobile as he was crossing Main street to the postoffice. He was rendered unconscious and suffered a slight concussion of the brain, together with severe bruises about the body. His condition was regarded as grave during Saturday night but this morning it was much improved and physicians advised his relatives he would recover.

The machine which struck Mr. Brown was owned and driven by F. McAlley of Chester. The story as given by some persons who witnessed the accident was to the effect that Mr. Brown crossed in front of the automobile and on seeing the machine became nervous, stood still and in backing away stepped in its path. Others said the machine was traveling fast and the man did not have a chance to get out of its way.

Mr. Brown is the father of Mrs. Gilbert Weaver of Glens Falls.

There were several minor accidents today in this vicinity. A Ford machine ran into a fence on the Thurman road, about two miles from the business center of Warrensburg. The car's windshield was broken and its four inmates were cut about the face and hands by the shower of glass but were not otherwise hurt. A similar accident took place on the Chester road near Tripp's Lake, where a machine collided with a fence. None of the occupants were hurt.

SOME FACTS ABOUT BEER.

A pint of beer contains eight-tenths of an ounce of alcohol, equivalent nearly to a tablespoonful of whisky.

While cold beer tastes cool and pleasant to a hot man, it does not cool him off.

It heats him up.

The alcohol and solids are burned into heat.

The effect of alcohol is to send an excess of blood to the skin.

Whenever a large amount of blood goes to the skin it causes a feeling of warmth.

When a man drinks beer he causes himself to feel hot.

He also actually increases his body heat.

He increases his chances of sunstroke at least 100 per cent.—Dr. W. A. Evans, Chicago.

FATAL AUTO WRECK

Leroy M. Starbuck, of Saratoga, Killed Near Chestertown.

PINNED UNDER CAPSIZED CAR

His Companions, Harry G. Underwood and John Dix Coffin, Escape With Minor Injuries — Road Obscured by Fog.

Sept 21 1916

Le Roy M. Starbuck, of Saratoga Springs, twenty-six years old, was killed in an automobile accident at 1 o'clock Tuesday morning, when a Dodge Brothers touring car he was driving overturned on the state road about one mile south of Chestertown. He was accompanied by Harry G. Underwood, of New York, and John Dix Coffin, of Albany, both of whom escaped with minor injuries.

Mr. Starbuck left Saratoga Springs at 6 o'clock for his camp at Fourth Lake to pass a few days fishing. Mr. Underwood and Mr. Coffin met him in Glens Falls. They stopped in Lake George and also at Alf Stone's Halfway house, two miles south of this village. They left the latter place at 12:30 o'clock. A heavy fog enveloped the road but the machine was running about thirty miles an hour when it rounded the curve near the Chester Rural cemetery near Chestertown. Failing to make the curve the car ran for some distance in the soft sand shoulder of the road. The driver applied the brakes and the car swerved to the other side of the road where it struck a pile of sand and turned over.

Mr. Starbuck and Mr. Underwood, who was also in the front seat, were caught under the automobile, the former being pinned squarely under the steering wheel in such a position that he was rendered unconscious and before the car could be lifted from him he died, within half an hour after the accident occurred. Mr. Underwood was pinned under the car with the back of the front seat resting on his chest and his legs under the dash board. It was a remarkable feature of the accident that he was not also killed. Mr. Coffin, who was in the rear seat, managed to extricate himself and found his companions beneath the car. He was unable to assist them alone and ran to the farmhouse of Clark Leggett for help. Several men were soon on the scene and jacks were secured and the wreck raised. Mr. Starbuck breathed his last as his body was being removed from beneath the steering wheel.

Dr. F. E. Aldrich, of Chestertown, was called and directed that the body be removed to the Leggett home. Later in the day it was taken to the young man's home in Saratoga. Messrs. Underwood and Coffin were taken in Dr. Aldrich's automobile to his office, where their wounds were dressed.

ERVIN J. SMITH HAS MADE SUCCESS

May 30 1916

Detective's Investigation of Family Tree May Lead to Big Law Suit

Stay

DOES WORK FOR ROOSEVELT

Recently Established 20 Branch Offices in Larger Cities—Has 36 Operatives at Work On Eastern Cases

Ervin J. Smith, president of the young but already widely known Smith Detective Agency of New York, has arrived in Glens Falls, his native city, to pass a needed week's vacation, following a strenuous and successful winter's work. Mr. Smith recently established twenty branch offices in *major cities of the United States and* his thirty-six operatives are attending to important work in all sections of the east. He recently placed 176 special officers as guards along the coast line of hotels in Atlantic City and nearby resorts.

Mr. Smith is recognized as one of the most successful detectives in the United States, having during the ten years he has followed the business, worked on many important cases, including the murder of Herman Rosenthal, for which Lieutenant Becker and four gunmen were sent to the electric chair; the Roosevelt robbery at Oyster Bay and the $25,000 necklace robbery in Chicago. He was in charge of Roosevelt's body guards throughout last election campaign. Mr. Smith provides all detective service required by the former president.

During his spare hours of the last few weeks, Mr. Smith devoted his time to tracing his family tree, and as a result, a big law suit may be started soon. Mr. Smith has ascertained that he is a direct descendant of Johannes Waldron, who was one of the twenty-three men to whom the grant of the new town of Harlem was made by Peter Stuyvesant, first governor of New York. The new town of Harlem, as it was then known, comprised all of the district from Seventy-fourth street and the East river, New York, across the island of Manhattan to the North river and 129th street, each block of which is now worth a million dollars or more. A question has arisen as to the validity of many of the present deeds, and thirteen years ago Mr. Smith's father received a letter from a law firm, which the detective has since learned is reliable, saying that if these deeds were not valid and the title should revert to the heirs of the twenty-three men to whom the original grant was made, each heir would receive approximately $180,000 as his share.

This property includes the Polo grounds, the New York speedway and the Jumel mansion, which was the Washington Heights headquarters of George Washington, and which is now owned by the Daughters of the American Revolution. Mr. Smith last evening said that he had interviewed a large number of his relatives and he expected to represent their interests. It is possible a petition will be made for a court order granting the privilege to examine certain records which are now refused him.

Whether he ever succeeds in gaining anything in a financial way, Mr. Smith believes that the results of his investigation are certain to prove a big help to him. In New York, when he applied for membership in clubs, his one answer to the question as to his identity was "Smith of Glens Falls, now New York detective." Now he can show he is descended from one of the oldest American families and on the strength of it he has applied for membership in the Holland club, which is one of the most exclusive organizations in New York.

Mr. Smith traces his relationship as follows: Johannes Waldron's daughter Elizabeth married M. McQuire, and their daughter Lucretia married Benjamin Harris, whose daughter Cornelia was wedded to Earl Smith, grandfather of the detective. In looking up his history, Mr. Smith has found that Johannes Walron was appointed by Governor Stuyvesant as attorney general and constable in the new town of Harlem, and the detective laughingly remarked, "I now realize from whom the detective instinct came."

Mr. Smith has never told the whole story of why he became a detective, but a part of it leaked out last night while he was talking with a reporter for The Post-Star. He left Glens Falls in 1901 and went into the real estate business in New York, meeting with ordinary success, until 1905, when he managed to "swing a big deal" and make a large commission. Like the other agents, his savings, over and above living expenses, were invested in the stock of the company for which they worked and substantial dividends were being declared to them until an officer suddenly "went south with the funds." Mr. Smith admitted that he desired to catch him, but would allow the conversation to drift no further along that line.

He ventured into detective work almost at once and within a year was working under the direction of Benjamin Drummond, former chief of the secret service of the United States, for which he did much successful work. Leaving the employ of Mr. Drummond, he took a position with William J. Burns, advancing step by step until he became the head of the Burns' New York office. Following successful work in that position, he saw the advantage of establishing himself in business and working along his own ideas, and last July he left Burns, and the Ervin J. Smith agency was founded. One success after another has followed this agency, and recently it took a part in the famous Dr. Waite case in New York, which resulted in the dentist confessing the Peck murders.

BURGESS WARREN HAS SUCCUMBED

Feb 8 1917 Times

Was Member of Company Which Erected Sagamore Hotel on Lake George.

Burgess Warren, one of the original stockholders of the company that purchased Green Island in Lake George and erected the popular summer hotel, "The Sagamore," at Bolton, died recently in Palm Beach, Fla. Mr. Warren was familiarly known in Glens Falls and vicinity as "Birch" Warren. He resided in this city for a number of years.

He left Glens Falls several years ago and went to Philadelphia where he organized a company known as the Warren Roofing company. This company manufactured various kinds of roofing and the business was a big financial success from the start.

Mr. Burgess was well advanced in life but spent all of his summers at his beautiful summer home on Lake George. He owned one of the fastest yachts on Lake George, "The Elide."

YOUNG PEOPLE'S CORNER.

Conducted by Laura Stafford for Guidance of the Rising Generation.

Dear Readers:—I wonder how many of you are contemplating city life. I hope my girl readers will give me their undivided attention for a few moments, and I shall explain what a working girl may expect in the crowded city.

A dingy boarding place and poorly ventilated rooms. In too many instances the girl does not receive wages that will pay for board, room and proper clothing. So many white faced city girls merely exist. They must accept small paying positions to prevent utter starvation; and it is then, when the girl is starving for food and pure companionship; even the girl with the strongest character weakens, and yields to the call of the city streets for food, clothing, pleasure and companionship of the questionable kind, when before she would turn from it all with horror and loathing.

Many a girl goes to the city more for good times than employment—and this is the girl who is easily changed from an innocent country girl to a hardened city woman.

Girlies, stay in the country—you can find employment and pleasure—and the old home will always afford a protection for you. You cannot realize the danger of city life until you have drained it to the last bitter drop—then you are a wreck. Oh, shame! that in our land of civilization and freedom, thousands of girls are continually fluttering to the goal of shame.
Continued.

Mar 11 1916

LAURA STAFFORD

EX-GOVERNOR JOHN A. DIX

times Mar 8 1916.

Inside History of the Life of Boy Toiler in Lumber Camp Who Rose to Wealth and High Honor--- Romance of His Marriage---Seeking Health On California Ranch

Shattered in health, his money gone, former Governor John A. Dix, who is known personally by many people here and hereabouts, has been forced to abandon his plans. He is now trying to regain his health on a ranch near Montecito, Cal.

In a talk to a California friend Mr. Dix for the first time unbosoms himself of his troubles and gives some inside history hitherto unrevealed. Part of his revelations pertain to his lumber operations at McKeever which are of special interest in this locality. He said, according to the Booneville Courier:

"Were I to be Governor of New York again I know of nothing which I would do differently than was done by me during my term.

"I went into office a strong, rugged man, and came back to private life shattered in health.

"It would take more than one man of iron to serve as Governor of New York state and not break down under the strain, unless he is willing to take the system as he finds it and go with the current."

The former Governor choose for his California retreat a home far up in the coast range mountains. He had just completed a game of whist with Natchez, the famed violinist. Continuing he said:

"Absolutely I have no plans for the future. Leaving the Governor's chair in ill health, I faced business entanglements brought about solely by the war, which tied up the lumber markets of the country. As I was not physically to take charge of my private affairs a trustee was appointed as has been the case with most of the lumber firms even on this coast, and I was ordered to Honolulu to recuperate.

Lemon Thompson was a neighbor of the Dix family in Glens Falls. Thompson had two pretty daughters. The elder, Gertrude, and the foundryman's young son had been playmates from early childhood. As boy and girl they had romped on the goose common of Glens Falls.

When the boy was away at college the girl went to Thompson to live with her father. The now prosperous village of Thompson was then a rough lumber camp.

A year of foundry work was all young Dix could stand. Two years of college life had bred in him ambitions for greater things. It was not long after he left the foundry that he became a clerk in the employ of Lemon Thompson, the old lumberman. He went to live at Thompson. Fate ruled the lives of Miss Gertrude Thompson and young Dix in storybook fashion. They were married and Dix became the active head of his father-in-law's business.

About that time the pulp industry sprung to life in that section of the Adirondacks. The old Thompson sawmill burned down, but there remained immensely valuable water power rights. A capitalist furnished the money to build a great mill at Thompson and the United Buckboard Company was formed, the Thompson interests receiving a minority of the stock in return for the water power rights. Shortly after that combination was formed Lemon Thompson died, leaving the bulk of his property and the control of his estate to Dix.

Dix at once launched forth on a successful business career. He gave up his holdings in the United Buckboard Company and built the great Iroquois Paper Mill, on a portion of the water power site he had retained when he went into the deal with the United. He acquired big interests in four other mills.

A tract of land Thompson had owned on the Moose River was used to supply the pulp wood for all the Dix mills. He also became identified with important banking institutions at Albany, Glens Falls and Schuylerville.

With financial success came social advancement. The Dixes took a house in Albany and began to entertain lavishly. Mrs. Dix soon became a social dictator. Mr. Dix, too, was proud of their success as social leaders.

Lake George Merchant Meets Death in Automobile Accident.

CAR SKIDS AND TURNS TURTLE

news April 6 1914

Body Pinned Down by Wrecked Machine and Life Is Instantly Crushed Out — No Witnesses of the Sad Fatality.

Dolphus J. Brown, a prominent and widely known resident of Lake George, was instantly killed about 4 o'clock Tuesday afternoon in an automobile accident which occurred on the Bolton road, about a mile from the village, near the Peabody place.

Mr. Brown was a candidate for Democratic committeeman for the town of Caldwell in the primaries and was engaged in transporting voters to and from the polling place. He was returning to the village after carrying some men to their homes and was alone. There was no one in the vicinity when the accident occurred therefore the exact manner in which the

unfortunate man met his death can only be surmised. It is believed that his car skidded on the wet road, whirled about, struck the fence by the roadside then crashed into a tree and overturned. Mr. Brown's body was pinned under the machine and was found with one side of the body resting on his head. There was a hole of considerable size in his skull over the right eye which is believed to have been caused by striking a board in the fence before the car overturned. If this was the case, it was this injury which caused his death.

The accident was discovered by M. L. C. Wilmarth, of Glens Falls, who passing in his automobile saw the wrecked car and stopped to investigate. He discovered a man's leg protruding from beneath the machine and tried to release the body but was unable to do so. He ascertained that the man was dead and then went for help. The machine was lifted and the body was removed to the Brown home on the lake shore in the village. Mrs. Brown was visiting in New York and was immediately informed by telegraph of her husband's horrible death. She left the city as soon as possible and arrived in Lake George yesterday morning.

The widow was formerly Miss Nellie Lewis, daughter of Mr. and Mrs. H. M. Lewis, for many years residents of Warrensburgh, but now of Glens Falls. The couple were married in Warrensburgh in the early 80's. They had three children, all of whom survive, Mrs. Fred N. Cooper and Miss Gwendolin Brown and Howard A. Brown, of Lake George. Mr. Brown also leaves three sisters, Mrs. Jessie Nichols, of Lake George and New York; Mrs. Elmer J. West and Mrs. W. J. Hunt, of Glens Falls.

Mr. Brown was fifty-three years old and a life-long resident of Lake George, and was well-known in other towns of the county. He was noted for his generosity and was a prince of good fellows in the best sense of the term, therefore had a large circle of friends wherever he was known. He was the senior member of the hardware firm of D. J. Brown & Company and was also engaged in lumbering. He was prominent in the Odd Fellows' fraternity, being one of the chief promoters of the organization of the Lake George lodge and one of its most active members. Two weeks ago he became a Mason when he received the third degree in Warrensburgh lodge, No. 425.

Automobile News. *1912*

Joseph P. Gabel, the local baker, whose automobile delivery truck was burned a few weeks ago, has replaced it with a second-hand Ford truck, purchased from a Troy firm. L. A. Mosher, the River street merchant, has also made a change, replacing his Saxon runabout with a new Saxon-six to be used in connection with his general merchandise store. *news*

-242-

CHARLES A. HOVEY DIES IN FLORIDA

Hardening of Arteries Fatal to Prominent Local Business Man

DEATH NOT UNEXPECTED

Glens Falls Resident Had Been Seriously Ill Since His Arrival Two Weeks Ago in Orlando—Body Expected Home Tomorrow

Nov 6 1916 Star

Charles Albert Hovey, one of Glens Falls' most widely known and most public-spirited citizens, died at 3:50 o'clock Saturday afternoon in his winter home in Orlando, Fla. Mrs. Hovey was at his bedside when he breathed his last but no other relatives were present. His daughter, Mrs. Edward Kenyon, departed from Glens Falls at midnight Thursday with her husband in response to a telegram telling of Mr. Hovey's serious condition, but she did not reach Orlando until three hours after her father's death.

Mr. Hovey's death was caused by the hardening of arteries near his heart, an affliction which had resulted in ill health during the last eight years and which had caused him to be critically ill on several occasions. z

Mr. and Mrs. Hovey departed from Glens Falls on October 19 for their winter home. At the time of their departure Mr. Hovey complained that he did not feel well and the long train ride to the south weakened him so greatly that he was confined to his home immediately after his arrival at Orlando and he never rallied. Last Wednesday evening, it was seen that there was little hope of his recovery and information was conveyed by a telegram to his family in this city.

Charles Albert Hovey was a self-made man and it is doubtful if there is a man in Glens Falls who was more deservedly popular than he. He was born October 31, 1851, in Victory Mills, the son of Charles and Huldah Sherman Hovey. When he was ten years old, his father was claimed by death and the boy at once became the support of his mother. Shortly after his father's death, Mr. Hovey moved to Glens Falls with his mother and he had since resided here.

After various occupations during his early boyhood, Mr. Hovey became a fruit peddler. In this venture he was very successful and as a result in 1879 he established the first produce store in Glens Falls and was the pioneer of northern New York in that business. With his splendid ability, he developed the business rapidly and twenty years ago he added the ice business to the enterprise, the combined venture being known as the Hovey Fruit and Ice company of which he was president.

For many years, Mr. Hovey was active in the real estate market and he built a large number of dwelling houses and business places in Glens Falls. About twenty years ago he made his first winter trip to the south and since that time he rarely missed passing the colder months in Florida. He established a winter home ten years ago in Orlando and acquired extensive real estate holdings in that city. He built many houses there and had planned further investments.

During his long and useful life Mr. Hovey served his home community as a commissioner of public safety, a village trustee and overseer of the poor. In the last named position he built up an enviable reputation.

His charitable disposition made him the ideal man for the position and the poor of the village were never better cared for than under his administration. His kindness to the poor was not confined to his term of office but it was one of his foremost characteristics throughout his life.

In this city today can be found families who are using barrels of flour sent to them by Charles A. Hovey. The homes of others are being warmed by coal that was put in their cellars at his expense. These kindnesses have been carried out for many years and are known only because of the stories which have been told by the recipients of them. His gifts were made with a free heart and he always preserved secrecy regarding them.

At times he has loaned and given money to the poor but he was more fond of contributing the necessities of life and it has been said that no man who asked him for provisions, fuel or clothing, was ever refused.

On July 19, 1876, Mr. Hovey was married to Caroline Irish of Lake George, who was his helpmate and adviser during his life and who survives him. He is also survived by his daughter, Mrs. Kenyon, four sons, C. A. Hovey jr., Darwin W. Hovey, Edward Hovey and Fred Hovey and a sister, Mrs. Henry Wester, all of Glens Falls.

Telegrams received here yesterday announced that the body would arrive in Glens Falls Tuesday afternoon or early Tuesday evening.

PREY OF THE ELEMENTS.

Utowana Hotel, Once Magnificent Structure, a Ruin at Blue Mountain Lake.

The Utowana hotel, at Blue Mountain Lake, built in the 80's and at that time one of the most magnificent summer resorts in the Adirondacks, has been empty and deserted for more than twenty years and is fast crumbling into ruins. During the recent heavy winds and rain about 100 feet of the structure was blown down and the remainder is tottering. The hotel was built by Fred Durant when Blue Mountain Lake was in high favor as a summer resort. It had accommodations for about 500 guests and was richly furnished. Everything was on the most elaborate scale and the place was opened with a great flourish, but the expected guests did not arrive in sufficient numbers to make the venture profitable. After a few years' struggle it was closed and never reopened. A few years ago the furniture was sold and the building has been allowed to go to ruin, a monument to the mistaken judgment of its owner.

RICHARD J. BROWN.

Richard J. Brown, for many years a prominent and highly esteemed resident of Bolton-on-Lake-George, died Friday afternoon at 5:15 o'clock, having suffered three strokes of paralysis, death came to him suddenly, as he had been able to walk around his room until about an hour before the end, when he was seized with convulsions. He leaves no relatives nearer than cousins. Mr. Brown would have been seventy-one years old today. He was born in Brooklyn and came to Bolton when he was fourteen years old. For more than forty years he conducted the Lake View house and made it one of the most popular summer resorts on the lake. Mr. Brown was an expert surveyor and was the oldest practitioner in that line in Warren county. When the law providing for county engineers went into effect Mr. Brown was appointed to that office and held the position until it was abolished. He was a man of great intellect and by his own unaided efforts acquired proficiency in many lines of endeavor. He was noted for his honesty and square dealing in business transactions and for his charity. His body was taken to Troy Monday and cremated at the chapel in Oakwood cemetery. The Rev. Dwight Parse, a former pastor of Mr. Brown, conducted the religious services. The ashes were brought back to Bolton for interment. *Jan 14 1917*

SUMMER HOME BOUGHT BY TICONDEROGA MAN

Jan 10 1917 Times

Three well known men, Melvin Barton, of Hague; W. J. Smith and F. B. Wood, of Ticonderoga, have purchased the summer home of the late Benjamin Day and the beautiful property surrounding it. The estate is one of the finest in the Town of Hague and it is reported that the price paid was $30,000. The late Mr. Day was the inventor of the "Benday" process for developing colored picture negatives.

Chester House Closed for the Winter.

The Chester house, in Chestertown, was closed January 1 for the winter. Extensive improvements will be made before it is reopened early in the spring. The hotel was established more than 100 years ago and has entertained many famous people of America and Europe. The present popular proprietor, Harry S. Downs, inherited the property from his father, who conducted it successfully for many years. *January 3 1917*

'BUFFALO BILL' IS NEAR DEATH

Plainsman Receives Announcement of His Physician Calmly

Jan 9 1917 Star

END TO COME WITHIN THIRTY-SIX HOURS

DENVER, Jan. 8.—Colonel William F. Cody ("Buffalo Bill") is dying in Denver tonight, facing death in the same manner that he has faced it many times on the plains of the west in conflicts that made his name famous. The colonel heard the warning

COL. W.F. CODY (BUFFALO BILL)

words of the approach of the end from his physician. He had summoned the physician to the home of his sister, where he is spending his last hours. When the doctor walked into his room, the colonel said: "Sit down, doctor, there is something I want to ask you. I want you to answer me honestly. What are my chances?"

The doctor turned to the scout:

"There is a time, colonel," he said, "when every honest physician must commend his patient to a higher power."

"How long?" he asked simply.

"I can't answer that," said the physician, "only by telling you your life is like the hour glass. The sand is slipping, gradually, slowly, but soon the sand will all be gone. The end is not far away."

Colonel Cody turned to his sister, Mrs. May Decker.

"May," he said, "let the Elks and Masons take charge of the funeral."

Then the man who made history in the West when it was young began methodically to arrange his affairs.

Death, it is said, will come within 36 hours. Hundreds of telegrams of sympathy from all over the country came today. Many boys from different parts of the country wrote.

"Won't you please send me a story of your life so I can be a scout like you," wrote one boy. "He is a typical American boy," said the colonel, as his face lighted with a smile.

HUNTERS MUST BE TAGGED.

Will Wear Big White Button to Show Possession of License.

Hunters, as well as automobiles, are to wear license plates next year. The Conservation commission has sent forth the edict which is to set the fashion for 1917, that the game warden may the easier spot the licenseless seeker of game.

According to the new rule, however, while the hunter must at all times wear his license plate in a conspicuous place on his clothing, he is required to wear only one and no provision is made as to the use of a cutout or rear light.

Dog and marriage licenses still continue in use and canines are supposed to be provided with license tags. Married women are, of course, tagged with the wedding ring, and there are those who would go so far as to attempt to compel the "head of the house" to display some sort of classifying identification other than the worried look. *Jan 2 1917. News*

As for the hunter's license tag—it is a two-inch white celluloid button with blue lettering and red numerals which is furnished free with each hunting and trapping license. The button may be held firmly in place on a hunter's jacket by a stub which screws on the back.

If the hunter loses the button he must buy a new license and button. Should he lose his license he should at once apply to the clerk who issues the license and who will furnish a statement to the effect that the license has been lost, this statement to be carried in lieu of a license.

The hunter who fails to wear a button bearing his license number will be required to forfeit his license.

Glens Falls Man Friend of "Buffalo Bill."

Charles Miller, of Glens Falls better known as "Broncho Charley," was for five years a member of the Wild West company of Col. William F. Cody, "Buffalo Bill," who died yesterday in Denver. Mr. Miller, with twenty other cowboys, accompanied the show to Europe some years ago. "Buffalo Bill" was a unique figure in American history and one of the best known men in the country. He was the friend of many men of national prominence. *Jan 11 1916*

Frank Harris Sells Village Milk Route.

Frank J. Harris, of Sunrise Farm, has sold his milk route in this village to Jeptha Ross, who has been staying at Mr. Harris' farm for some time. Mr. Ross formerly had a route in Bolton and is therefore thoroughly at home in the business. He took possession Monday. *Jan 18, 1917.*

BUFFALO BILL DIED A POOR MAN

Made Three Millions in the Show Business, But Saved Comparatively Little.

Jan 20 1917 Star

Much of the success of the Buffalo Bill show was due to the business abilities of Nate Salsbury, Col. Cody's manager, and to Major Burke, his publicity man.

On the first of November, 1911, Buffalo Bill announced his retirement from the show business, at a time when it was said he had made from it as much as $3,000,000. Certain it is that whatever had been his earnings up to that time, his extreme generosity and fondness for good living had materially depleted them. He could not remain long in retirement at Cody, Wyo., however, and was soon back again with his show.

In July, 1913, began bitter times for Col. Cody. He had joined forces with Gordon W. Lillie, called Pawnee Bill, who had had a wild west show of his own, under the name of "Buffalo Bill's Wild West and Pawnee Bill's Far East." Attachments for some $66,000 were filed against the show while it was in Denver.

Then came quarrels between Col. Cody and Lillie about the terms of settlement of the judgment, and Col. Cody charged Lillie with having cheated him systematically out of a part of the gate receipts. Things went from bad to worse, and finally the celebrated show was sold under the hammer. The Indians had been sent back to a reservation. There was one bright spot for Col. Cody, however. His famous white horse, Isham, which he had ridden for twenty-five years, was bought in for him by Col. Bills of Lincoln, Neb., an old friend of Buffalo Bill.

After these troubles, however, the great scout kept a good courage and announced his intention to raise money on some Canadian timber land which he held. A little later he said he would join the Sells-Floto circus, which held a $20,000 loan of the old Buffalo Bill show.

Col. Cody is survived by Mrs. Louise Cody and their two daughters. For some years he and his wife were estranged, but a reconciliation took place a few years ago one Christmas. Most of his resting time was spent on a large ranch in Wyoming, where he instituted many improvements and took a pride in the growth of the community.

BUFFALO BILL'S WILL IN PROBATE COURT

Jan 25 1917 Times

CODY, Wyo., Jan. 25.—The will of the late William F. Cody, (Buffalo Bill), has been brought here for filing in the Probate court, probably today. The estate is valued at $65,000 and the bulk will go to the widow. This does not include a valuable collection of trophies which also will go to her.

POPULATION OF MEXICO CLASSIFIED

Thirty-Eight Per Cent Pure Indians, Nineteen Per Cent Whites

Ap 20 1916

DESCENDENTS OF AZTECS

Sun

WASHINGTON, April 19—There are more Indians living today within the territory originally comprising Mexico than ever existed at any one time in all the rest of the Western Hemisphere combined, according to a bulletin issued today by the National Geographic Society of Washington.

"Of the 15,000,000 inhabitants of Mexico, fully 38 per cent. are pure Indians, and 48 per cent. of mixed blood, only 19 per cent. being whites," continues the bulletin.

"These six million Indians, many of whom are descendants of that wonderful race, the Aztecs, are divided into many linguistic families and tribes, the number varying according to the standards of differentiation adopted by each enthnologist. Some authorities group them into fourteen families, with fifty-one languages and sixty-nine dialects, while others make sixteen family divisions, subdivided into one hundred, thirty-two tribes.

"The pure-blooded Indian of the remote regions untouched by civilization is more frequently than otherwise a stalwart individual of upright character, moral, honest and loyal.

Madam Homer Building in Lake George.

news 1919

The Schermerhorn Construction company, of Lake George, has secured the contract to build a handsome residence for Madame Louise Homer, the famous grand opera singer, on Bixby's point, on Lake George, recently purchased by the singer from W. K. Bixby for $25,000. Work has been begun and the house will be ready for occupancy at the opening of the summer season. Ludlow & Peabody, of New York, are the contractors.

William Owens. *news*

The funeral of the late William Owens, proprietor of the Palisodes hotel at Brant Lake, was conducted today. The body was taken from Brant Lake to Chestertown this morning and funeral services conducted by Rev. Father Crowe in the Chestertown Roman Catholic church. The body was then taken to Warrensburg and placed aboard a special Hudson Valley car and with twenty-five mourners conveyed to the Union cemetery in Hudson Falls, where interment was made.

BOLTON LANDING.

Harry Barber, of the University of Pennsylvania, spent the holidays with his parents.

The new residence of Owen K. Maranville is nearing completion under the skillful supervision of Ormsby Brothers. *Jan 3 1917*

The George R. Fish place at Bolton has been purchased by Dr. W. H. Becker, of Brooklyn, from Iaez B. Fish, of Glens Falls. Mr. Becker has also bought the Gates property on the Huddle Bay and property adjoining it on the south owned by Mrs. P. Fuller, of Bolton. Dr. Becker intends in the spring to build a handsome summer home on his newly acquired Gates property overlooking the lake, also to remodel the Fish homestead into a house for his caretaker. *news*

William Tobin's new house is nearly ready for the roof. When completed it will be an ornament to the village.

The skating on the lake, which has been excellent for a week past, has been spoiled for a time by the arrival of about two inches of snow.

Myron O. Brown has been quite ill of grip but is so far recovered as to be able to sit up in a chair part of the time. Mr. and Mrs. Brown are domiciled at I. E. Stafford's.

Miss Ella Lenox died Sunday morning, at her home at the Huddle. She had been in poor health for a number of years. Funeral Tuesday and interment in Bolton cemetery. Miss Lenox is survived by her aged mother, with whom she lived; two brothers, Thomas and Robert, and three sisters, Mrs. Anna Dearstyne, Mrs. Fred R. Smith and Mrs. Henry Wilson.

She Fights for Indians

FLORENCE ETHERIDGE

Miss Florence Etheridge, of the Indian Bureau, is Uncle Sam's guardian of the property of Indian heirs, and her keenness has discouraged many unscrupulous persons who prey on Indian credulity. Her specialty is to see that Indian heirs get justice. She is an expert on wills, a member of the bar of the District of Columbia and of the United States Supreme court. *Dec 13 1916 Sun*

SNEEZING OMENS.

At One Time to Sneeze Was Regarded as a Death Warrant.

Sneezing from very remote times has been regarded with superstition.

Our forefathers went to bed again if they sneezed while putting on their shoes. A sneeze to the right was deemed lucky; to the left, of evil portent. To sneeze near a burial place was very unlucky.

Tradition has it that sneezing was at first a fatal sign—every human being sneezed but once and then died—but Jacob petitioned the Creator to remove the sneezing ban and succeeded. Thence arose the once universal custom of saluting a sneezer with "God bless you!" or "May you live long!" The custom still obtains in some parts of Europe.

In England not only was a sneezer blessed, but friends raised their hats to him as well. In an old book, "The Code of Conduct," it is directed that "if his lordship sneezes ye are not to bawl out, 'God bless you!' but bow to him handsomely." All over the world the sneeze was recognized. Whole nations were under orders to make exclamations when their king sneezed.

Sneezing was believed to be a sure cure for hiccough and was also looked upon as a sign of sanity. If ancient and universal belief goes for anything it is good to sneeze.—London Tele-

---

How Fast Can You Say This?

A pickle peddler pushed his pushcart full of pickles o'er a puddle but ne'er a passer purchased e'er a piddling pickle from that pushcart in the puddle as the passers passed. Peeved at this, the pickle peddler pushed his pickle pushcart into a passer who, the pickle peddler, promptly punched, praying petulantly as the prostrate pickle peddler picked a pickle from his pushcart, poised and in a passion put the pickle in the passer's paunch with such a punch that that poor person punted o'er the puddle and on the prostrate pickle peddler's pushcart fell.

Pausing importunate, the pickle peddler peeled to paste the passer who had pushed his pickle pushcart in the puddle and pertinent proposed to pickle that poor passer so that pickle peddlers might a puddle pass without a passer pausing e'en to push a pickle peddler's pushcart full of pickles o'er—

We pause here in this illustration of the great virtue in the letter P to remark that the only intention of this proem of pickles is to attract YOUR attention to the fact that the great 24-page illustrated Magazine and Story Section of the Sunday World is really the best thing in its way ever produced by a daily newspaper. Get next Sunday's World and see for yourself.

HERMIT GOES TO JAIL

Orlando Bryant Sent to Albany Penitentiary for Five Months.

CONVICTED OF STEALING CHICKENS

news nov 19

Caught in Act of Gently and Quietly Removing Unsuspecting Fowls From Alf Stone's Yard at the Halfway House.

1916

Orlando Bryant, the hermit of Harrington hill, was arraigned before Justice John T. Bryant yesterday morning, in Lake George, convicted of larceny and sentenced to five months imprisonment in the Albany penitentiary. He was taken to that institution by Constable Melvin H. Wilcox on the afternoon train. Bryant, who, by the way, is not a relative of the justice who sentenced him, was accused of stealing chickens from the hen yard of Alf Stone's Halfway house on the Lake George-Warrensburgh road. Mr. Stone caught him in the act one day last week and caused his arrest on a charge of larceny. Orlando had rigged up a trap into which he lured the unsuspecting fowls by means of attractive bait. He then transferred them to a bag, without disturbing their serenity of mind, and therefore so quietly as to attract no attention and transported them to his shack on Harrington hill. Mr. Stone believes this has been going on all summer and he estimated his loss at 150 fowls.

Orlando is a character. Of repulsive appearance he might be taken for a man of low intelligence, but this is far from being the case. He is shrewd and calculating and is never caught napping. He has been accused of poisoning animals and other minor crimes, but this is the first conviction that has been secured against him, except for intoxication and disorderly conduct.

For some years Orlando has lived alone in a hut on his farm on Harrington hill. He was formerly married but his wife divorced him and remarried in a western state. He has a daughter living but she has no communication with him. A son grew to vigorous young manhood and enlisted in the United States army. He was sent to the Phillipine Islands and became one of the most expert sharpshooters in the army and a soldier of reckless bravery. His career was cut short by disease, to which he succumbed after a brief illness. His body was brought home. The boy was the last of the family to leave his father and after his departure Orlando was left alone. He lived in unspeakable filth, defying all sanitary laws. When they clean him up at the penitentiary it will be a great surprise to his system and a shock, perhaps, which may disturb his health.

The hermit's departure from his squalid abode will greatly relieve the mind of Overseer of the Poor John J. Archer, who has ploughed through huge snow drifts for several winters to go to his relief. Mr. Archer has tried to induce the old man to go to the county home, where he would be comfortable during the winter months, but he refused to go fearing that by so doing he would be obliged to forfeit his property to the county. In his house he had a dozen or more cheap clocks of various patterns, strewn about the one room in which he lived, and kept them all running to hear them tick. This, he said, relieved the loneliness of his situation.

From the bounty on hedge hogs and hen hawks, paid by the Board of Supervisors, Orlando had for several years derived a considerable revenue. He claims to possess the power of charming animals and to this method he attributes his success in luring them into his snares. He profess to be a student of the occult and boasts of his dealings with the devil. His neighbors fear him and will sleep easier the coming five months while they know he is safely locked up in Albany.

FRIDAY, APRIL 27, 1917

S. R. STODDARD AT JOURNEY'S END

Resident of Glens Falls for More Than Half a Century

WIDELY KNOWN AS TRAVELER AND WRITER

Seneca Ray Stoddard died at 2 o'clock yesterday afternoon at his late home, 17 Harlem street. He had nearly rounded out a full three years more than the span of three score and ten, having been born at Wilton. Saratoga county, May 13. 1844.

Mr. Stoddard's illness dates back more than two years, at which time, without pronounced disease, the failing forces appeared to be more mental than physical. Up to a year ago an indomitable spirit refused to admit weakness though physical failure made it plain. Since late last fall Mr. Stoddard had been confined to the house and to the bed since Christmas. He fought valiantly through all the successive stages of his physical decline until at last, like the clock running down, he gave up and gently, peacefully he fell into the long sleep.

As a young man, Mr. Stoddard went to Troy where he learned his "trade," which consisted of interior decorating as applied principally to railway coaches. Shortly afterward he came to Glens Falls where he has since made his home. Then came years full of continued effort where his own interests were but little considered; where the commercial possibility was almost wholly sacrificed to the artistic in his toil for the upbuilding of the great north woods—his beloved Adirondacks and this community. For more than a half a century, Mr. Stoddard has preached the glories of this great northern country by means of his camera and pen, in poetry and song, on the lecture platform, in guide and art books, by map and by chart has he given to the atlas world much knowledge of a region glorified.

Close upon the heels of Adirondack Murray, being one year after, Mr. Stoddard made his first trip through the Adirondacks in the summer of 1872, and the following year his first guide book appeared which he continued to issue every year thereafter up to and including the 1915 edition.

The "Northern Monthly" published in 1906-7-8 was another periodical devoted to community and Adirondack interests.

In 1894 he made his first long trip which was to Alaska, following this in '96 to the Holy Land, Russia and the Orient, contributing as a result of these trips and others made later—one notably to the "Midnight Sun"—much to the lyceum platform and to literature.

Mr. Stoddard's last big effort which he undertook alone, was the compilation of the art book in commemoration of the Warren County Centennial four years ago.

Mr. Stoddard was a sturdy friend to those he called friends. He saw only the good in people and remained always silent if this could not be expressed. Thoroughly unselfish he lived, while gentleness appeared to govern his conduct throughout life and right to the end, it appeared to control his advent to the Great Beyond.

Mr. Stoddard was twice married. His first wife was Helen Augusta, the daughter of Thomas A. Potter, a former resident of Glens Falls. Two sons came of this marriage, Chas. H., a lawyer and LeRoy R., a physician, both of New York city.

In 1908, he married Miss Emily Doty of this city, who with the two sons, a brother and two sisters in the West, survive him.

The funeral will be held at the late home on Sunday at 2:30 o'clock and interment will be Pine View cemetery.

BOLTON LANDING.

Jan 24 1912

Mrs. Mary J. Goodman is the victim of a severe cold.

H. E. Barber is ill of a severe cold and confined to the house.

Frank Clark suffered an attack of heart trouble Saturday night.

Mrs. Anna Frazier, who has been ill of grip, is some better at present.

Dr. E. J. Wilson has been confined to the house by a severe cold and pleurisy, but is now recovering.

Wm. P. Gates

WARRENSBURGH (N. Y.) NEWS

OBITUARY.

Dec 11   1921

Johnathan Streeter Gates

Johnathan Streeter Gates, a life-long resident of Bolton, well known and highly respected, died suddenly at his home at about 8:30 o'clock Sunday evening, December 11, of neuralgia of the heart, having been in his usual health up to the time of his death. Coming so suddenly, Mr. Gates' death was a shock not only to his family but to the entire community. He was born in Bolton, in the vicinity known as Coolidge Hill, about seventy-five years ago, the son of Mr. and Mrs. John Gates, early settlers of the town. On September 27, 1873, he married Miss Zilpha E. Ferriss, who died several years ago. Their only child, Walter E. Gates, died January 17, 1919, of influenza. His death was a severe blow from which the stricken father never recovered. Mr. Gates is survived by one brother, Dodge S. Gates, of Diamond Point, and four grandchildren, Ferris, Zilpha, Robert and William Gates; four nieces and four nephews, all of Bolton. For many years, Mr. Gates was postmaster of Bolton, conducting also a general store there and later, in company with his brother and son, conducting a store also at Bolton Landing, which property he owned at the time of his death. The funeral was held Tuesday afternoon at his late home, the Rev. George Robinson, pastor of the Methodist church at Bolton Landing, officiating. Interment was made in Bolton cemetery.

Gates Falls, Lake George, Bolton, N. Y.

Articles in this book were collected from the following newspapers:

Albany Journal
Benson Correspondent, Fair Haven, VT
Brooklyn Eagle
Chicago News
Chicago Record-Herald
Chicago Tribune
Detroit Tribune
Glens Falls Daily Times
Glens Falls Post
Glens Falls Post Star
Glens Falls Star
Glens Falls Times and Messenger
Hague Correspondent
Houston Post
International News
Kattskill Bay Correspondent
Knickerbocker Press
Lake George Mirror
Mail and Express
National Magazine
New York Globe
New York Times
Patriotic Publishing Company
Philadelphia Press
Taylor County, Kentucky Enquirer
The "Globe"
The Christian Instructor
The Corinthian
The Morning Star
The Press
The Technical World Magazine
The Whitehall Times
The Youth's Companion
Ticonderoga Sentinel
Toronto Telegram
Troy Times
Utica Saturday Globe
Warrensburg News
Woman's Home Companion

INDEX

B

"Baby Raliance V"
(Boat), 197
"Baby Speed Demon II",
197
"Beer" Facts, 240
"Bet-a-million" GATES,
167
"Bird, The Little," 230
"Buffalo Enquirer"
(Boat), 197
B & S Garage, 199
Backus, Alexander, 202
Bailey, Mr., 81, 108
Bain, James H., 42, 48
Bain, Supervisor, 64
Baird, John, 20
Baker Farm, 17
Baker, 71, 81, 108
Baker, Bernard, 158
Baker, C.H., 140
Baker, Charlie, 88, 96,
106
Baker, Clarence, 167
Baker, Cordelia, 178
Baker, Dick, 106
Baker, Ella, 167
Baker, Henry, 223
Baker, Leonard, 237
Baker, Miles, 146
Baker, Mrs. Benjamin, 66
Baker, Mrs. Caleb, 200
Baker, R. D., 59
Baker, Sam C., 140
Bakers Falls, 55
Bakers Mills, 84, 88, 96,
128, 147
Baldwin, 10, 26, 46, 72,
75, 129, 140, 217
Baldwin, Calvin, 16
Baldwin, Captain, 156
Baldwin, Eliza Jane, 56
Baldwin, James, 214
Ballston Lake, 233
Ballston Spa, 129, 176,
198, 233
Baltimore, 83, 109
Bangs, John K., 230
Bank (Lake George), 40,
41, 49, 58
Bank Square, 166, 171,
174, 225

Banker, George, 36
Banking Device, 66
Banks, David, 75
Banner, Star Spangled,
194
Baptists, 15, 35, 42, 64,
66, 86, 99, 103, 104, 107,
117, 127, 162, 167, 168,
185, 193, 205, 218, 223
Barber Bay (Lake George),
43, 143
Barber, Amy, 64
Barber, Cicero, 87
Barber, Clayton A., 140
Barber, Cromwell, 115
Barber, Dr. Isaac, 87
Barber, Fred, 14
Barber, H.E., 246
Barber, Harry, 245
Barber, Henry W., 203
Barber, Hosea, 159
Barber, Hulda, 158
Barber, Jesse A., 188
Barber, Lucille, 188
Barber, Moses, 87
Barber, Mrs. H., 181
Barbour, Annie, 64
Bargain Hunter, 42
Barge Canal, 223
Barger, Mrs. Charles H.,
139
Barker, Atty. John H., 204
Barnes, Mrs. Joseph, 103
Barnum, Ethel, 187
Barnum, P.T., 202, 215
Barrigan's Café, 79
Bartlett, Dispatcher, 158
Bartlett, Ezra, 111
Bartlett, Gillette, 111
Bartlett, Henry, 111
Bartlett, Huldah, 111
Bartlett, John, 111
Bartlett, William, 224
Barton, Joseph, 29
Barton, Melvin, 243
Bascomb, W.S., 53
Baseball, 141, 233
Basin Bay, 48, 60
Batcheller, Florence, 35
Batcheller, George A., 117
Bates Cemetery, 19
Bates, C.J., 63
Bates, George W., 127,

159
Bates, Rev. Francis, 133
Bates, Rev. H.H., 89
Batesville, 28, 165
Batterson, Henry W., 145
Batty, Benjamin, 51
Baumann, J.P., 16
Bay Road (Street), 17, 25,
36, 37, 48, 49, 97, 127,
154, 157, 162, 166, 167,
218, 225, 229, 230
Bay Street Cemetery, 36,
77, 92
Bayle, George F., 237
Bayruth, 32
Bayview (Estate), 93
Bazinet (County Trea-
surer), 69
Bazinet, John, 140
Be Kind to Loved Ones at
Home, 215
Beach, Claude, 19
Beach, Louis Napoleon,
115, 147, 149
Beach, Mary A., 175
Beadenell, Sarah, 3
Bean, Tarleton H., 205,
222
Beanes, Dr. Wm., 194
Bear Swamp, 205
Beardsley, W.H., 27, 37,
49
Beaudett, Julien, 57
Beaver River, 8
Beckers, Dr. William, 245
Becker, Lt., 241
Beckwith, John Francis,
138, 174
Beebe, Warren, 104
Beecher, Henry Ward,
202
Beekmantown Road, 206
Belden, Charles, 178, 218
Belden, Oscar, 178
Bell Point, 6
Belvedere Restaurant
(Glens Falls), 146
Bemis Heights, 161
Bemish, Postmaster, 235
Ben Starbuck Stage Line,
37
Benday Film Process, 243
Benedict, Charles E., 74

Bennett, Alfred, 117
Bennett, Eliza, 4
Bennett, Frank L., 49
Bennett, Jeptha, 141
Bennett, Joel F., 69
Bennett, John, 4, 197
Bennett, Melvin, 115
Bennett, Mrs. Charles, 145
Bennett, Mrs. Gordon, 237
Bennett, Mrs. William, 33
Bennett, R.J., 115
Benson, Jacob, 138
Bentley, Forester, 166
Bentley, Fred A., 18
Bentley, Harry E., 224
Bentley, Jesse, 58
Bentley, John, 27
Bentley, Walter, 103
Bentley, Wellington, 166
Bentley, Wilbur, 40
Benton, 103
Benton, S., 185
Bergen, Oswald, 135
Berlin, Connecticut Iron
Bridge Co., 148
Berne, NY, 87
Bertold, Herman, 45
Beswick, Albert, 112
Beswick, Byron, 13
Beswick, Delbert, 13
Beswick, Eliza, 13
Beswick, Herbert, 13
Beswick, Leonard, 112,
175, 217, 239
Beswick, Mary O., 64, 65
Beswick, N. Lester, 226
Beswick, Reynolds, 226
Bevins, M.S., 17
Bibbey & Ferguson Brew-
ers, 140, 144
Bibbey & McNaughton,
144
Bibbey Hose Co., 140, 144
Bibbey, Dr. George, 210
Bibbey, Leonard, 23, 81,
140, 144
Bibbey, Walter, 140
Bickley, Joseph P., 14, 71,
217
Bidwell, Fred H., 172
Bidwell, Sedgewick W.,
172
Big Bay, 203

13, 22

Brown, John and Martha, 109

Brown, John B., 175

Brown, John Carter, 151

Brown, John Nicholas, 151

Brown, Johns daughter, 109

Brown, Lee, 22

Brown, Louis M., 54, 64, 148, 206

Brown, Mark, 240

Brown, Mary J., 186

Brown, Milon U., 50, 224

Brown, Mrs. J.L., 139

Brown, Myron O., 17, 22, 23, 24, 36, 123, 168, 227, 245

Brown, Percy, 72

Brown, R.J., 120, 136, 159, 182, 236, 243

Brown, Ralph, 22, 63

Brown, Richard, 27

Brown, S. (Judge), 24

Brown, Sanford, 74

Brown, Sarah, 109

Brown, Stewart, 3, 213

Brown, Sylvester (Sheriff), 225

Brown, Truman, 92, 184

Brown, W.W., 16, 22, 168

Brown, Willard, 22, 36

Brown's Hotel, 39, 40

Brownelle, Ella, 127

Brownelle, Lester, 9

Bruder, Charles H., 106

Brunelle, Arthur, 228

Bryant, G. Frank, 65, 81, 117, 159

Bryant, Justice John T., 217, 246

Bryant, Orlando, 246

Buchanan, James, 97

Buckbee, Mrs. Duane, 3

Buckingham, W.W., 42

Buckley, Constable Cornelius, 51

Buckley, Henry, 224

Budden, Captain, 165

Buell, Judge, 173

Buffalo Bill Cody, 31, 107, 202, 244

Buffalo Yacht Club, 197

Buffalo, NY, 107, 126, 201, 223

Bull, Charles, 91

Bull, G.N., 146

Bull, John, 91

Bull, Mr., 24, 26

Bull, Theodore, 91

Bullards Undertaking, 36

Bullion, Royal, 229

Bullis, Dr. Edgar L., 5, 36

Bump, Game Protector, 230

Bungalow (Poem), 130

Burbank, Daisy, 224

Burbank, Helen, 185

Burbank, Rose, 224

Burdett, Elliot, 86

Burdett, William E., 86

Burdick (John, Anna, Mary, Jewett), 162

Burds, Mrs. Alexander, 143

Burds, Mrs. Allen, 117

Burge, Jane A., 227

Burge, Miles, 227

Burge, Mrs. Stephen, 227

Burger, R.E., 170, 218

Burgess, Lewis, 19, 69

Burgess, Minerva, 63

Burgoyne, General, 87, 119, 138, 162

Burke, Major, 244

Burke, Patrick, 203

Burleigh, H.G., 23

Burlesque Circus, 228

Burlington Free Press, 98

Burlington, VT, 83, 96

Burnans, Charles F., 208, 238

Burnans, Viola H.P., 36

Burnham, Cyrus, 173

Burnham, George, 173, 190

Burnham, James, 173

Burnham, John, 173

Burnhams, Charles H. & Fred, 186

Burnhamville, 17

Burns, Robert, 151

Burns, W.J. (Detective) 168, 185, 189, 219, 238, 241

Burt, Dr. C.K., 24, 44, 84, 96, 118, 164, 181, 183, 194, 199

Burt, John, 66

Burton, W.W., 34, 43

Burtt, Mrs. Julius R., 127

Butler, Albert, 217

Butler, Dr. G.R., 100

Butler, Dr. Glentowrth, 179

Butler, Edward, 134

Butter, To Make, 197

Butterfield Lake, 213

Butterfield, Daniel (Governor), 131

Byrne Property (Glens Falls), 128, 174

C

"Calypso" Boat, 185

"Carol II" (Boat), 195

"Cleo" (Boat), 37, 44

"Cynthia" (Steamboat), 156

Cadillac Auto, 193, 202

Cady, J.R., 115

Cady, Merch, 115

Calamity Jane, 102

Calamity Point, 38

Caldwell (Lake George Village), 3, 5, 6, 7, 9, 10, 11, 13, 14, 15, 27, 35, 37, 38, 64, 66, 71, 82, 86, 118, 121, 134, 142, 156, 176, 195, 196, 208, 211, 224, 229, 233, 237, 242

Caldwell, James (Boat), 20, 38, 75, 86

Caldwell, William, 14, 75

Calf Without Legs, 237

California, 108, 236, 239

Callanan & Prescott Co., 197, 217

Calumet Lodge, 90, 93

Cambridge Valley Agricultural Society, 130

Cambridge, MA, 161

Cambridge, NY Fair, 123

Cambridge, NY, 28, 56, 93, 123, 130, 214

Cameron, D.E., 210

Camp, John, 198, 209

Canada (Steamboat), 156, 233

Canada Street (Lake George), 48, 149, 236

Canada, 98, 109, 147, 162

Canal Street, 173

Canfield, Richard, 78

Cannon, Henrietta, 4

Cannon, Joseph G., 90

Cannon, Le Grand, 4

Canonball, 91

Canton, NY, 222

Cape May, 197

Capitol Building (Albany), 169

Capone, Joseph, 233

Capone, Nicholas, 233

Capron, William O., 113

Captain's Daughter (Poem), 69

Cardiff Giant, 44

Cardinal, Frank & Joseph, 155

Cardle, David, 111

Cardle, Milo, 4, 237

Cardle, Robert, 63

Carey Arid Land Act, 202

Carey, Charles, 195

Carey, Charles, 203

Carney, Bruce, 53

Carpenter House, 91, 95

Carpenter Mountain, 220, 221

Carpenter, Ben, 19

Carpenter, Gilbert, 13, 17, 19

Carpenter, William, 224

Carpenter's Tannery (Glens Falls), 113

Carr, Charles, 112

Carr, Hosea F., 75

Carr, Joseph B., 131

Carr, L., 73

Carson Hotel, 102

Carson, J.R., 72

Carter Towing Car, 143

Carter, Nathaniel, 161

Cary, James, 117

Cary, John, 117

Casavant Building (Glens Falls), 113

258

I

61

272

X

Y

Z

Epilogue

I often wondered why my great-grandfather labored for decades to read, select, cut, paste, and safeguard his scrapbooks. I further wondered if he ever waded back through them and reread all of the articles. It was Mark Frost who solved my mystery. He said, "Jonathan knew that *you* would come along someday and know what to do with them."

I hope that Jonathan would be pleased if he knew about this book – and I sincerely hope that you have enjoyed it as much as I have enjoyed putting it together.

William Preston Gates